國家圖書館藏古文字學
與古史研究稿本叢刊

甲骨叢編

第一集

董作賓 ◎ 著

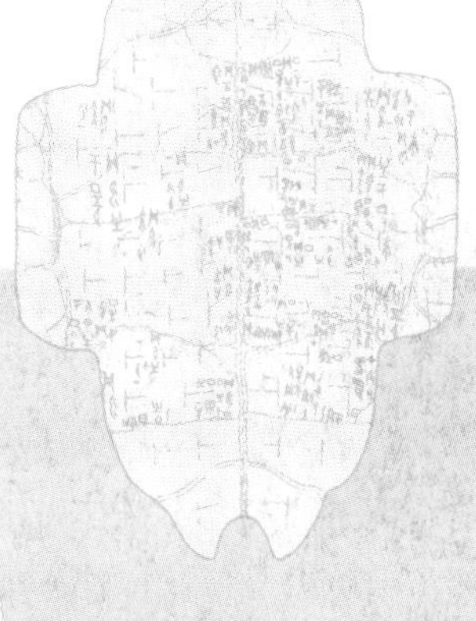

北京大學出版社
PEKING UNIVERSITY PRESS

圖書在版編目(CIP)數據

甲骨叢編.第一集 / 董作賓著; 國家圖書館編.—北京:
北京大學出版社, 2024.3

(國家圖書館藏古文字學與古史研究稿本叢刊)

ISBN 978-7-301-34736-2

Ⅰ.①甲… Ⅱ.①董… ②國… Ⅲ.①甲骨文–研究 Ⅳ.①K877.14

中國國家版本館CIP數據核字(2024)第004849號

書　　名　甲骨叢編(第一集)
　　　　　JIAGU CONGBIAN(DI-YI JI)
著作責任者　董作賓 著
　　　　　國家圖書館 編
策劃統籌　馬辛民
責任編輯　魏奕元
標準書號　ISBN 978-7-301-34736-2
出版發行　北京大學出版社
地　　址　北京市海淀區成府路205號　100871
網　　址　http://www.pup.cn　新浪微博: @北京大學出版社
電子郵箱　編輯部 dj@pup.cn　總編室 zpup@pup.cn
電　　話　郵購部 010-62752015　發行部 010-62750672
　　　　　編輯部 010-62756694
印 刷 者　三河市北燕印裝有限公司
經 銷 者　新華書店
　　　　　787毫米×1092毫米　16開本　35.25印張　290千字
　　　　　2024年3月第1版　2024年3月第1次印刷
定　　價　198.00元

目録

前言

董作賓（1895—1963），著名考古學家、古文字學家。原名作仁，字彦堂，又作雁堂，號平盧。祖籍河南南陽（今南陽市），1949年遷居臺北，直到去世。董作賓一生致力於甲骨文研究，是一位在甲骨文研究上頗有建樹的學者，被譽爲「甲骨四堂」之一。他曾於1928—1934年間多次主持並參加殷墟科學發掘，並親手整理大量的出土甲骨資料。董作賓撰述豐富，堪稱著作等身，有專著十餘種，學術論文200餘篇；研究範圍涉及甲骨學、古文字學、商代文化與歷史、曆法、民俗等諸多領域，尤其對甲骨學與殷商史貢獻良多。董作賓主要學術論著可見於《董作賓學術論著》（世界書局，1962年）和《平盧文存》（藝文印書館，1963年）。另有《董作賓先生全集》十二册（藝文印書館，1977年），收録了大部分著述。但是，董作賓於20世紀40年代初曾編著有一部《甲骨叢編》，却因故未能刊行。

這部鮮爲人知的未刊手稿，現存於中國國家圖書館。

抗日戰爭爆發後，國民政府以重慶爲陪都，四川成爲抗戰大後方。中央研究院作爲當時的最高學術研究機構，也跟隨國民政府西遷。經過長途奔波，史語所最終落脚在偏遠的四川省宜賓市郊李莊鎮。《甲骨叢編》（第一集附考釋）是董作賓於1941年在李莊鎮板栗坳完成的一部甲骨文研究著作。

抗戰時期，國立北平圖書館同樣避居西南，館長袁同禮率領同仁竭力爲西南聯大及各科研機構提供研究書籍。袁同禮策劃了「國立北平圖書館考古學叢刊」項目，以出版中國考古學家在戰時的研究成果。《甲骨叢編》稿本封面題「國立北平圖書館考古學叢刊第五種」，表明書稿屬此項目成果之一。當時陳夢家也積極參與促成此事，並高度讚賞董作賓的書稿。董作賓在書稿「自序」中寫道：「客秋偶與陳夢家先生談及此業，出寫本示之，以告袁守和先生（袁同禮，字守和），願爲出貲印刷並力促其成，高誼至爲可感。乃於遷川期間，發憤編此第一集。」另外，1937年陳夢家與董作賓通信中也提到：「《殷墟文字外編》編成後似可續編此書，將來全書告成，實契學空前之大著也。」〔一〕

遺憾的是，戰亂導致出版停頓。書稿完成後十餘年，董作賓自己已不明原稿的下落，一度認爲書稿遭遇毀滅了。1954年董作賓在《殷曆譜的自我檢討》中寫道：「我在民國三十年曾計劃把甲骨文字分期分類編纂起來，名爲《甲骨彙編》，全部由我摹寫，照原大小付石印，以供整理時拼合復原之用。北平圖書館長袁同禮先生願意替我刊印。當時我曾先作了一本，共一百頁，外有釋文考證一本，已送上海付印。以後停頓了，原稿一去不返，渺如黃鶴了。許多經我摹寫過的孤本，也都跟着犧牲掉。」〔二〕此處《甲骨彙編》與《甲骨叢編》的書名存在一字之差，大概時隔多年董作賓自己也記憶模糊了。總之，《甲骨叢編》（第一集附考釋）的書稿完成於1941年，因故未能正式出版，學界至今無緣得見其真容。

這部書稿爲紙撚毛裝，共四大册。從序文中可知，董作賓原計劃將《甲骨叢編》編纂成一部十集的巨著，擬將當時所有存世的私

〔一〕陳遠：《信劄之美，源於自由》，《同舟共進》2017年第4期，第19—22頁。

〔二〕董作賓：《殷曆譜的自我檢討》，《大陸雜誌》第9卷第4期（1954年）。後收入《大陸雜誌·史學叢書》第一輯第二册「先秦史研究論集」（上）；又收入《董作賓先生全集》乙編第五册，藝文印書館，1977年。選入劉夢溪主編：《中國現代學術經典·董作賓卷》，河北教育出版社，1996年，第393頁。

家收藏甲骨文材料，按照五期分期，分甲、骨兩類編纂完竣。《甲骨叢編》第一集第一、二册爲甲骨文摹寫圖版，摹寫於硫酸紙上，然後貼附於宣紙書葉上。第三、四册爲釋文及考釋，先鈎摹甲骨片輪廓，然後在原字對應位置寫出釋文。所有甲骨摹本均爲董作賓親手摹寫，對殘片或綴合片補出完整骨形，釋文則用箭頭和編號標出各辭左行右行方向及先後順序。按五期編排，各期再按材質分「甲」「骨」兩類。各類下以「專題」編排。一個專題下收甲骨若干片，然後針對具有重要史料及考證價值的典型甲骨片，或逐片或同類分組，進行詳細的考釋。專題内容主要有：「大龜四版」與龜版復原及曆譜排譜，羅振玉藏大肩胛骨與骨版復原及卜辭前後順序等文例，同文異版，何遂雲南所得甲骨拓本三張，牛胛骨文例，卜王卜辭，總述三期、四期卜辭特徵，日祭卜辭，征人方卜辭，五種祀典，卜夕卜旬卜辭等方面。書稿用毛筆小楷書寫，清晰流暢；1090 幅（1005 號）甲骨摹本製作工整精良，各期甲骨文字形變化及甲骨上的鑽鑿、卜兆等細節特徵均得以淋漓盡致地展現。

在《甲骨叢編》中，董作賓運用《甲骨文斷代研究例》中五個時期和十項標準來對那些缺乏地層依據的甲骨刻辭進行分析和研究。爲了進一步闡發甲骨文斷代研究方法，董作賓利用實例推演，意在示範運用十項斷代標準來研究那些非科學發掘的甲骨材料也能實際操作，進一步檢驗五個時期和十項斷代標準的可行性。除此之外，董作賓還在考證部分開展諸多開創性研究實踐。譬如：其一，書稿中可見多處運用新材料推算殷曆的成果。董作賓的殷曆研究是根據甲骨卜辭記日、旬、月、年的資料排譜編纂，依卜辭中有關天文曆法的紀録解決殷商年代問題。這項研究始於 1930 年，直至 1945 年他纔費盡心力終於著成《殷曆譜》。其二，董作賓在書稿中提到在殷代祀典中，以祖甲及帝乙帝辛，即二、五兩期最爲嚴肅，其中翌、祭、壴、劦、彡五種祀典，具有系統和組織性，先祖妣依日祭祀，井然有序。這就是董作賓發現的殷商最重要的祭祀制度，即周祭制度。其三，關於商代地理的程途研究。在 20 世紀 40 年代，董作賓是商代地理研究成績最顯著的學者之一，他對黄組卜辭的征人方地理進行系統整理，排比地名，按干支繫聯，考釋其地望，並繪出路線圖。在本書稿中，董作賓關於商代地理的研究已初現端倪。其四，在書稿中，董作賓對一些甲骨片依據殘辭予以補釋，對甲骨進行復原，並拼綴了很多版甲骨。大多數的補釋和拼綴都與當今學者新的綴合研究成果不謀而合，這些都表明他對甲骨材料以及不同類别的契刻文例和規律等掌握得相當精準。

倘若該書稿當年得以按時刊行，勢必對甲骨學研究與發展産生强大的推動作用。時光荏苒，80 餘年後的今天，這部書稿仍具有極高的學術價值。書稿中關於甲骨學與殷商史諸多問題的討論，至今仍能給我們帶來新的啟發，依然值得我們繼續深入學習和研究。

此次藉「古文字與中華文明傳承發展工程」及其子項目「國家圖書館藏古文字研究類稿本整理」（G1415）的支持，我們對書稿加以整理，並影印出版，以供廣大學者進一步研究和利用，確爲一大幸事。同時感謝國家圖書館古籍館領導和同事的鼎力支持，以及北京大學出版社編輯的辛勤工作，助力書稿順利刊行。

胡輝平

书籍 1002
04845

採 號
甲骨叢編
四册

甲骨叢編

第一集

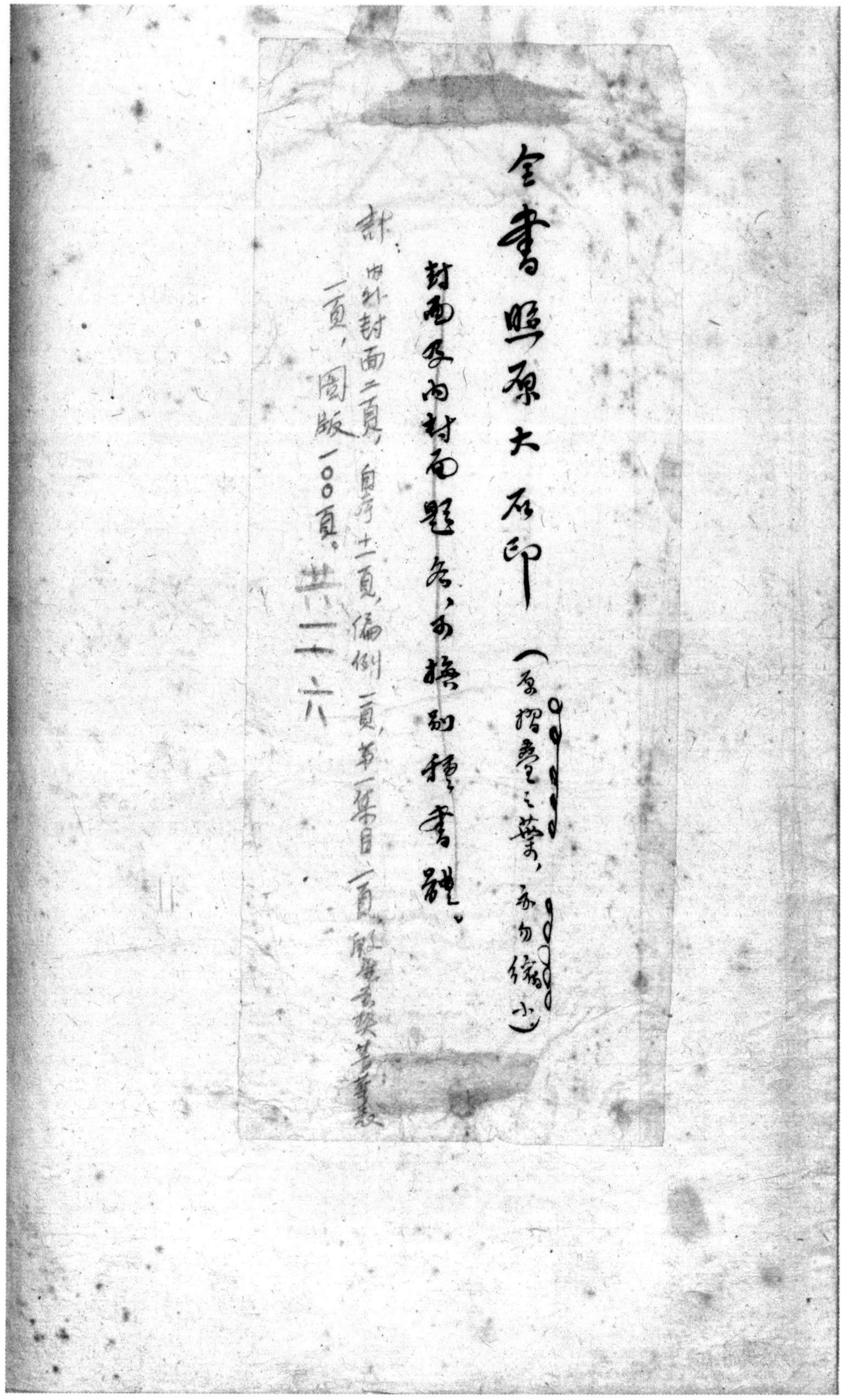

全書照原大石印（參摺疊之葉，不另縮小）

封面及內封面題名，另換別種書體。

計：內外封面二頁，自序十二頁，編例一頁，第一集目一頁，殷虛書契菁華表一頁，圖版一〇〇頁。共一一六

國立北平圖書館考古學叢刊第五種

甲骨叢編

第一集 附考釋

甲骨叢編

自序

殷虛甲骨文字之出土，自清光緒二十五年(公曆一八九九)迄于今(民國三十年，一九四一)，四十三年矣。其發見採掘，約可分為三期：

一曰偶然發見時期。光緒二十五年以前屬之。此期因耕種而偶然發見甲骨文字，已數十年，村人以為龍骨，售之藥材店。曇花一現，瞬即毀滅，出土之物，殆無幸存。

二曰土法採挖時期。光緒二十五年至民國十六年(一九二七)屬之。其時村人已知藥材之為骨董，可得善價而沽也，則羣起挖取之，廿餘年間，搜括幾徧。估客亦麕集相市，重貲購求，以轉售之平滬。私家收藏，海外流布，皆此期出土之甲骨文字也。

三曰科學發掘時期。民國十七年(一九二八)至民國二十六年(一九三七)屬之。此期已知甲骨文字為重要古物，應歸國有，乃由國立中央研究院遴派考古專家，組織發掘團，從事工作。前後十年，發掘十五次，除十至十二次為殷代陵墓外，採掘甲骨者十二次，總計所得，大小凡二萬餘版。

以上三期，第一時期無論矣，第二、三期所出土之甲骨文字，中外公私所收藏，見於著錄之專書，已有三十三種，並未著錄者而統計之，號稱十萬版也。

甲骨文字乃新興學問之一，自孫詒讓作栔文舉例始（光緒三十年，一九〇四），至民國二十五年止，（一九三六）凡三十三年之間，甲骨之編纂論著，三百三十三種，其中三分二以上，又為近十年作品，則斯學之昌明，誠如雨後春筍，萬長怒發，日新月異，蔚成大觀也。其有關考釋者，專書，通論，散見，凡六十四種，有關專題研究者，文字，歷史，考古，社會，禮制，曆法之論著，凡一百五十二種，參加研討之中外學者一百三十四人（以上統計，均據甲骨年表）。創見傑作，觸目而是，可謂極一時之盛矣。

由此言之，十萬版甲骨文字，因皆經治此學者鑽研摩挲，索隱探賾，發為宏論，著成專書，似已登峯造極，嘆觀止矣。然吾可以正告讀者：此過去三十餘年之研究，猶不免東鱗西爪之見，縱橫擘合之作，乃此學之發軔，非此學之終的，蓋此學研究，尚未入於正軌也。山窮水盡，疑已無路，柳暗花明，實別有村，吾今將引君至一嶄新之境界，一觀甲骨學之新園地，可乎？

余之從事發掘工作也，或躬親探檢，實地觀察，或兀坐一室，苦思冥索，積之既久，乃發明斷代研究之法，斷代研究法，固此新園地之鑽鑰也。乃發表以來，又經十載，而採用此法以澈底全部整理甲骨文字者，猶無其人。今此編之作，乃導君入其門徑，至一新境，以探甲骨文字之秘。換言之，亦即課入吾人日夕鑽摩之牛角尖中一角落也。於此，不能不舊事重提，畧述斷代研究之法。

在甲骨文斷代研究例中，余曾舉十種標準：

一、世系　二、稱謂　三、貞人　四、坑位　五、方國

六、人物　七、事類　八、文法　九、字形　十、書體

十標準之主要者為「稱謂」，其次「貞人」與「坑位」。「世系」則稱謂之所資，餘皆由前三者推演而出者也。今於此舉世系與稱謂。貞人已散見於本編各期卜辭中，坑位關係，限於科學發掘之材料，均從畧。

殷人祖妣世系圖　①至(33)祖次　㊀至㉓妣次

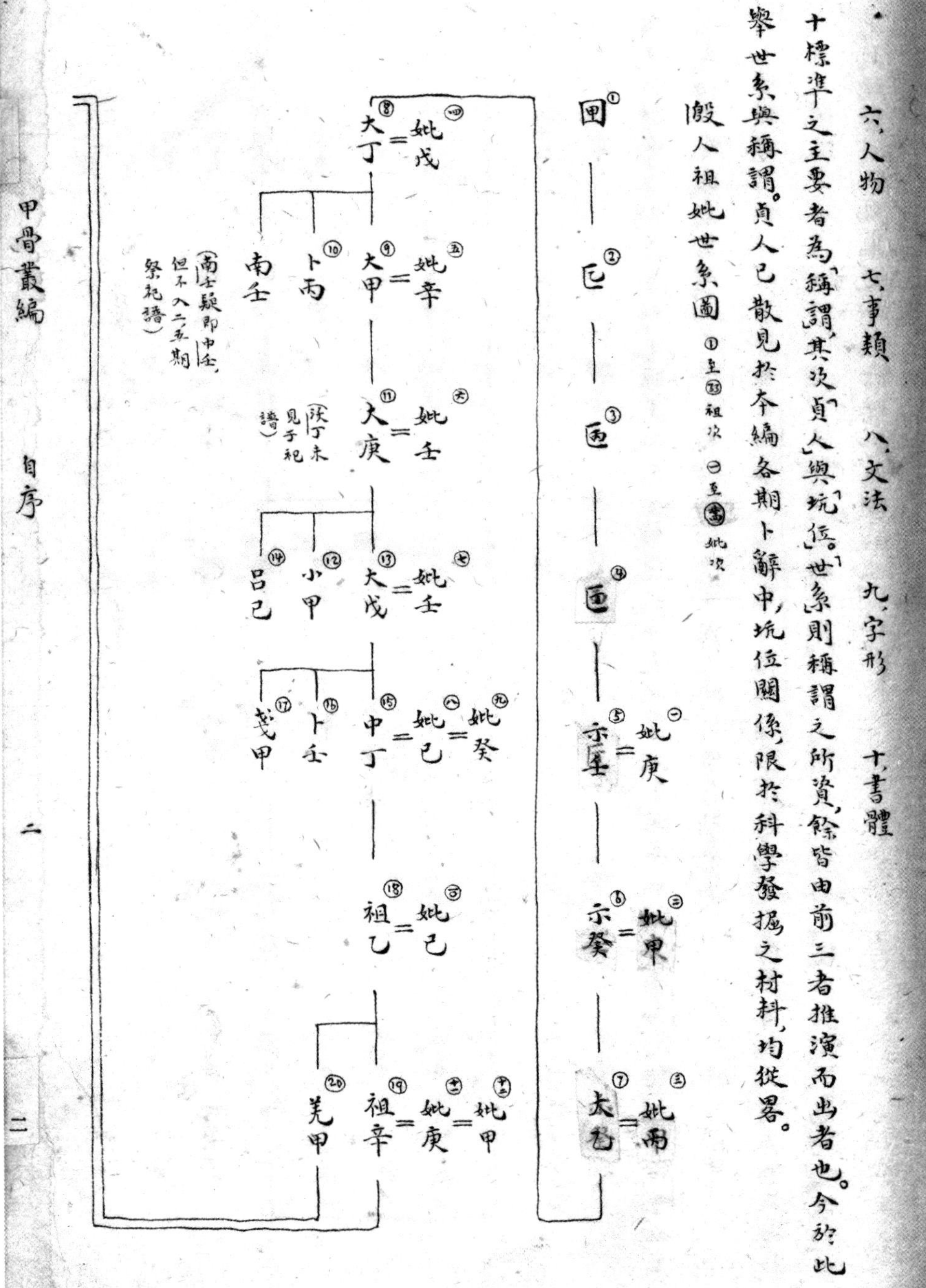

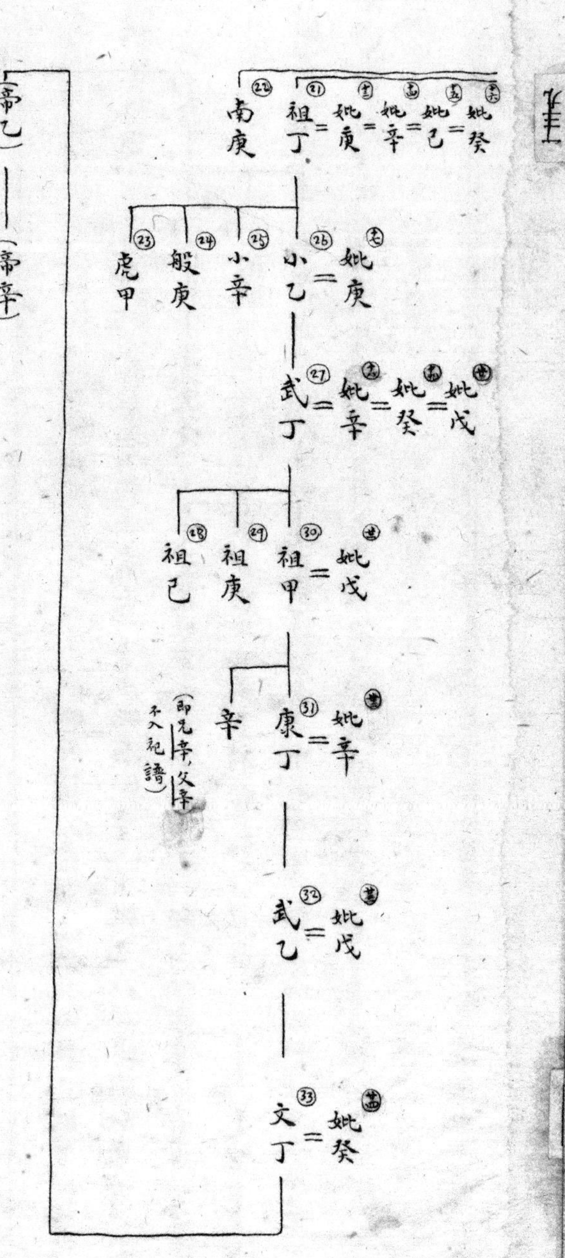

右表乃據第五期帝辛時先祖先妣之五種祀譜中之次第列之，並參以祖甲帝乙之譜。此譜上甲以上之遠祖不祀，故表未列。且上甲之前，除高祖夒、王亥之外，均當存疑也。

余於斷代例一文中，曾作自祖乙至文丁九世稱謂圖，此圖應補充者尚多，每期均有不入五種祀典之人，如父某、母某、兄某、子某，一一詳列，必待各期祭祀卜辭全部理出之後，今尚不能為之也。僅就習見之稱謂，足以助斷代研究者，增訂原圖如次。

卜辭稱謂表

被祭者	第一期 般庚—小乙 武丁	第二期 祖庚	第二期 祖甲	第三期 廩辛	第三期 康丁	第四期 武乙	第四期 文丁	第五期 帝乙	第五期 帝辛
大乙	唐	唐	大乙	大乙	大乙	大乙	大乙	大乙	大乙
祖乙	祖乙		祖乙	中宗祖乙		高祖乙		祖乙	祖乙
妣己	高妣己		妣己					祖乙奭妣己	祖乙奭妣己
祖辛	祖辛		祖辛	祖辛				祖辛	祖辛
妣庚	高妣庚							祖辛奭妣庚	祖辛奭妣庚
祖丁	祖丁			祖丁				祖丁	祖丁
妣庚	妣庚							祖丁奭妣庚	祖丁奭妣庚
妣己	妣己							祖丁奭妣己	祖丁奭妣己
妣癸								祖丁奭妣癸	祖丁奭妣癸
虎甲	父甲		虎甲				虎甲	虎甲	虎甲
般庚	父庚		般庚					般庚	般庚
小辛	父辛		小辛					小辛	小辛
小乙	父乙		小祖乙、乜、后祖乙	小乙		后祖乙	小乙	小乙	小乙

妣庚 兄丁 兄戊 武丁 妣辛 妣癸 妣戊 祖己 祖庚 祖甲 妣戊 廩辛 康丁 妣辛 子癸

母庚 兄丁 兄戊

兄己

妣庚 父戊 父丁 母辛 兄己 兄庚

妣庚 祖戊 后祖丁 后妣辛 父己 父庚 父甲 母戊 兄辛 子癸

祖丁 父辛 父丁 母辛 兄癸

后祖丁 祖己 祖甲 父辛 父癸

小乙奭妣庚 武丁 武丁奭妣辛 武丁奭妣癸 武丁奭妣戊 祖己 祖庚 祖甲 祖甲奭妣戊 康丁 康祖丁 康丁奭妣辛

小乙奭妣庚 武丁 武丁奭妣辛 武丁奭妣癸 武丁奭妣戊 祖己 祖庚 祖甲 祖甲奭妣戊 康丁 康丁奭妣辛

武乙	父乙	武祖乙 武乙	武乙
文丁	文丁	文武丁	文武丁
母癸	母癸	妣癸	

上表所可注意者，大乙之稱，始于祖甲；武丁之稱，始于帝乙；文武丁之名，始于帝辛；由其名稱，可以確定其時代也。其餘每期均有特殊之稱謂，此表雖不完備，而綱要畧具，讀者可以隅反矣。

各王卜辭，固有可以細別者，為研究之便，仍當分五大期也。茲依斷代例所舉，加注今定年數：

壹　第一期　盤庚十四年(自遷殷始)　小辛廿一年　小乙廿一年　武丁五十九年（前三期不易分出，今見卜辭以武丁時為多。）

貳　第二期　祖庚七年　祖甲三十三年（此期庚甲易分，祖甲時卜辭為多。）

叁　第三期　廩辛六年　康丁八年（此期不易分。）

肆　第四期　武乙四年　文丁十三年（此期乙丁可分。）

伍　第五期　帝乙三十五年　帝辛五十二年（此期乙辛尚可分。）

本編以大寫數字為分期記號，故列于上端。各期年數有多寡懸殊者，故卜辭之分量不同。五期雖可更作各王之分，然亦有兩期近似易相混亂者，如二期祖庚時，除貞人外，字形稱謂，皆易與武丁時不分。又三四期亦有不易分者，至於殘片細小，僅餘貞卜干支之字，亦難斷定時期。但大多數卜辭之時代既定，專題研究，有所取資，隻字片文，附之存疑，蓋已無關宏恉矣。

吾人誠能以斷代研究，為治甲骨學之第一方法，則進一步之工夫，即為甲與甲骨與骨之拚合，使之復其舊觀。則一切問題，自然披陳於目前，且隨時可以解決，而許多意想不到之成果，亦絡繹不絕，應手而來也。夫一甲一骨，猶人之有每一家族也，其在殷代，其在地下，固屬同居共處，精誠團結也，而一旦出現於斯世，有如大難臨頭，分崩離析，父子不相見，兄弟妻子離散矣。今欲使其儘可能範圍之內，重圓破鏡，一家團聚，寧非幸事？故吾人整理甲骨文字，有最後之目的焉：

第一目的，各王各期之卜辭，皆分類集合，使其各歸于原存甲骨之檔。

第二目的，每一版卜辭，皆使之還其在甲或骨上之本來地位。

如此理董完竣，吾人可以指示於讀者，此武丁時某年某月存牛胛骨之檔也。此又祖甲時某年卜祀之辭之第幾龜腹甲也。如此理董完竣，再有發現一殘片者，吾人可以之接兑於帝辛時卜多祭先祖之第若干龜背甲右半，曰此第三肋甲中部之殘版也。任何一片，如非贋品者，不應於若干骨若干甲之中，無所歸宿也。此非完全出于理想，倘能集衆力以赴之，兩目的者，未嘗不能計日而達也。

拚合之法，本編第一集有舉例數版，畧供參考。於此須注意者：即龜與骨各部分之鑑定識別及甲骨上貞卜刻辭之公例也。先述鑑別之法。

龜腹甲及背甲，各期皆用之。欲別腹背之異，須看其版片上之齒縫與盾紋。生龜於甲外被有角質盾版，猶骨之有皮，盾版相接處，深嵌甲面，雖剖磨之，不能泯滅，吾人謂之「盾紋」。龜既剖分為腹背兩面，背甲更中分之為左右兩半，施鑽鑿于反面(即内面)而後灼用之。其破裂也，必在卜兆或「齒縫」處，卜兆易坼，齒縫易散。今試取一片，可見其必有兩甲接處之「齒縫」，否則腹甲中部，四邊皆緣兆坼而破裂之小片也。知「盾紋」與「齒縫」，在腹背甲之不同，更證以左右行之文例，未有不能定其部位者也。

牛胛骨之鑽鑿部位，較為單簡，即分别其左右，視其原邊緣之屈曲情形，參以卜兆向背，文例左右，刻辭先後，即得之矣。

今揭龜骨圖及其普通之文例圖，以便對照。

龜腹甲

此為縮小一倍之圖，原大見「任甲二〇七」標準甲。

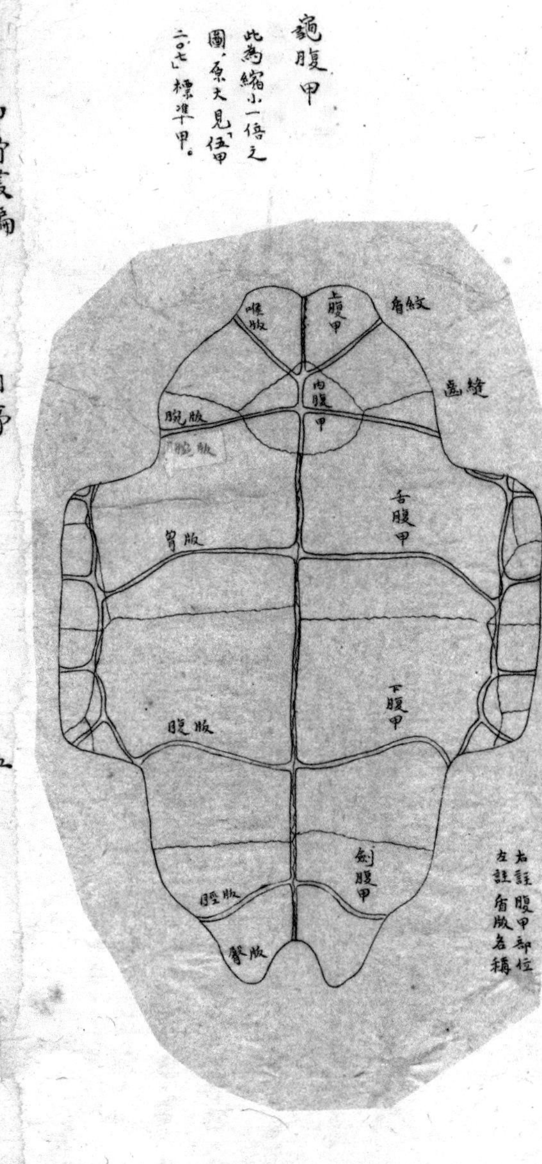

此為腹甲公式圖：
四行八段式
虛線示每卜辭之區域。
數字示全版卜辭之次序。
矢形，示卜辭左右行。
卜，示卜兆之方向。
以下甲骨公式同。

四行七段式一

腹甲文例一
（壹甲四）

腹甲文例二
（貳甲一）

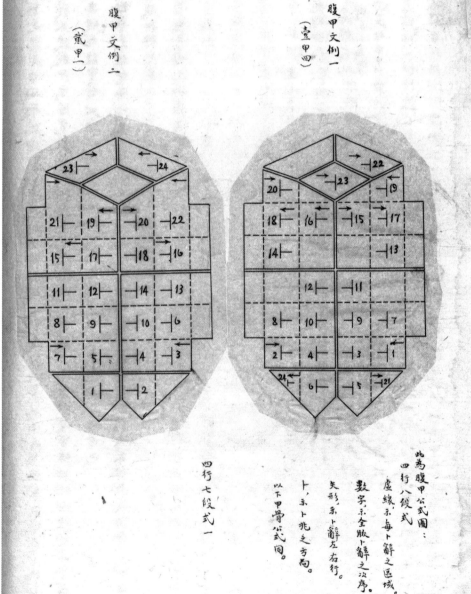

腹甲文例三
貳甲三一至三七
三九　六五

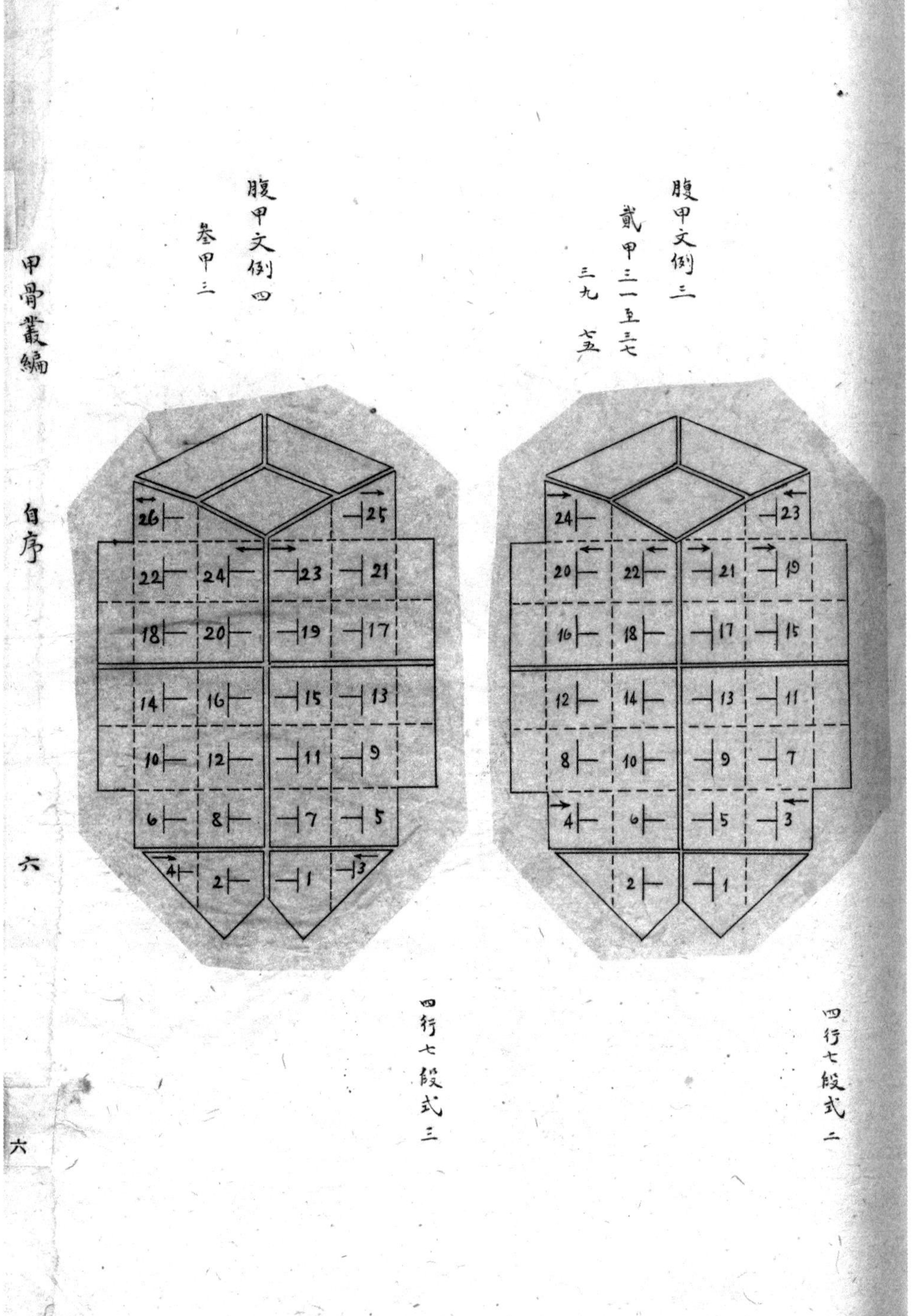

四行七段式二

腹甲文例四
叁甲三

四行七段式三

腹甲文例五
伍甲二〇七

六行九段式

腹甲文例六
伍甲二七四

八行九段式

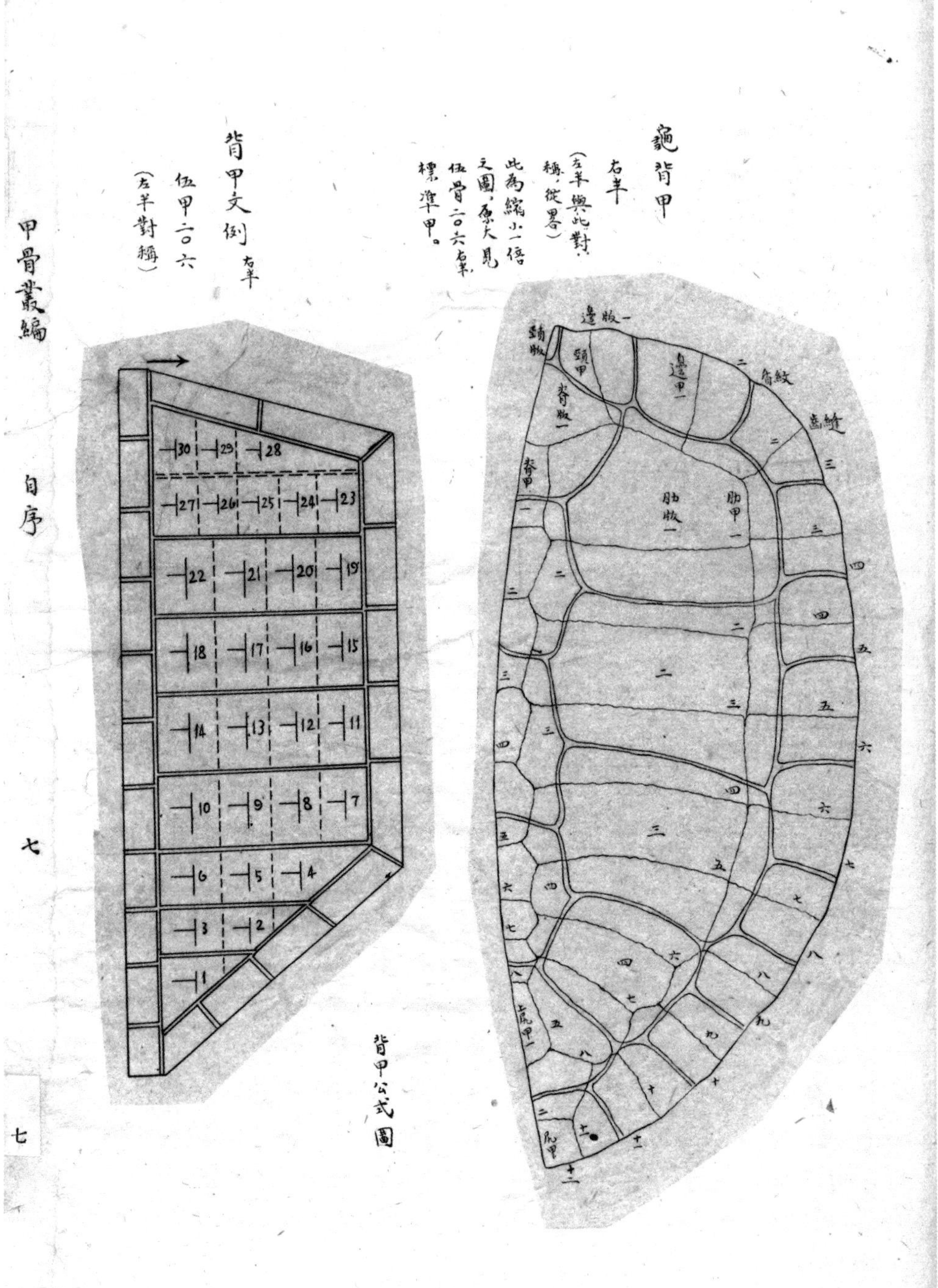
甲骨叢編
自序
七
背甲文例 右半
伍甲二〇六
（左半對稱）
龜背甲
右半
（左半與此對稱，從畧）
此爲縮小一倍之圖，原大見伍骨二〇六右半，標準甲。
背甲公式圖

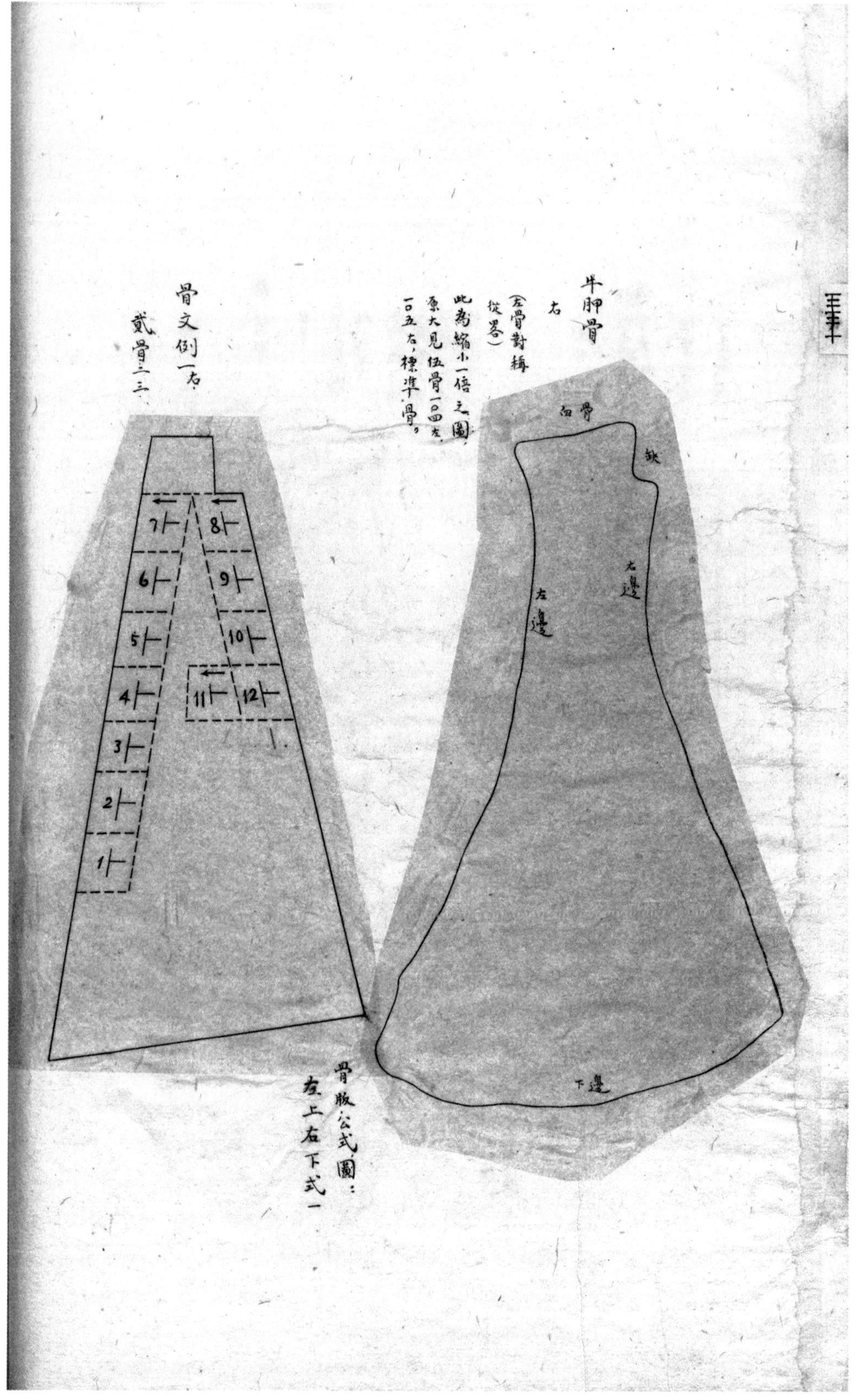
牛胛骨
右
（左骨對稱從略）
此為縮小一倍之圖，
原大見伍骨一四左，
一〇五右，標準骨。
臼骨
缺
右邊
左邊
下邊
骨版公式圖：
左上右下式一
骨文例一右
貳骨二三
1
2
3
4
5
6
7
8
9
10
11
12

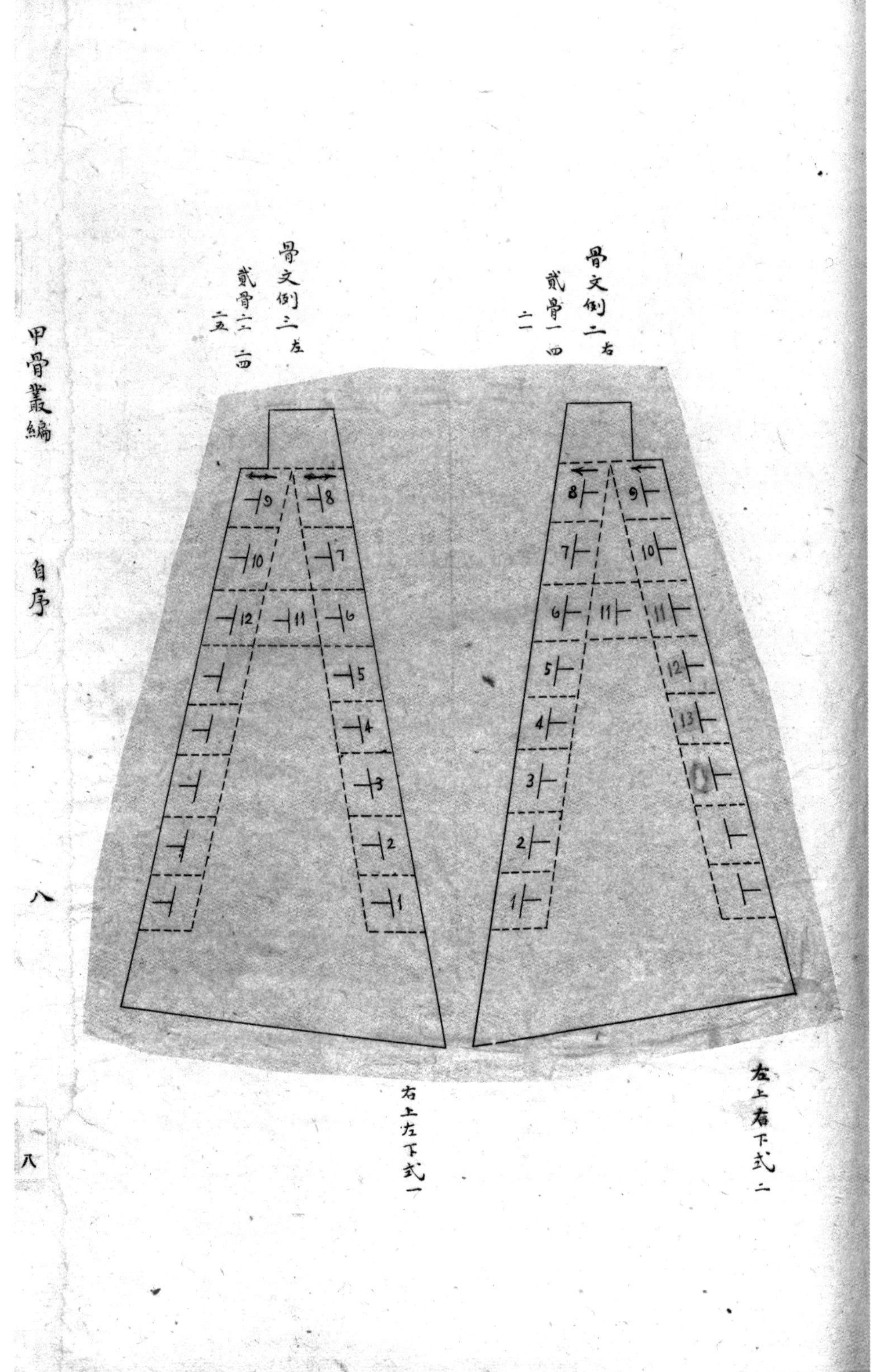
骨文例二右
貳骨一四
二
骨文例三左
貳骨二一四
二五
右上左下式一
左上右下式二
甲骨叢編
自序
八
八

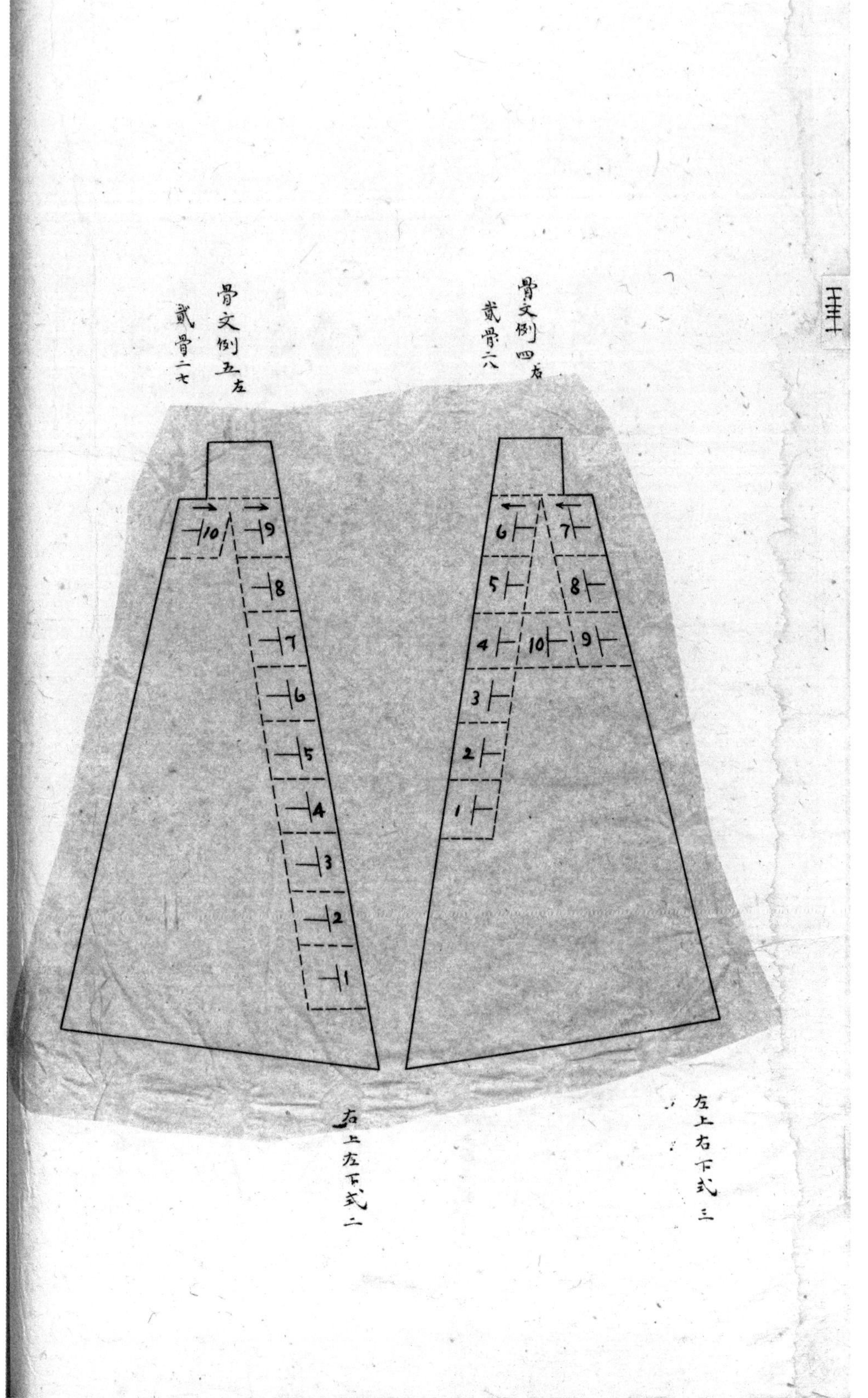

骨文例四右
貳骨六八
骨文例五左
貳骨二七
左上右下式三
右上左下式二

骨文例六右
伍骨二

骨文例七左
伍骨一

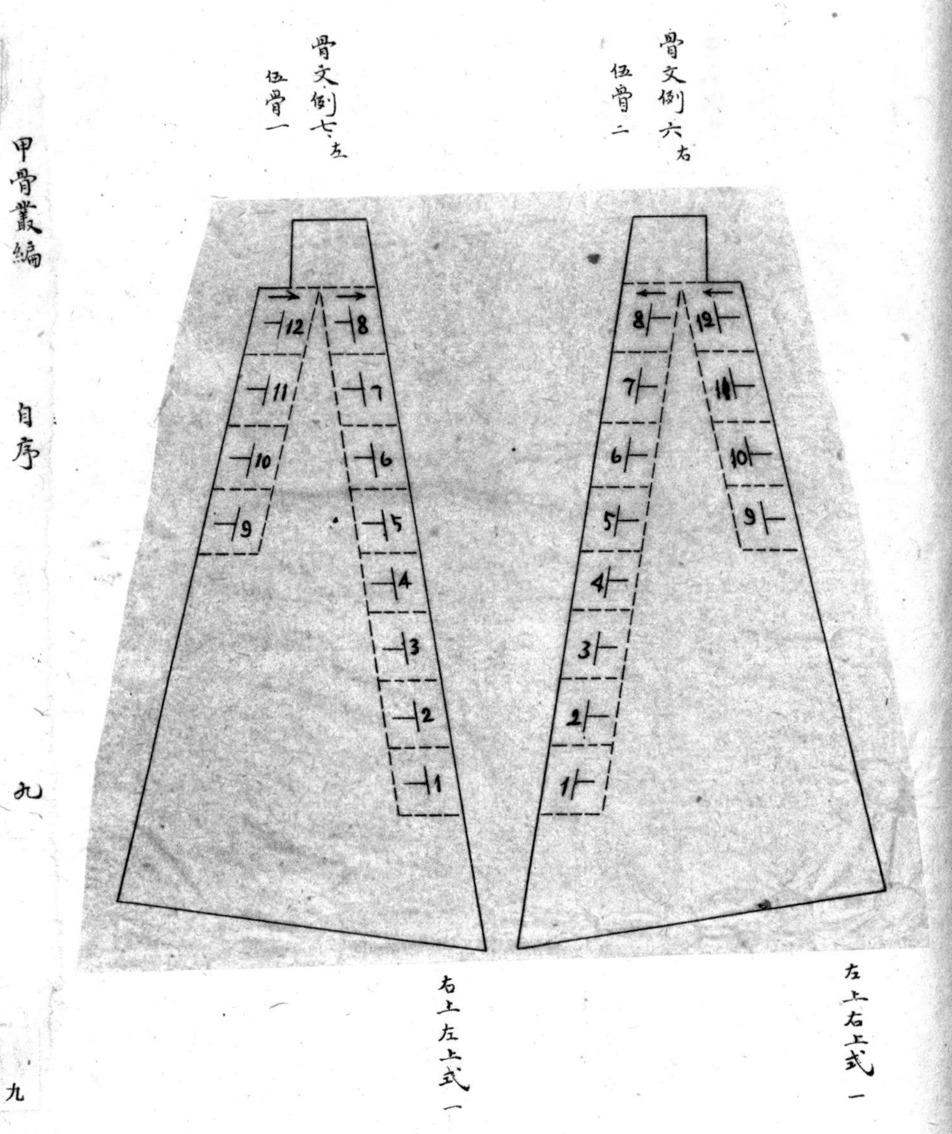

左上右上式一

右上左上式一

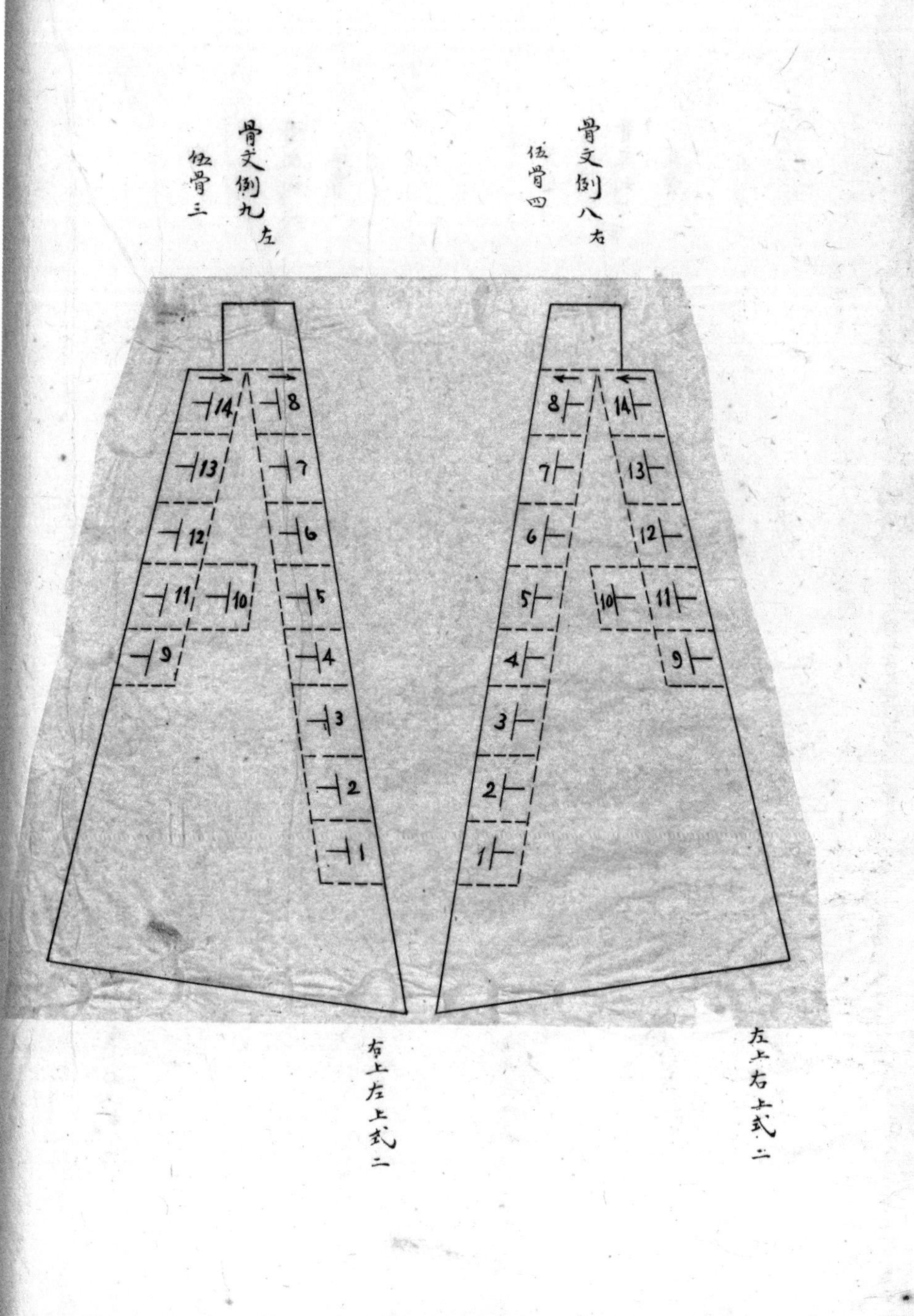
骨文例八右
伍骨四
骨文例九左
伍骨三
左上右上貳二
右上左上貳二
1
2
3
4
5
6
7
8
9
10
11
12
13
14

右所揭舉，為甲骨之一般刻辭公式，大多數卜辭皆可觸類而旁通者也。此類文例之求得，多出于卜旬、卜夕、卜王之版，向不為編者所重視，而實則此三者乃治甲骨學者入門之鎖鑰。蓋甲骨之完整者少，殘碎者多，不易見其全版之組織，今據此類有聯系性之卜辭，排其部位，補其干支，審其次第，則甲骨全版文例，可得而知。比較多版，得其公式，拼合殘片，易如反掌矣。

依斷代法，分其時期；依鑑別法，定其部位，更依卜事之種類，使相集合；有干支以排其次序；有詞句以求其貫連；有文例公式以證其在甲若骨上之關係；如是而本屬一版，後經離散，但有著錄，尚在人世，而曰不能復其原形，吾不信也。

編中拼合復原之版，僅舉其例，乃余偶一為之者，全部理董，尚未遑為之也。古詩云「鴛鴦繡手從君看，不把金針度與人」。余則不然，本編所揭斷代研究各例，余之鴛鴦繡手；而斷代之標準甲骨之公式，實為余之金針。材料豐盈，方法具在，讀者其有意乎？

考證部分，多為余最近研究之所得。約畧舉之：

一、為曆法之探討。近五年來余嘗集中精力作古曆之研究，成殷曆譜一書。其涉及本編材料者，輒舉以為例。如武丁五十年之旬譜（壹甲四），祖庚七年之夕譜（貳骨四至六），帝辛十年之日譜（伍骨一至四），皆其顯例也。

二、為祀典之說明。殷代祀典，以祖甲及帝乙帝辛，二王兩期，最為嚴肅。如彡翌祭壹劦五種祀典，皆有系統之組織，而先祖妣之依日祭祀，秩然不紊。如祖甲時之彡祭（貳甲一、二）帝乙時之翌祭（伍骨五、八），乙辛時之日祭（伍甲一至一六○），足見一斑。

三、為史實之聯貫。如壹骨五至一七，所輯各辭，以四事為綱，更以同版同文，互資接綴，於殘簡斷編千創百孔之中，各事之線索，猶能一目了然，如讀武丁實錄也。

四、為時期之分劃。第三期卜辭，著錄甚少，第四期卜辭鑒別甚難。今於此兩期，特加注意，述其分劃之標準。此兩期能辨別之，其餘三期，更易為力也。

五、為坑位之考求。坑位之紀錄，惟科學發掘之材料有之。今據吾人之經驗，以考求前後出土之物，如壹骨一至四，著華之大骨，貳骨四至六，卜夕之全版，皆能得其出土之地。三四期之多出於村中，更可因其存儲之庫，以推求私家收藏之品。

此外如同文異版之例（壹骨七至一二），正反銜接之文（壹骨一至一七），甲骨部位名稱之標準（伍甲二○六、二○七，伍骨一○四、一○五）卜辭互相拚合之方法（壹骨五、六，伍骨一至四），演變中之字形（壹骨一八至三○），程途中之地理（伍骨一至四），小王之名（叁骨一），卜月之辭（伍骨九至三五），皆一得之見，或涵新義，治甲骨之學者，可供參考研究之資者也。

本編所收寫本，有為最近影摹者，有為十年以來隨時積存者，故工有精粗，筆有新舊，紙有厚薄，墨有濃淺，不能齊同。然其出於忠實態度，則始終如一。雖不足與原刻比，讀者作鈔本觀可也。國難以來流離再四，此類材料，珍藏行篋，時有散佚毀滅之虞。每擬粘貼成冊，又須待全部寫成，分類理董之後，而全部理董，則非短時期內所能為也。客秋偶與陳夢家先生談及此業，出寫本示之，以告袁守和先生，願為出貲印刷，並力促其成，高誼至為可感。乃於還川期間，發憤編此第一集。杜君士雄，時於工餘相助，於此誌謝。此集考證文字，多屬匆促中一次寫定，未作草稿，但求達意，不暇修詞，有時興致甚好，揮毫直書，瑣瑣不休，有時神思既倦，秉筆乏生，數行了事，或天寒指僵，字畫生澀，或菜油燈昏，行列斜欹，讀者倘責其行文蕪雜，書字草率，所不敢辭。如於研究方法，有所商討，加以是正，跂予望之。

民國三十年三月一日。董作賓自序於西川之板栗坳寄廬。

編輯凡例

一：本編每集輯錄甲骨卜辭影寫本百葉。釋文百葉。考證文字若干葉。

二：本編所收，採用寫本者：因拓本付印不易，成書價昂；且未著錄者多無拓本，已著錄之寫本亦須全收，故決用寫本，以求一致。又拓本有模糊不清晰者，有無字處被剪裁者，有但拓有字部分不及全形者，有甲縫、盾紋、邊緣、卜兆不可辨者，寫本能免此諸弊。

三：初擬每集中平均分配五期甲骨，每期甲與骨各佔十葉。及着手編纂，頗感困難，因甲骨之分量，多少有殊；各王之年數，修短各異；版片之遺存，大小不一；整齊排比，勢不可能。如第四期骨多甲少，第三期甲骨皆少，一集縱能勉湊，二集以下，即難為繼。故決定不計分量多寡，以每集各期甲骨均有為原則。

四：每葉中縫，以大寫數字，記五期之分；其下記甲類或骨類；再下記本葉所收版片之號數起訖。甲骨版片右上方，不再加註期、類，僅註編號。此號繼續至全部各期甲骨，分類編錄完竣為止。

五：本編問世後，徵引甲骨文字者，每片註其期、類、號，即得。如「壹骨四五」或「1骨45」，即可知為甲骨叢編第壹期，骨類第四十五片也。有此總號，可免重複。

六：本編輯錄卜辭，以全部收入為最終目的，片字隻詞，不使遺漏。惟每集在不悖期、類之原則下，因材料之便，或以類相從，或以事聯系，或一書全收，初無一定標準。俟全書編就，別作分類檢字，檢詞，人名，地名，專書之各種索引，以為剪裁，拼合，檢查研究之便。

七：本編第一集中，已將殷虛書契菁華一書，全部收入，附索引示例。以後各集，如某一專書編完，即附以此書之索引，以便對證原書。

八：本編甲骨寫本，均注意圖繪一準確之輪廓。甲類凡腹背甲有齒縫，盾紋可見者，均繪出之。骨版注意其邊緣兆坼。卜兆可知者，甲骨均摹之。間有圖繪全形，以示其部位所在。

九：本編甲骨寫本，乃編者廿年來隨時影摹之片，書寫工具及興致不同，故前後如出兩人之手。惟以忠實態度為之，不敢忽畧。如有謬誤，承讀者指正，尤所企盼。

甲骨叢編第一集目

本集共編錄甲骨文字一〇〇五號，一百葉。五期甲骨之分配如次：

分期	分類	編號	葉數
壹	甲	一—三三	四
壹	骨	一—四五	一八
貳	甲	一—一〇三	一〇
貳	骨	一—二三一	二〇
叁	甲	一—七	六
叁	骨	一—三三	四
肆	甲	一—五六	二
肆	骨	一—一八三	一七
伍	甲	一—二〇七	一〇
伍	骨	一—一〇五	九

以上第一集採録自專書或未著録者三十一宗，計甲骨文字殘片一〇九〇。除本集所編之一千零五號之外，其餘八十五片，爲各號甲骨之反面或互相拚合之版。

殷虚書契菁華

全書版片與甲骨叢編號數對照表

葉	版	號	版	號	版	號	版	號
一	一	壹骨一						
二	一	壹骨二						
三	一	壹骨三						
四	一	壹骨一反						
五	一	壹骨三反						
六	一	壹骨二反						
七	一	壹骨四						
八	一	壹骨四反						
九	一	壹骨三一	二	貳骨一七	三	伍骨一六	四九三合	伍骨一六
	五	叁骨一三	六	肆骨一七二	七	壹骨三三	八	壹甲一六
	九	伍骨一四	一〇	伍骨一六七	一一	伍甲一六八	一二	伍甲一六九
	一三	伍骨一	一四	伍甲一七〇	一五	伍骨一三	一六	伍骨二

甲骨叢編　　殷虚書契菁華表　　一

一〇　一　伍骨二〇　二　伍甲一七一　三　伍骨九　四　伍骨一七

五　壹骨一八　六　壹骨三二　七　壹骨三四　八　壹骨三五

九　壹甲三六　一〇　伍骨一二　一一　壹骨三七　一二　壹骨三八

一三　伍甲一七二　一四　貳骨一八　一五　貳骨一九　一六 九五合　叁骨一三

一七　貳骨二〇　一八　伍骨一〇

一一　一　壹甲一七　二　壹甲一八　三　壹甲一九　四　壹甲二〇

五　壹甲二一　六　壹甲二三　七　壹甲二二　八　壹甲二四

九　壹甲二五　一〇　壹甲二六　一一　壹甲二七　一二　壹甲二八

一三　肆甲五五　一四　壹甲二九　一五　壹甲三〇　一六　壹甲三一

一七　肆骨一七三　一八　肆骨一七四　一九　肆骨一四九　二〇　肆骨一七五

二一　肆甲五六　二二　肆甲五四　二三　肆骨一七一　二四　壹甲三二

二五　壹甲三三　二六　伍甲一七一

全書十一葉，著錄甲骨六十八版。入第二集，編為六十二號。

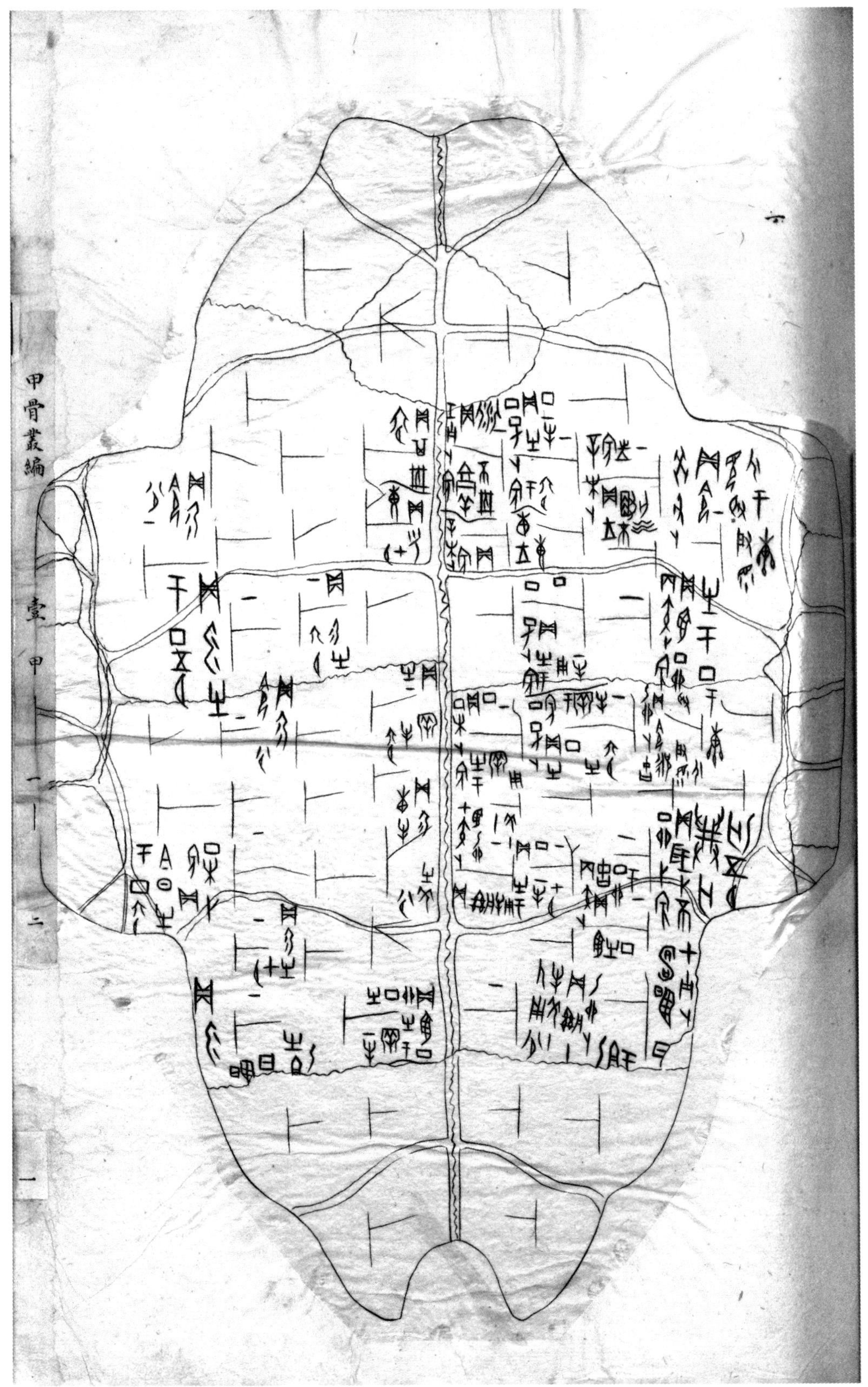
甲骨叢編
壹 甲

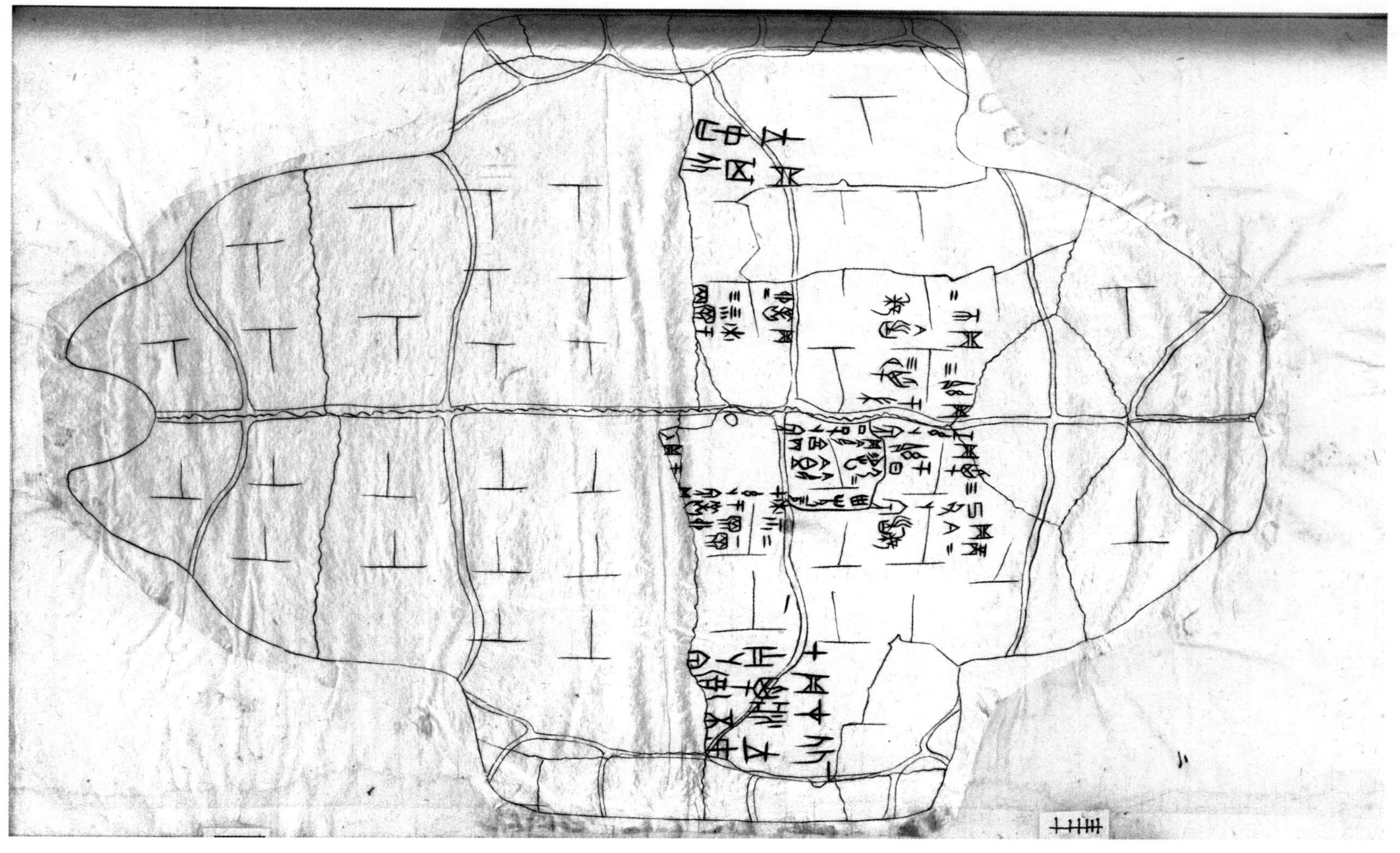

壹　甲

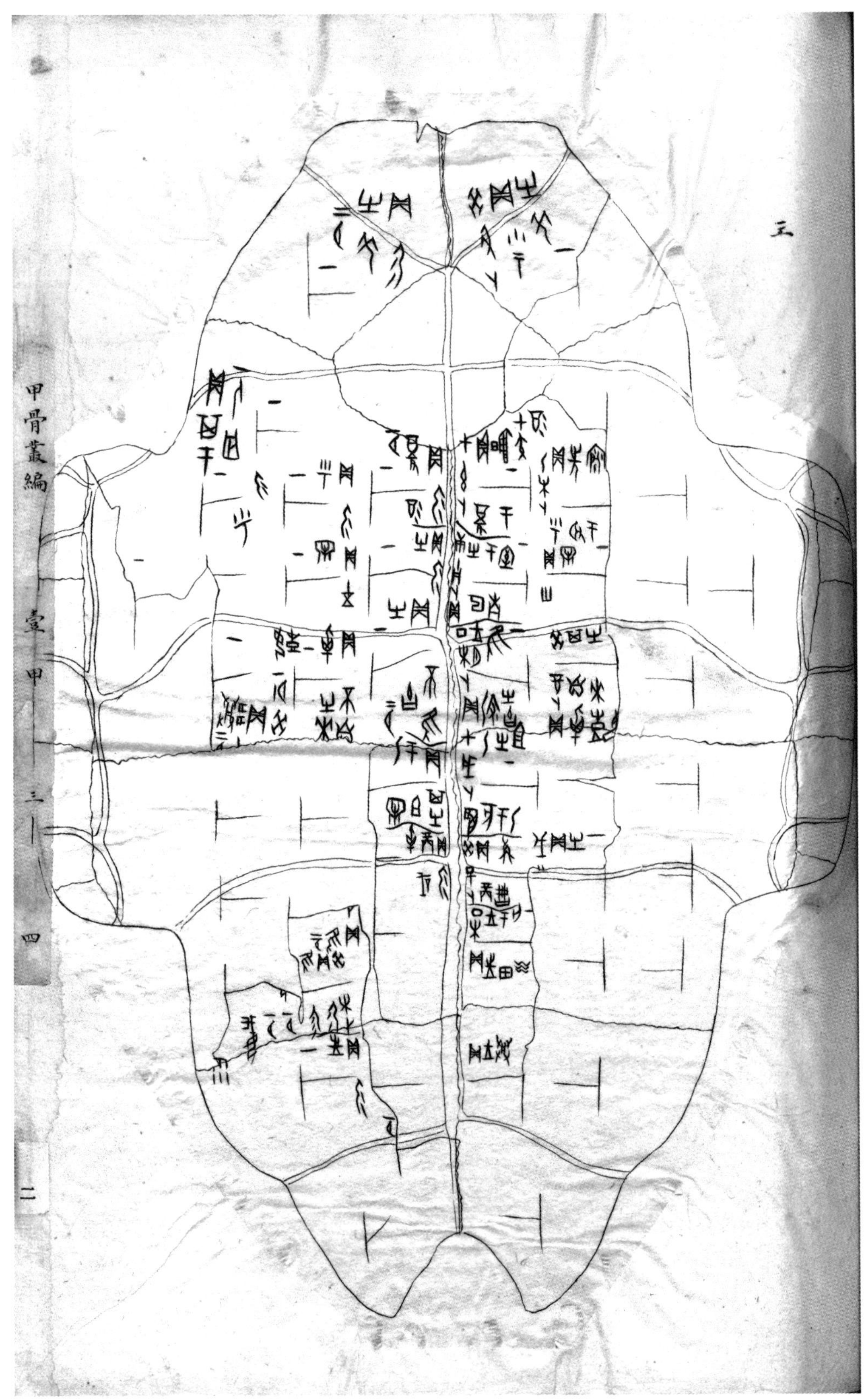

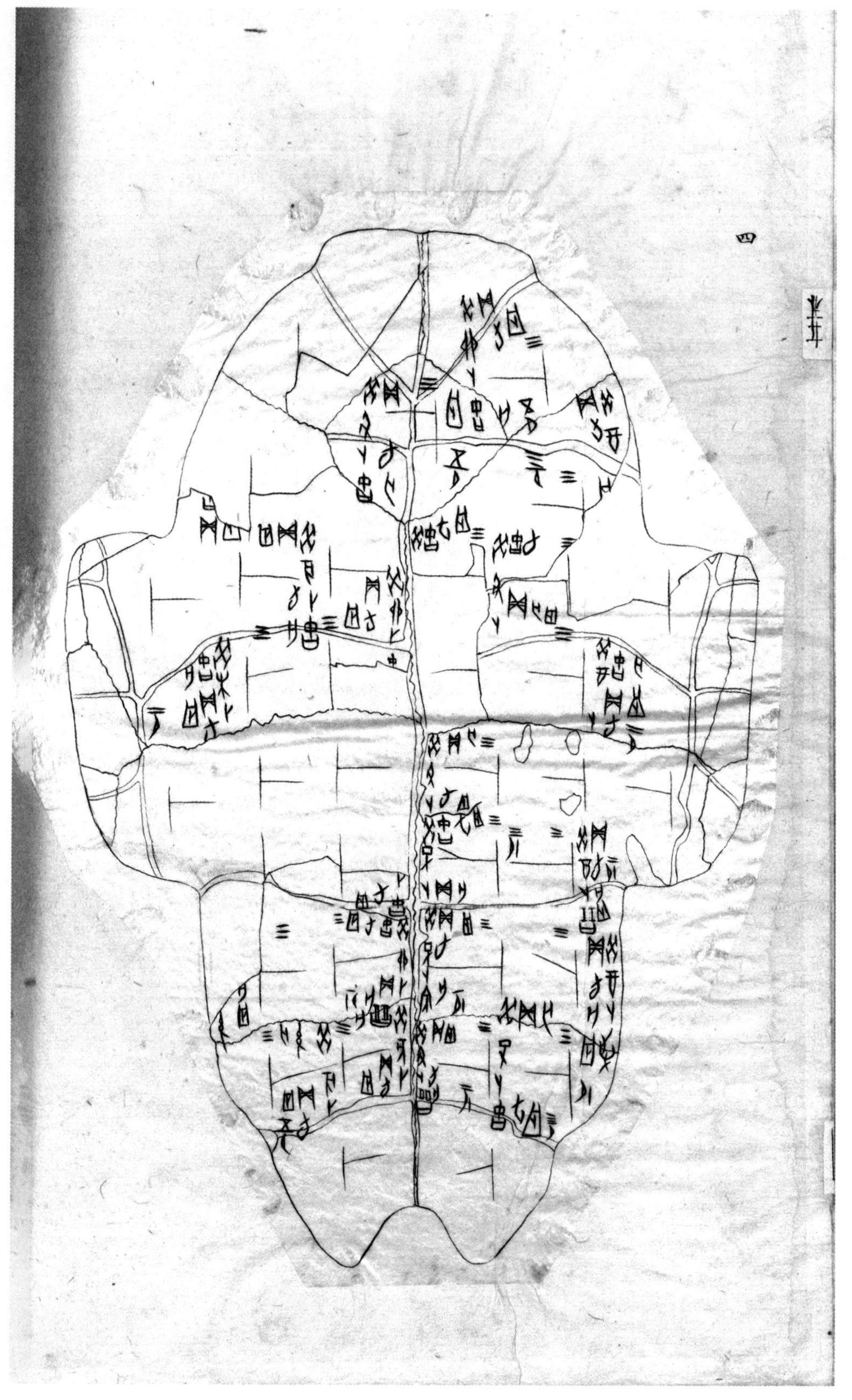

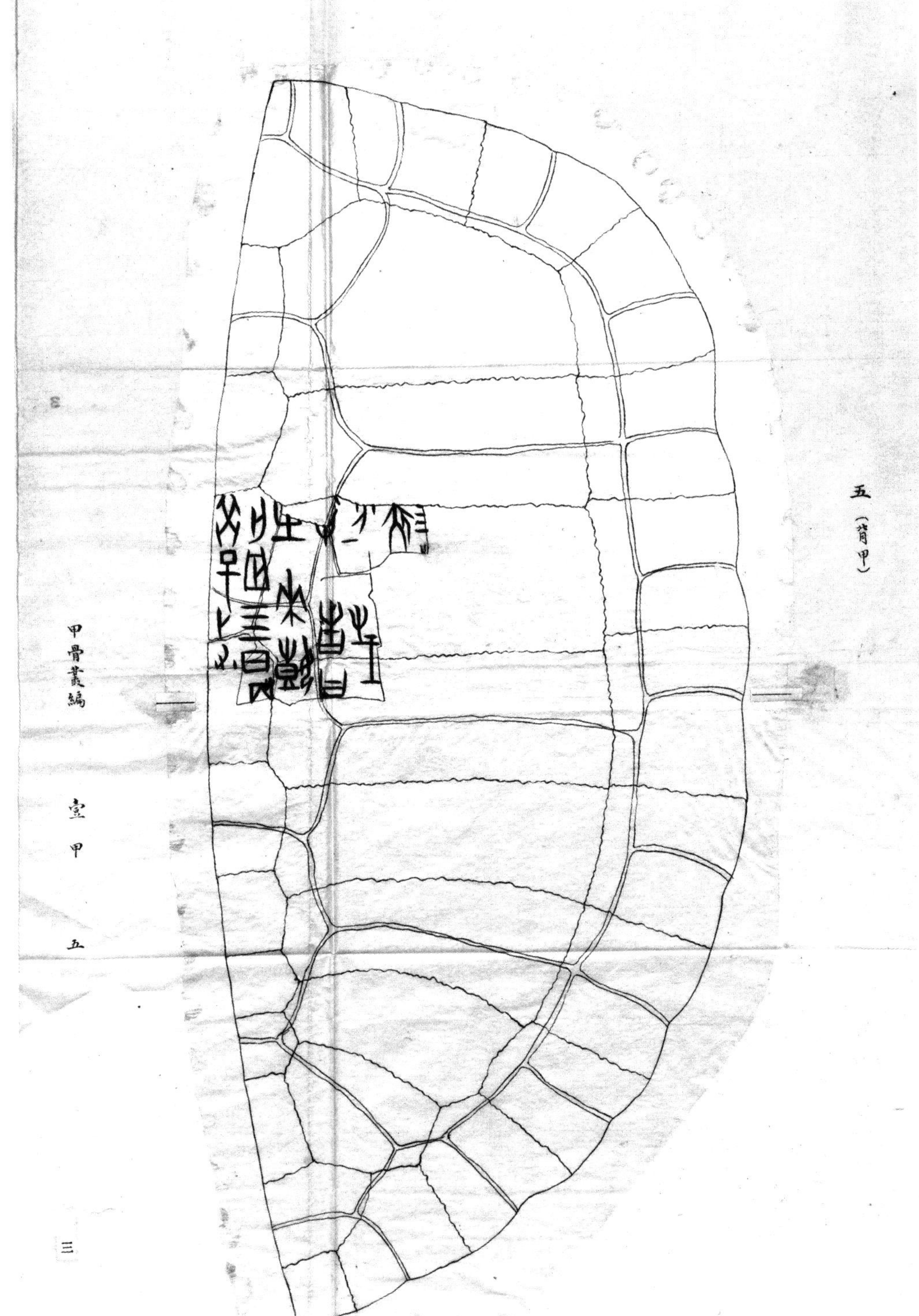

五（背甲）

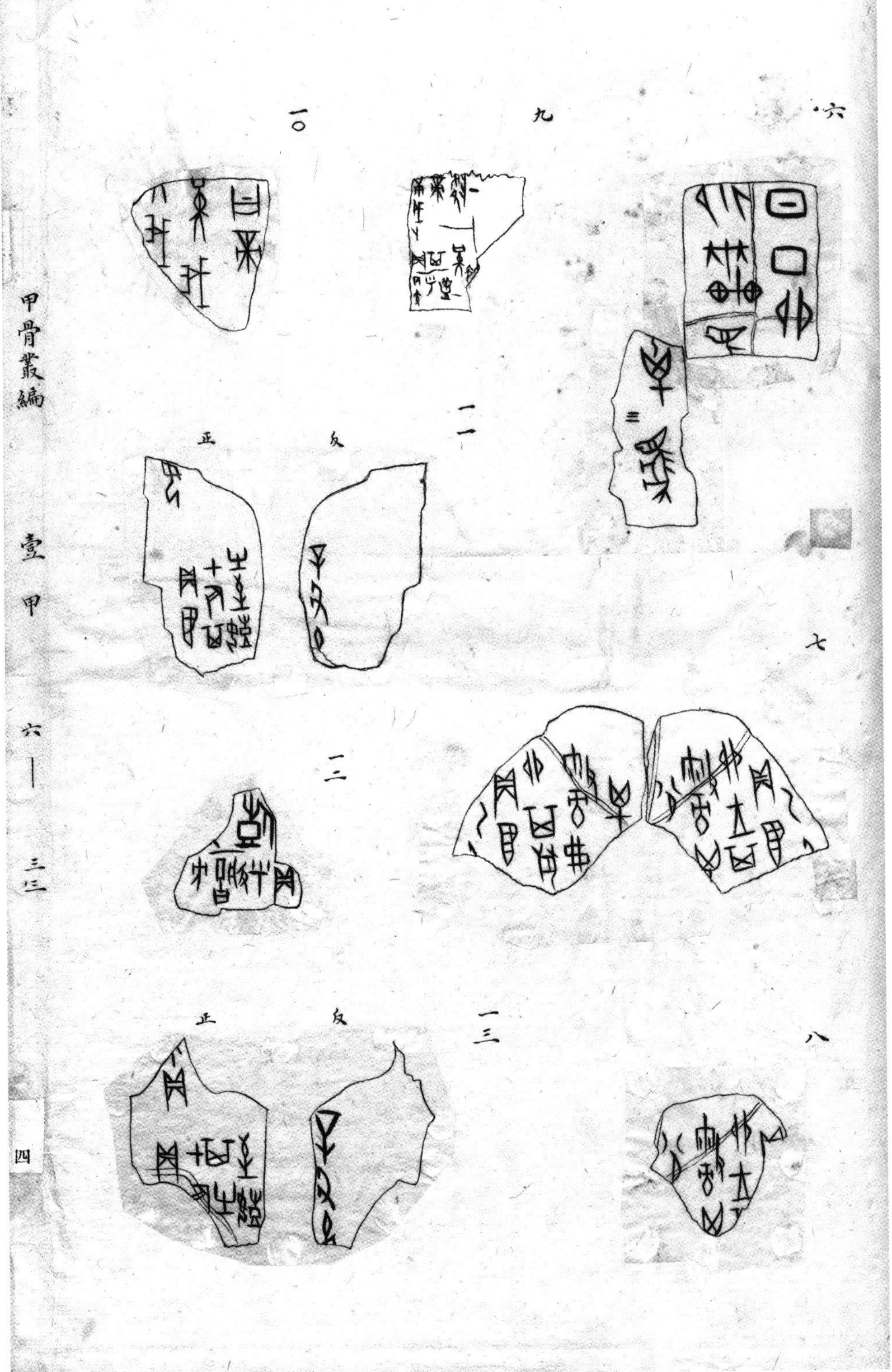
六
七
八
九
一〇
一一
正
反
一二
一三
正
反
甲骨叢編
壹 甲
六——三三
四

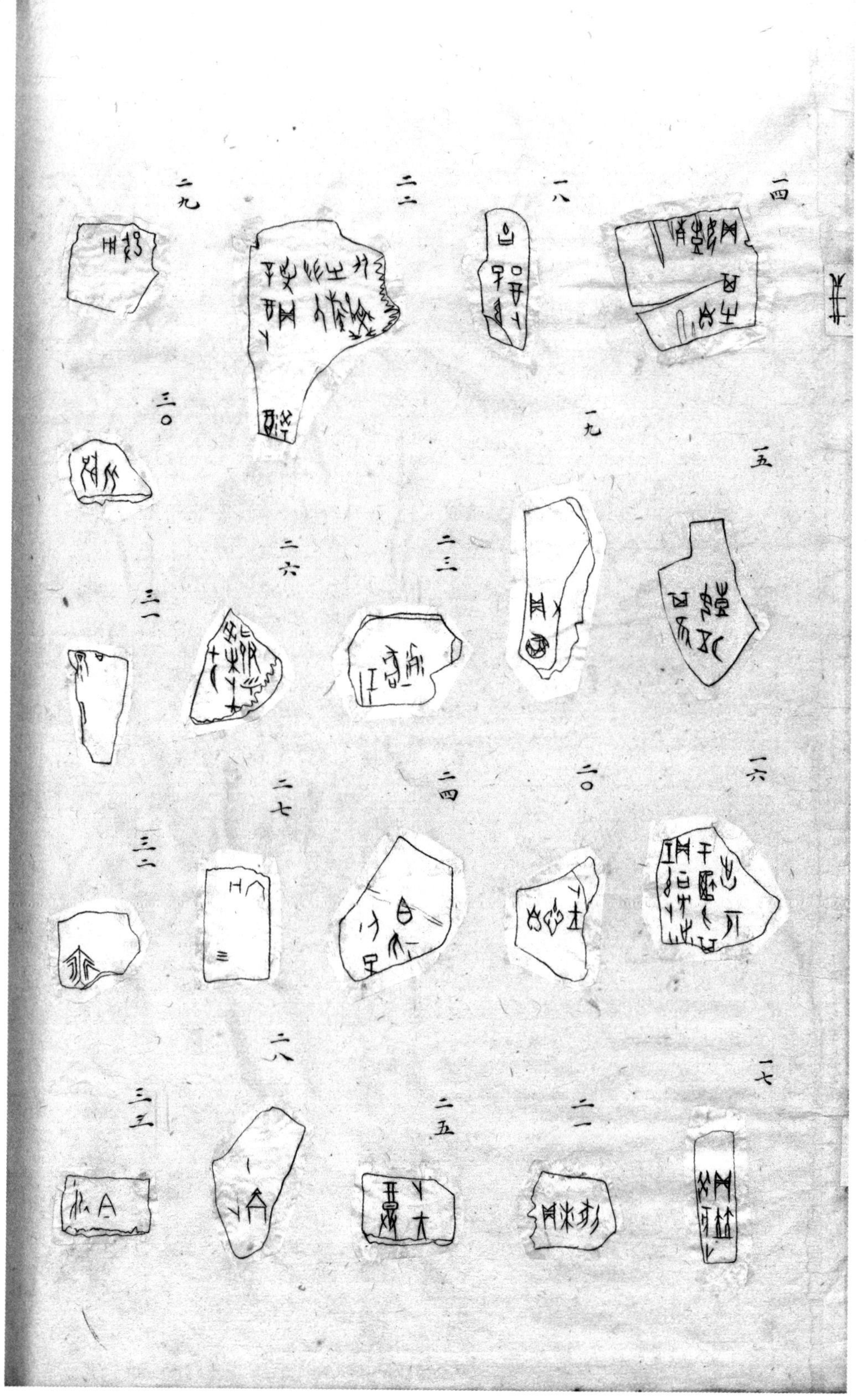
一四
一五
一六
一七
一八
一九
二〇
二一
二二
二三
二四
二五
二六
二七
二八
二九
三〇
三一
三二
三三

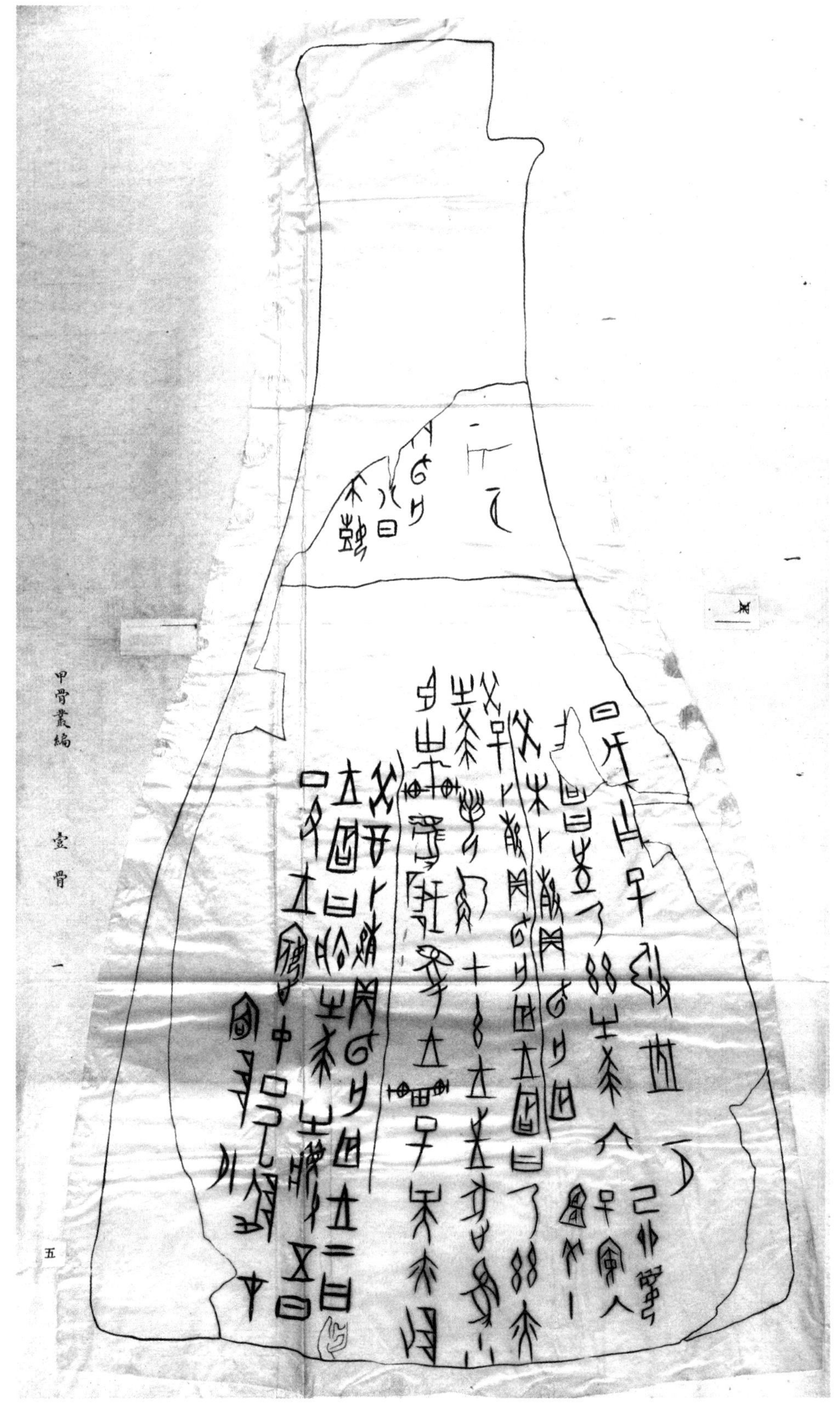
甲骨叢編　壹骨　一
五

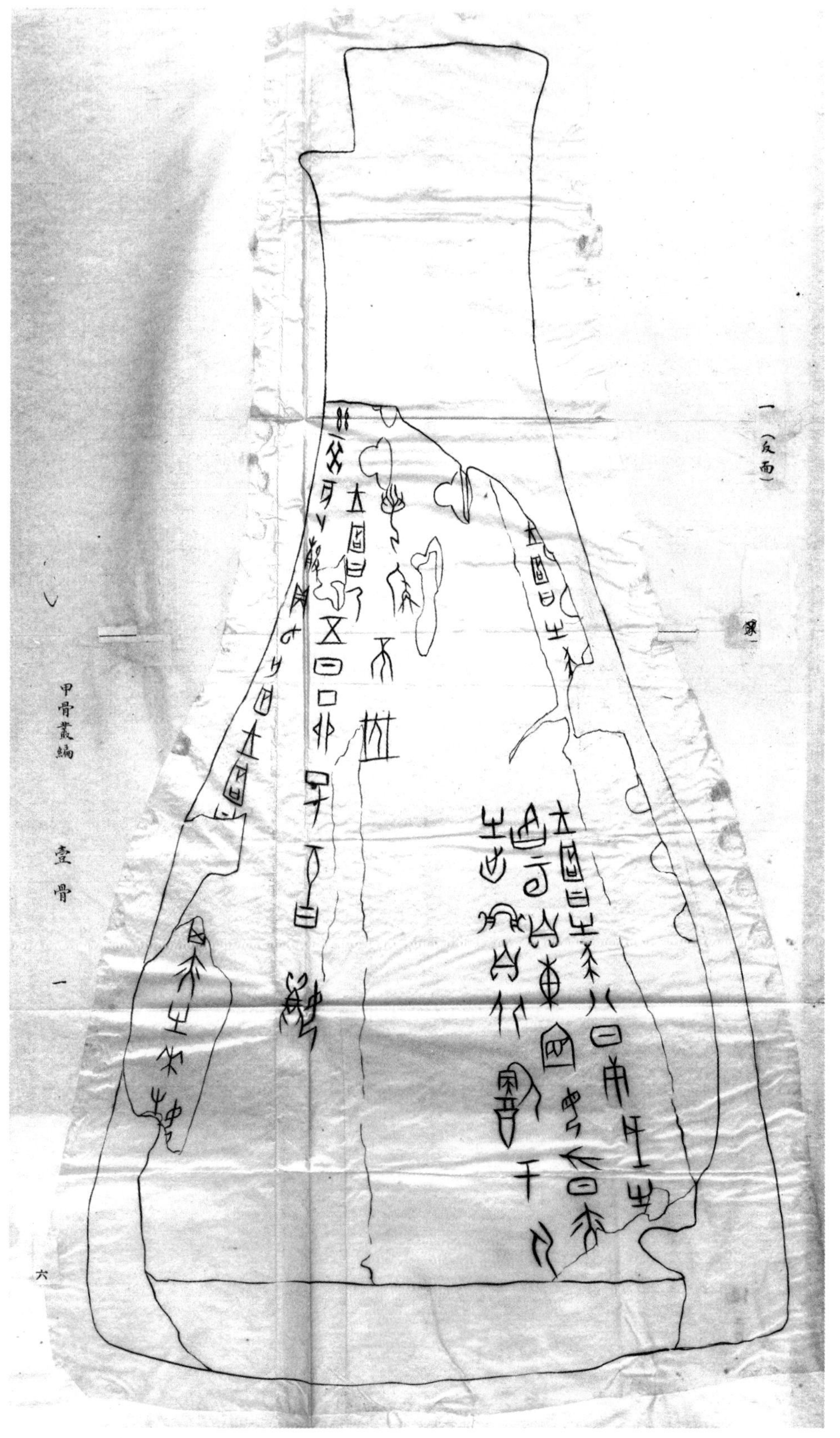
一（反面）
甲骨叢編
壹骨
一
六

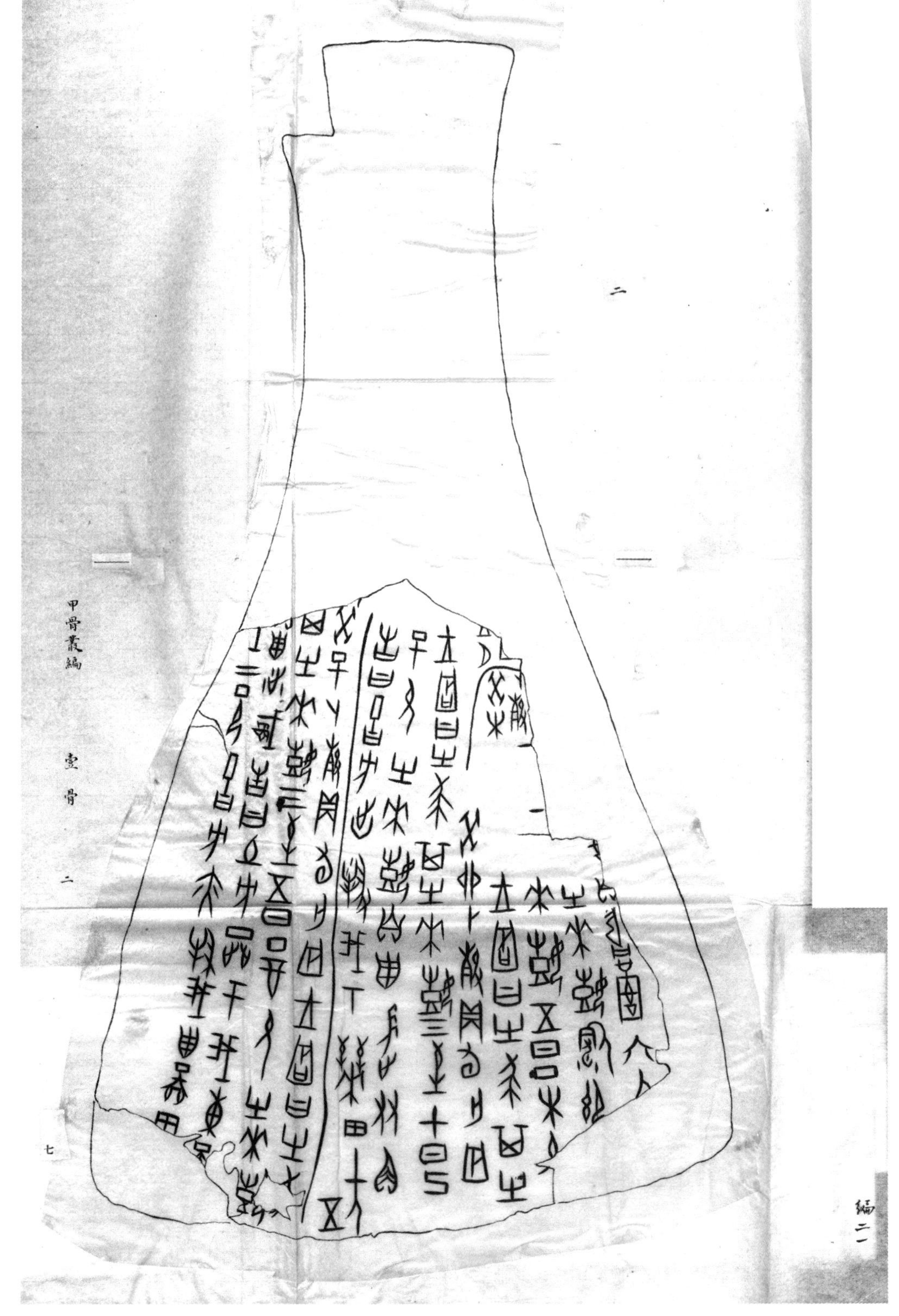
甲骨叢編　壹骨　二
編二一

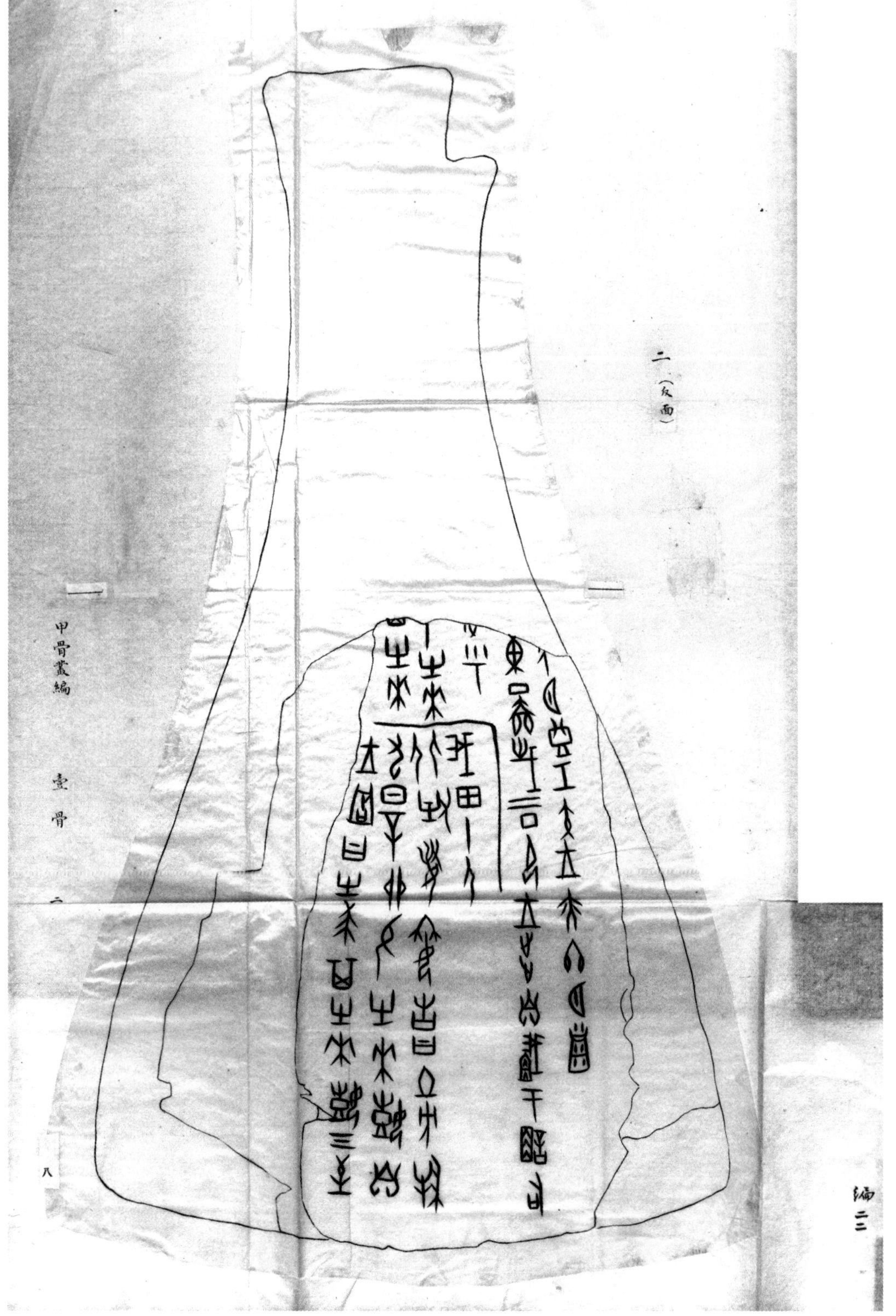

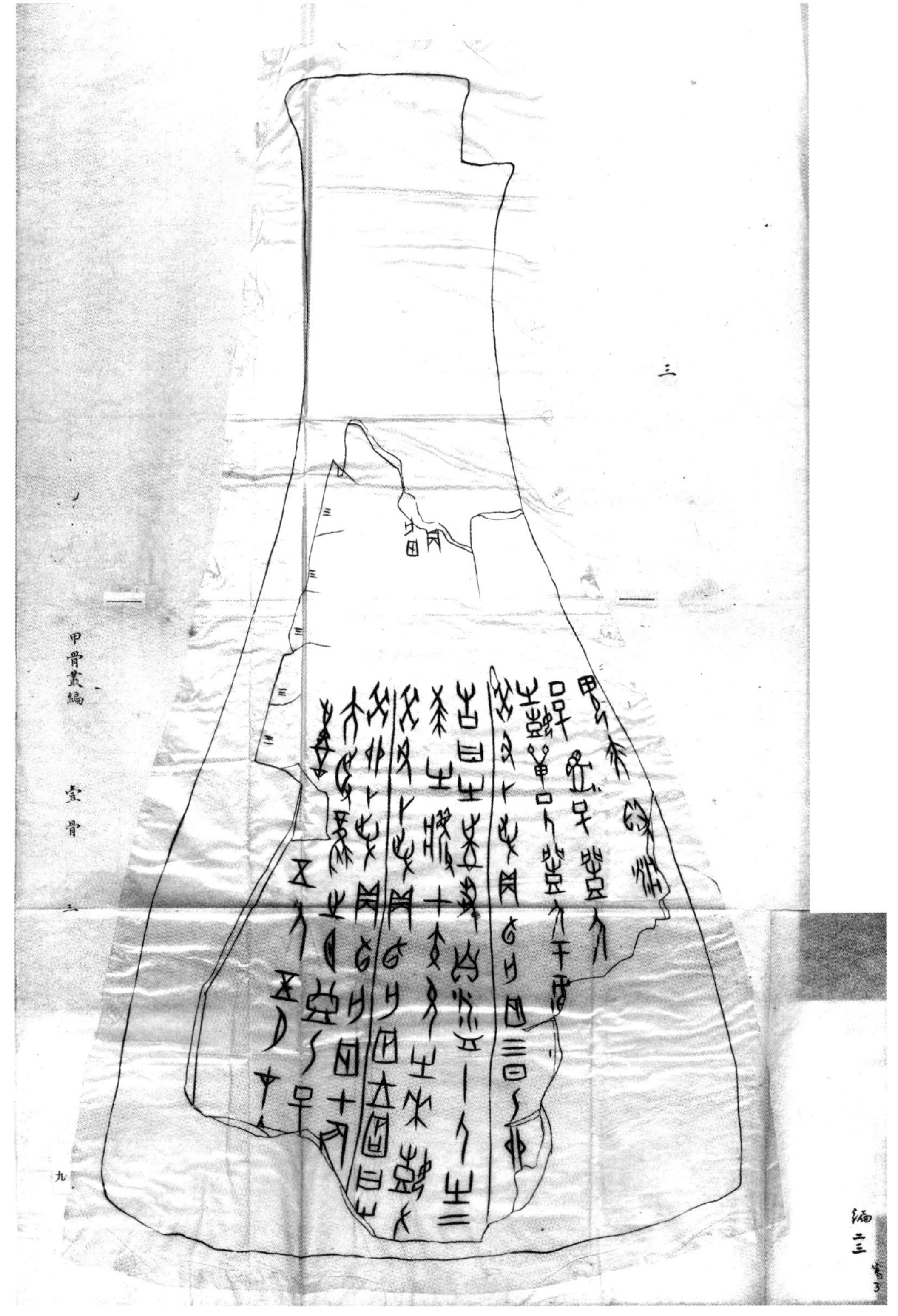
甲骨叢編
壹骨

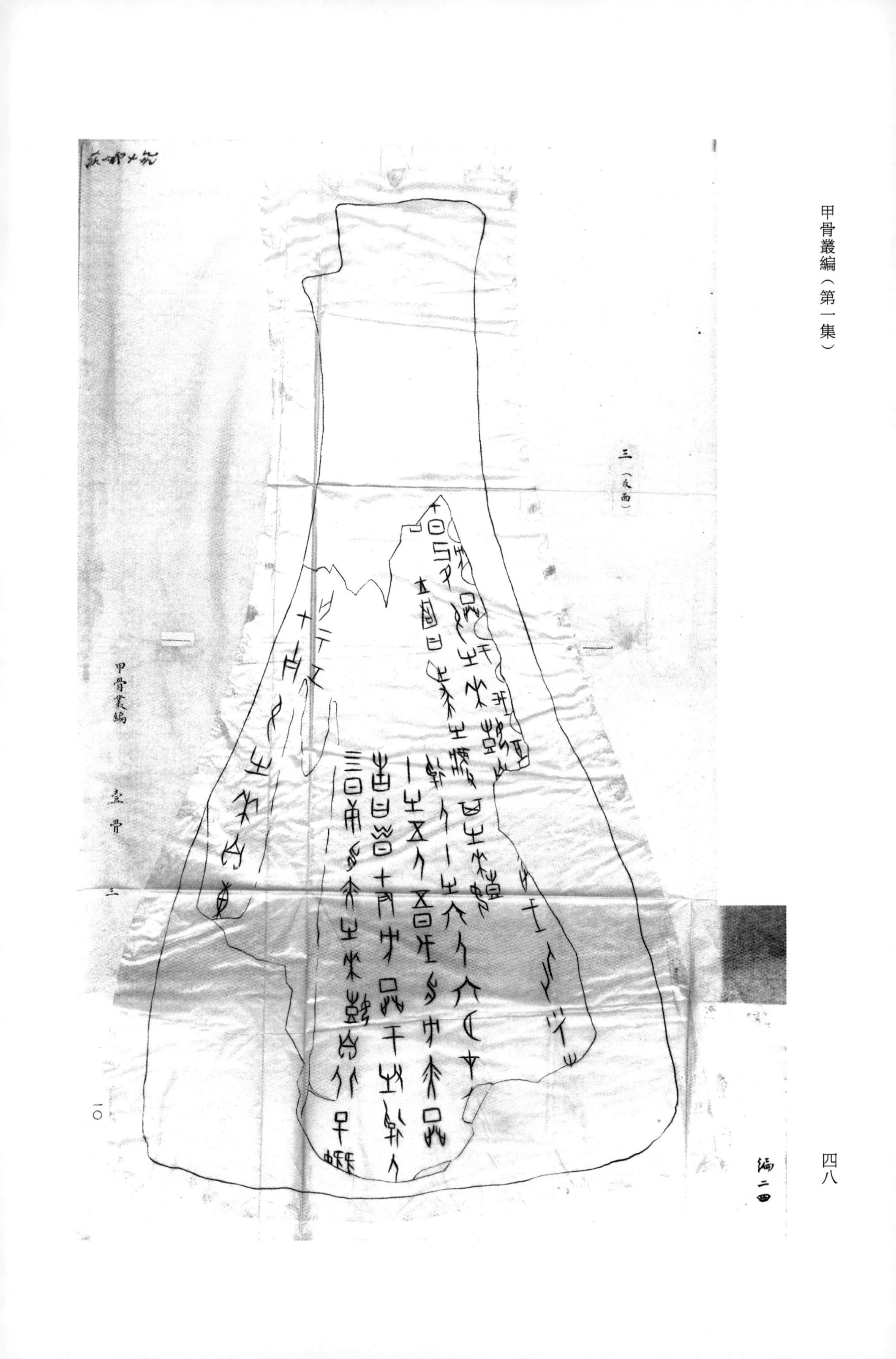

三（反面）

甲骨叢編 壹 骨 三

一〇

編二四

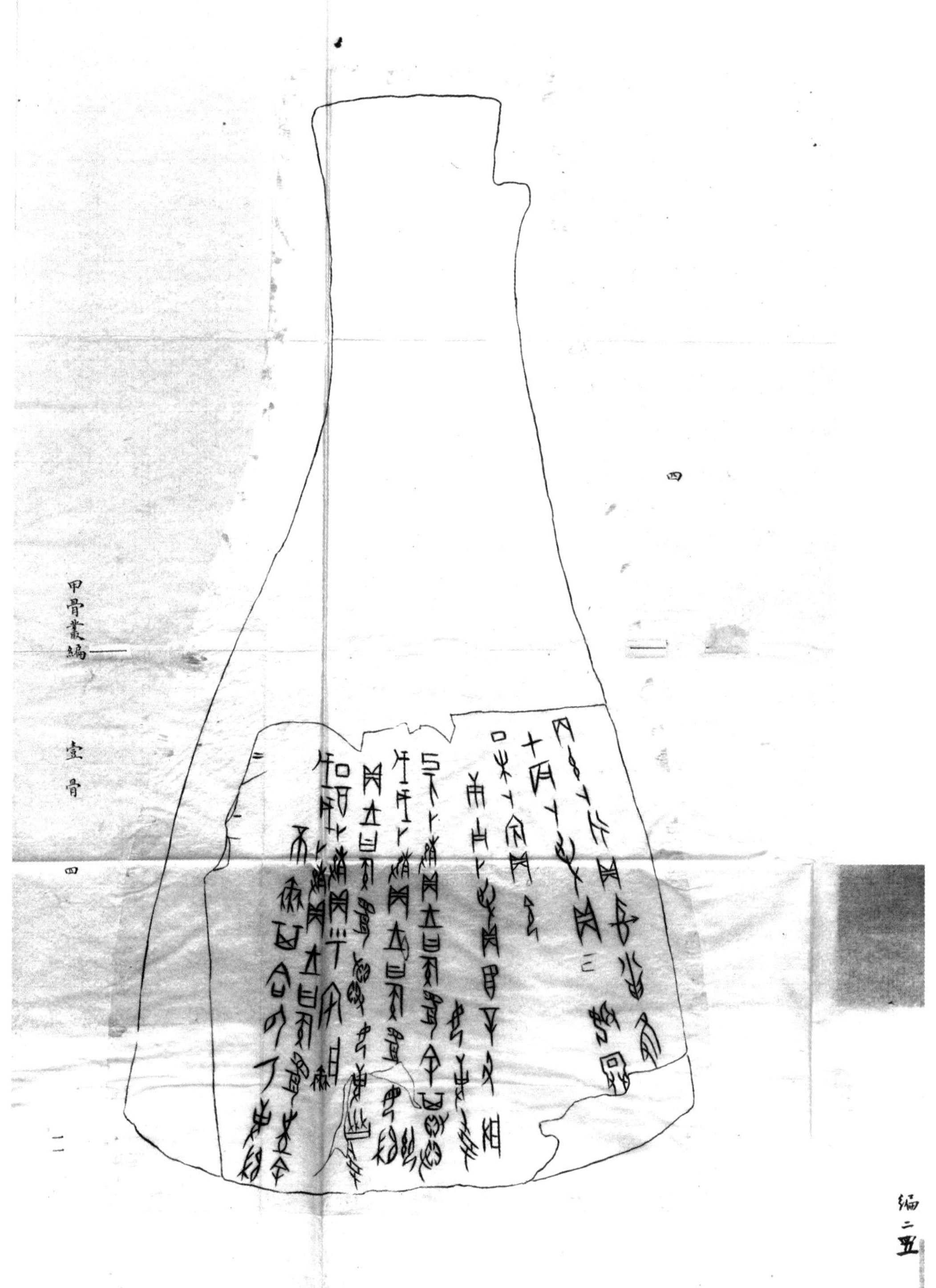
甲骨叢編一
壹骨
四
二
四
二

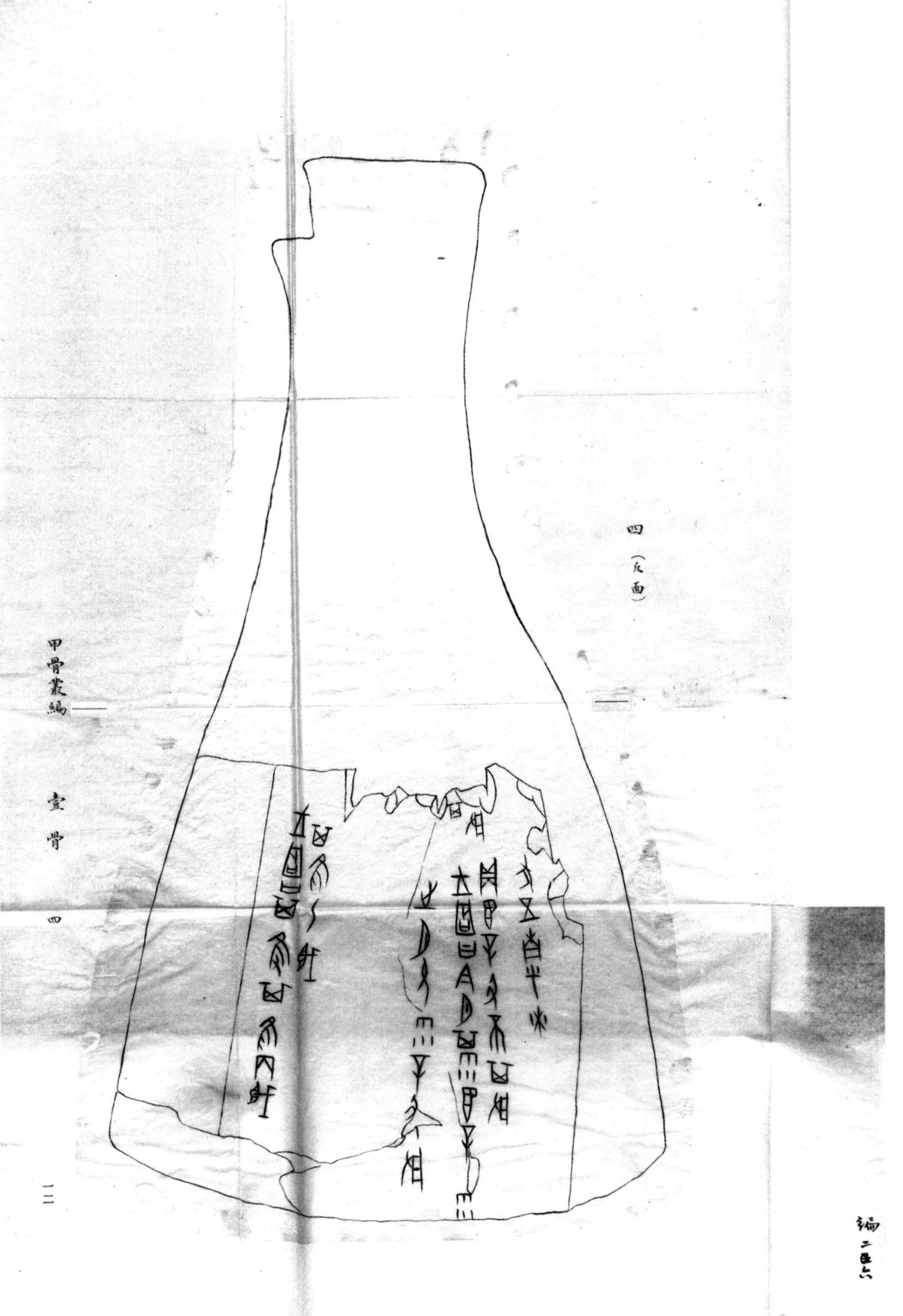
四
（反面）
甲骨叢編
壹骨
四
二

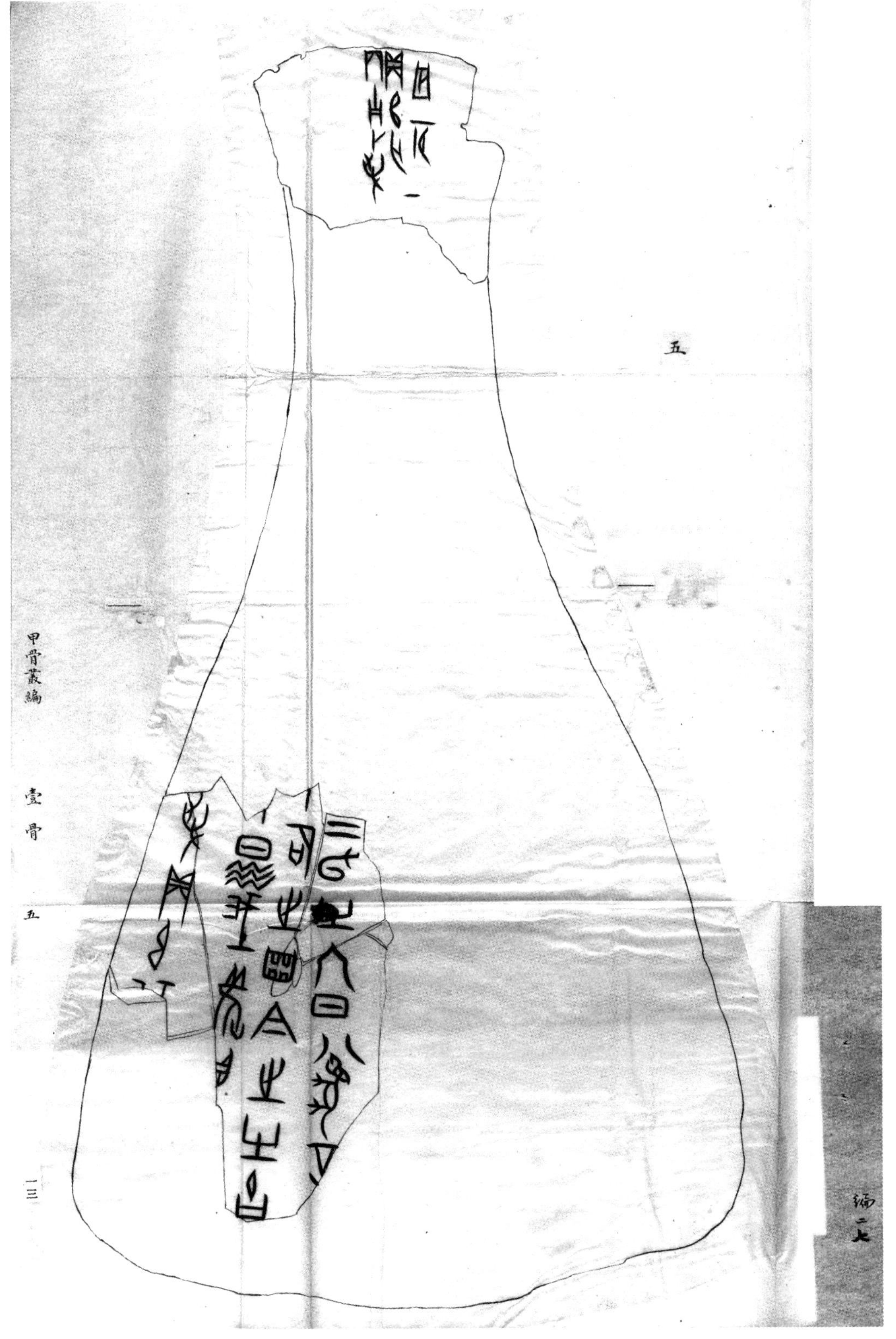
甲骨叢編
壹骨
五
一三
五
編二七

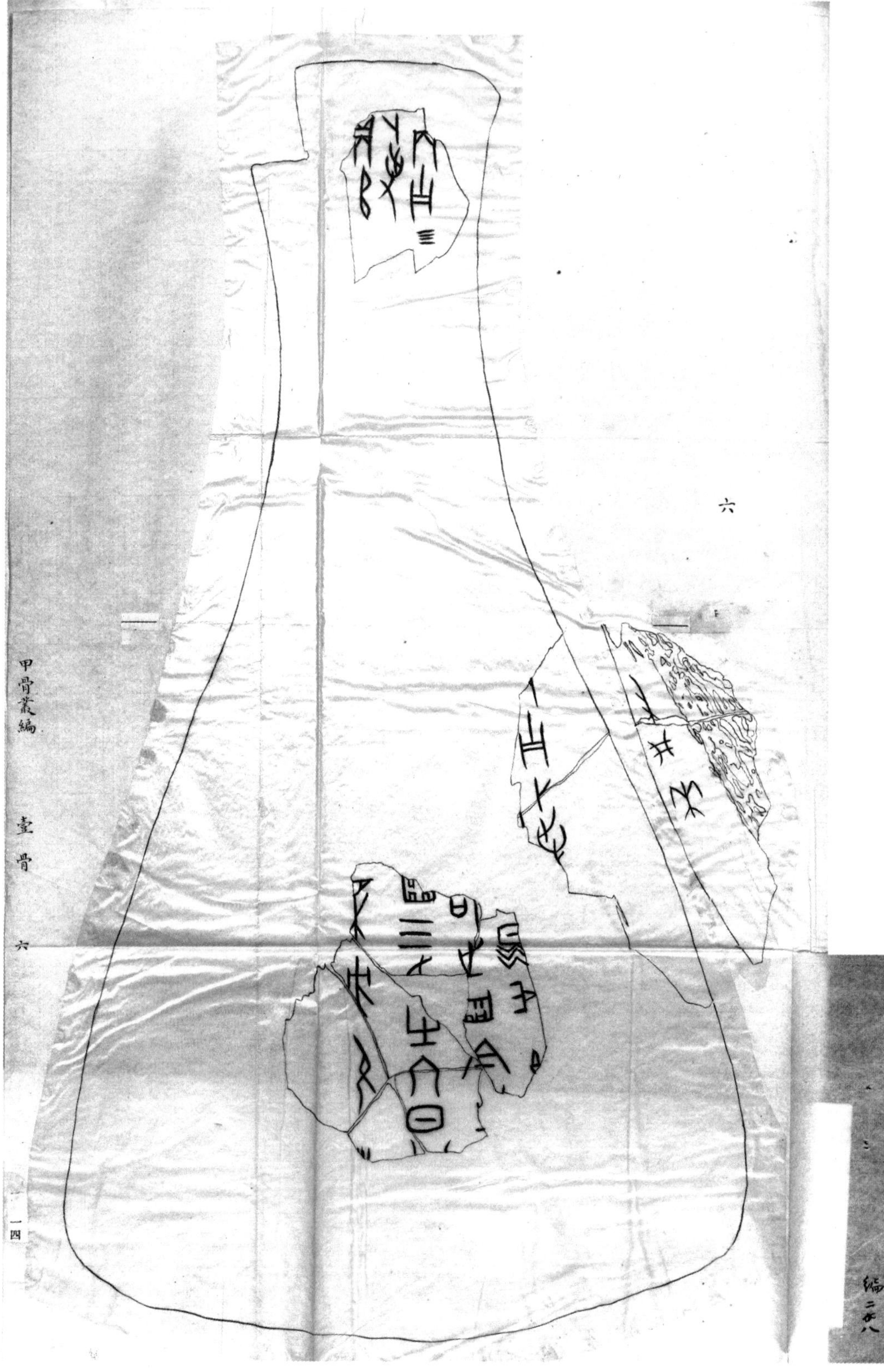
甲骨叢編
壹骨
六
一四
六
編二九八

甲骨叢編 壹骨 七

七

一五

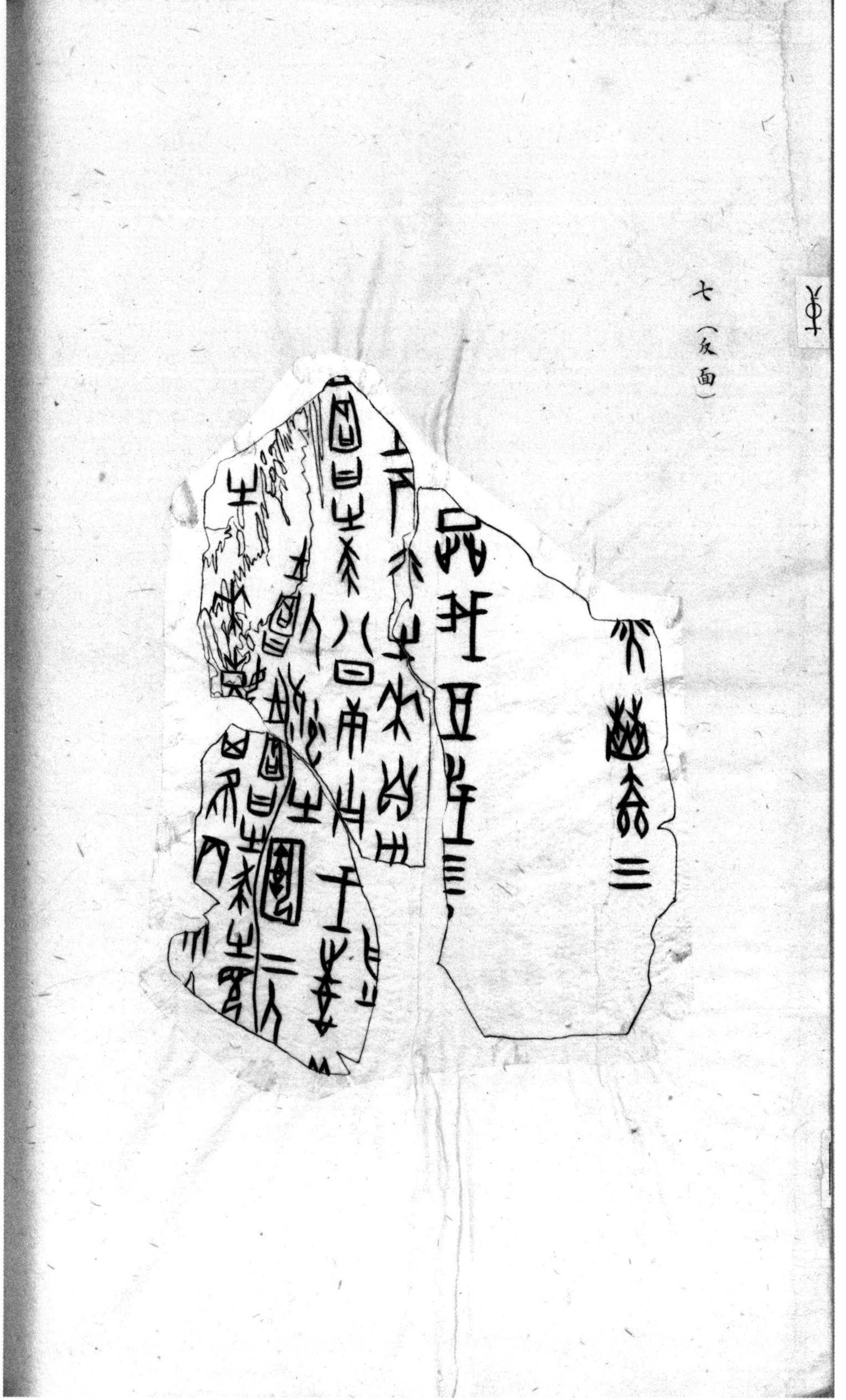

七（反面）

甲骨叢編　壹骨　八

八

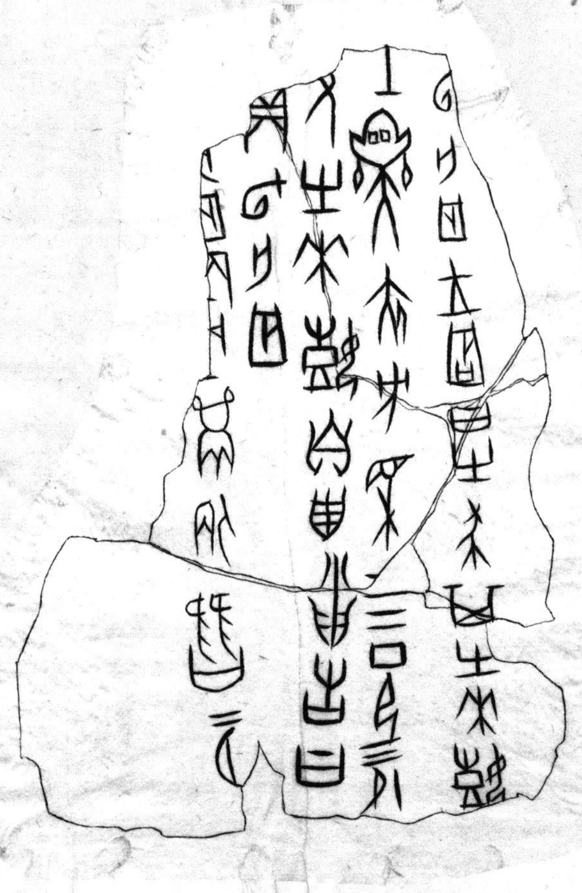

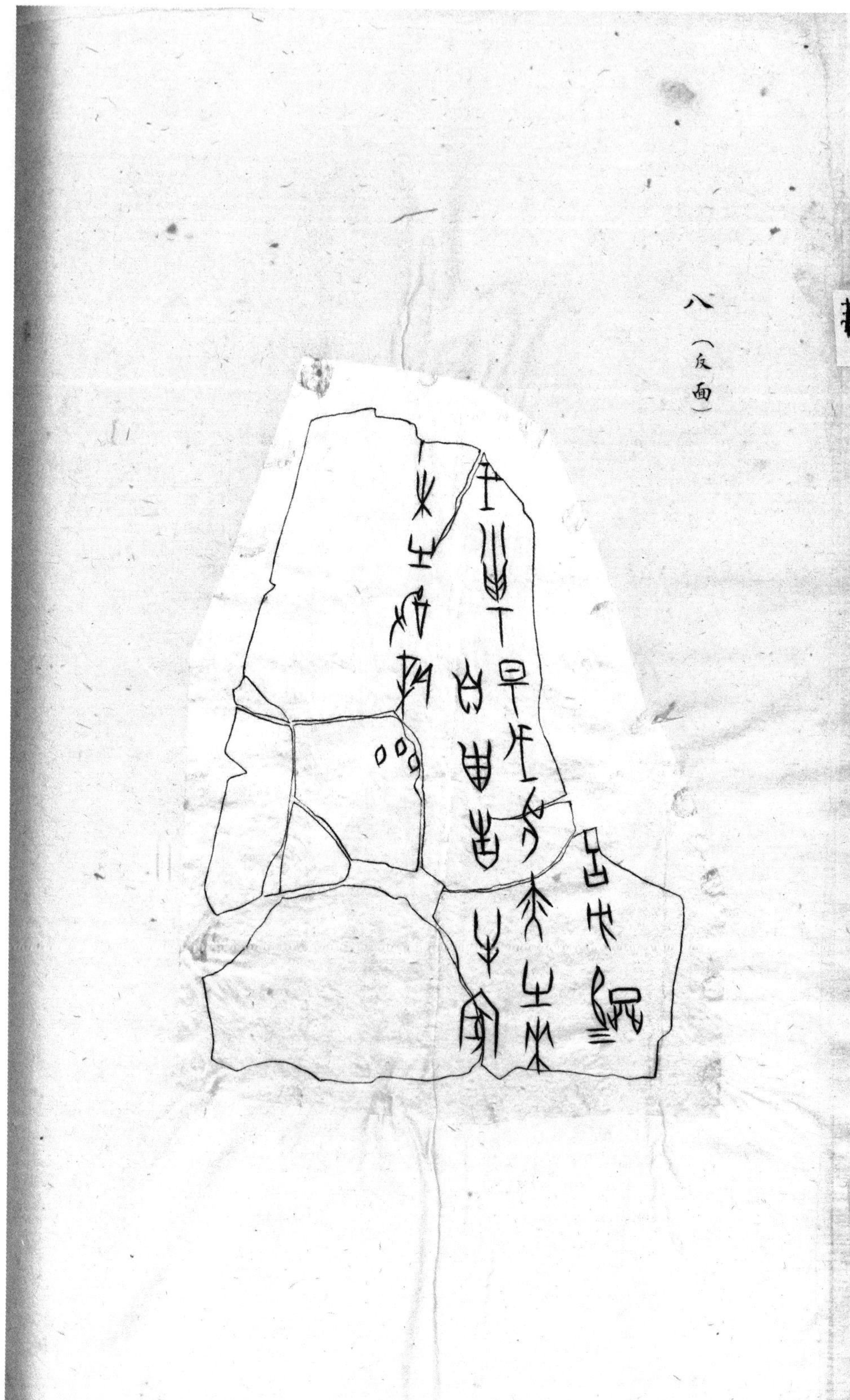
八（反面）

九

（反面）

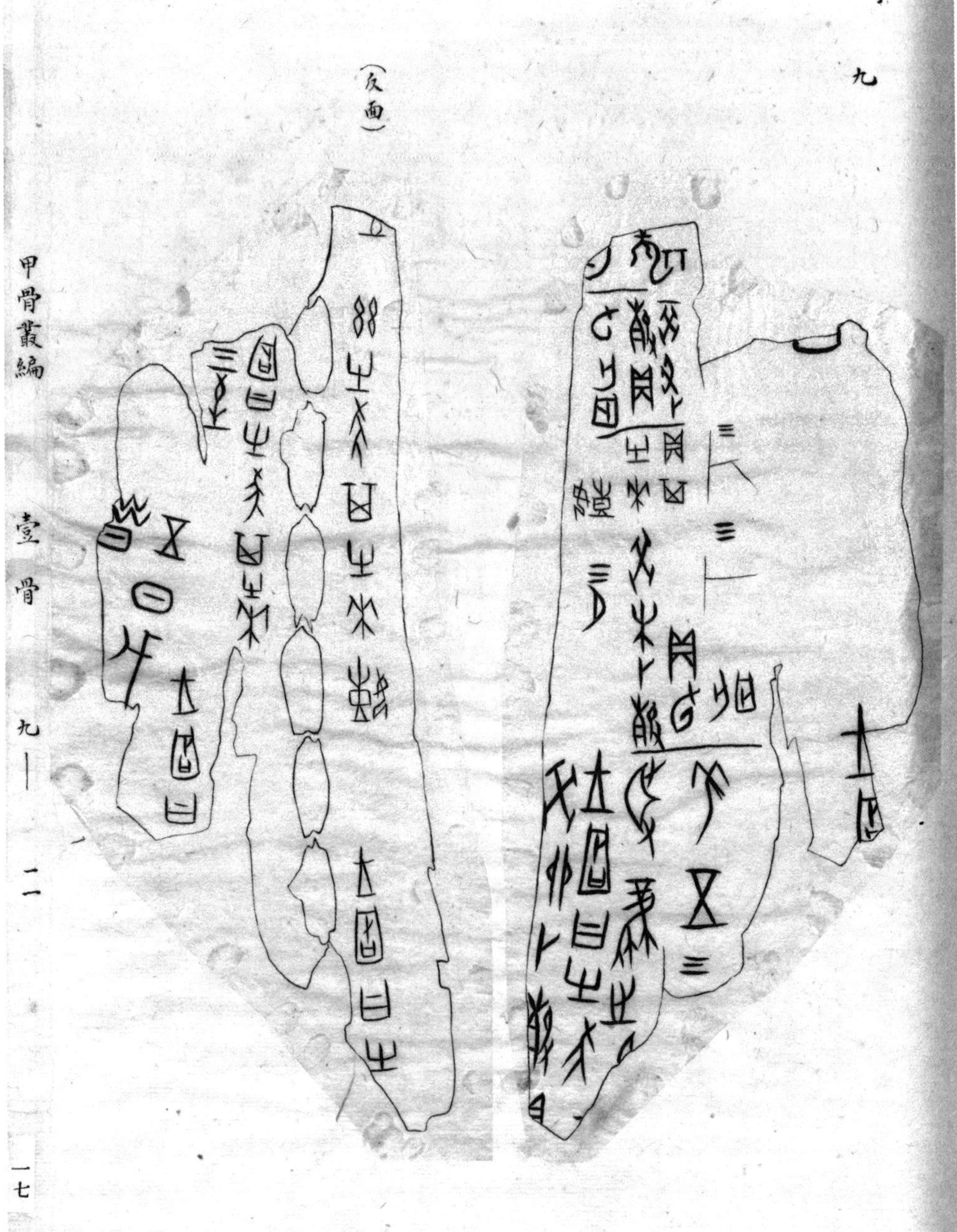

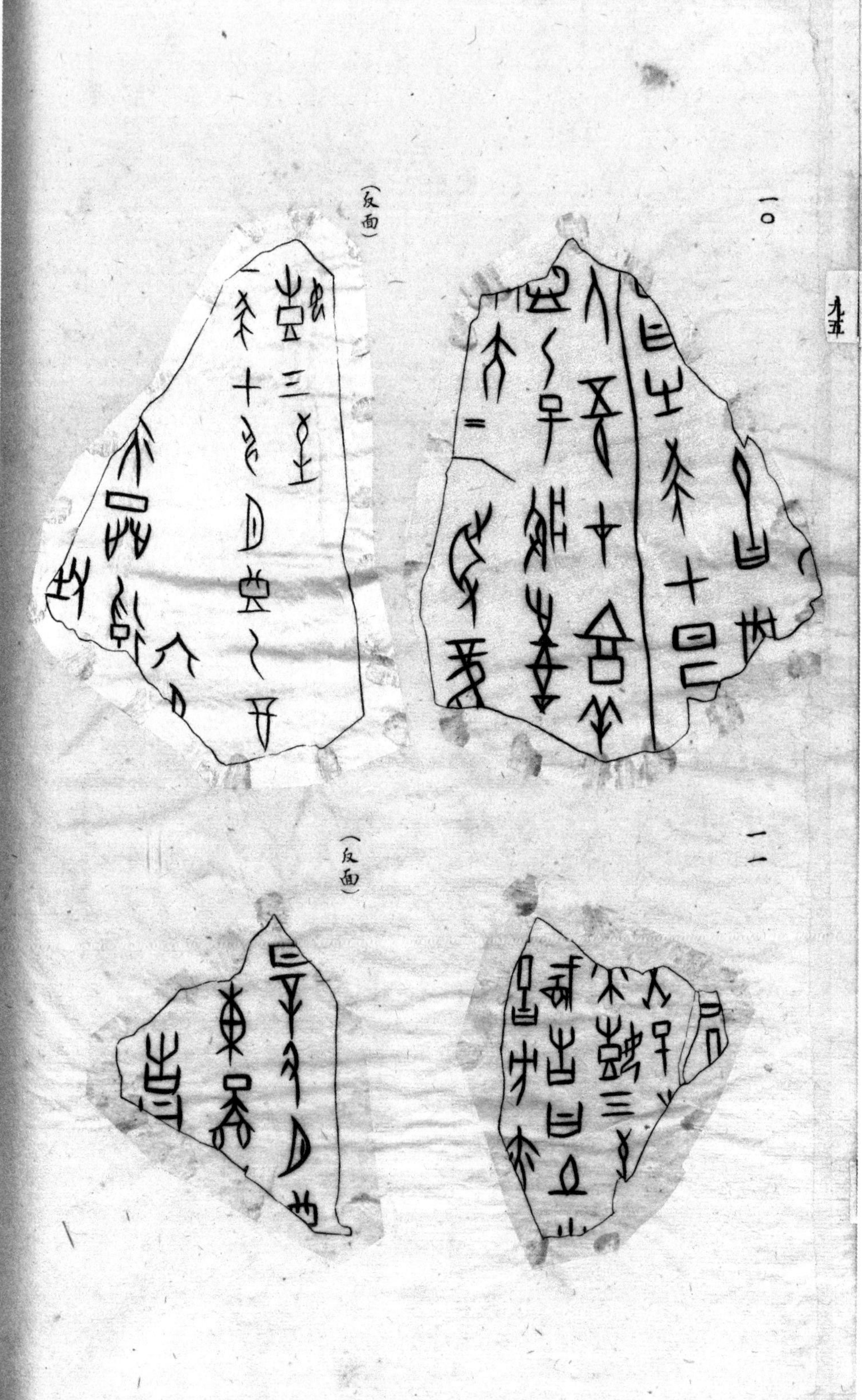
一〇
（反面）
一一
（反面）

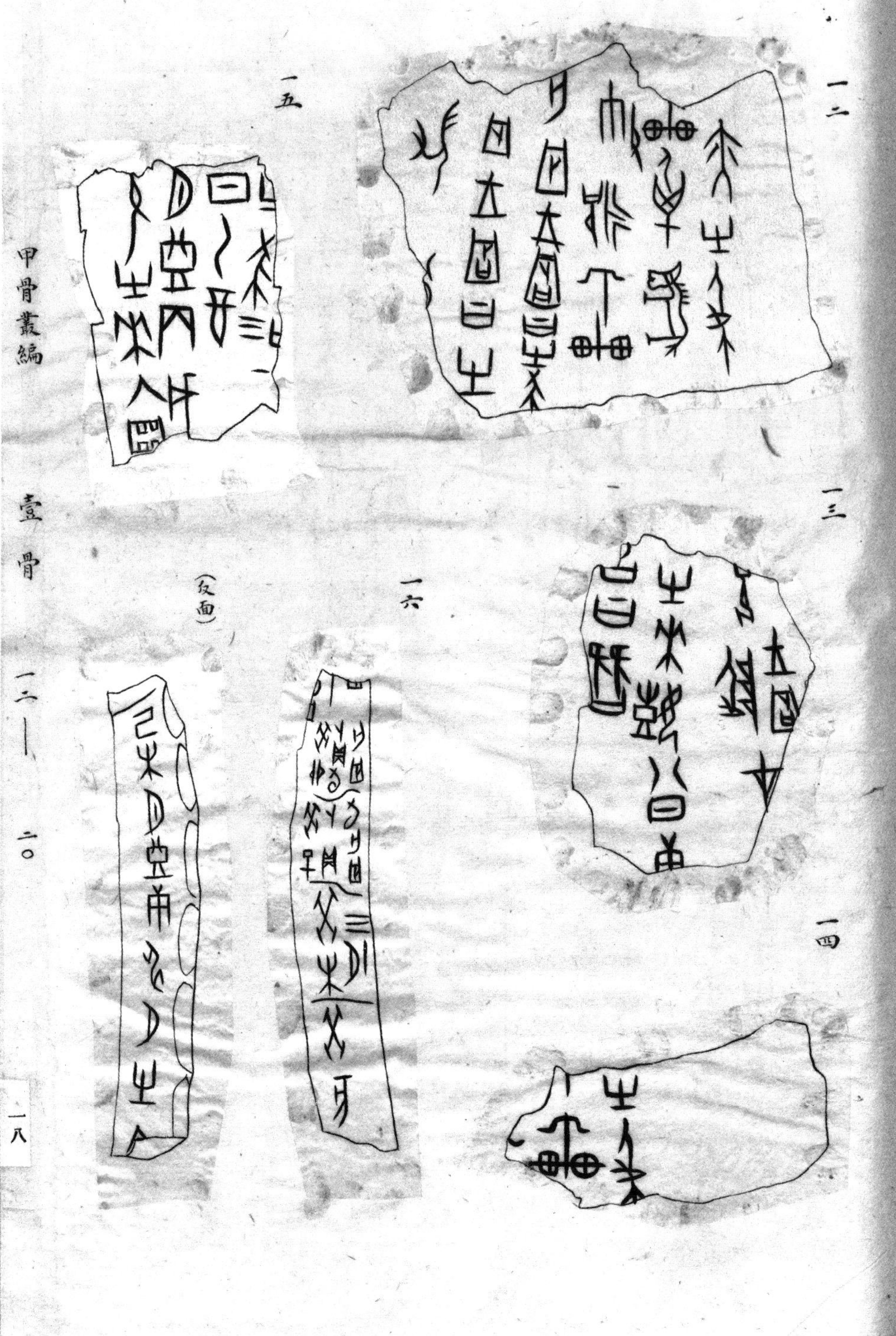

甲骨叢編　壹骨　一二—二〇
一二
一三
一四
一五
一六
（反面）
一八

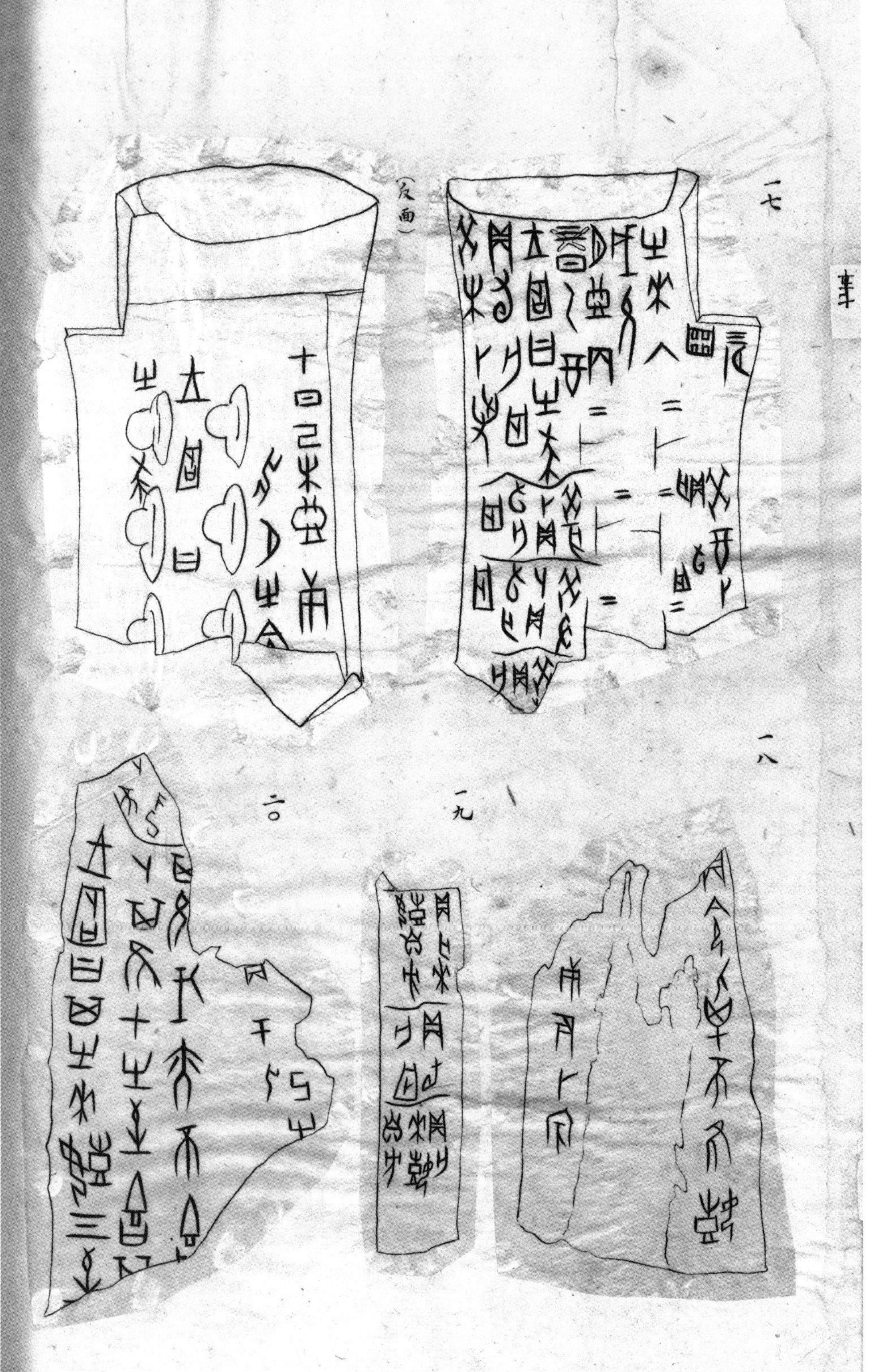
一七
（反面）
一八
一九
二〇

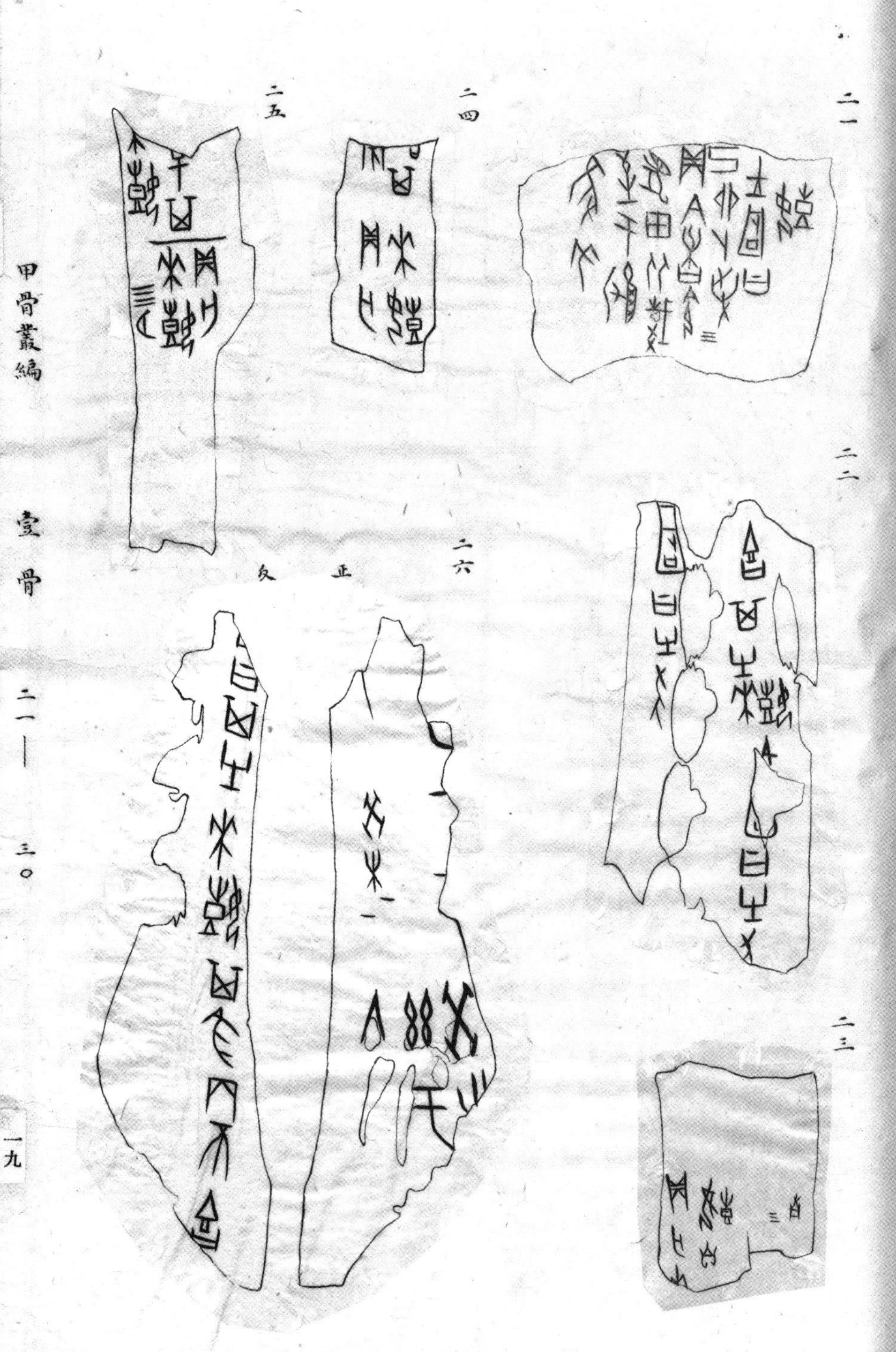
二一
二二
二三
二四
二五
二六
正
反
甲骨叢編 壹 骨 二一——三〇
一九

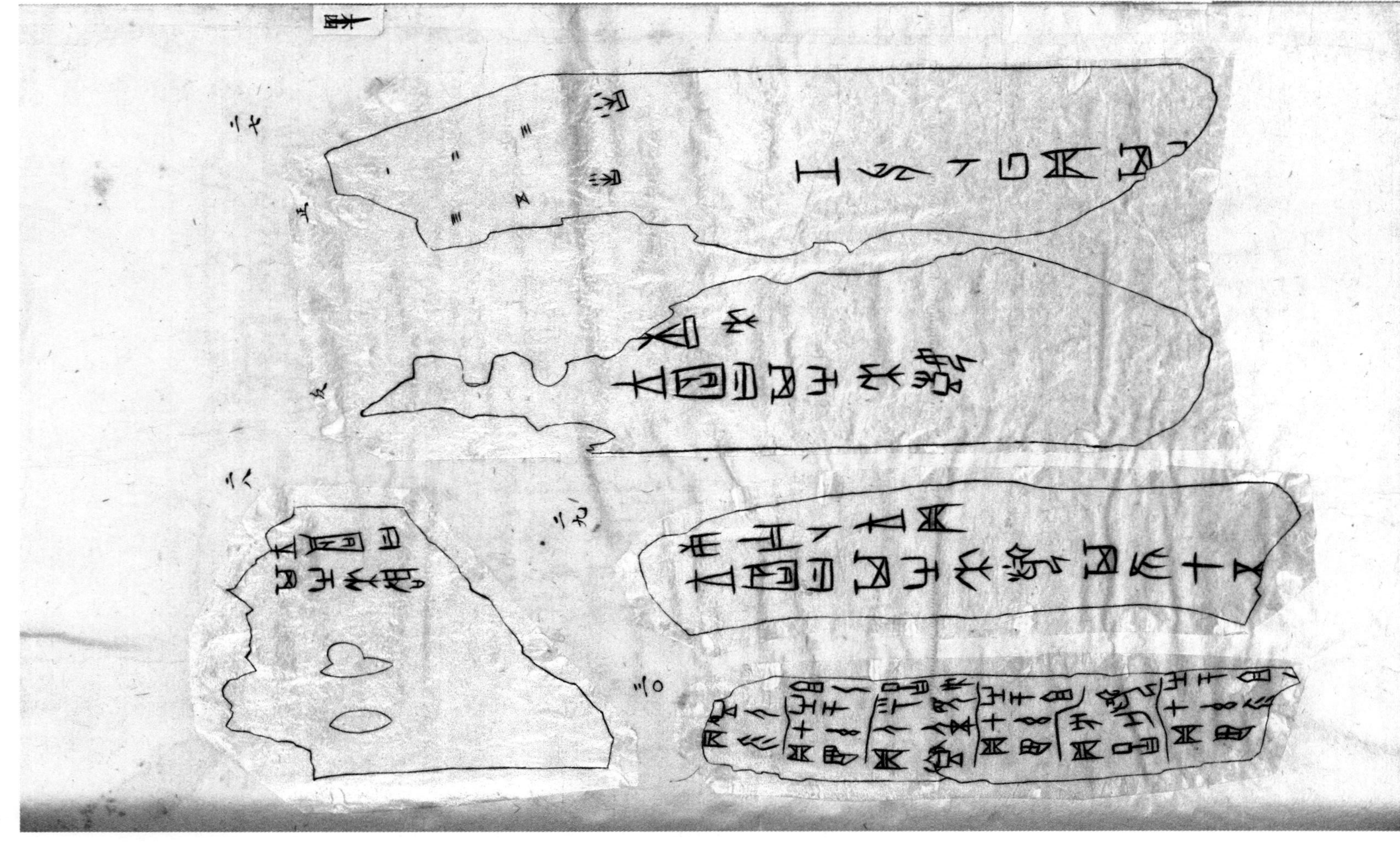

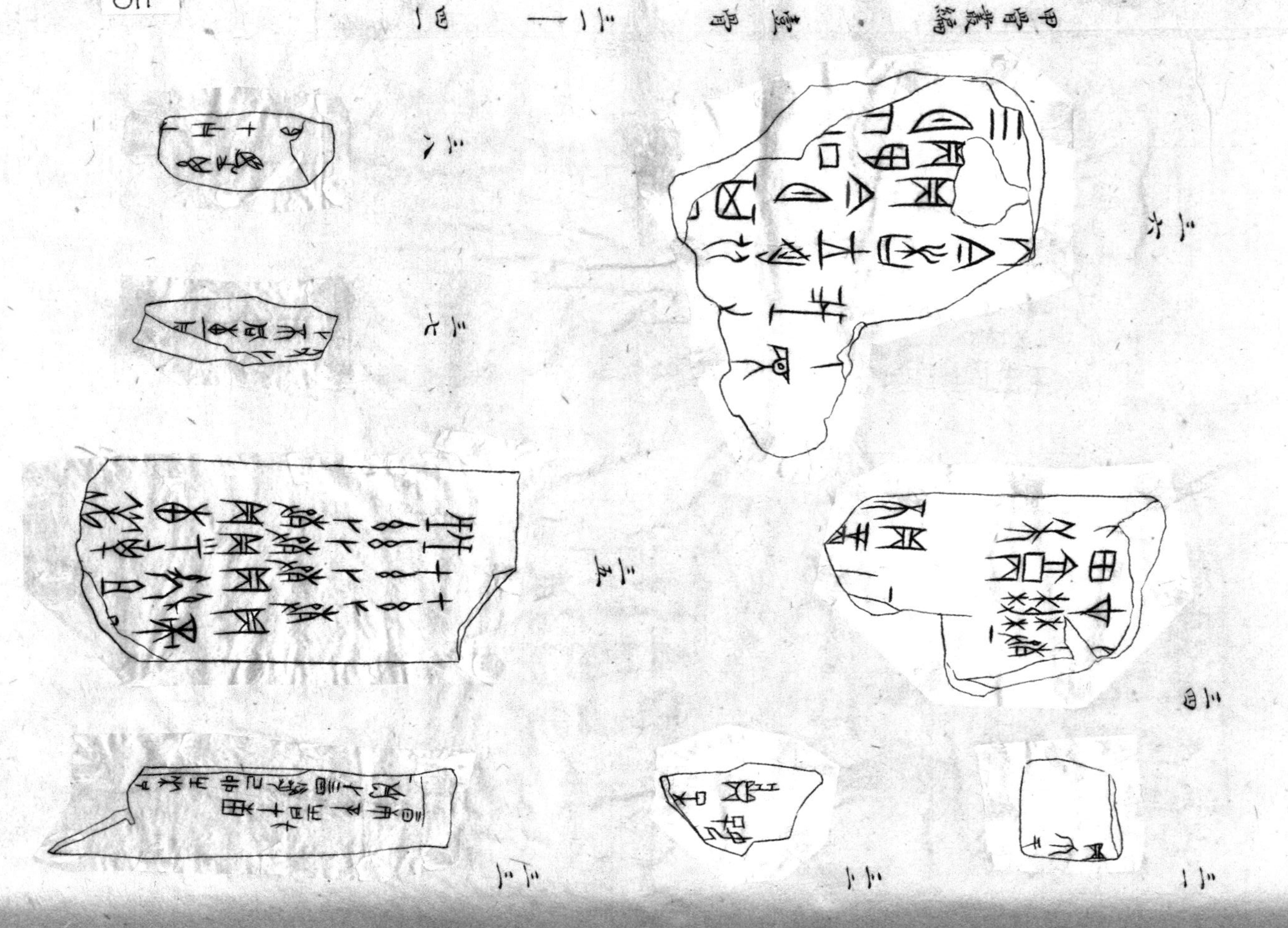

110
甲骨叢編 · 臺骨

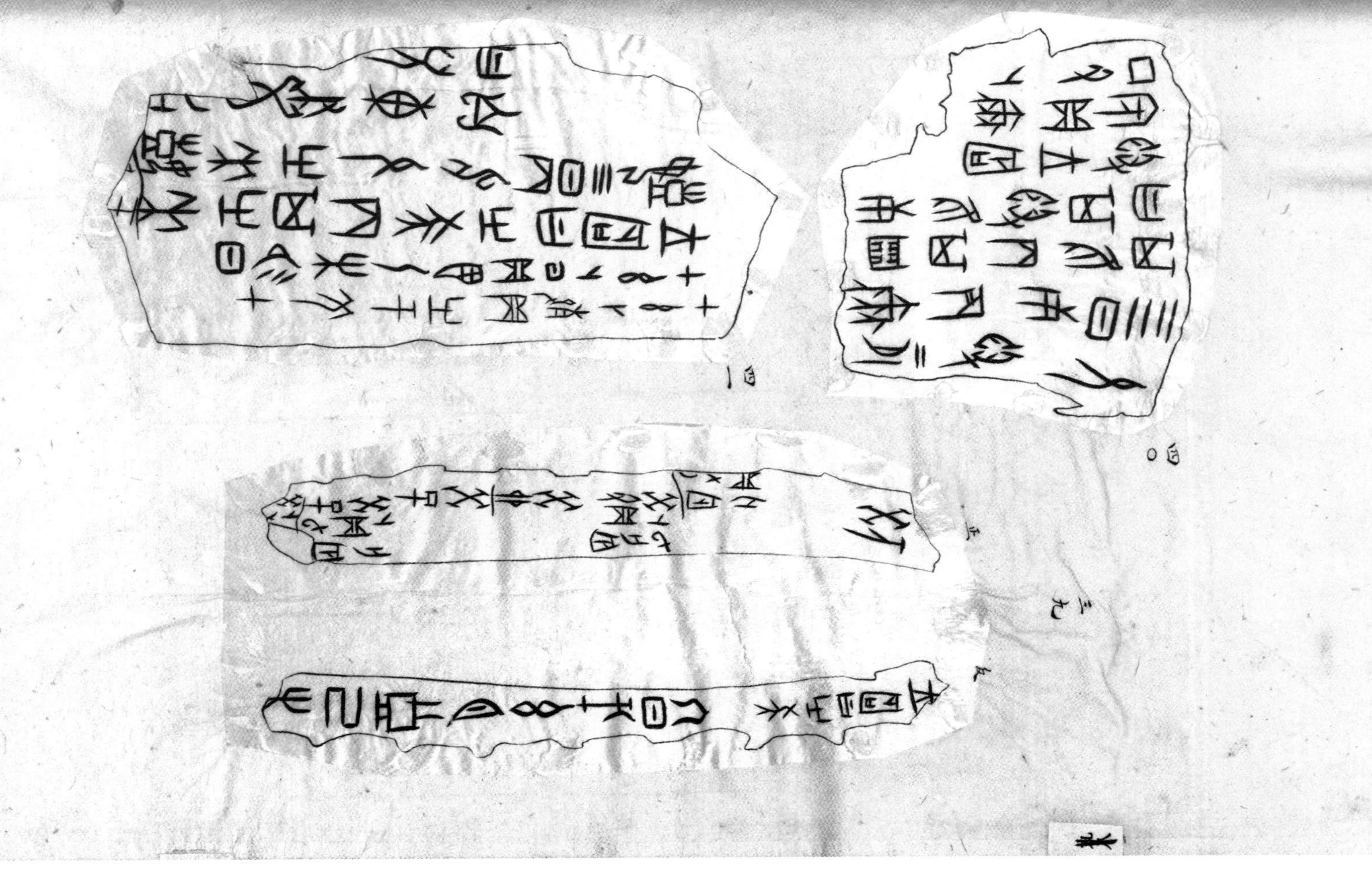

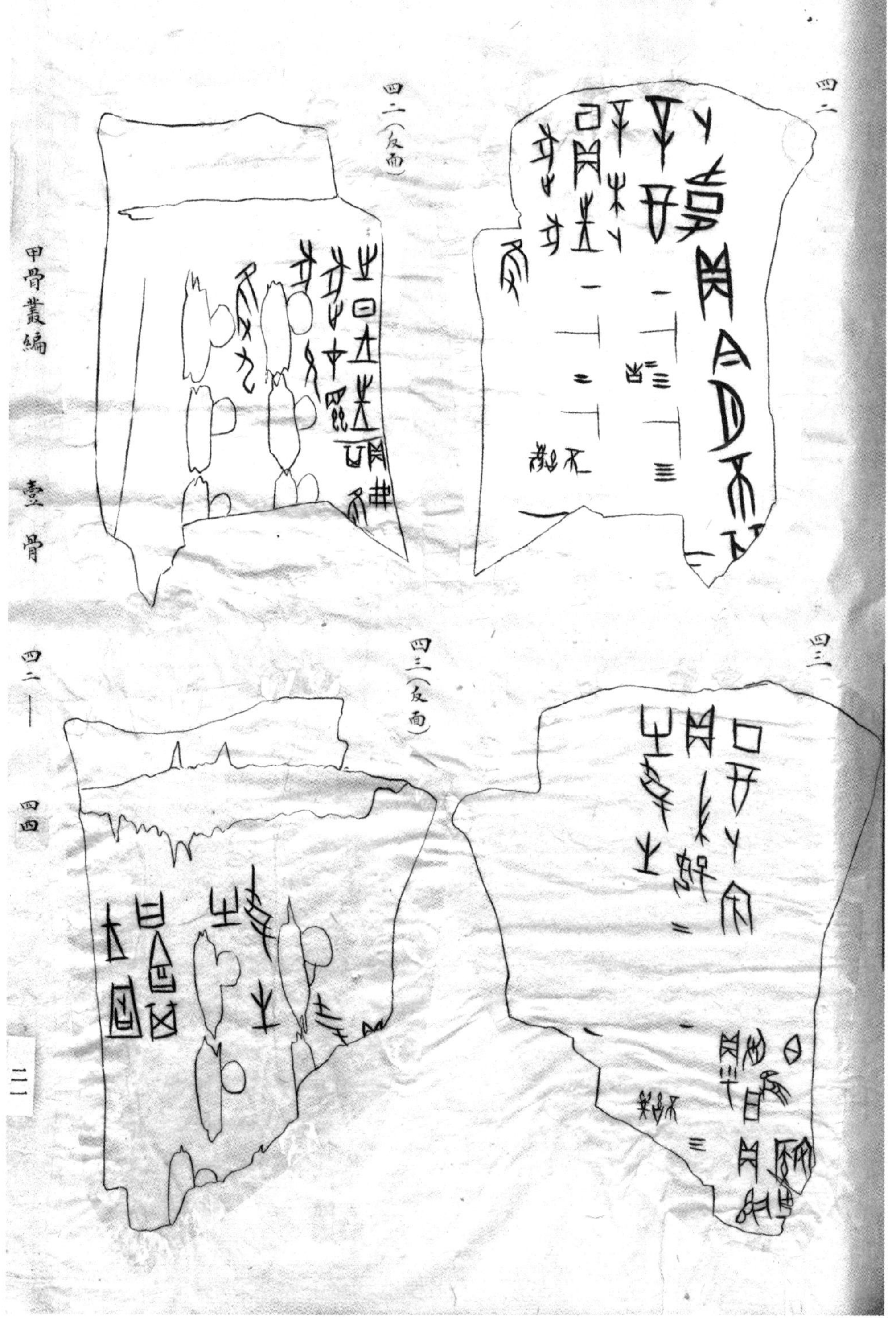

二一

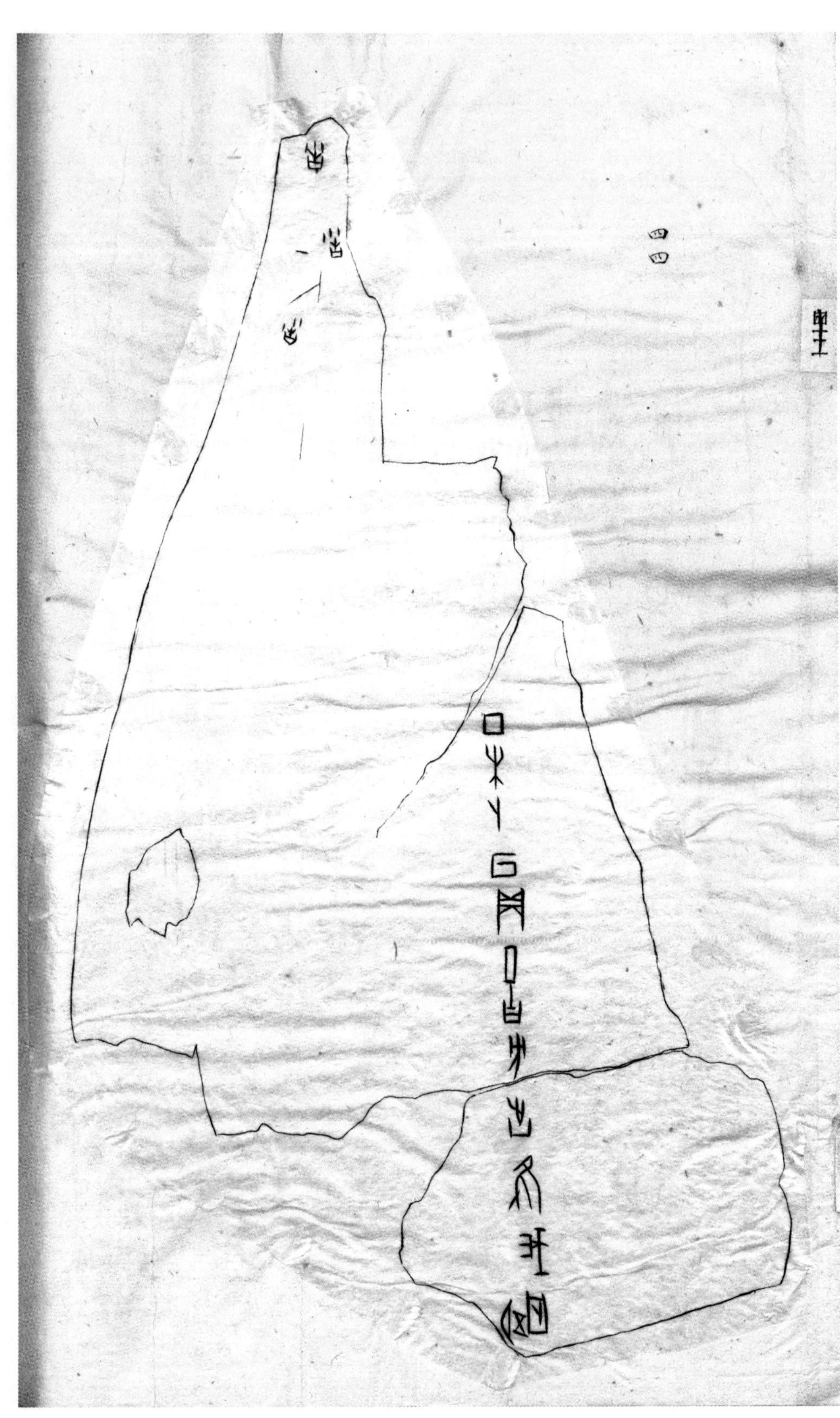

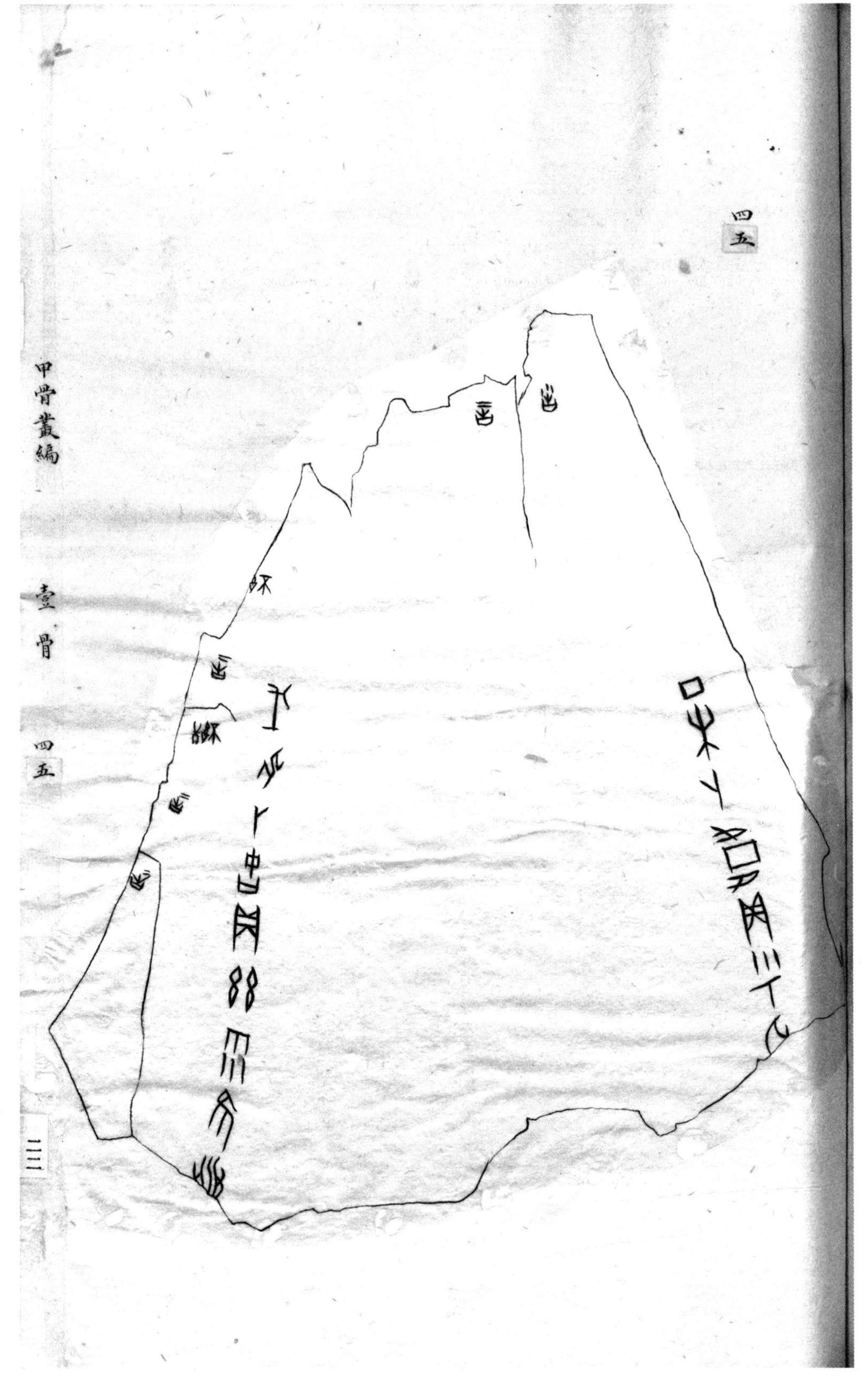

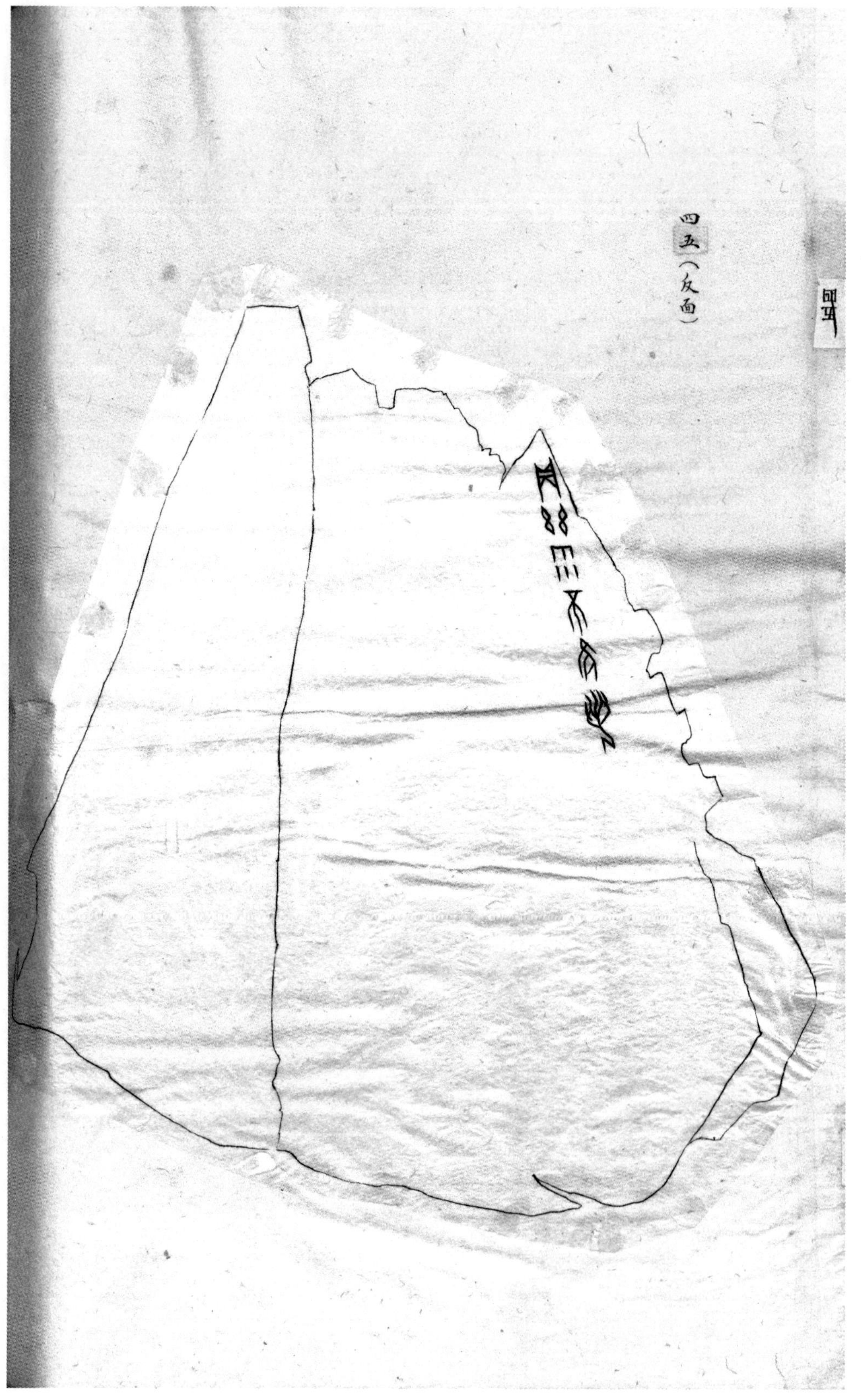
四五（反面）

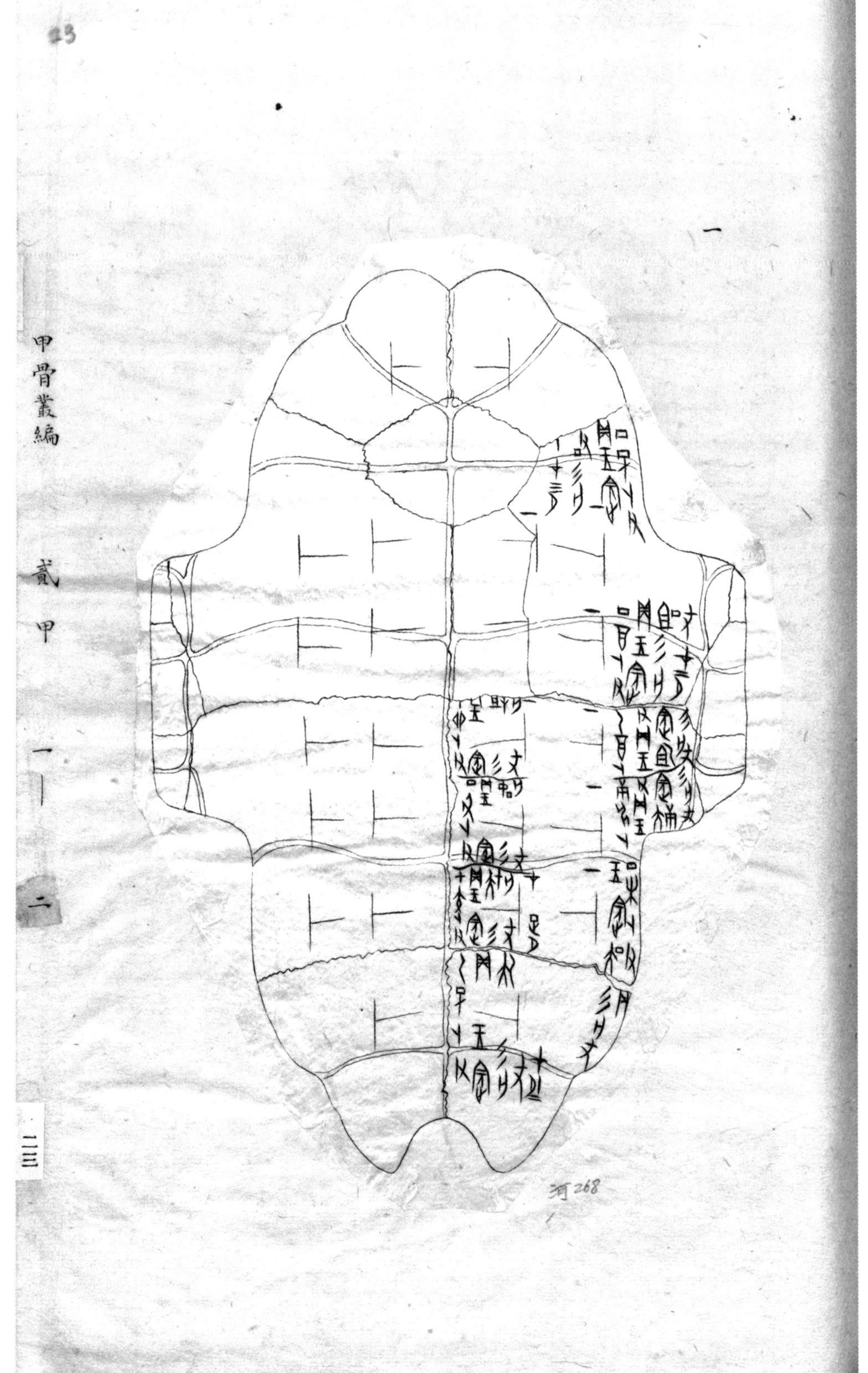
23
甲骨叢編
貳甲
一一二
二三
河268

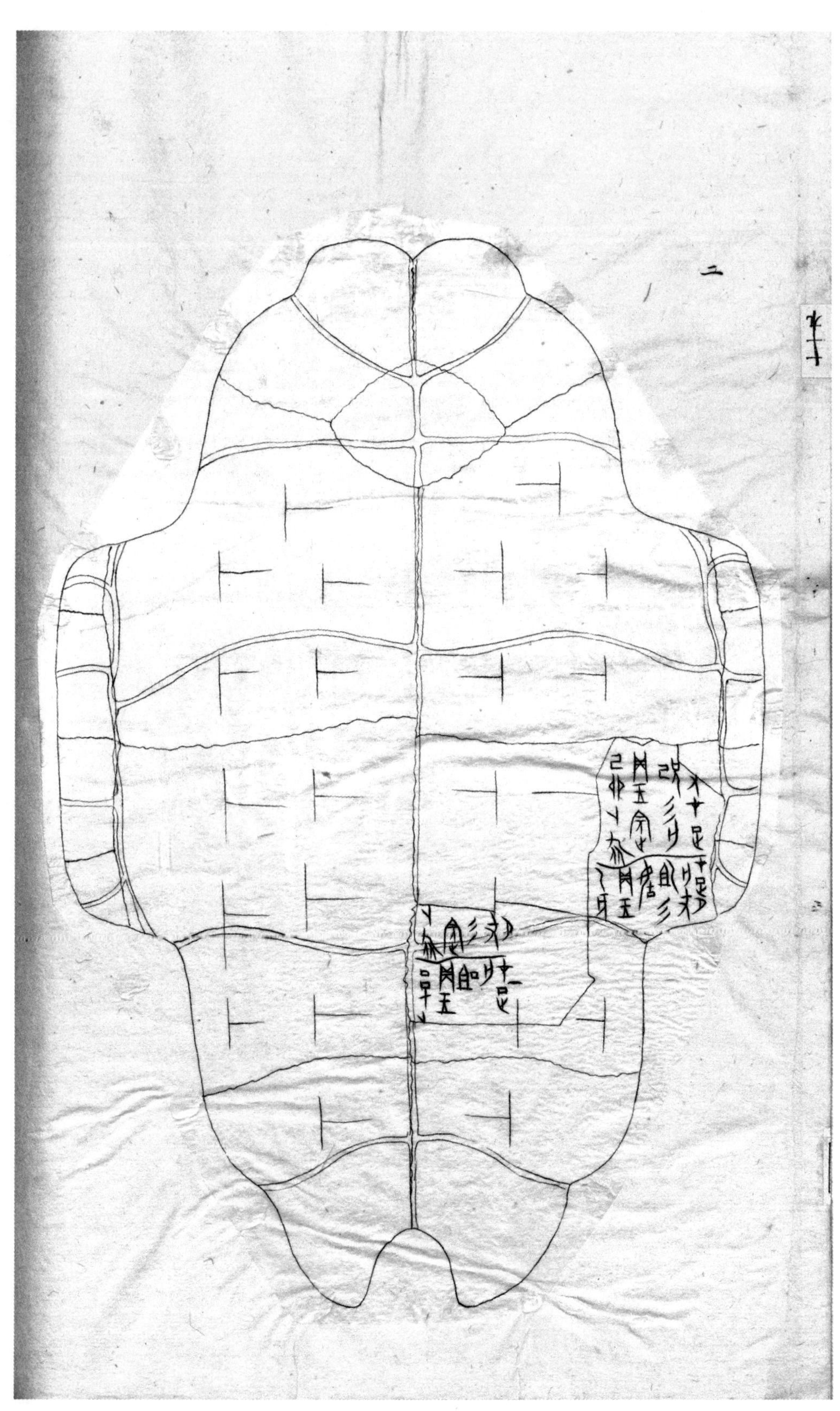

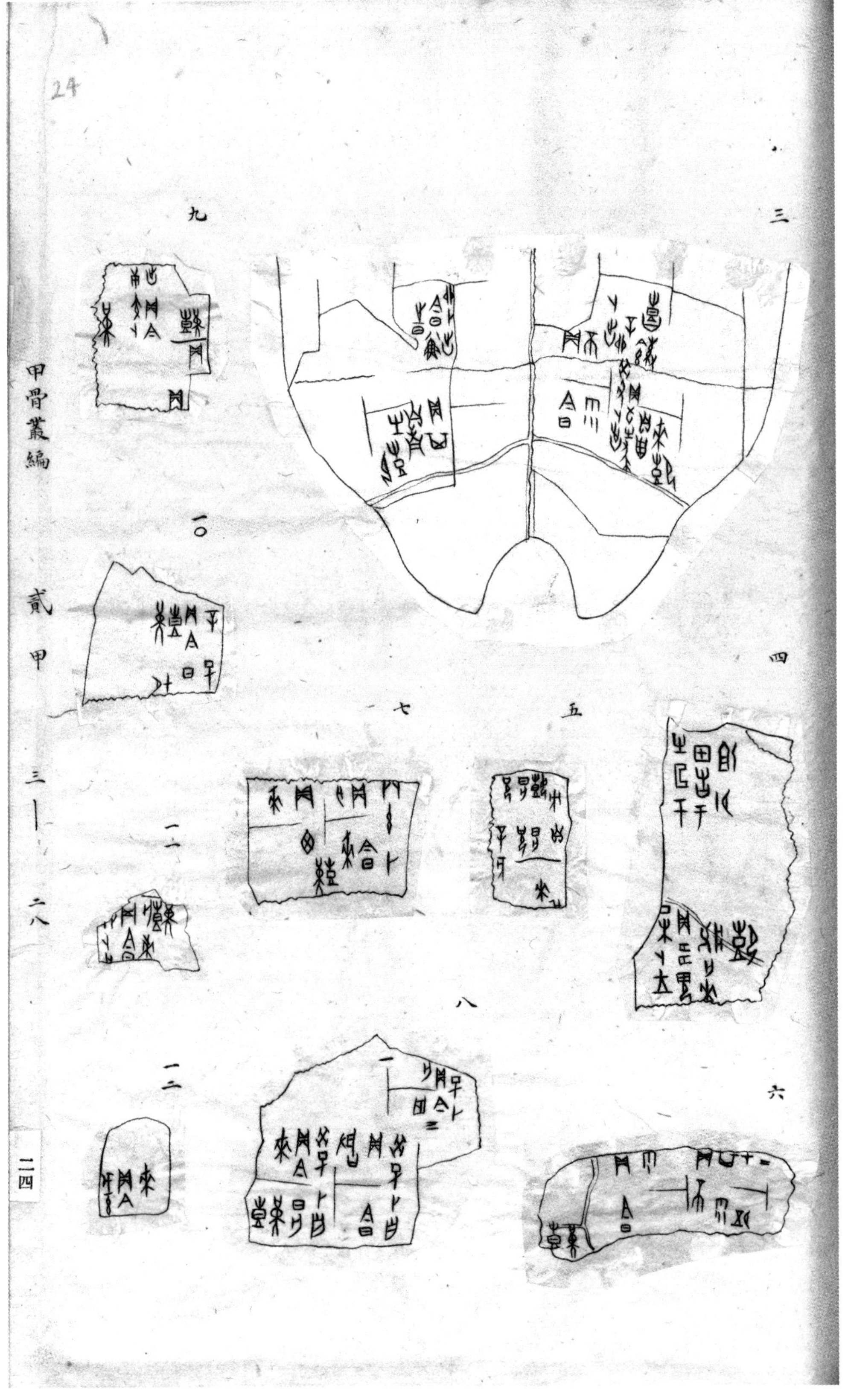
24
九
三
甲骨叢編
一〇
貳甲
三一二八
四
七
五
一一
八
一二
六
二四

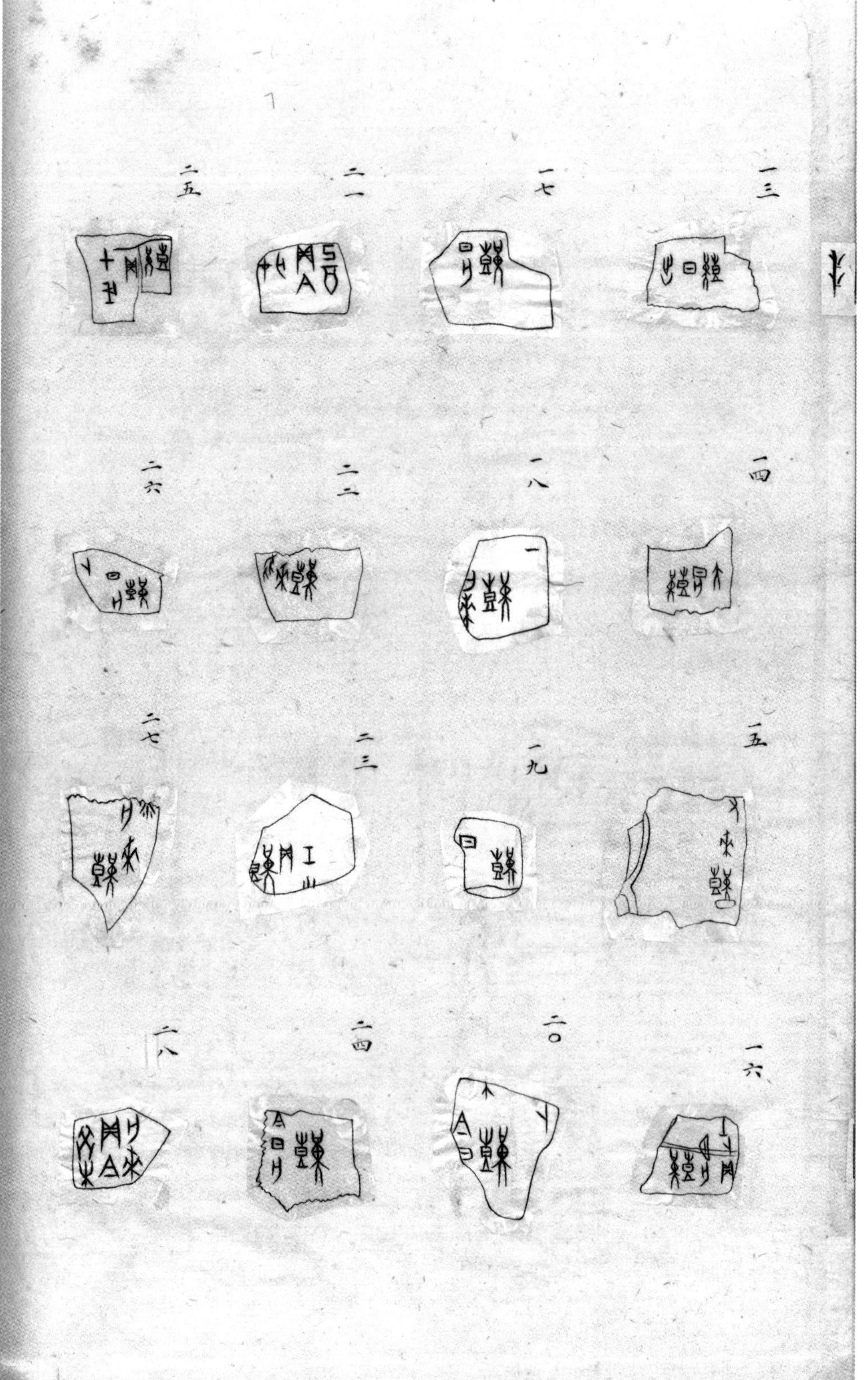

一三
一七
二一
二五
一四
一八
二二
二六
一五
一九
二三
二七
一六
二〇
二四
二八

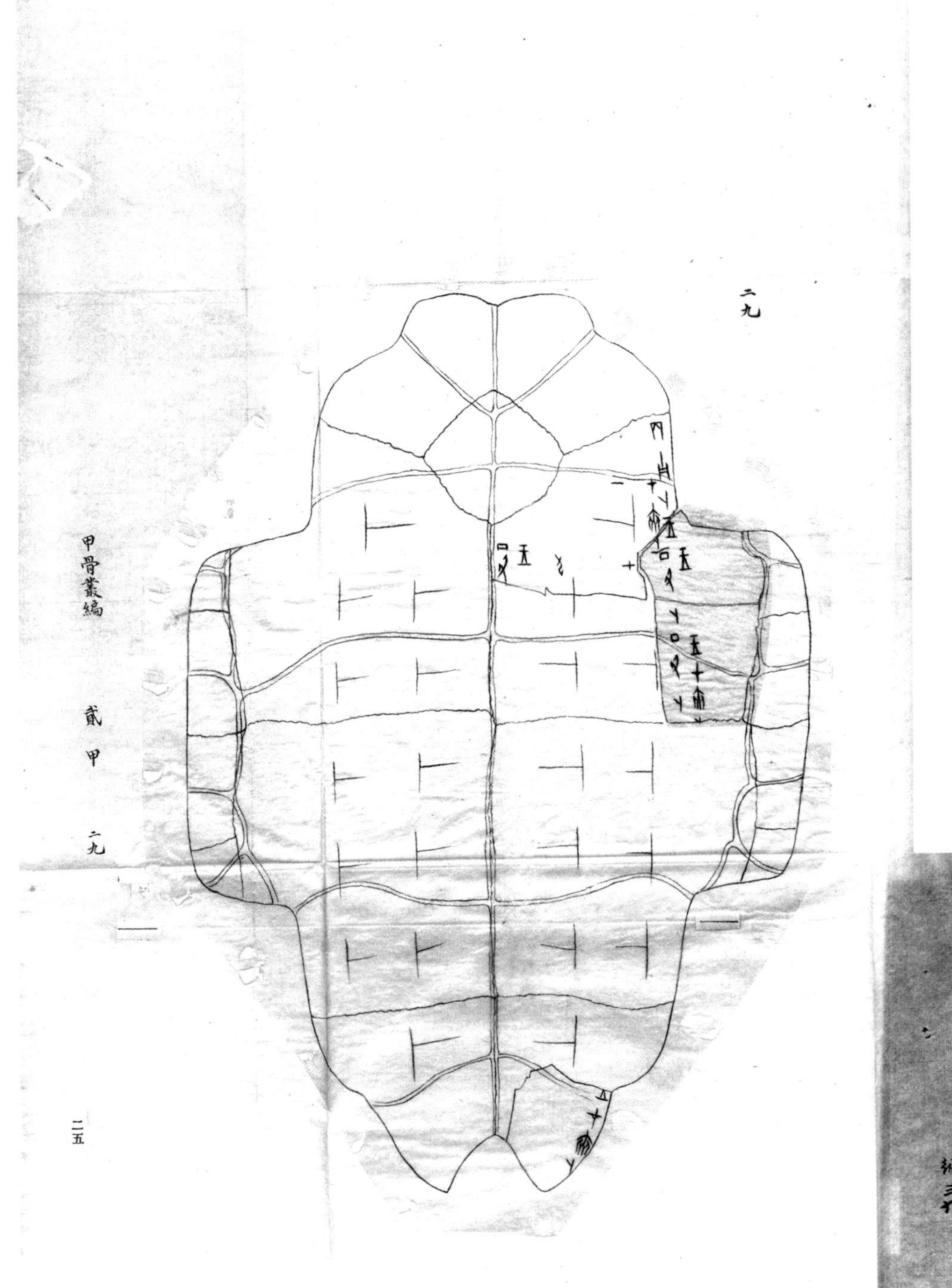
二九
甲骨叢編 貳甲 二九
二五
編三九

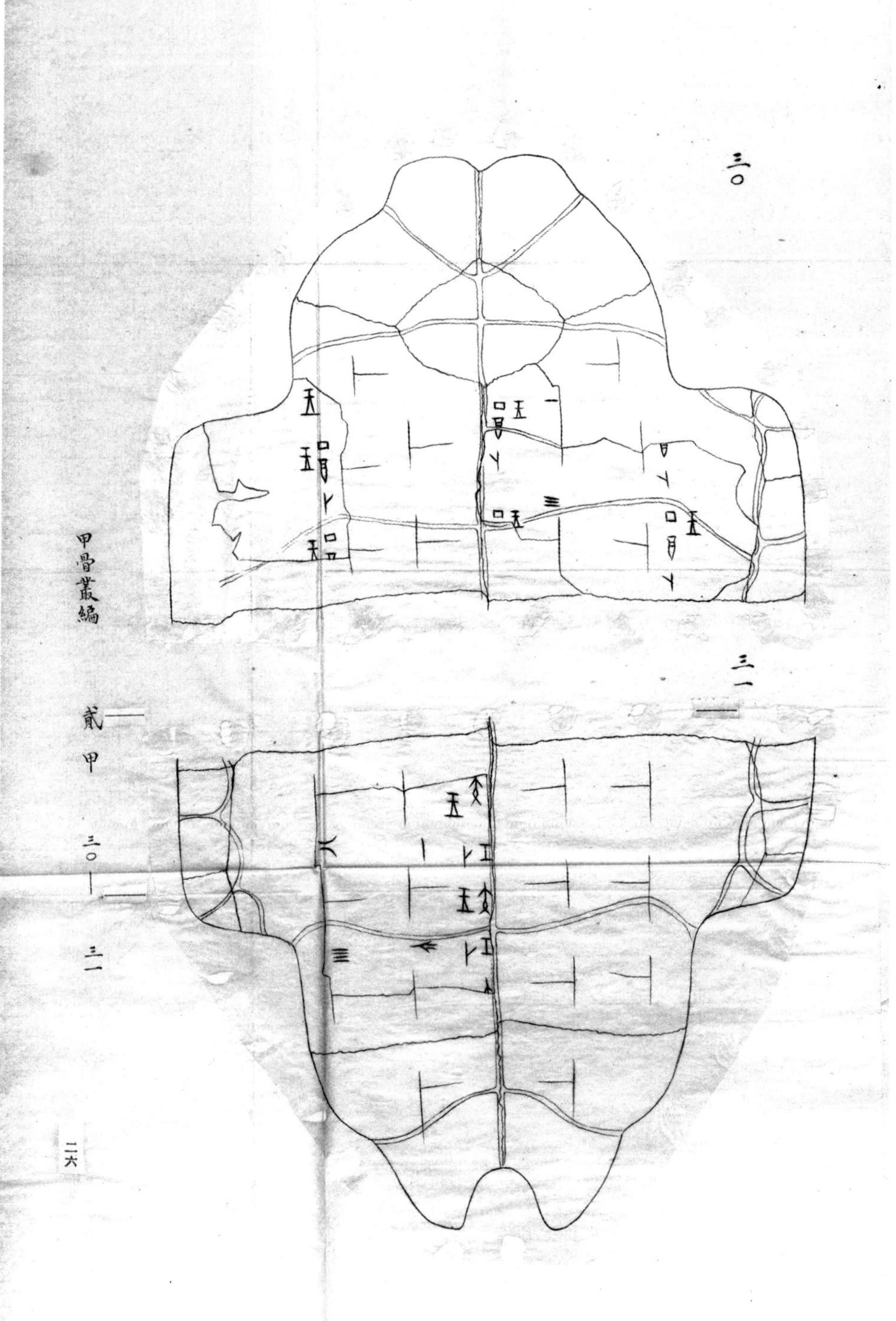
三〇
三一
甲骨叢編
貳甲
三〇—三一
二六

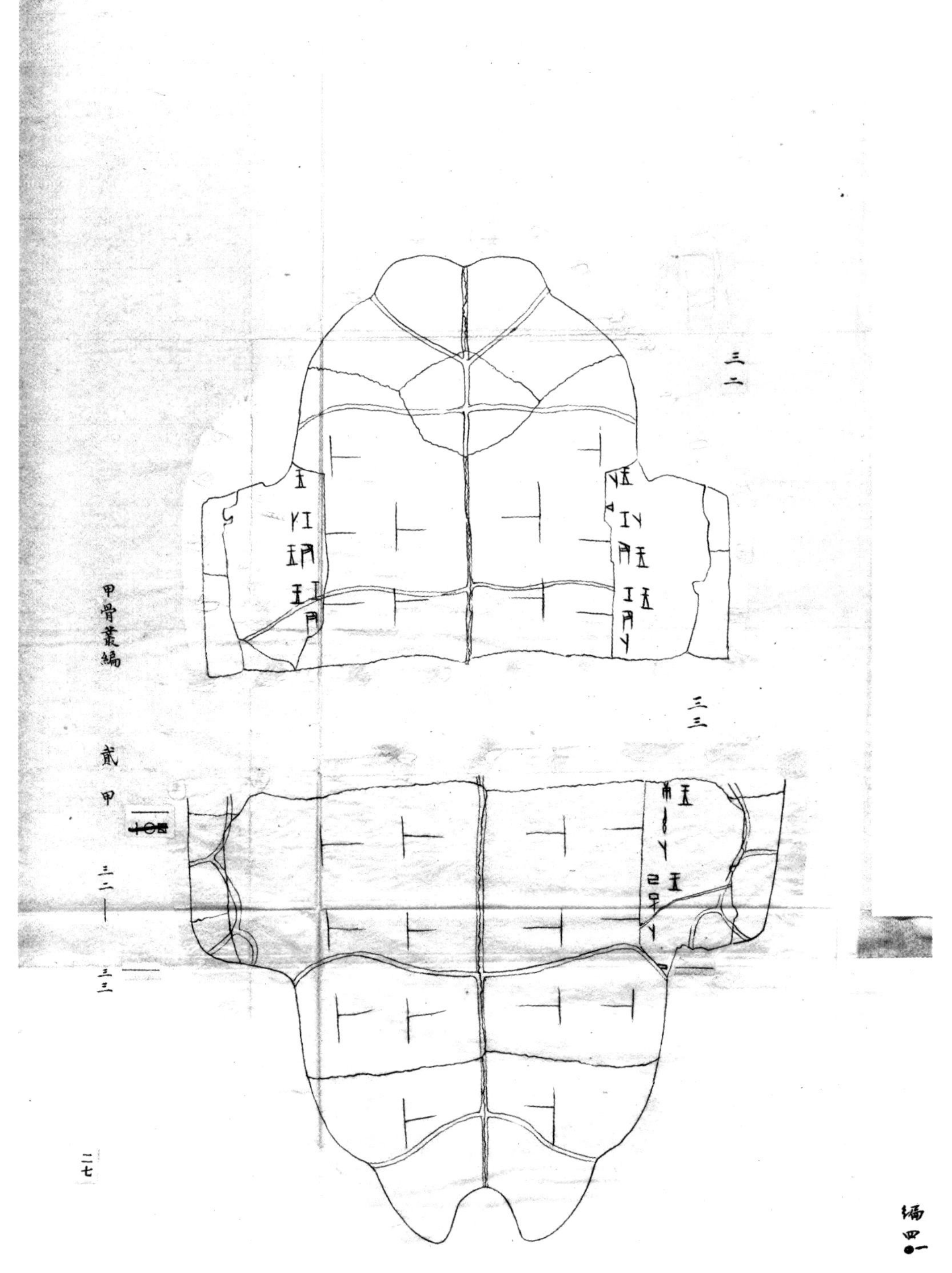
三二
三三
甲骨叢編
貳　甲
三二一
三三
二七
緬四一

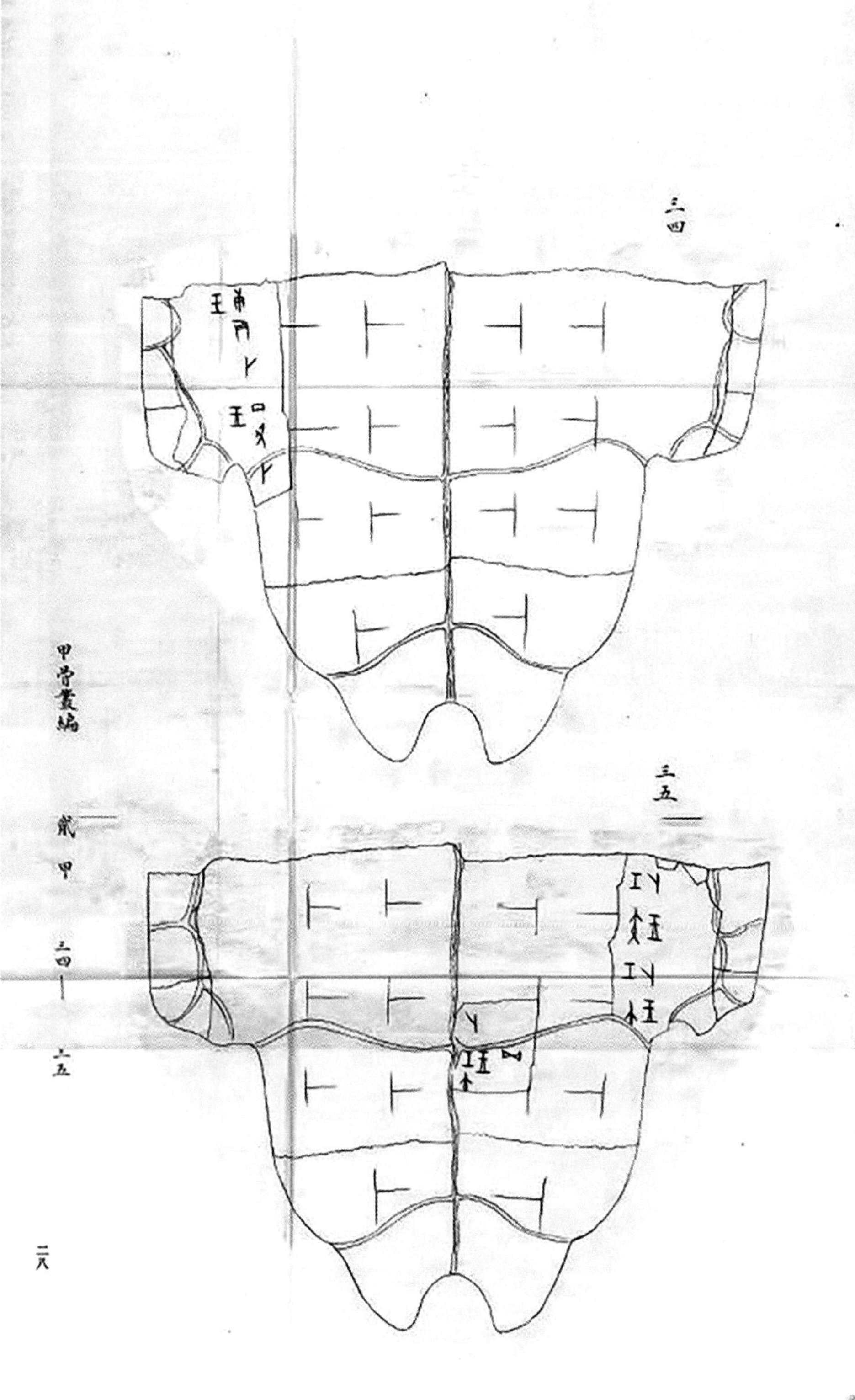

二四
二五
甲骨叢編 貳甲 二四—二五
二八
編四二

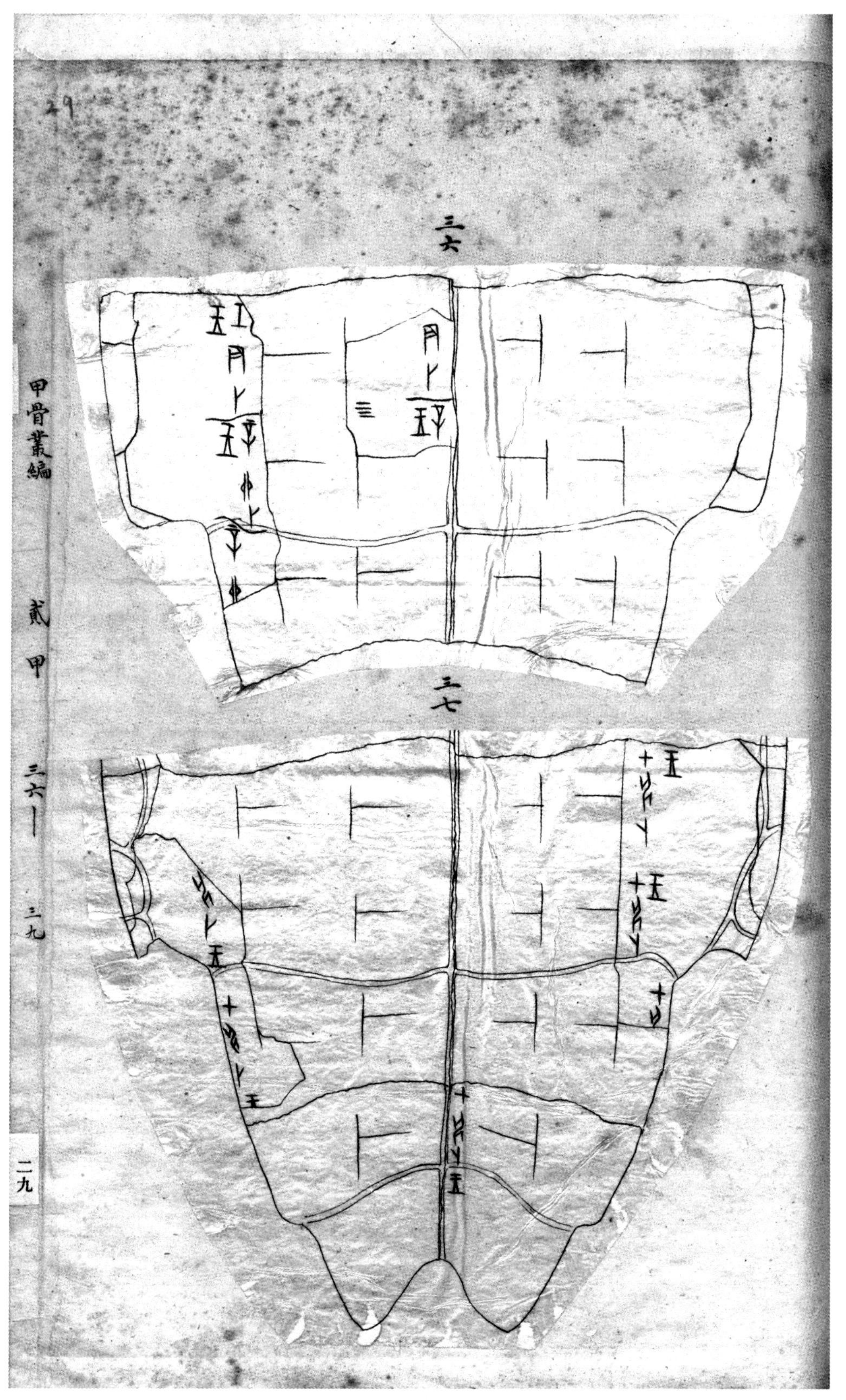

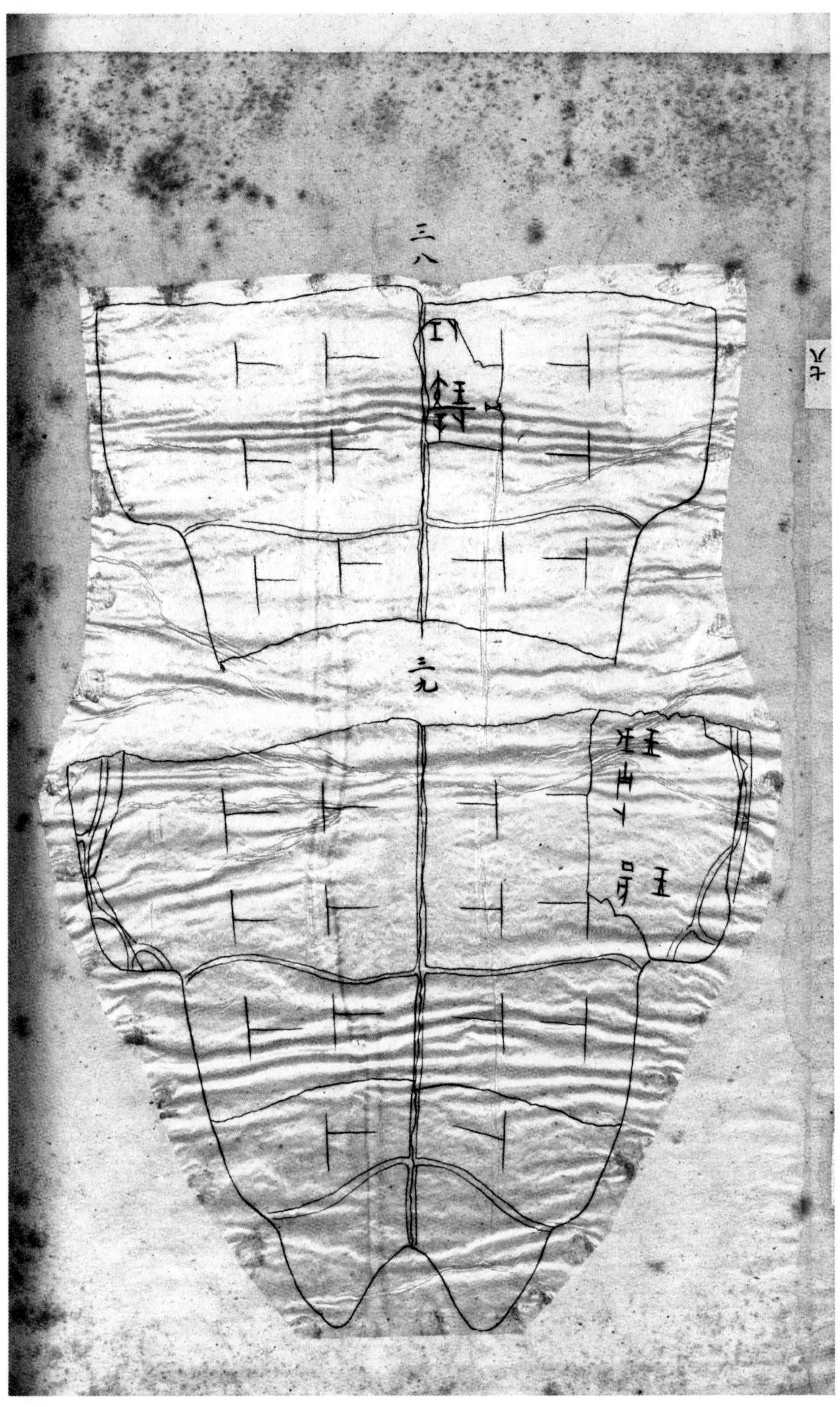

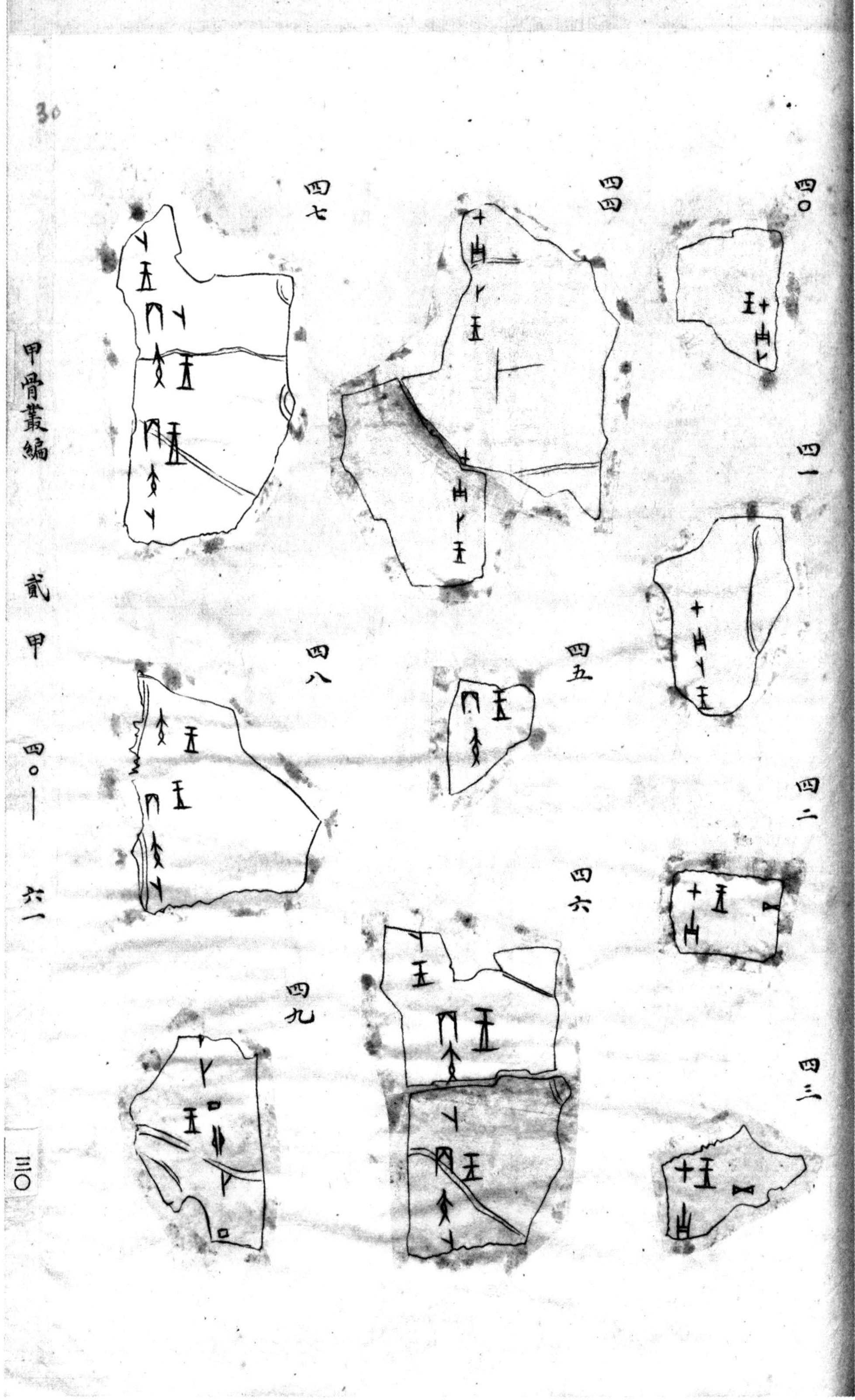
甲骨叢編　貳甲　四〇—六一
三〇
四〇
四一
四二
四三
四四
四五
四六
四七
四八
四九

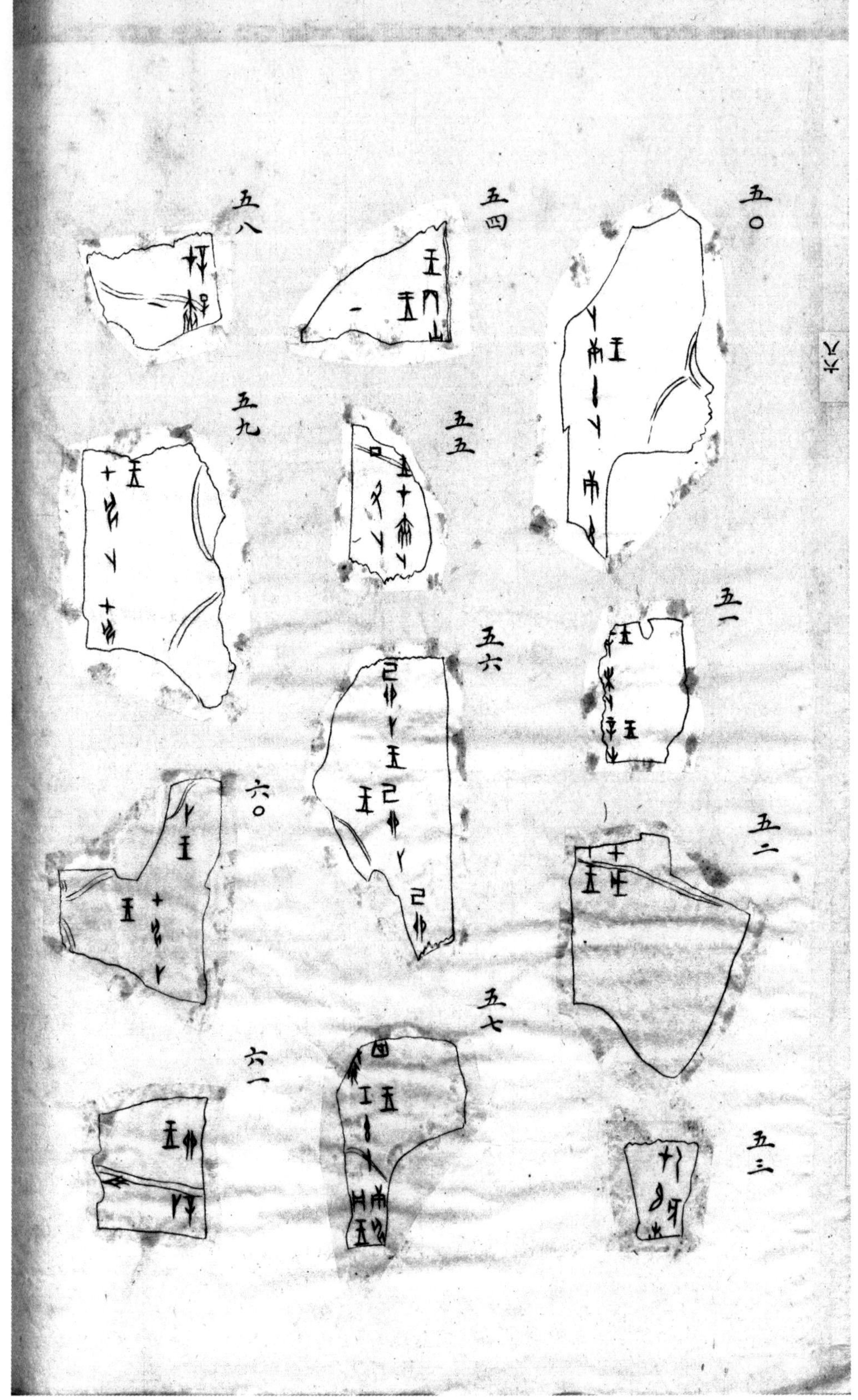
六八
五〇
五一
五二
五三
五四
五五
五六
五七
五八
五九
六〇
六一

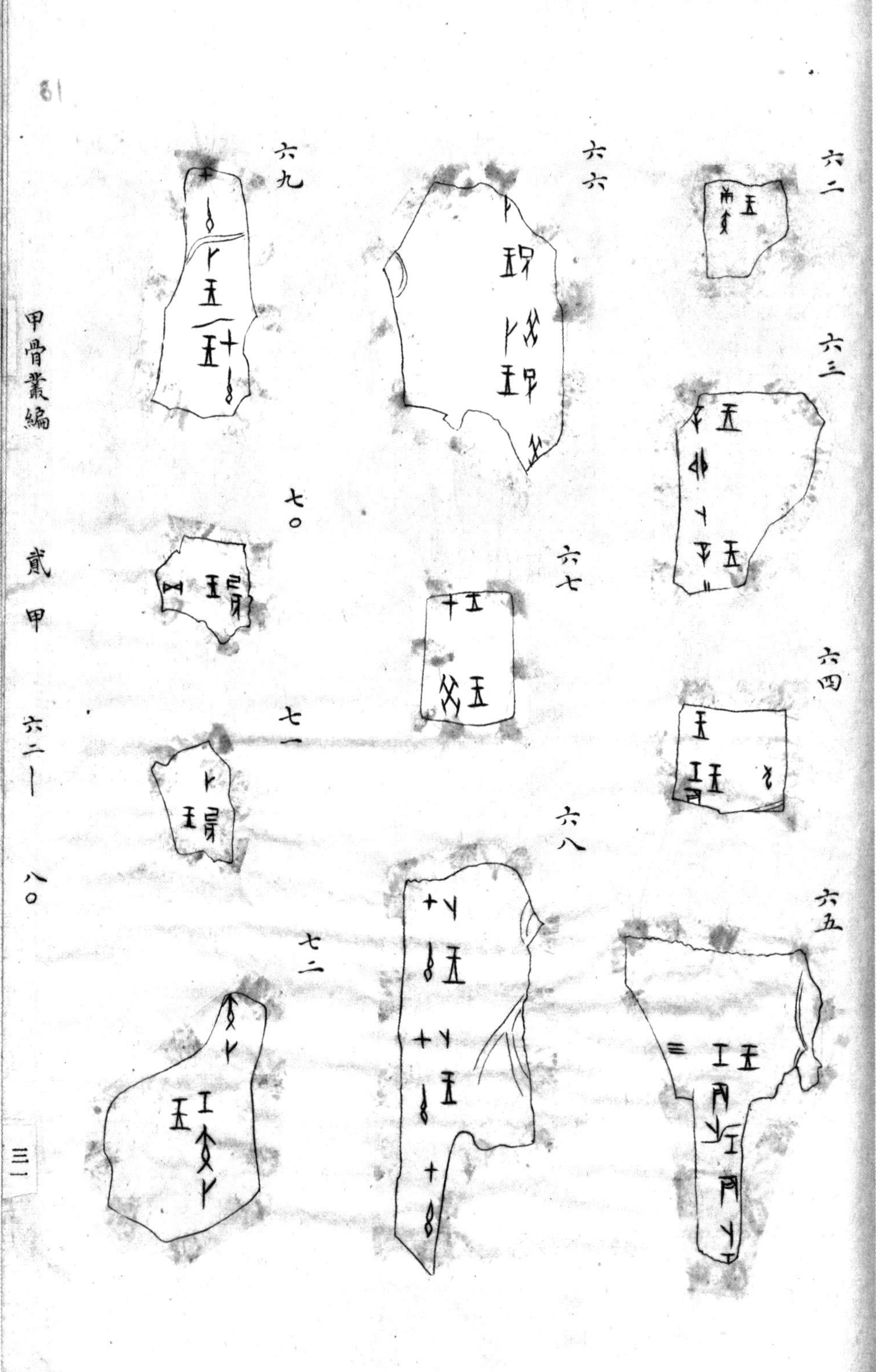

甲骨叢編 貳 甲 六二—八〇

三一

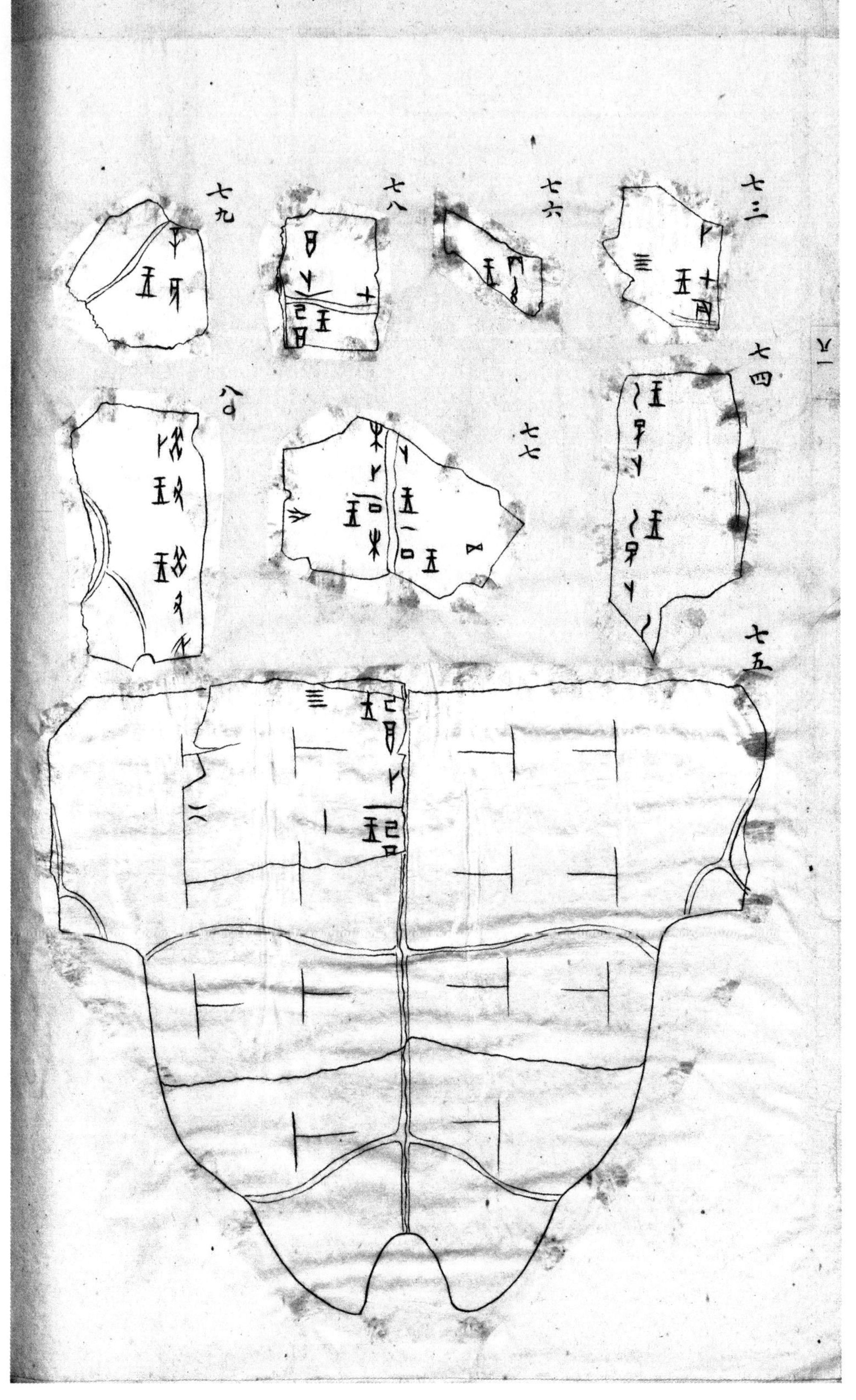
一八
七三
七四
七五
七六
七七
七八
七九
八〇

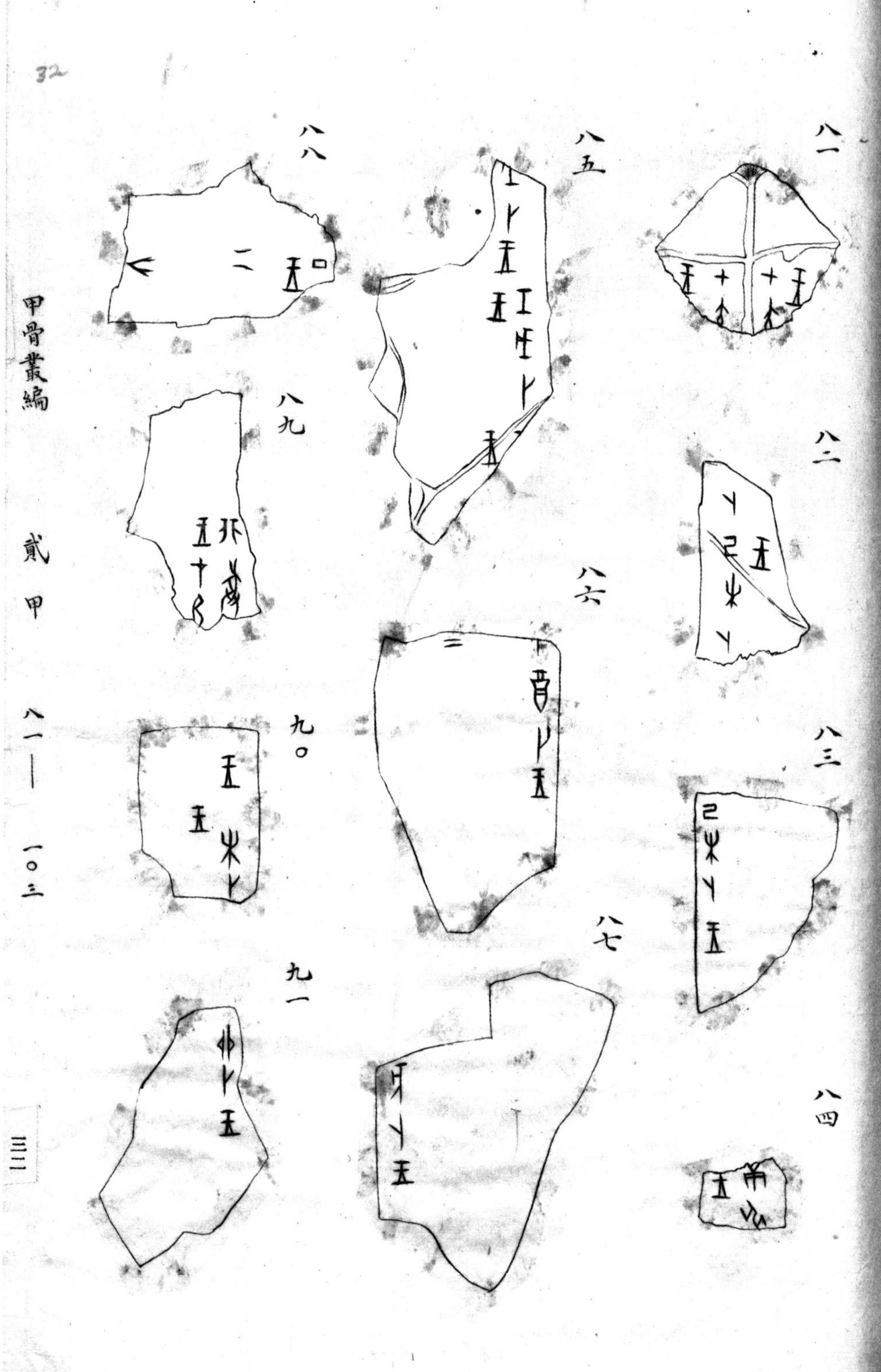

甲骨叢編 貳 甲 八一—一〇三

三二

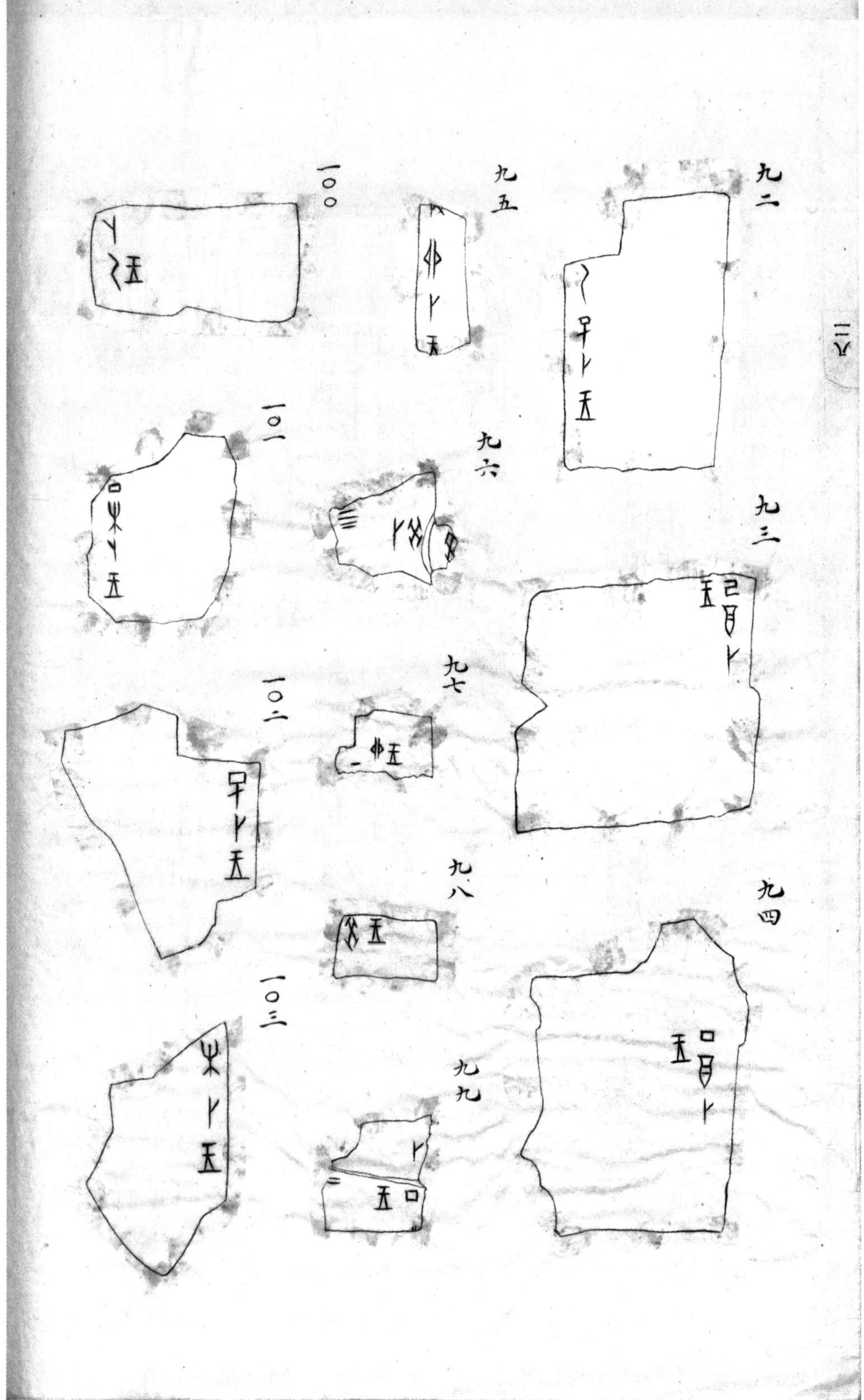
九二
九三
九四
九五
九六
九七
九八
九九
一〇〇
一〇一
一〇二
一〇三
八二

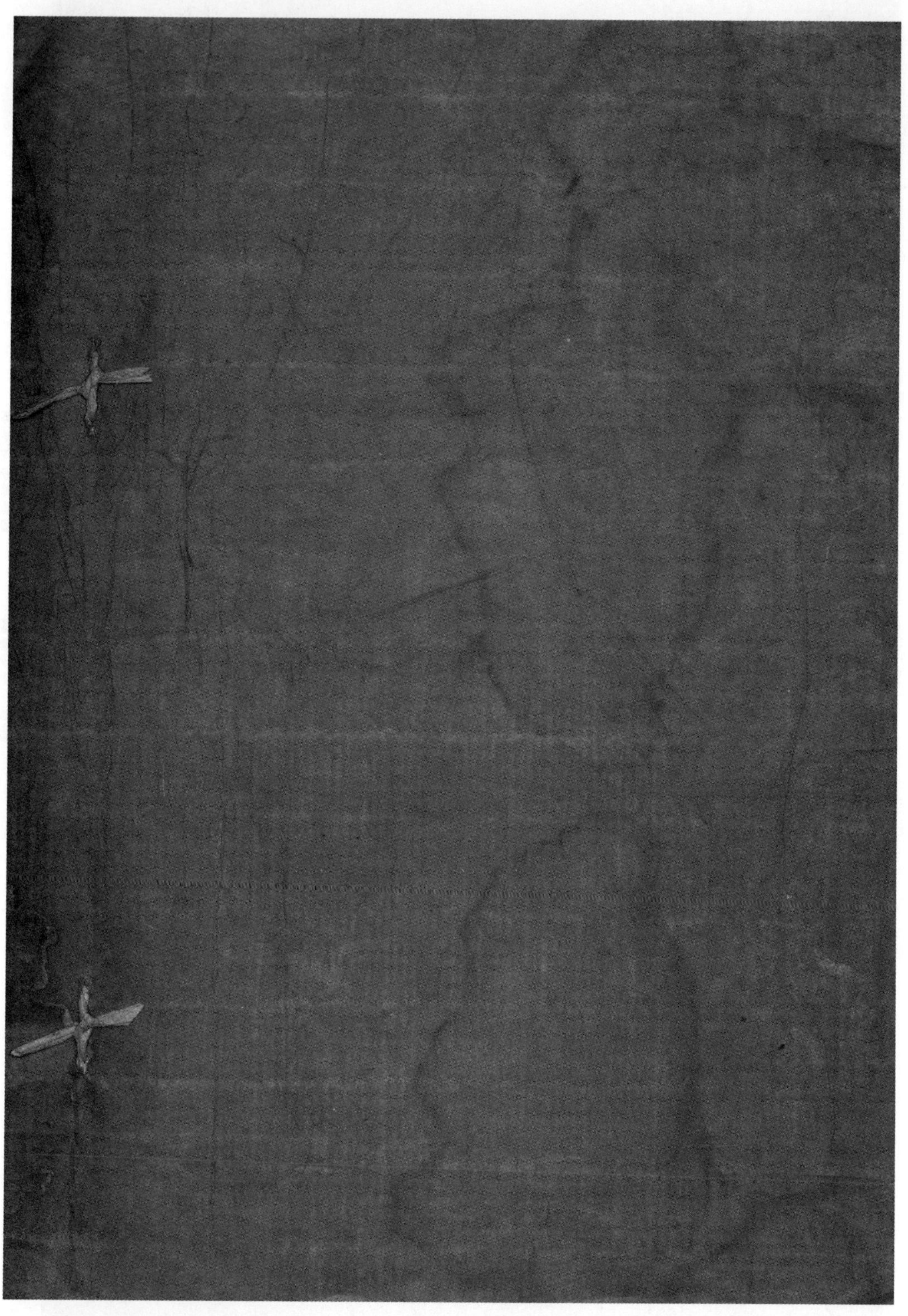

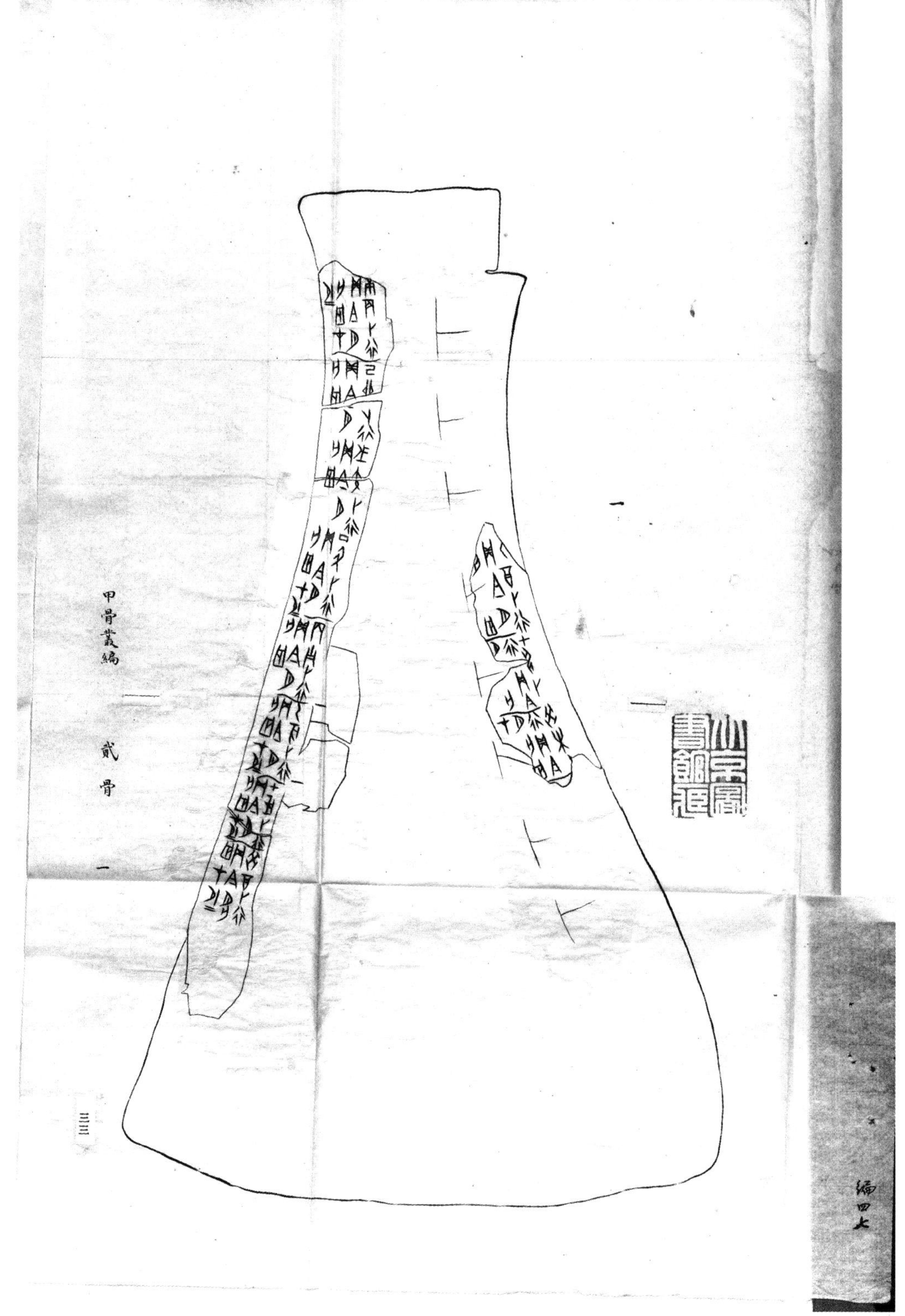
甲骨叢編
貳骨
三三

案：此頁及下頁爲上頁之局部放大。以下類此者十數頁，不再出校。

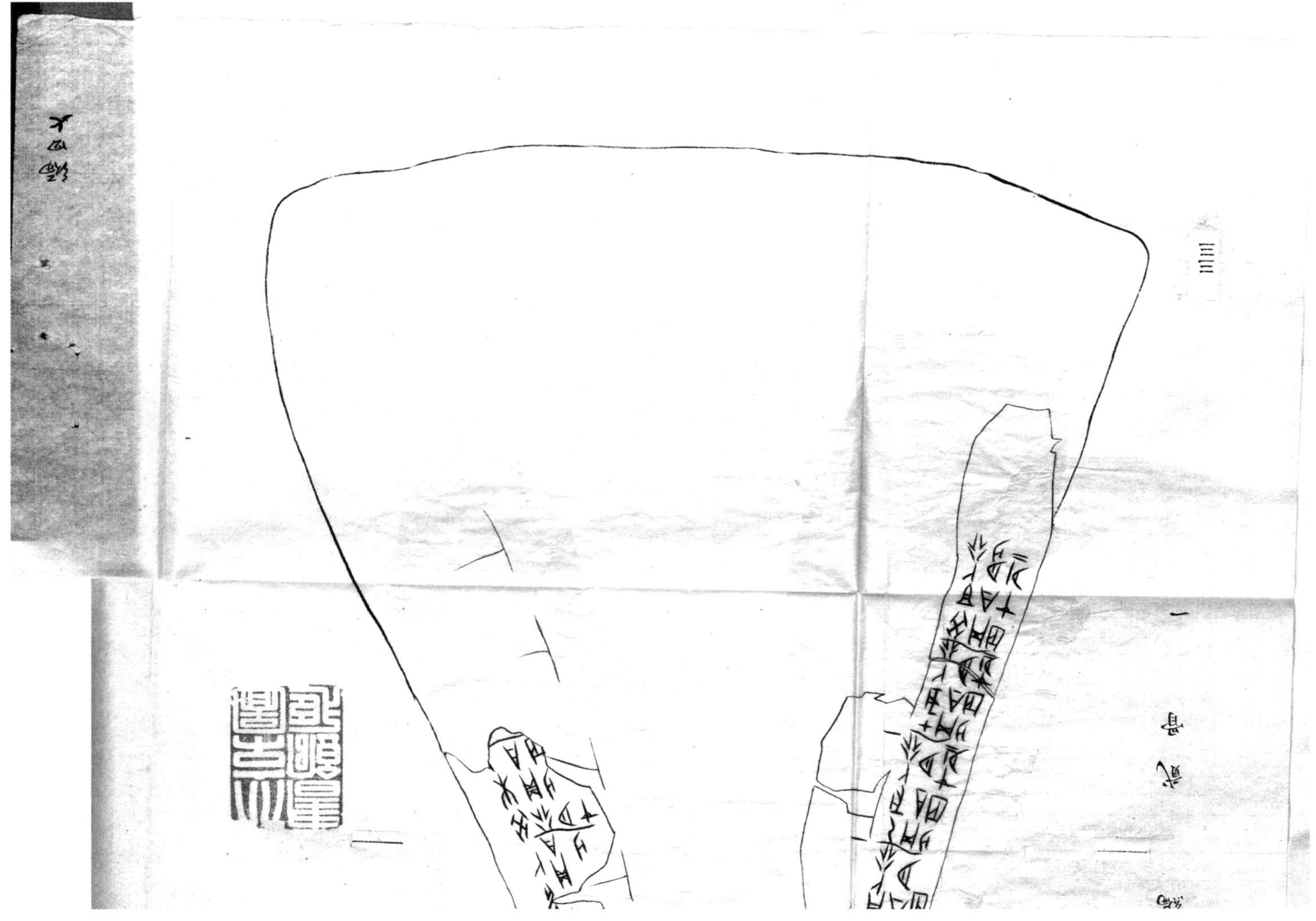

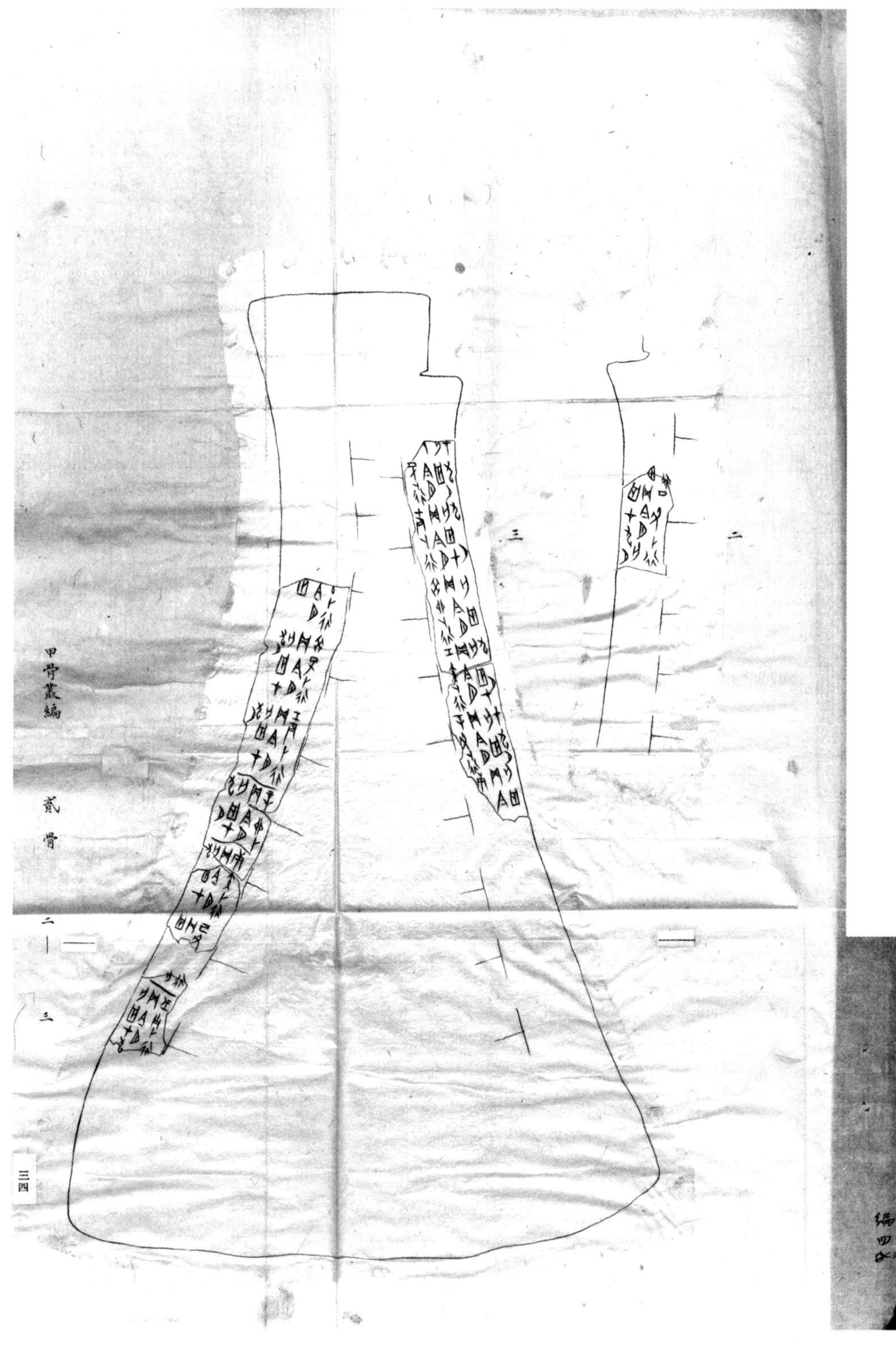

甲骨叢編 貳骨 二一三
三四
編四八

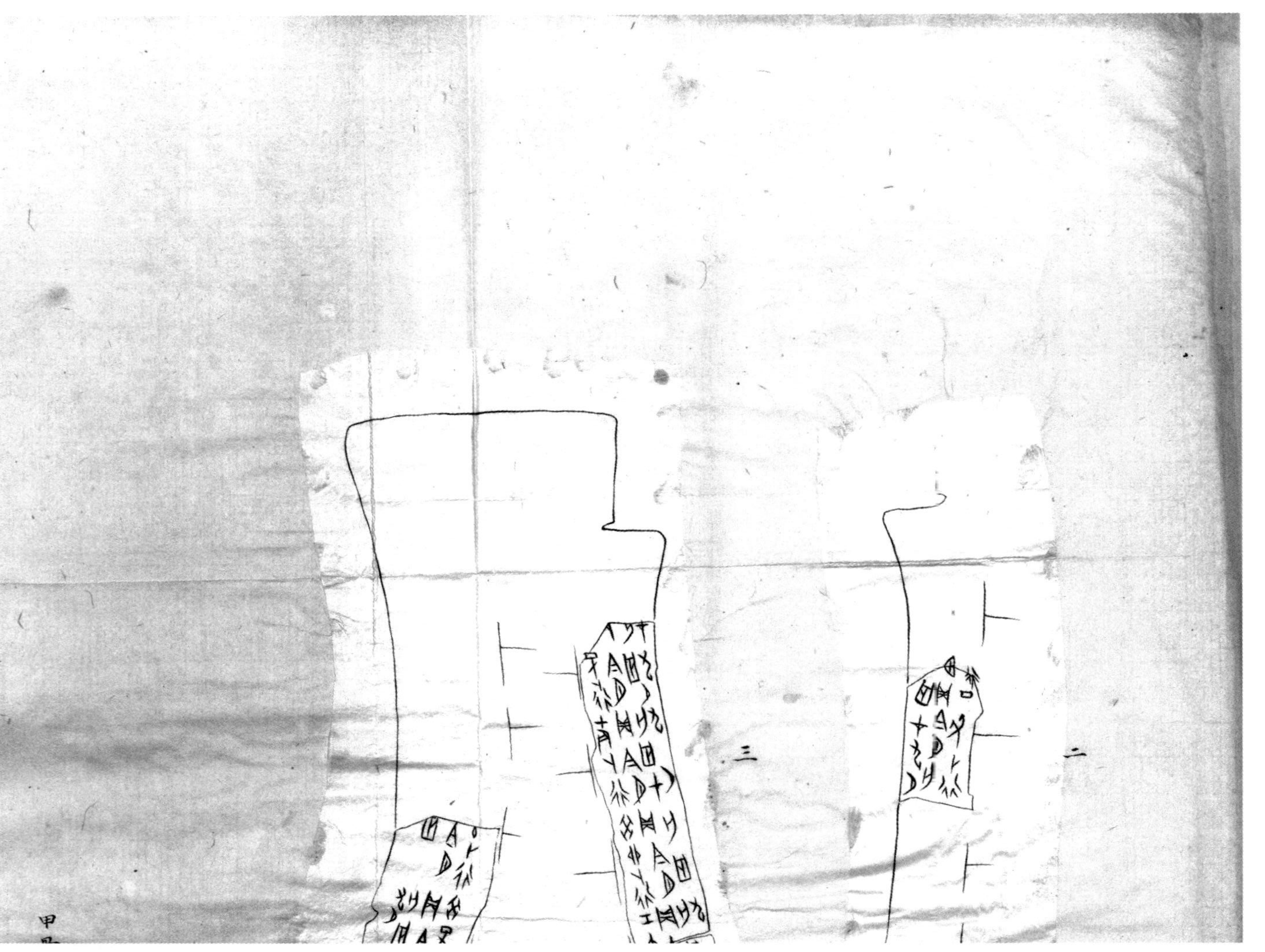

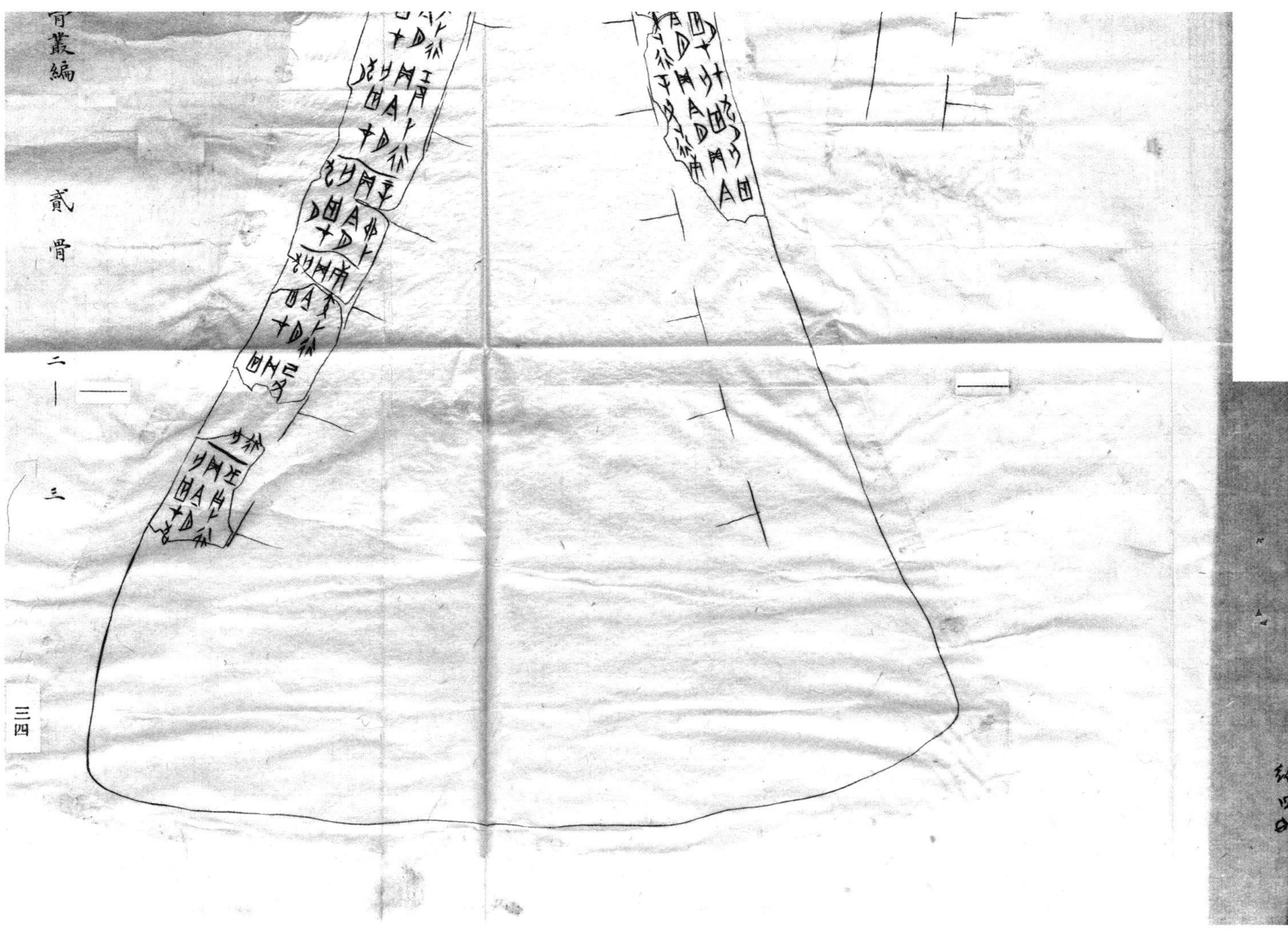
貳 骨 二一三
三四

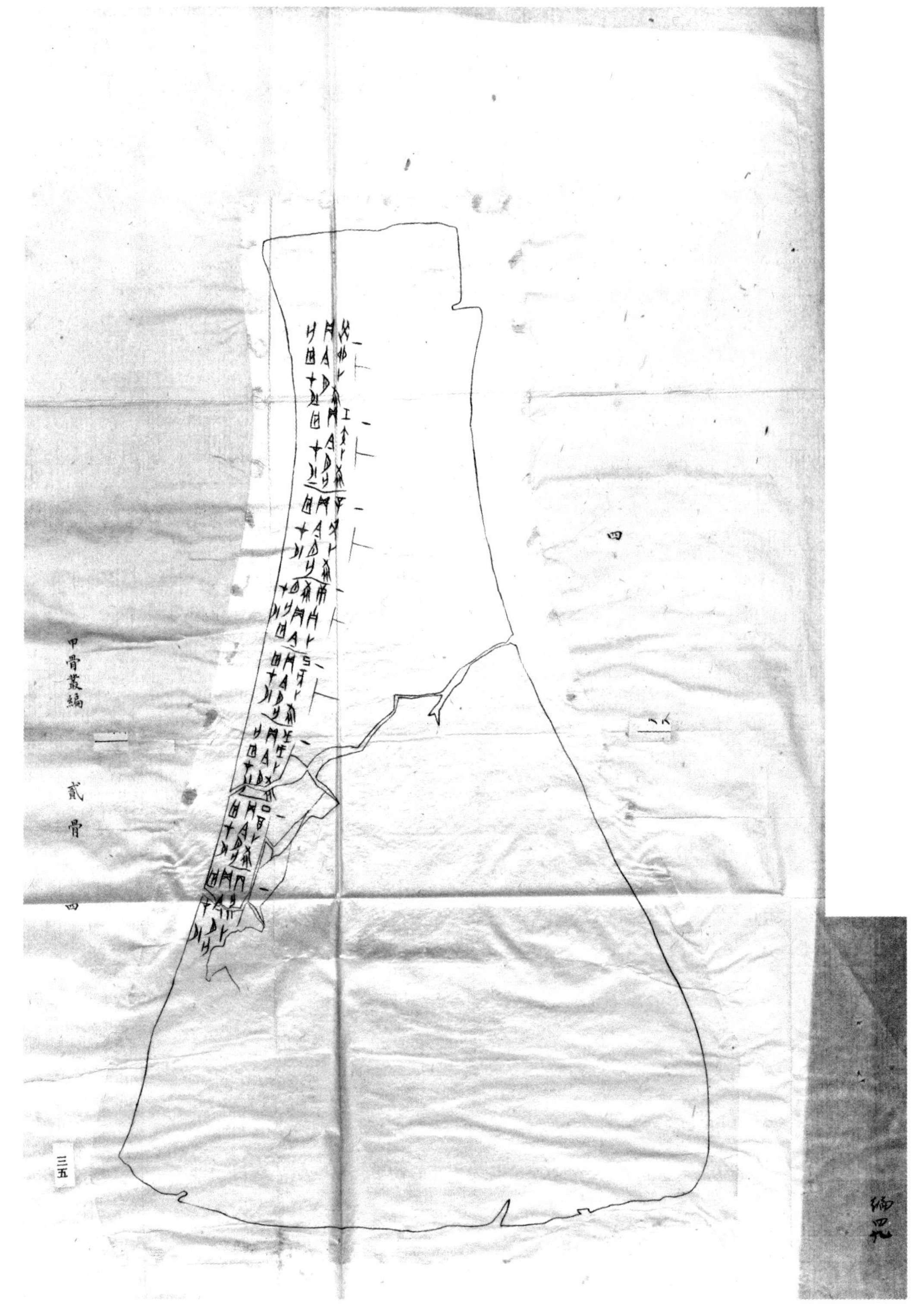
甲骨叢編
貳骨
四
三五
四
二八

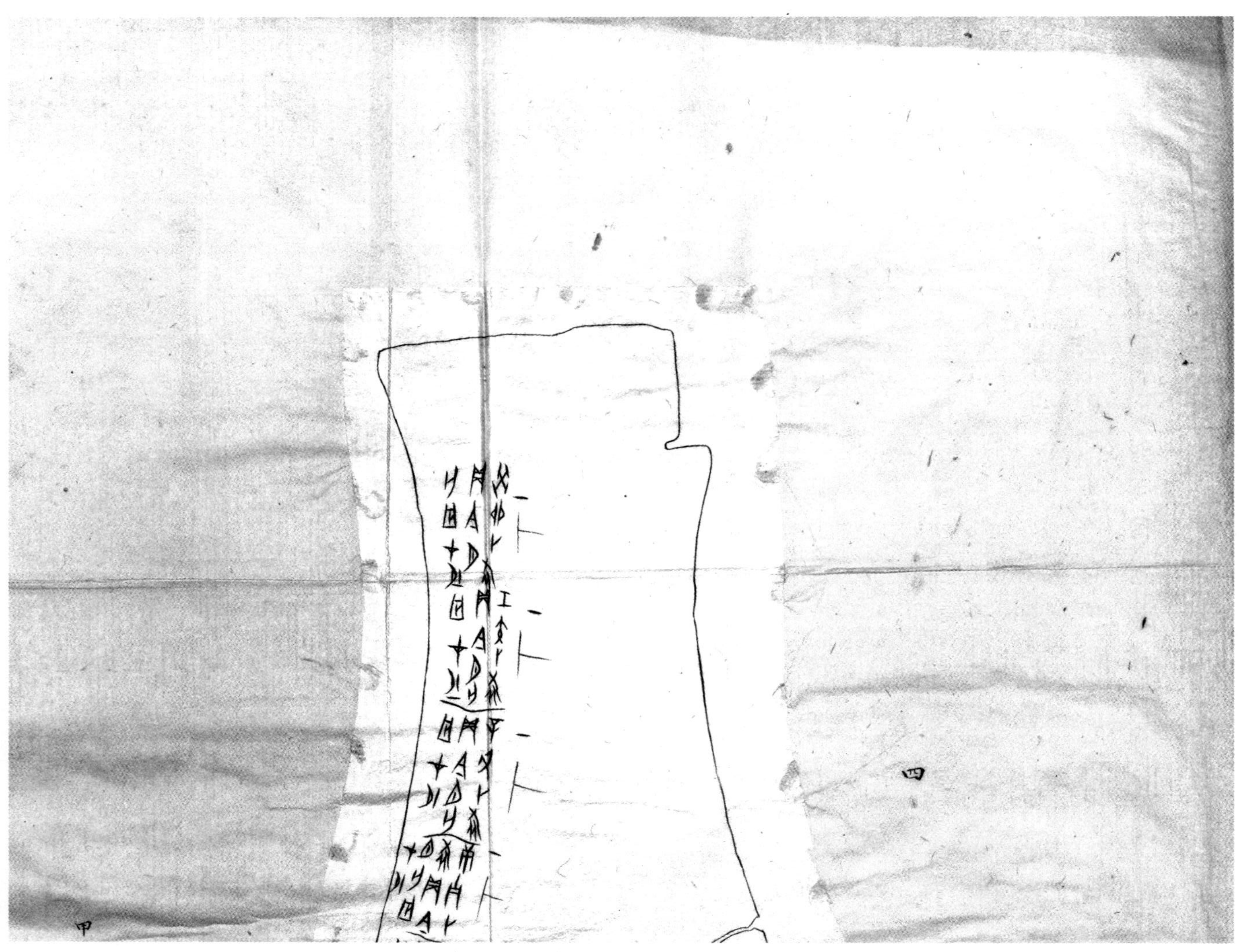

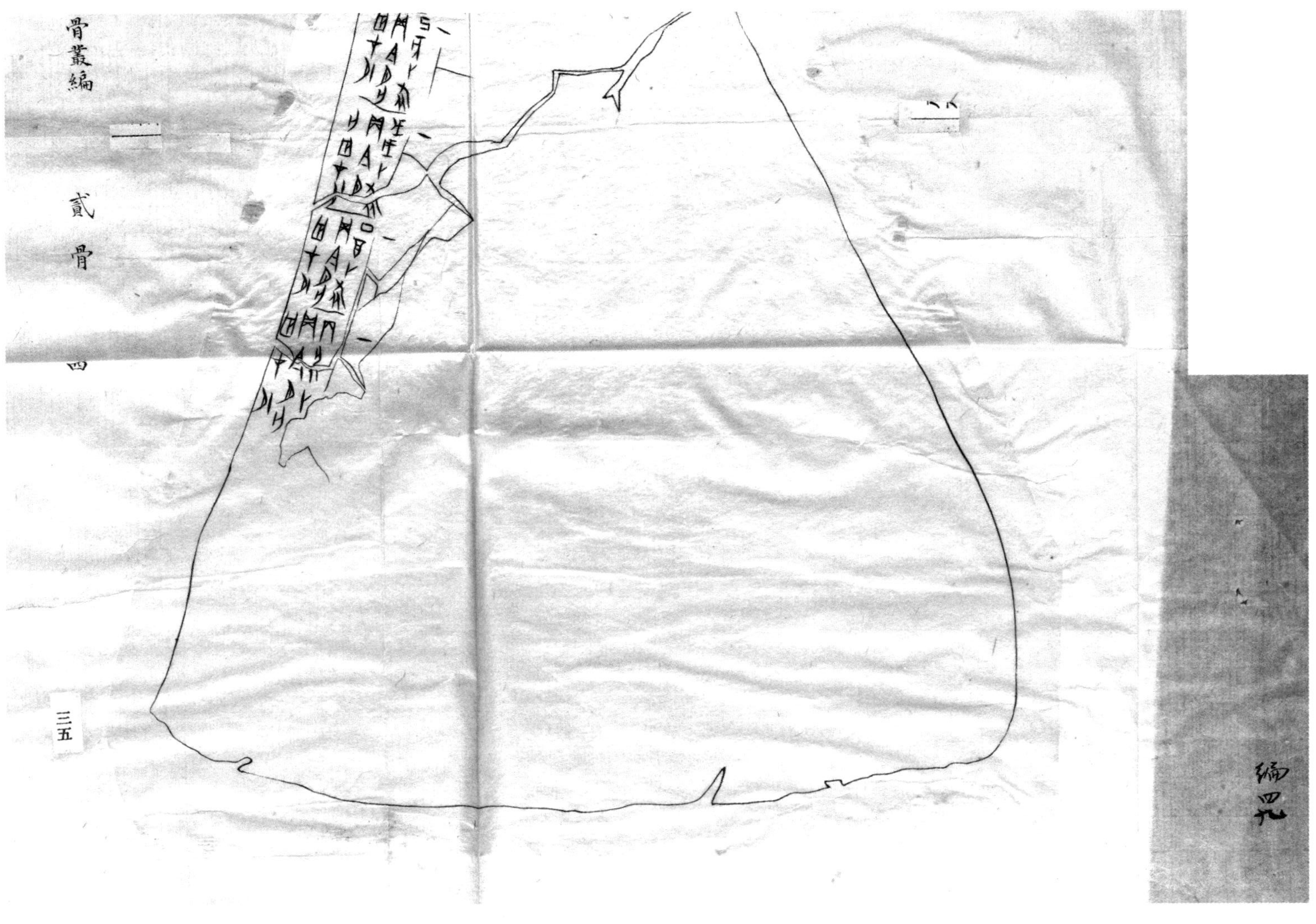
骨叢編
貳
骨
四
三五
編四

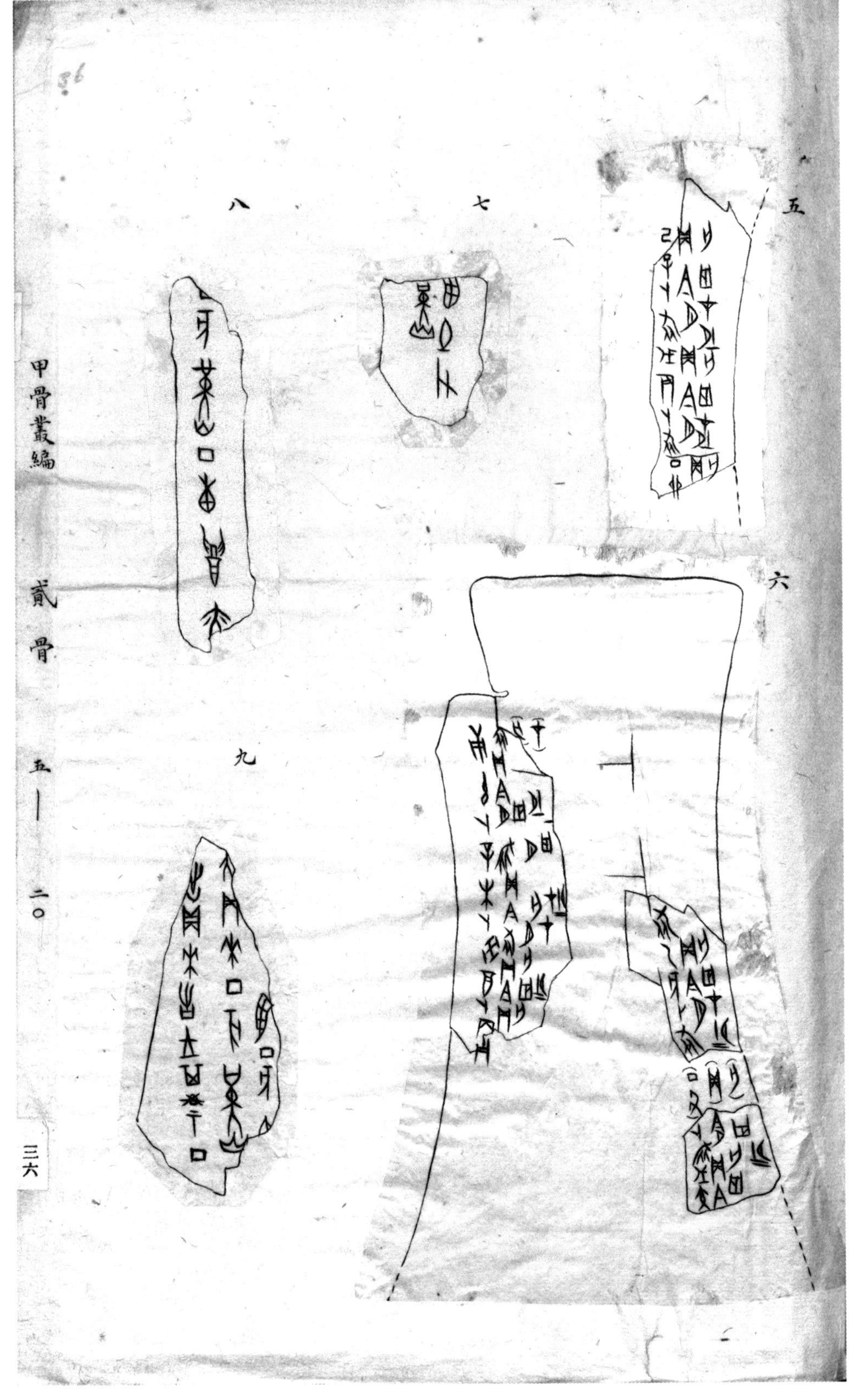
五
六
七
八
九
甲骨叢編　貳骨　五一二〇
三六

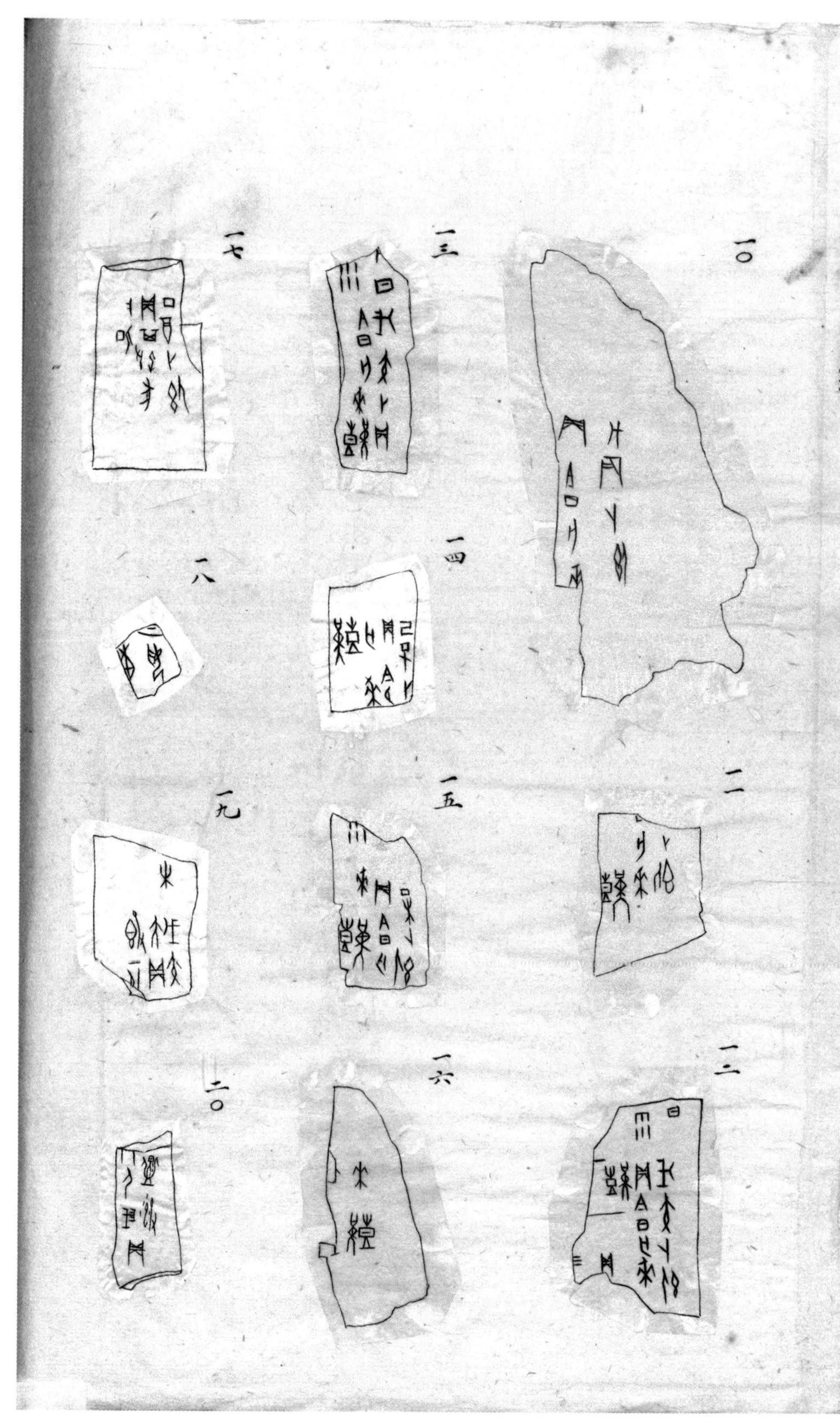

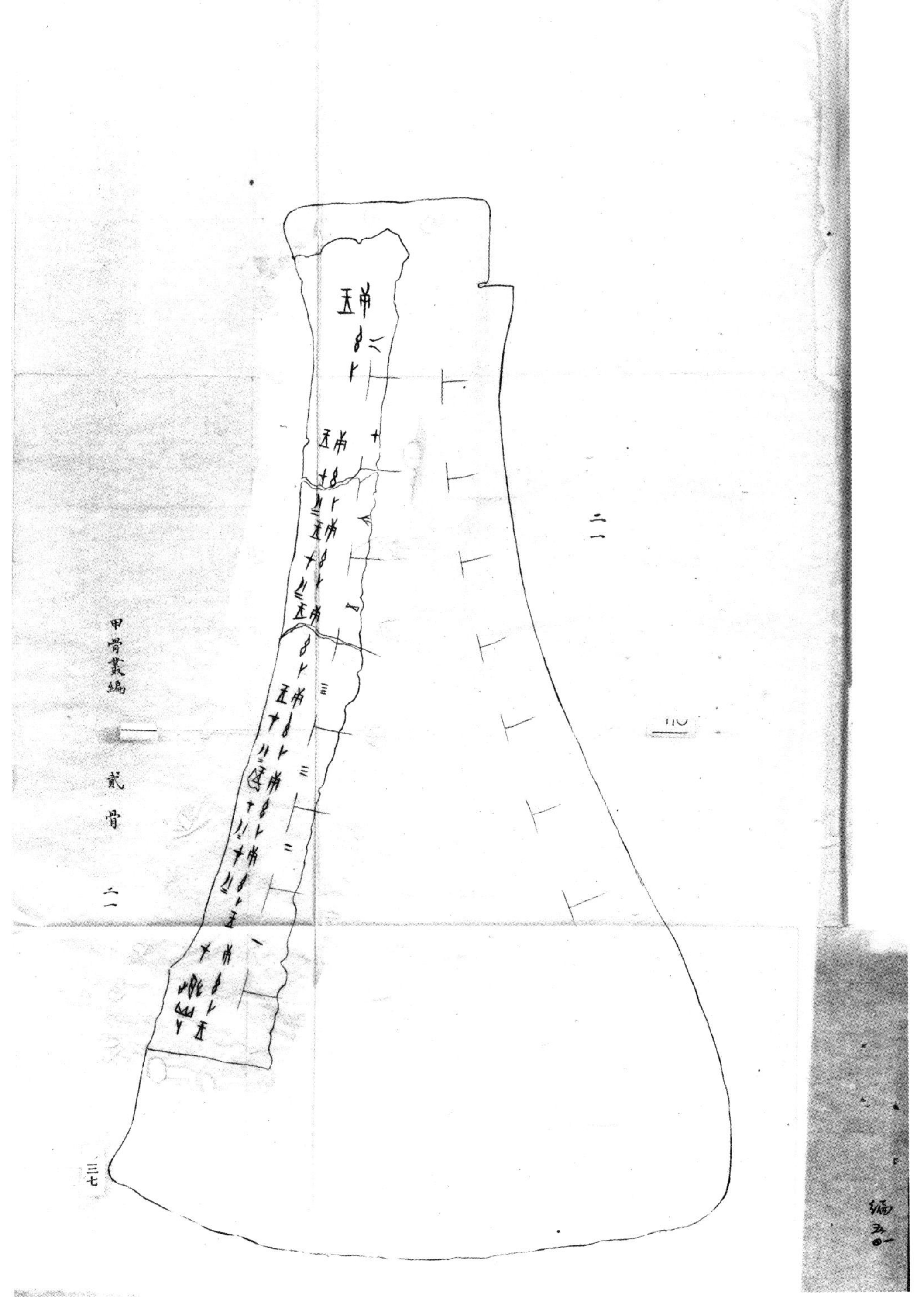
甲骨叢編
貳骨
二一
二一
三七
110

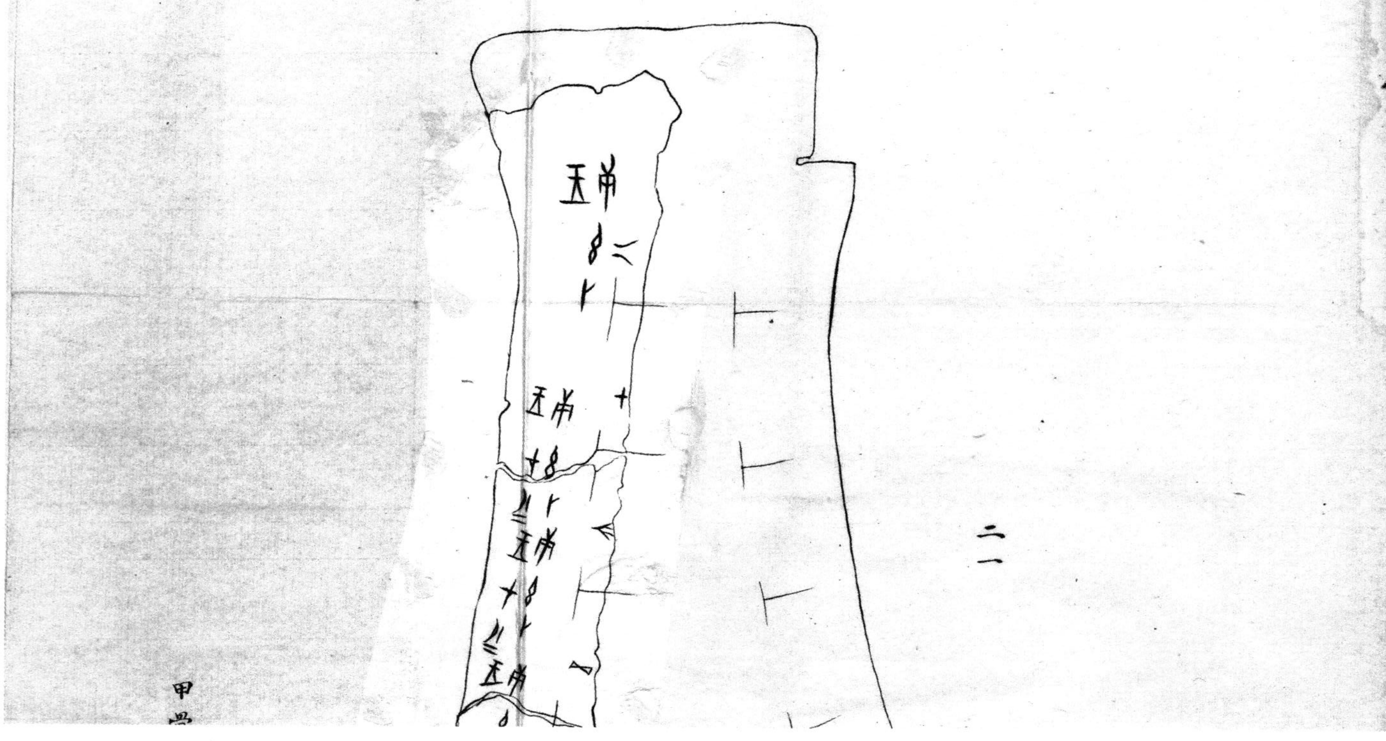

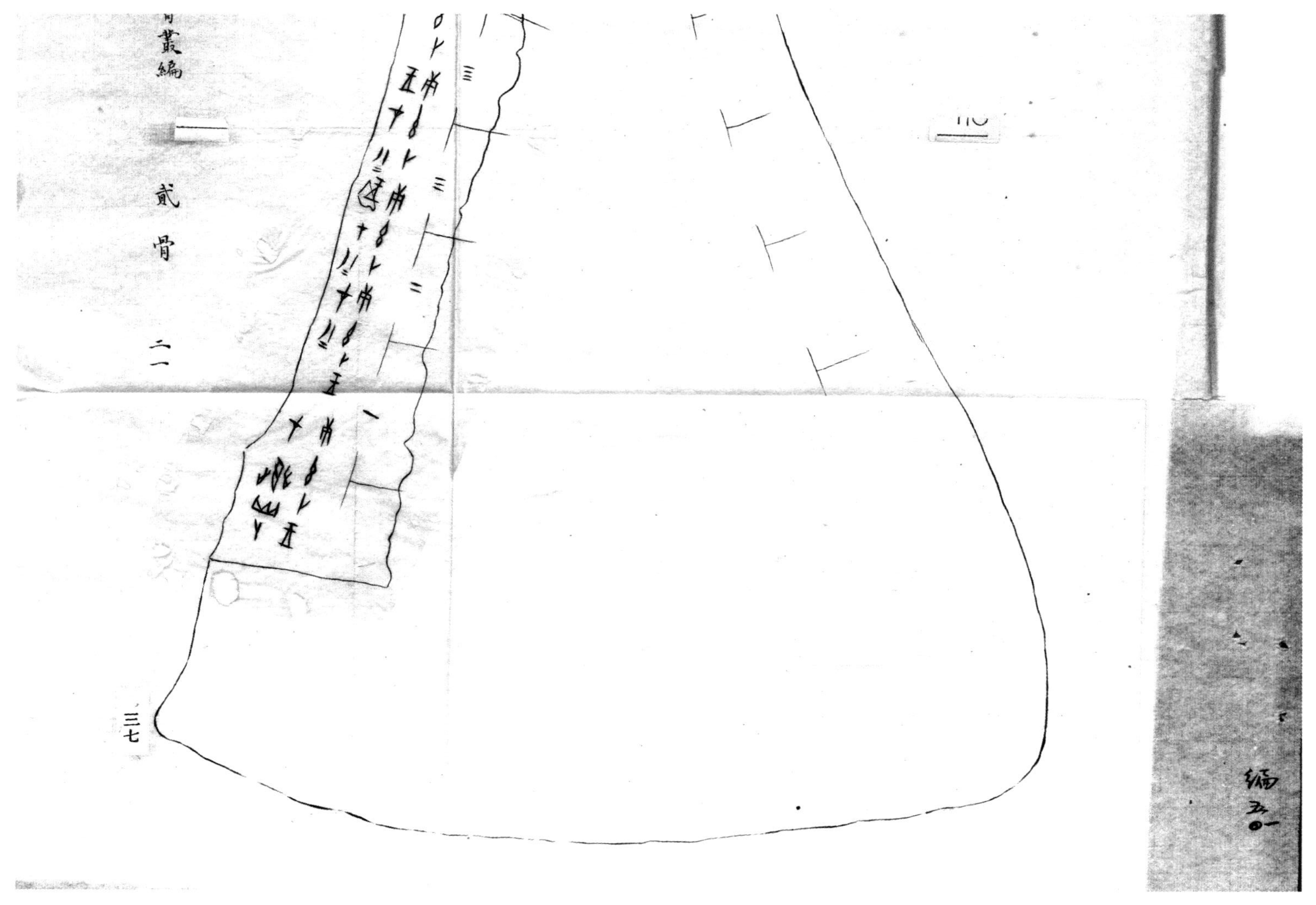
叢編
貳
骨
二一
三七

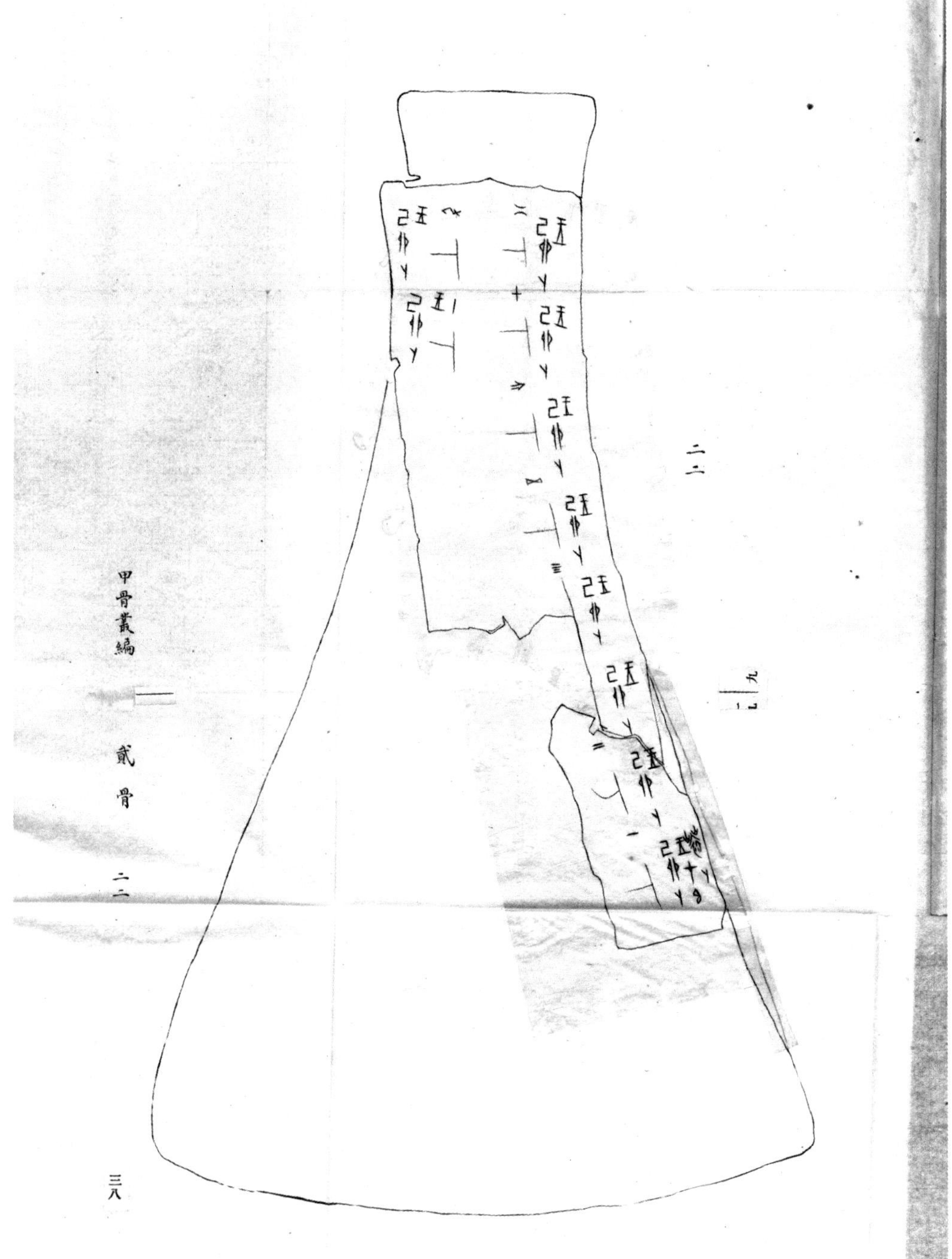
甲骨叢編 二 貳骨 二二
二二
三八

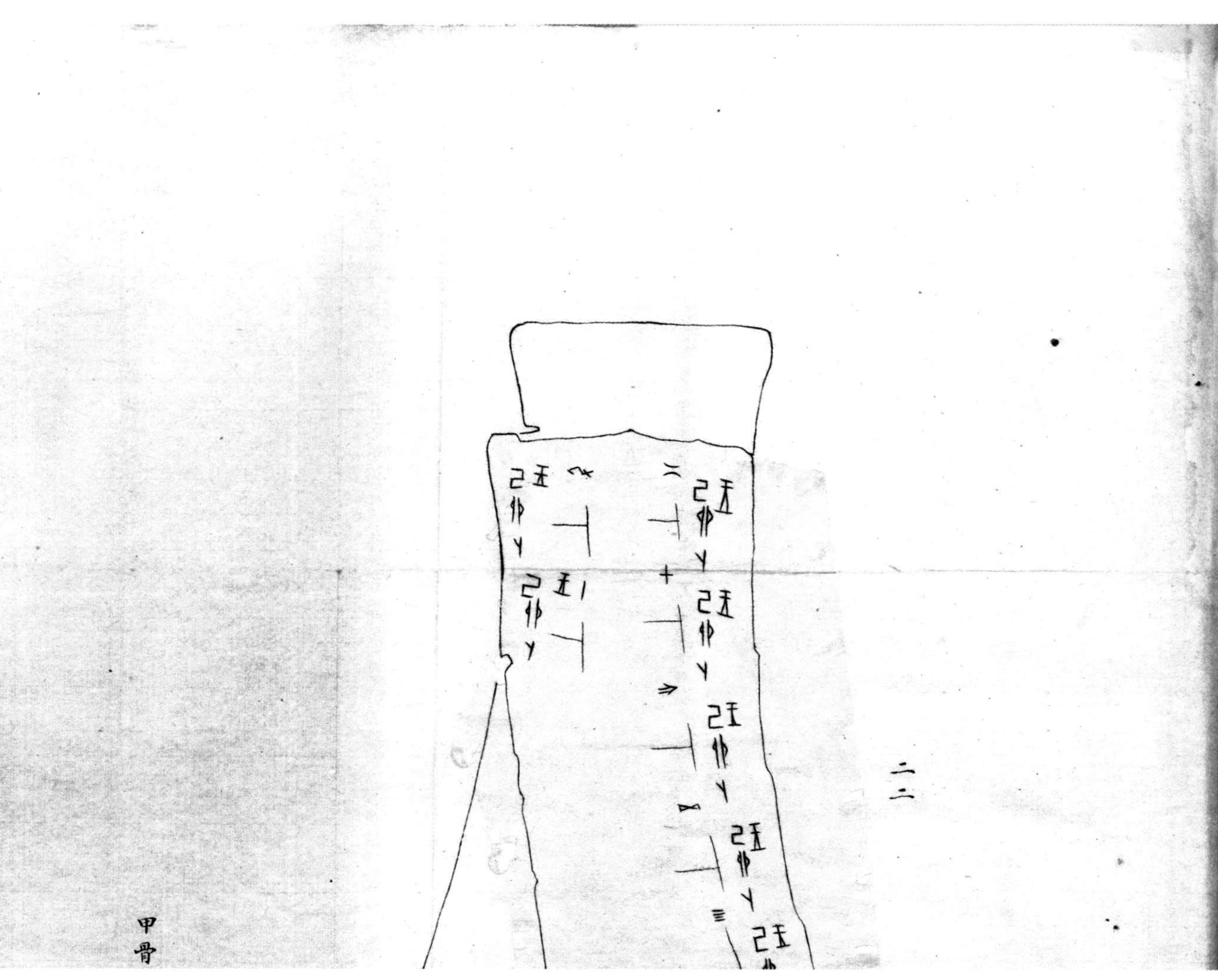
二二
甲骨

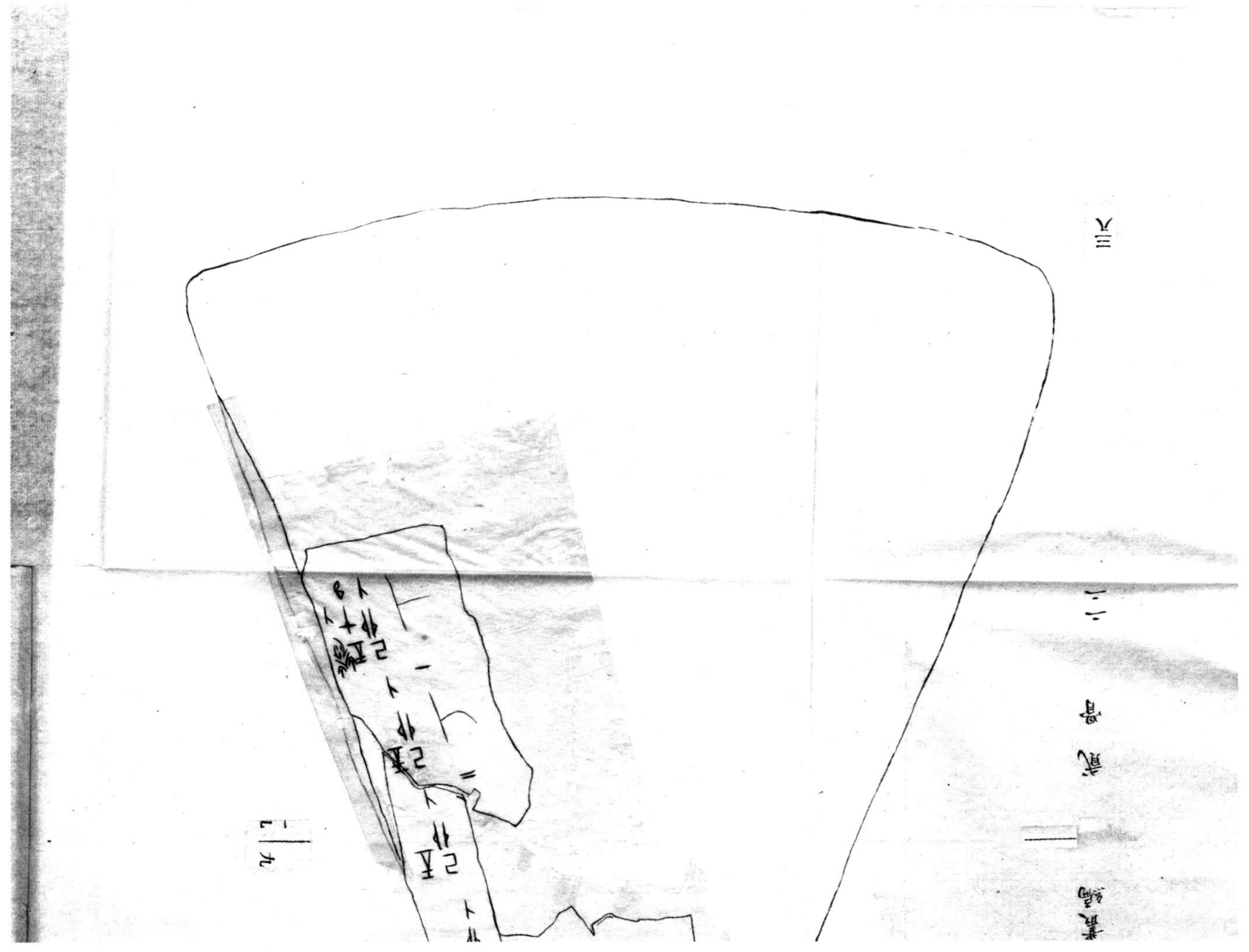
叢編
一
貳骨
二二
三八

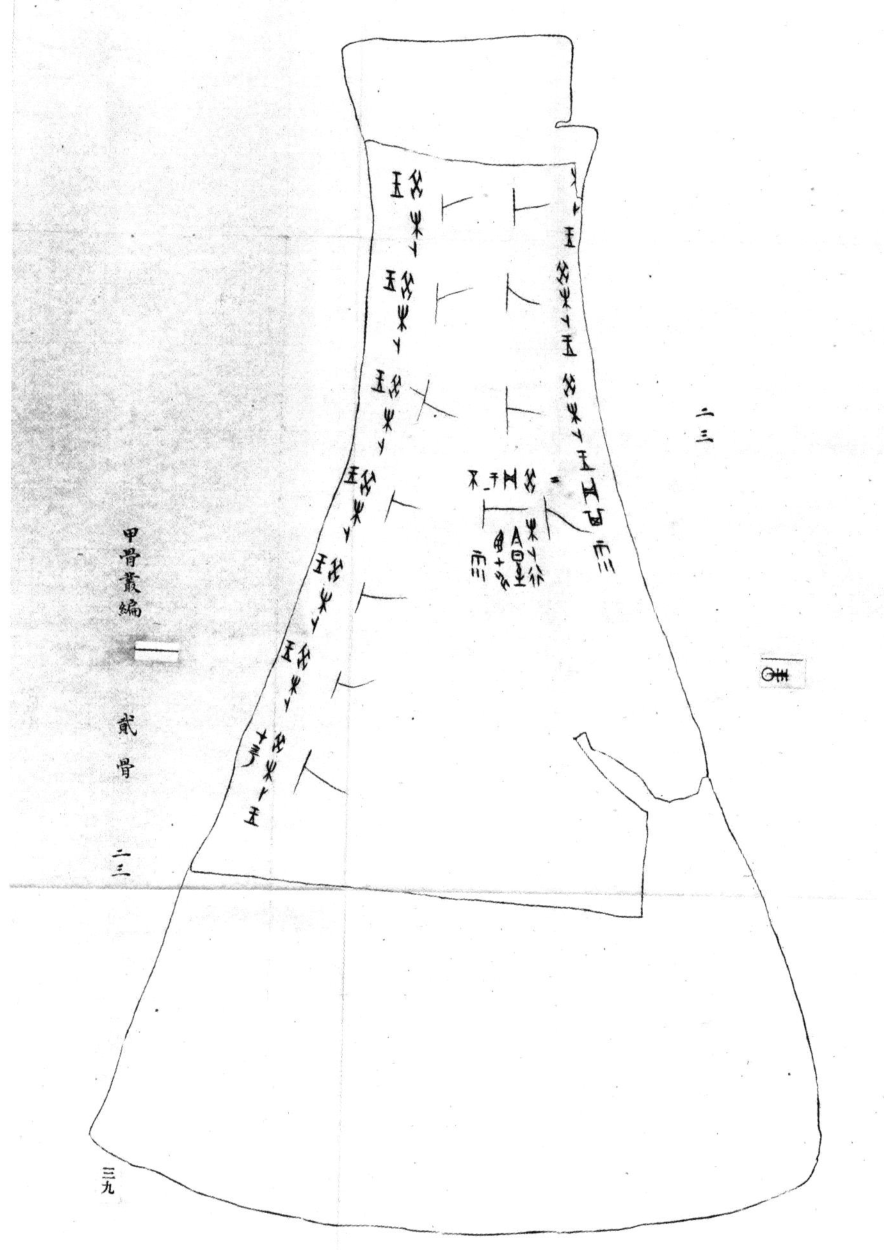
甲骨叢編
貳 骨
二三
二三
三九

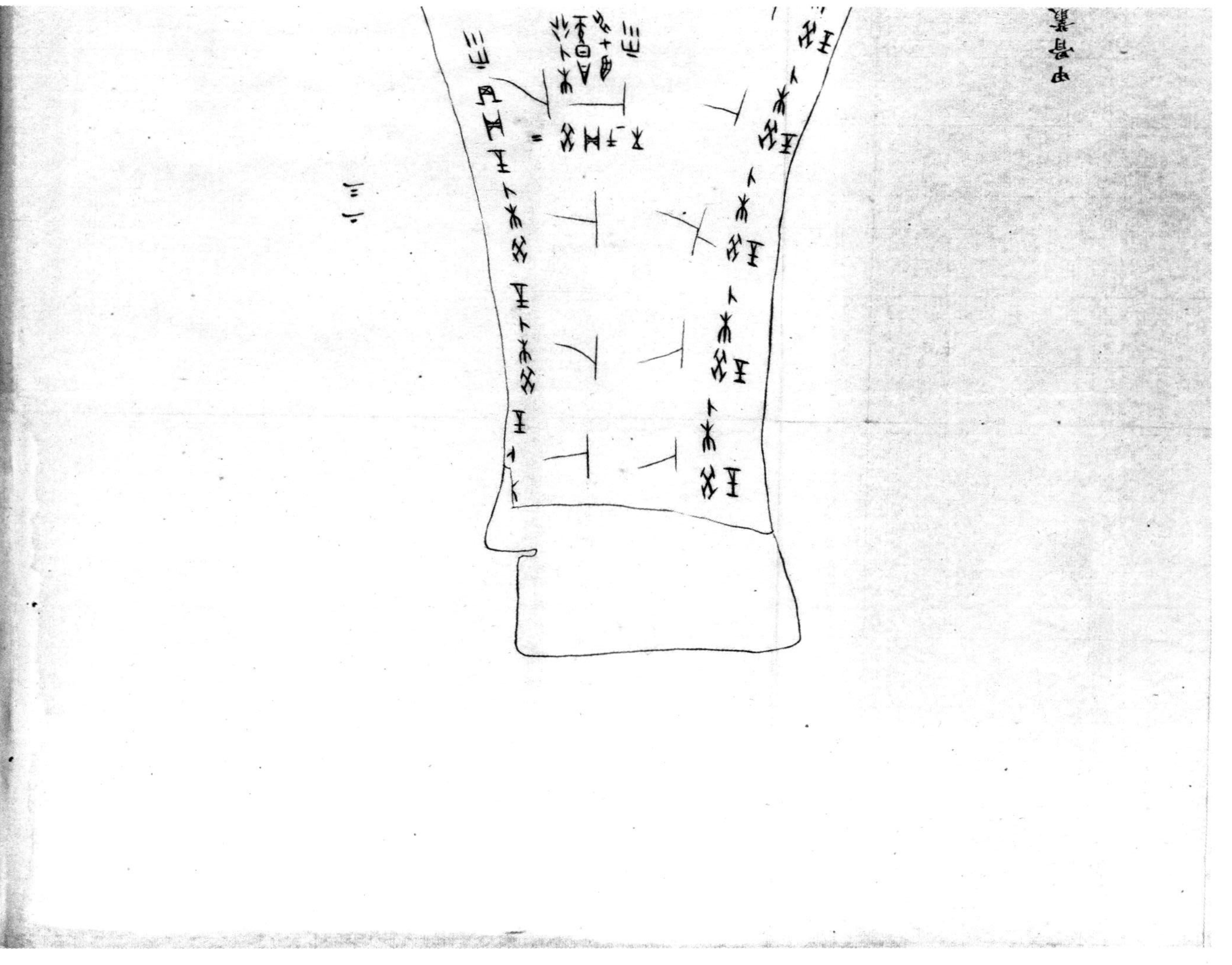

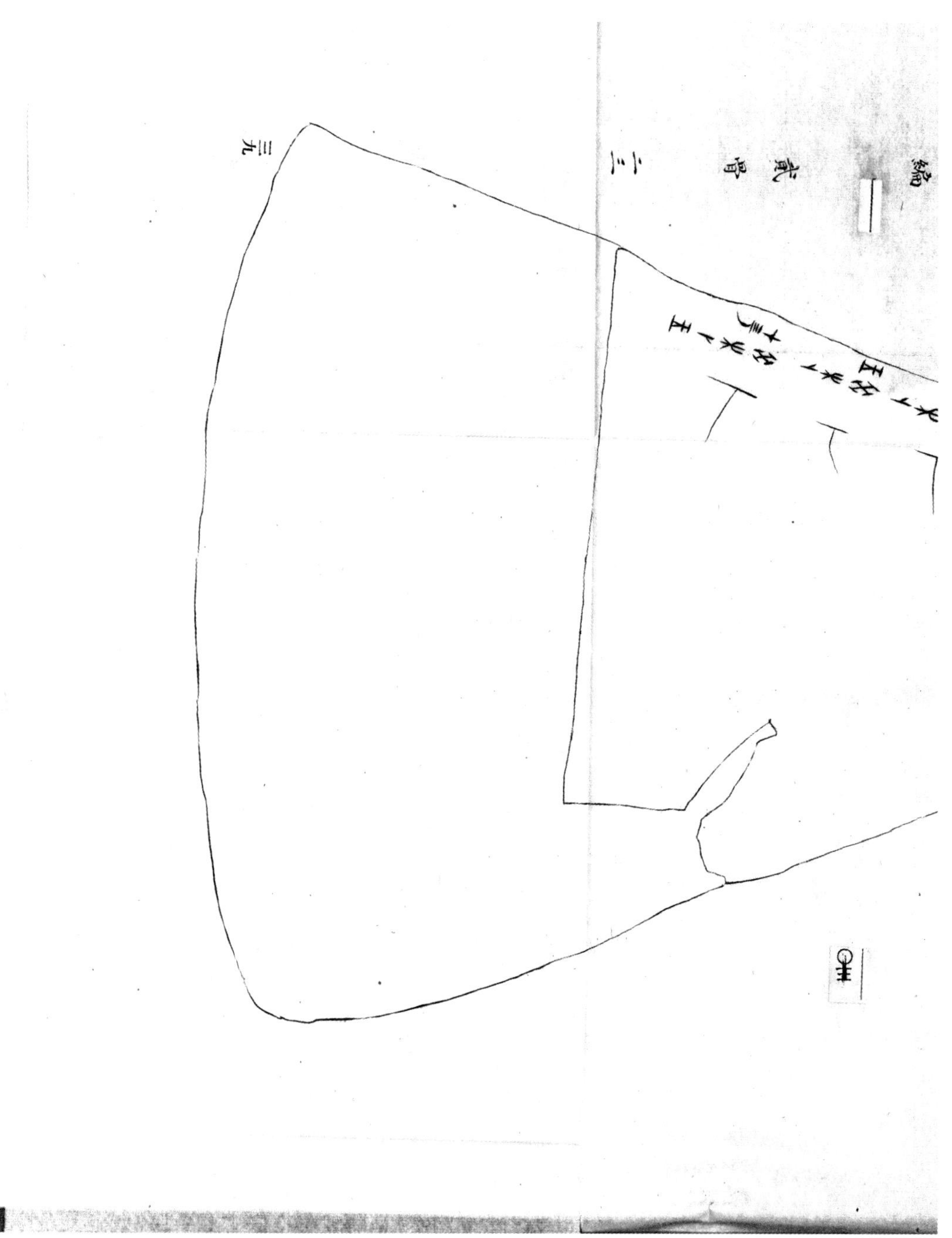
編
貳 骨
二三
三九

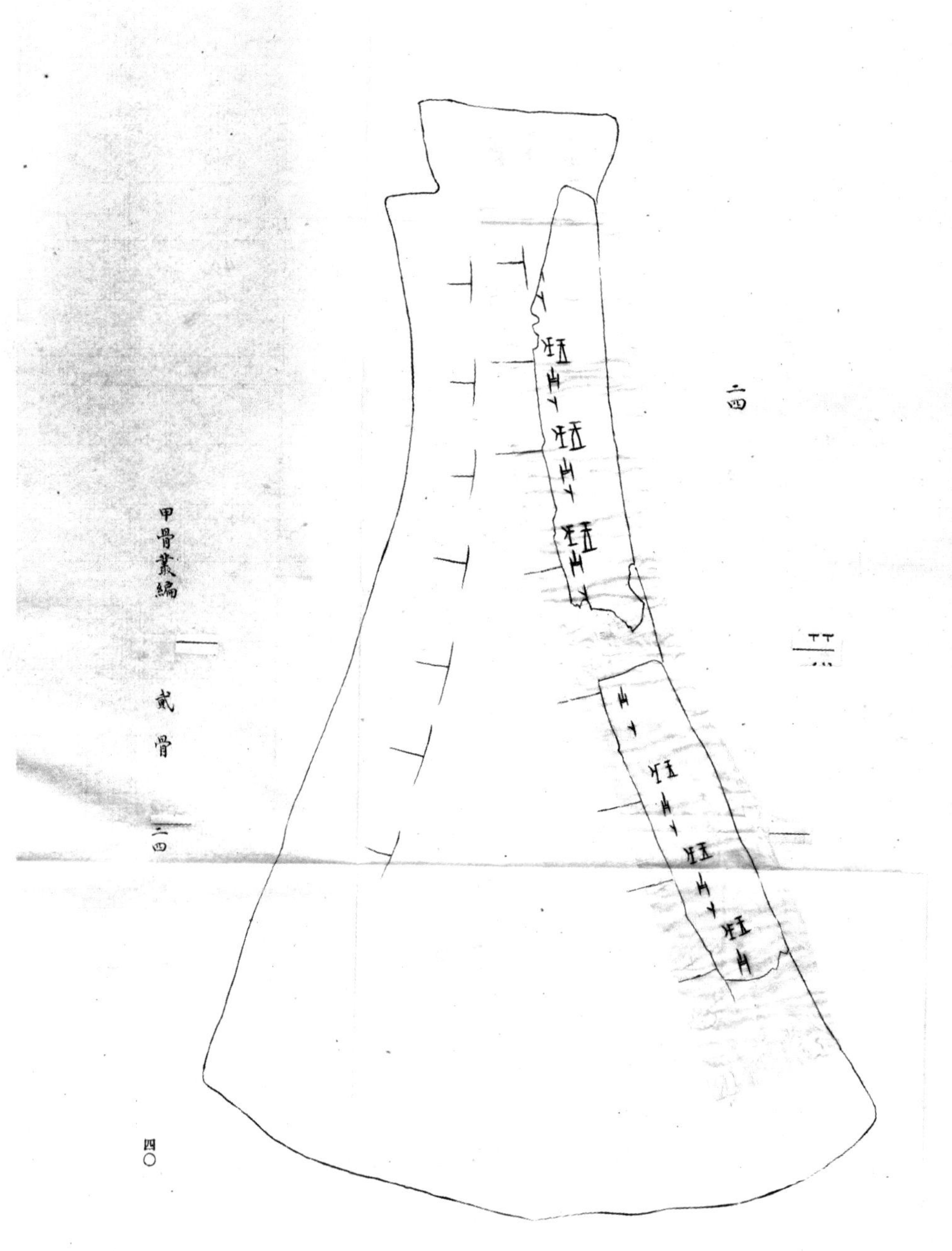
二四
甲骨叢編 貳骨 二四
四〇

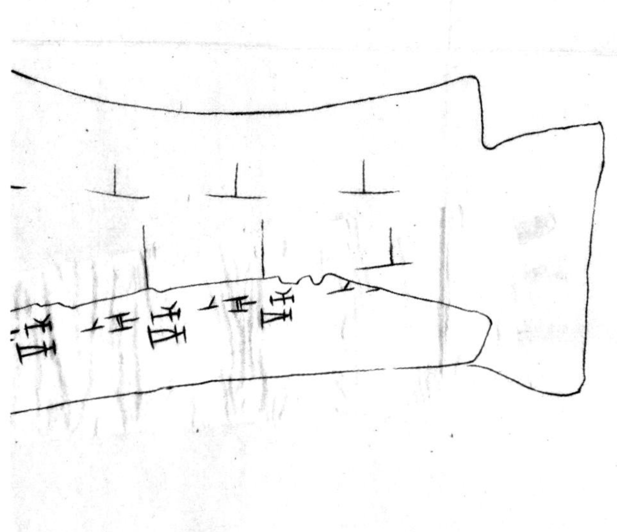

四〇

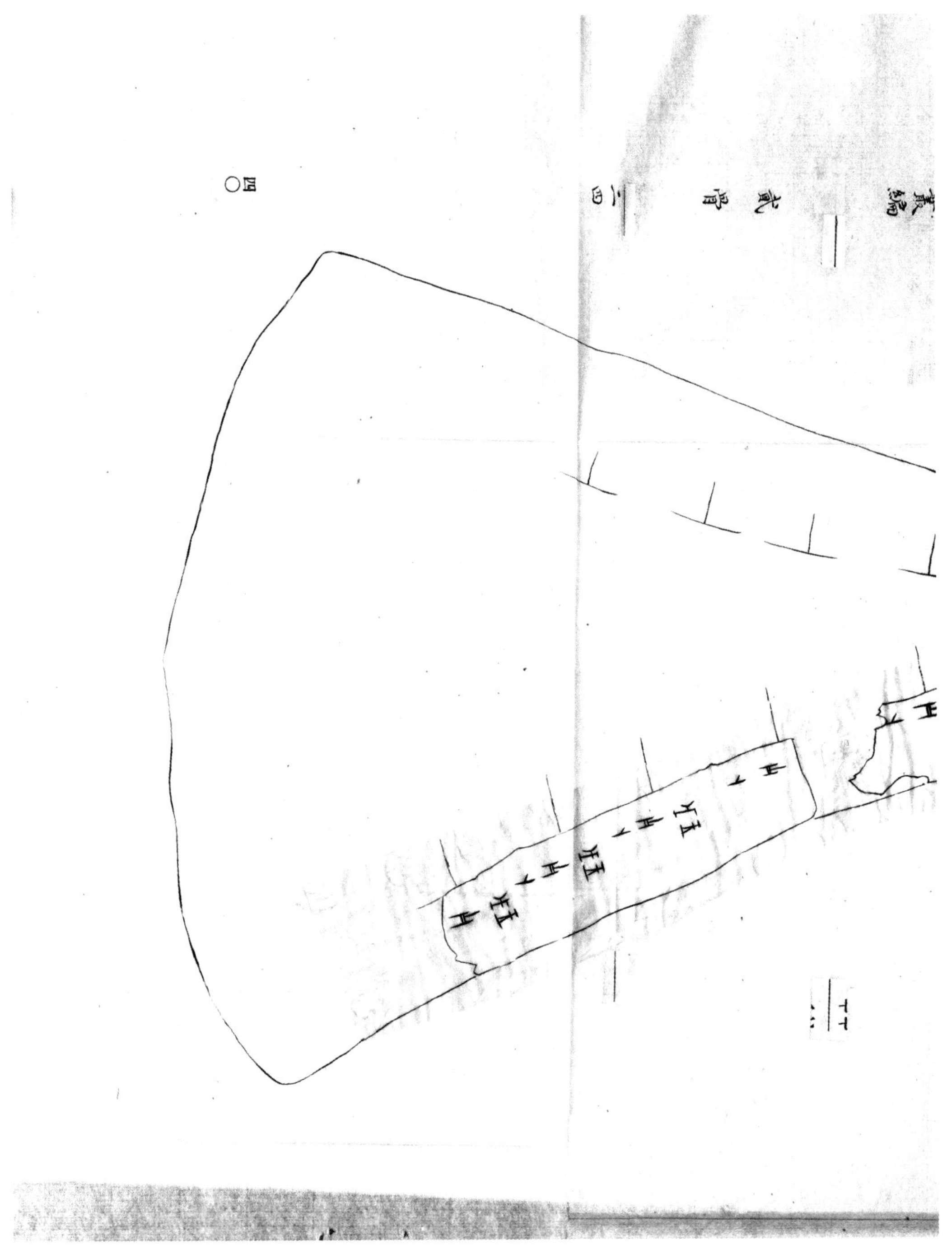

二五

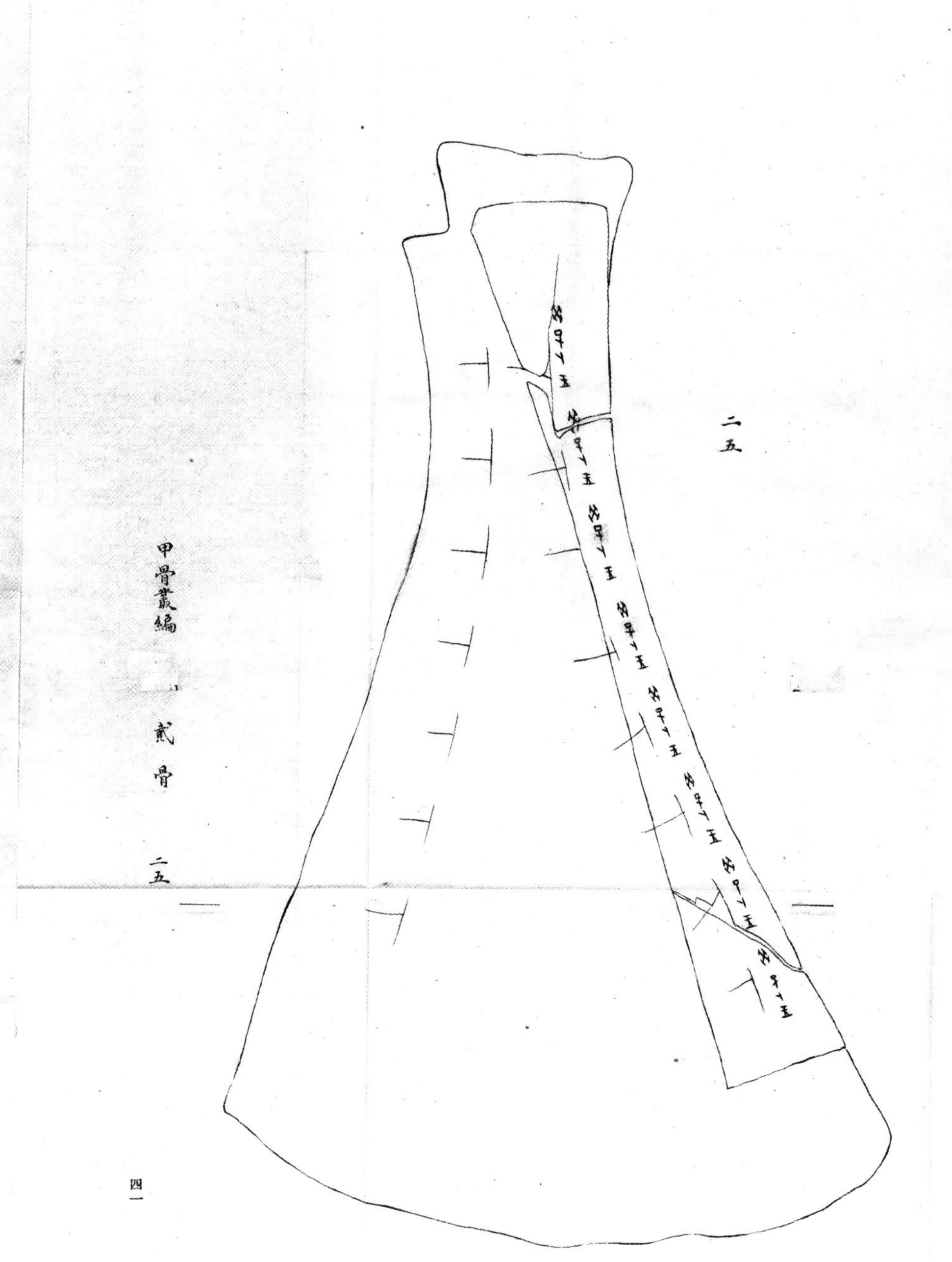

甲骨叢編　貳骨　二五

四一

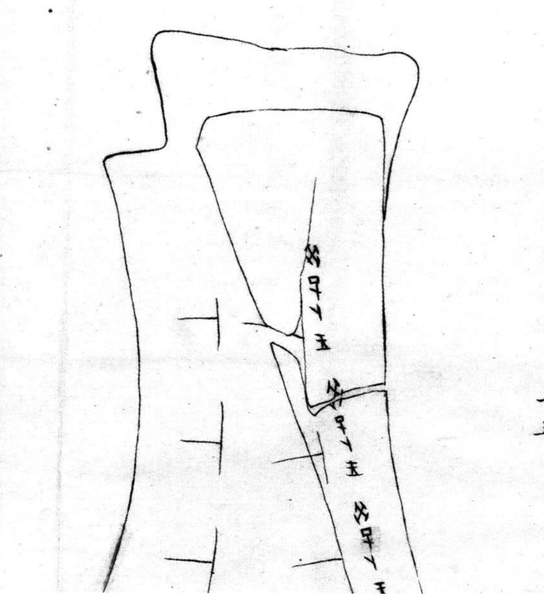
二五

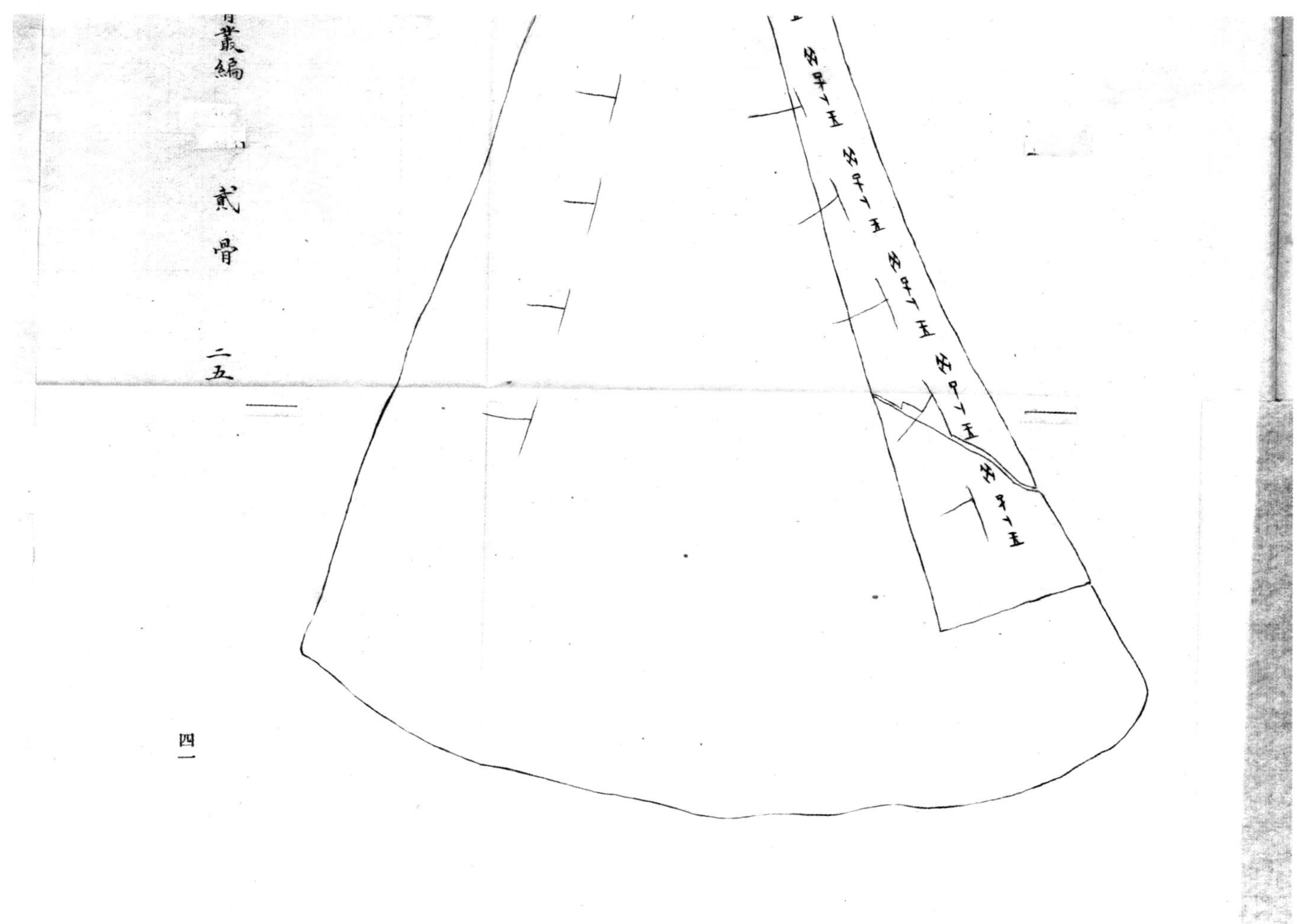
叢編
貳骨
二五
四一

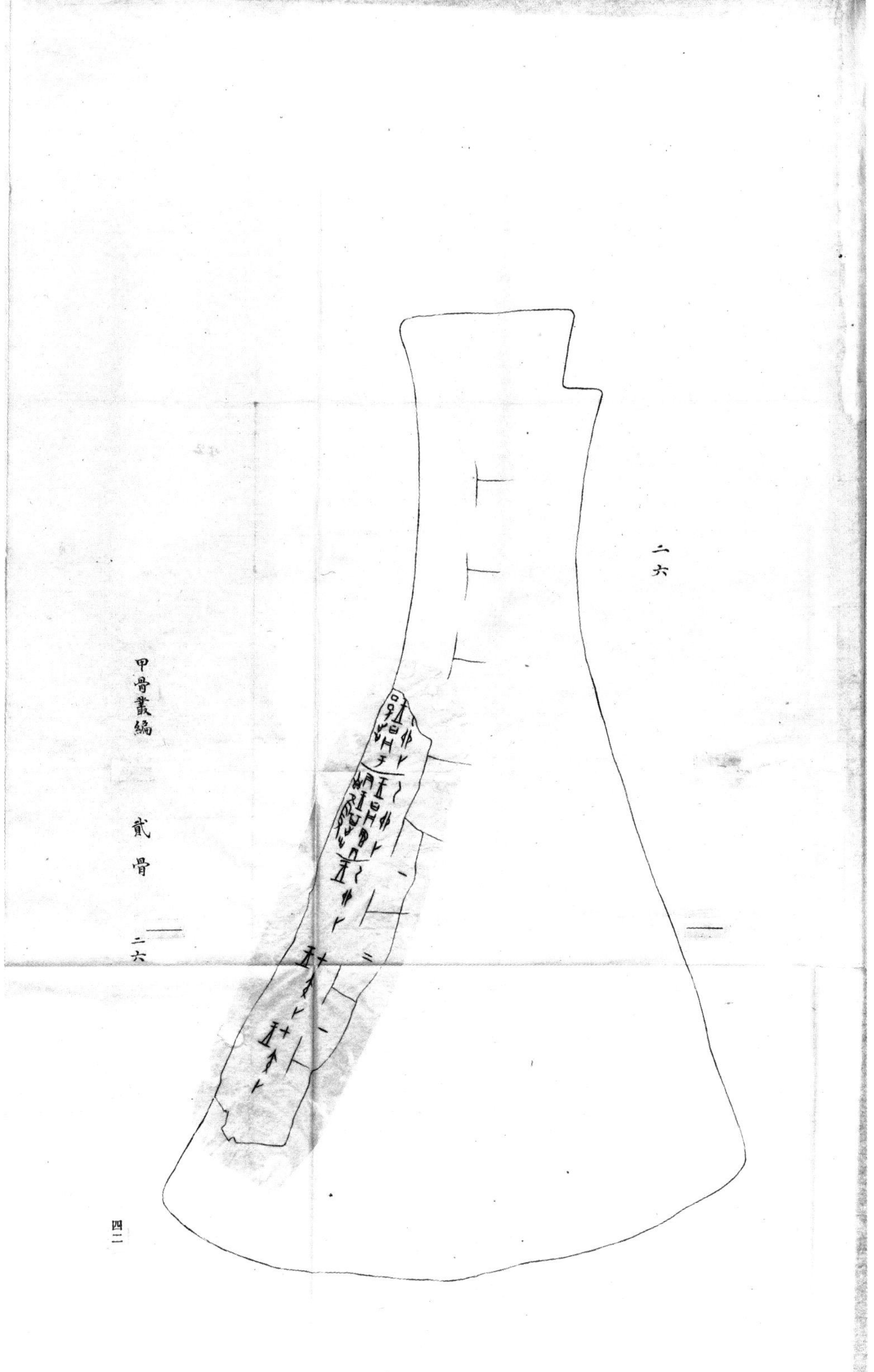
二六
甲骨叢編　貳骨　二六
四二

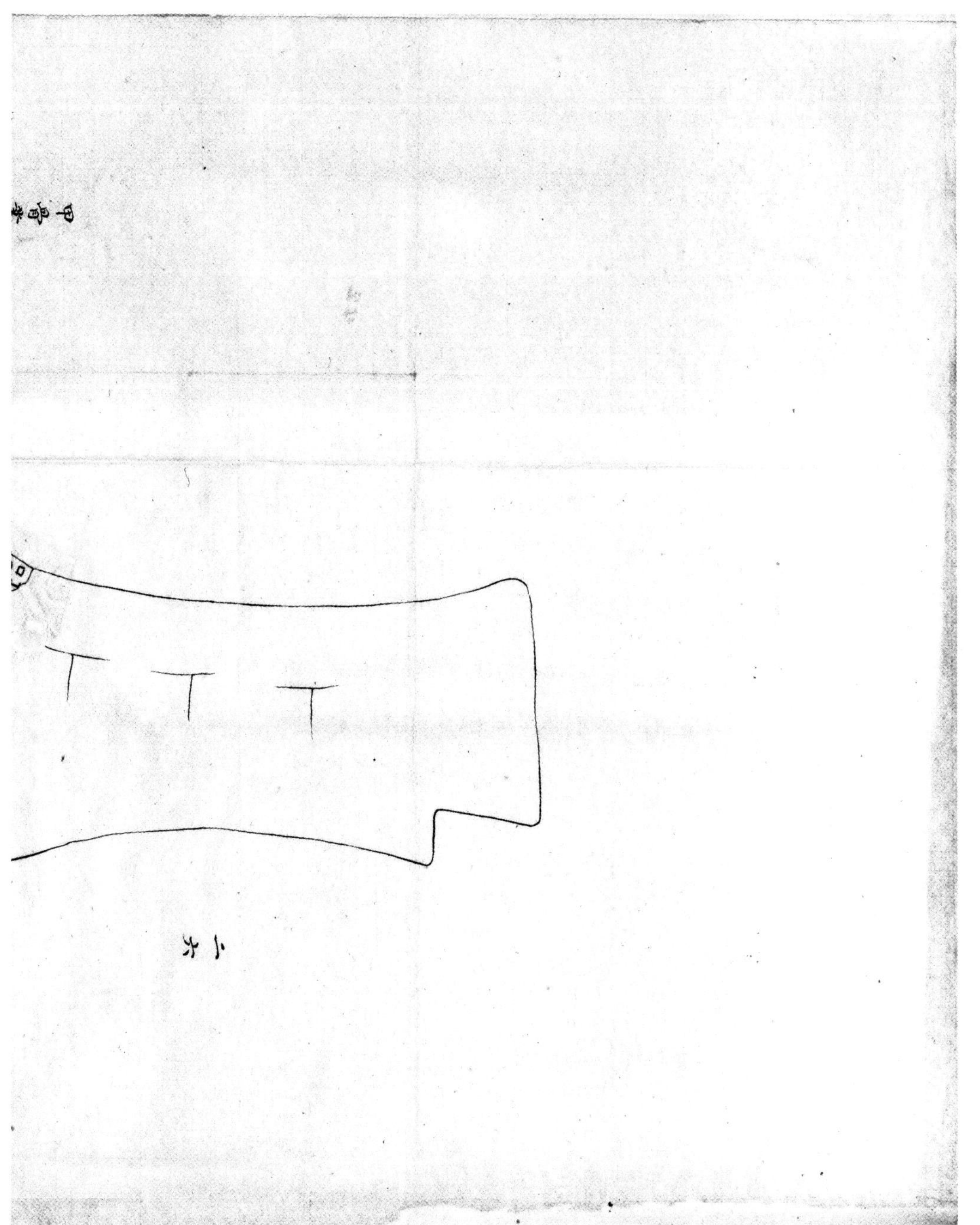

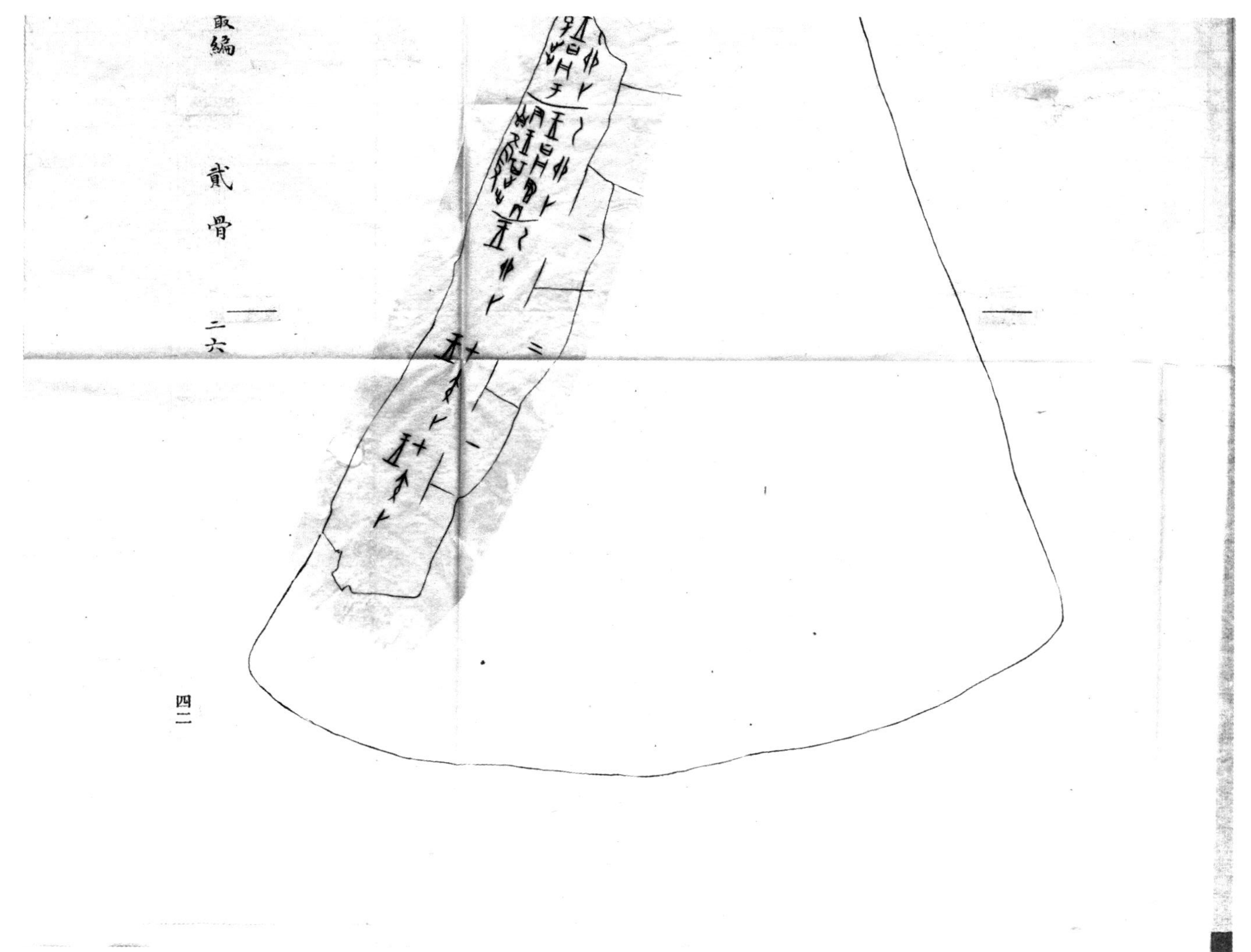

取編

貳骨

二六

四二

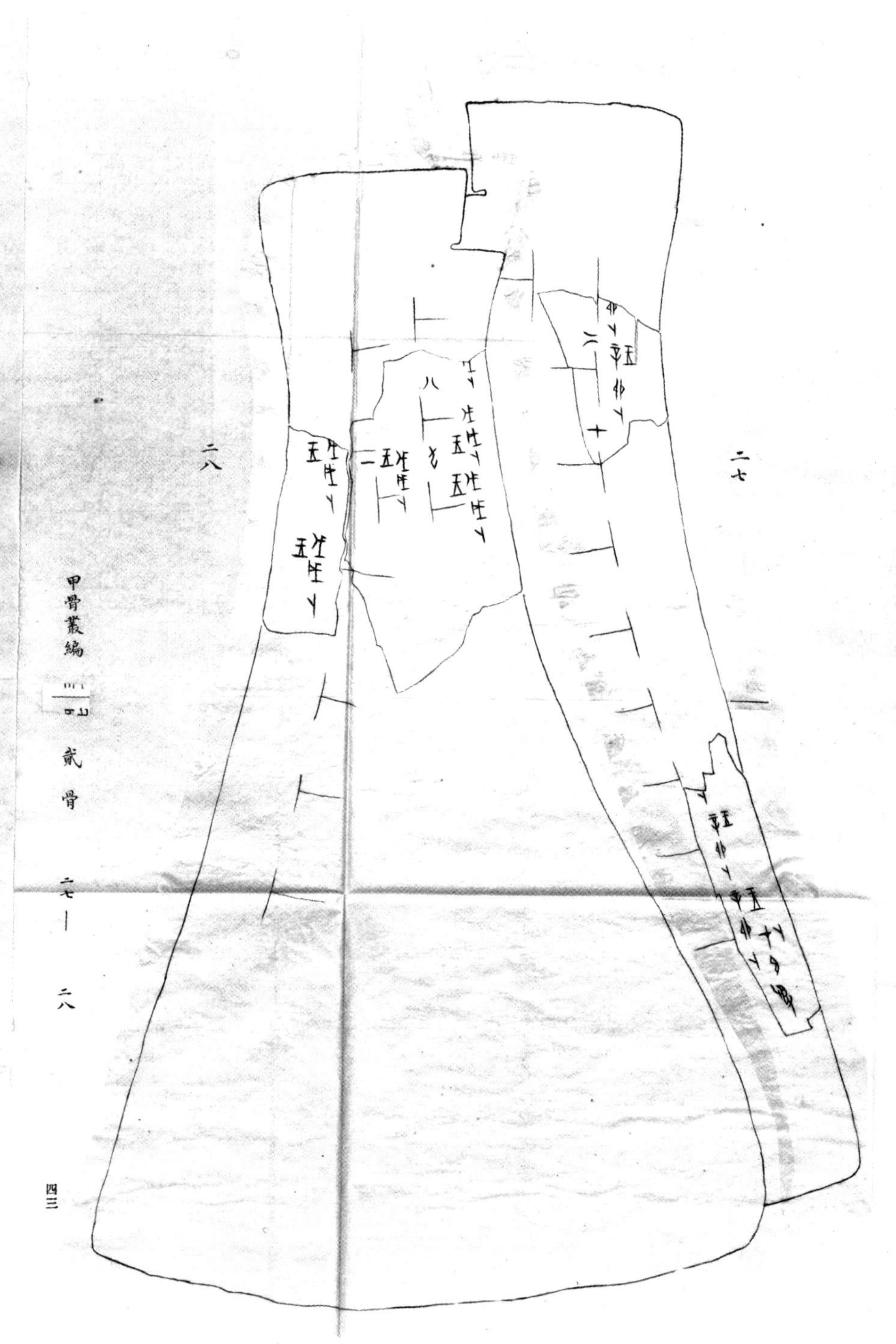

二七
二八
甲骨叢編 貳骨 二七— 二八
四三

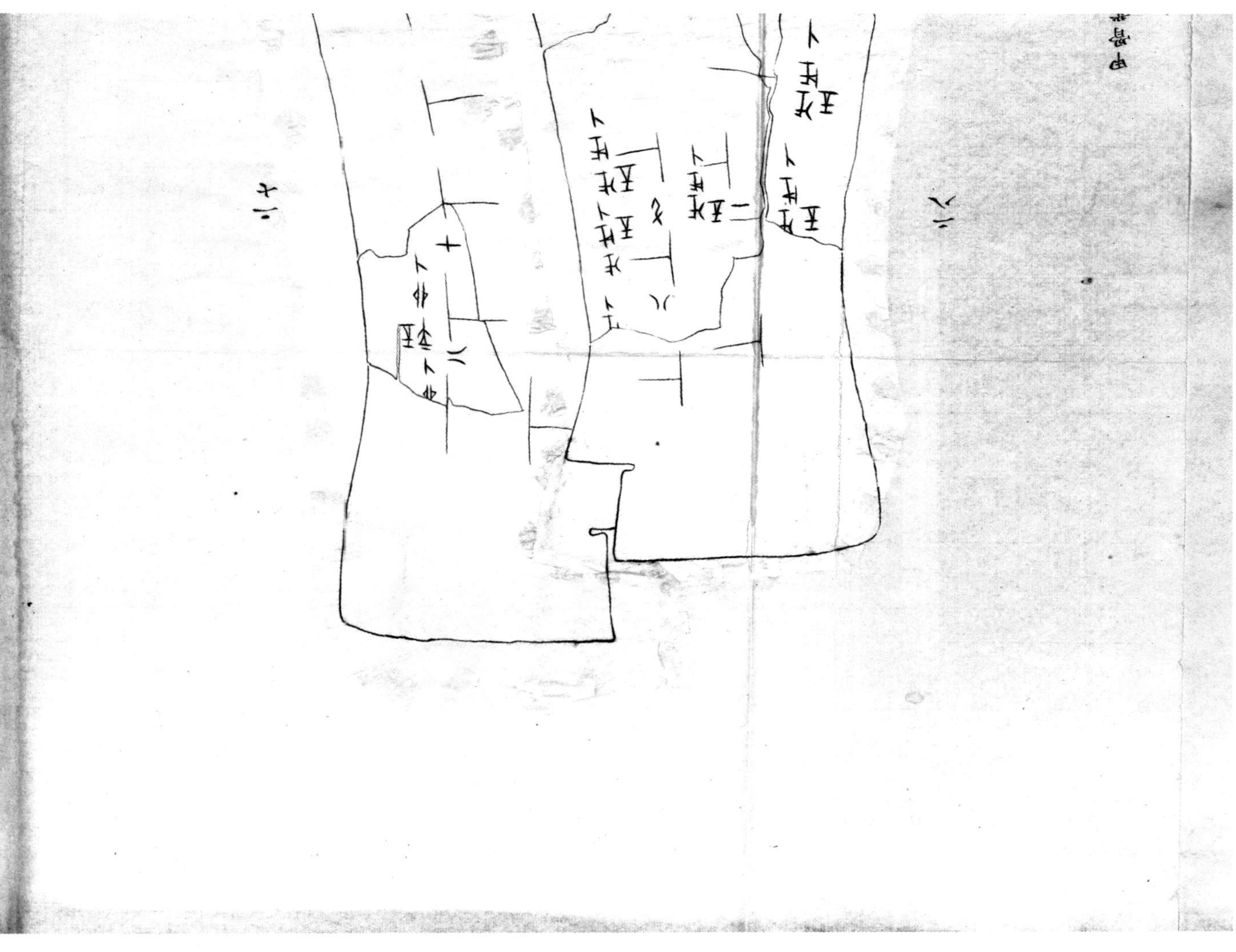

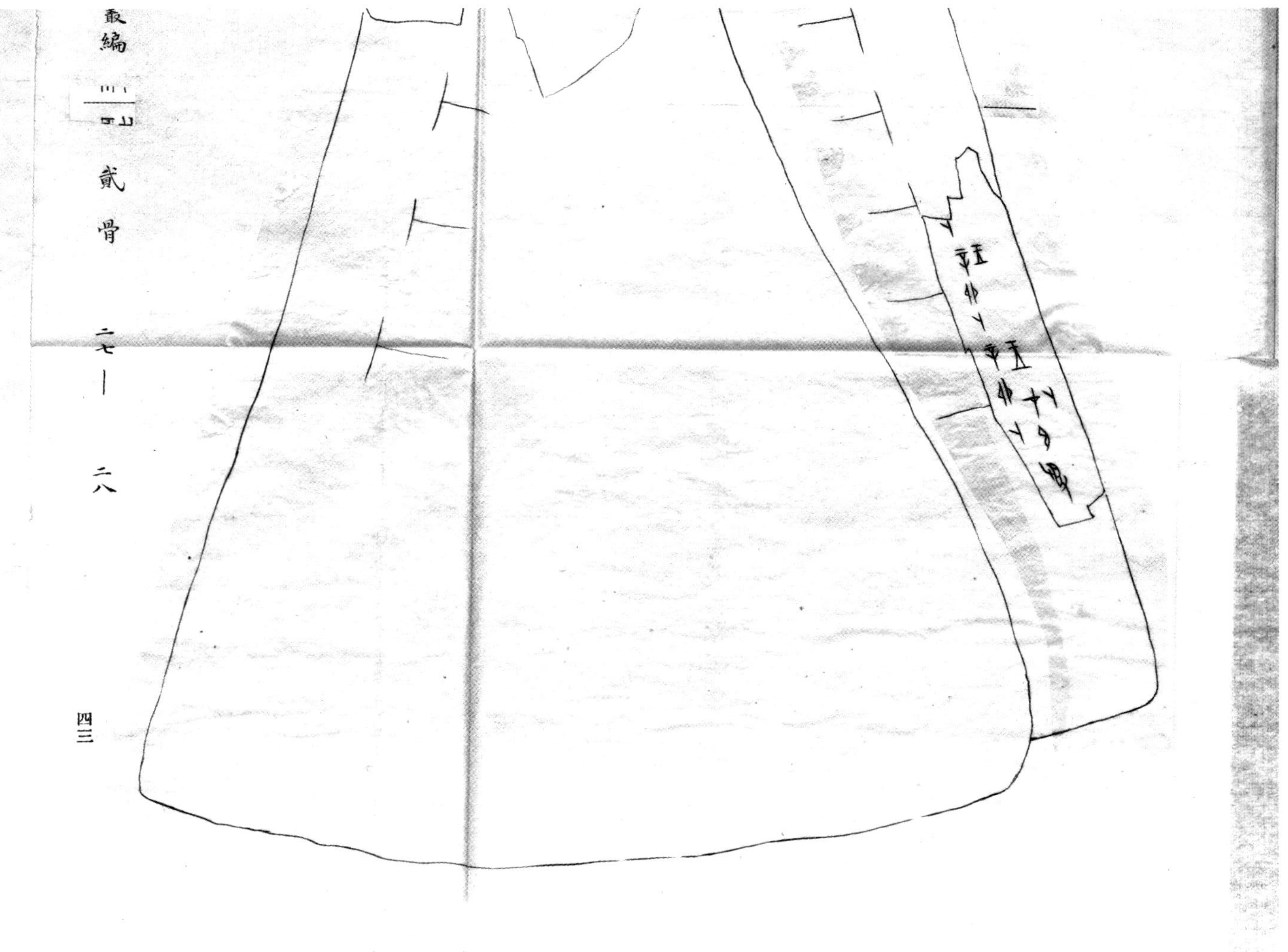
甲編
三四二三
貳骨
二七一
二八
四三

甲骨叢編　貳骨　二九一　四六

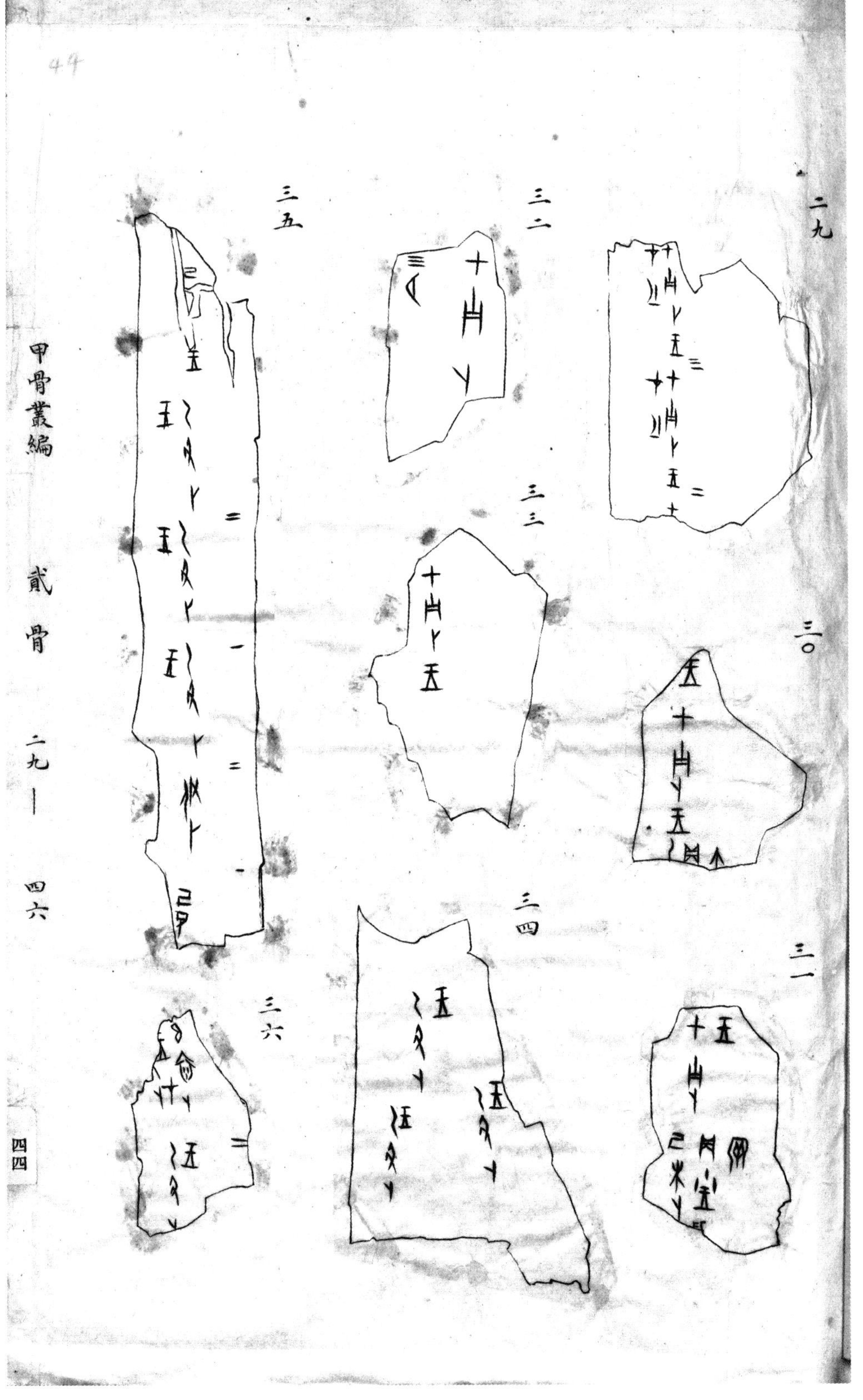

四四

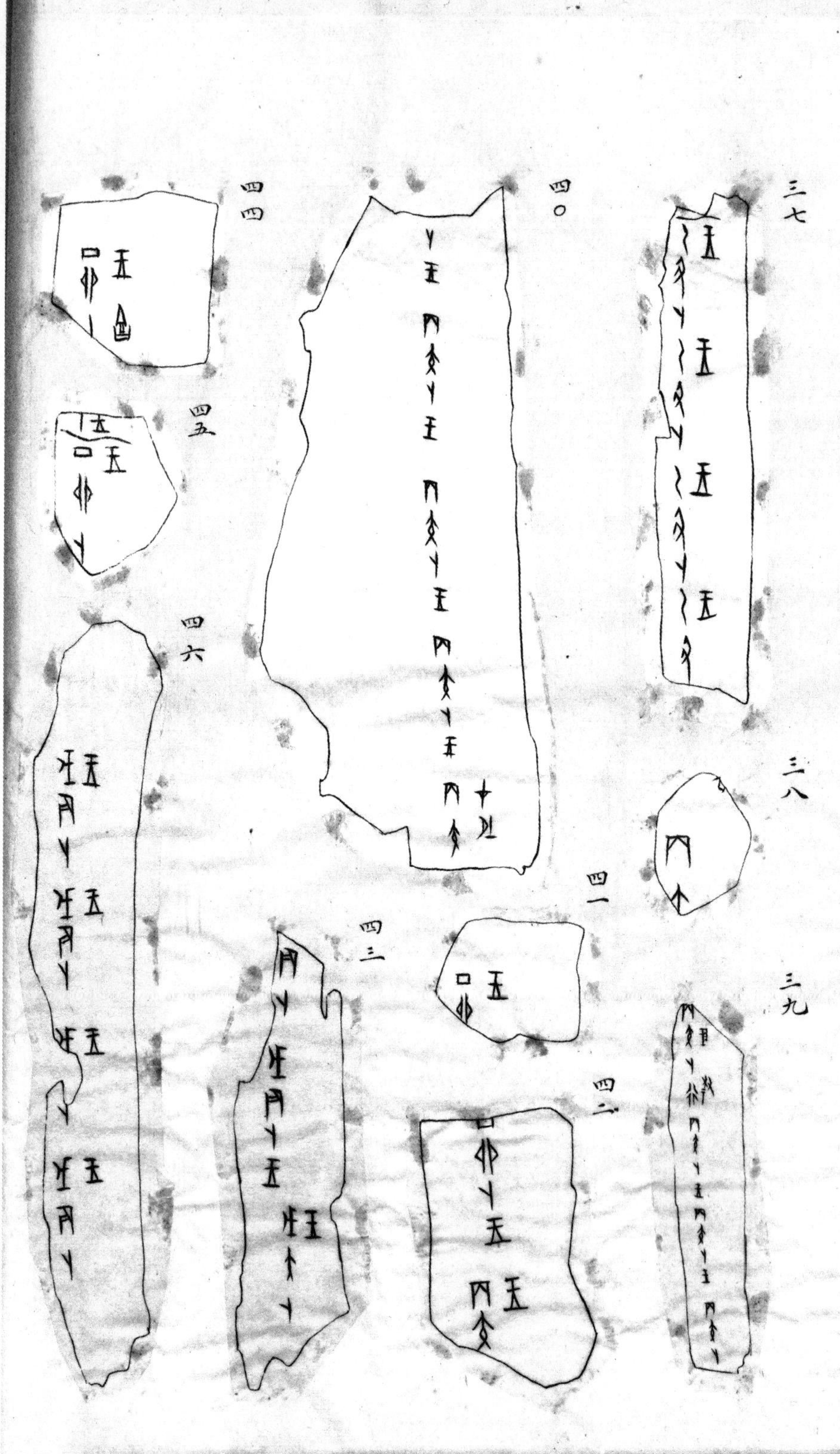
三七
三八
三九
四〇
四一
四二
四三
四四
四五
四六

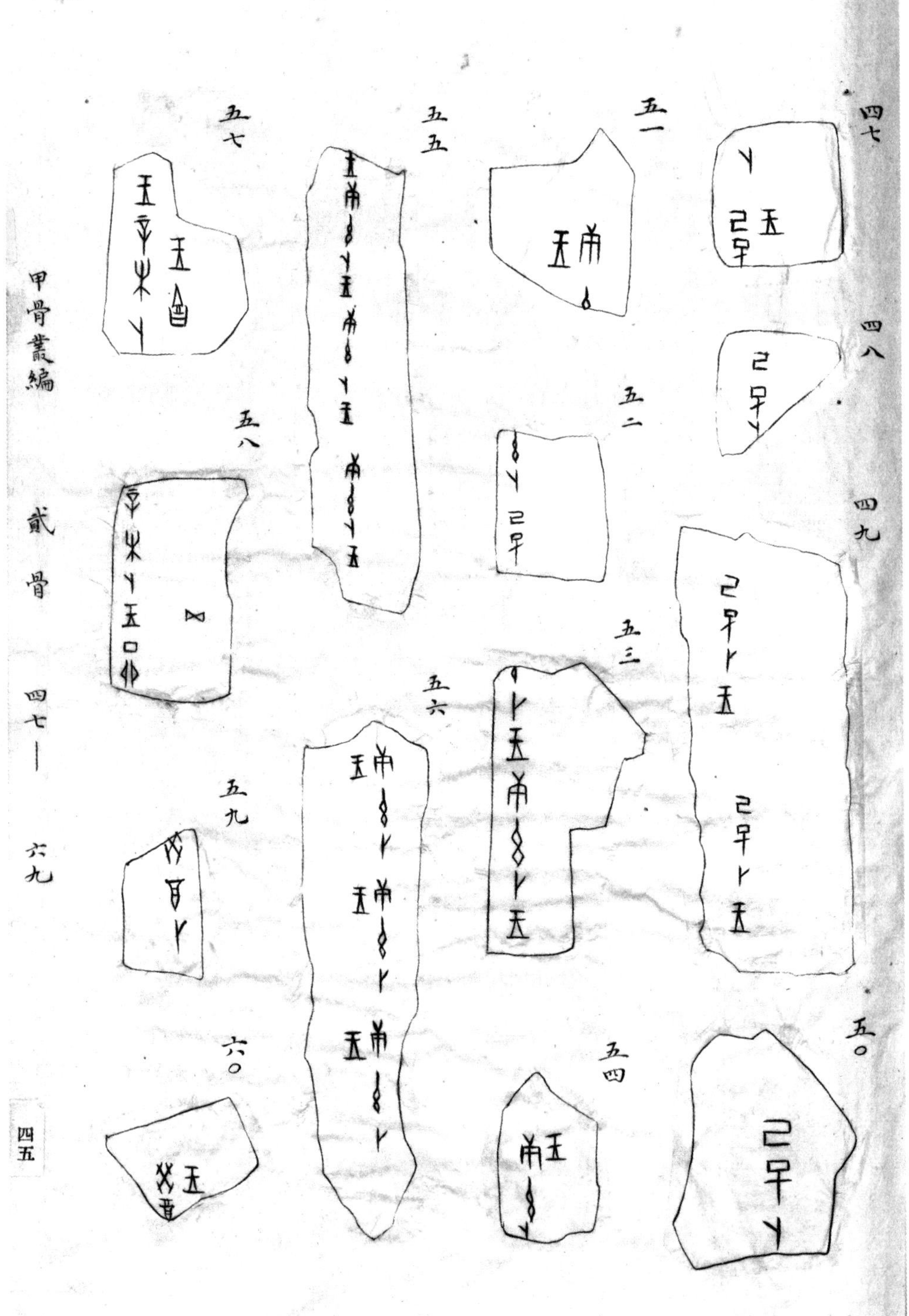

甲骨叢編　貳　骨　四七—六九

四五

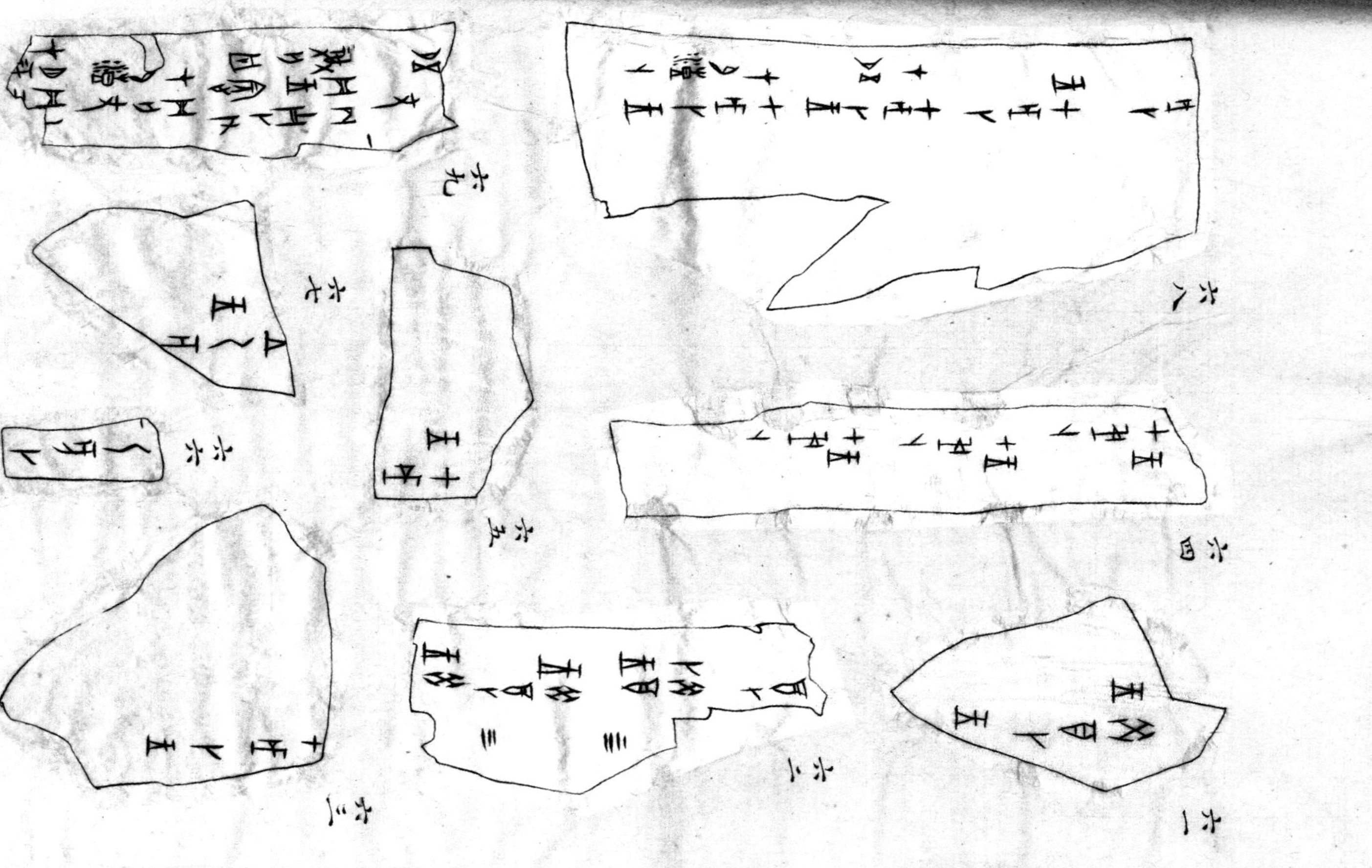
六一
六二
六三
六四
六五
六六
六七
六八
六九

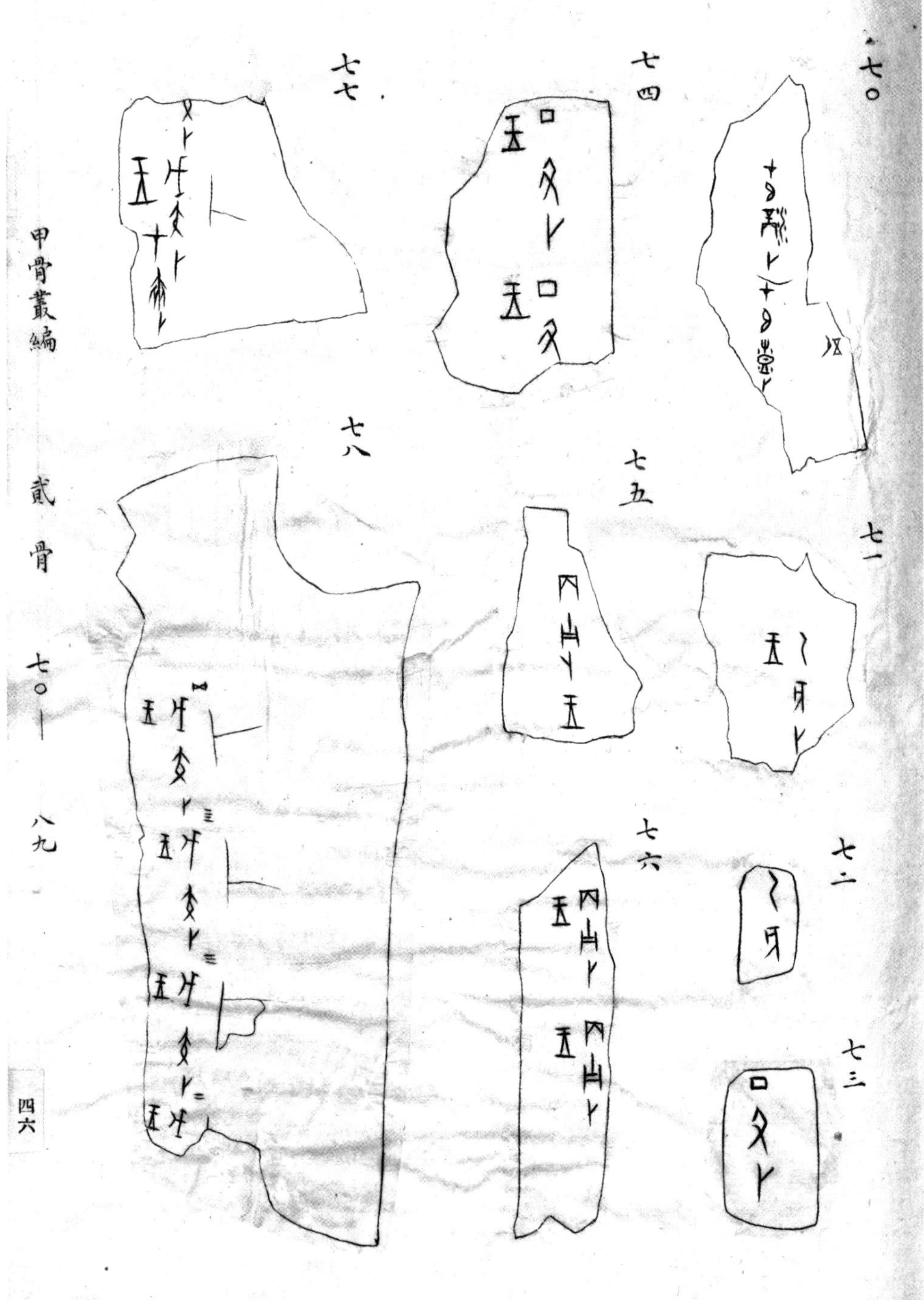

甲骨叢編 貳 骨 七〇—八九

四六

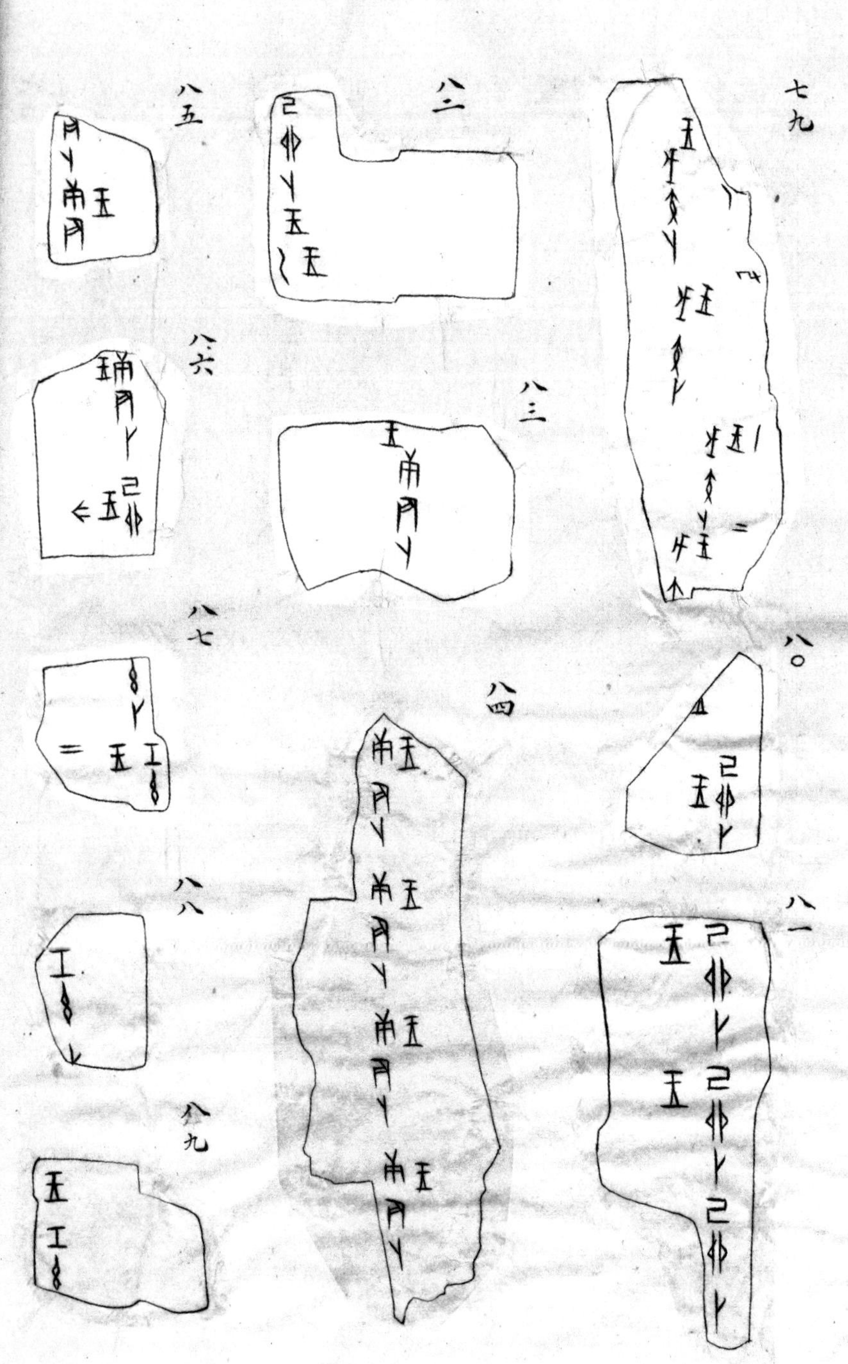
七九
八〇
八一
八二
八三
八四
八五
八六
八七
八八
八九

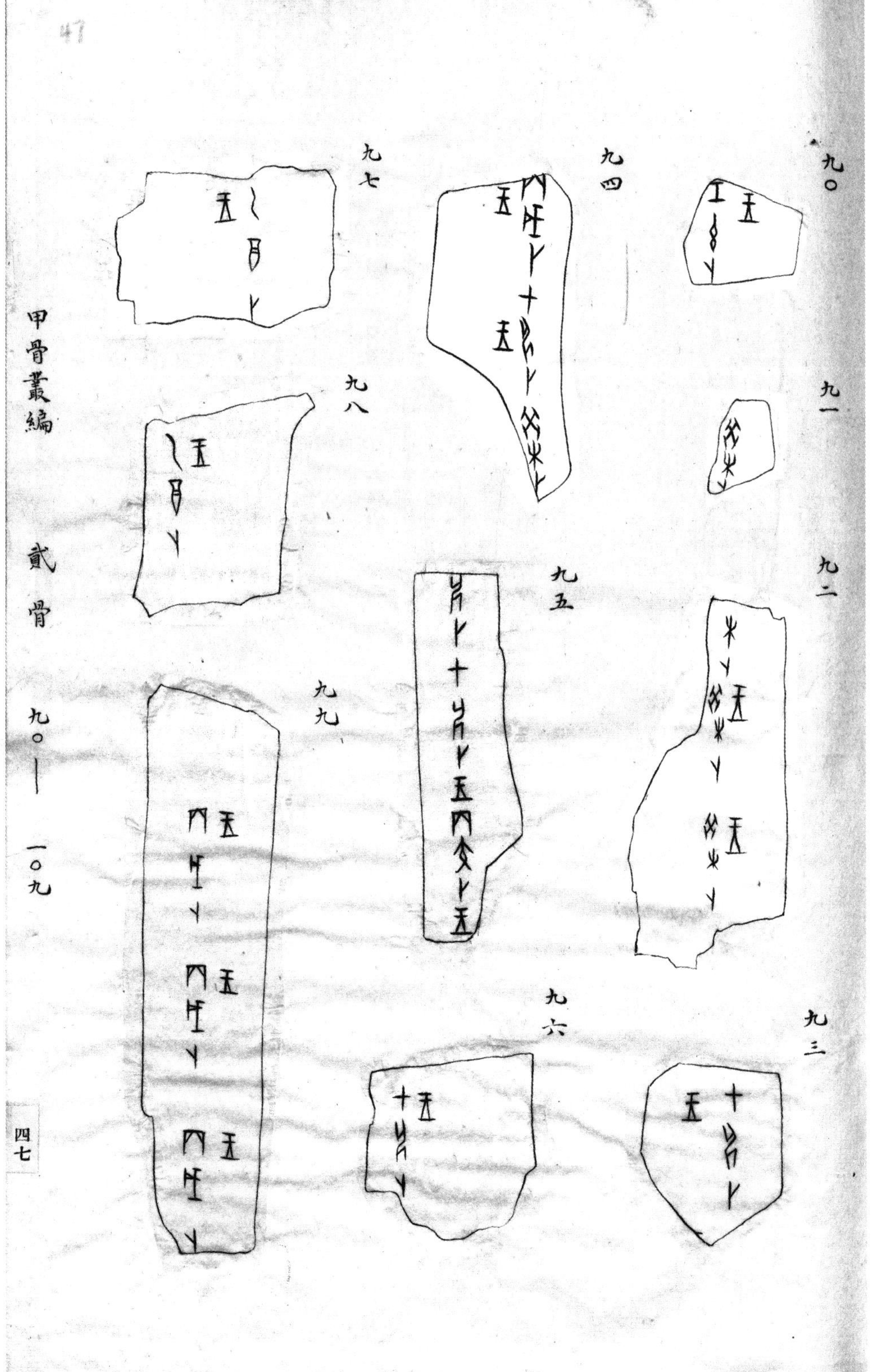
九〇
九一
九二
九三
九四
九五
九六
九七
九八
九九
甲骨叢編
貳骨
九〇——一〇九
四七

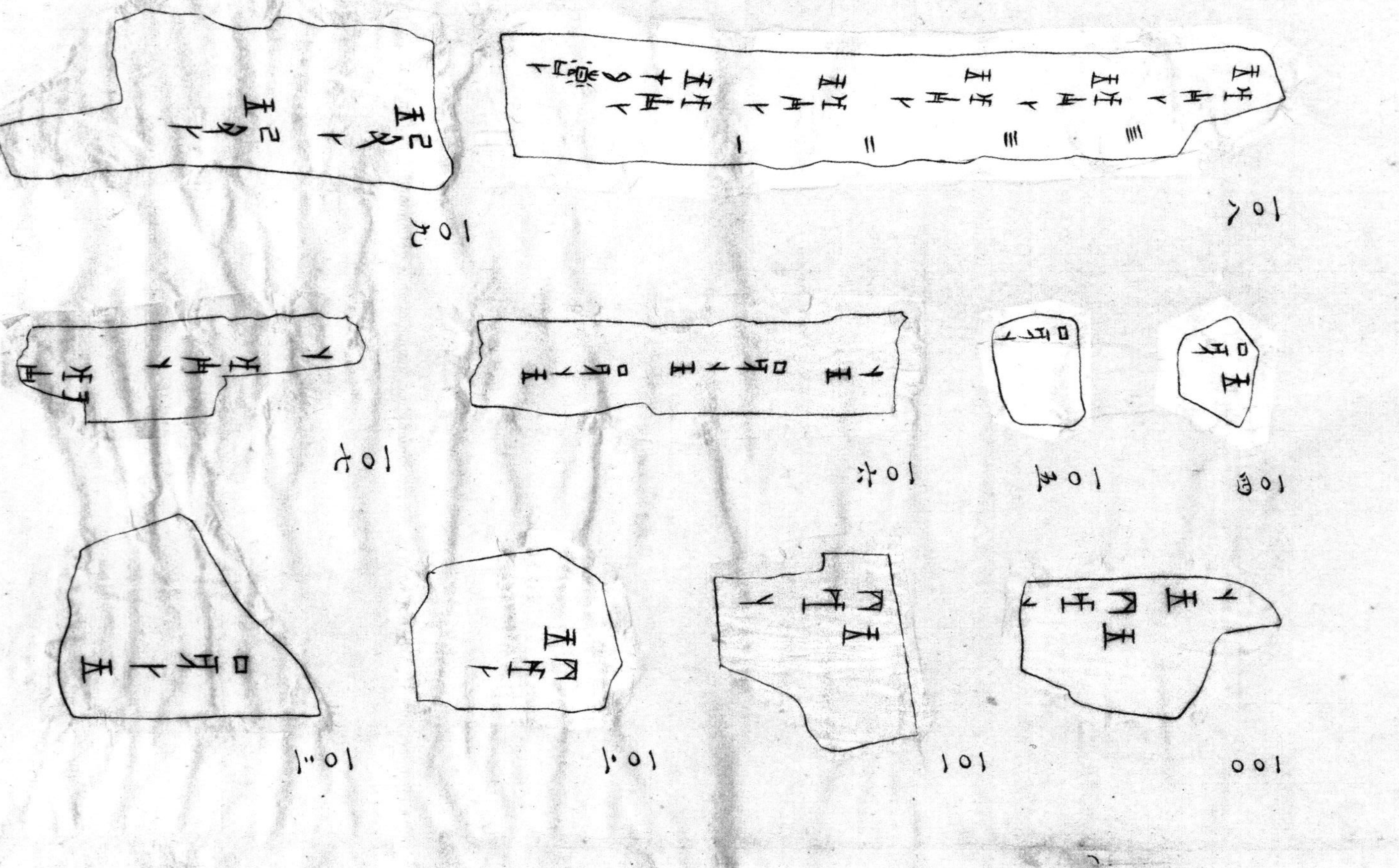
一〇〇
一〇一
一〇二
一〇三
一〇四
一〇五
一〇六
一〇七
一〇八
一〇九

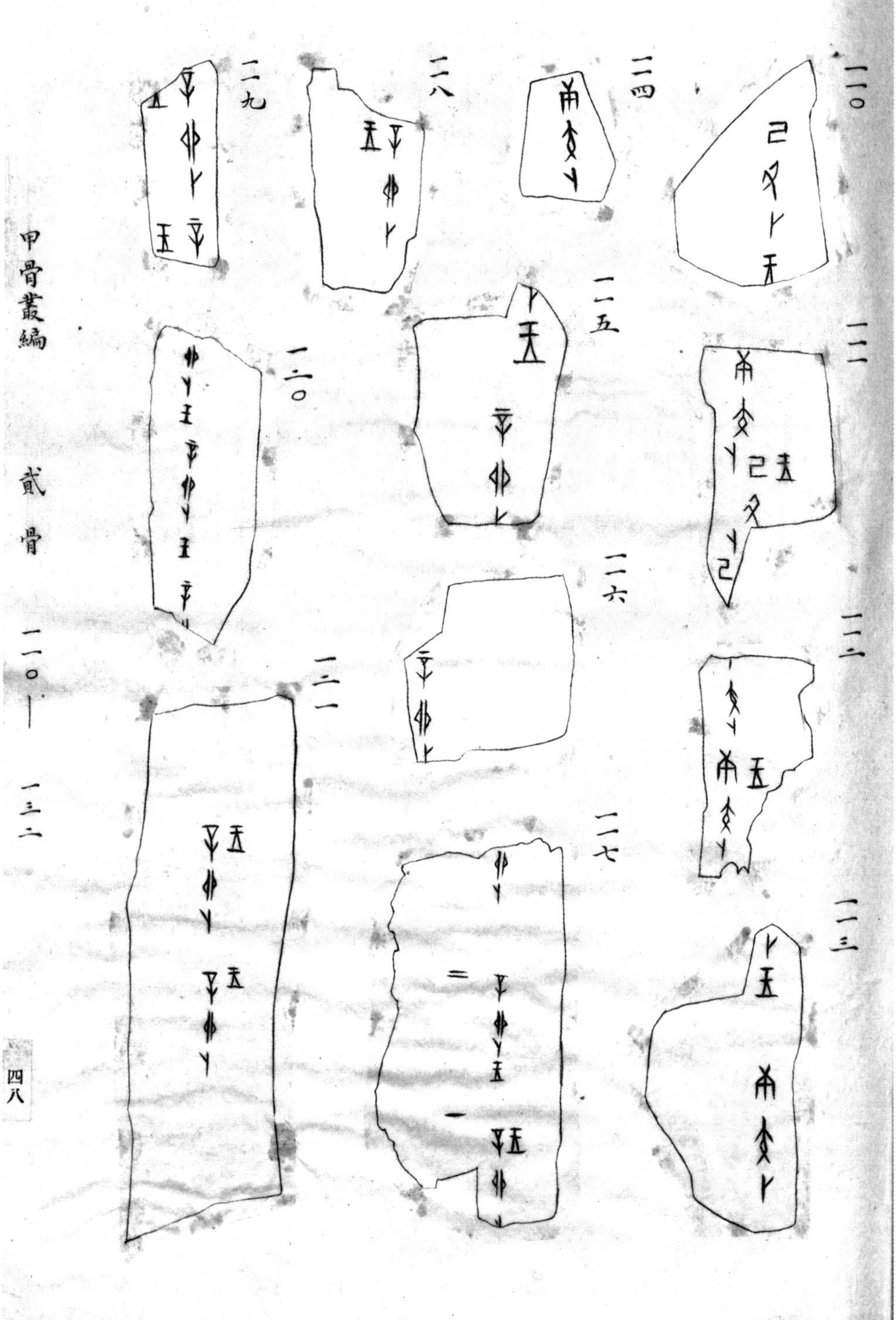

46
甲骨叢編　貳骨　一一〇一　一三二
一一〇
一一一
一一二
一一三
一一四
一一五
一一六
一一七
一一八
一一九
一二〇
一二一
四八

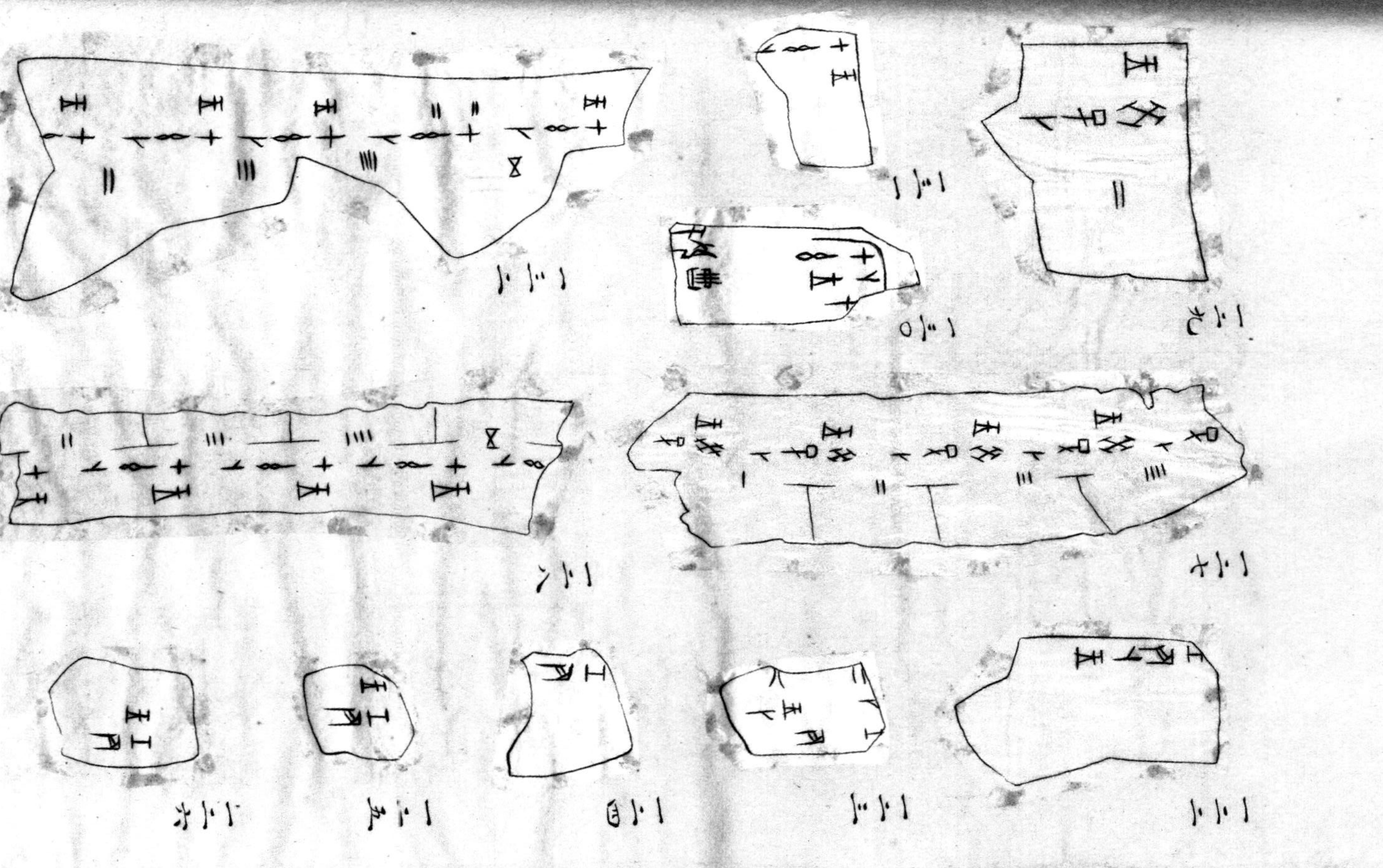

甲骨叢編　貳骨　一三三—一五五

四九

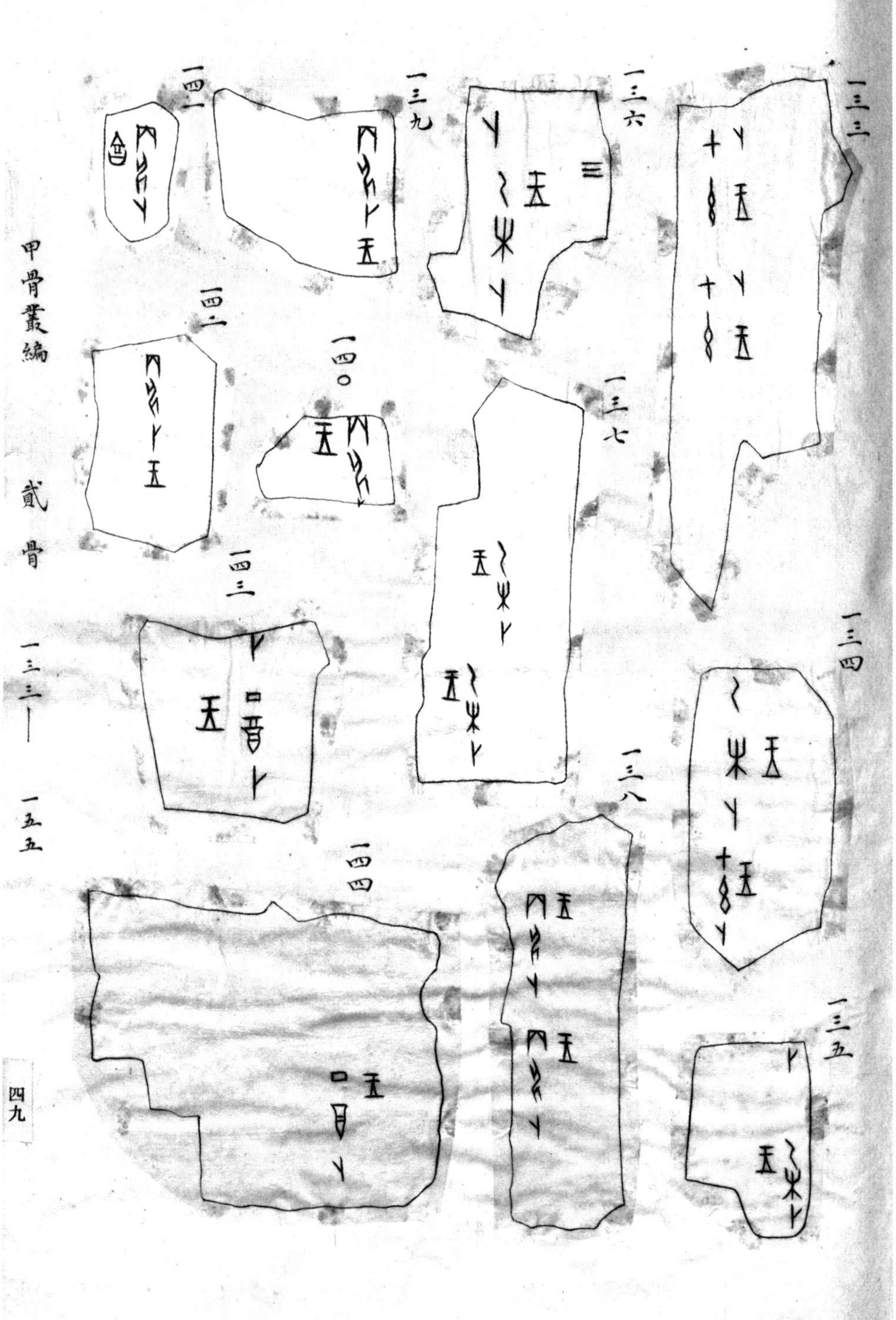

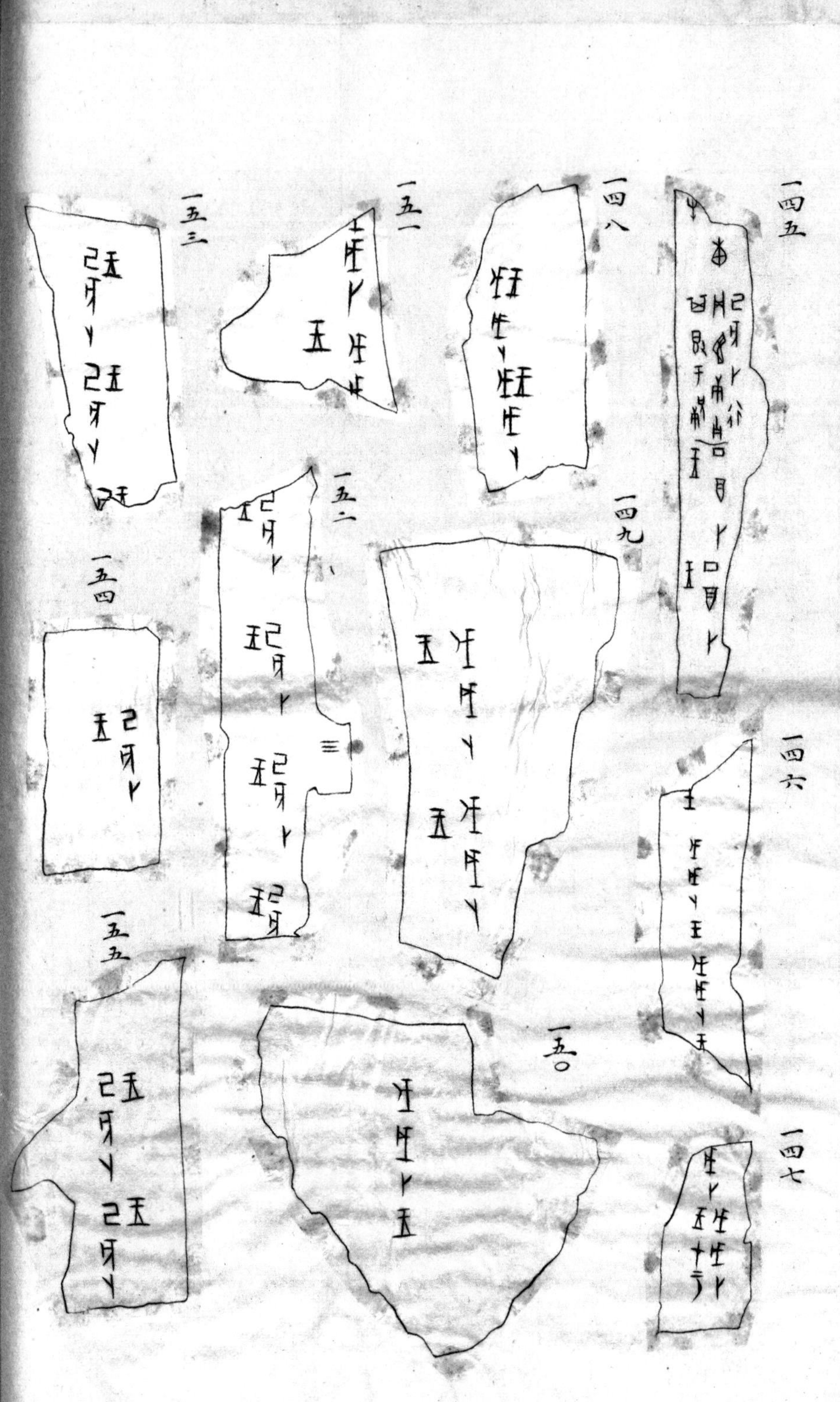
一四五
一四六
一四七
一四八
一四九
一五〇
一五一
一五二
一五三
一五四
一五五

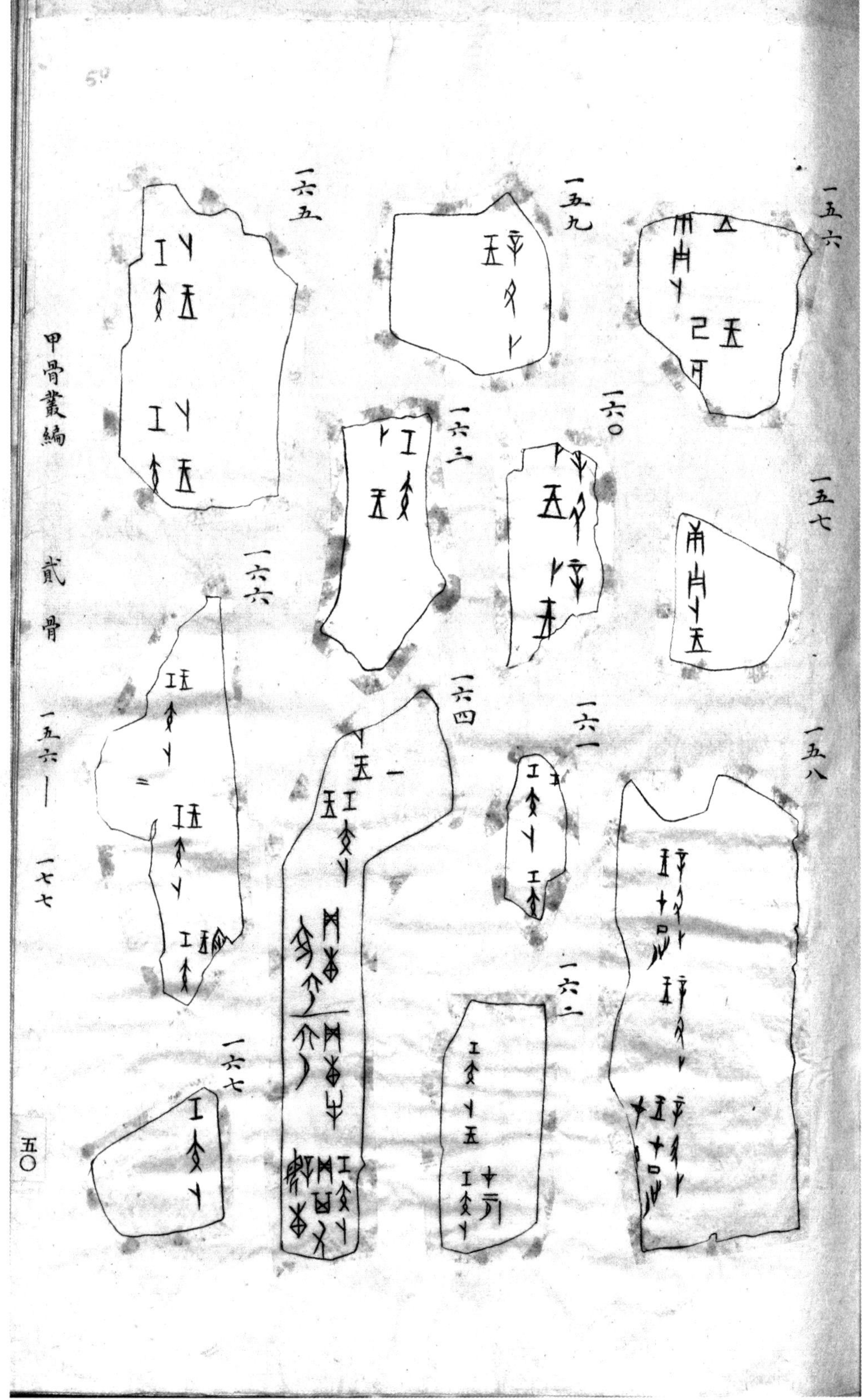
一五六
一五七
一五八
一五九
一六〇
一六一
一六二
一六三
一六四
一六五
一六六
一六七
甲骨叢編　貳骨　一五六—一七七
五〇

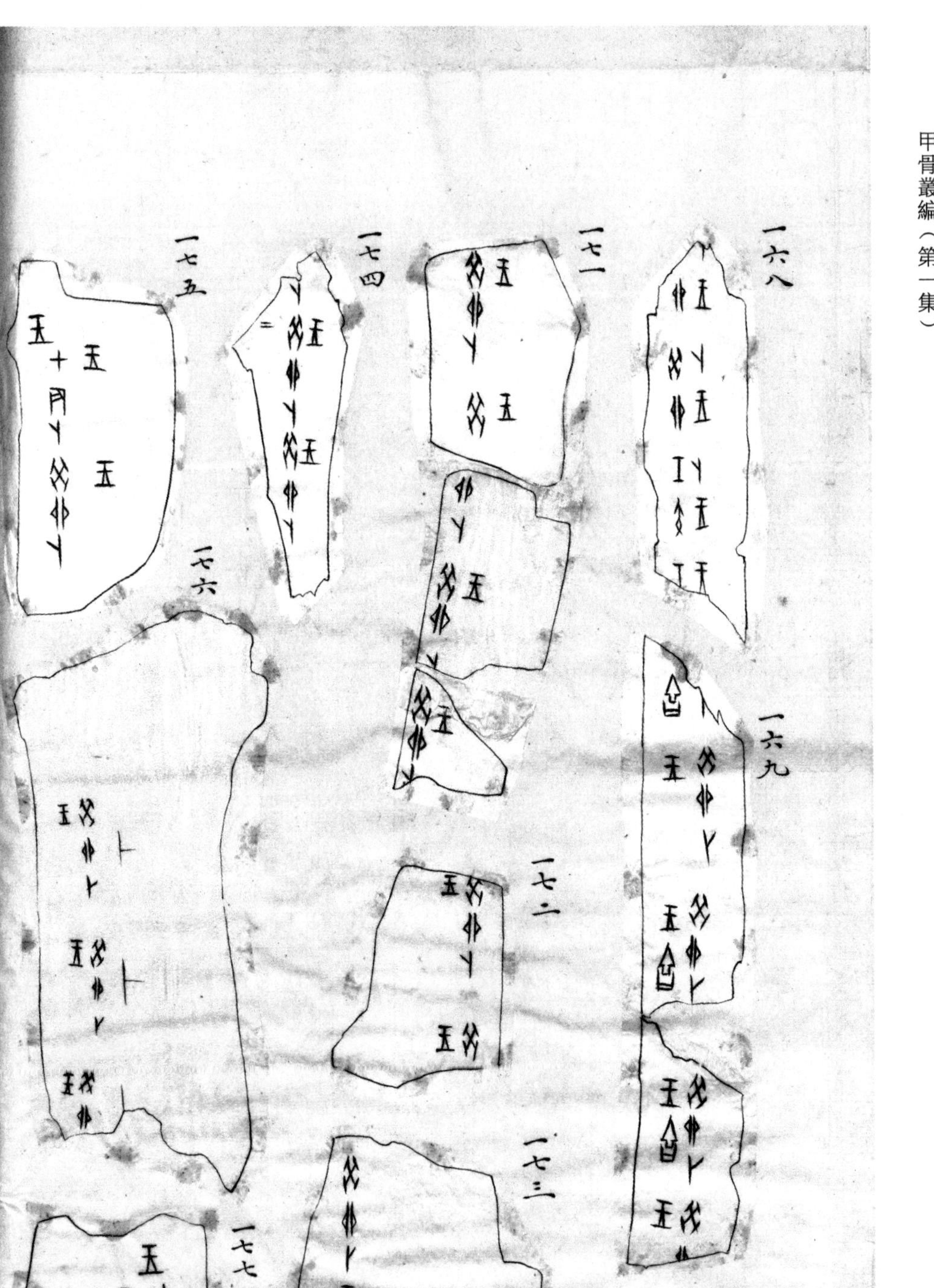
一六八
一六九
一七〇
一七一
一七二
一七三
一七四
一七五
一七六
一七七

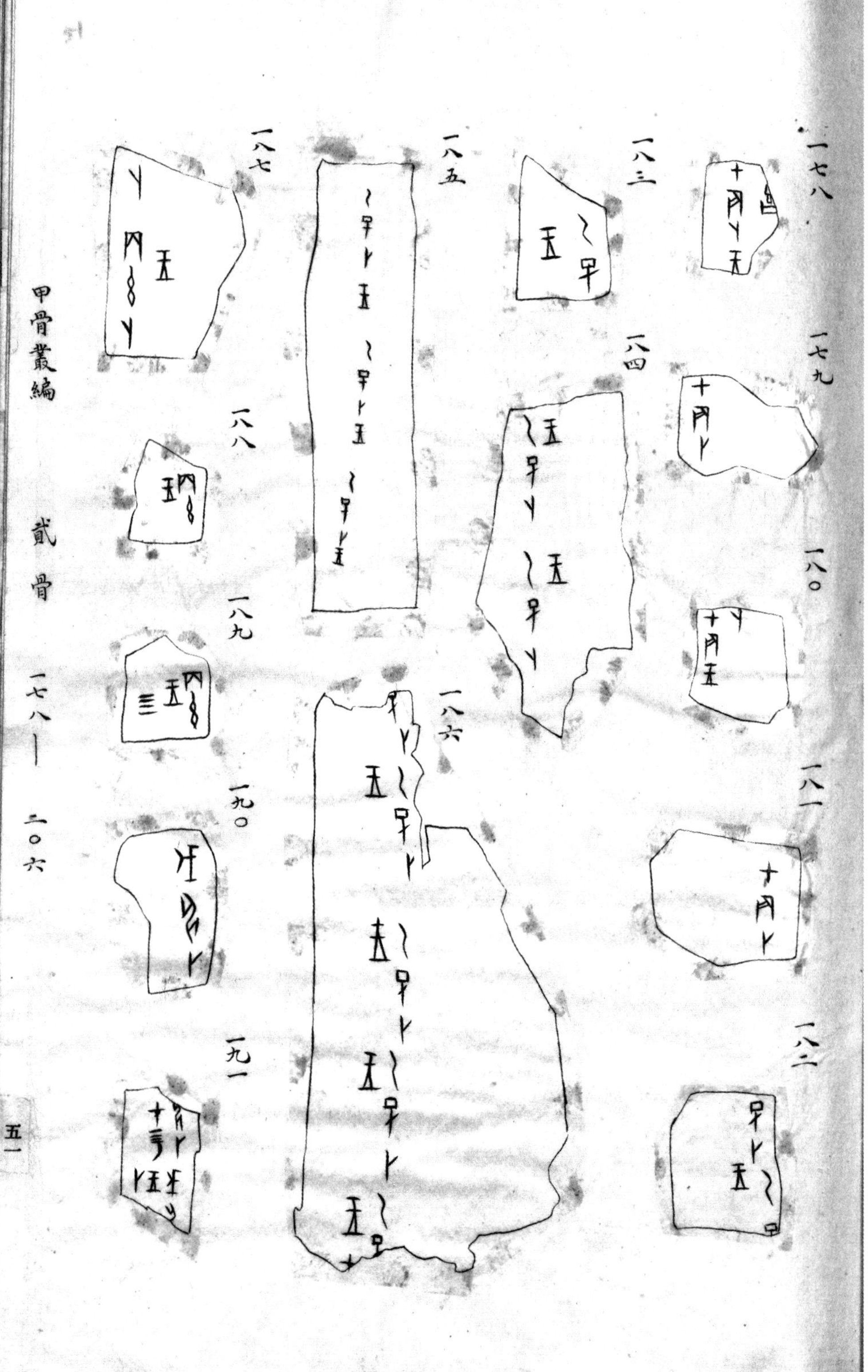
甲骨叢編　貳骨　一七八—二〇六
五一

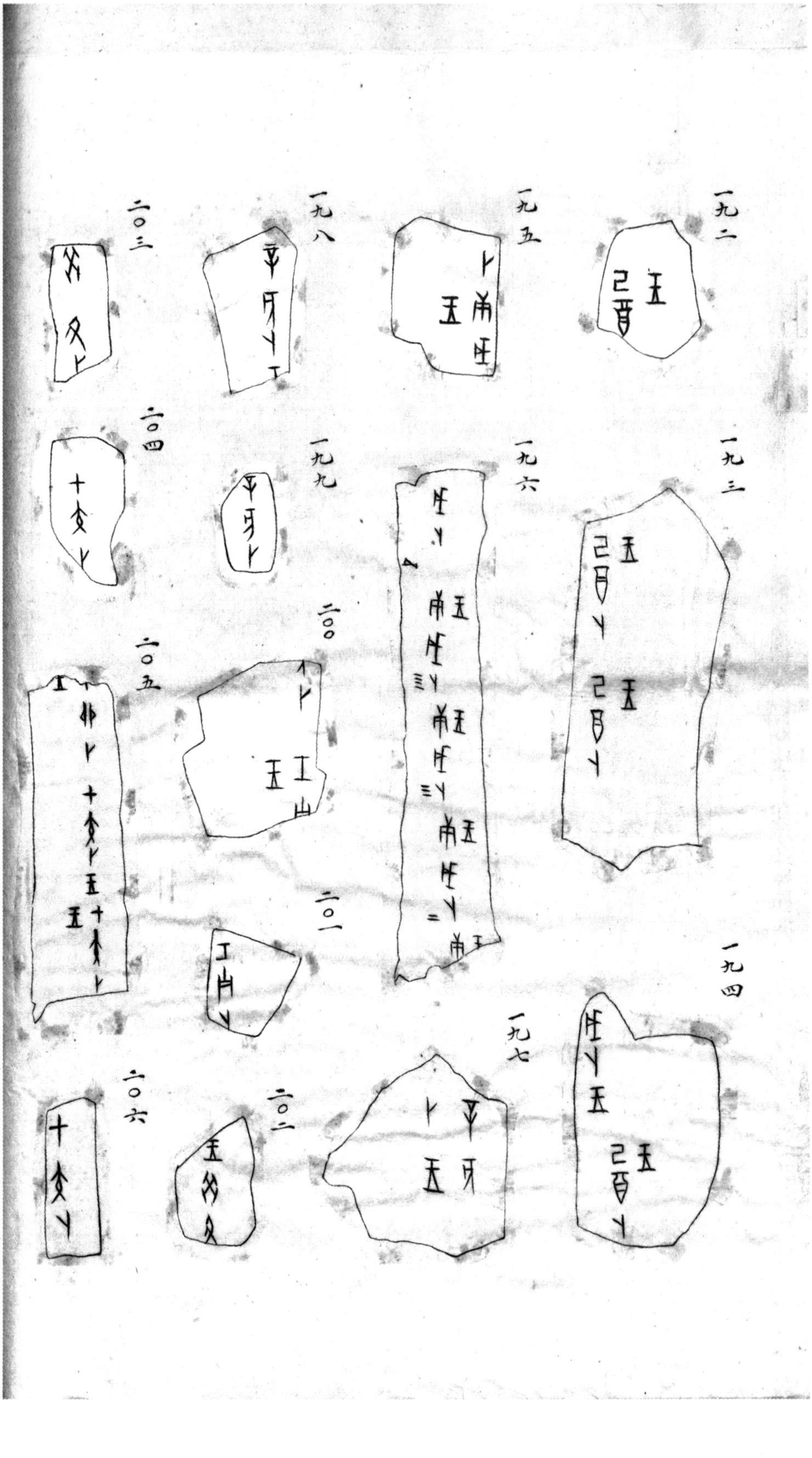

一九二 一九三 一九四 一九五 一九六 一九七 一九八 一九九 二〇〇 二〇一 二〇二 二〇三 二〇四 二〇五 二〇六

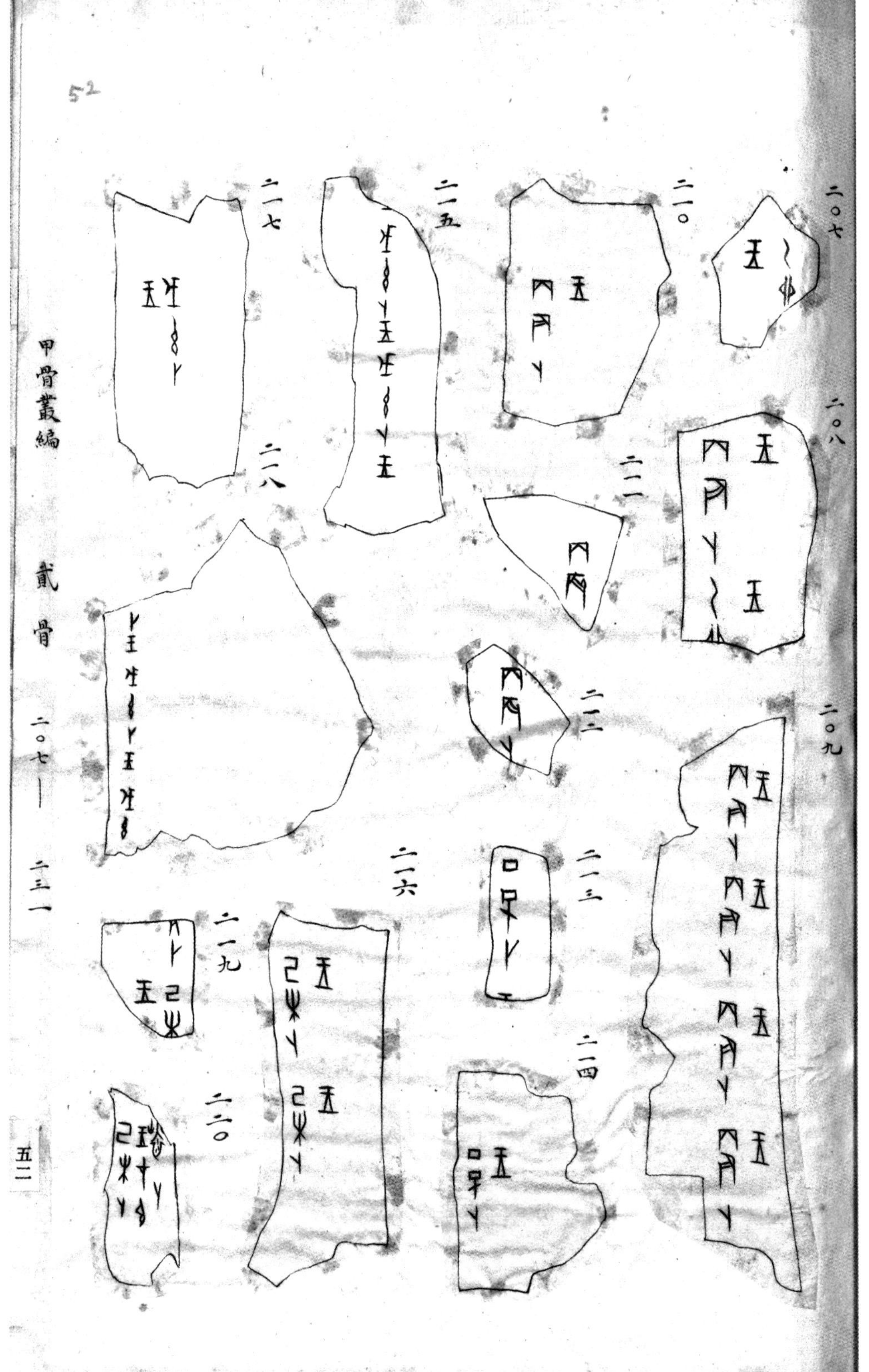
二〇七
二〇八
二〇九
二一〇
二一一
二一二
二一三
二一四
二一五
二一六
二一七
二一八
二一九
二二〇
甲骨叢編　貳骨　二〇七—二三一
五二

二二一

二二二

二二三

二二四

二二五

二二六

二二七

二二八

二二九

二三〇

二三一

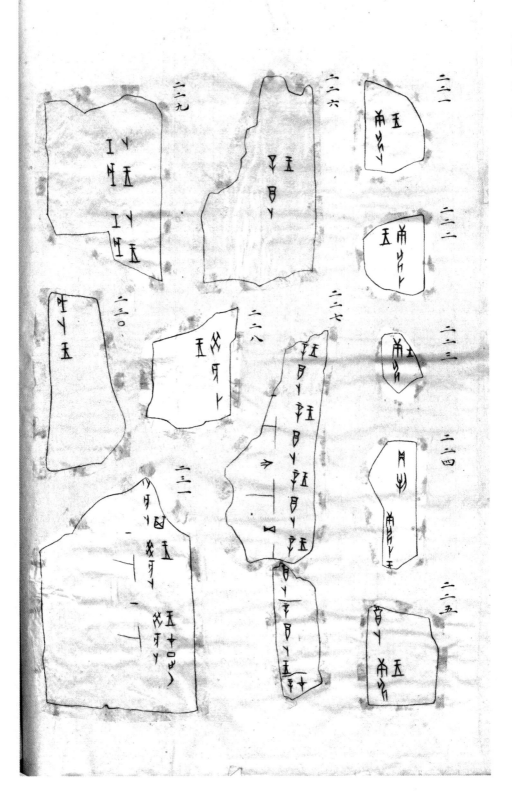

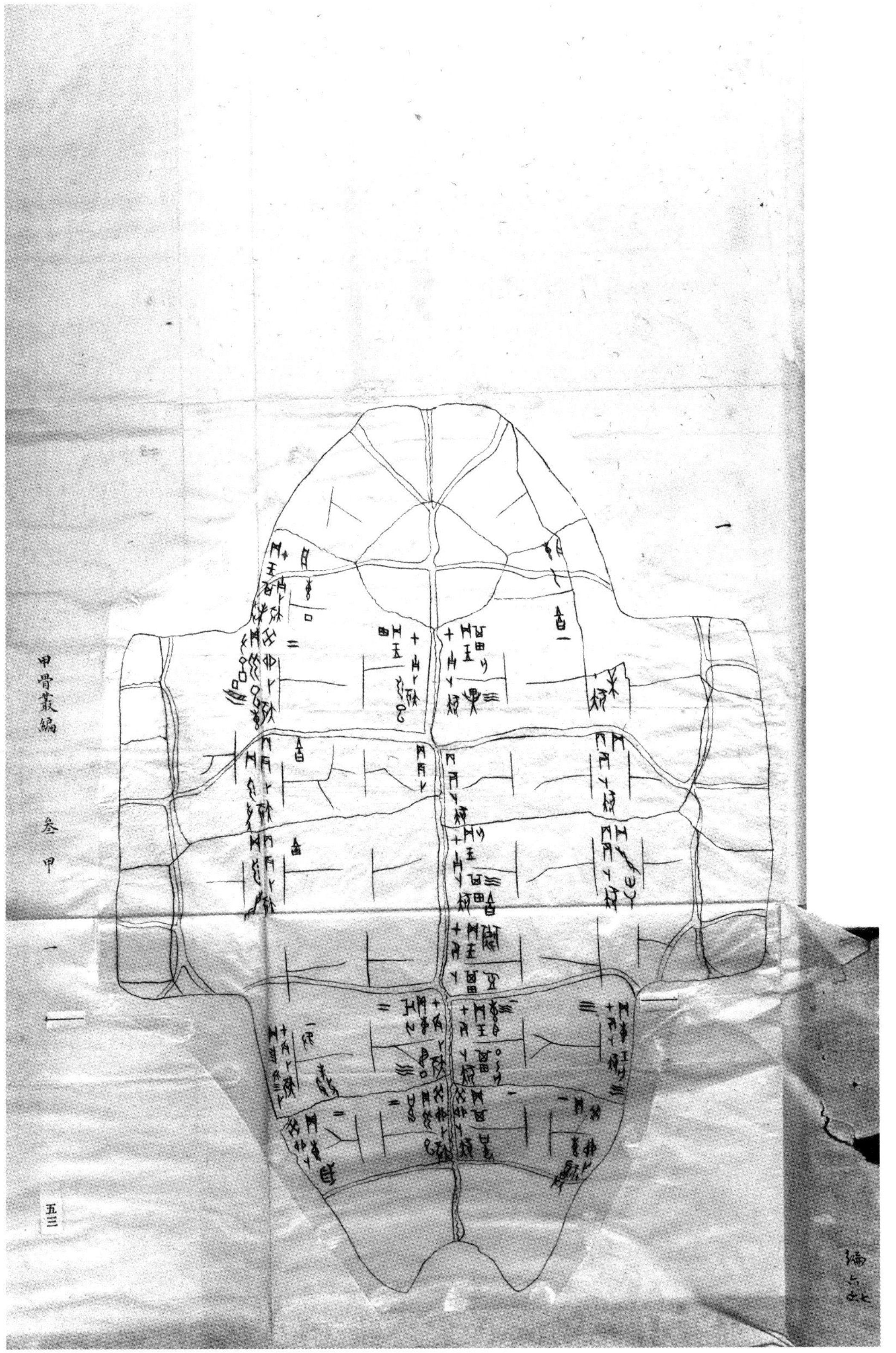
甲骨叢編
叁甲
一
五三

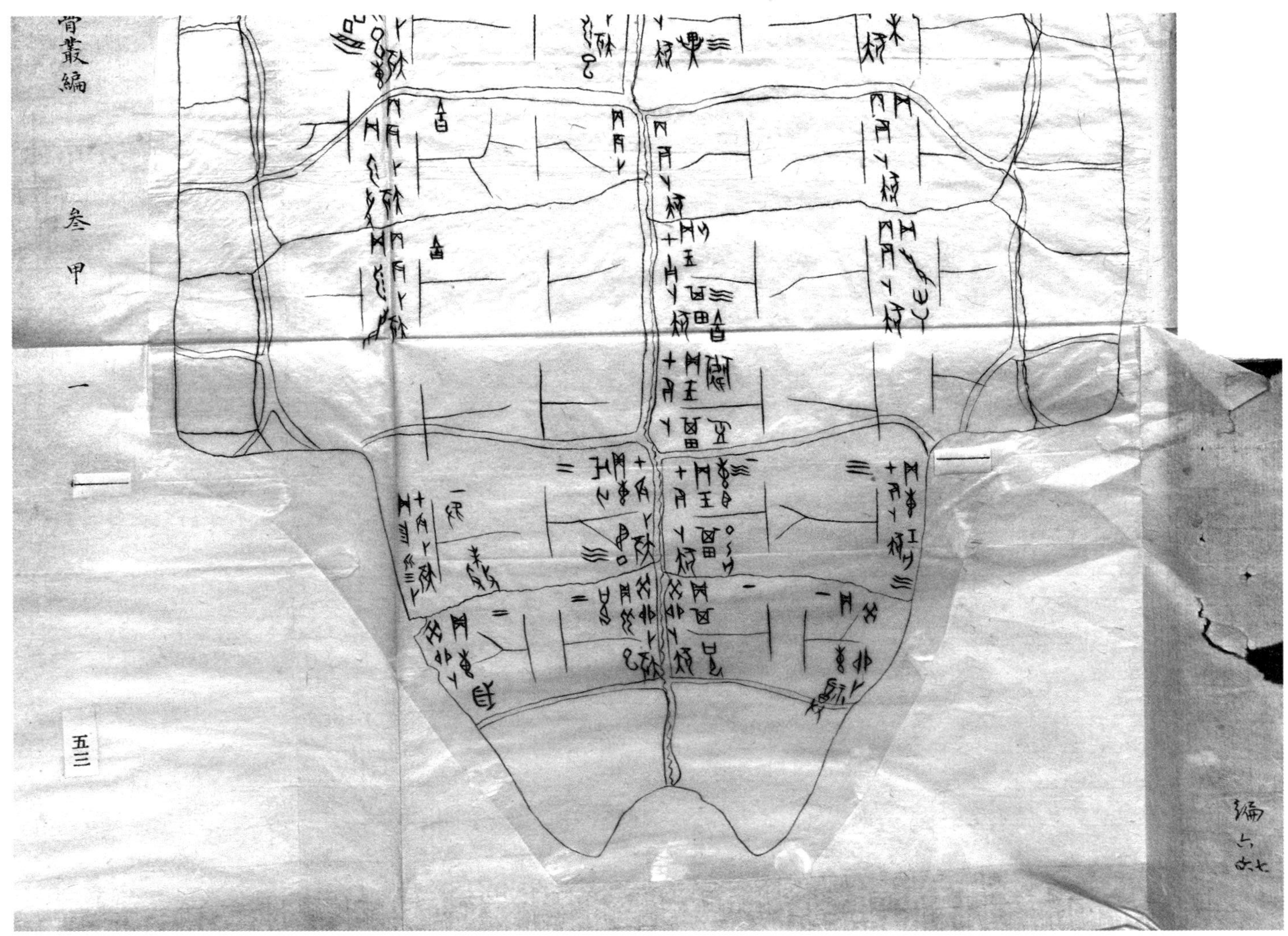
骨叢編
叁
甲
一
五三

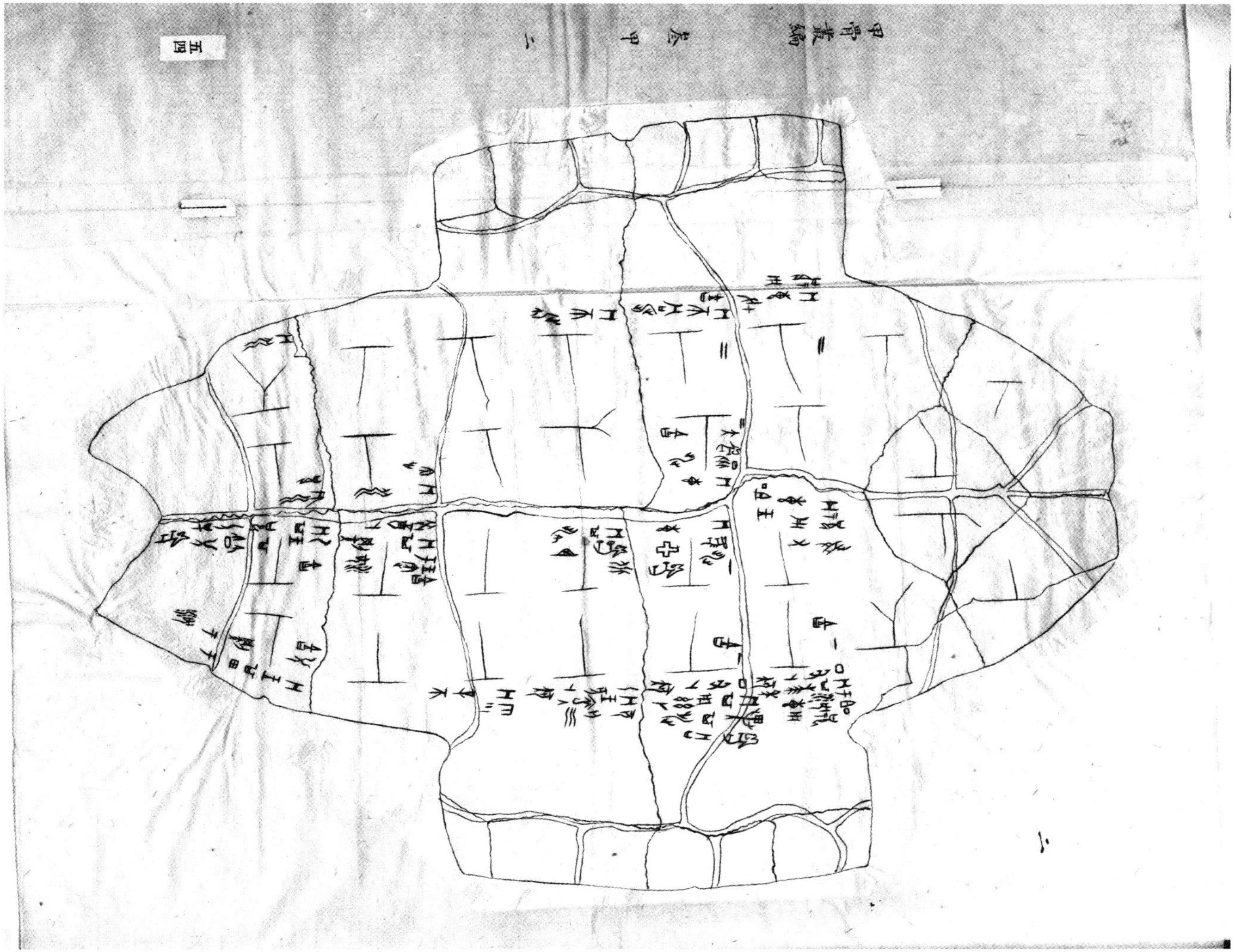

甲骨叢編 叄甲 二

五四

二

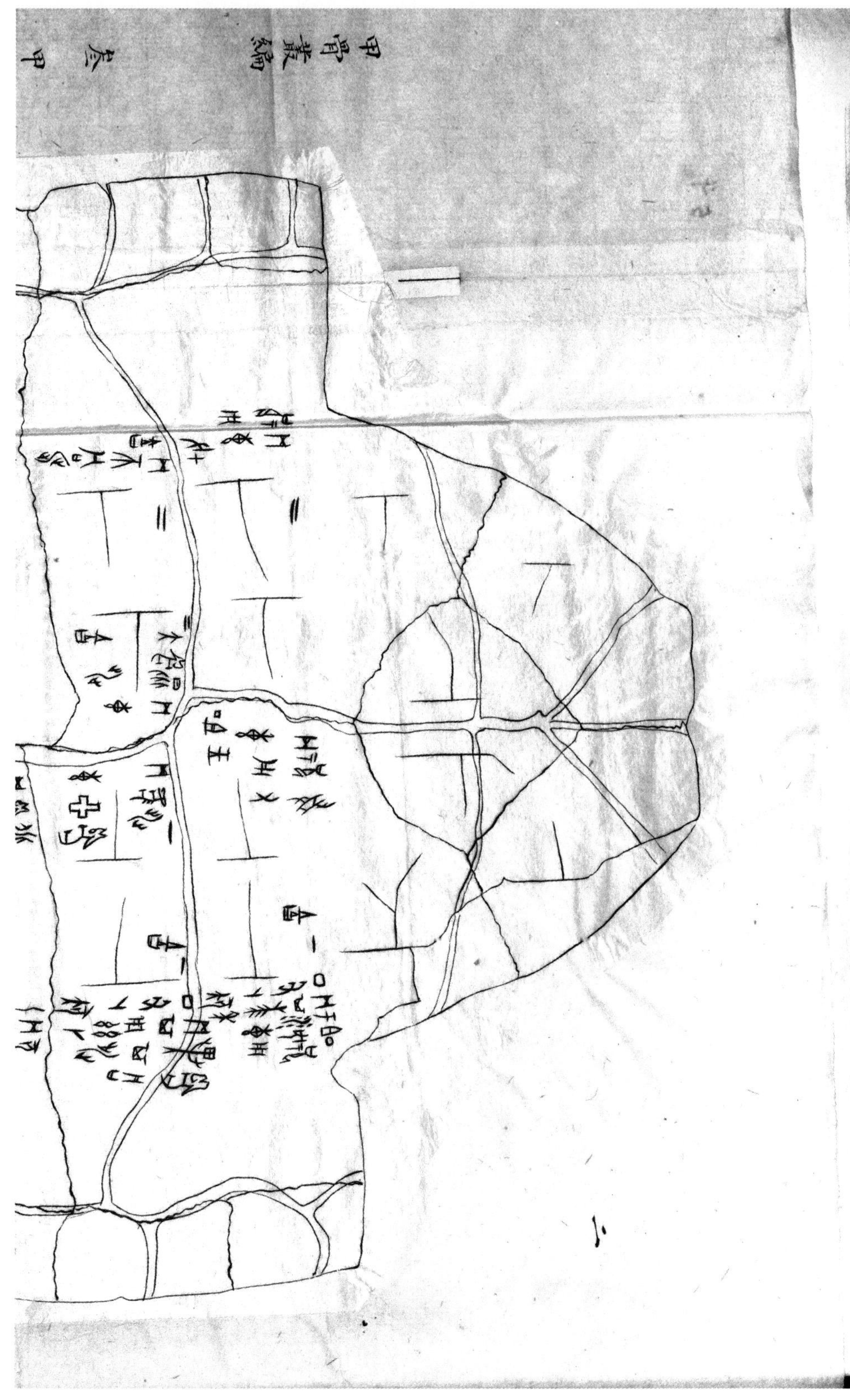
甲骨叢編
卷甲

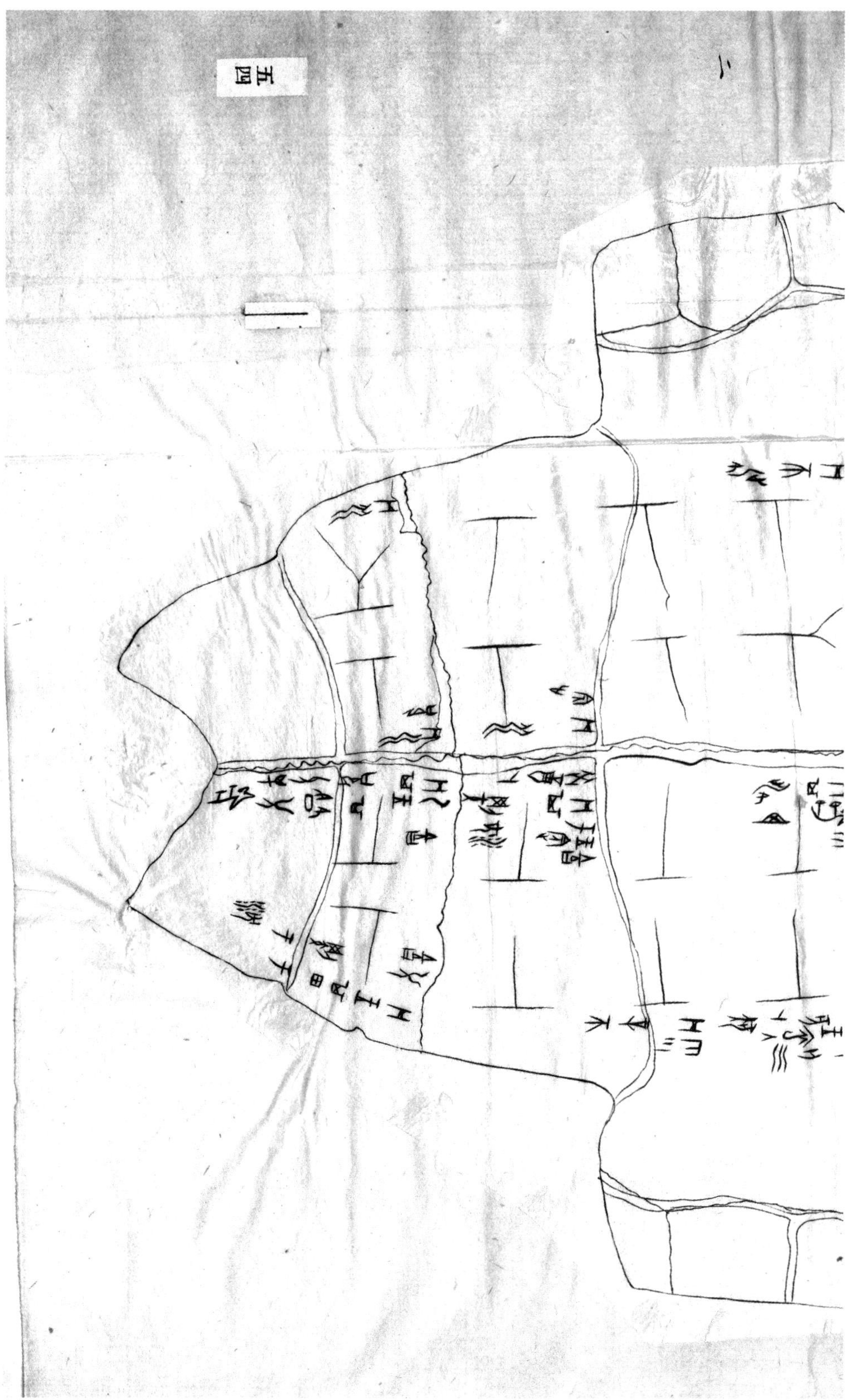
五四

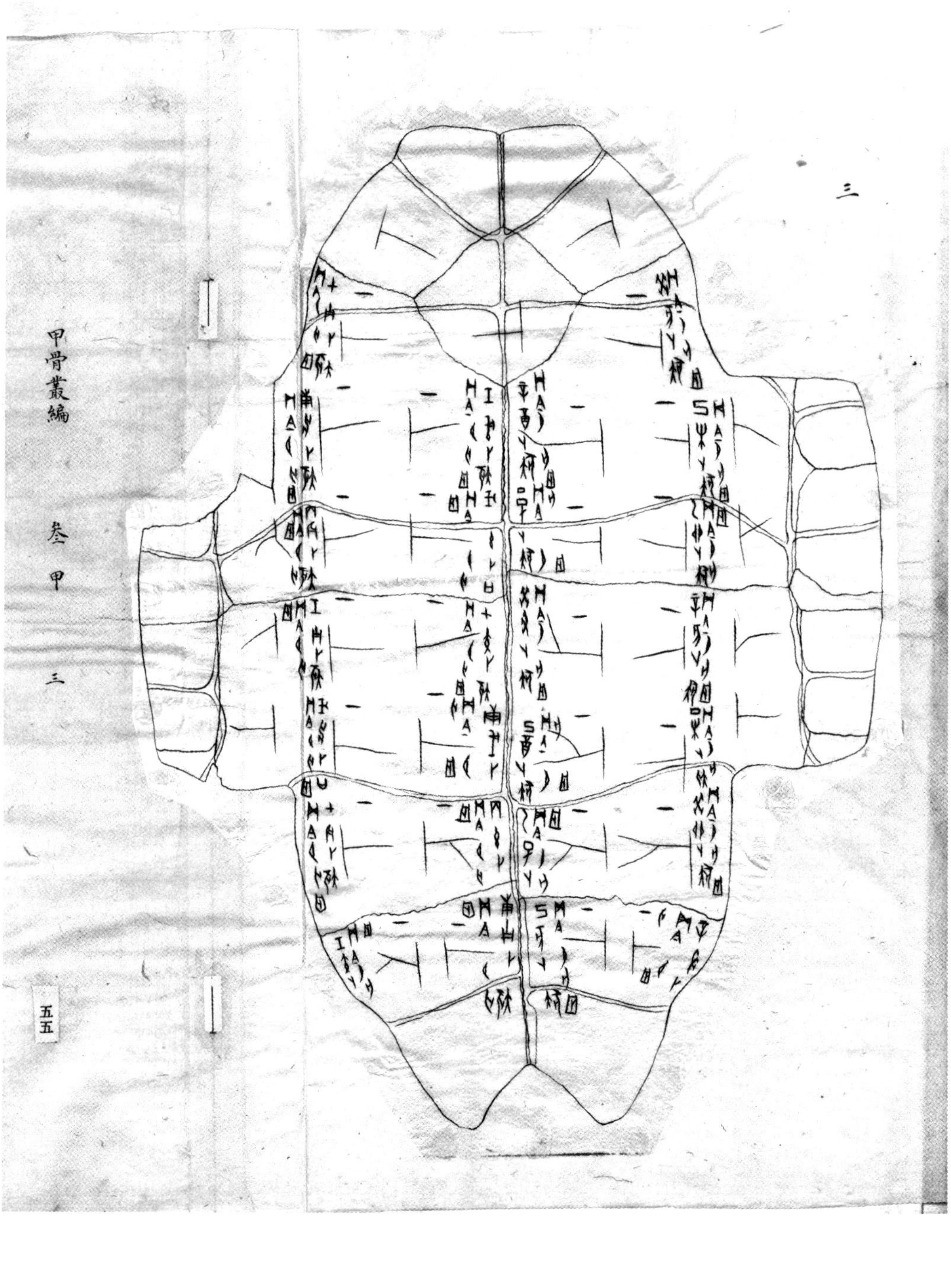

甲骨叢編　叄甲　三

三

五五

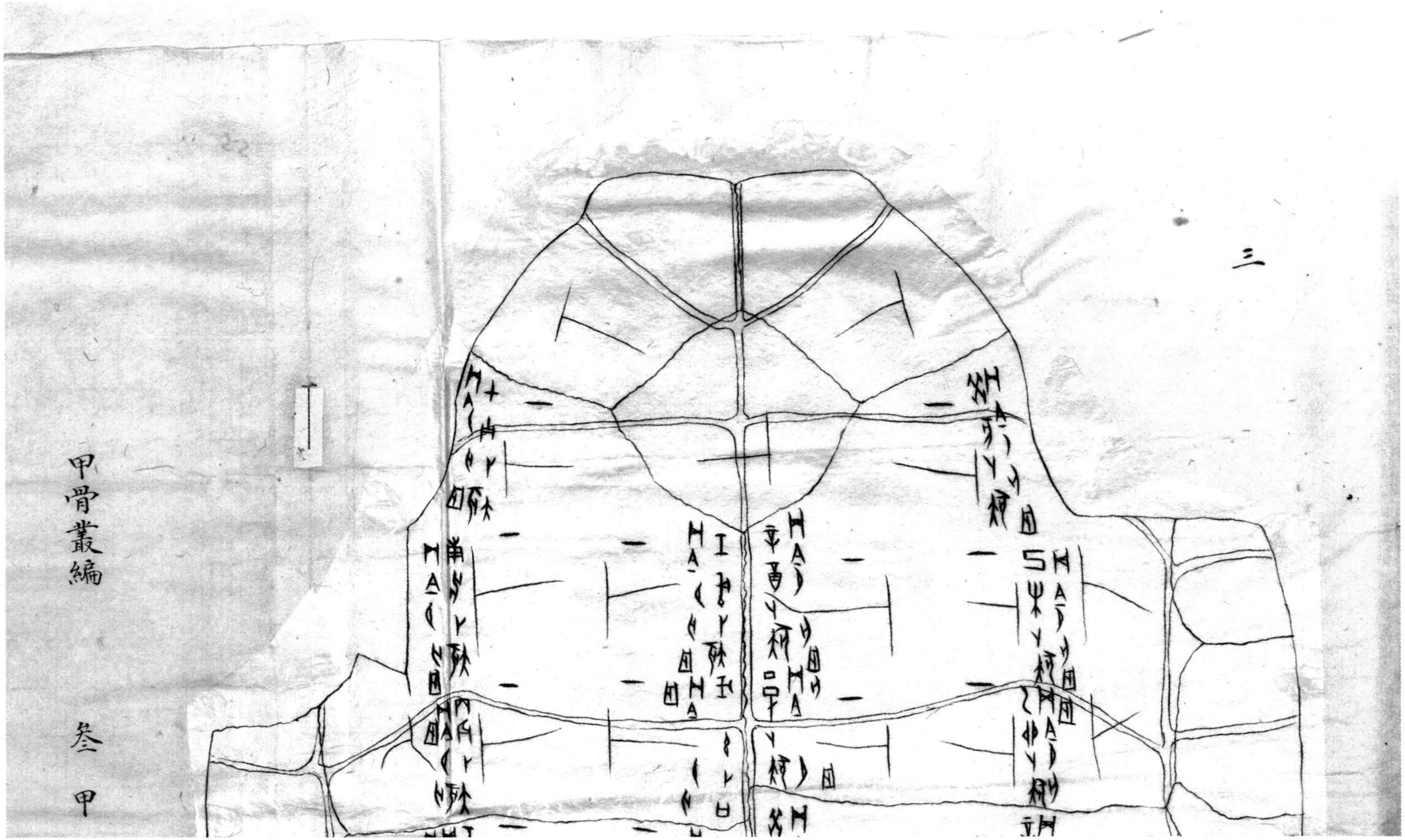

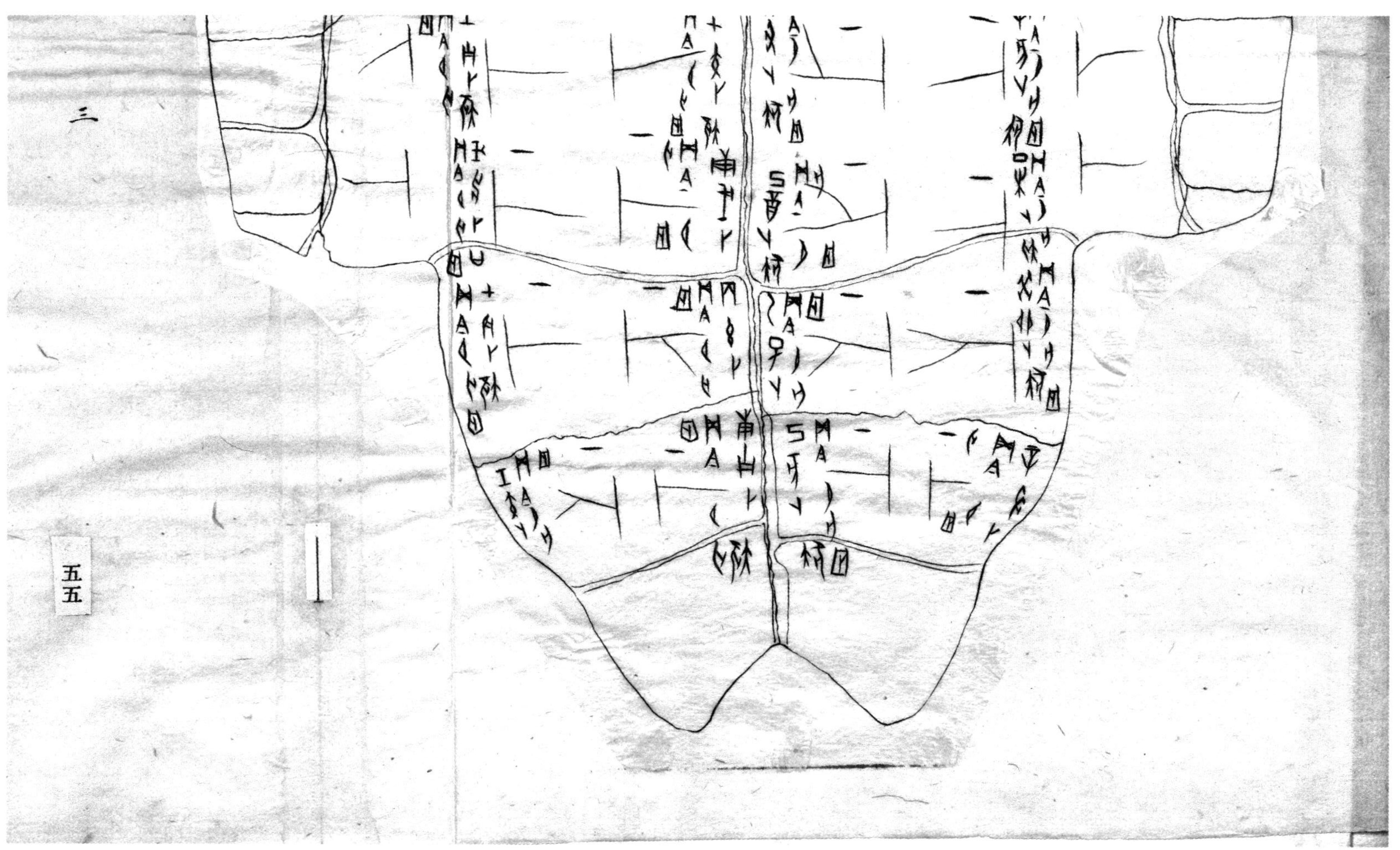
三
五五

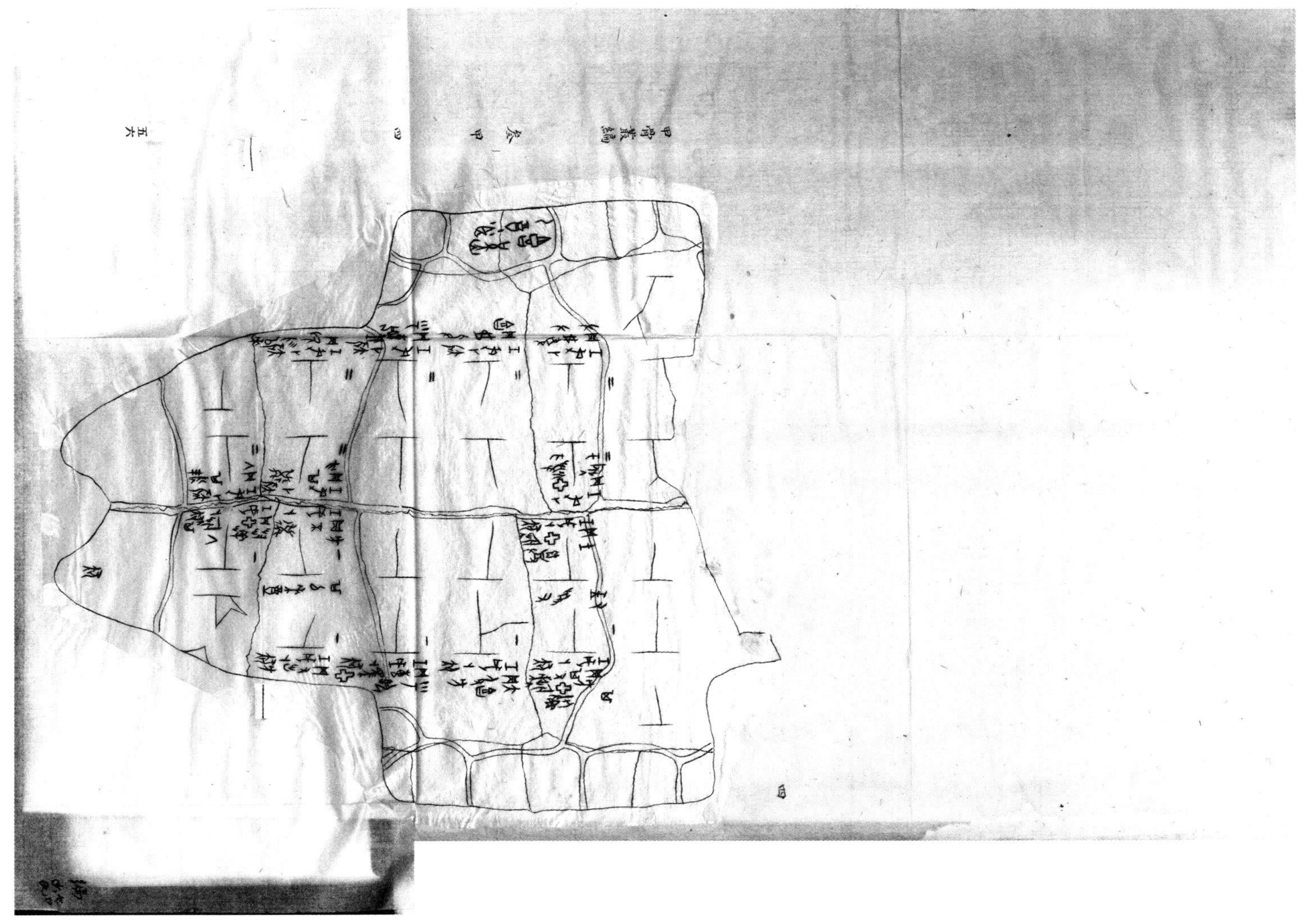

甲骨叢編
叁 甲 四
五六

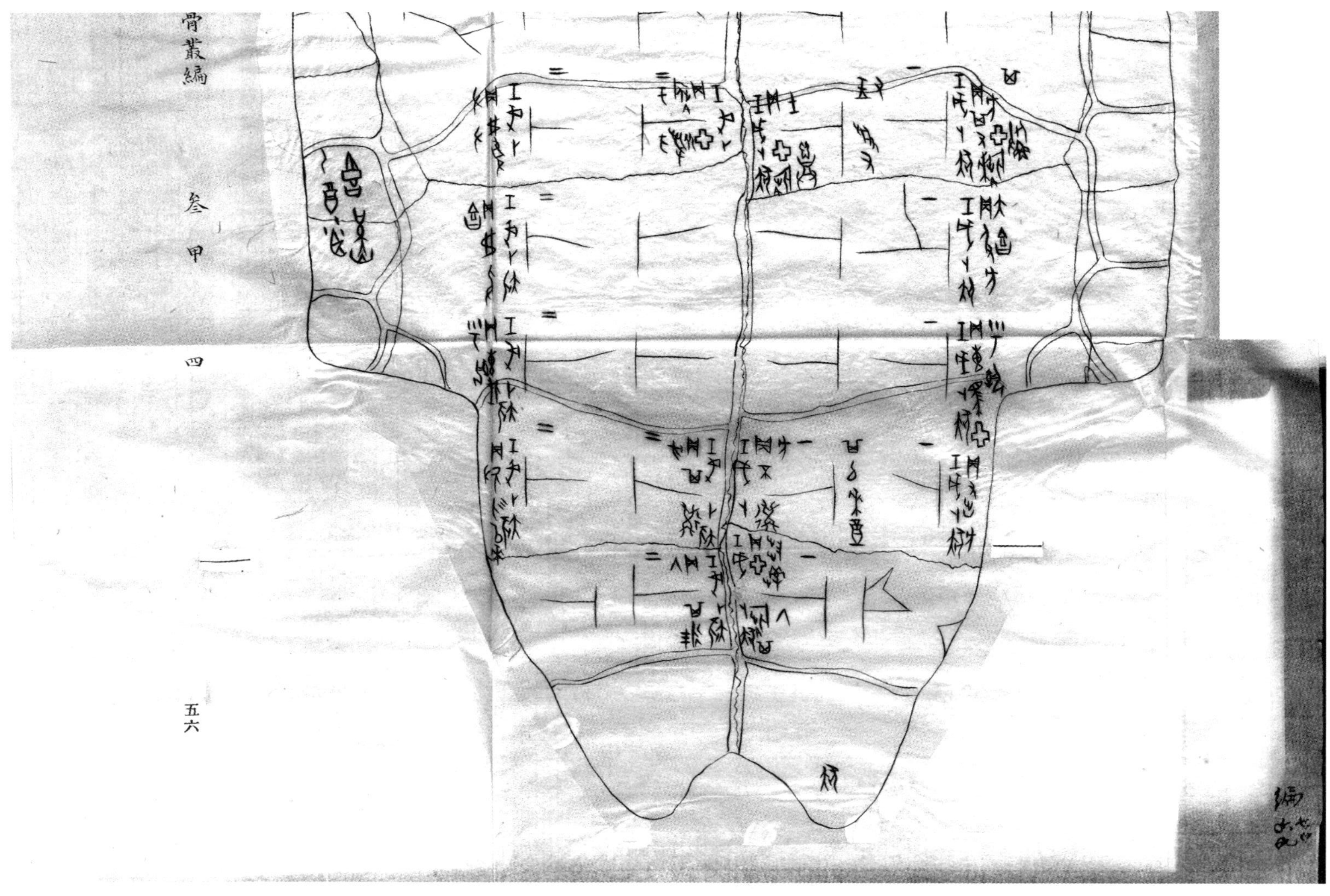
骨叢編
叁甲
四
五六

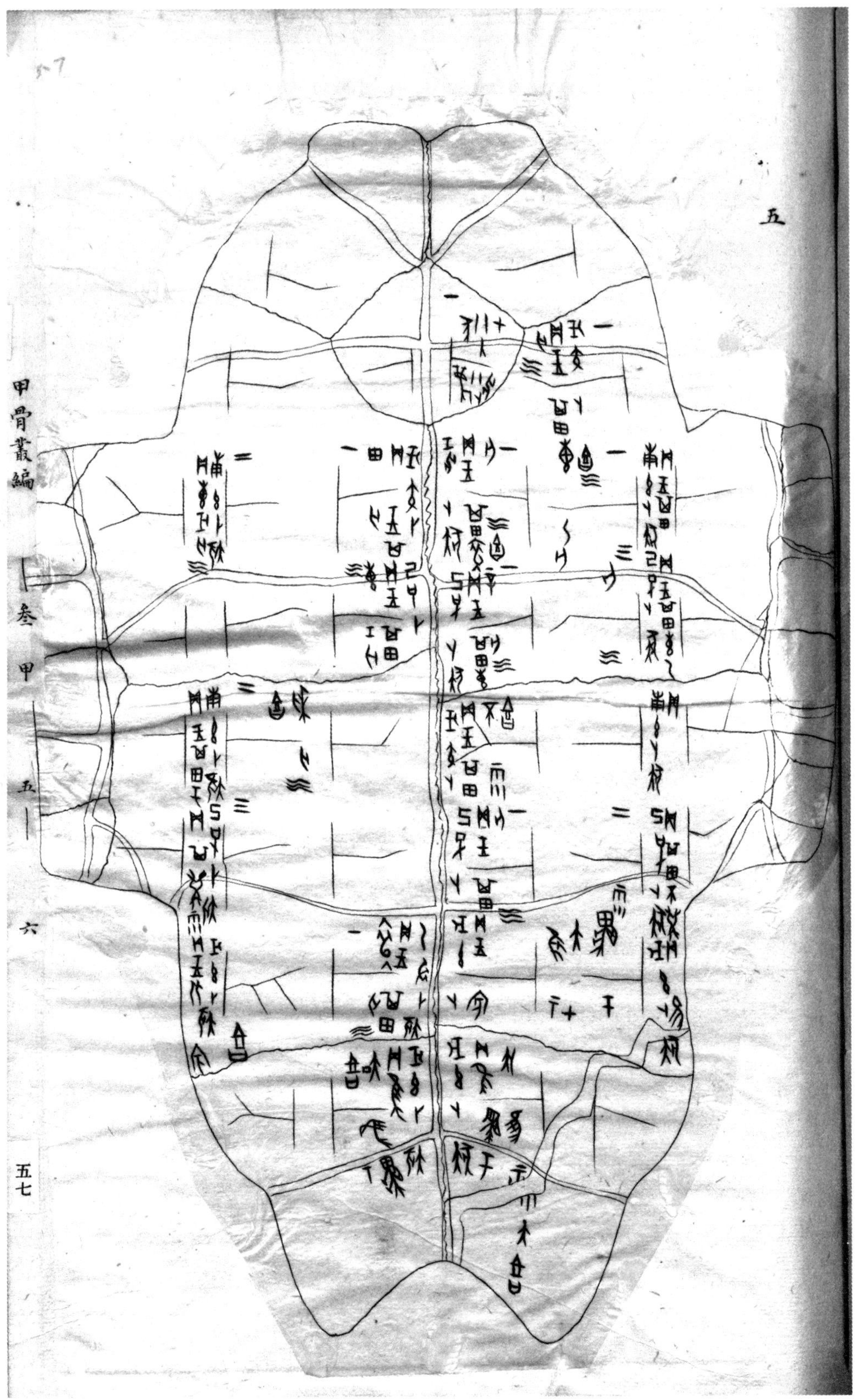

甲骨叢編
叁甲
五
一
六
五七
五

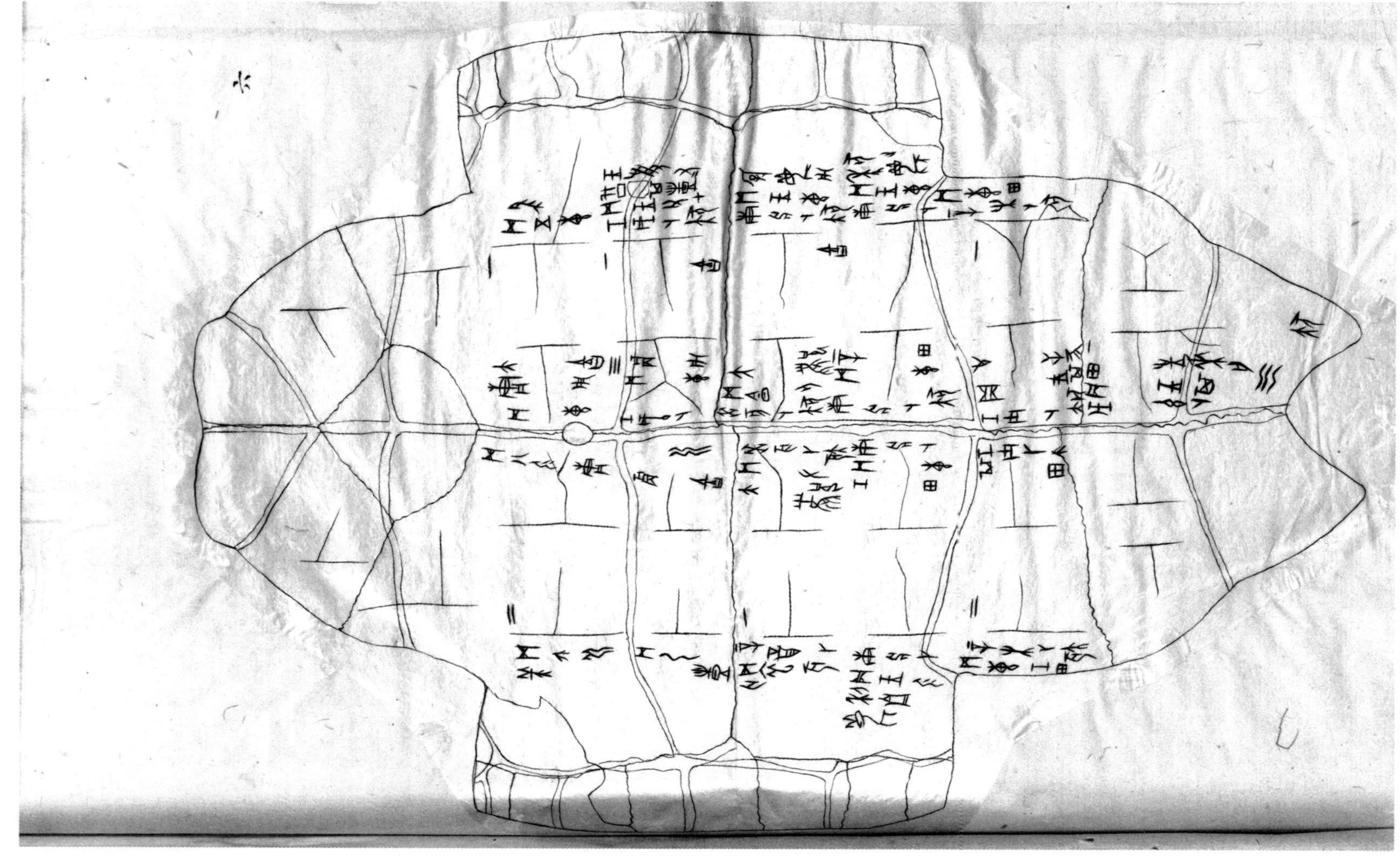
六

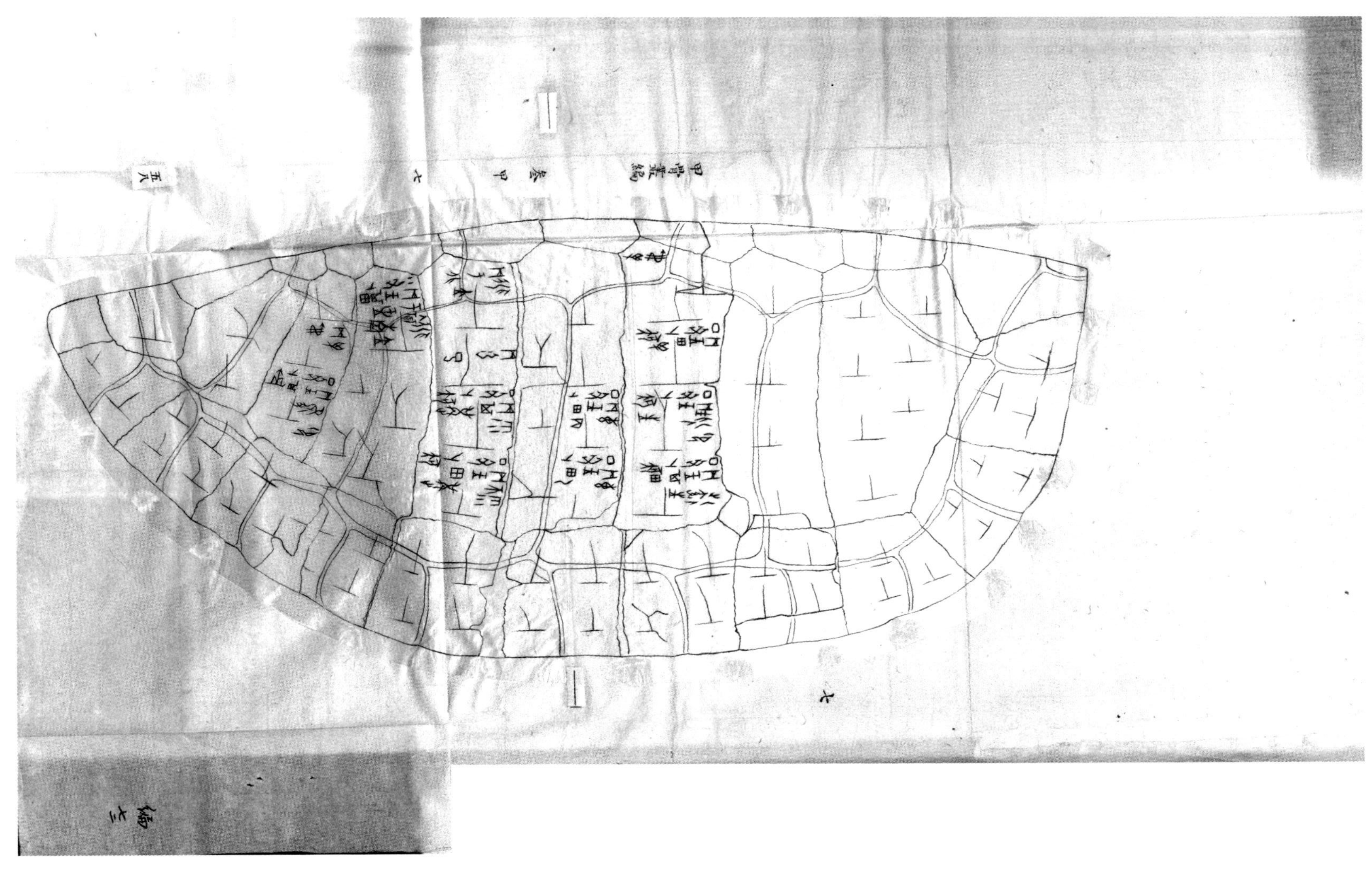
甲骨叢編
叁 甲
七
五八
編七三

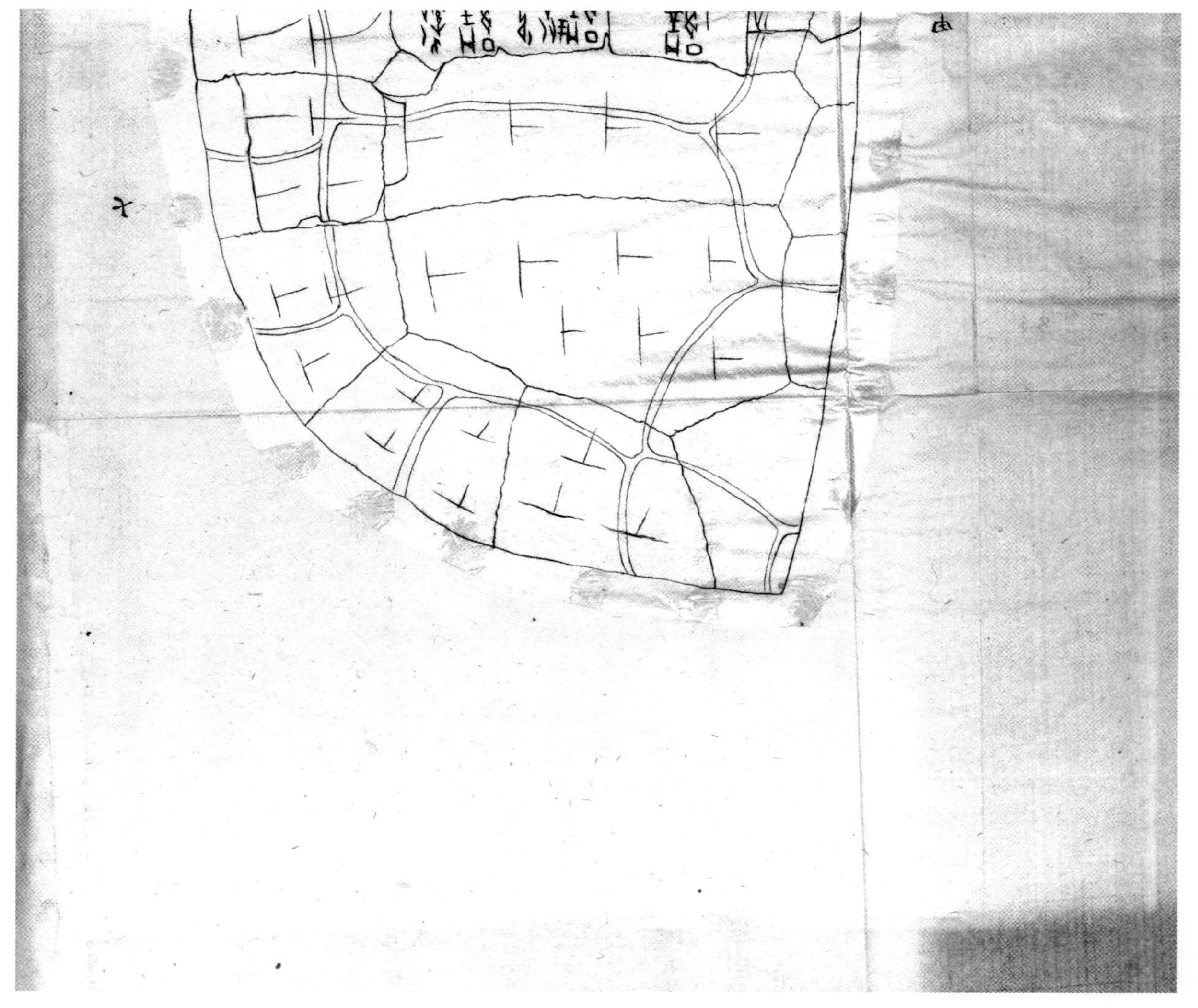

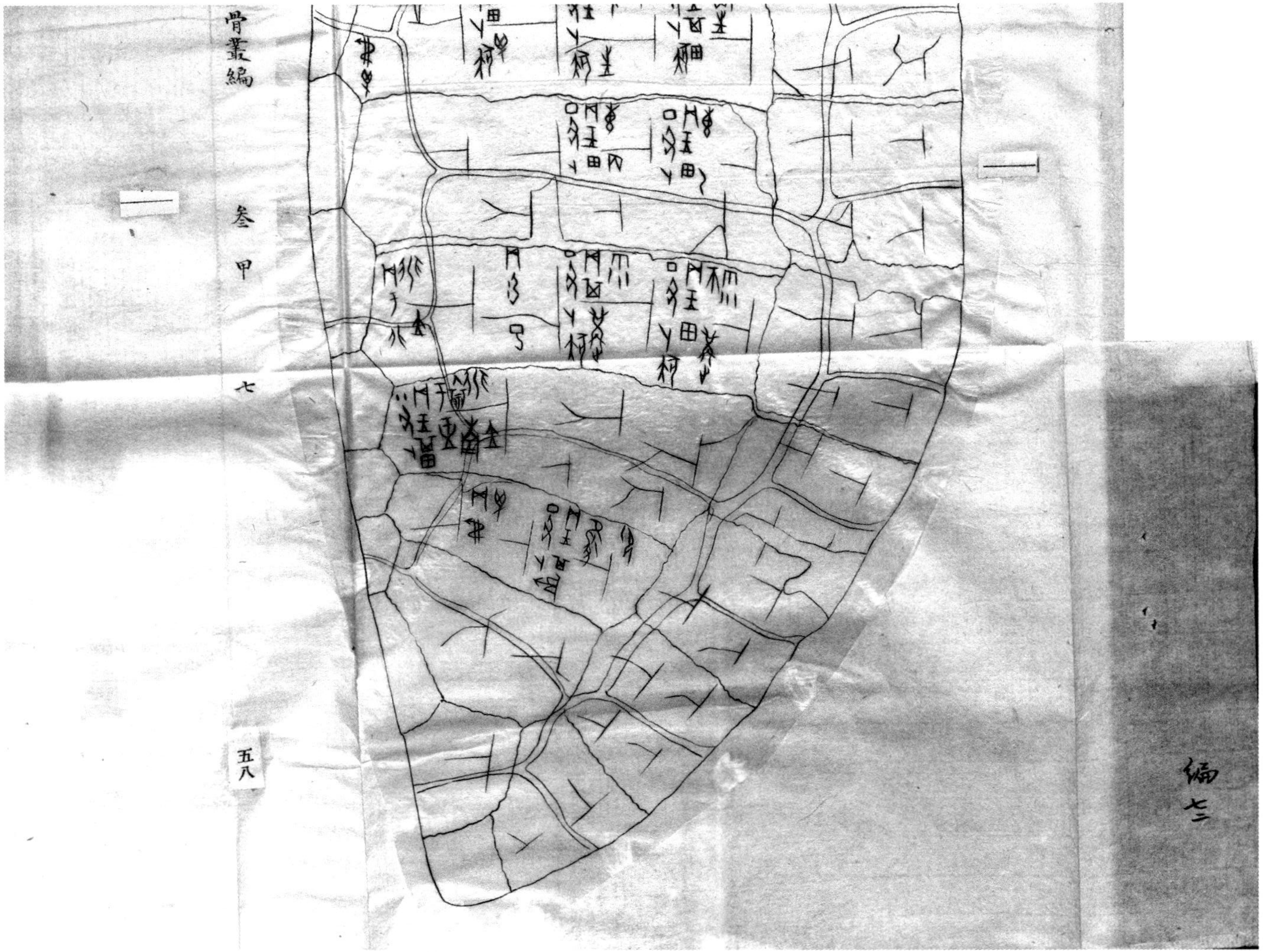

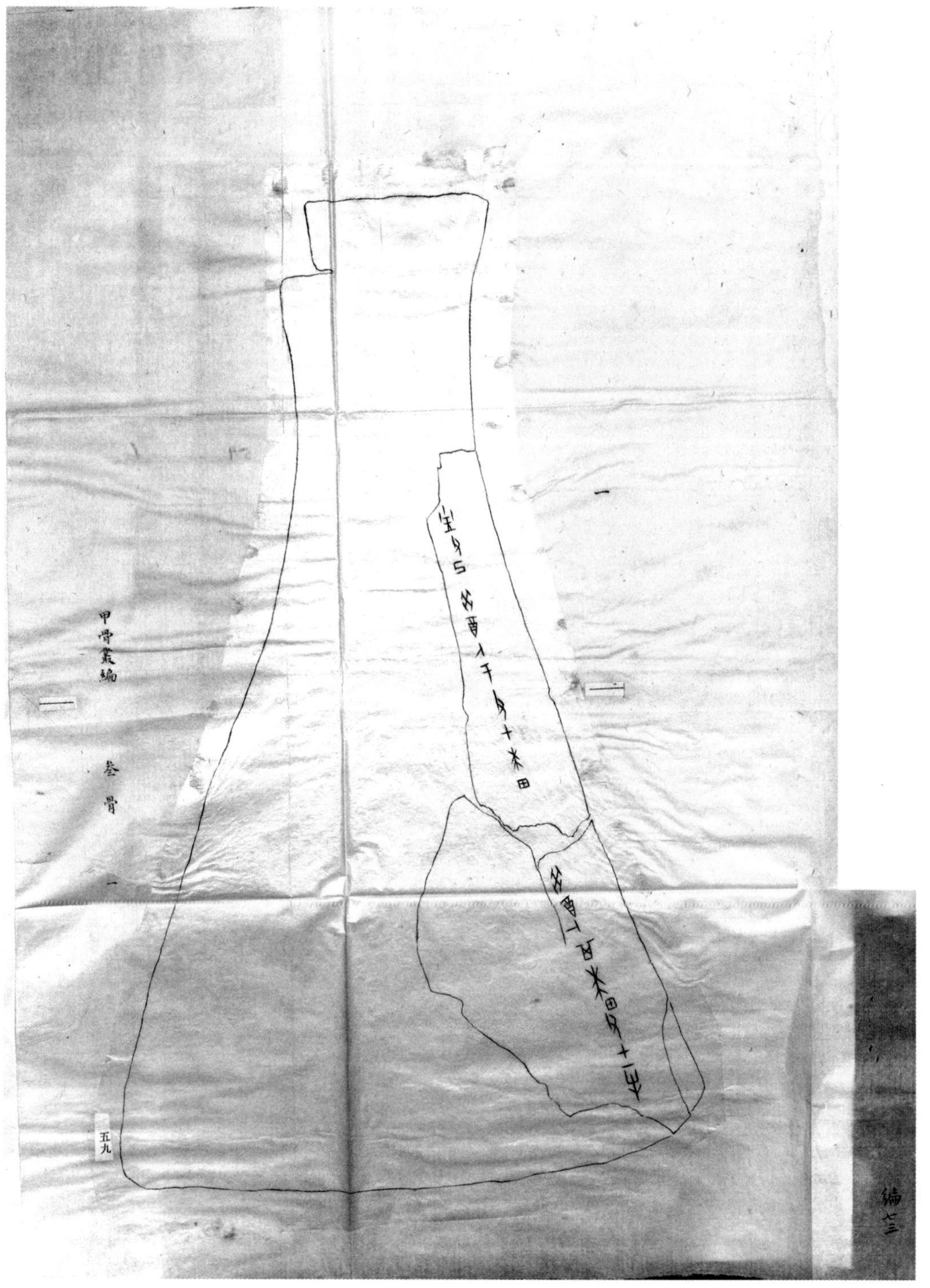
甲骨叢編
叁 骨
五九
編七三

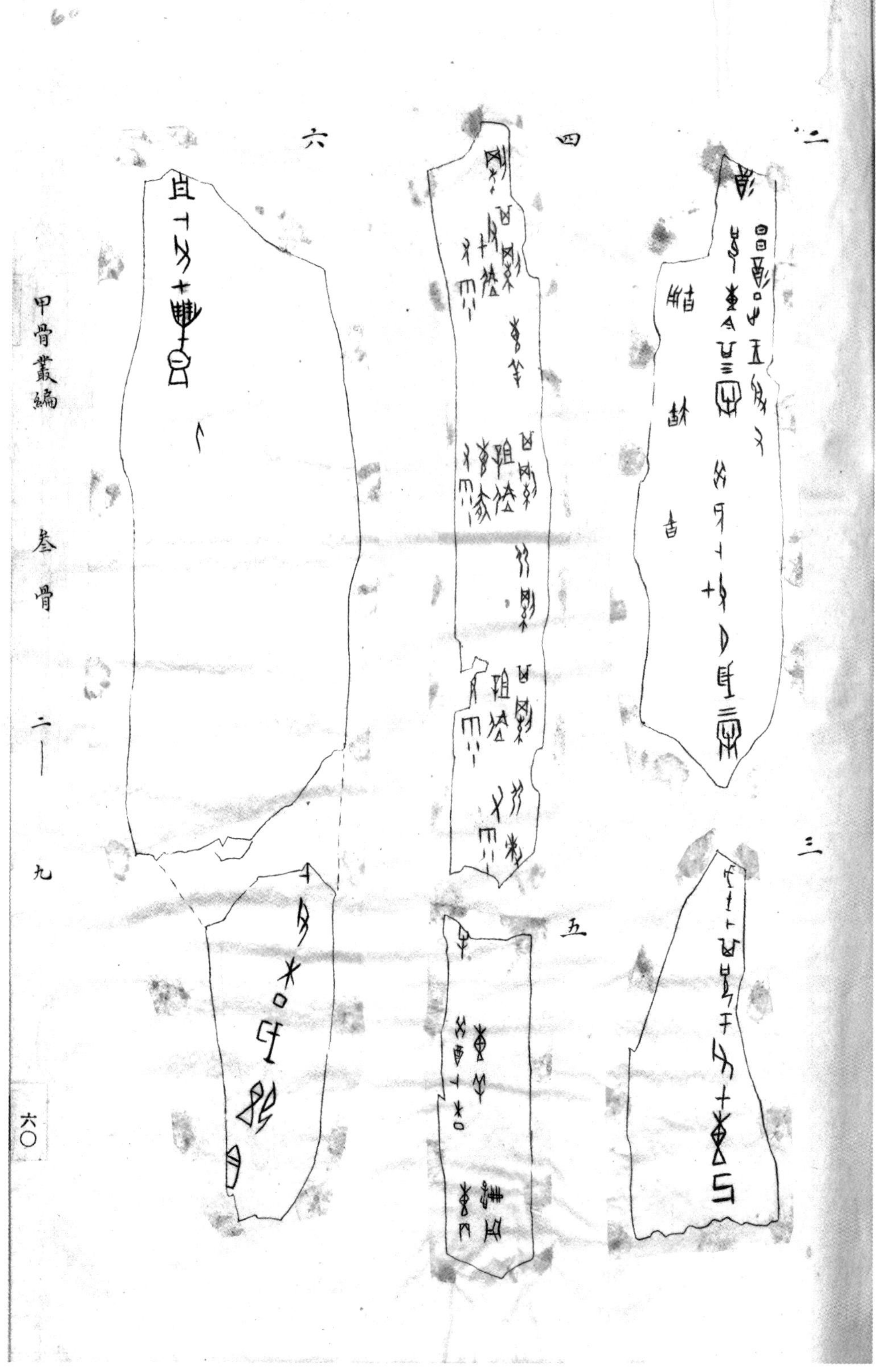
二
三
四
五
六
甲骨叢編 叁骨 二一 九
六〇

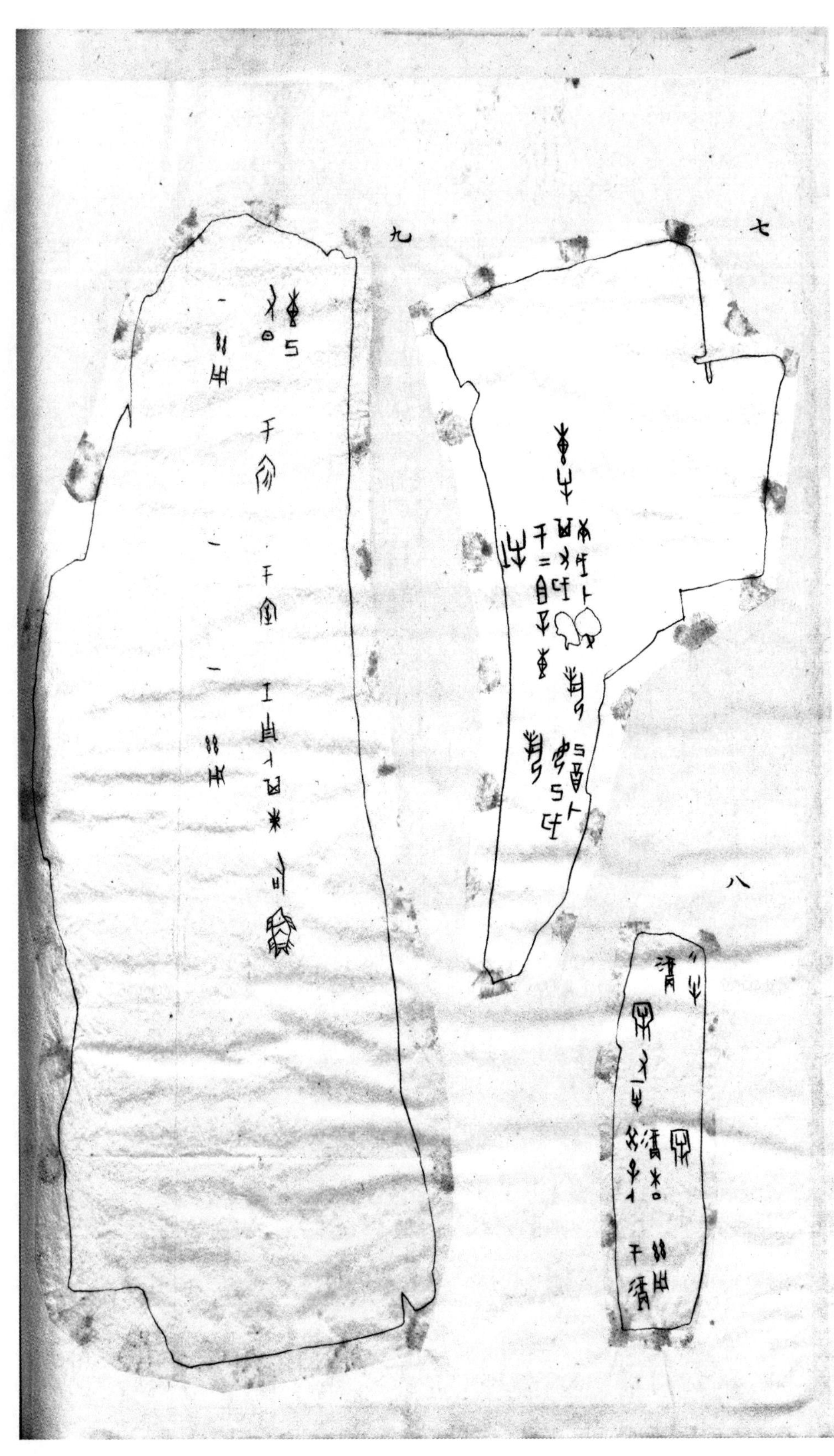
七
八
九

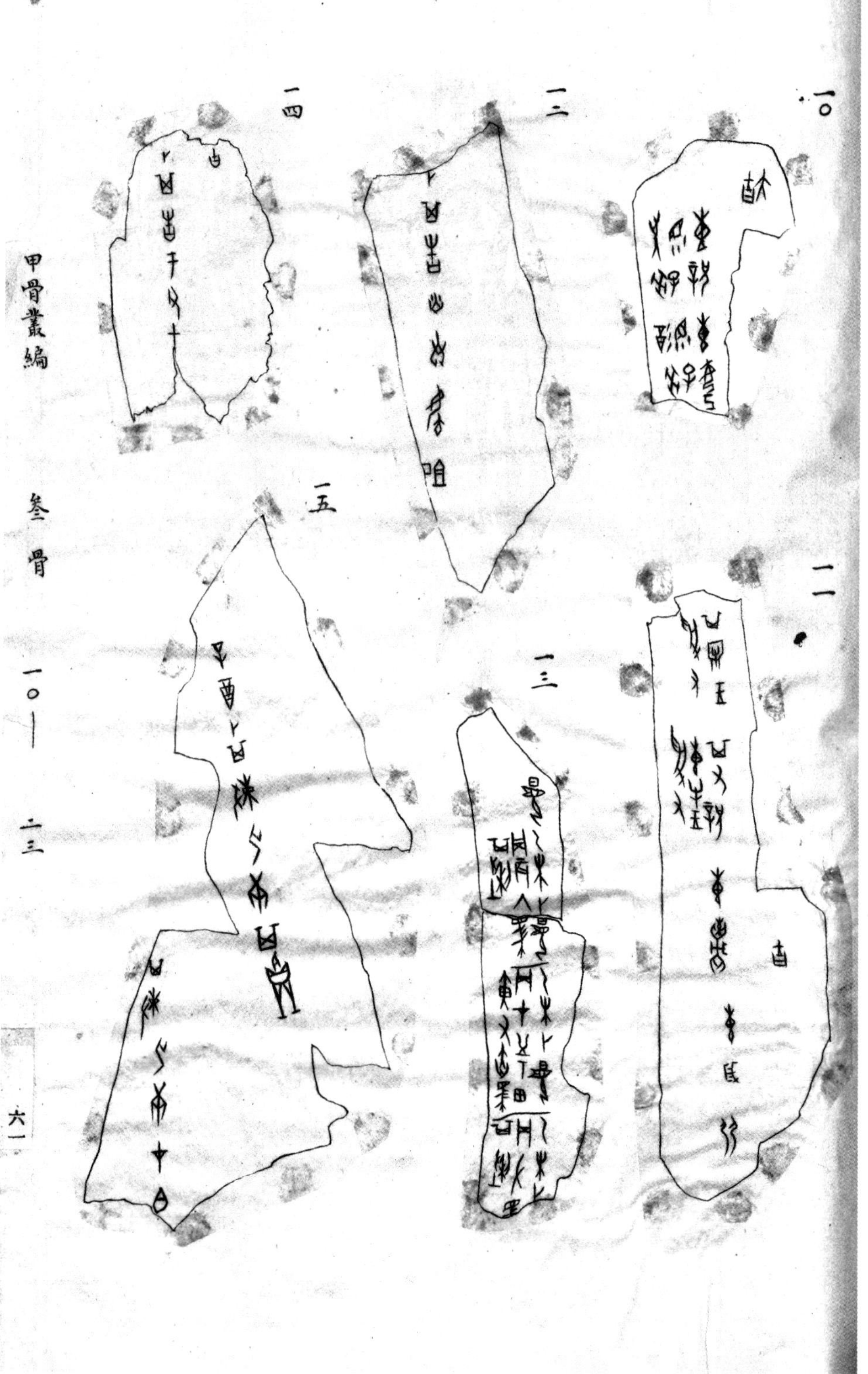
甲骨叢編　叁骨　一〇一　一三
六一
一〇
一一
一二
一三
一四
一五

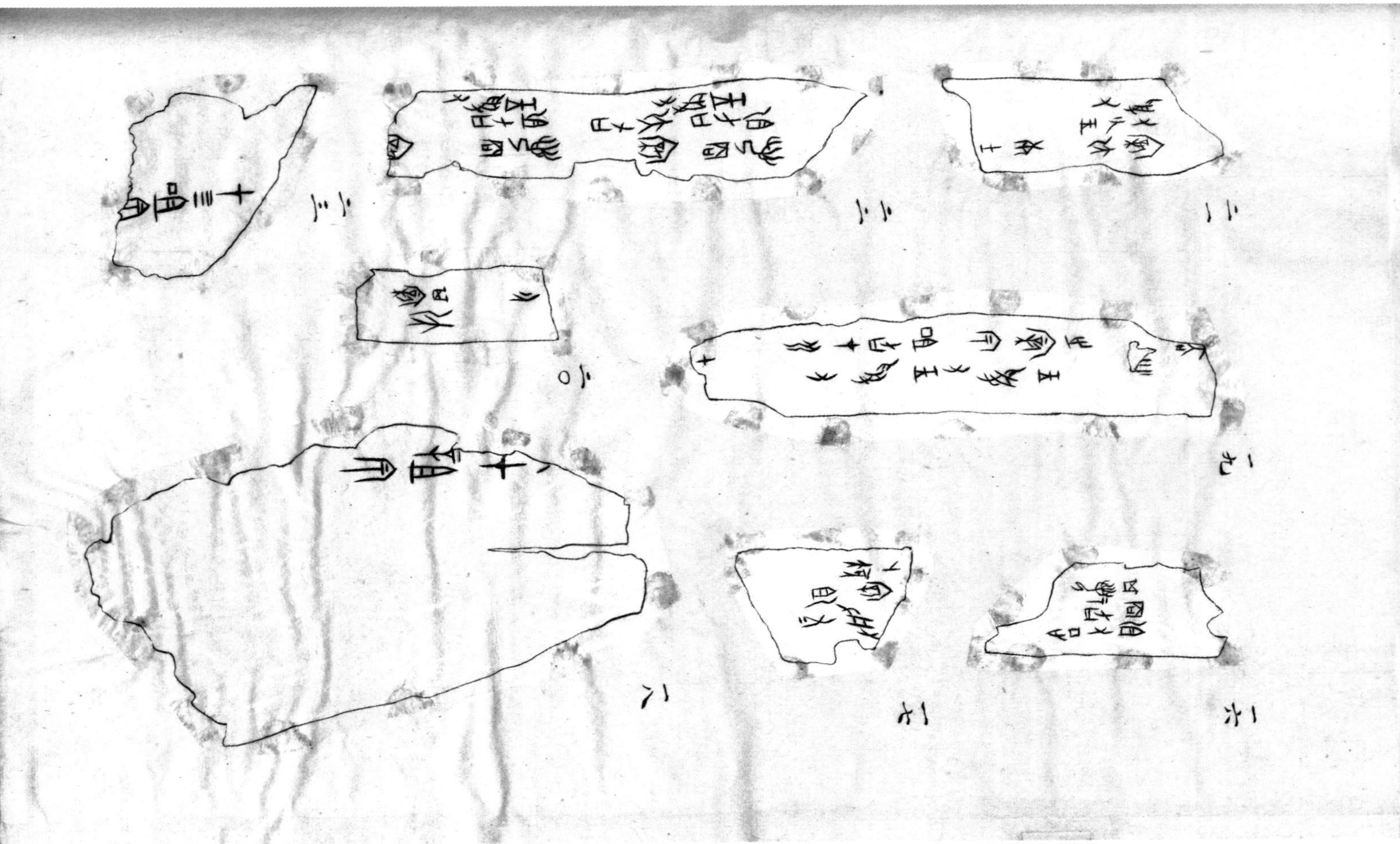

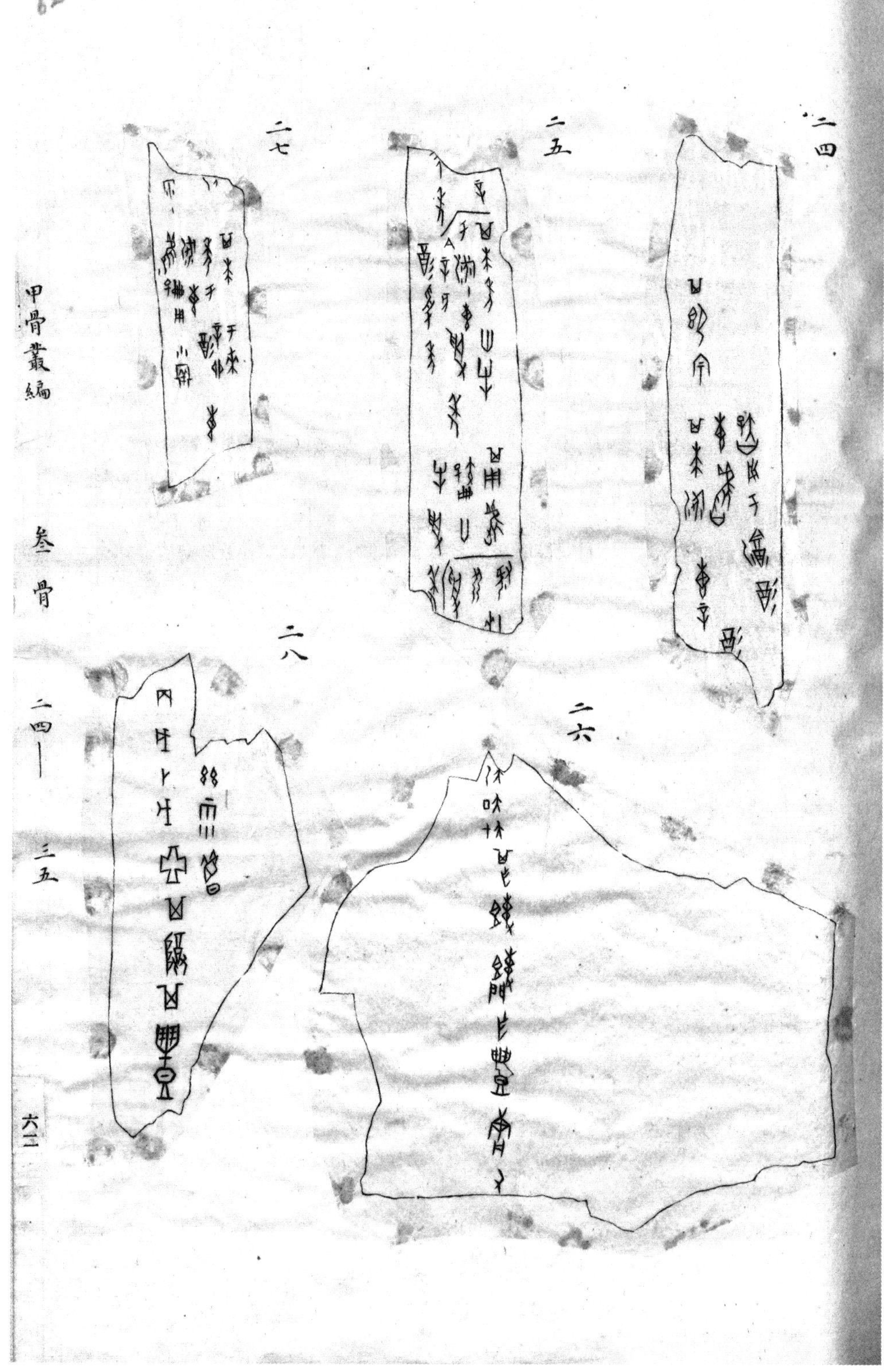
甲骨叢編　叁　骨　二四—三五
六二
二四
二五
二六
二七
二八

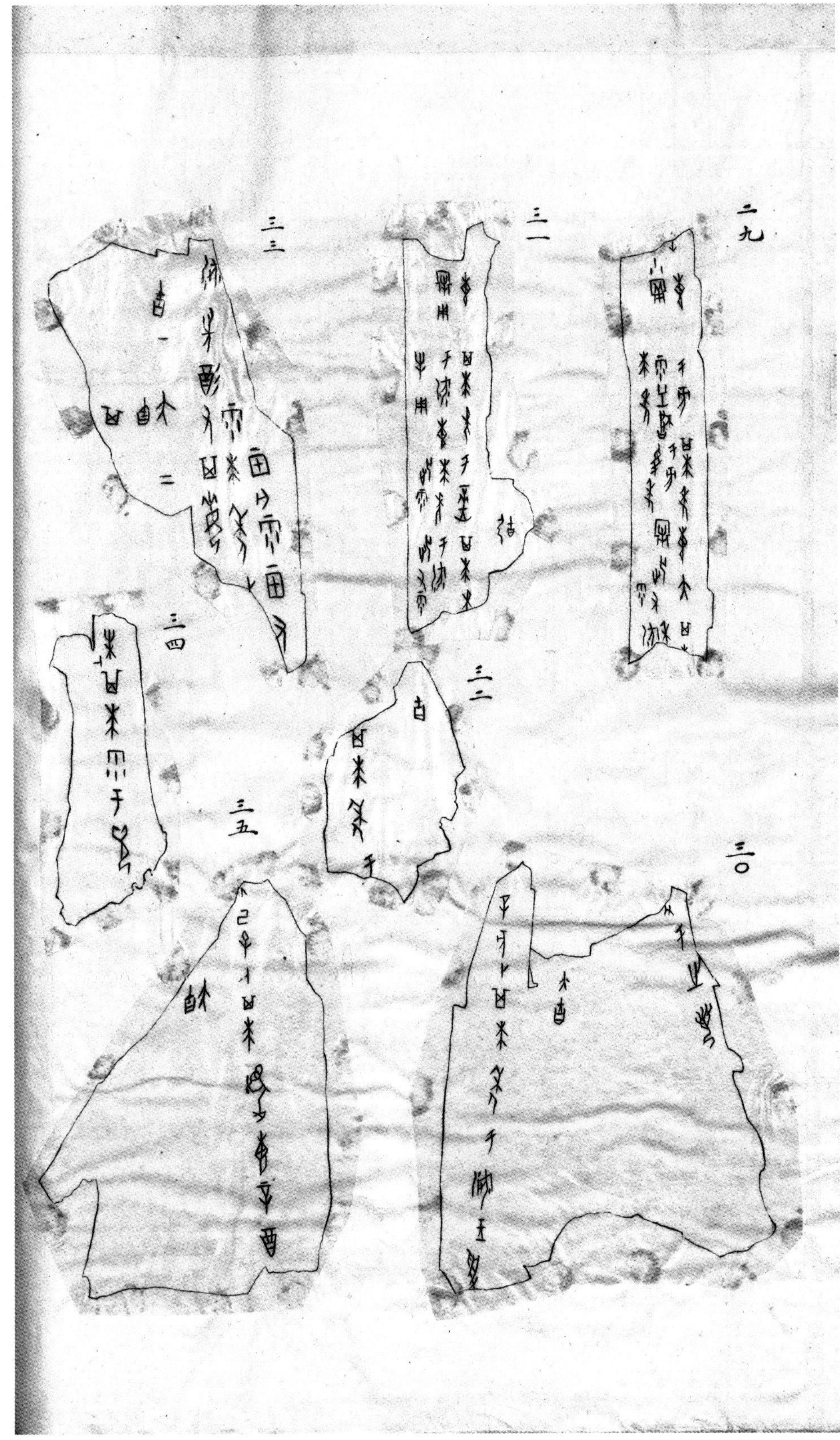
二九
三〇
三一
三二
三三
三四
三五

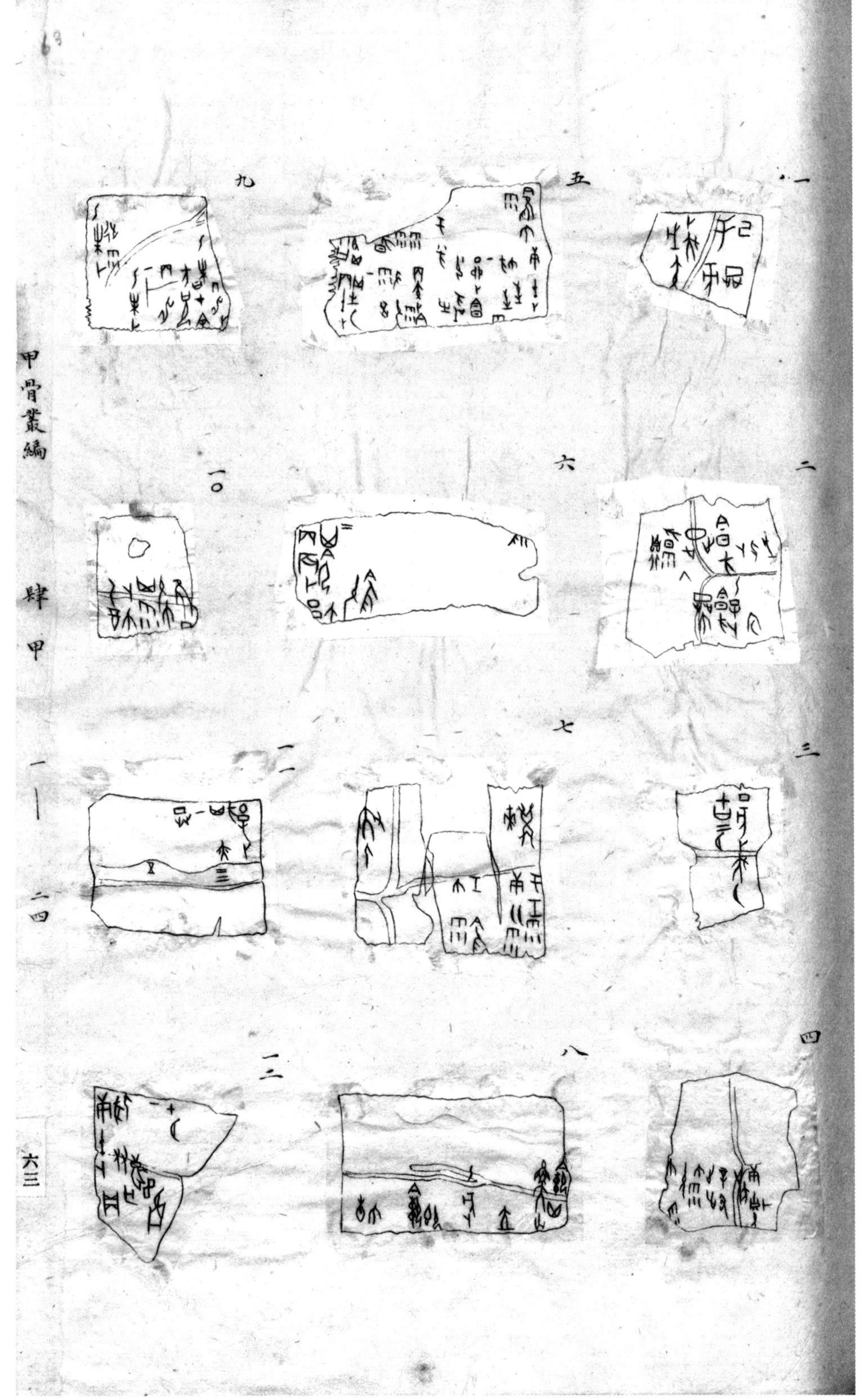
一
二
三
四
五
六
七
八
九
一〇
一一
一二
六三

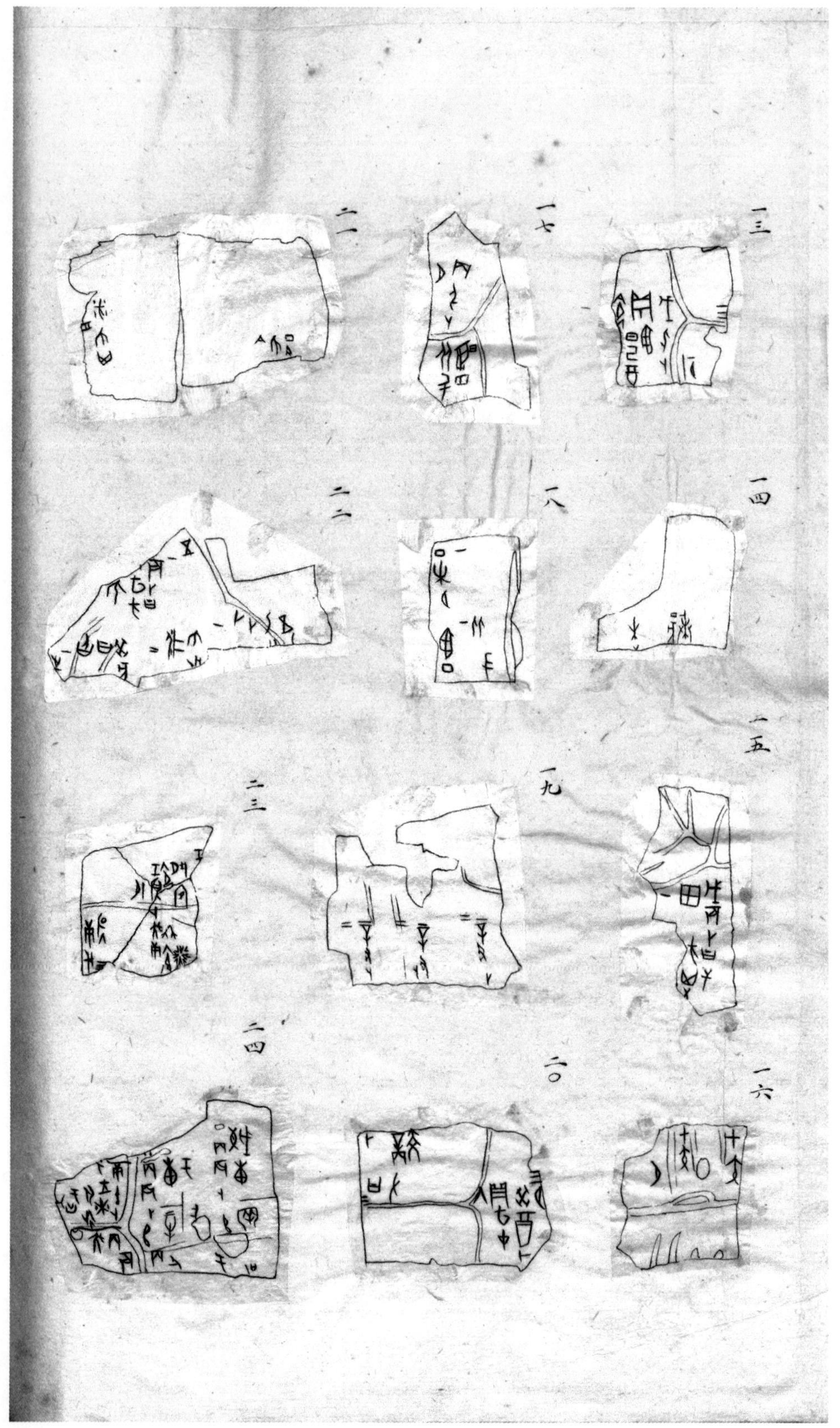
一三
一四
一五
一六
一七
一八
一九
二〇
二一
二二
二三
二四

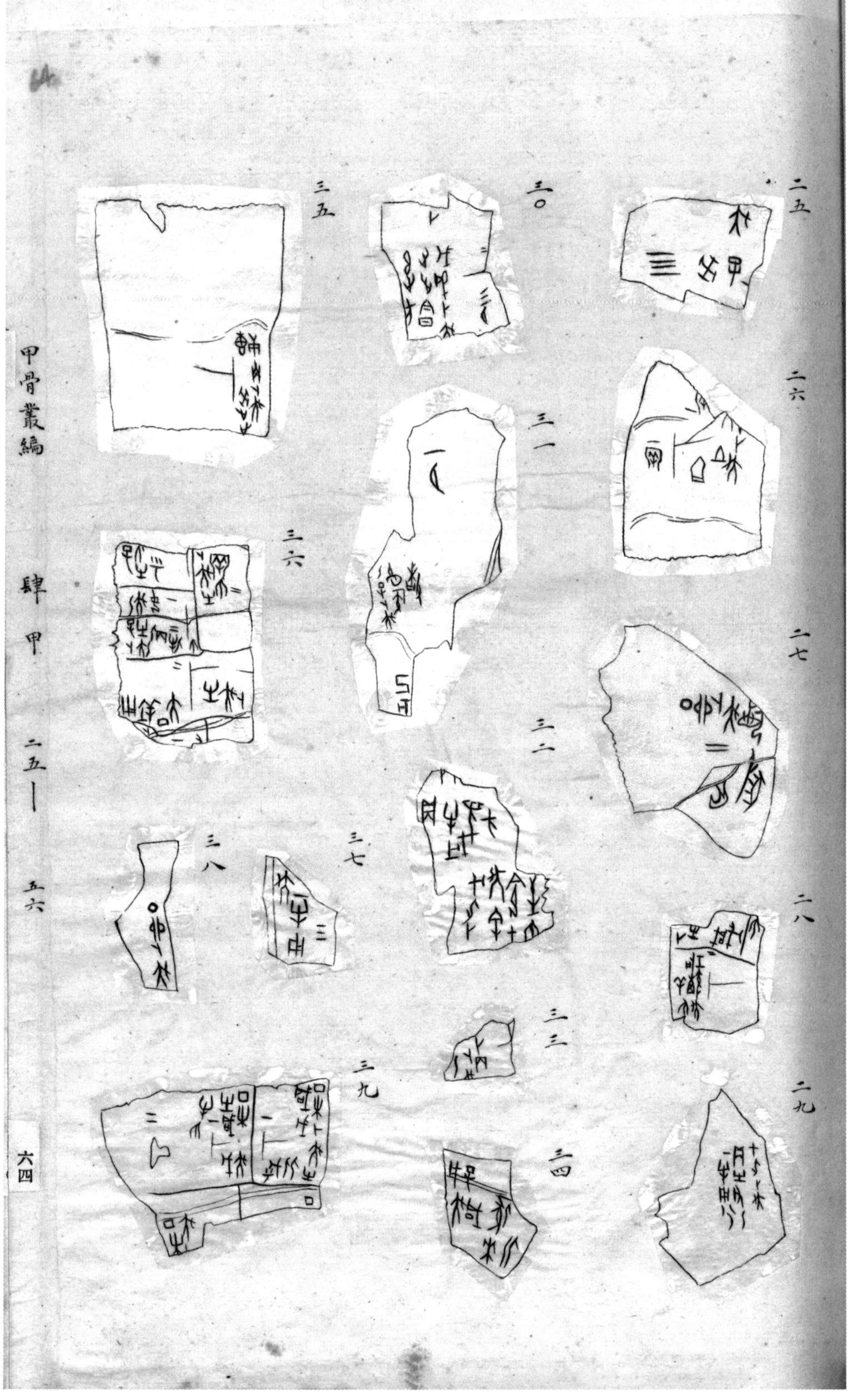
甲骨叢編
肆甲
二五一
五六
六四
二五
二六
二七
二八
二九
三〇
三一
三二
三三
三四
三五
三六
三七
三八
三九

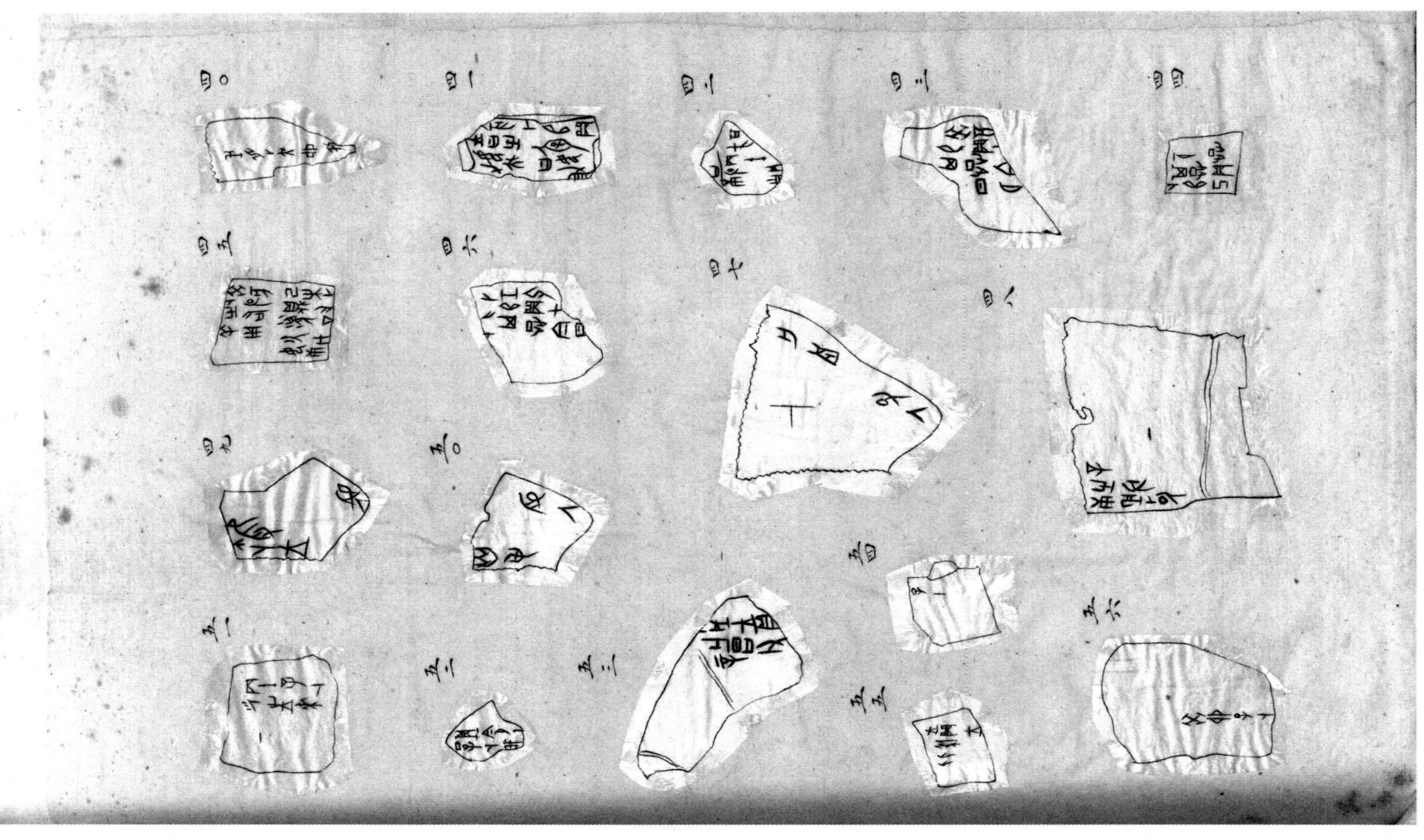
四〇
四一
四二
四三
四四
四五
四六
四七
四八
四九
五〇
五一
五二
五三
五四
五五
五六

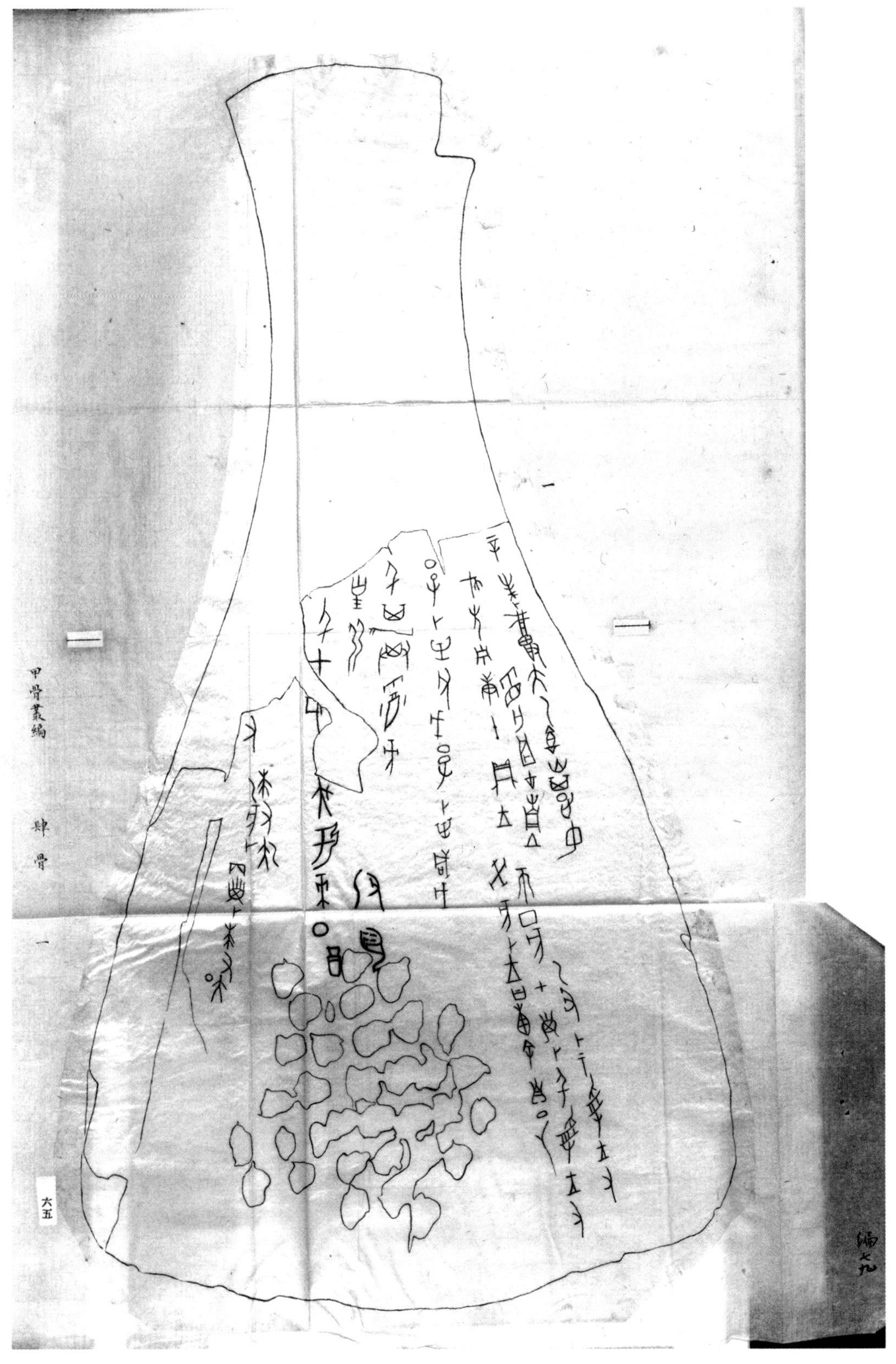
甲骨叢編　肆骨
六五
編七九

甲骨叢編　肆骨　一

六六

一（反面）

编六八九〇

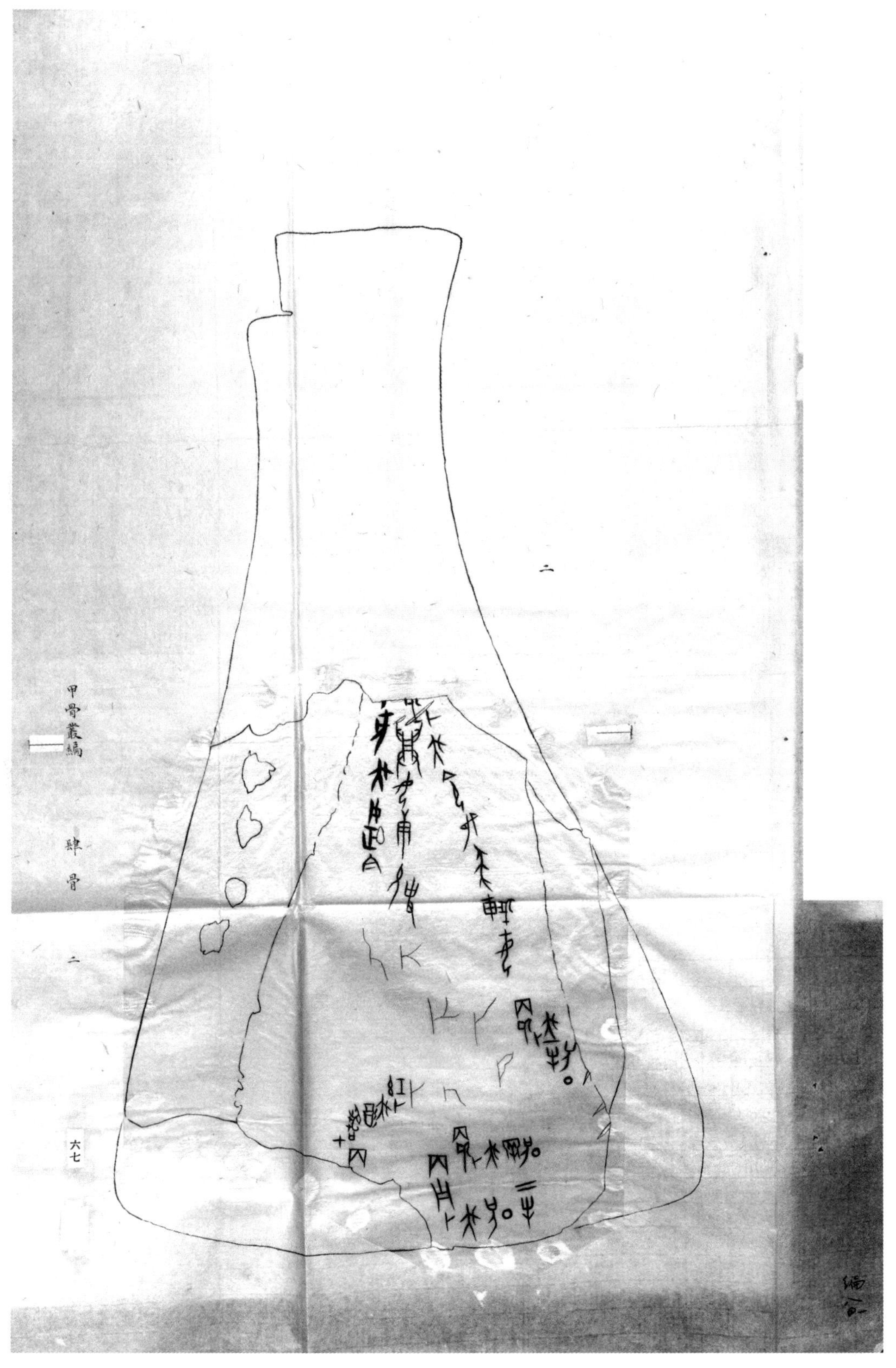
甲骨叢編　肆骨　二
六七
二
編合

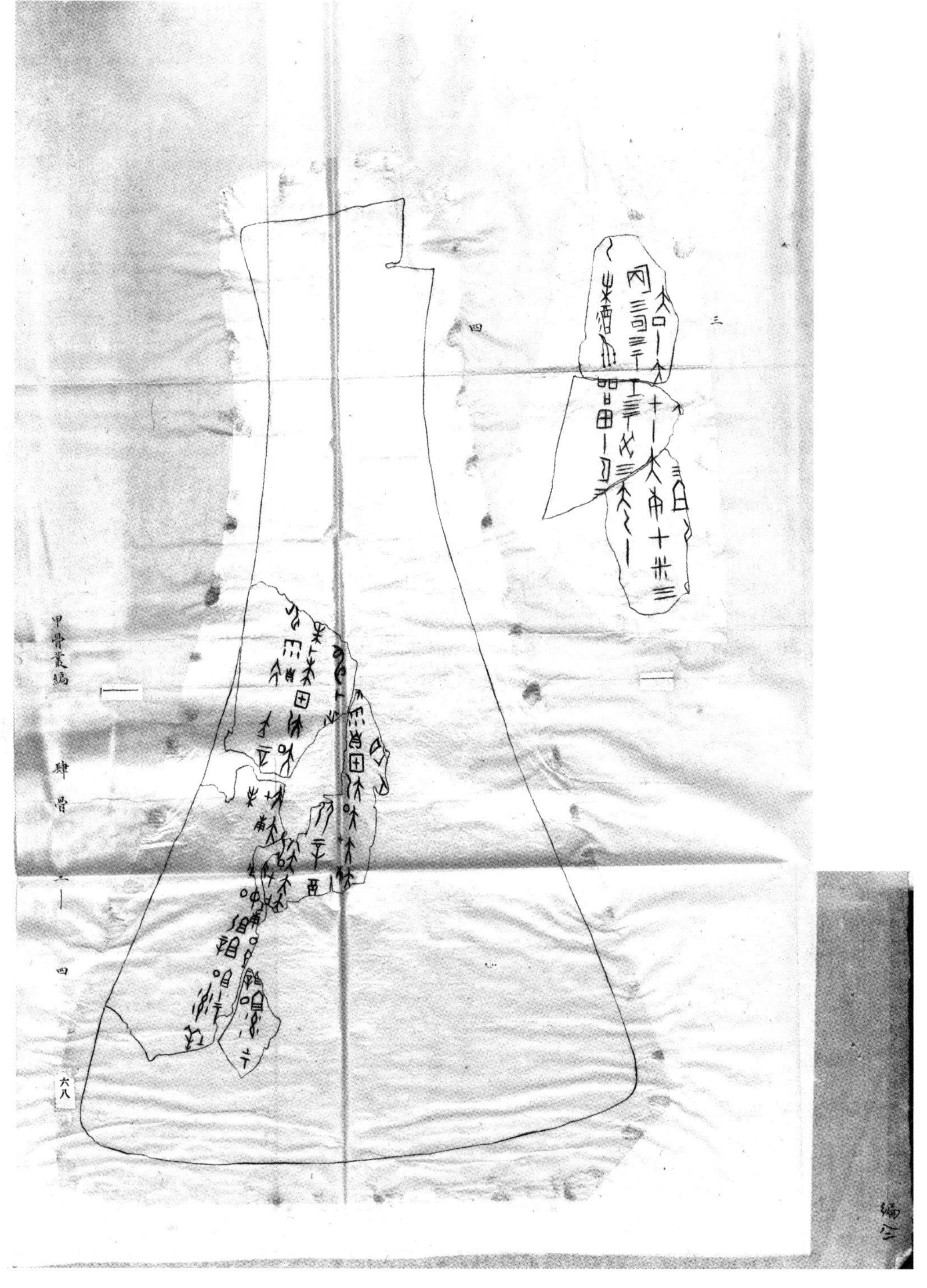
甲骨叢編　肆骨　一一四
六八
四
三
編八三

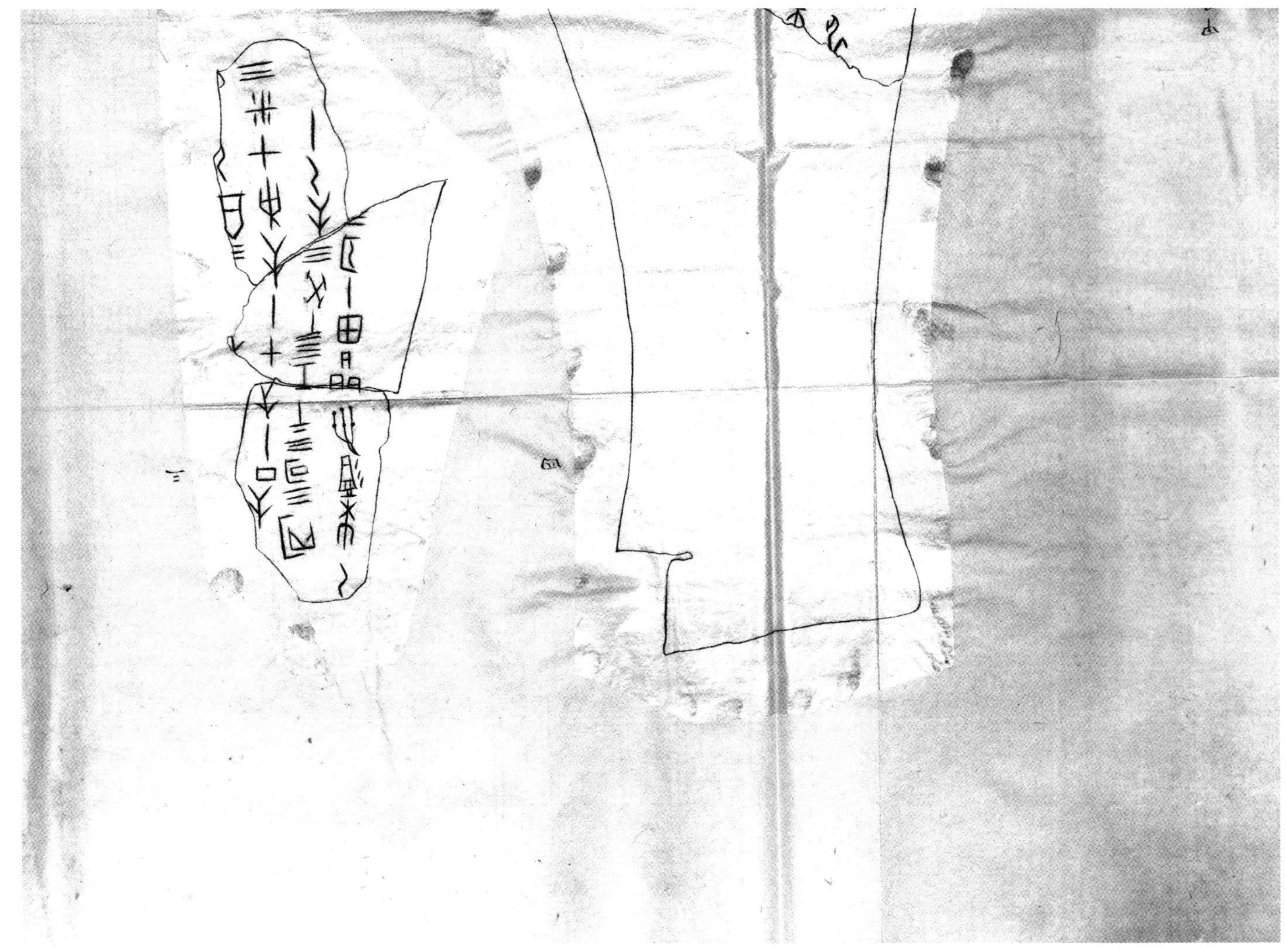

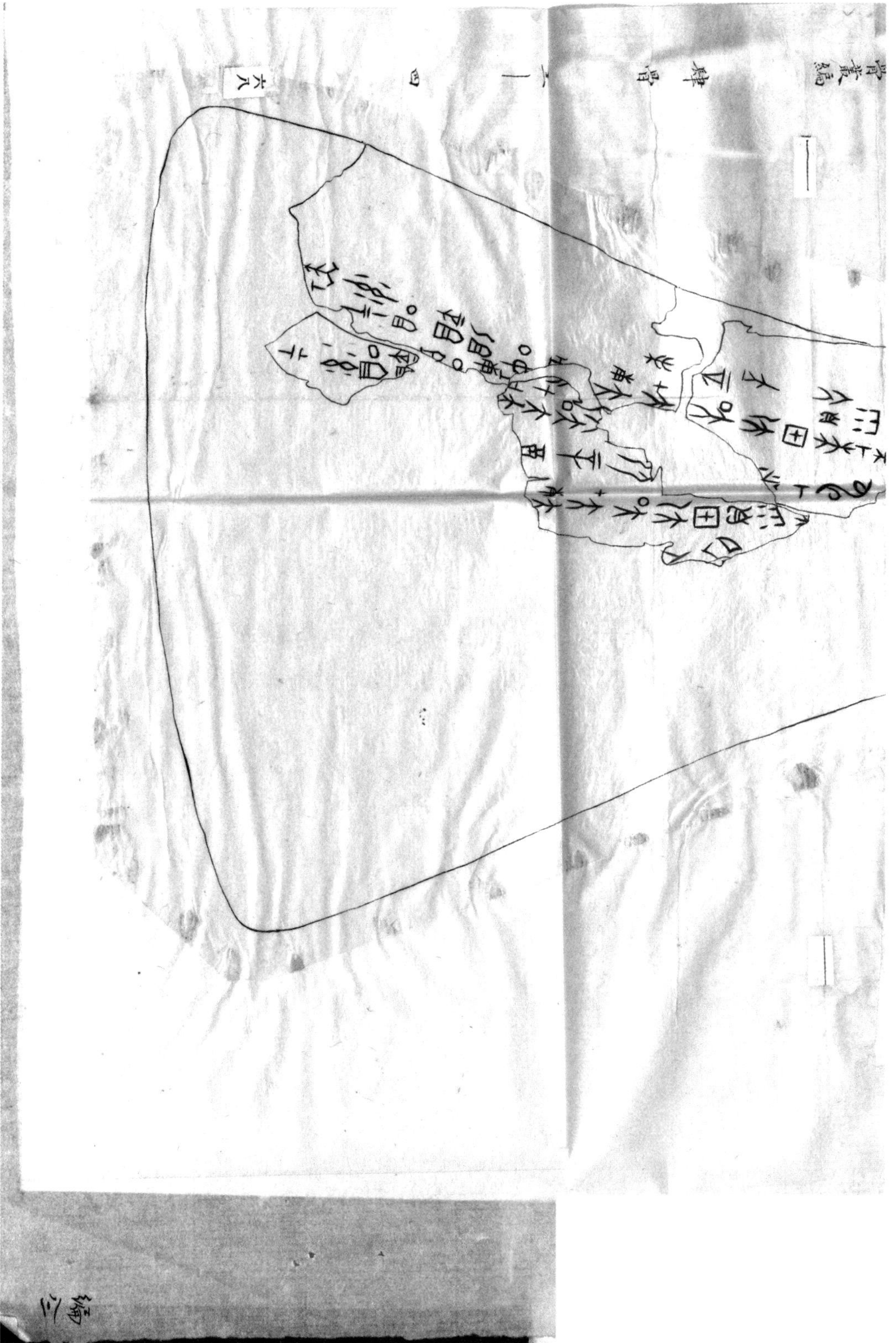

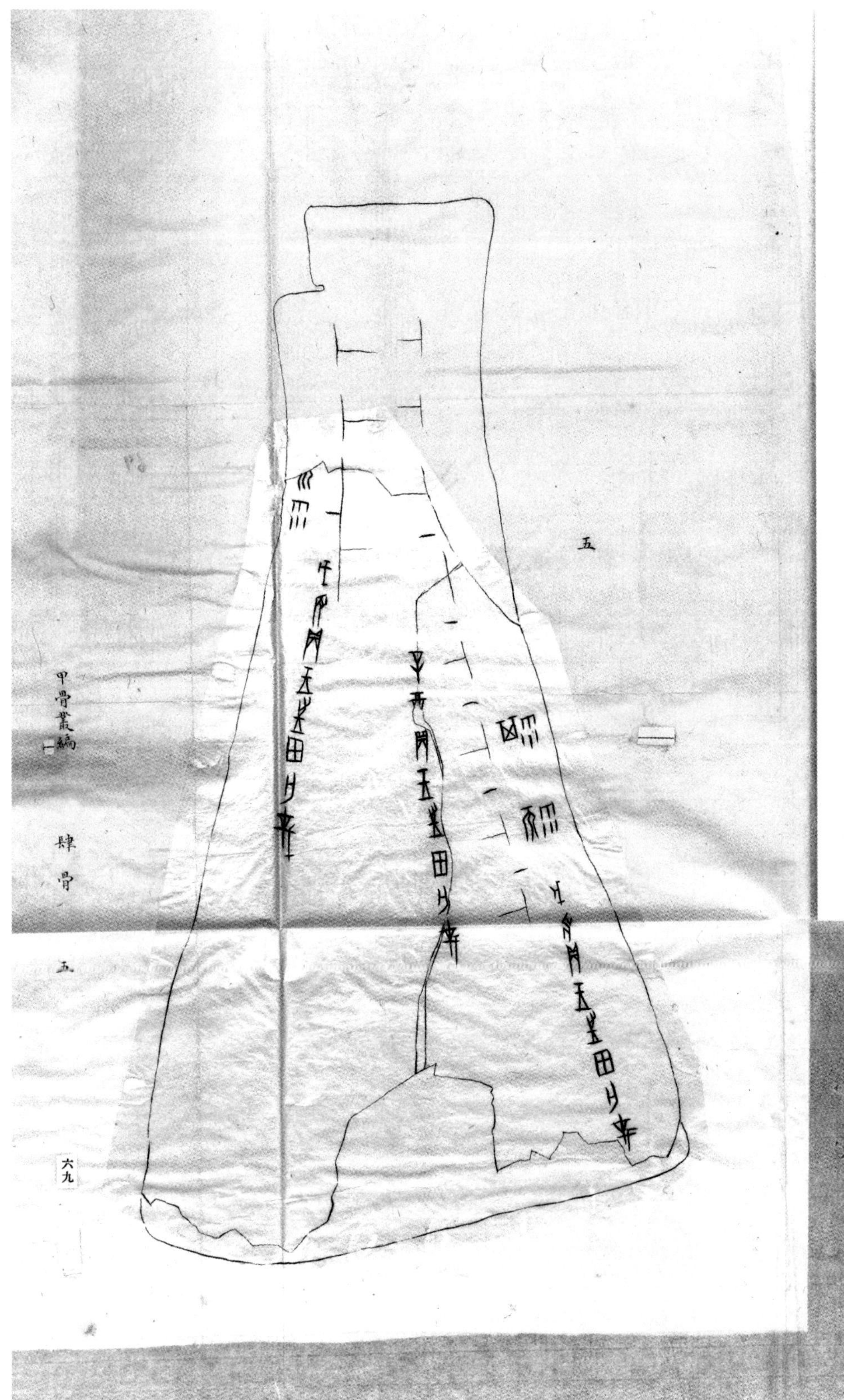
甲骨叢編
五
六九
編入三

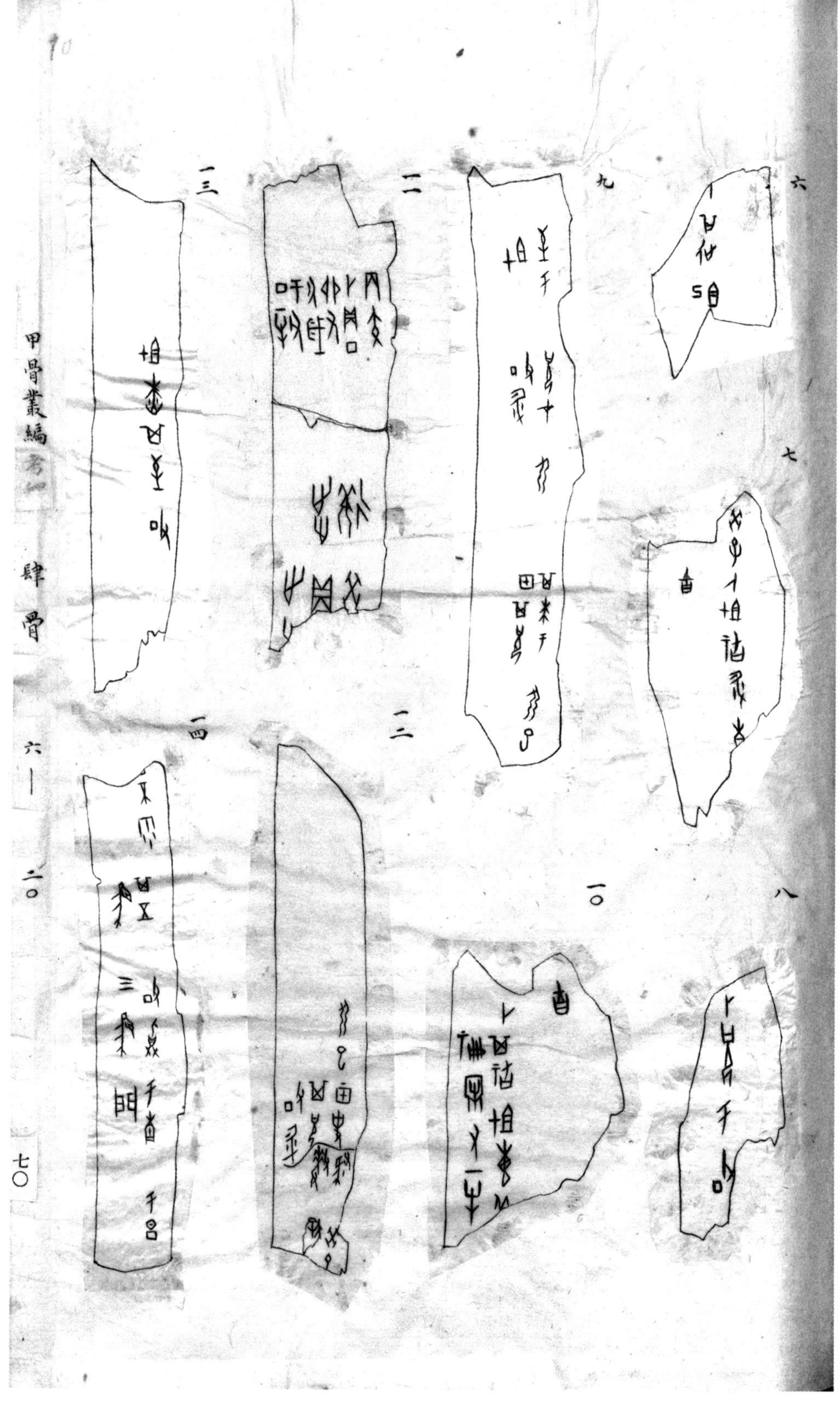
甲骨叢編 考四 肆骨 六一 一二〇 七〇
六
七
八
九
一〇
一一
一二
一三
一四

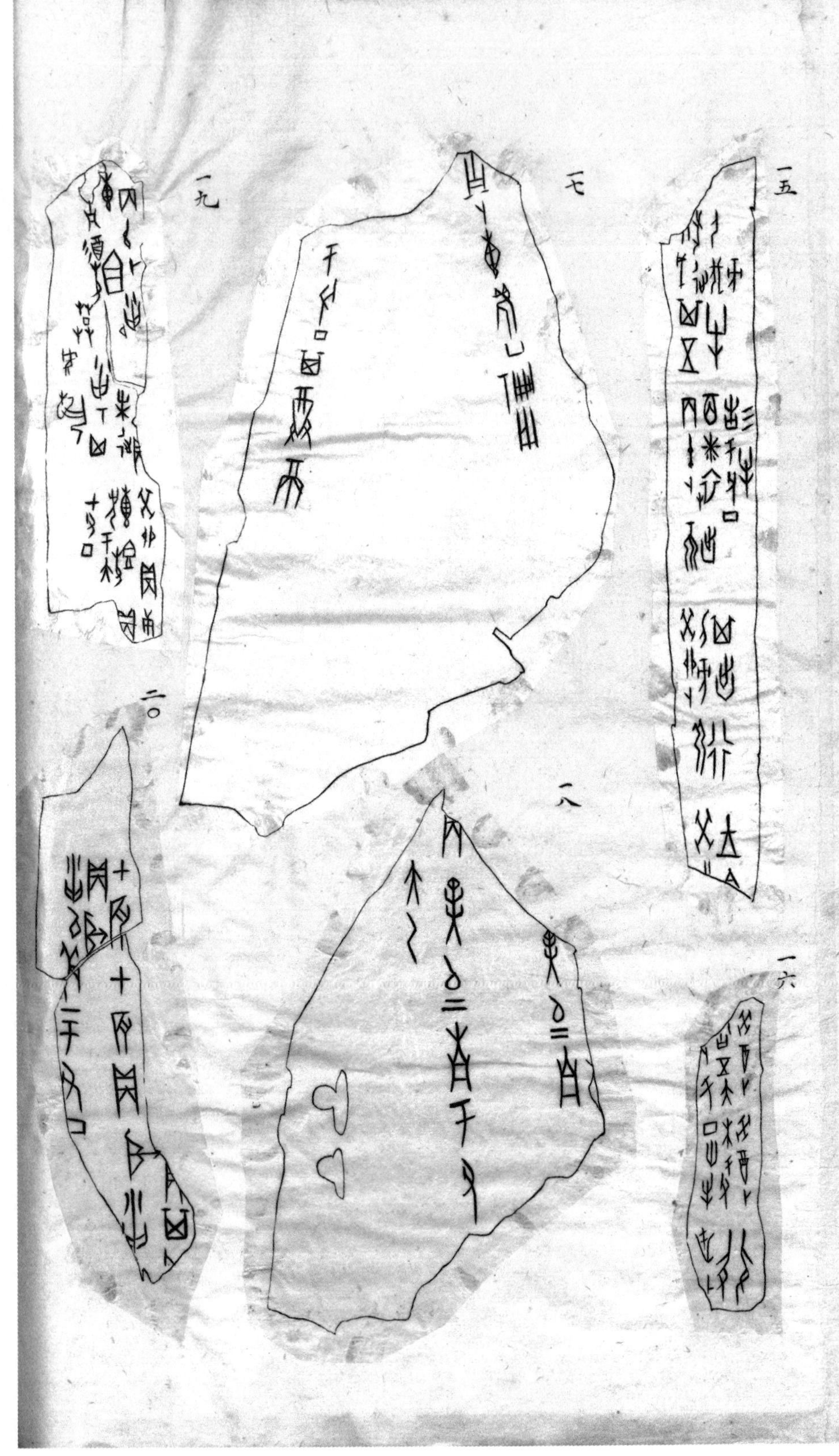
一五
一六
一七
一八
一九
二〇

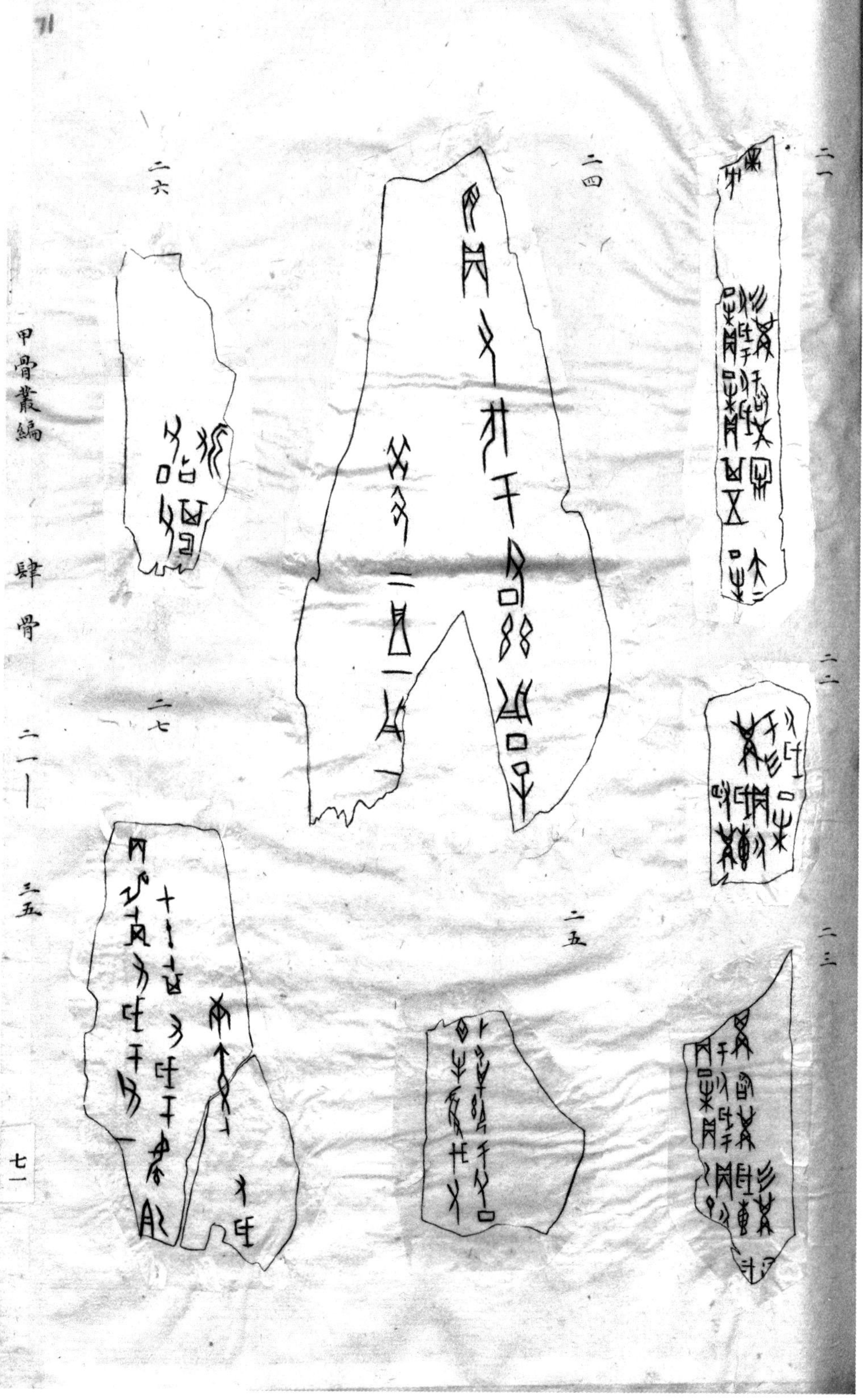
甲骨叢編　肆骨　二一一　三五
七一
二一
二二
二三
二四
二五
二六
二七

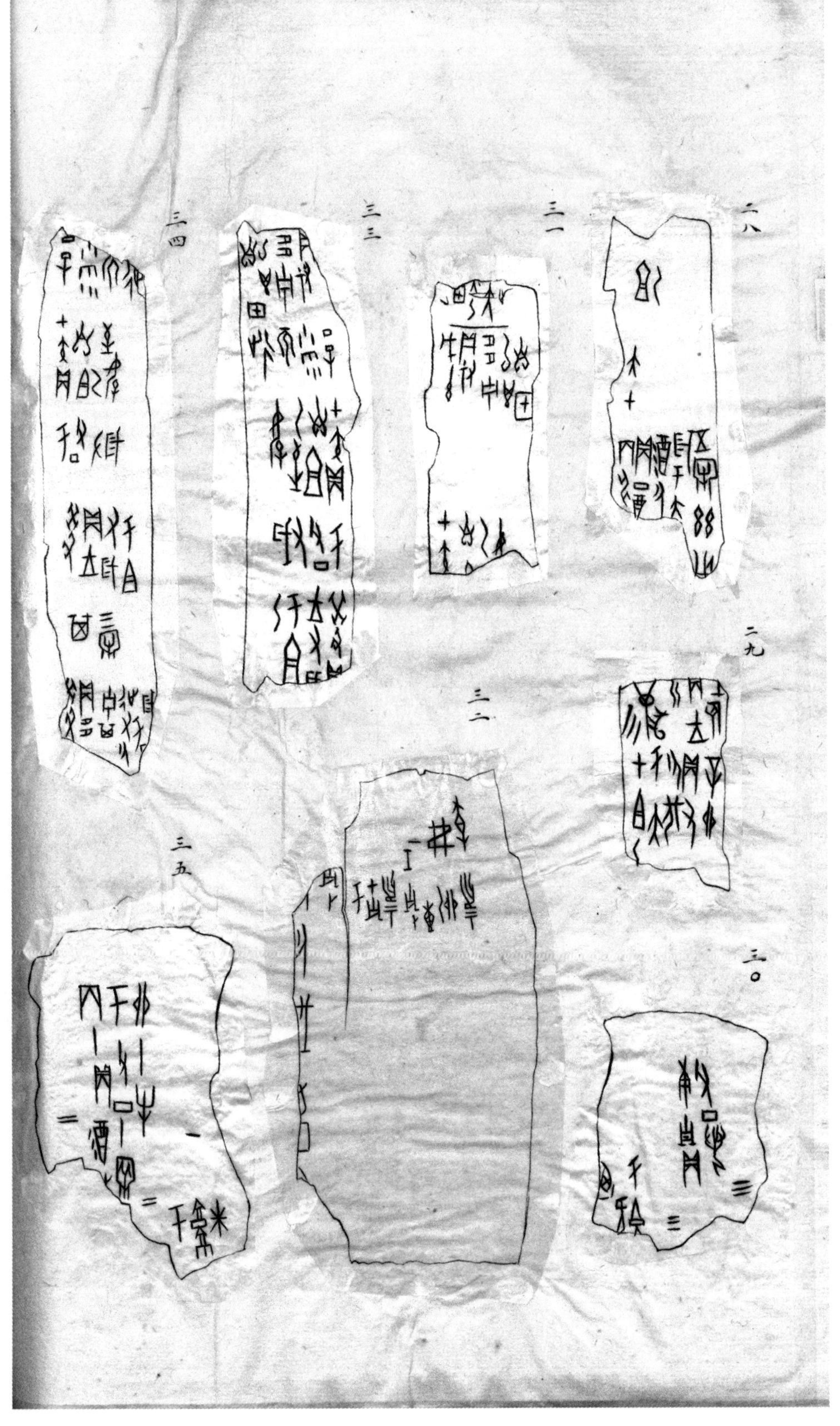

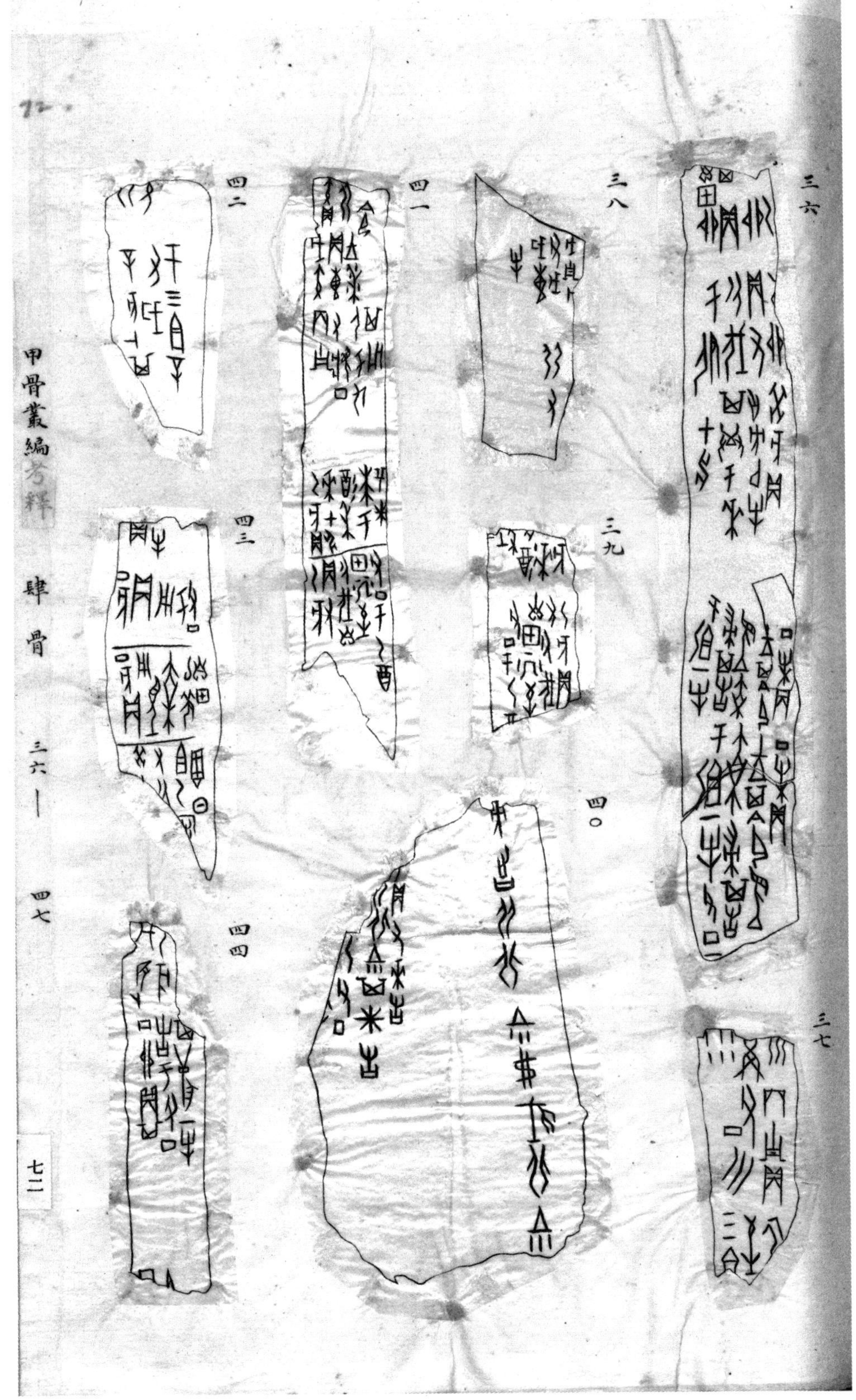
甲骨叢編考釋　肆　骨　三六—四七
七二
三六
三七
三八
三九
四〇
四一
四二
四三
四四

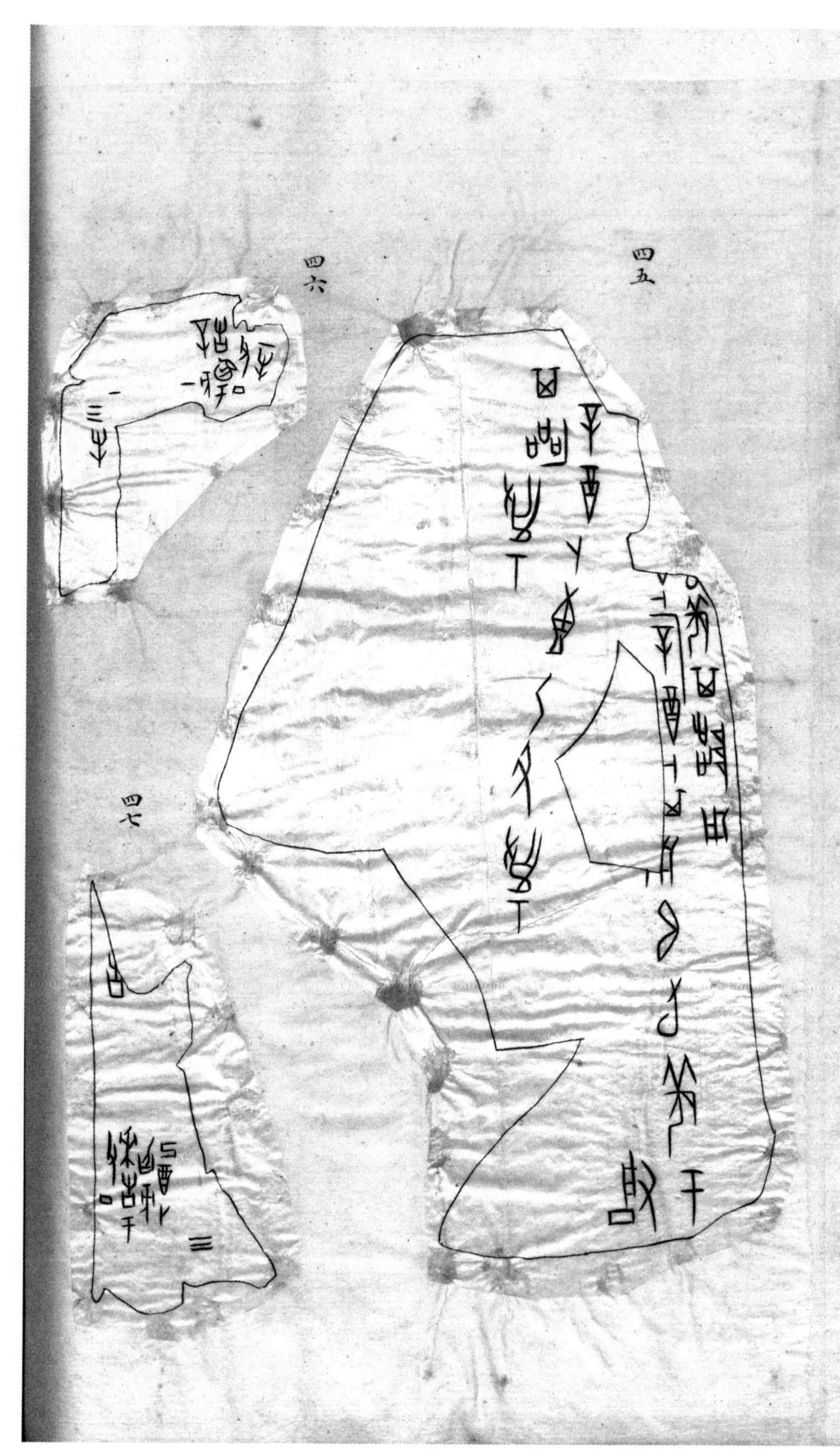
四五
四六
四七

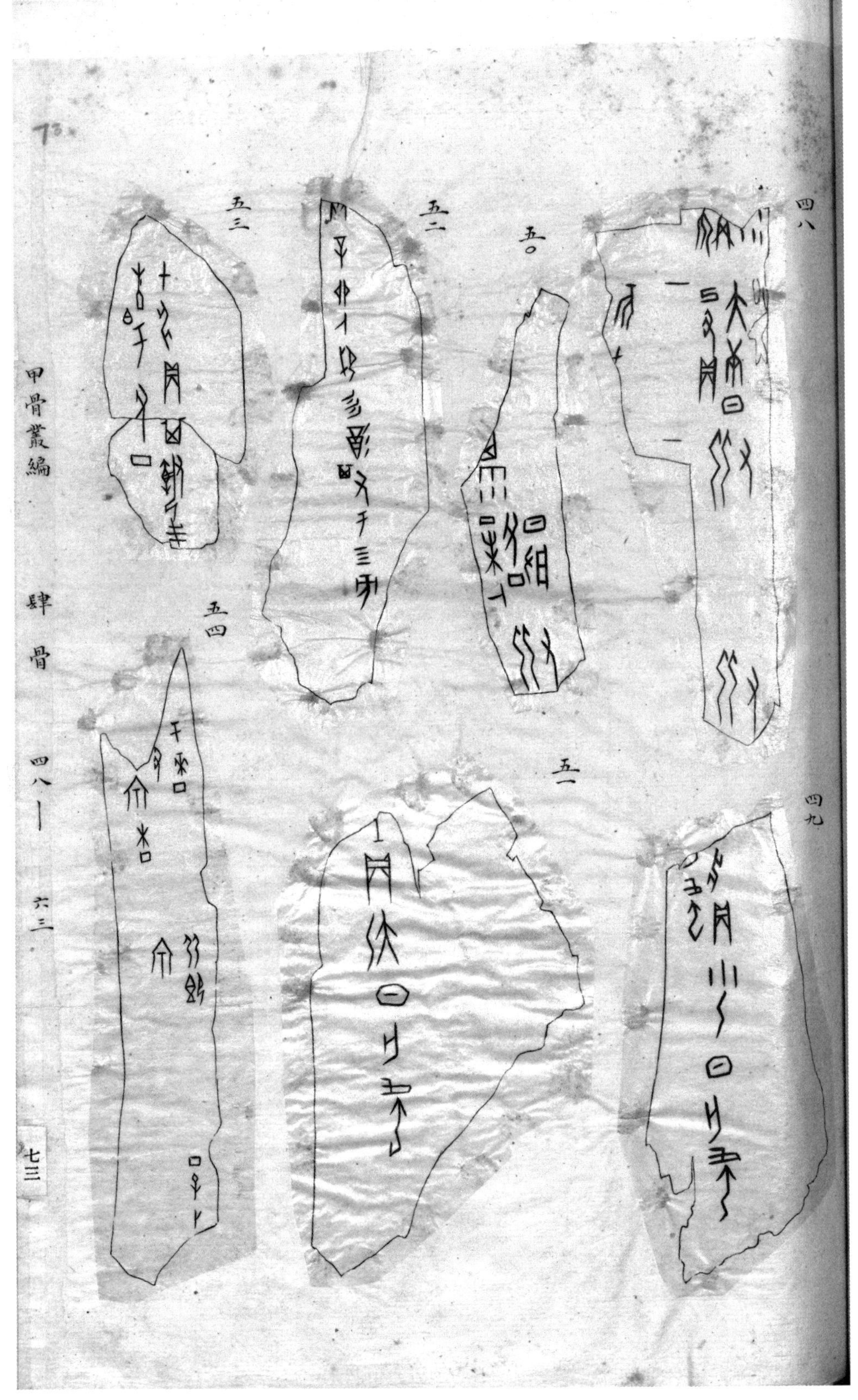
甲骨叢編 肆骨 四八一 六三
七三
四八
四九
五〇
五一
五二
五三
五四

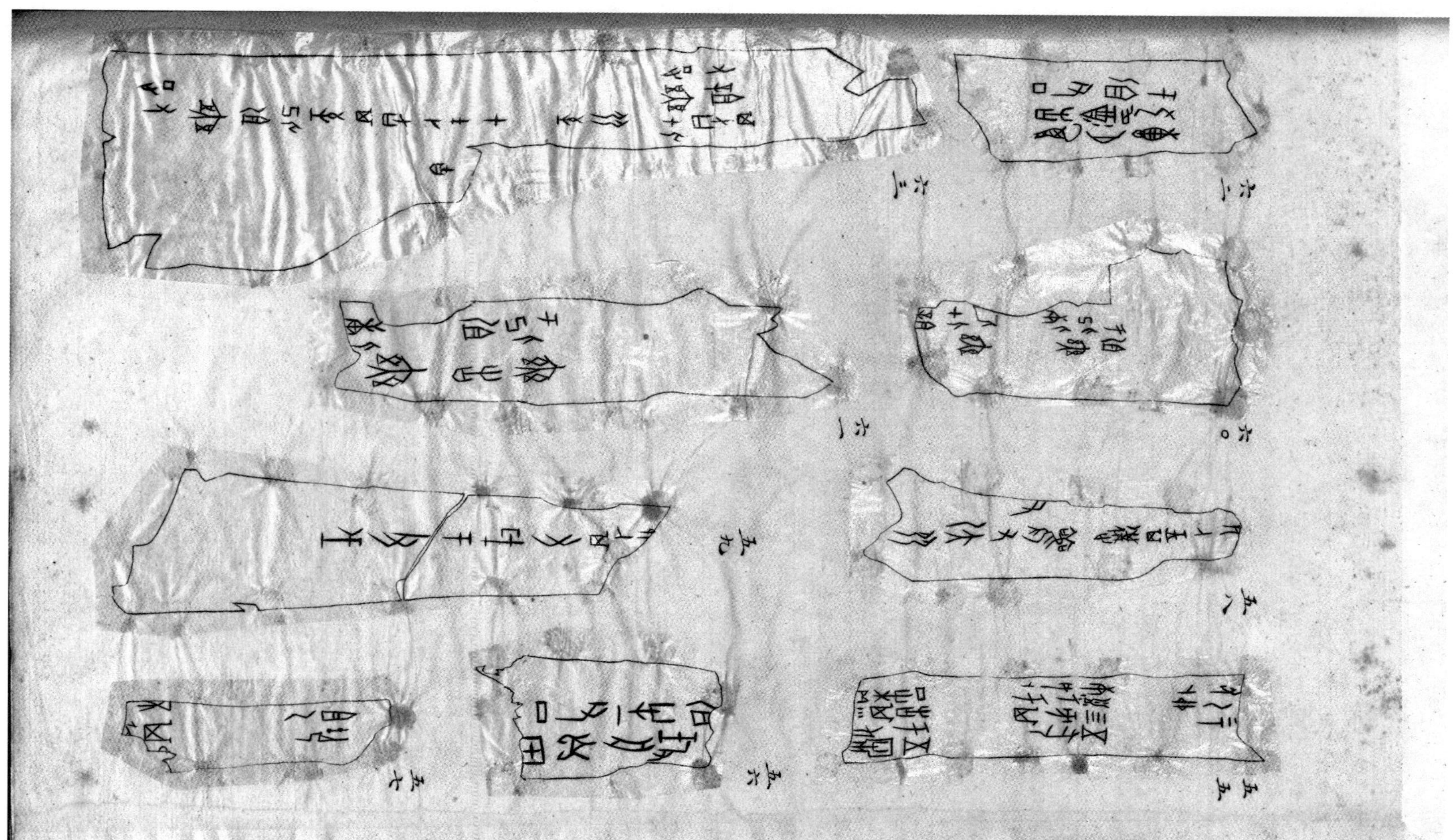
六二
六三
六〇
六一
五八
五九
五五
五六
五七

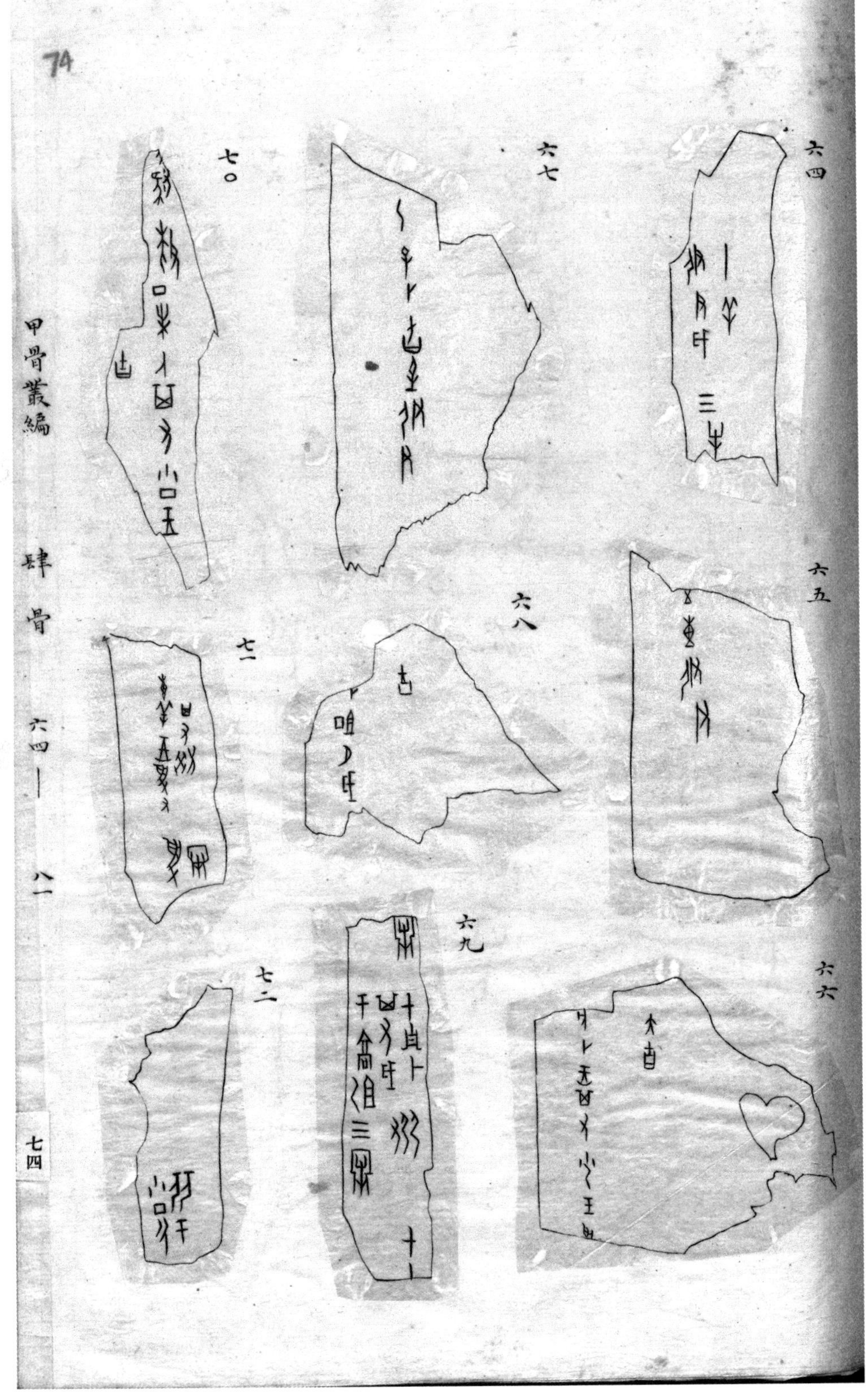
六四
六五
六六
六七
六八
六九
七〇
七一
七二

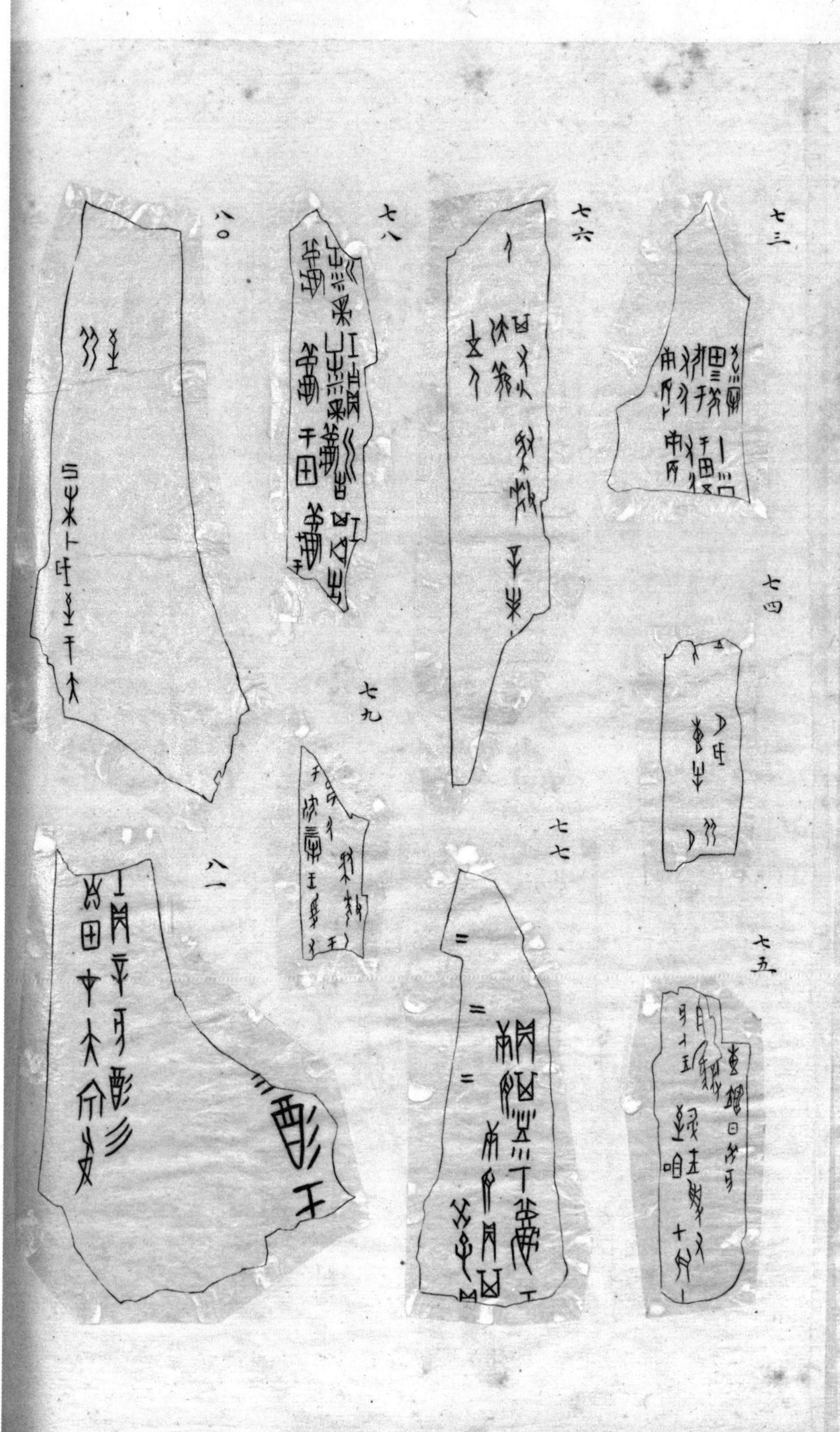

七三
七四
七五
七六
七七
七八
七九
八〇
八一

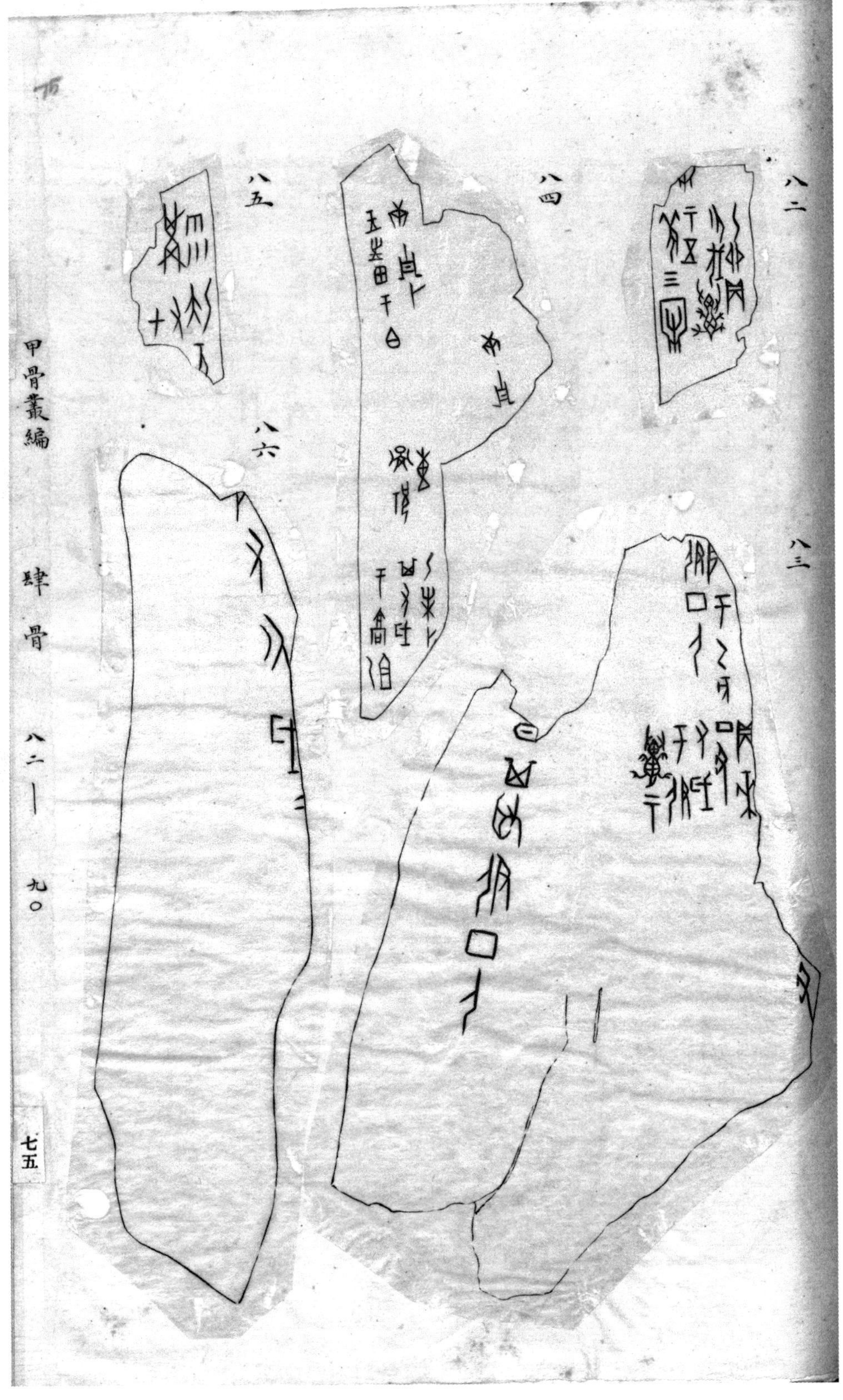
八二
八三
八四
八五
八六
甲骨叢編 肆骨 八二—九〇
七五

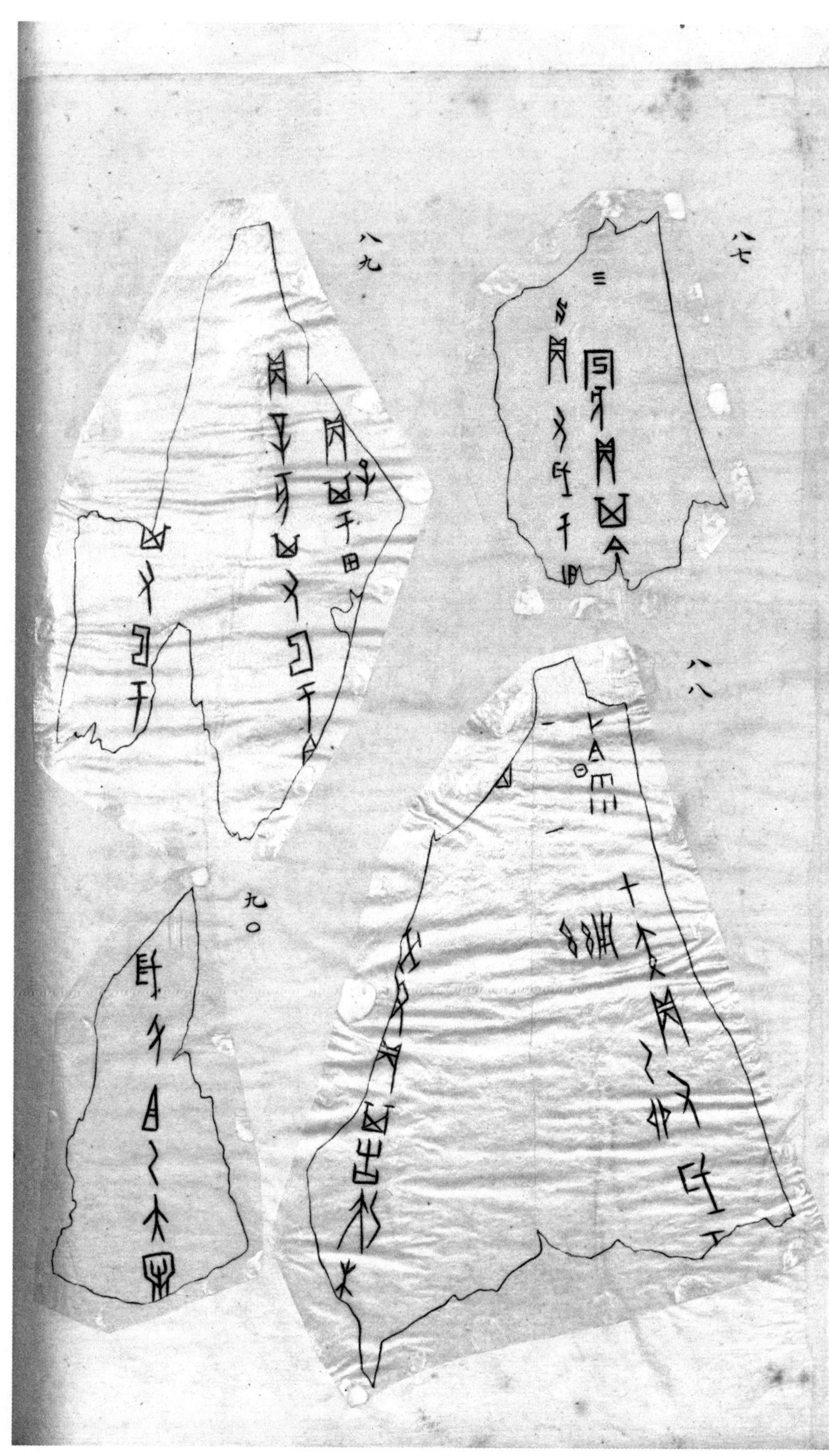
八七
八八
八九
九〇

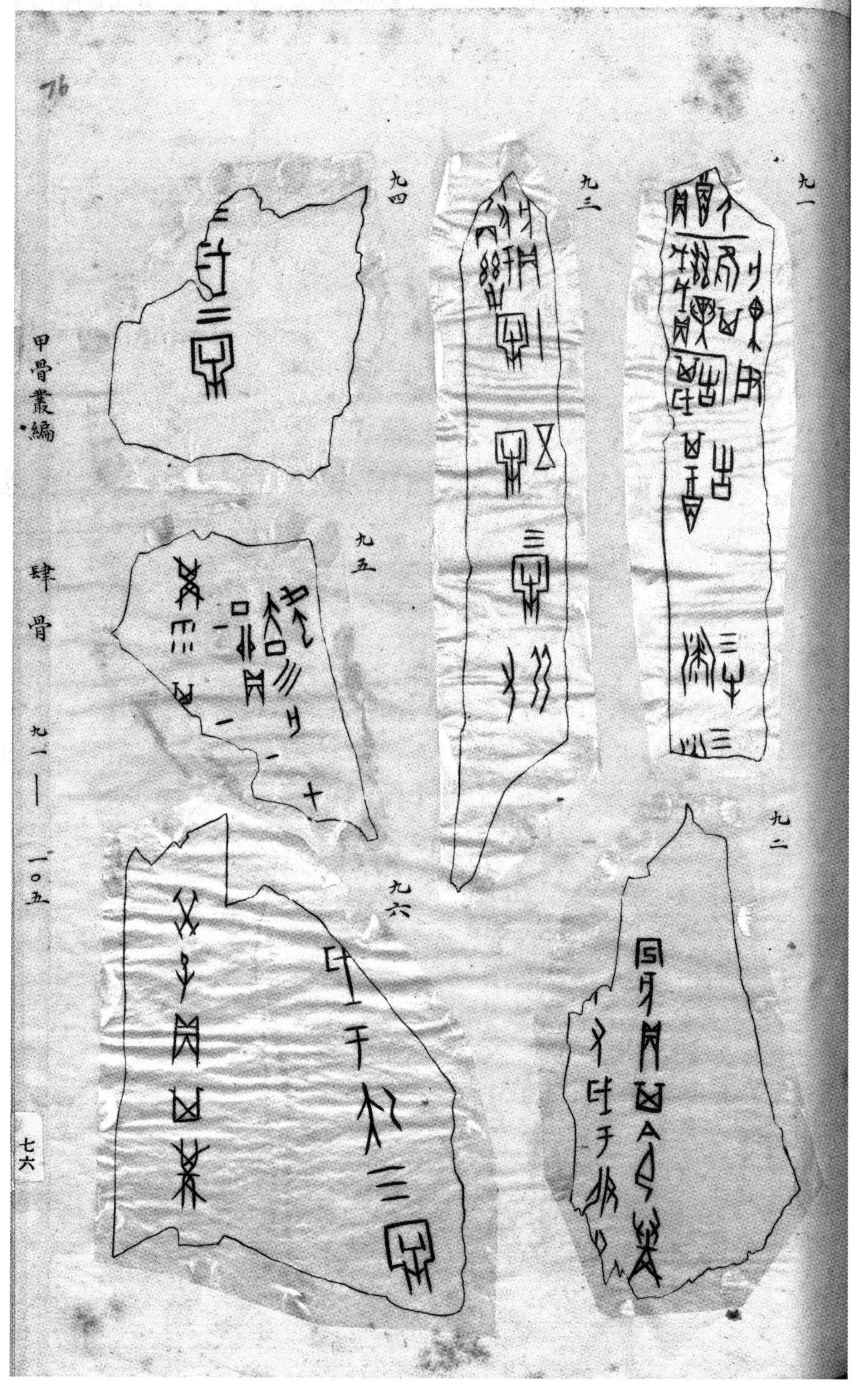
76
甲骨叢編·肆骨 九一——一〇五
七六
九一
九二
九三
九四
九五
九六

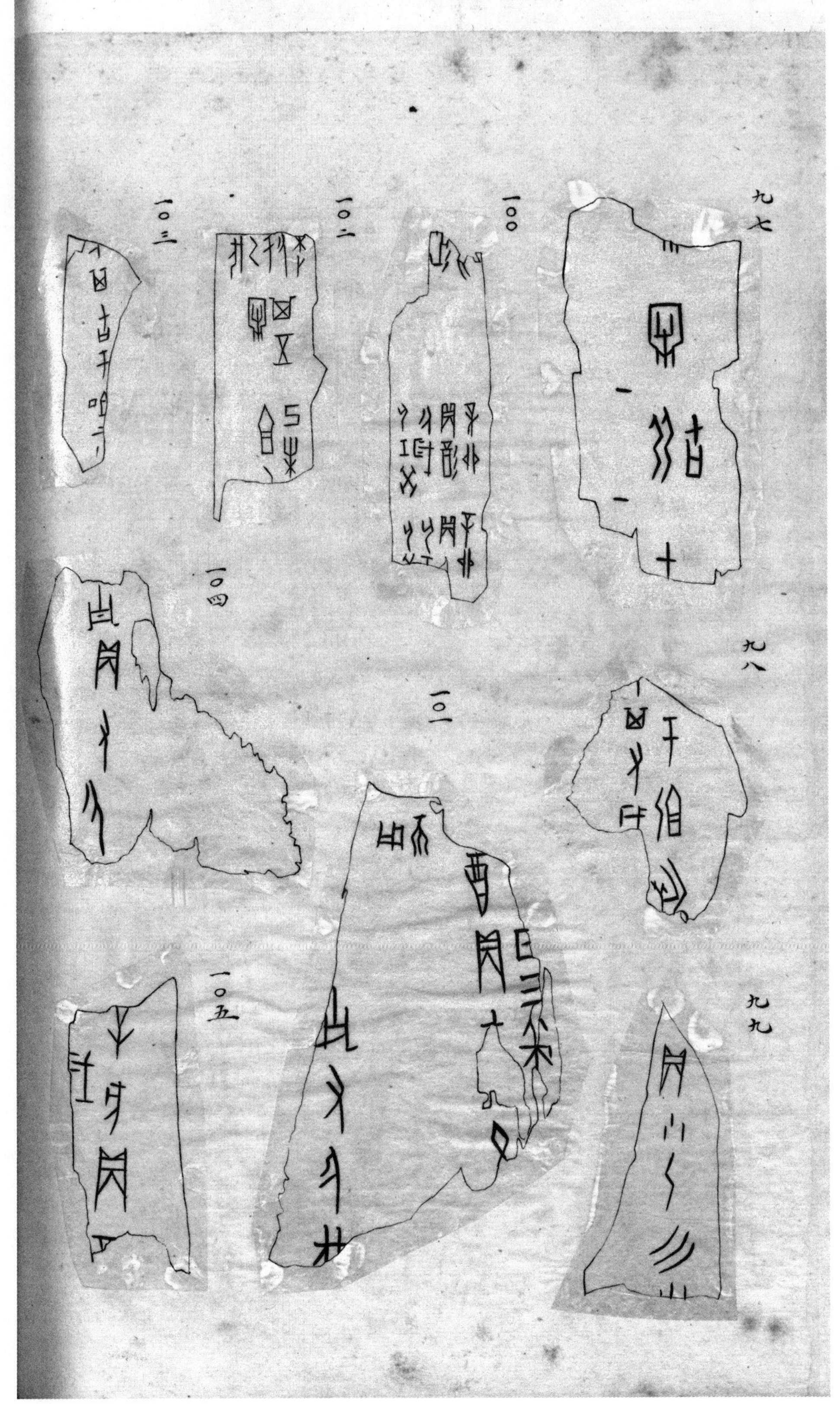

九七
九八
九九
一〇〇
一〇一
一〇二
一〇三
一〇四
一〇五

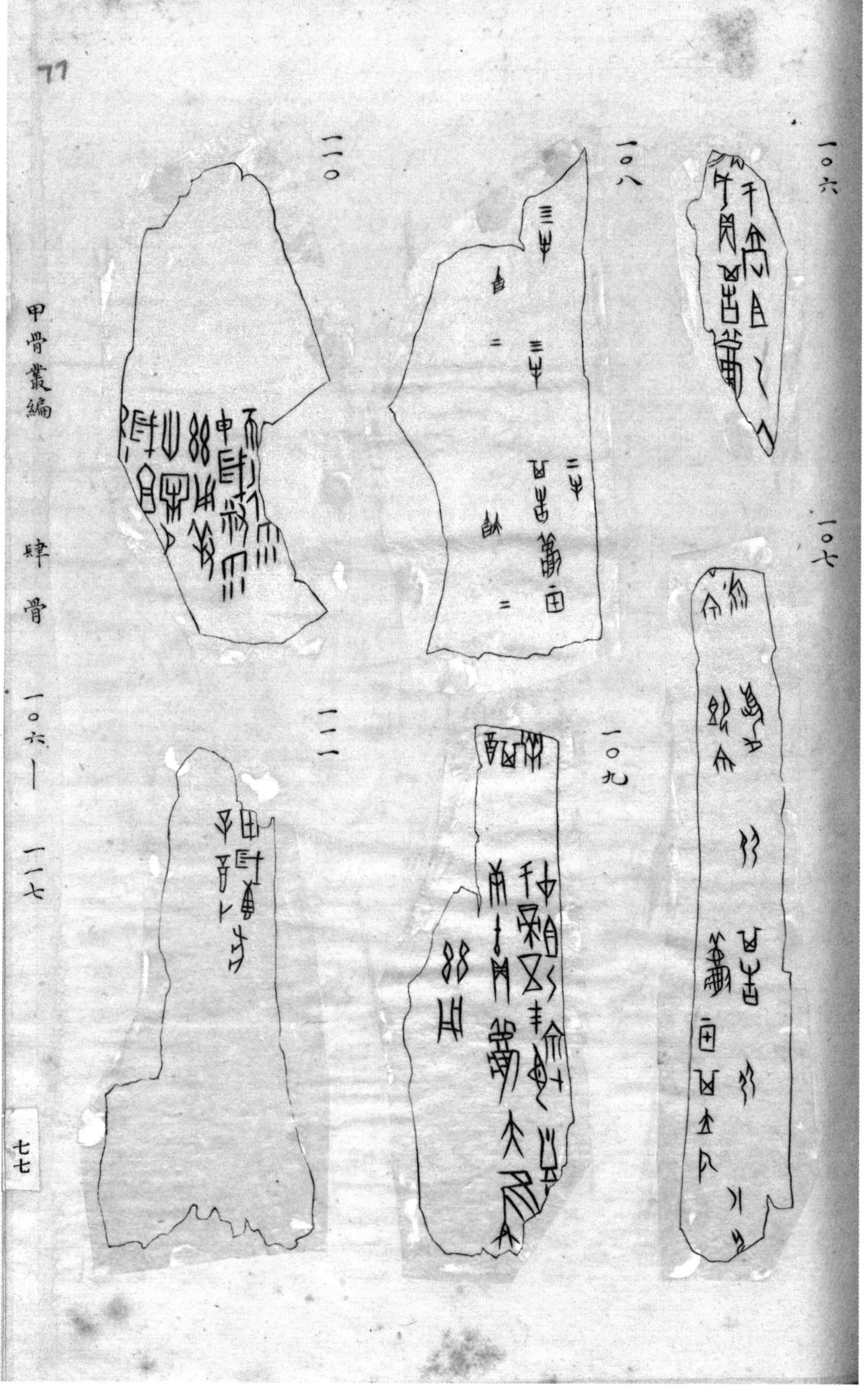
77
一〇六
一〇七
一〇八
一〇九
一一〇
一一一
甲骨叢編　肆骨　一〇六—一一七
七七

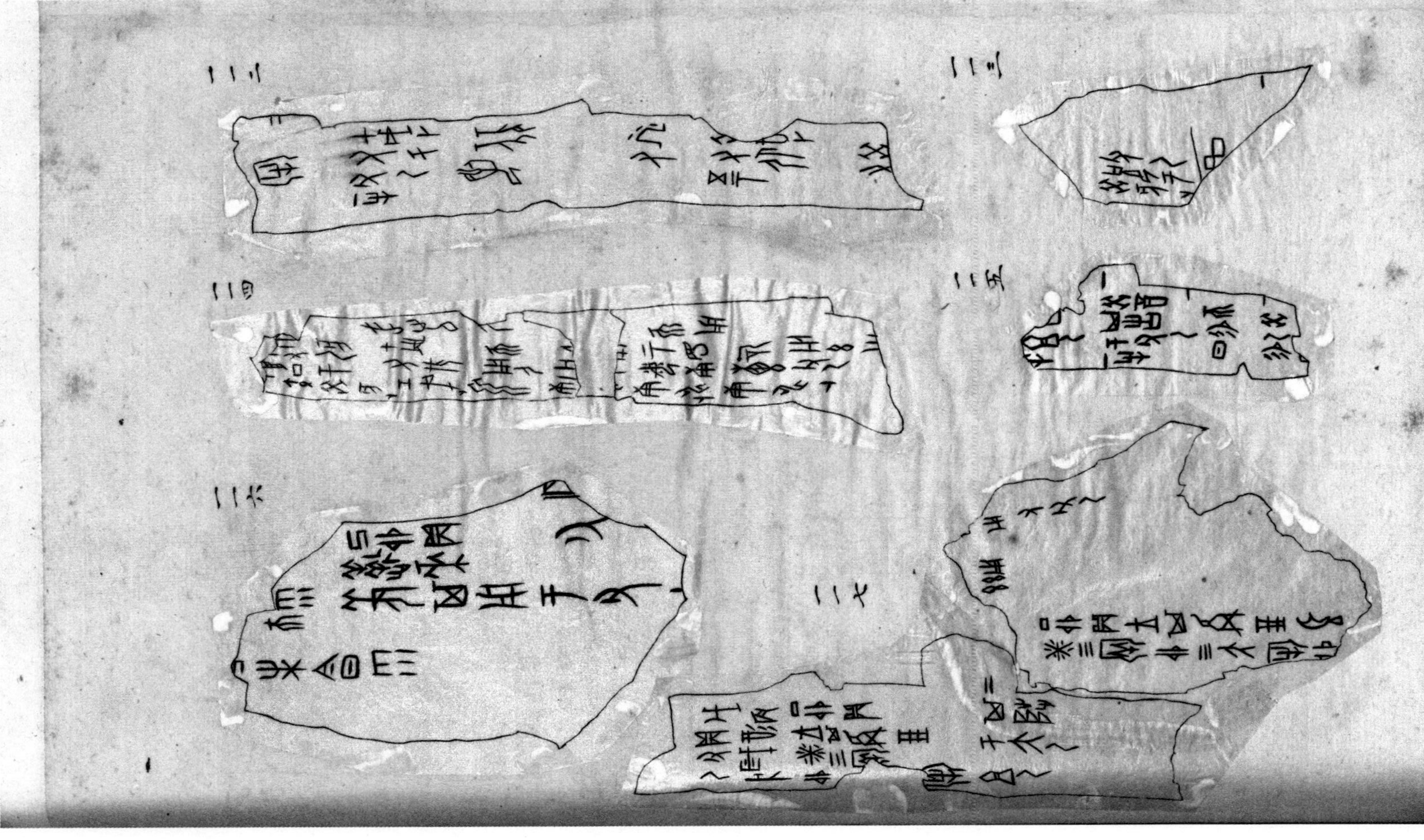
二一二
二一三
二一四
二一五
二一六
二一七

甲骨叢編　肆骨　一一八—一三一

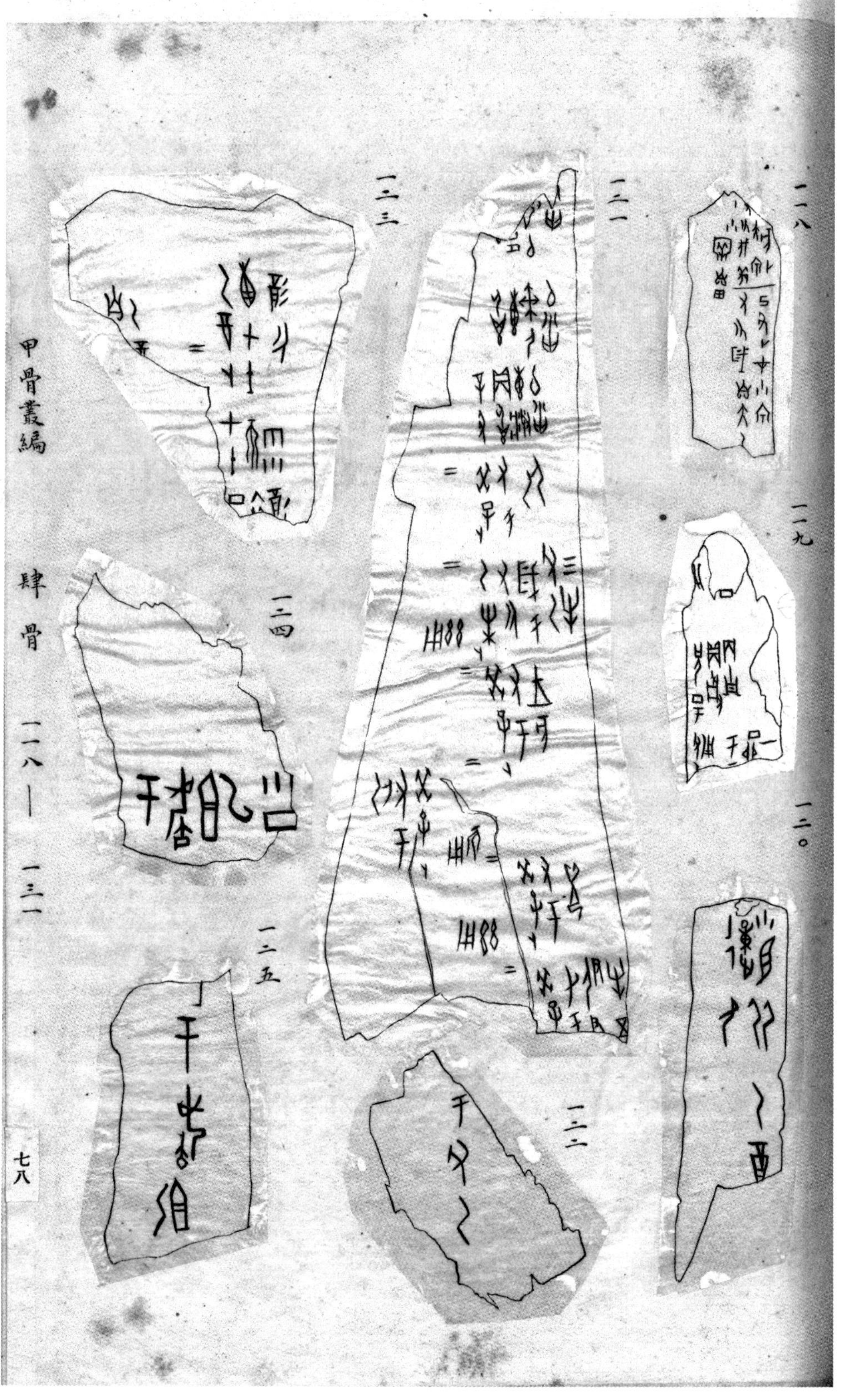

七八

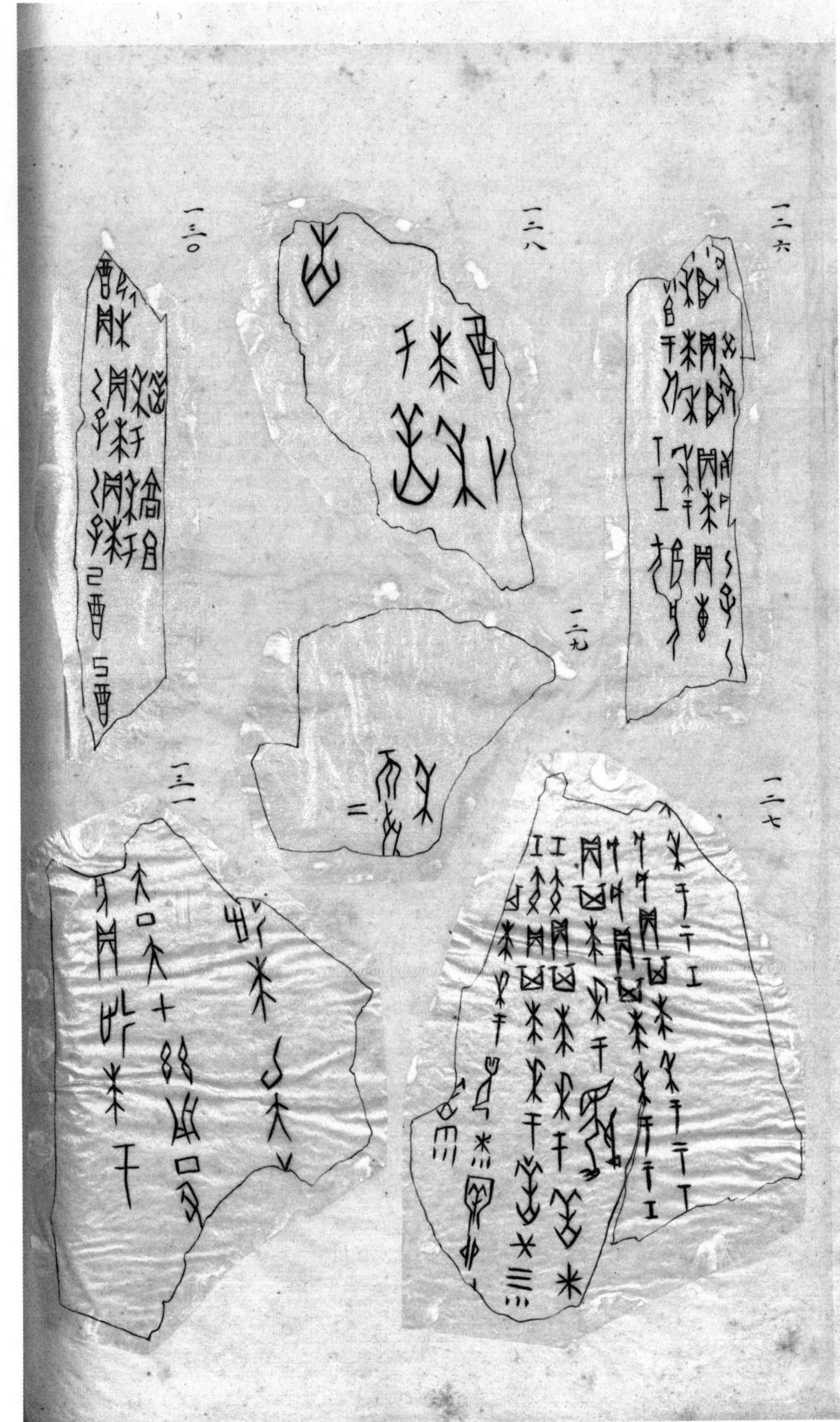
一二六 一二七 一二八 一二九 一三〇 一三一

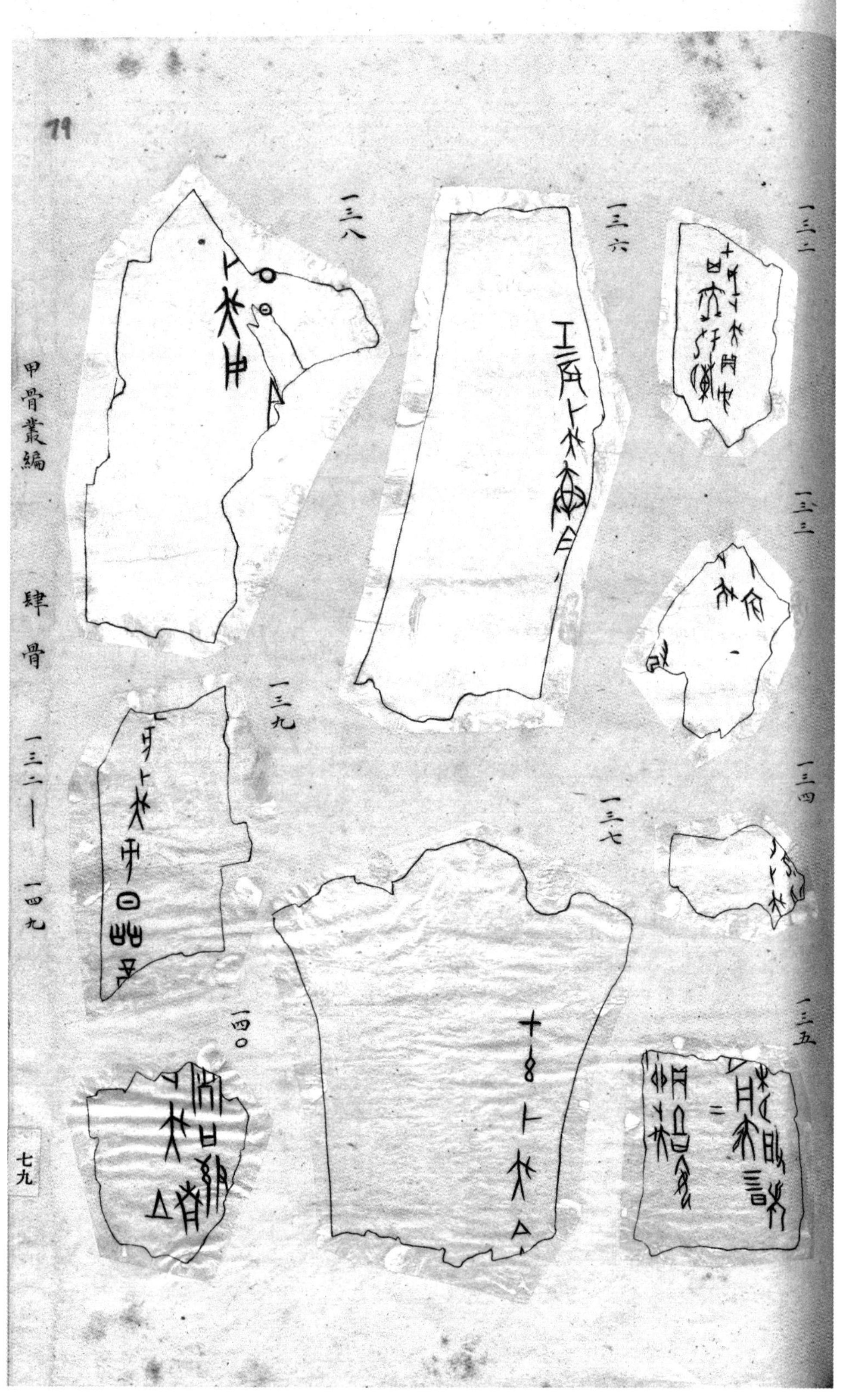
甲骨叢編　肆骨　一三二—一四九
七九
一三二
一三三
一三四
一三五
一三六
一三七
一三八
一三九
一四〇

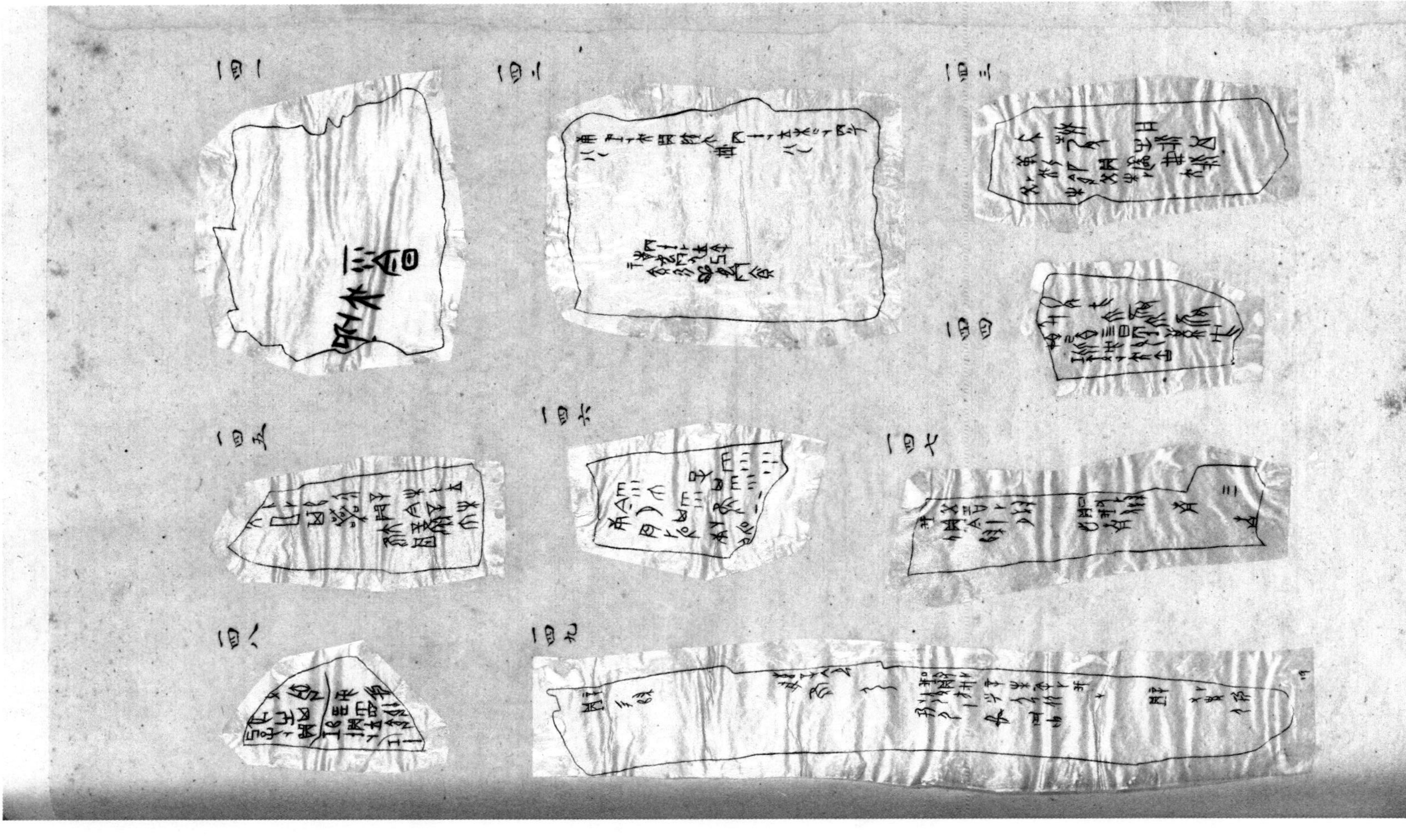
一四一
一四二
一四三
一四四
一四五
一四六
一四七
一四八
一四九

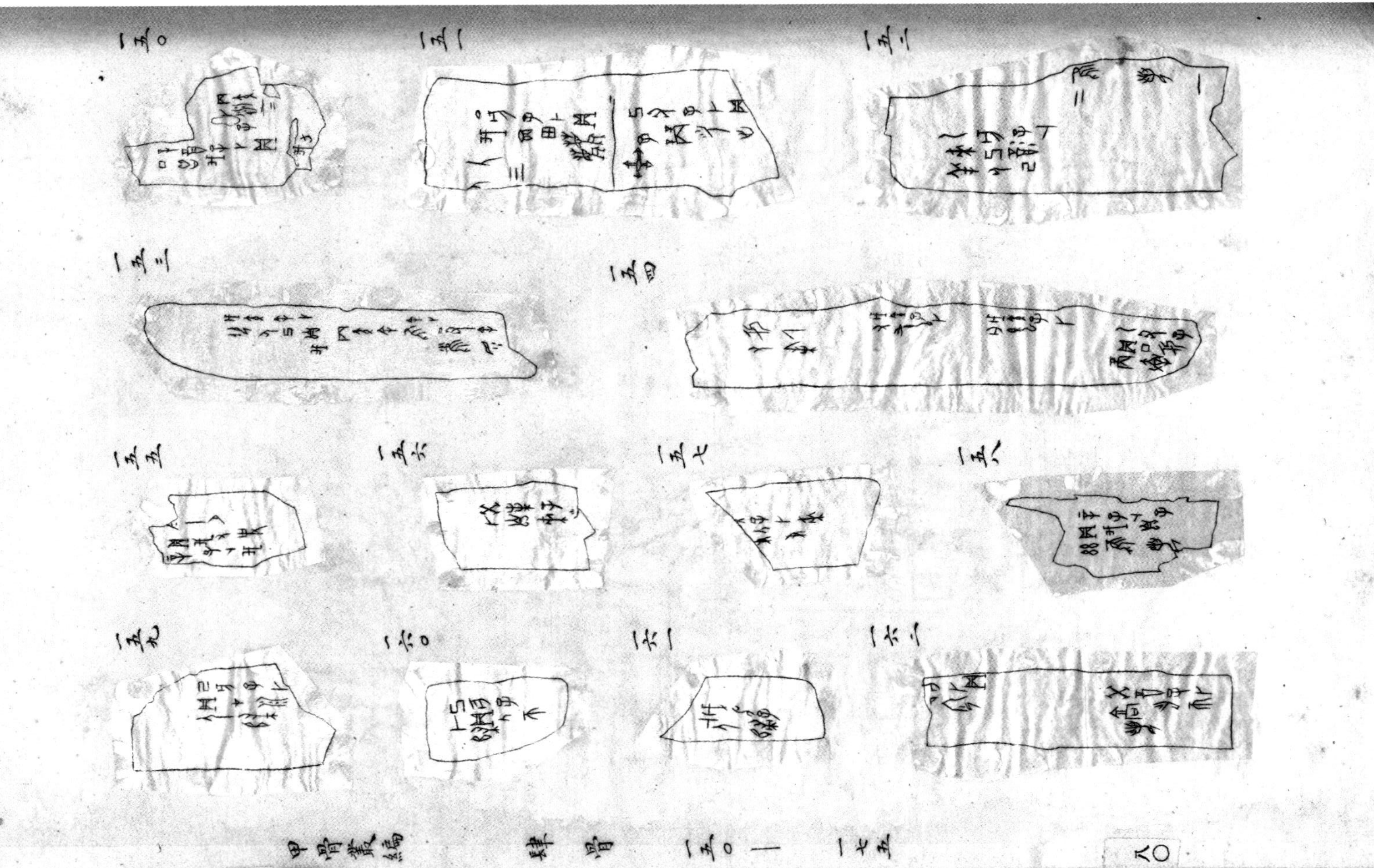

甲骨叢編 肆骨 一五〇——一七五 八〇

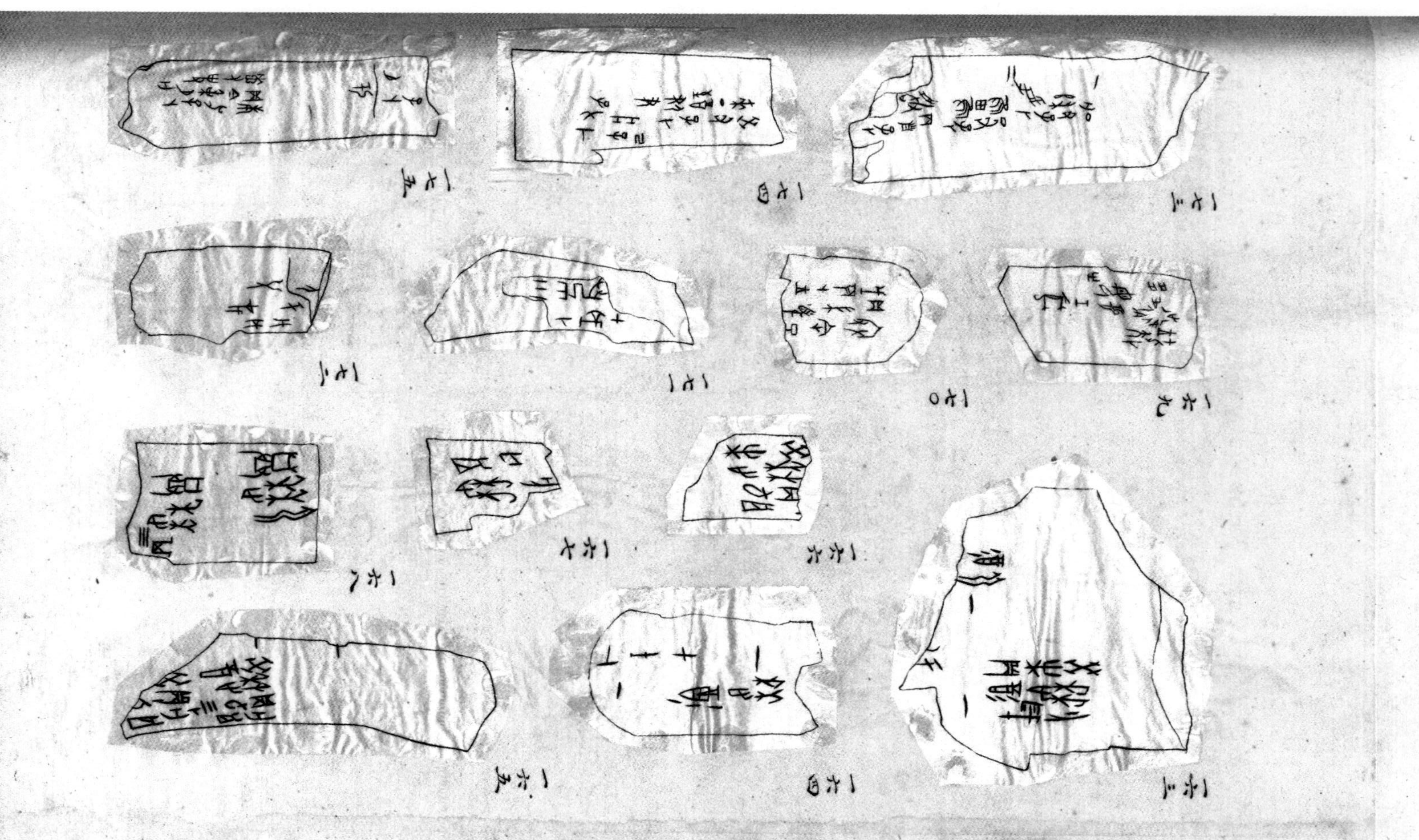
一六三
一六四
一六五
一六六
一六七
一六八
一六九
一七〇
一七一
一七二
一七三
一七四
一七五

一七六

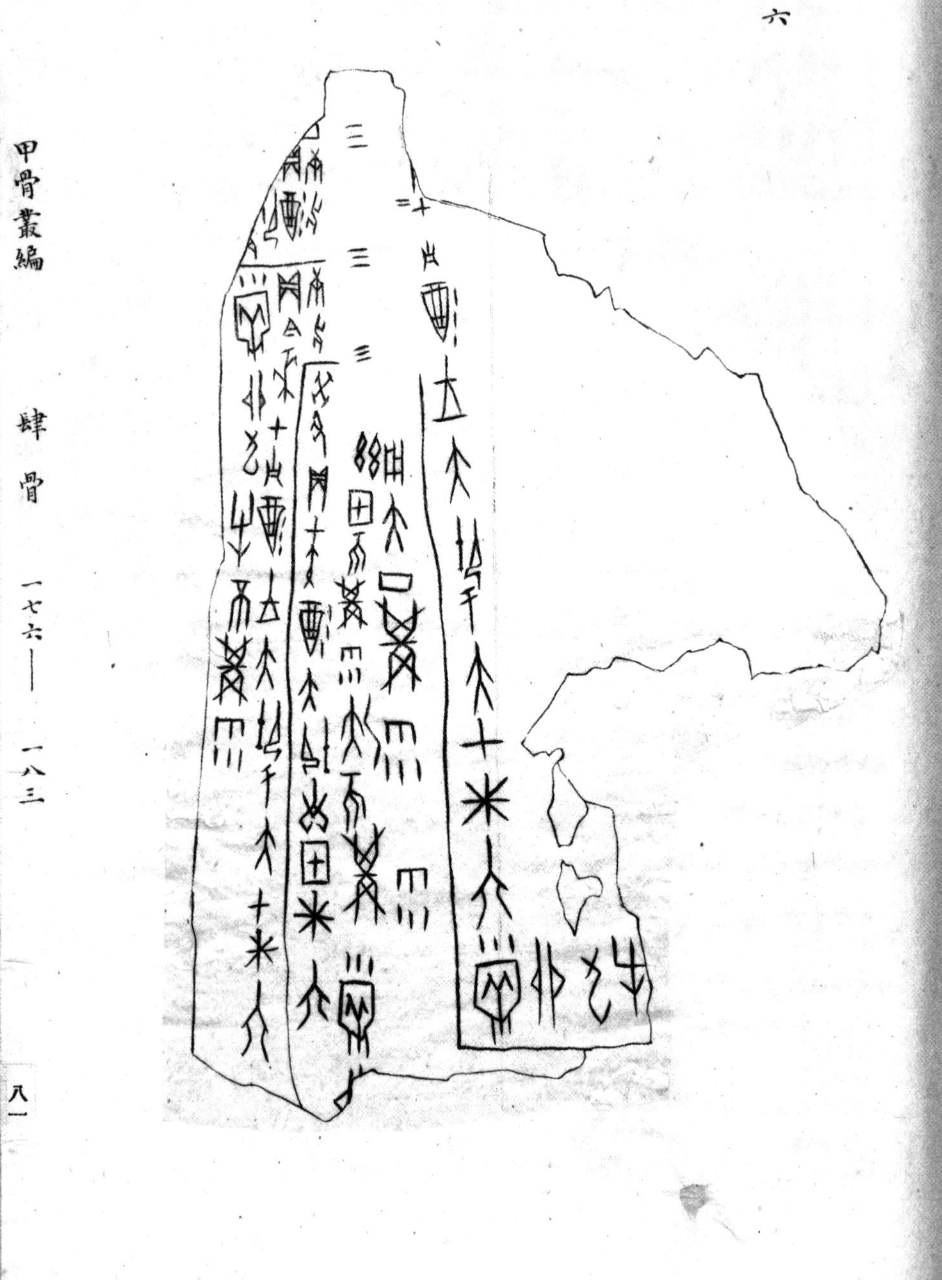

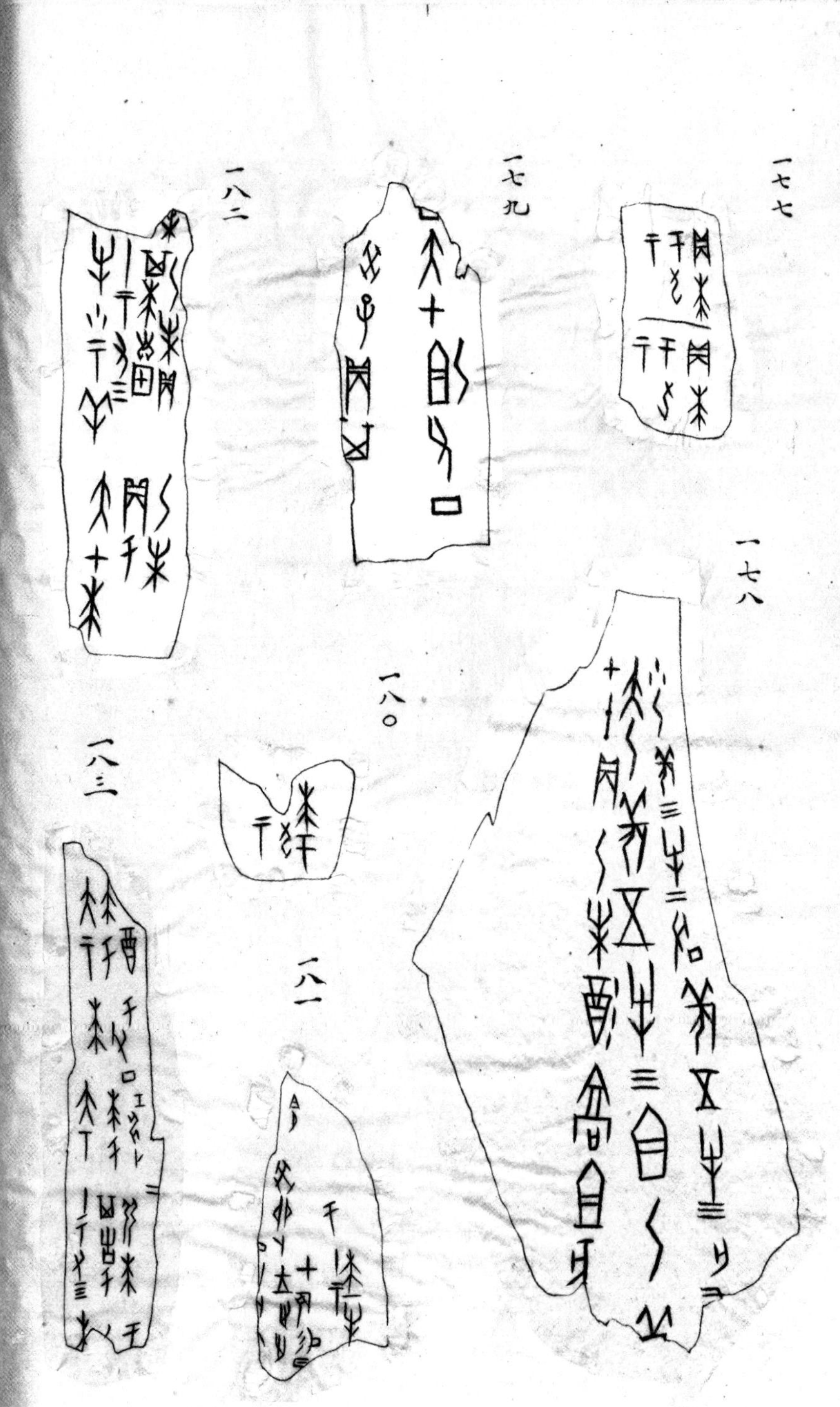
一七七
一七八
一七九
一八〇
一八一
一八二
一八三

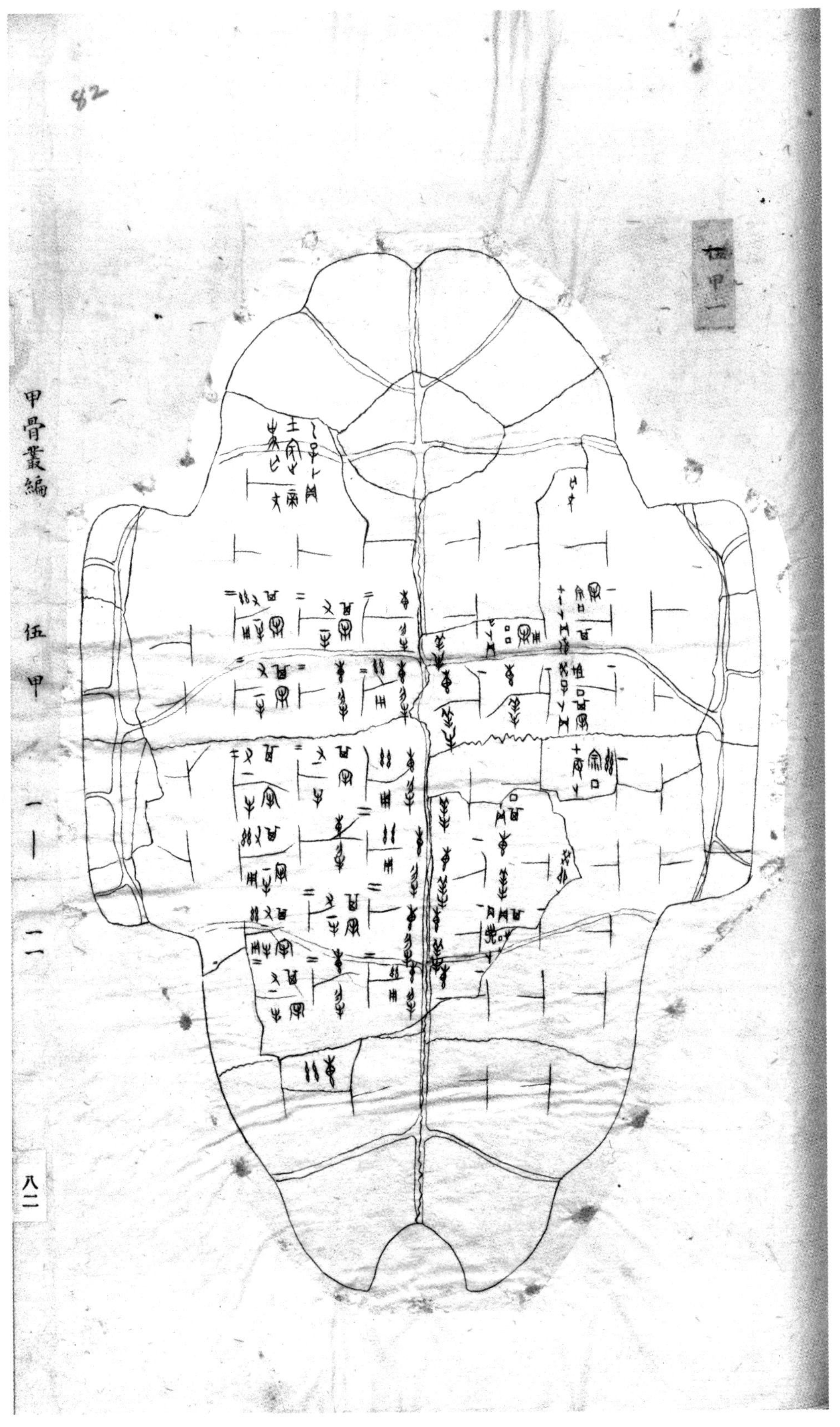
甲骨叢編　伍　甲　一一一
八二
伍甲一

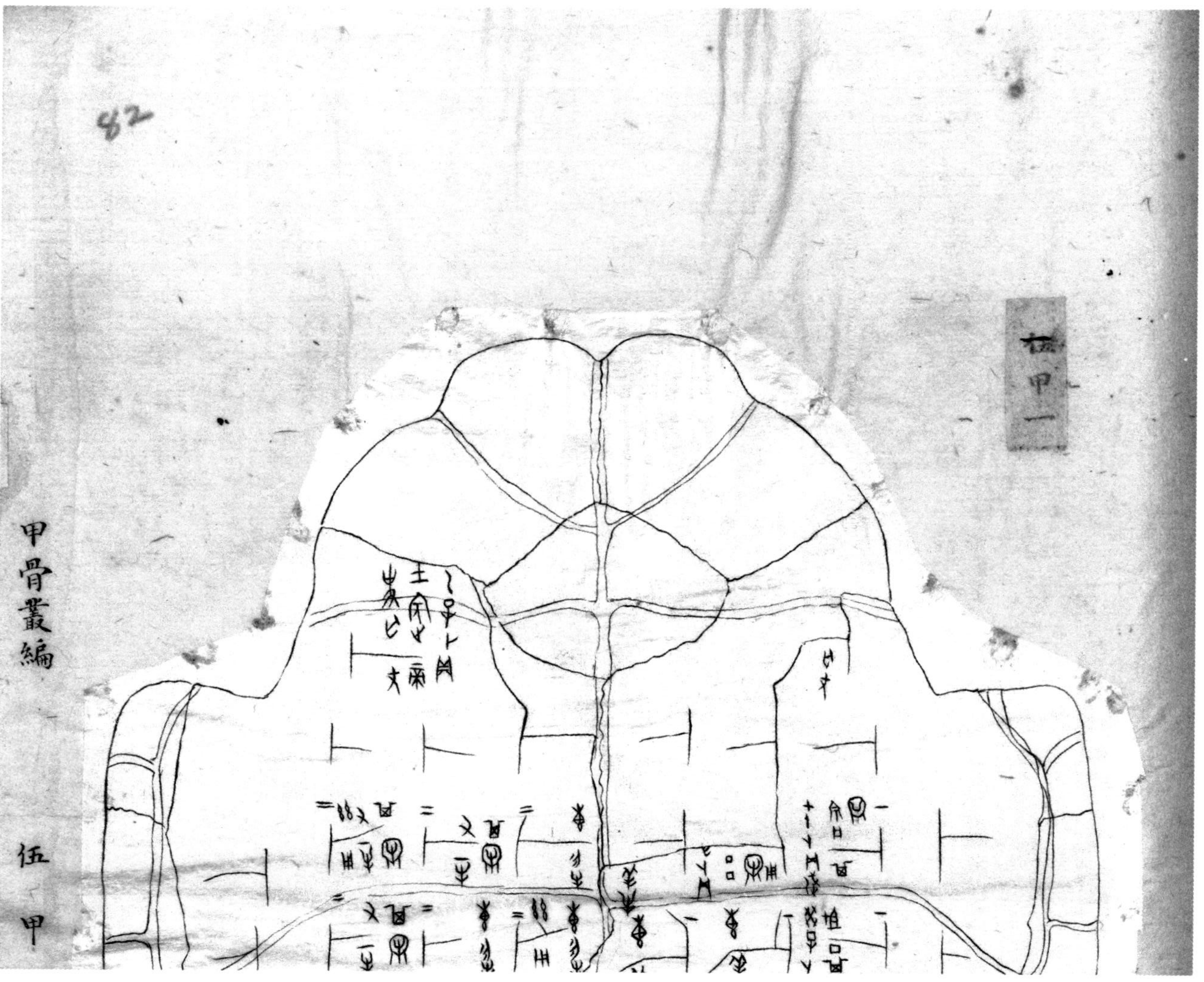

甲骨叢編
伍 甲
伍 甲 一
82

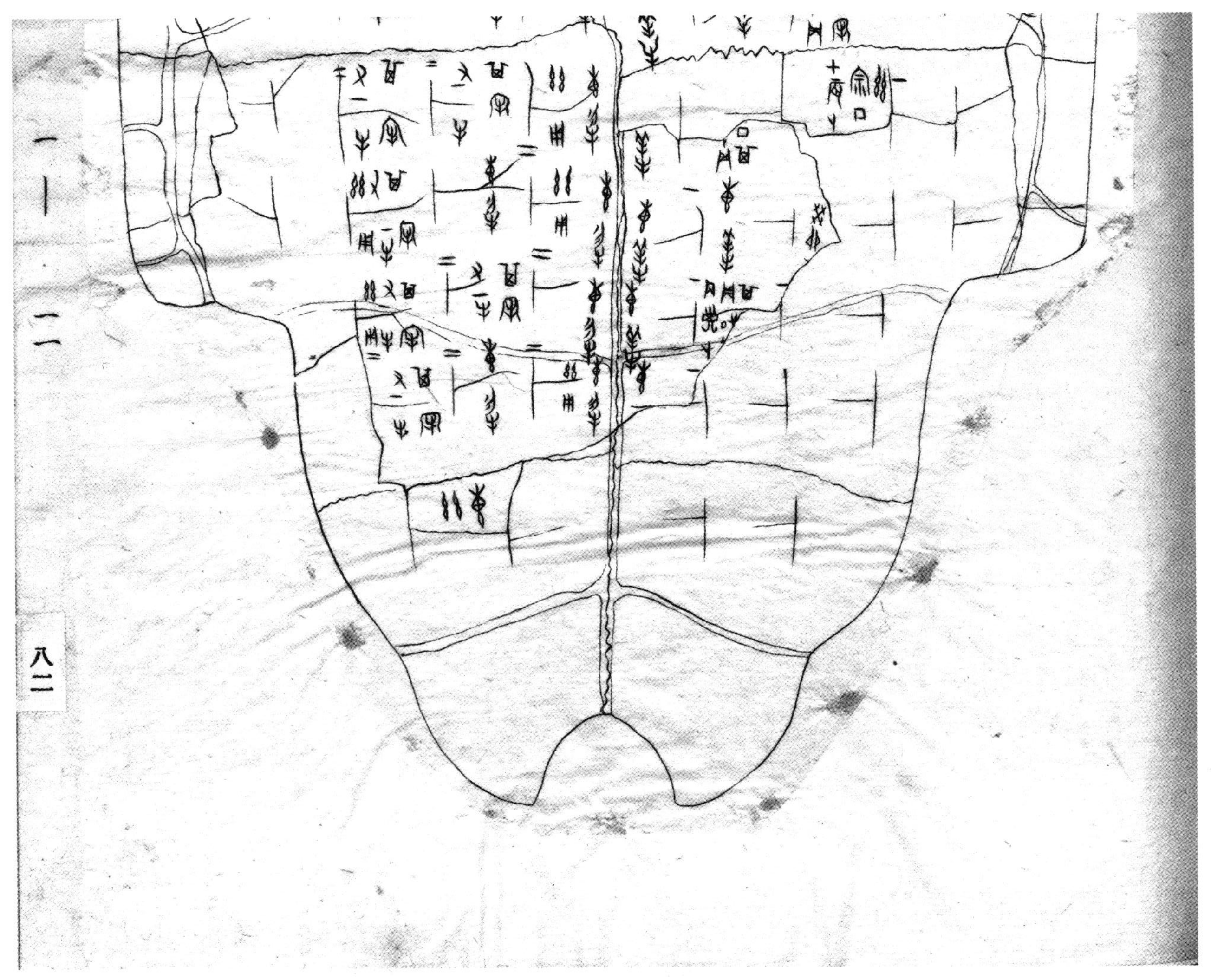
八二

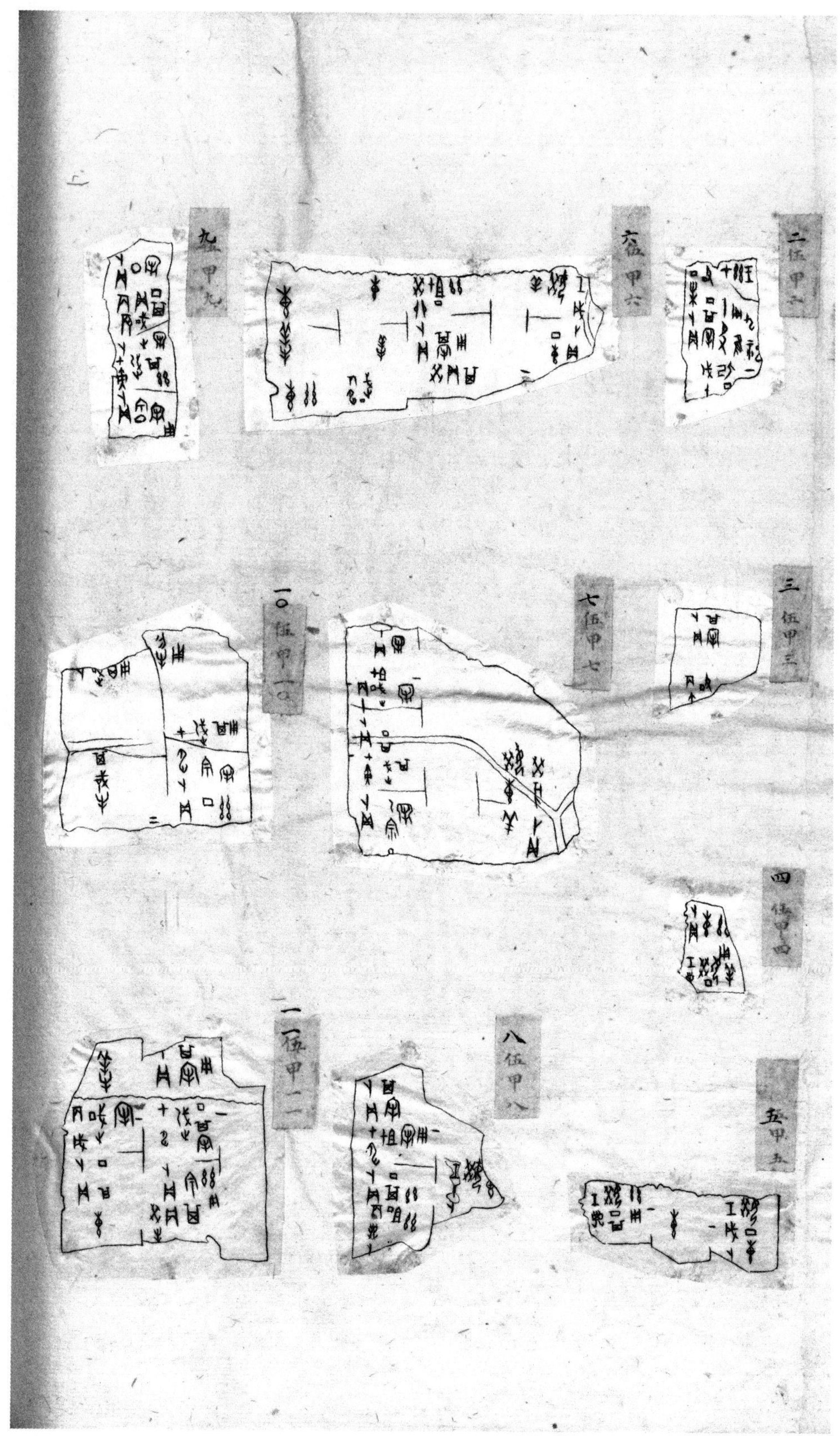

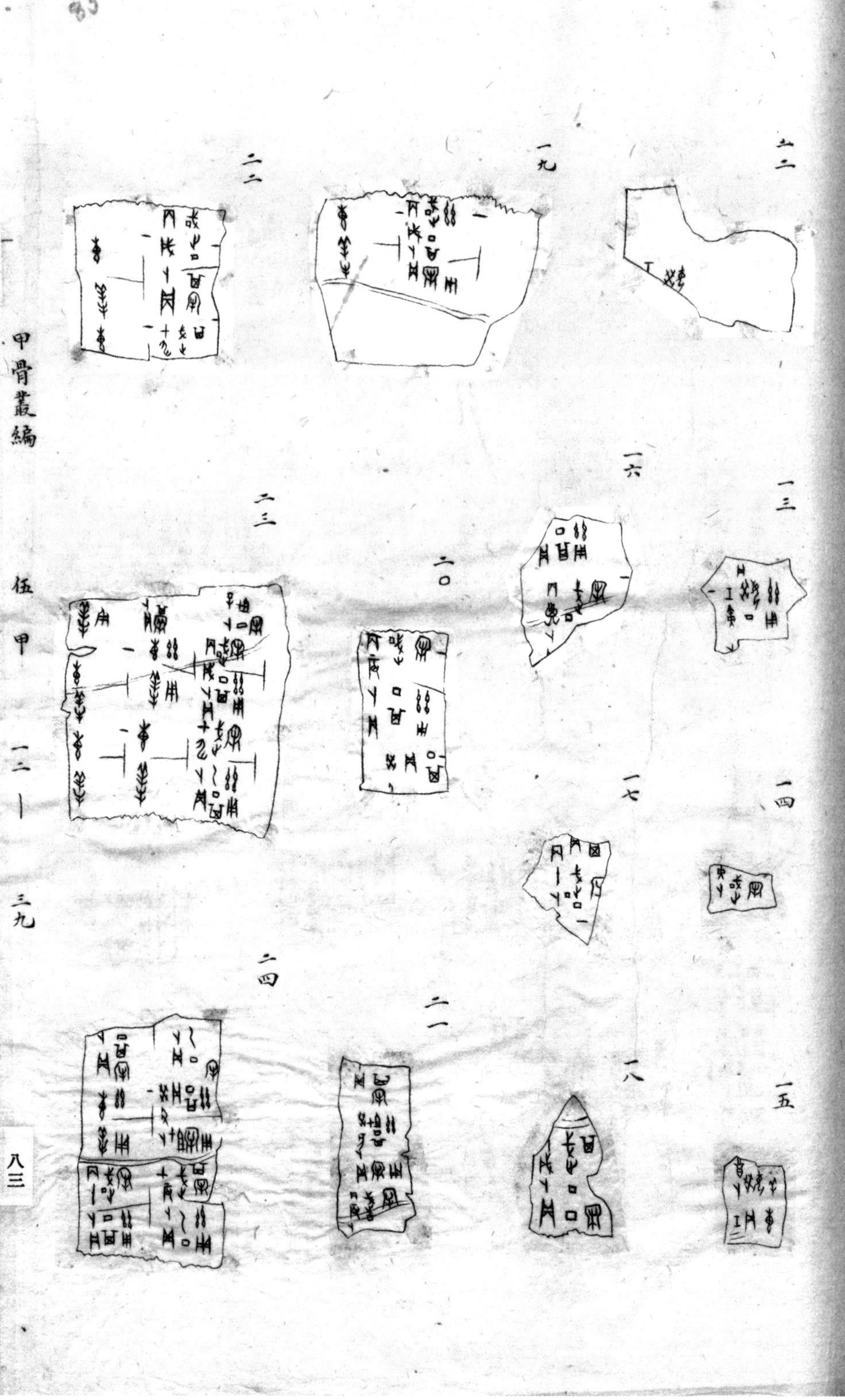
甲骨叢編 伍 甲 一二一 三九
一二
一三
一四
一五
一六
一七
一八
一九
二〇
二一
二二
二三
二四
八三

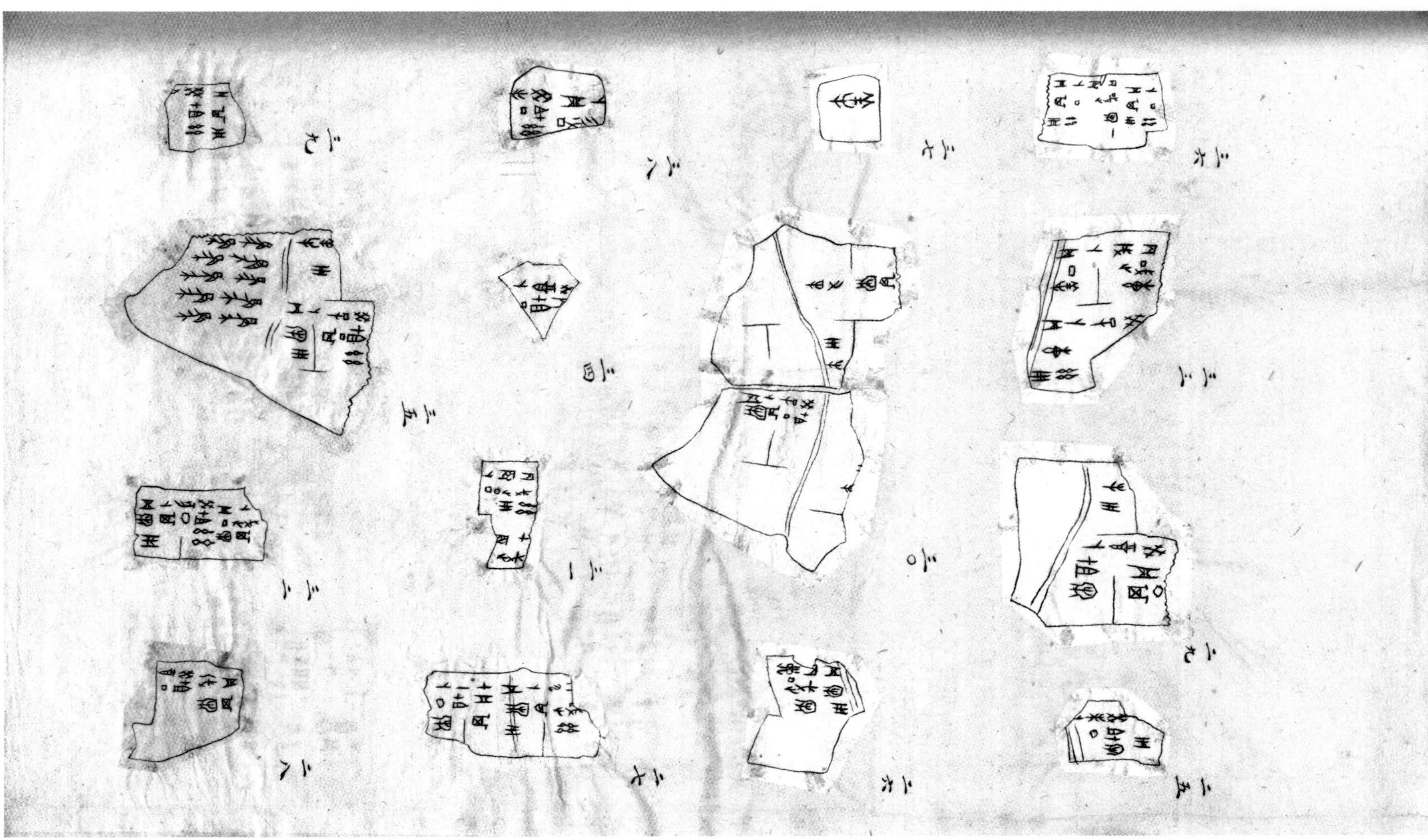

二五
二六
二七
二八
二九
三〇
三一
三二
三三
三四
三五
三六
三七
三八
三九

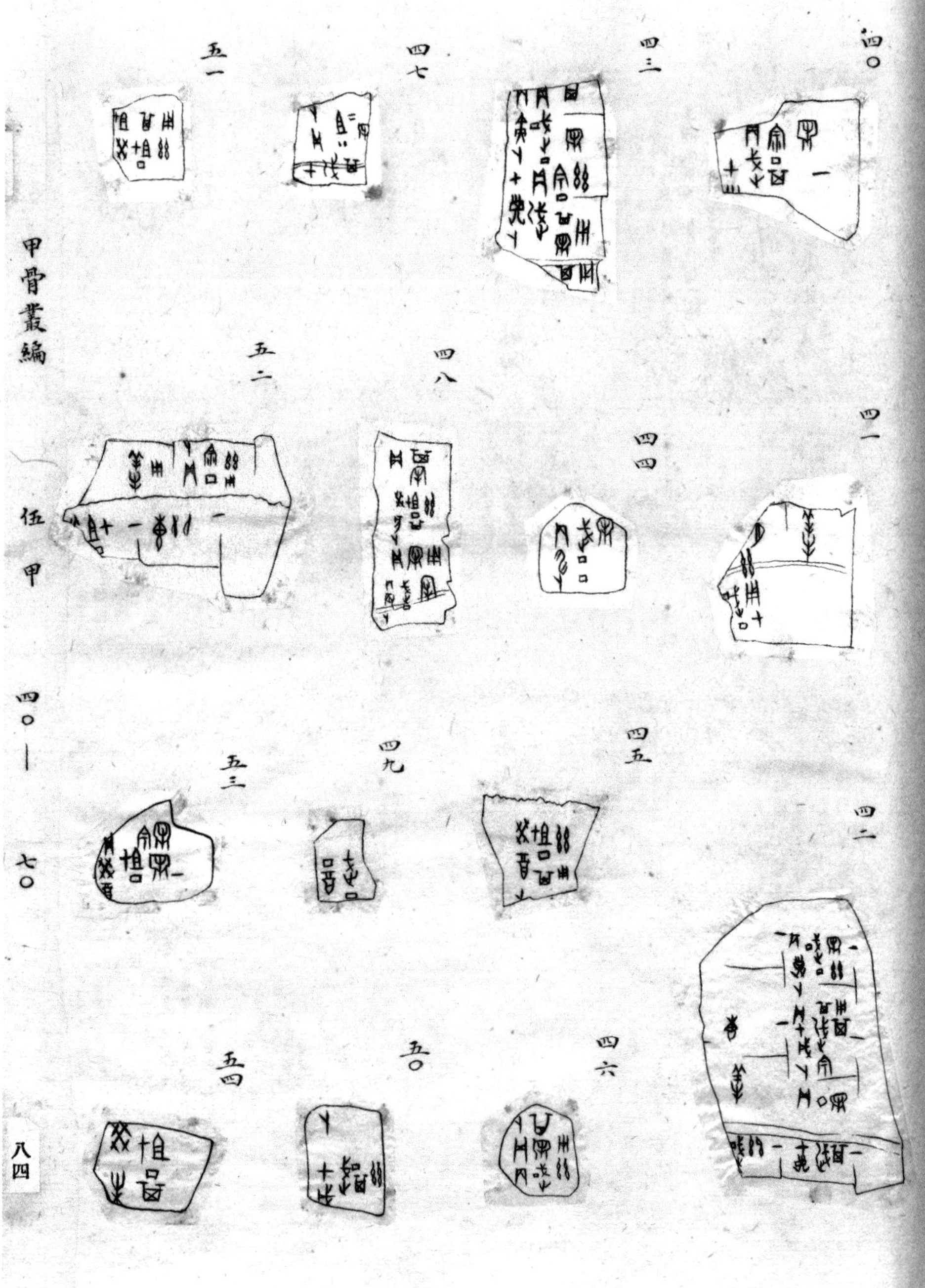

甲骨叢編 伍甲 四〇一—七〇

八四

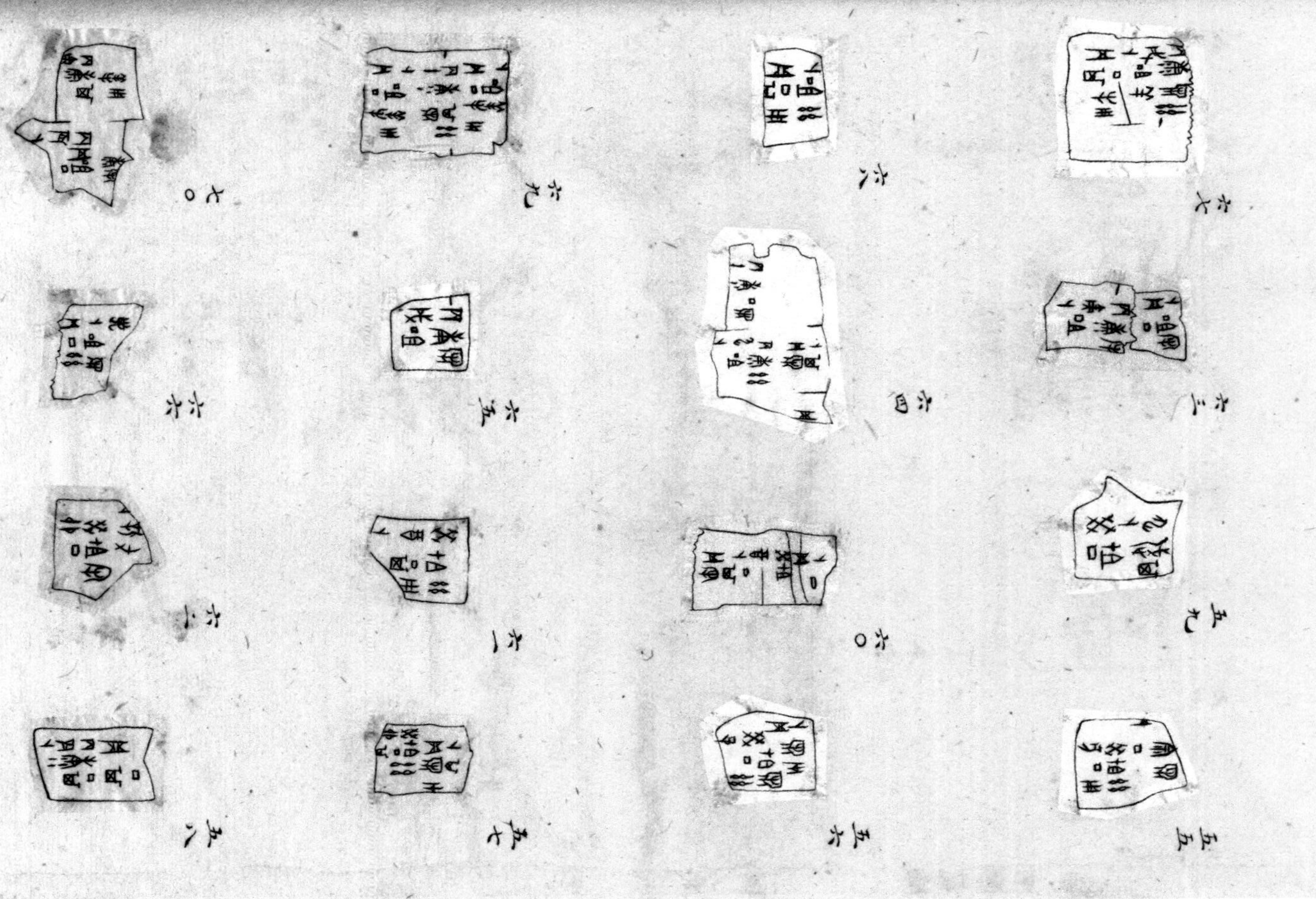
五五
五六
五七
五八
五九
六〇
六一
六二
六三
六四
六五
六六
六七
六八
六九
七〇

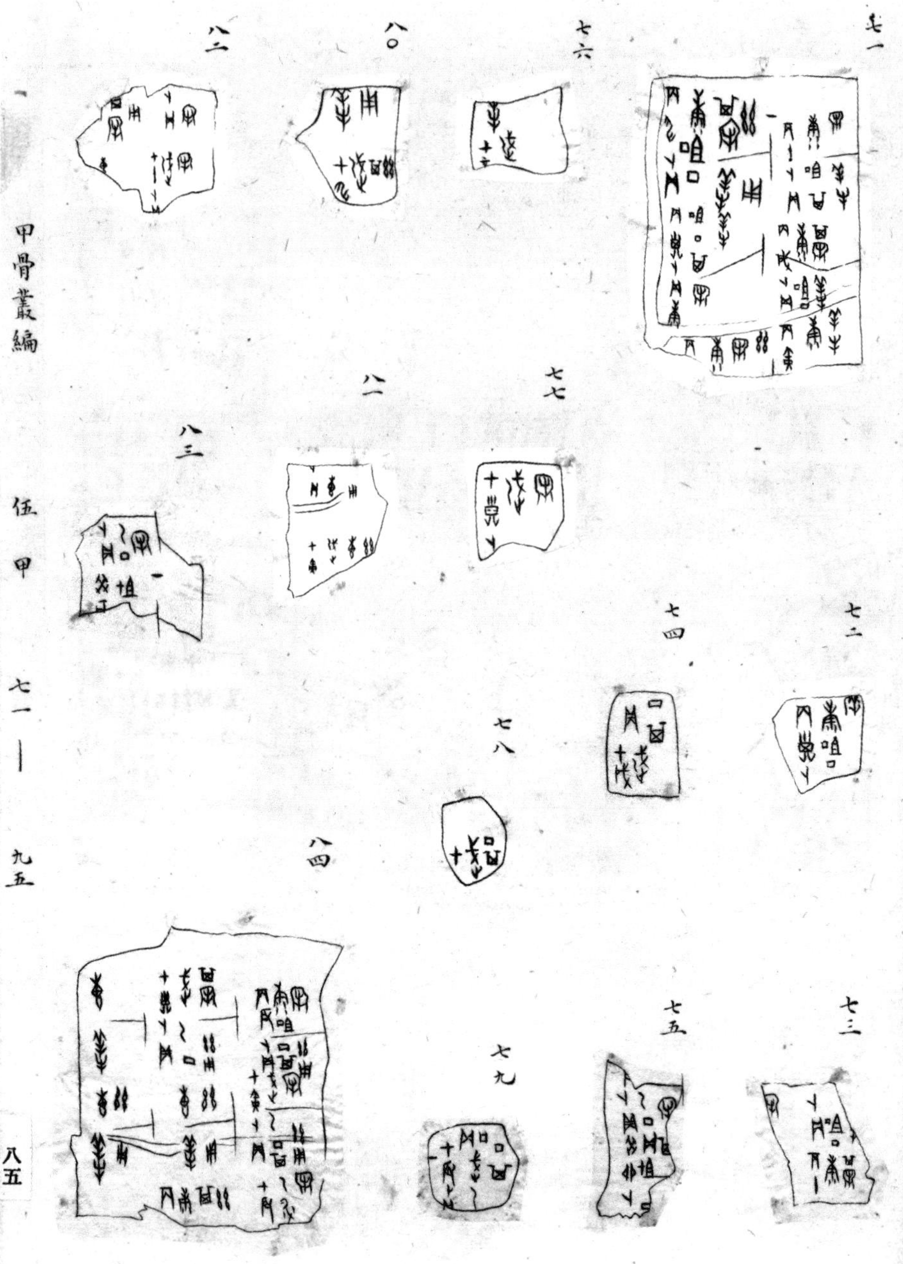
七一
七二
七三
七四
七五
七六
七七
七八
七九
八〇
八一
八二
八三
八四

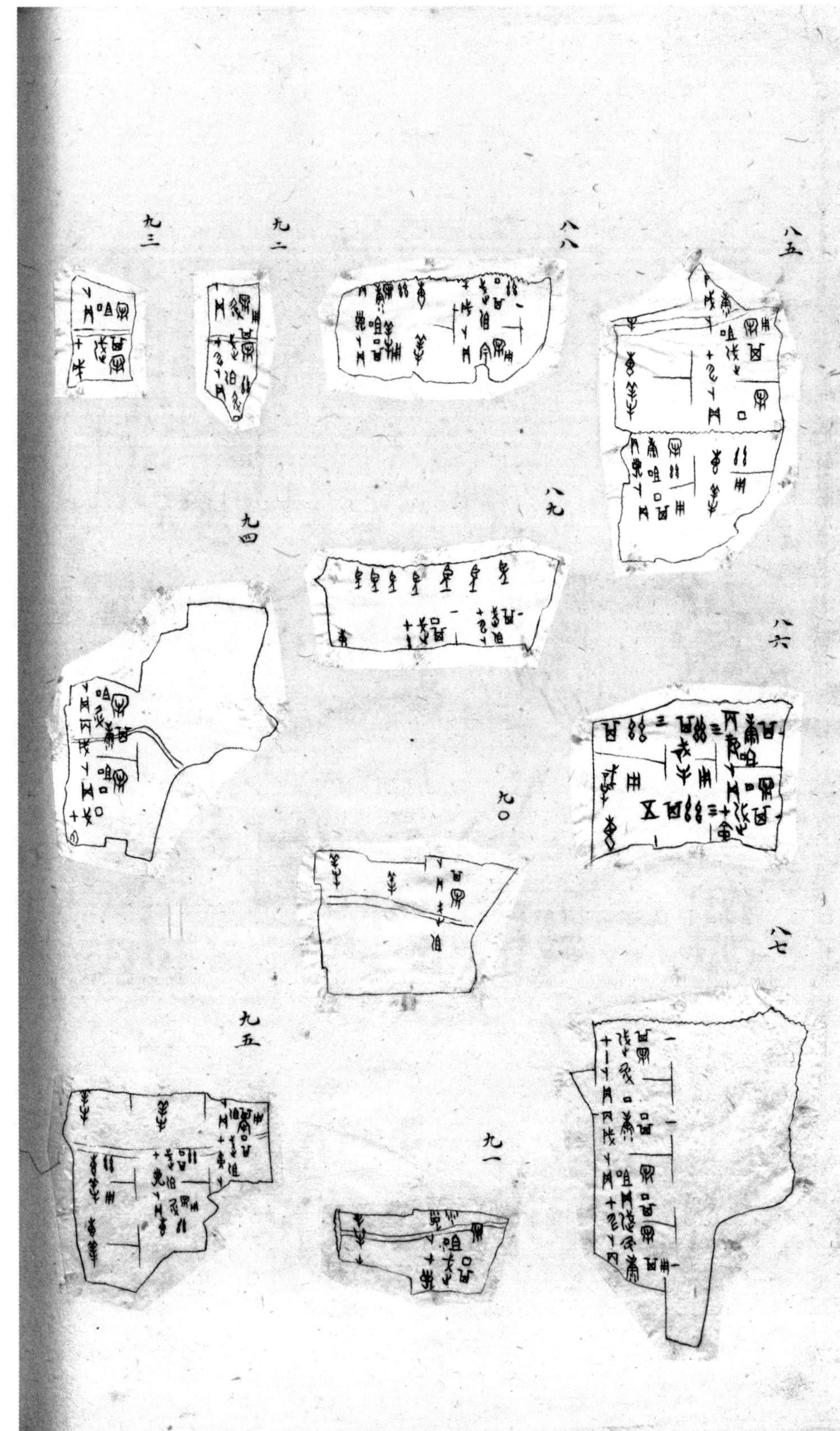

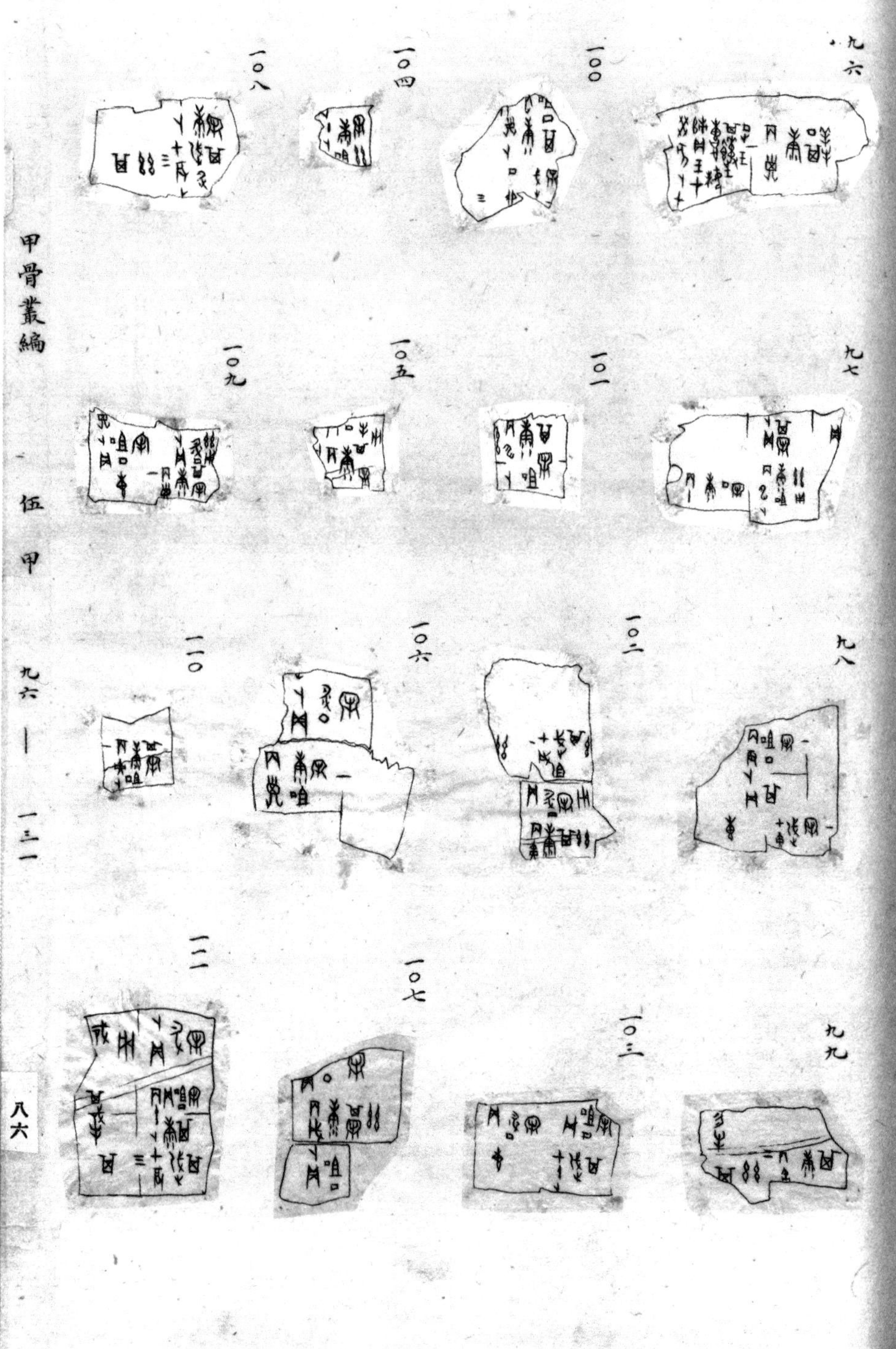

八六

一一二

一一三

一一四

一一五

一一六

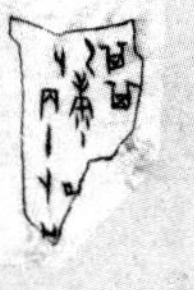

一一七

一一八

一一九

一二〇

一二一

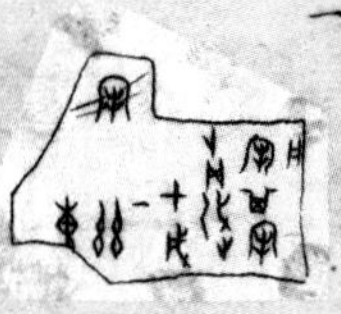

一二二

一二三

一二四

一二五

一二六

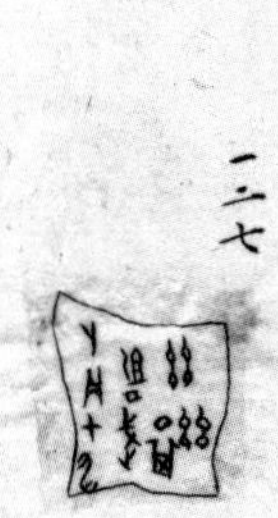

一二七

一二八

一二九

一三〇

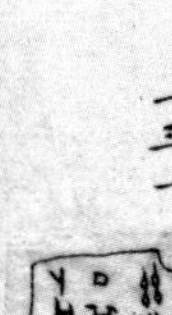

一三一

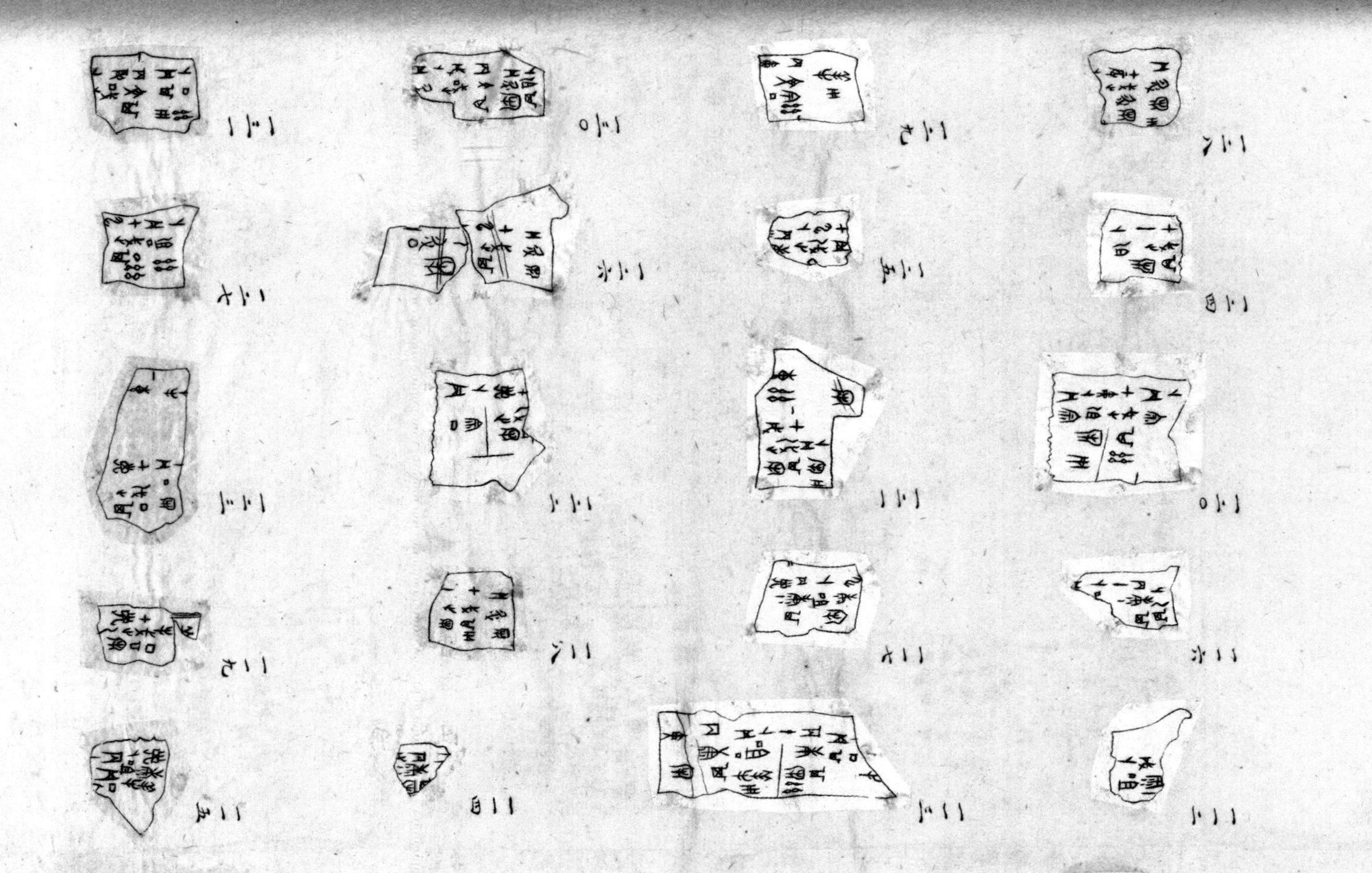

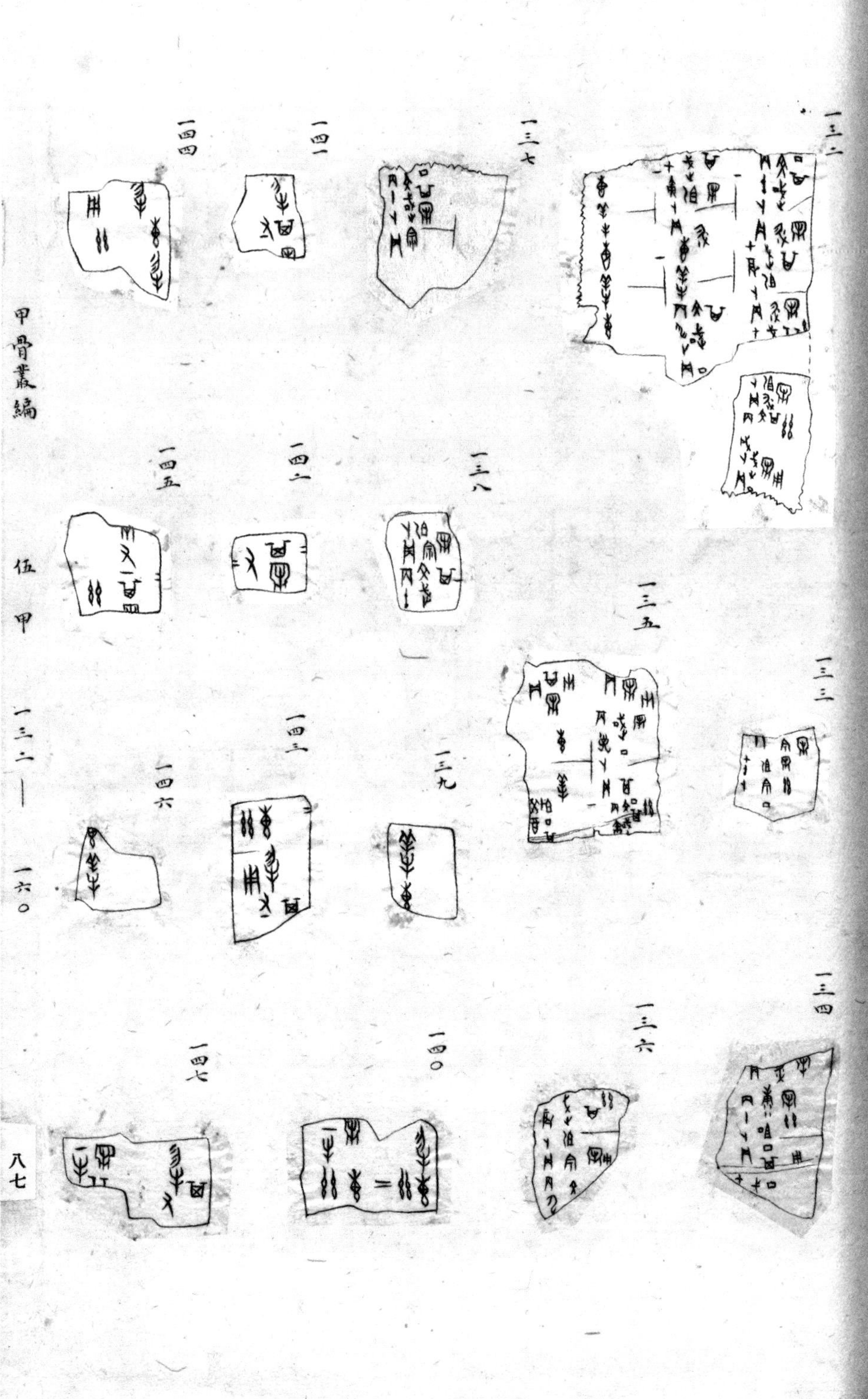
甲骨叢編　伍甲　一三二—一六〇
八七
一三二
一三三
一三四
一三五
一三六
一三七
一三八
一三九
一四〇
一四一
一四二
一四三
一四四
一四五
一四六
一四七

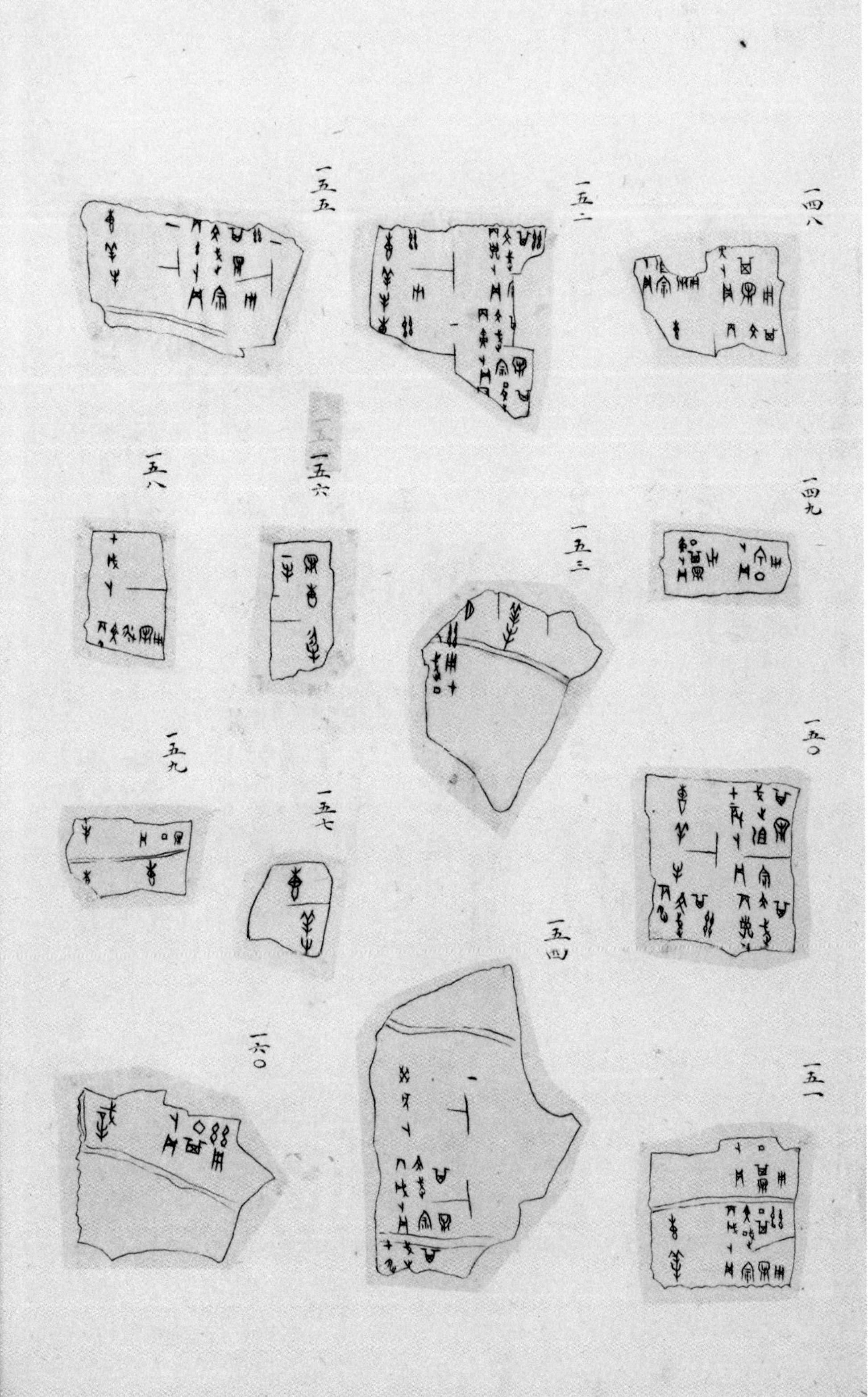
一四八
一四九
一五〇
一五一
一五二
一五三
一五四
一五五
一五六
一五七
一五八
一五九
一六〇

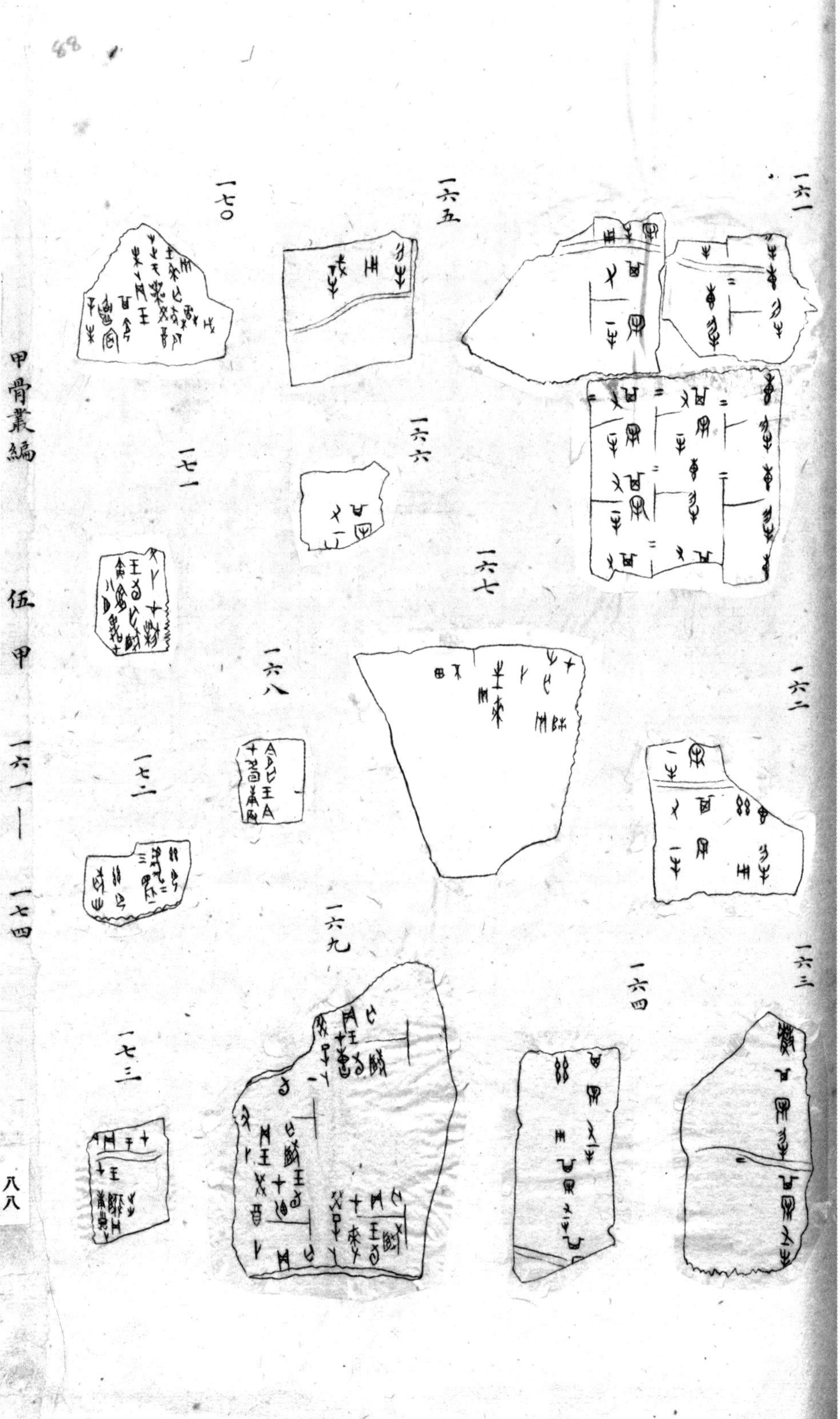
一六一
一六二
一六三
一六四
一六五
一六六
一六七
一六八
一六九
一七〇
一七一
一七二
一七三
一七四

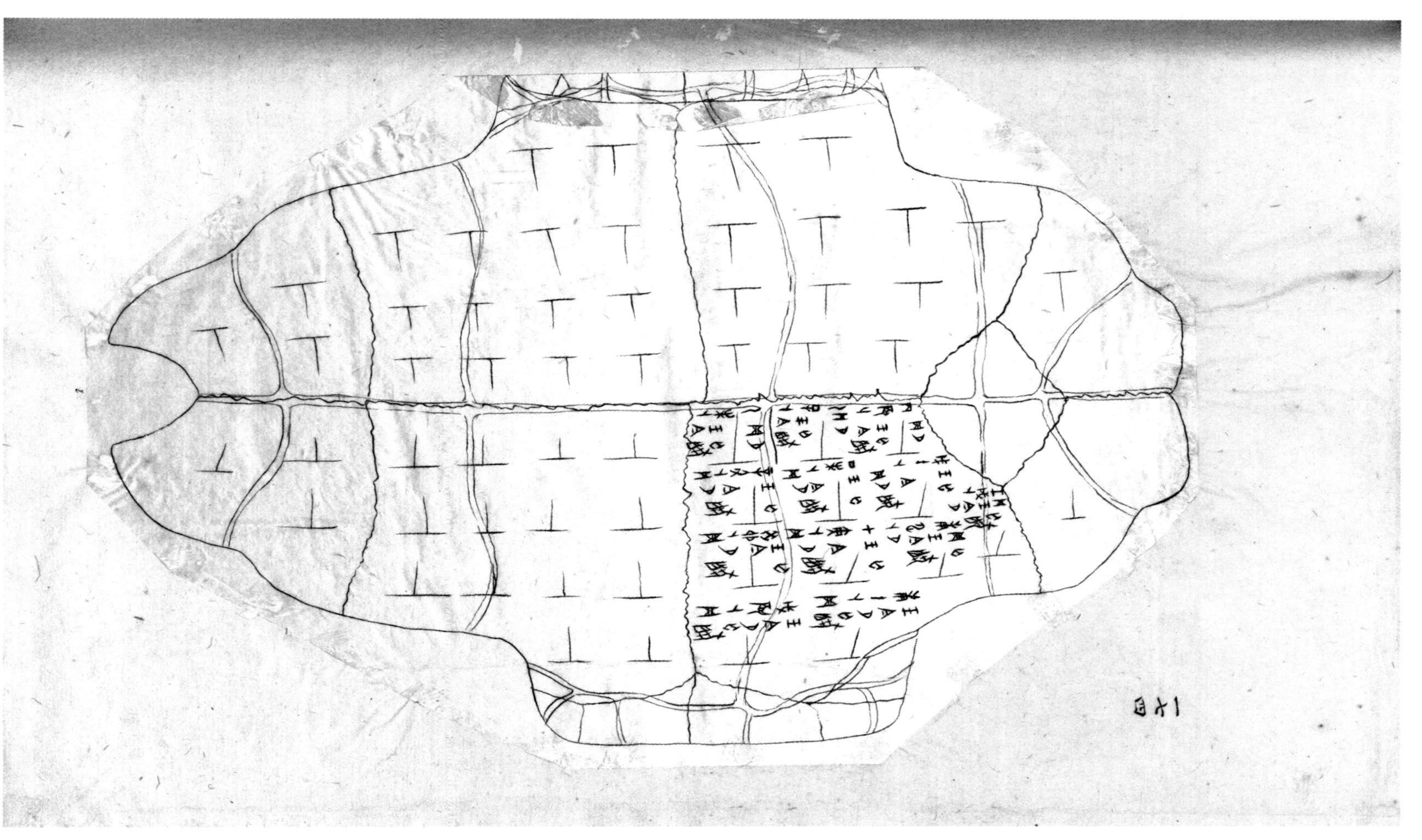

一七四

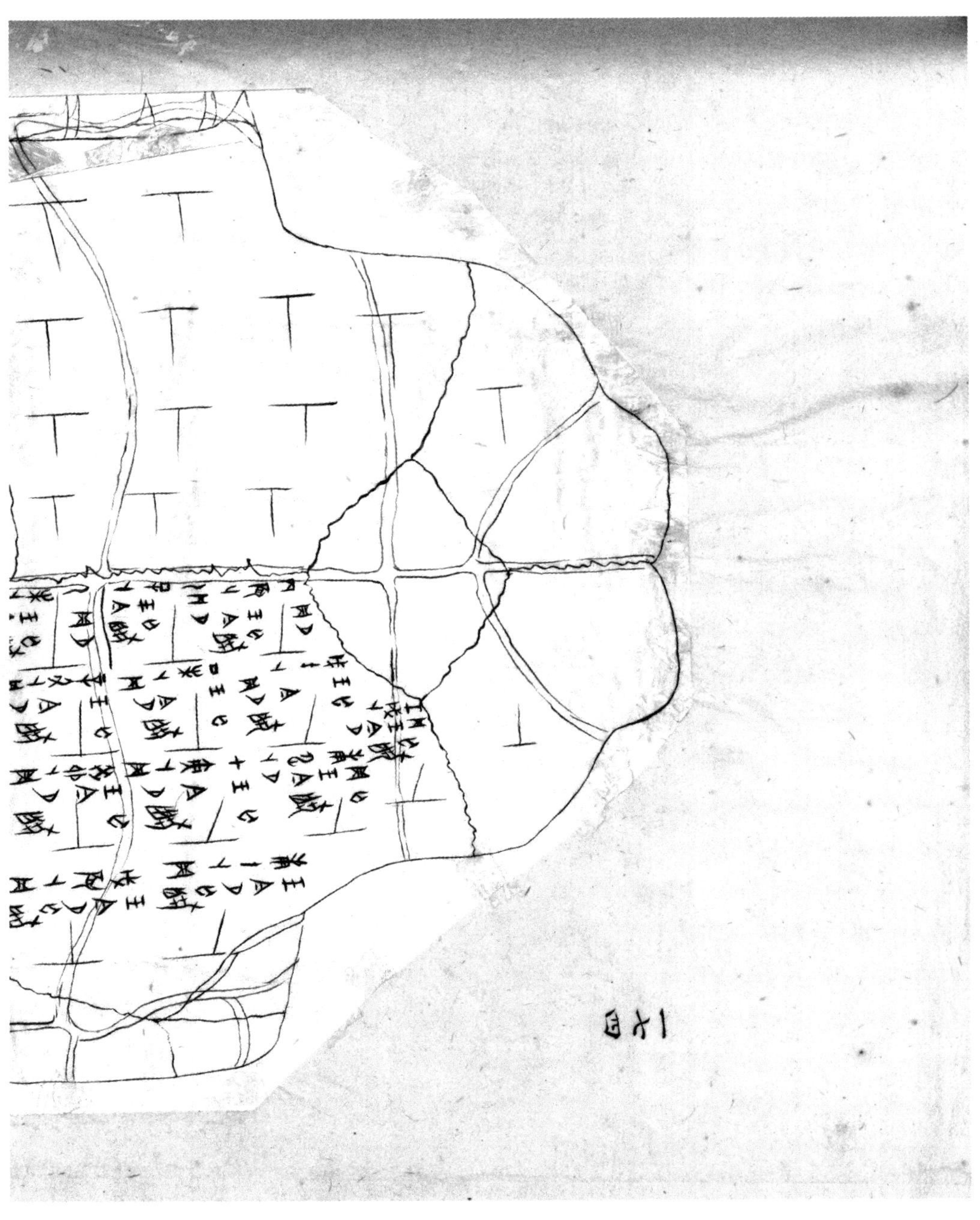

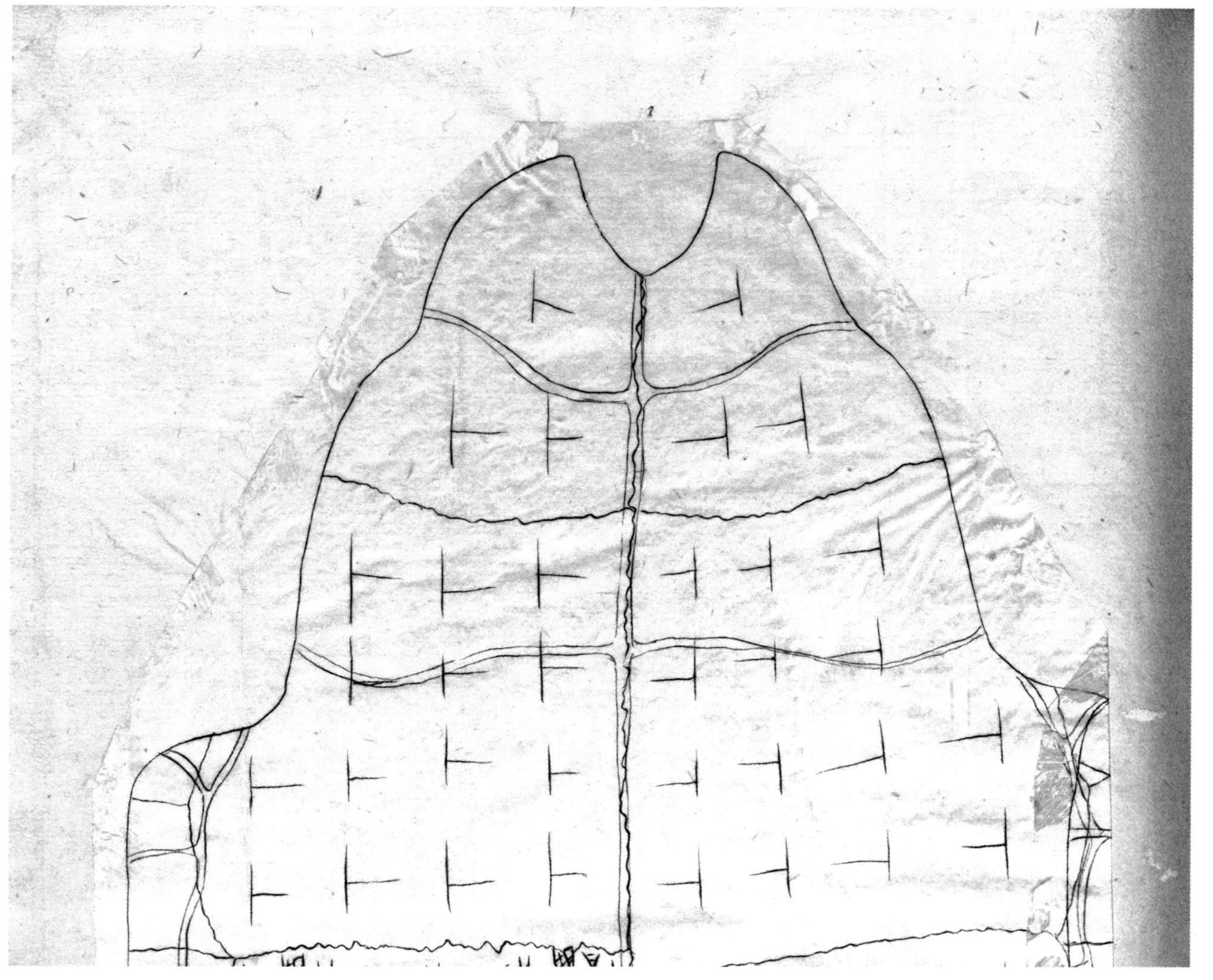

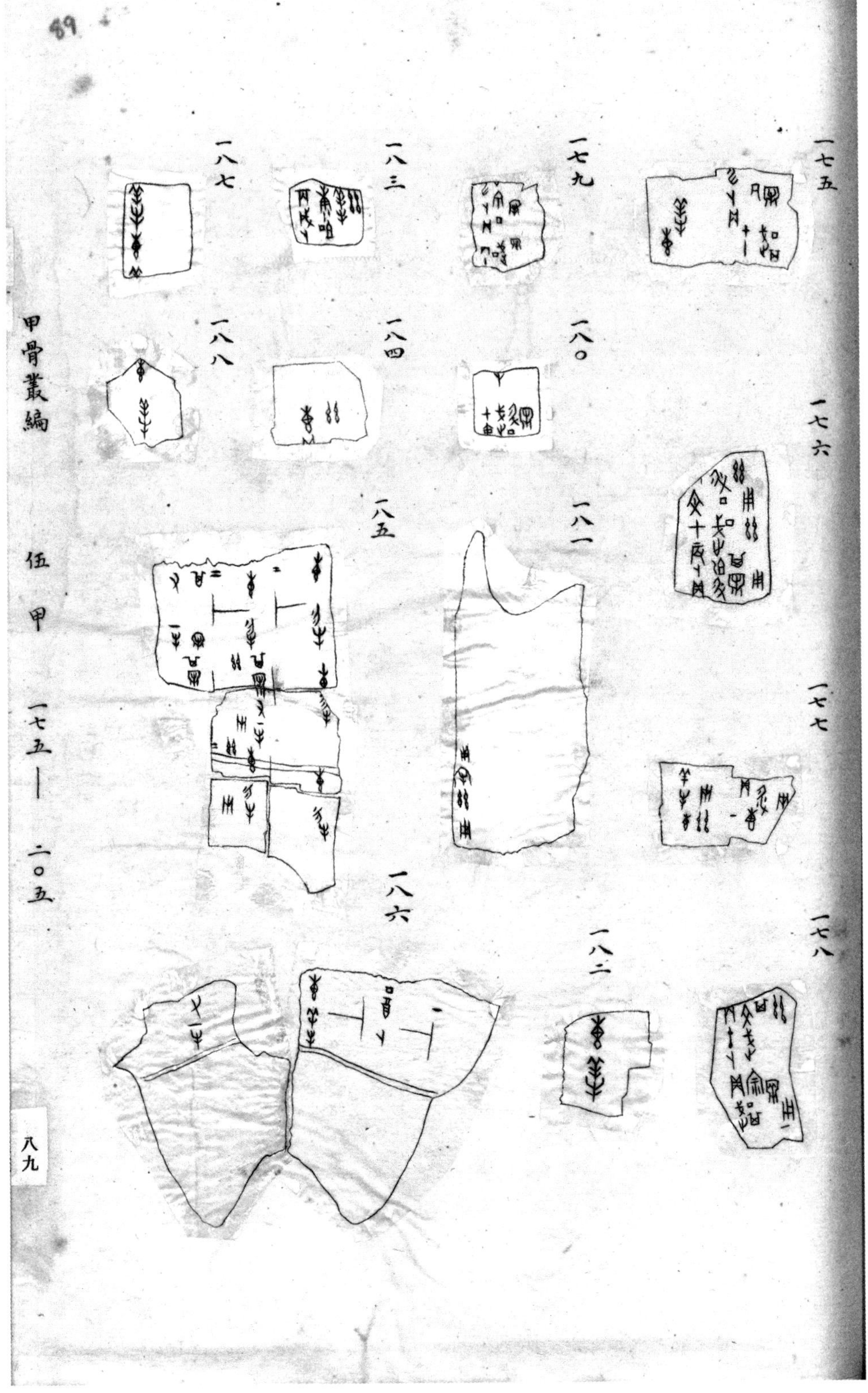

八九

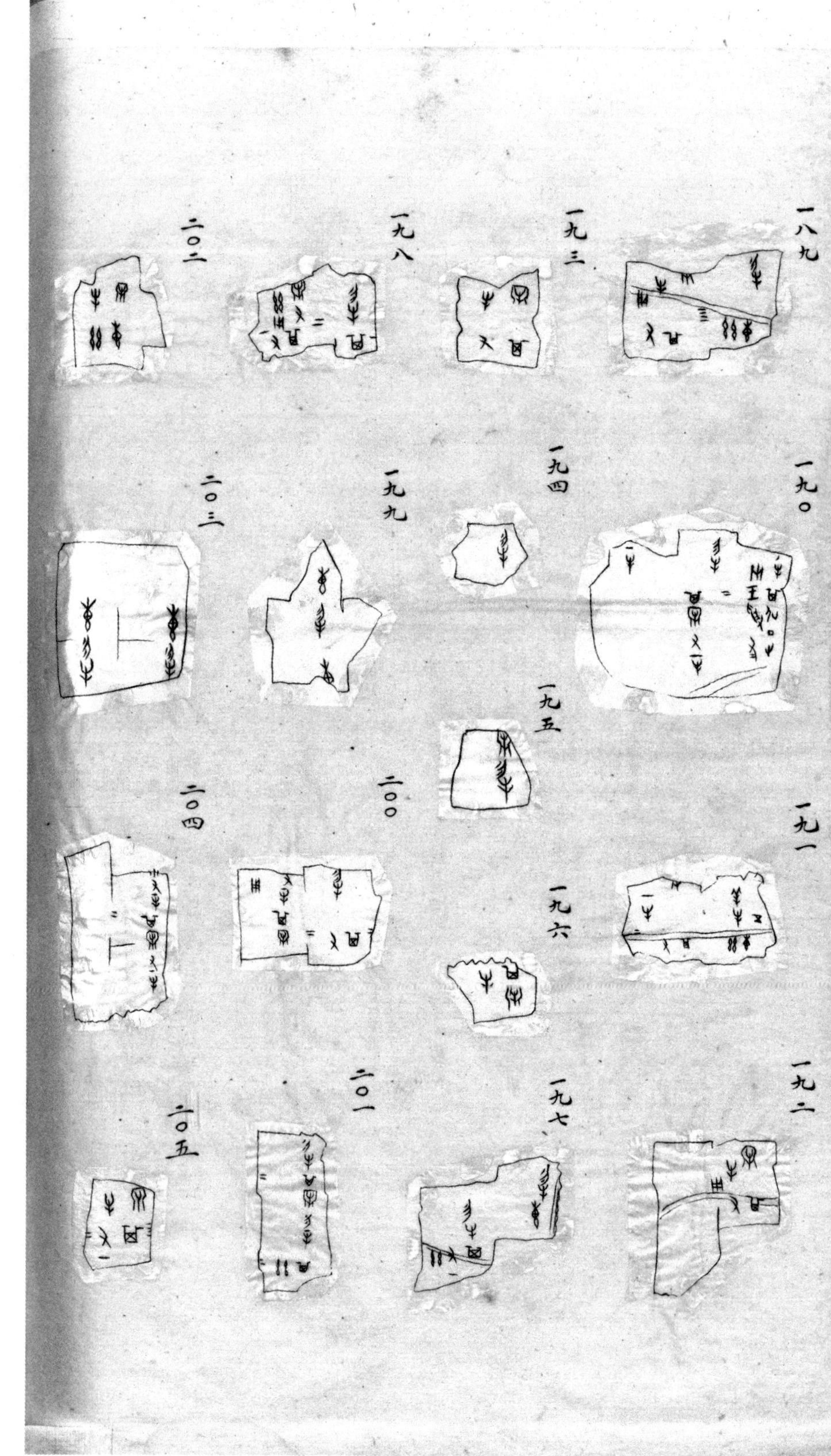
一八九
一九〇
一九一
一九二
一九三
一九四
一九五
一九六
一九七
一九八
一九九
二〇〇
二〇一
二〇二
二〇三
二〇四
二〇五

二〇六 標準甲（龜背甲 右半） 曲線：—— 甲縫 雙線：‖ 角質盾版紋

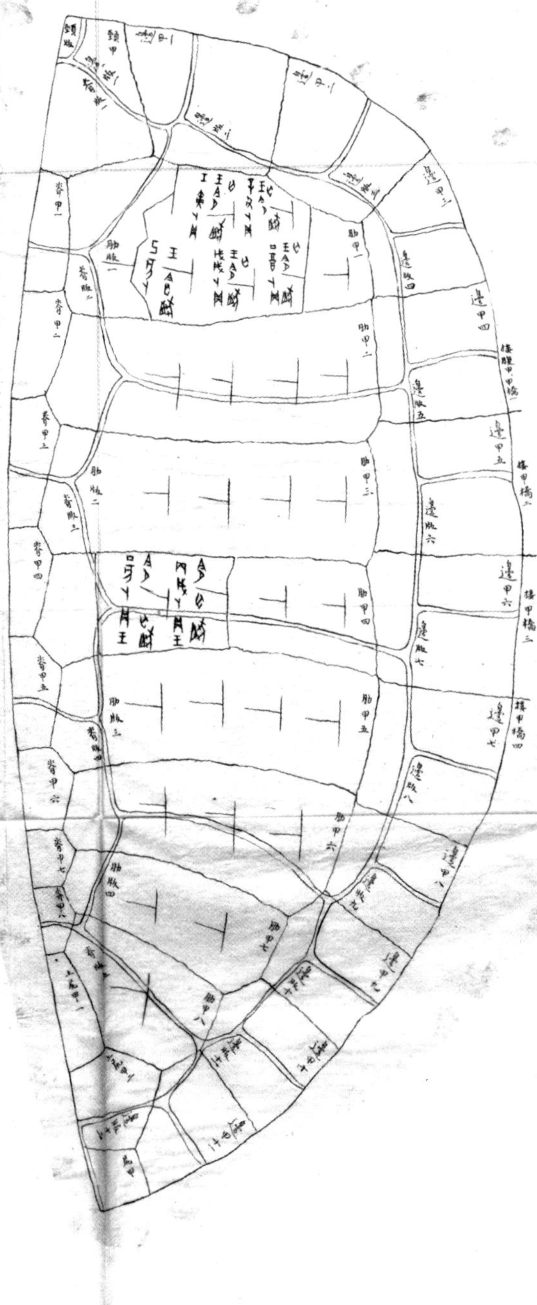

甲骨叢編 伍甲 二〇六

九〇

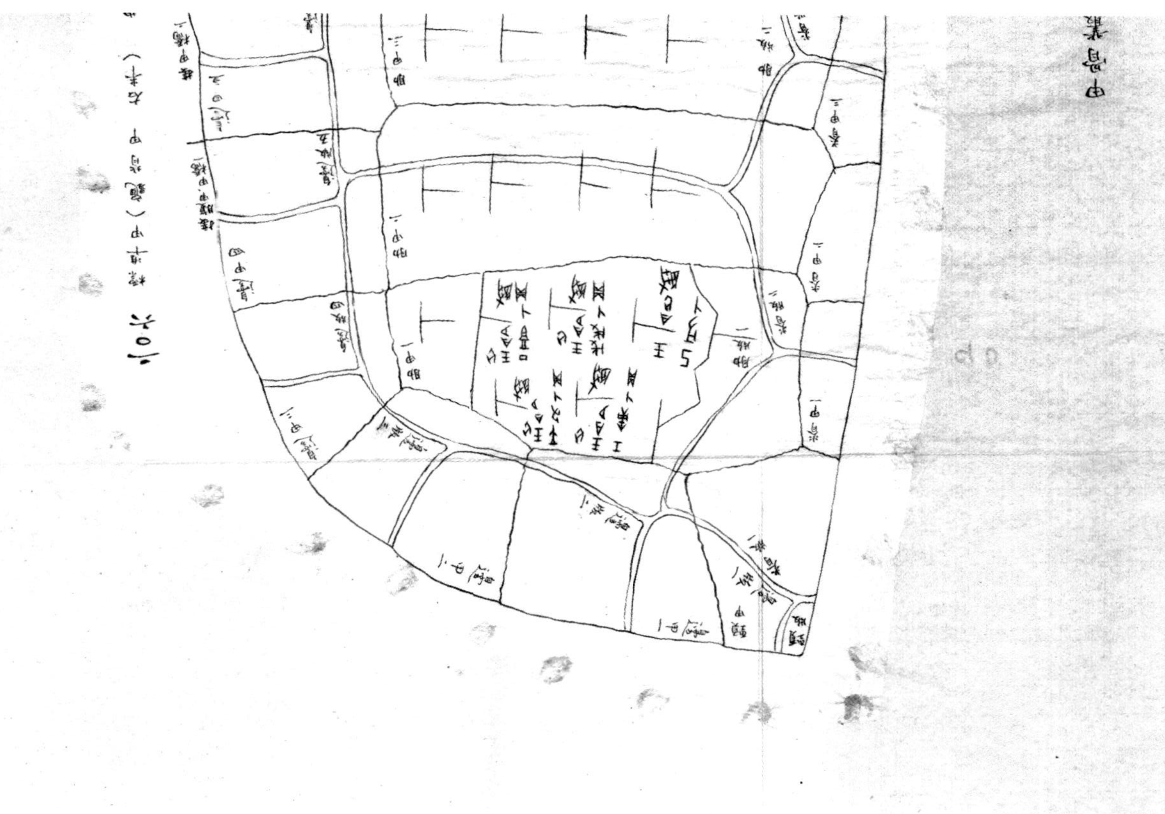

編
伍　甲　二〇六
九〇
單線：——甲縫
雙線：‖角質盾版紋
編一〇四
邊甲六
接甲橋三
邊版七
接甲橋四
邊甲七
邊版八
邊甲八
邊版九
邊甲九
邊版十
邊甲十
邊版十一
邊甲十一
肋甲四
肋甲五
肋甲六
肋甲七
肋甲八
肋版三
肋版四
脊甲四
脊甲五
脊版四
脊甲六
脊甲七
脊甲八
脊版五
尾甲

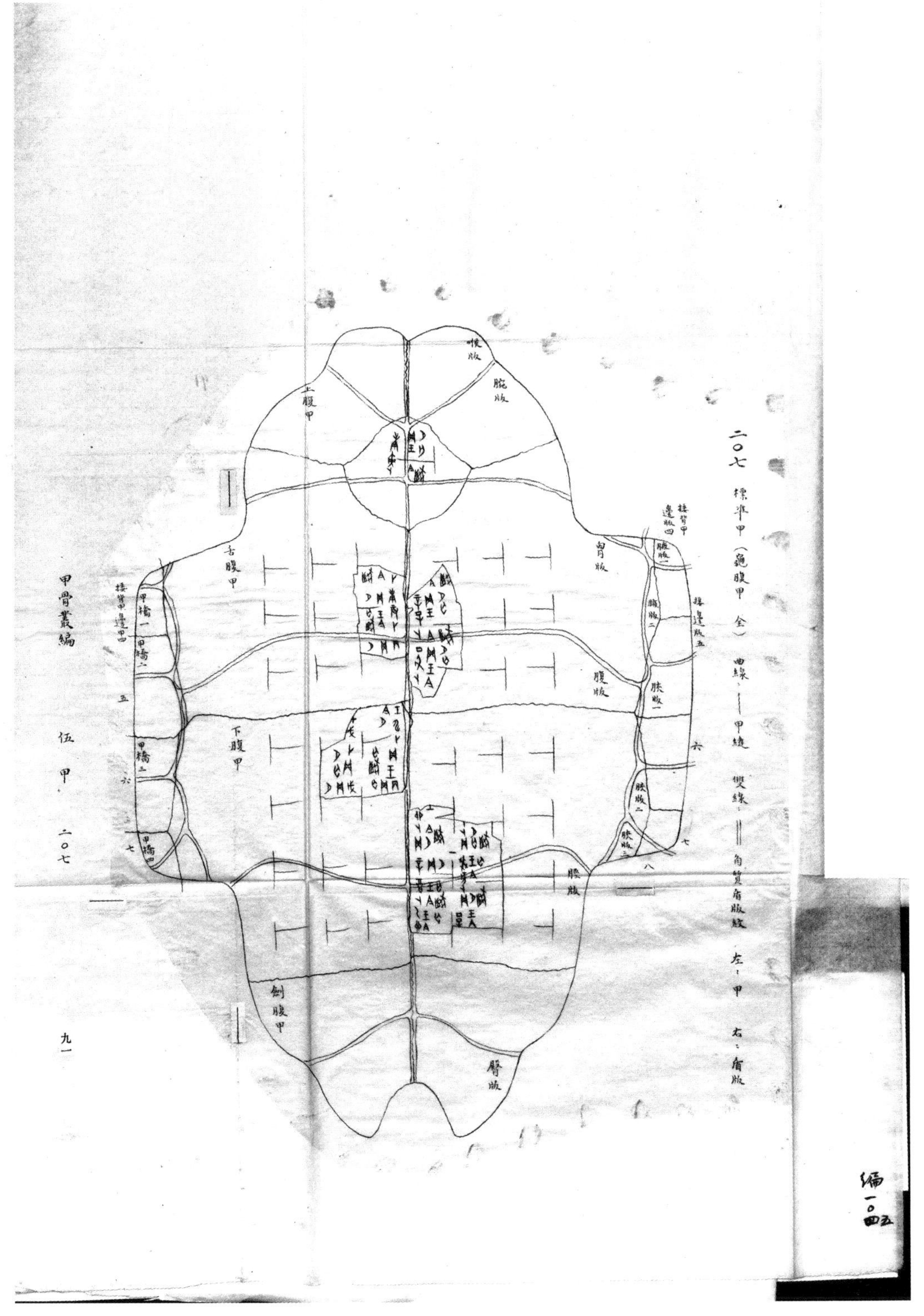
二〇七
標準甲（龜腹甲 全）
曲線、——甲縫　雙線、══角質盾版紋　左、甲　右、盾版
甲骨叢編　伍　甲　二〇七
九一
上腹甲
古腹甲
下腹甲
劍腹甲
喉版
腕版
胸版
腹版
股版
臀版
甲橋一
甲橋二
甲橋三
甲橋四
接背甲邊甲四
接背甲邊版四
接邊版五
肱版一
肱版二
肱版三
五
六
七
八

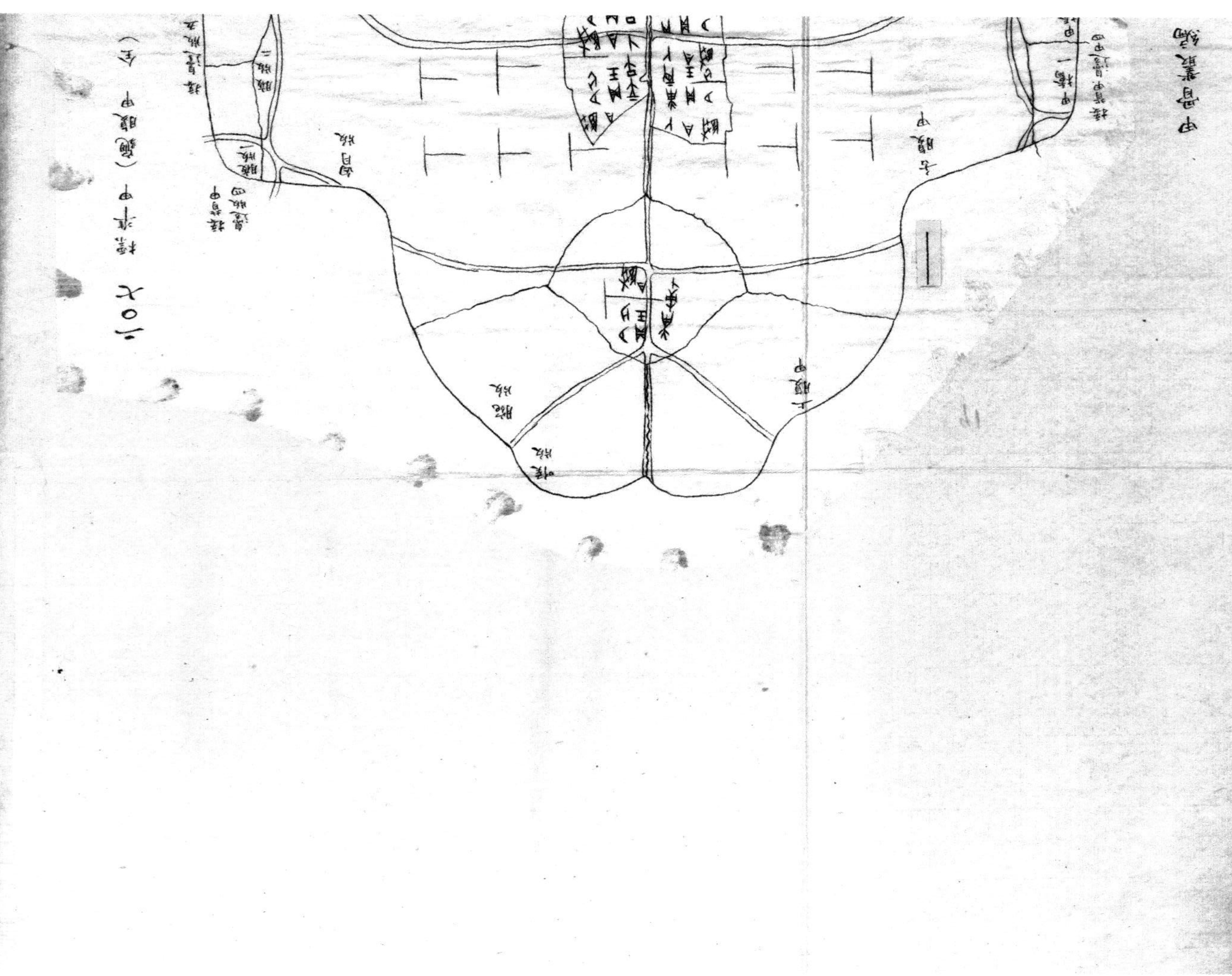
二〇七
標準甲（龜腹甲 全）

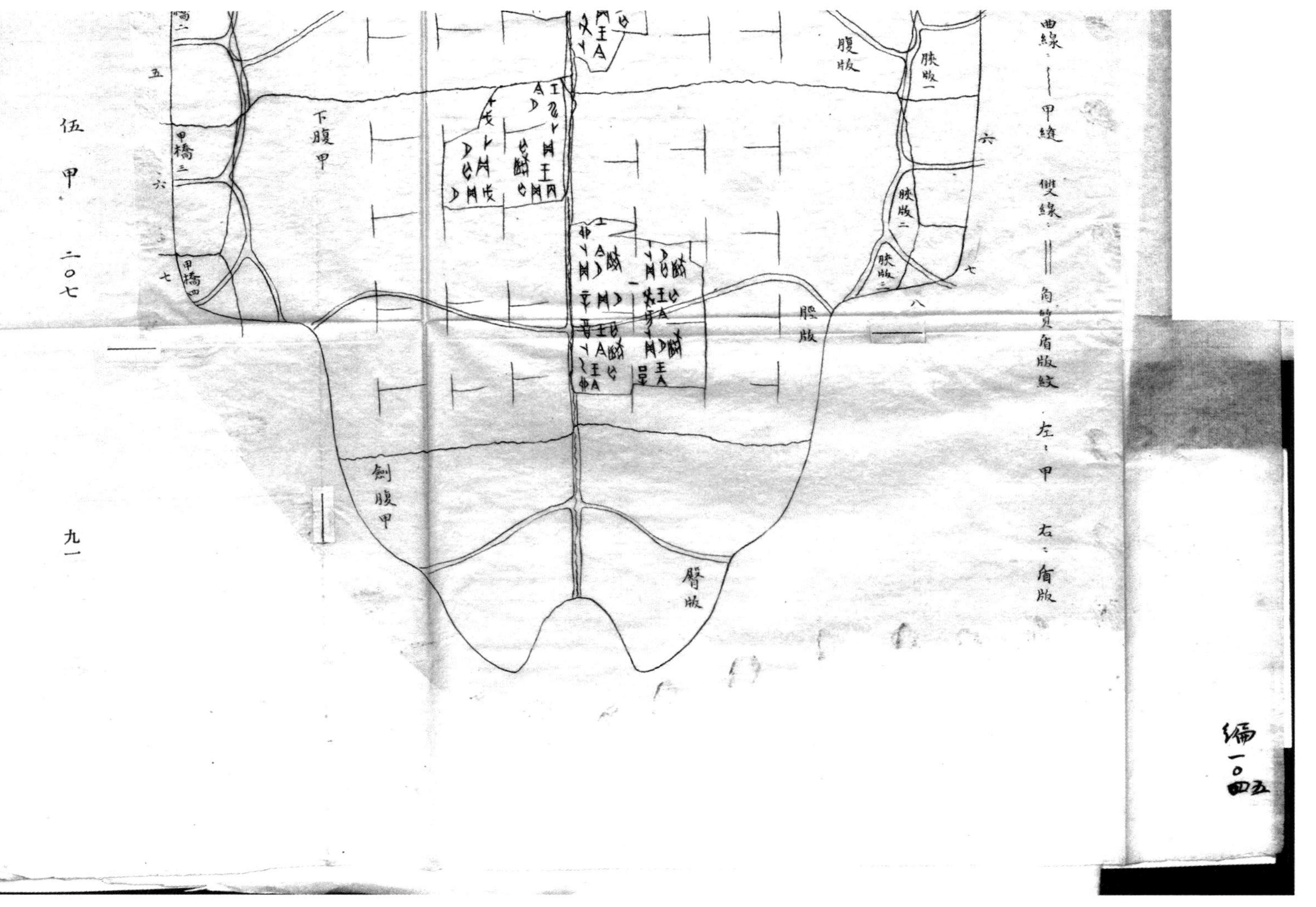

伍甲二〇七
九一
曲線：～甲縫
雙線：‖角質盾版紋
左：甲
右：盾版
下腹甲
劍腹甲
腹版
股版
臀版
胅版一
胅版二
胅版三
甲橋三
甲橋四
編一〇四五

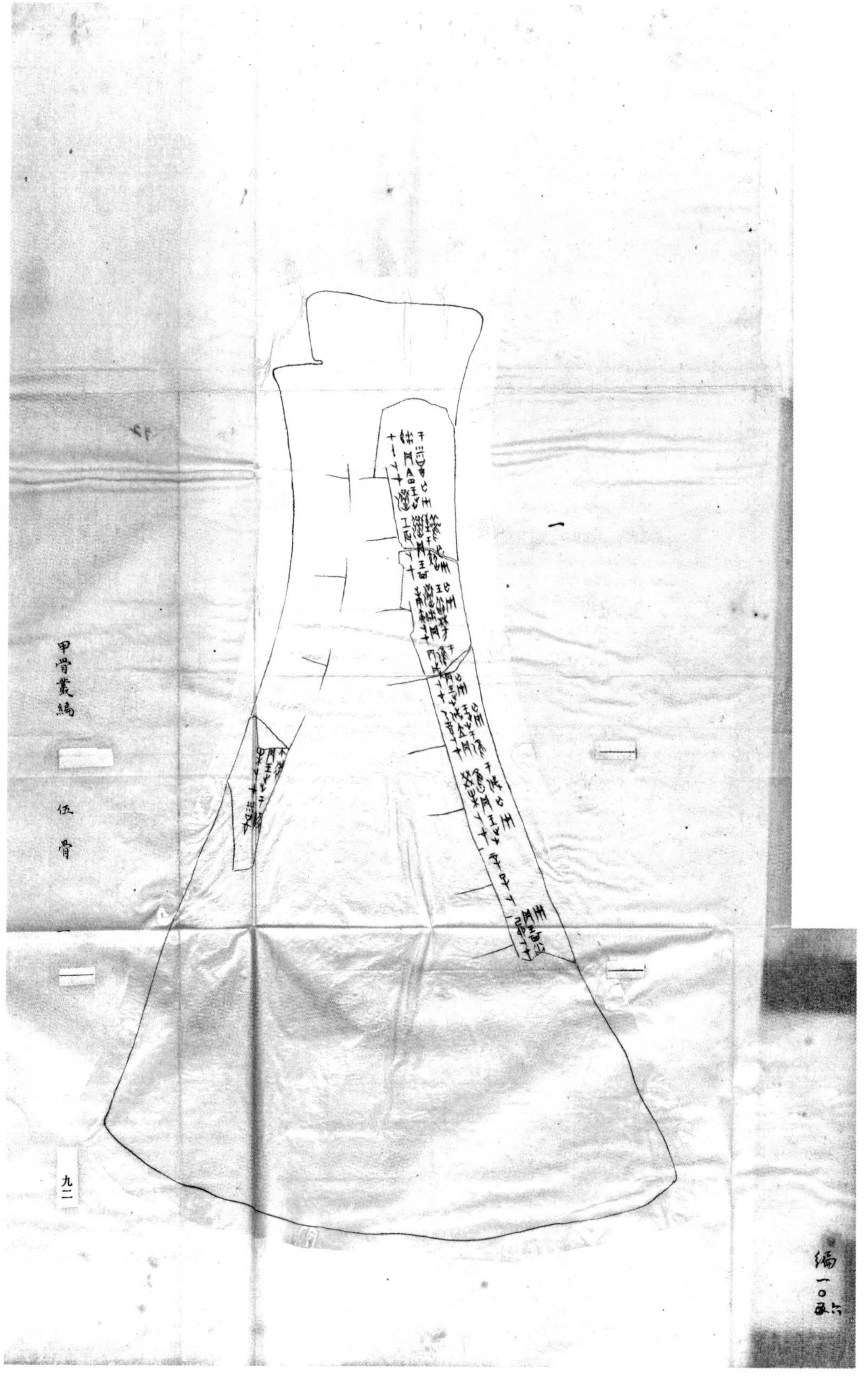
甲骨叢編
伍 骨
九二
編一〇五六

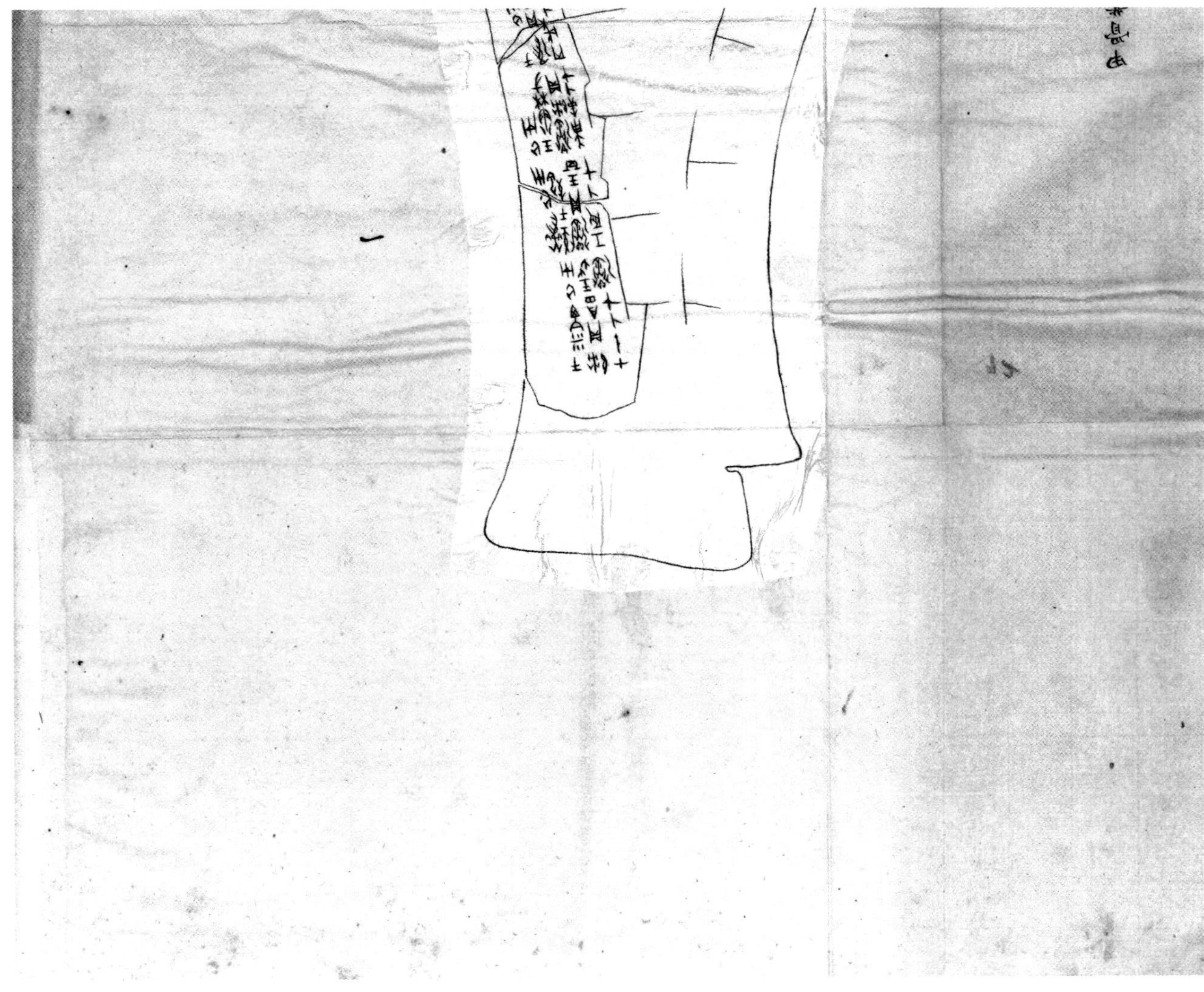

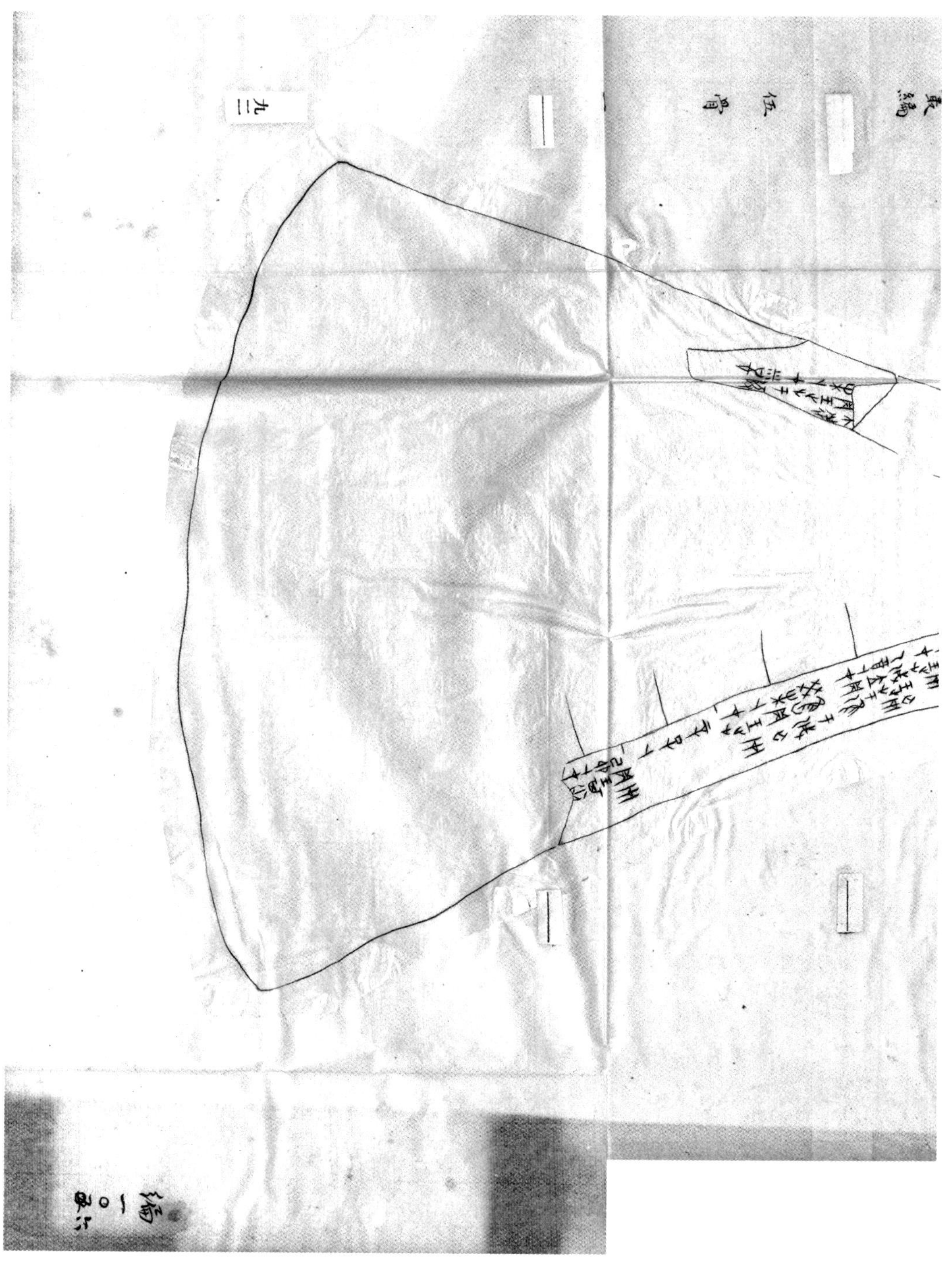
九二

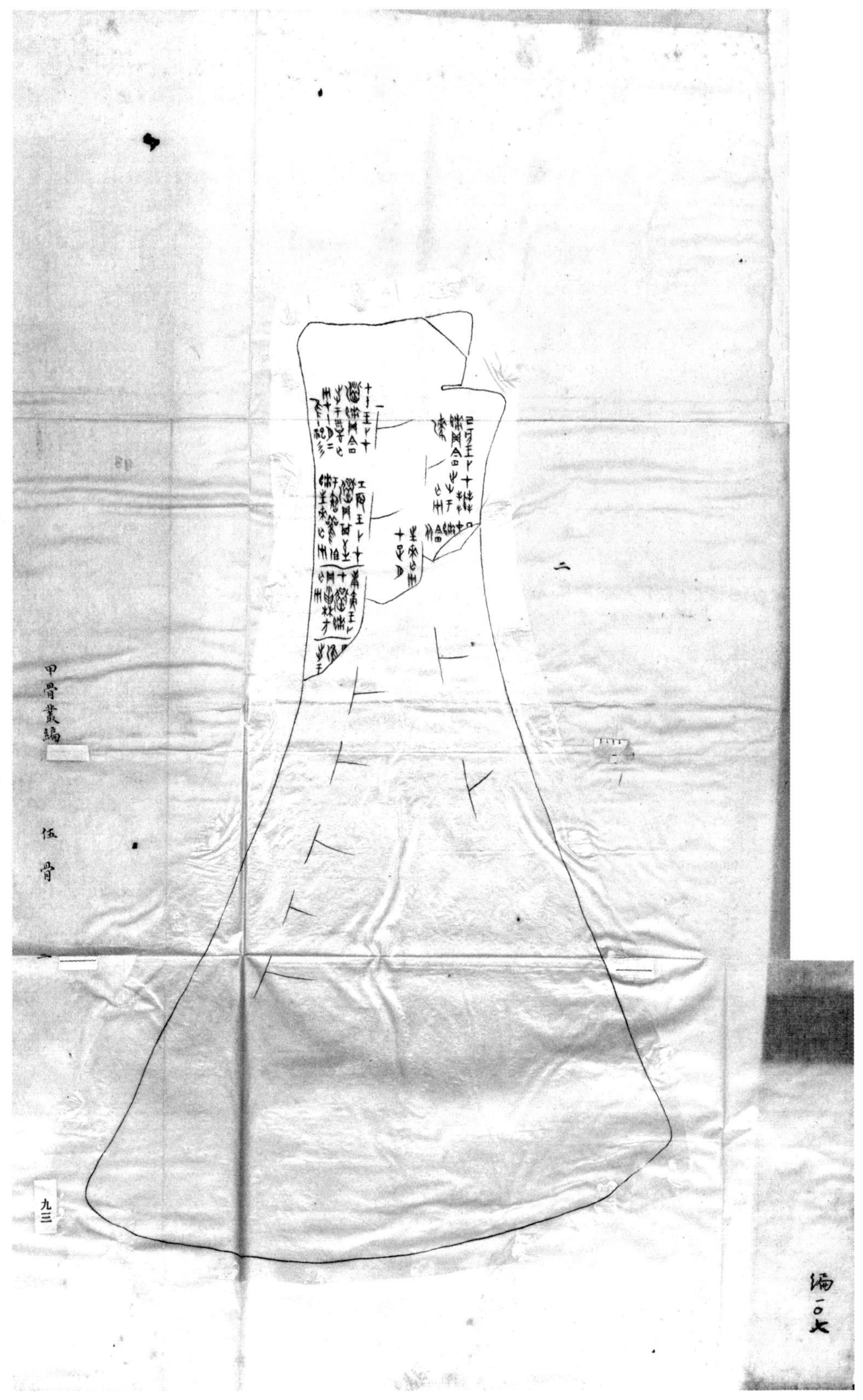
甲骨叢編
伍骨
九三
編一〇七

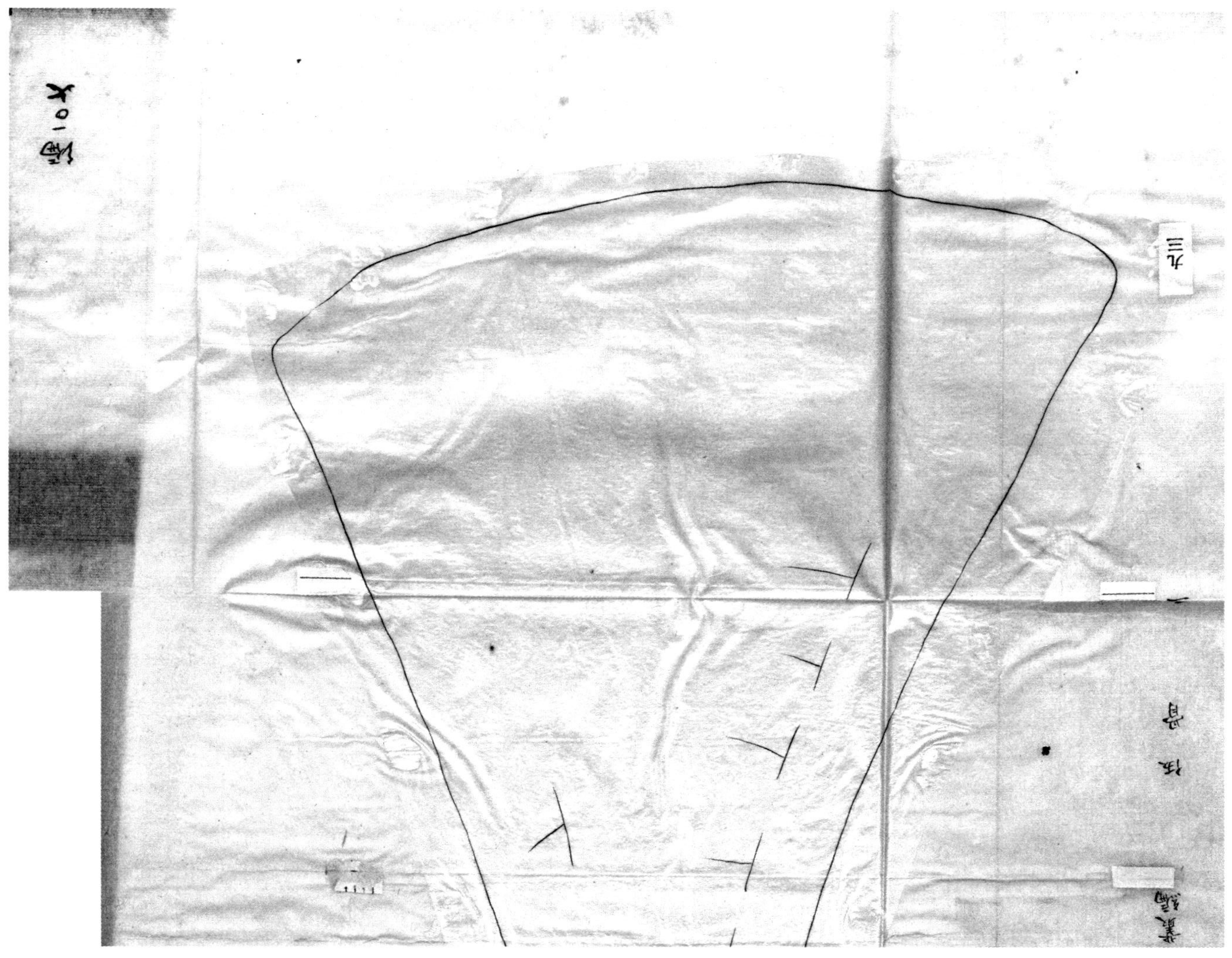

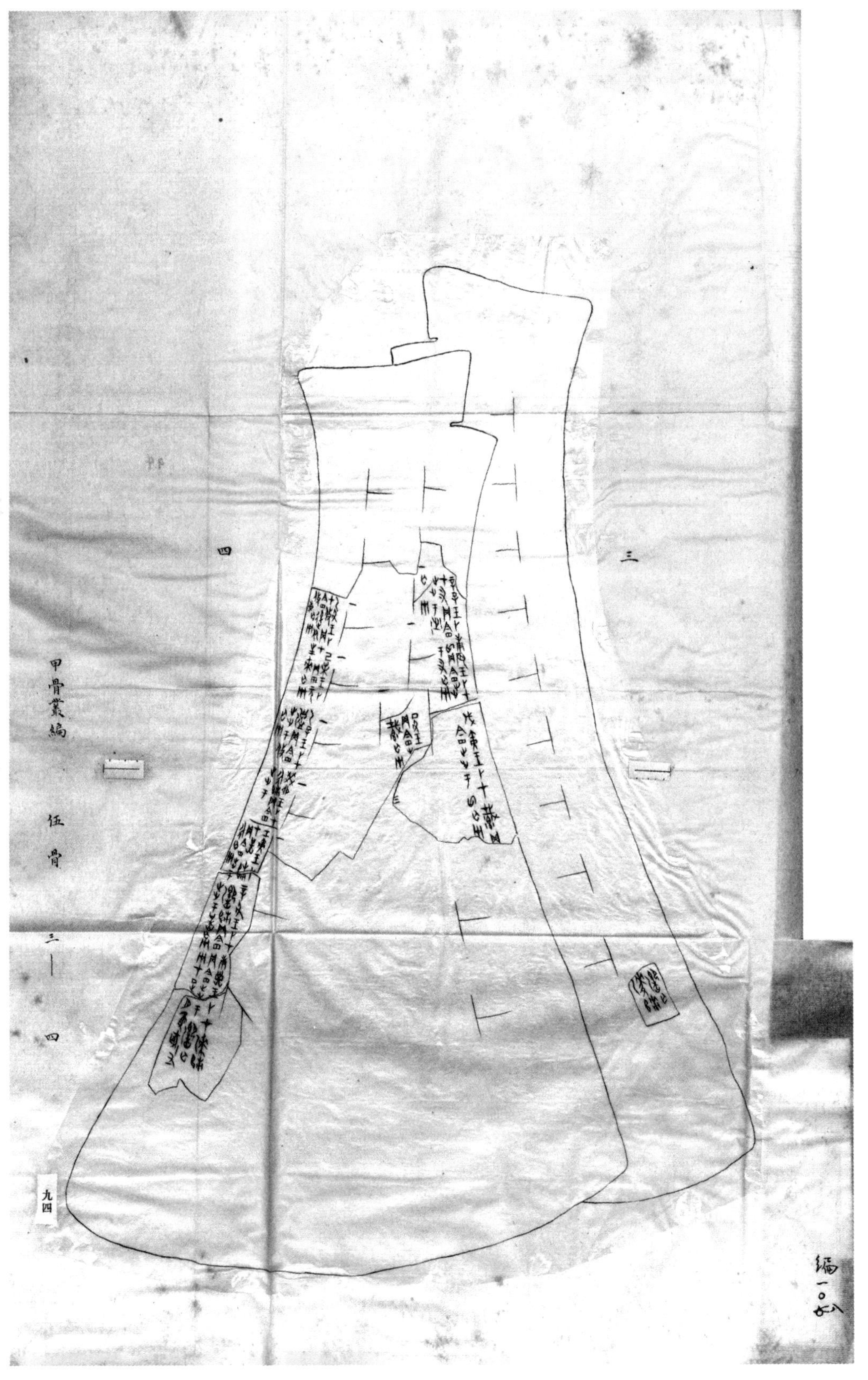
甲骨叢編 伍骨 三一四
三
四
九四
編一〇八

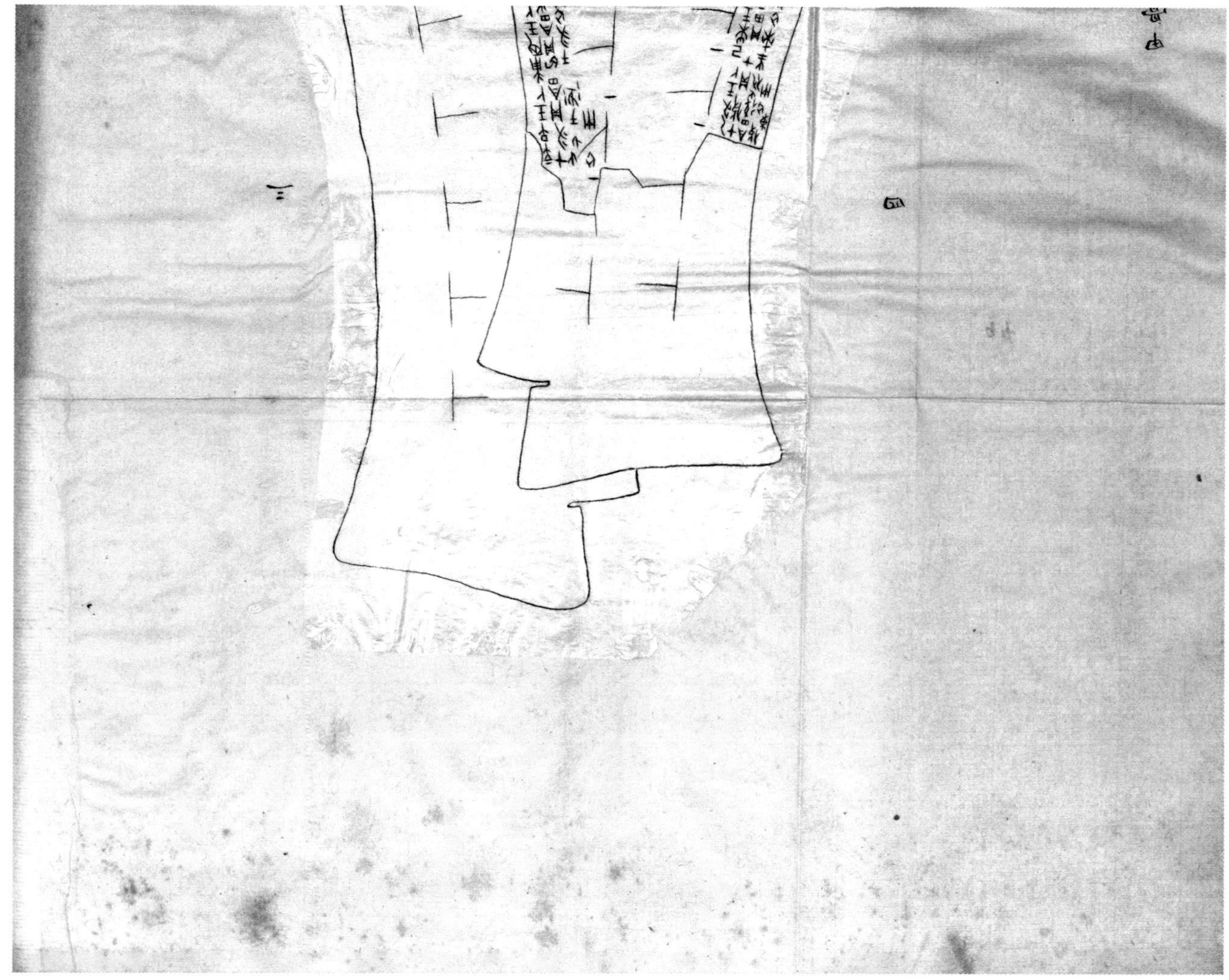

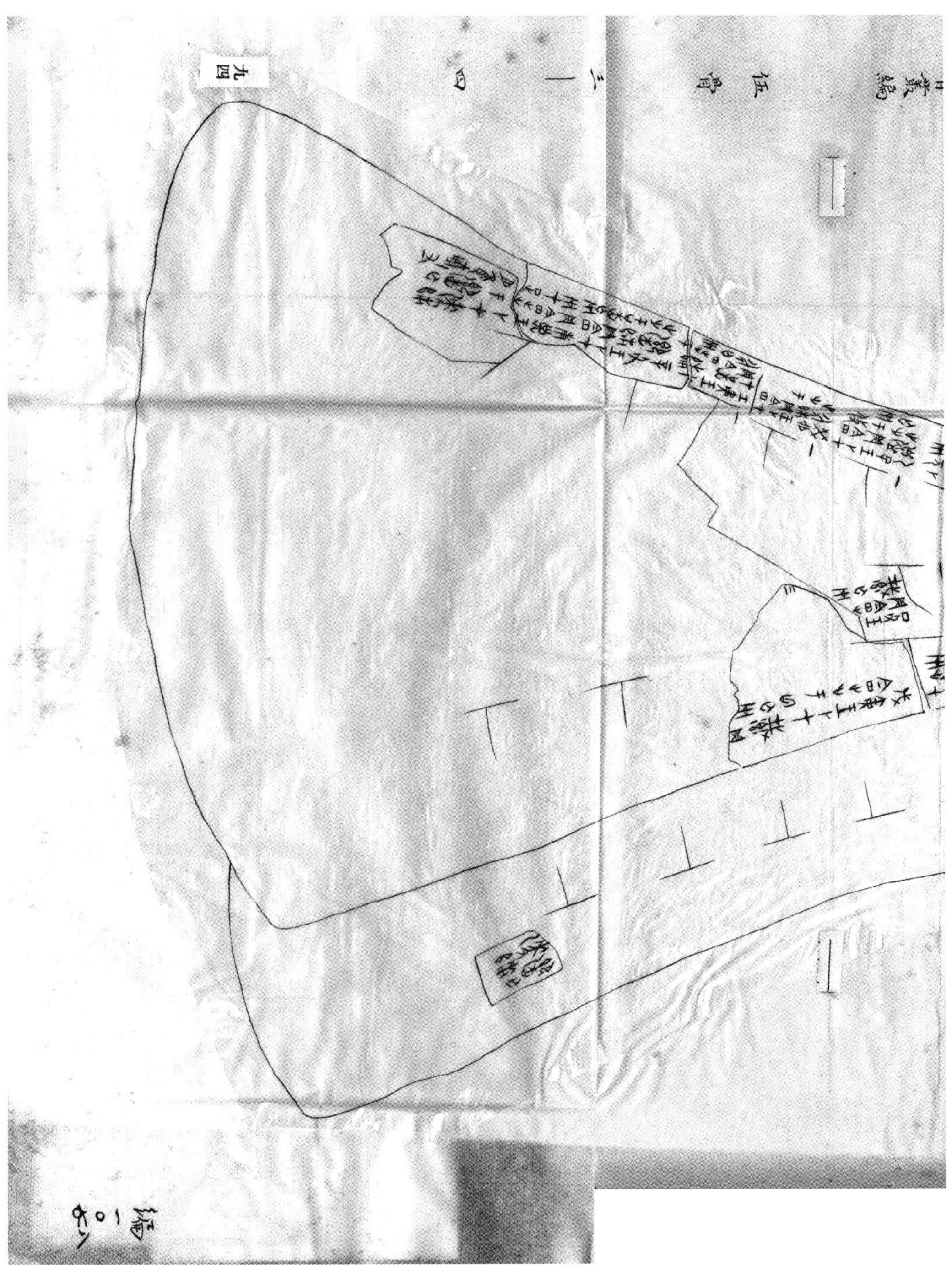

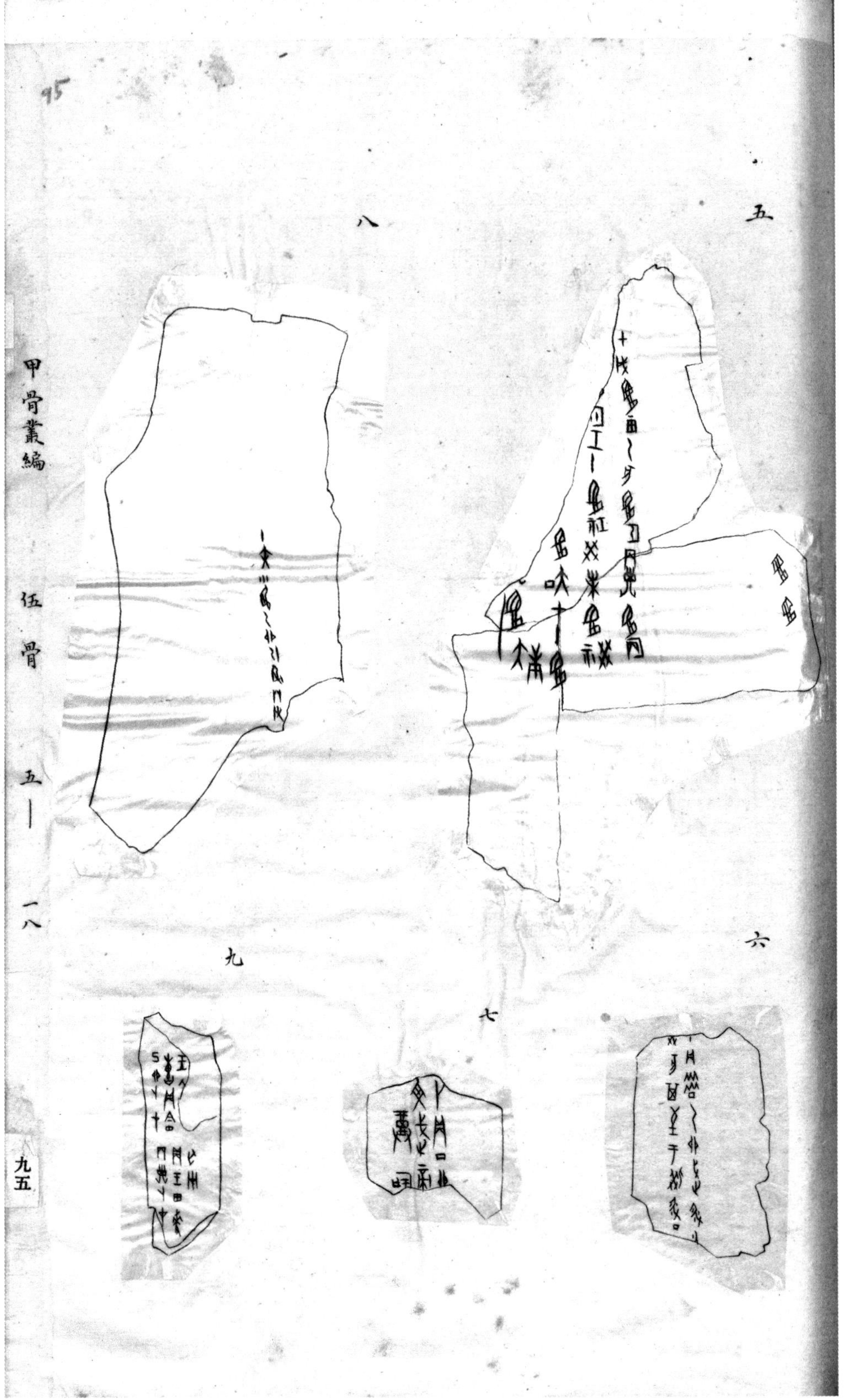
95
甲骨叢編　伍骨　五一　一八
九五
五
六
七
八
九

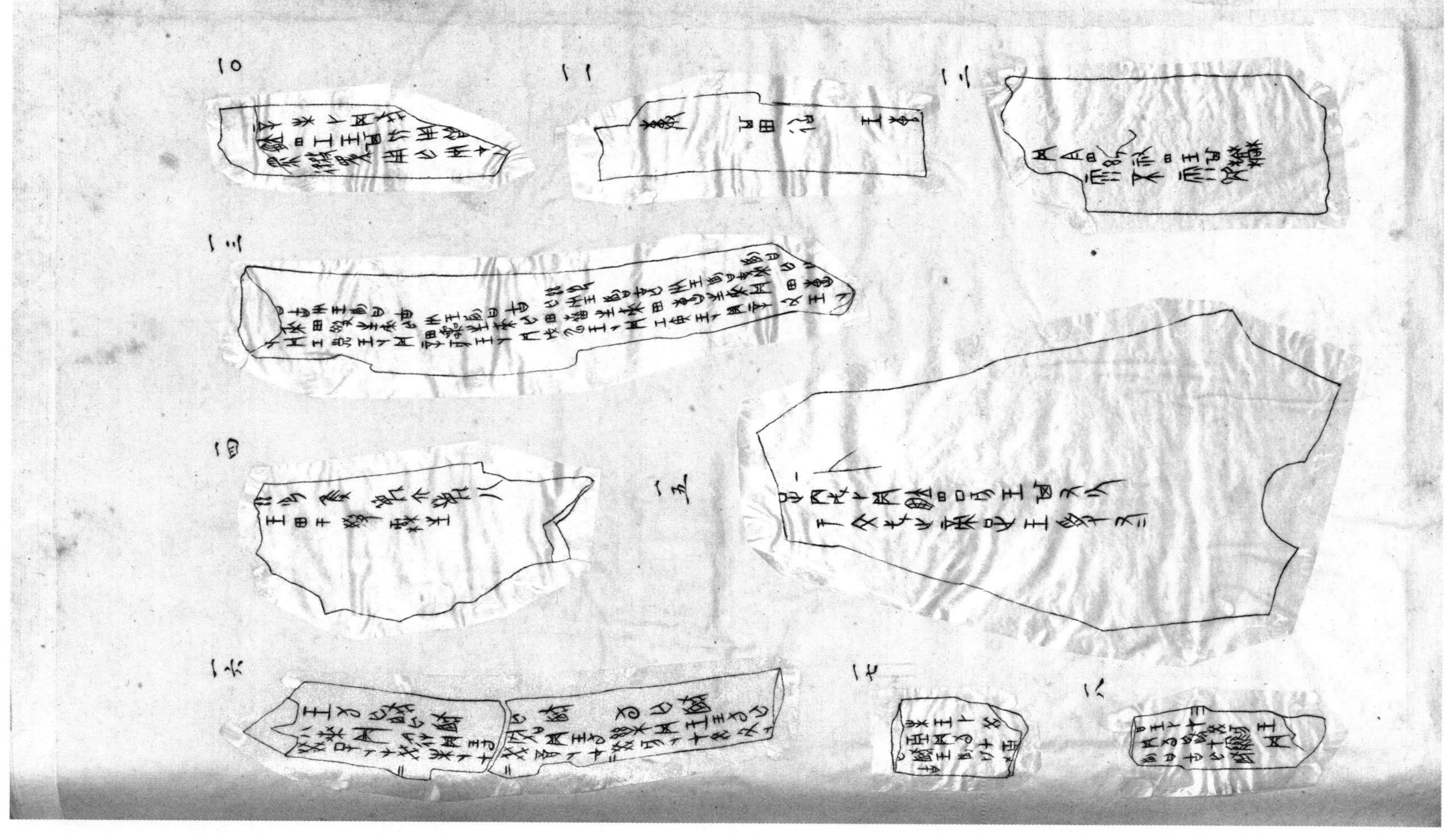

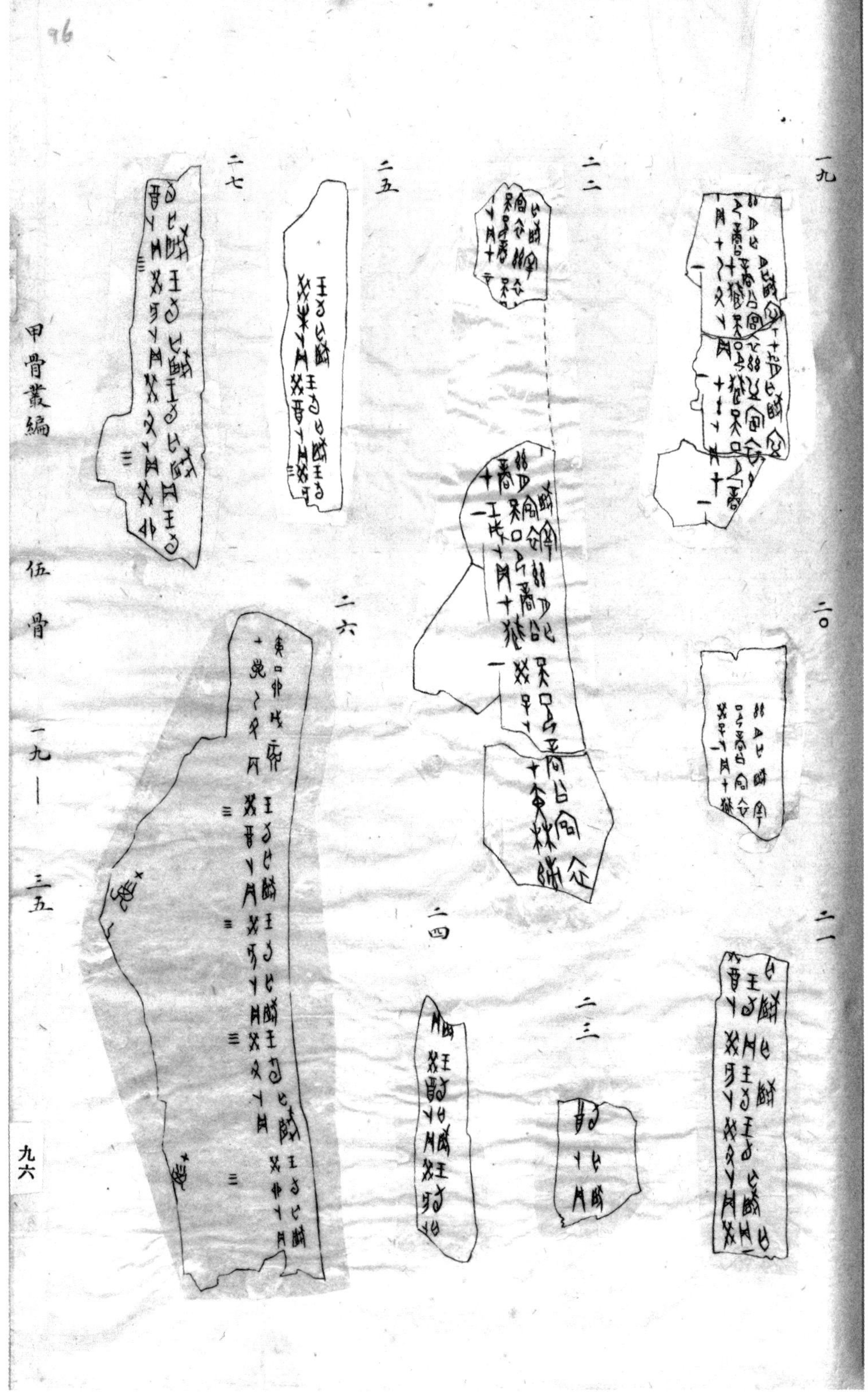
甲骨叢編　伍　骨　一九——三五
九六
一九
二〇
二一
二二
二三
二四
二五
二六
二七

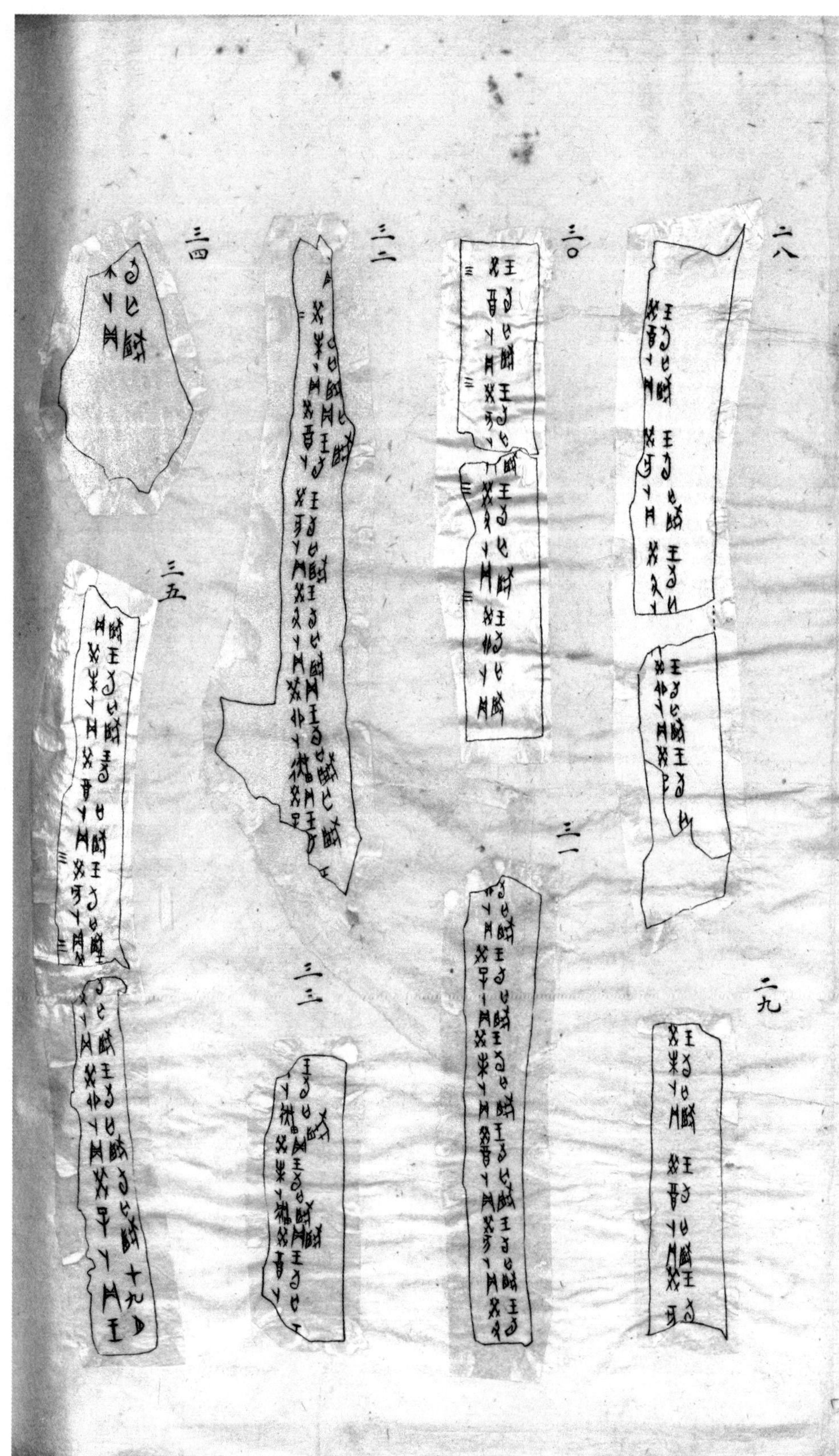
二八
二九
三〇
三一
三二
三三
三四
三五

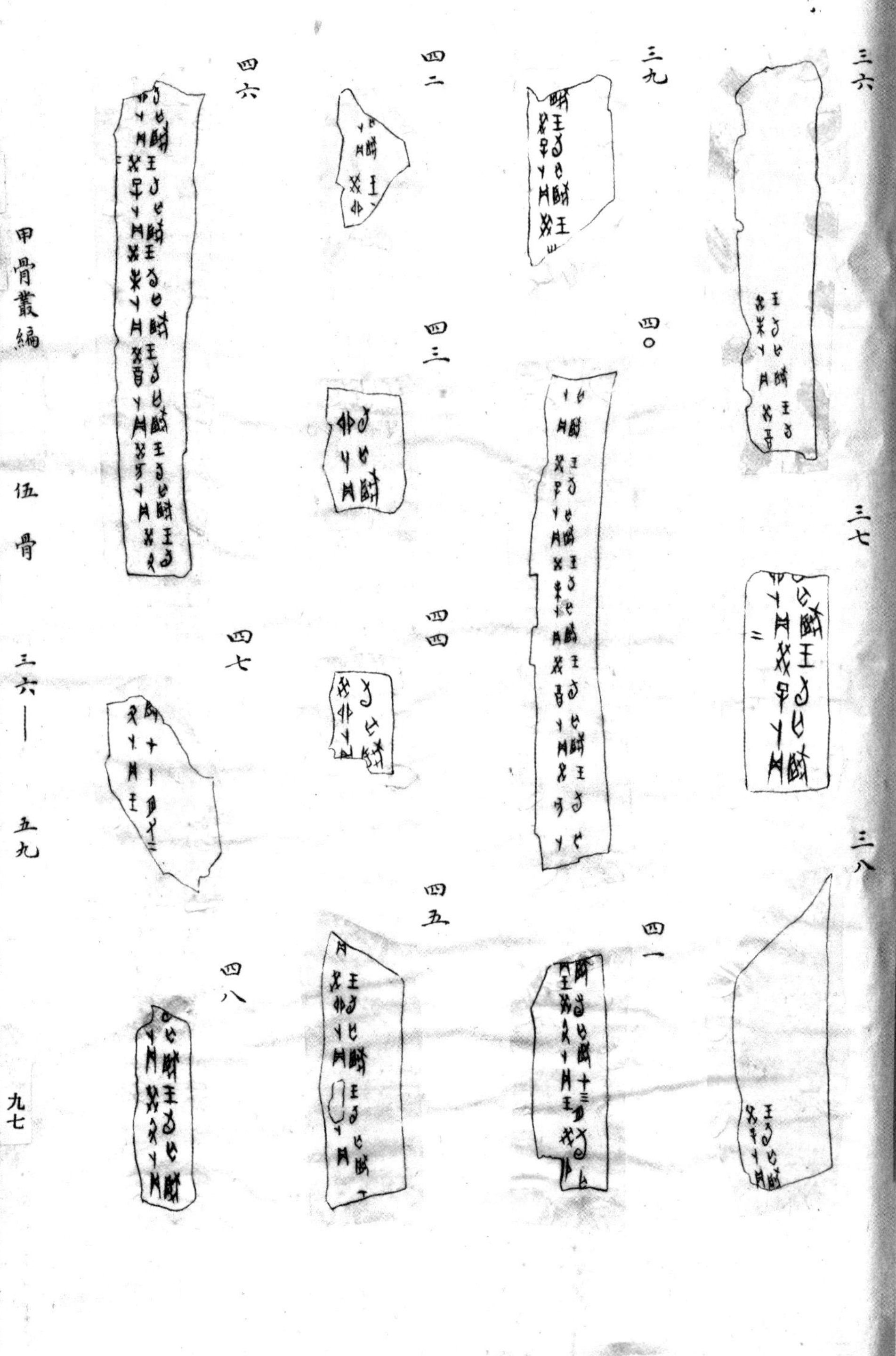
三六
三七
三八
三九
四〇
四一
四二
四三
四四
四五
四六
四七
四八

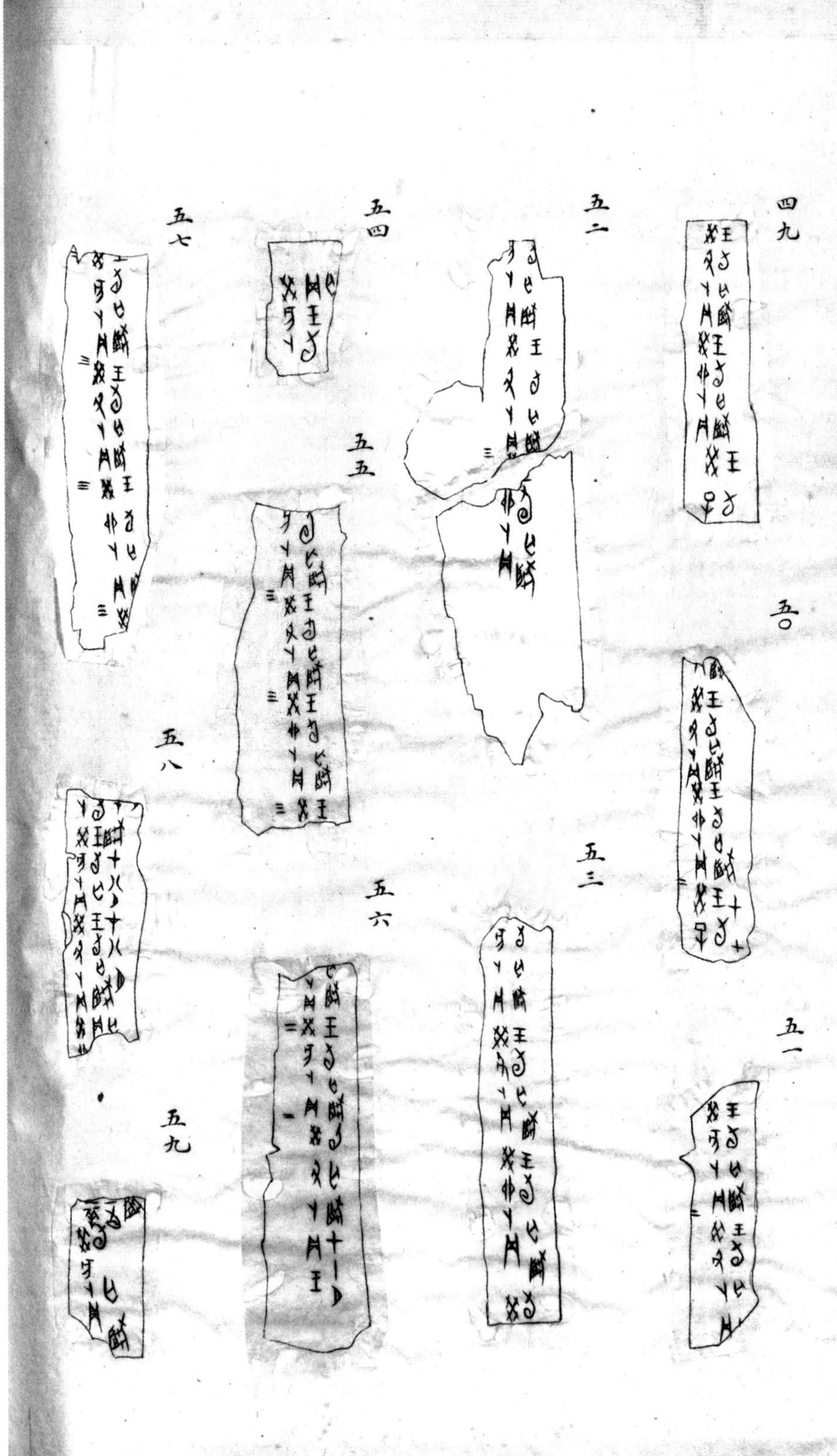
四九
五〇
五一
五二
五三
五四
五五
五六
五七
五八
五九

伍　骨

甲骨叢編　伍骨　六〇—八二

九八

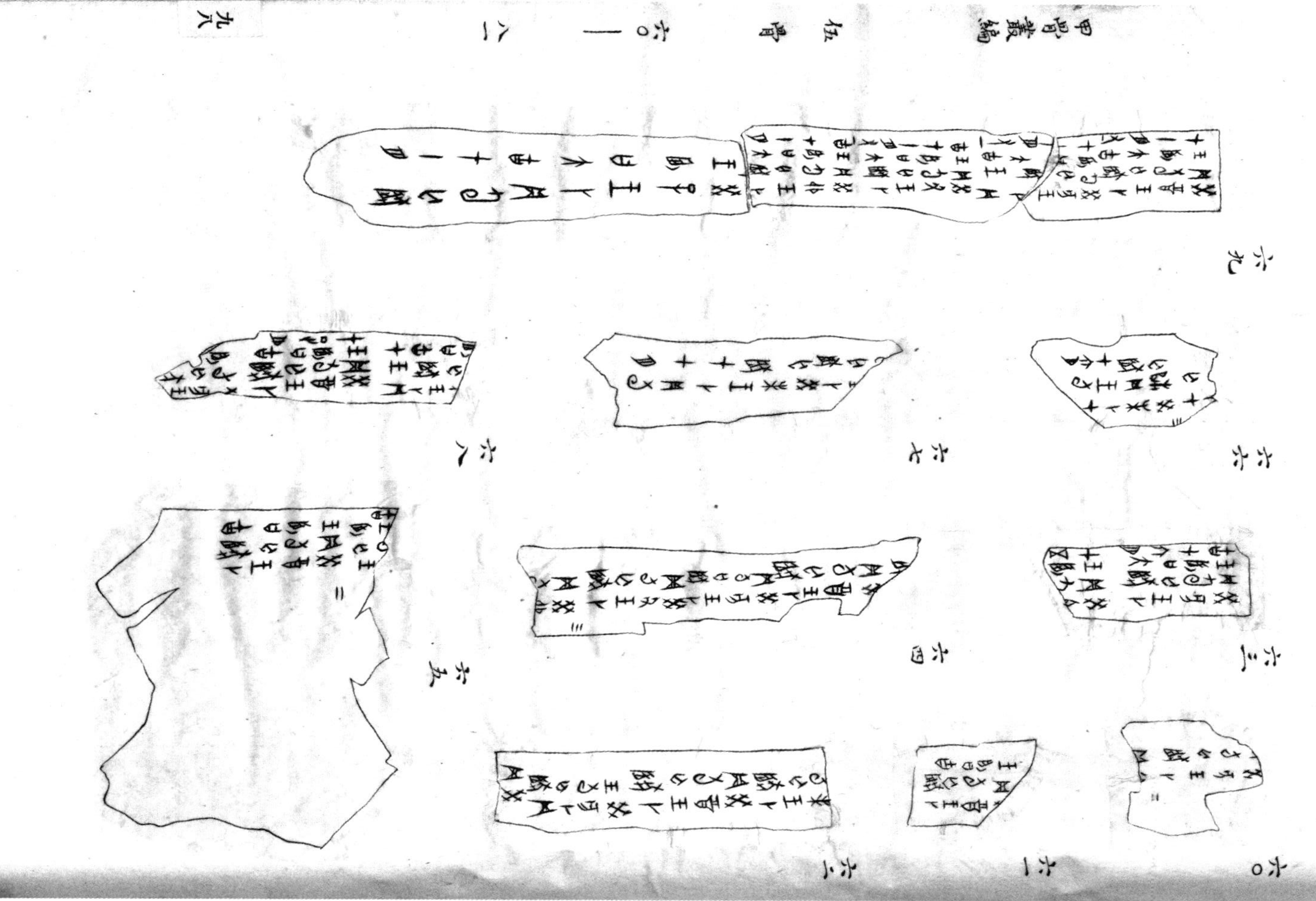

六〇　六一　六二　六三　六四　六五　六六　六七　六八　六九

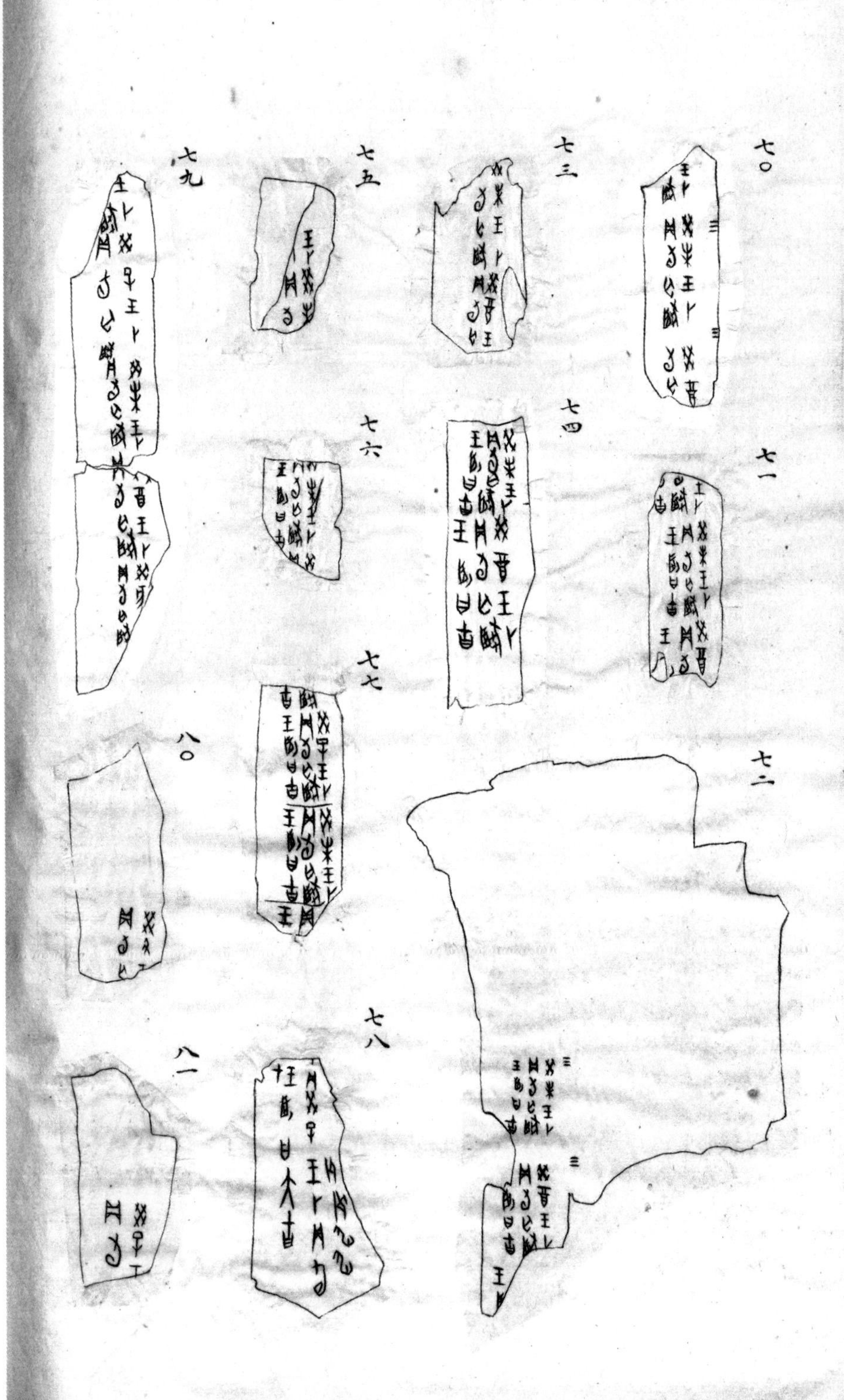
七〇
七一
七二
七三
七四
七五
七六
七七
七八
七九
八〇
八一

99

甲骨叢編　伍骨　八二——一〇三

九九

八二

八三

八四

八五

八六

八七

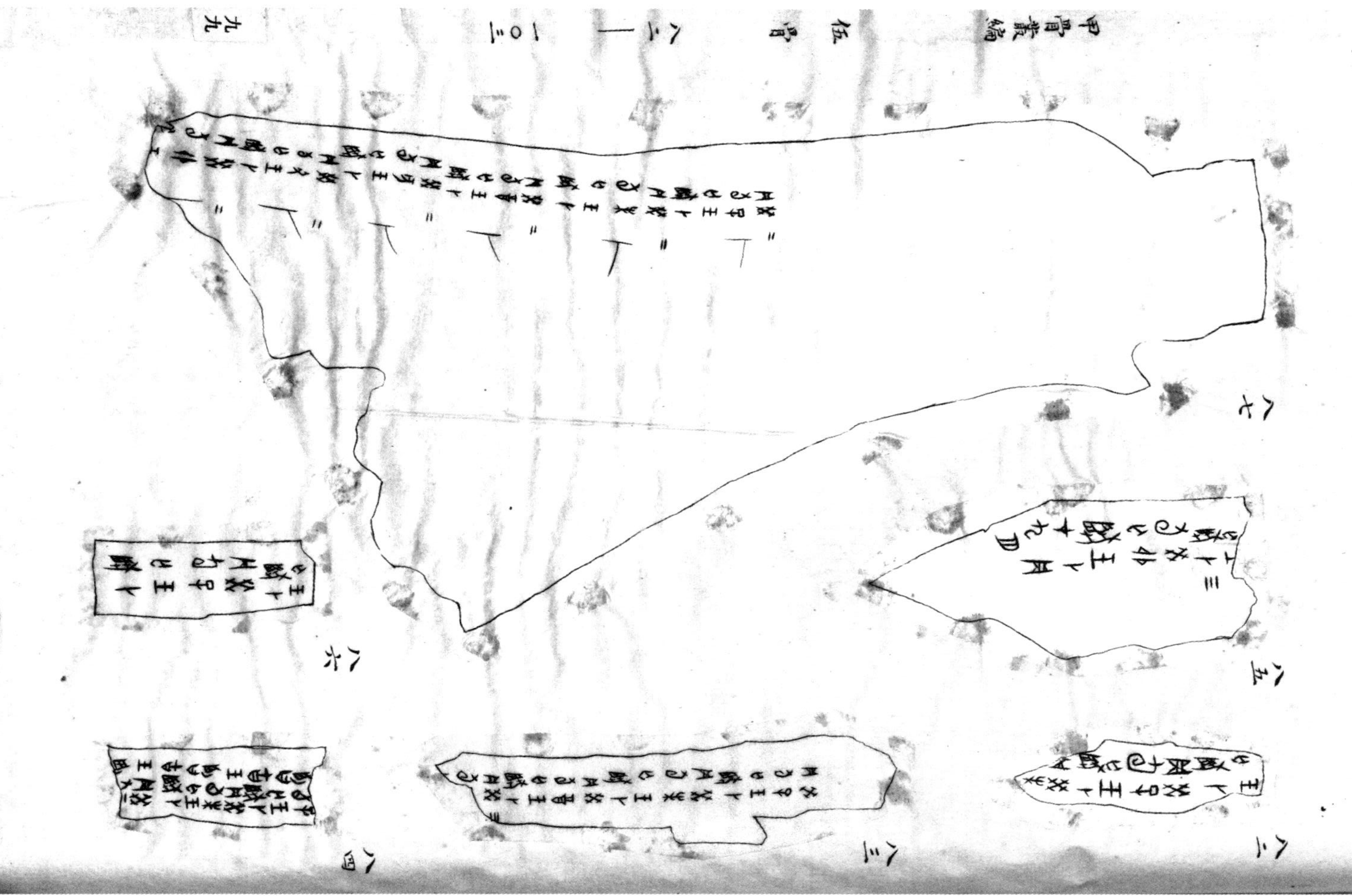

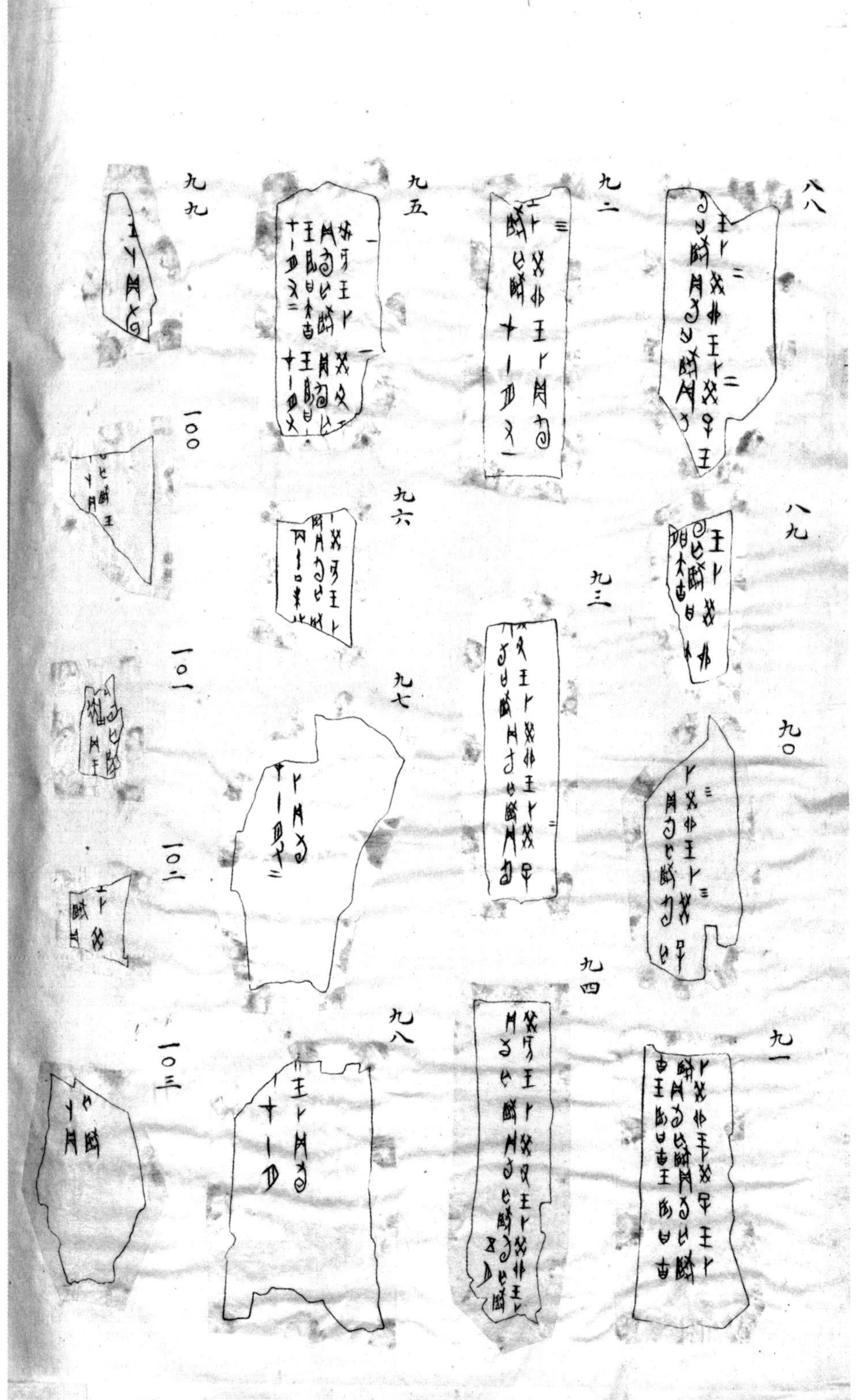
八八
八九
九〇
九一
九二
九三
九四
九五
九六
九七
九八
九九
一〇〇
一〇一
一〇二
一〇三

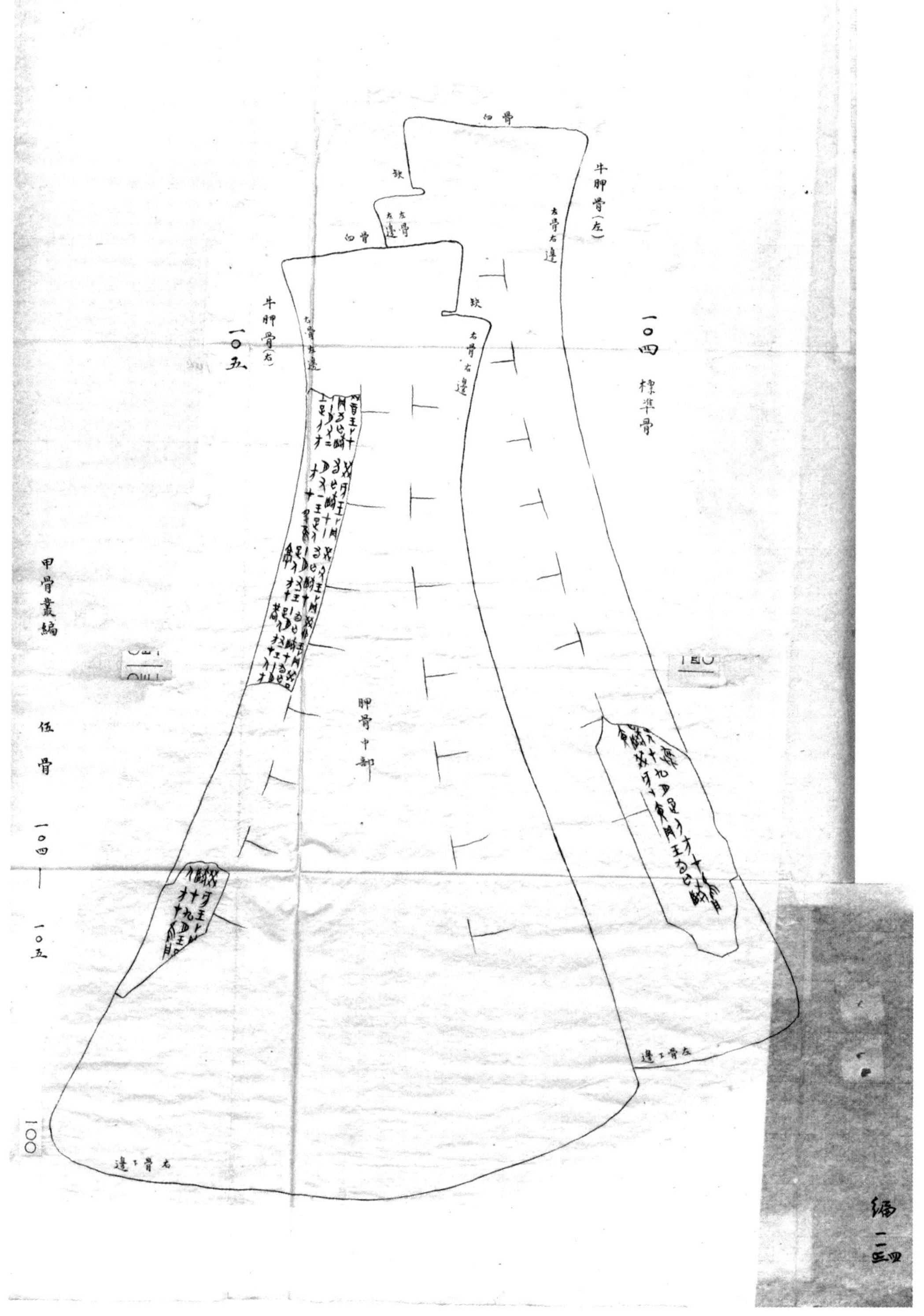
一〇四
標準骨
牛胛骨(左)
右骨右邊
右骨左邊
臼骨
缺
一〇五
牛胛骨(右)
右骨左邊
右骨右邊
胛骨中部
左骨下邊
右骨下邊
一〇〇
甲骨叢編
伍 骨
一〇四—一〇五

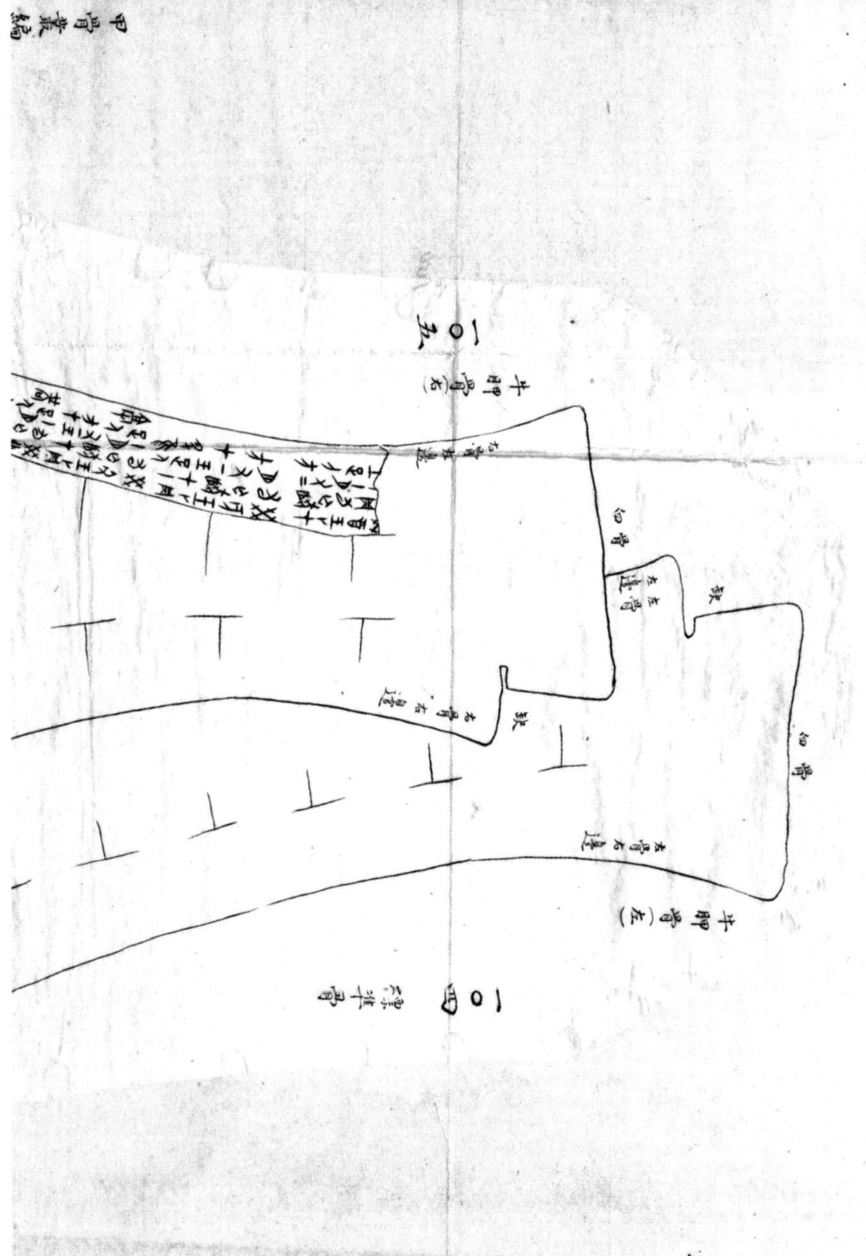
一〇四
牛胛骨（左）
一〇五
牛胛骨（右）
甲骨叢編

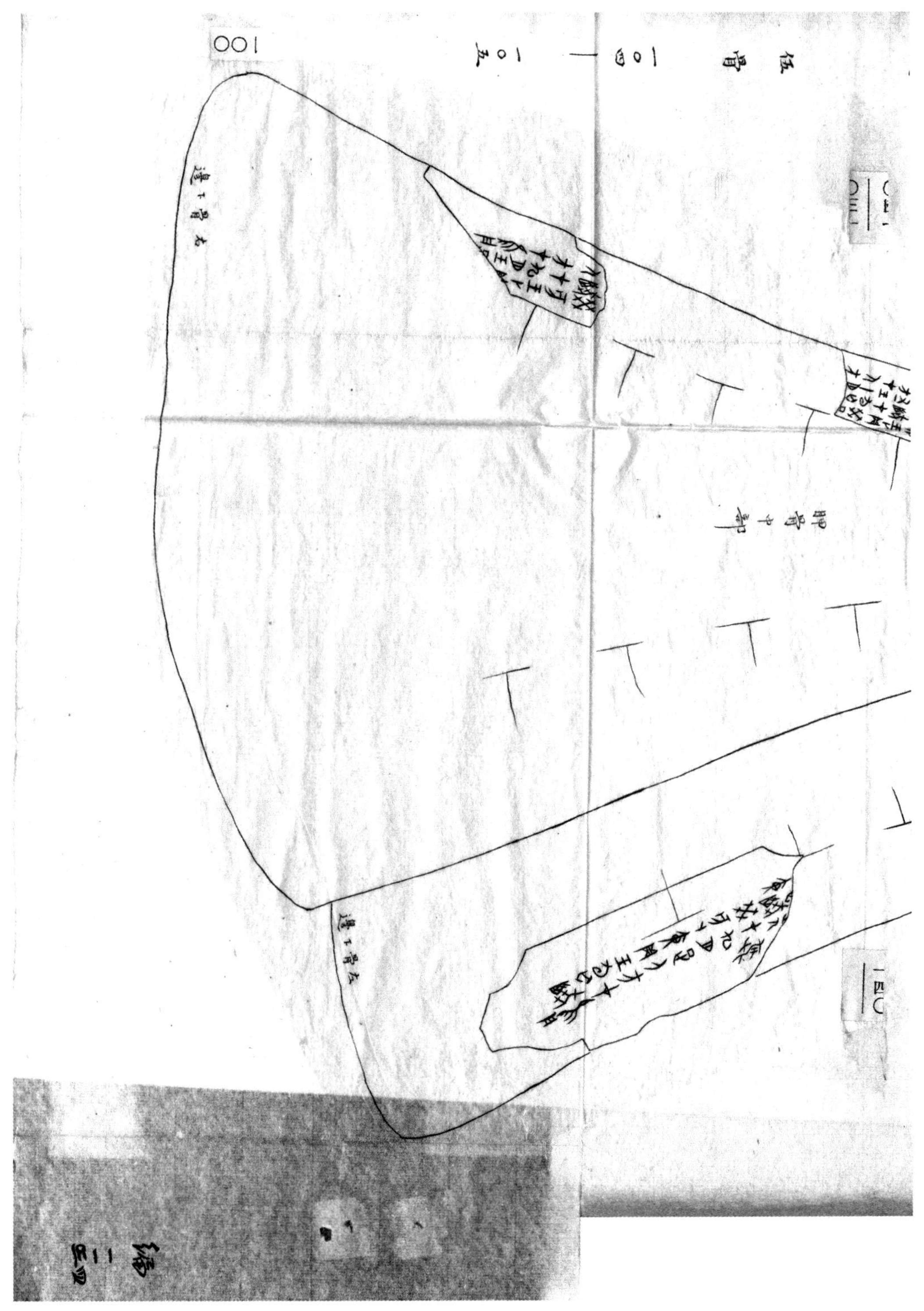

甲骨叢編

第一集

考釋

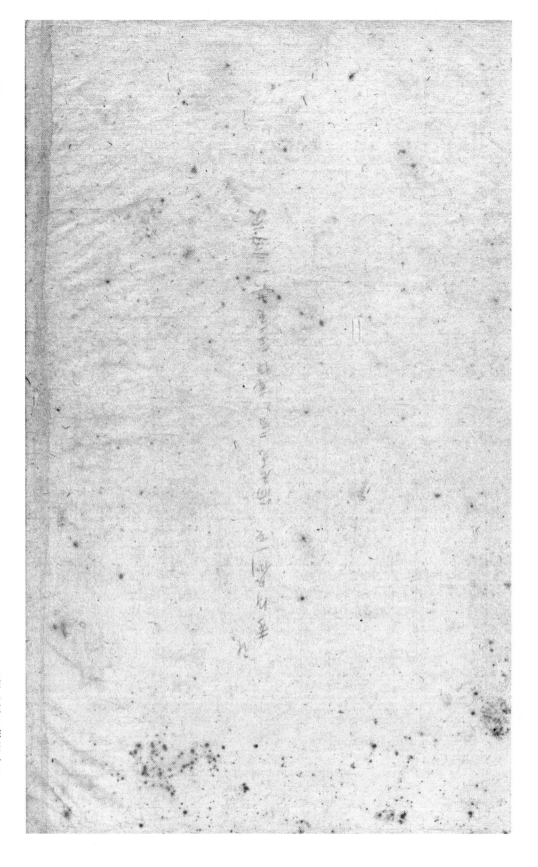

考釋凡例

一：本編考證部分，或因一片有特殊價值者；或因一字有沿革變化者；或成組之卜辭，關係一時之重要史實者；或全部之卜辭，關係一期之分劃鑑别者；或舉禮制；或述曆法；隨時隨處，提示研究之例，初無定格。

二：本編釋文部分，每版皆繪出原形，譯為今字，俾同文異版之辭，易於分辨。譯文以「約定俗成」為原則，不識之字，改書今體，為便省覽，非關考定，讀者諒之。

三：甲骨殘版，有須繪出全形，以見其部位所在及文例關係者，間或為之，以示其例。

四：卜辭之左右行，於辭上方以矢形示之。下行者不標記號。

五：卜兆與卜辭之關係及其範圍，以虛線界劃之。辭與辭之區分，可以一目了然。

六：以數字加圈圍之，示卜辭在本版上之先後順序。

七：殘缺之辭，今為補出者，皆作括弧於上下以識别之。未補者加點號於殘缺處以識别之。

八：本編材料來源，悉註於釋文片下。第一字為書名或收藏者簡號，第二數字為分卷，第三數字為葉數，第四數字為版片。亦有第二字註其類别或原書甲骨之號數者。

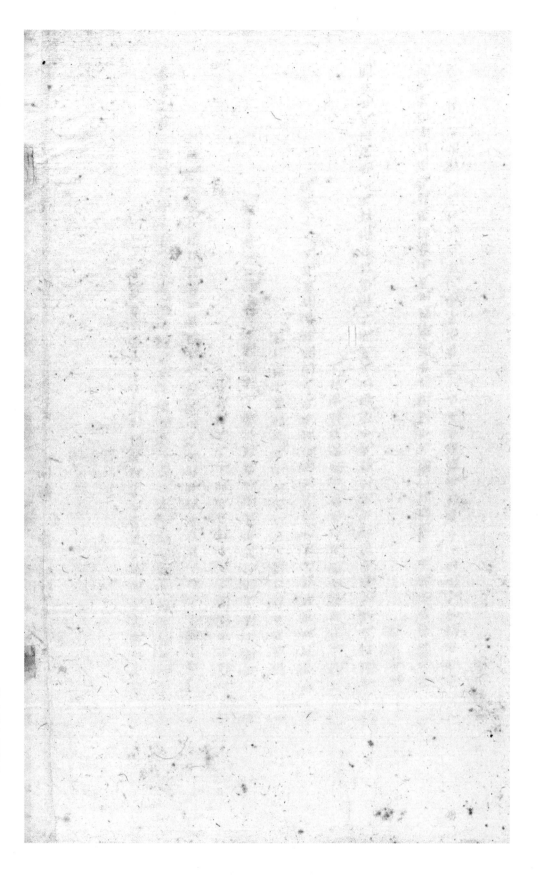

甲骨叢編採錄材料簡名對照表

簡名	全名	編著或收藏者	出版年月
鐵	鐵雲藏龜	劉鶚	清光緒二十九年
*前	殷虛書契前編	羅振玉	民國二年十二月
*菁	殷虛書契菁華	羅振玉	民國三年十月
餘	鐵雲藏龜之餘	羅振玉	民國四年
*後	殷虛書契後編	羅振玉	民國五年三月
圖	殷虛古器物圖錄	羅振玉	民國五年
*卜	殷虛卜辭	明義士	民國六年三月
*戩	戩壽堂所藏殷虛文字	姬佛陀	民國六年五月
*龜	龜甲獸骨文字	林泰輔	民國十年十二月
*徵	簠室殷契徵文	王襄	民國十四年九月
拾	鐵雲藏龜拾遺	葉玉森	民國十四年
*新	新獲卜辭寫本	董作賓	民國十七年
*真 河真	殷虛文字存真第一集	關葆謙	民國二十年六月

福*	福氏所藏甲骨文字	商承祚	民國二十二年四月
絜*	殷絜卜辭	容庚、瞿潤緡	民國二十二年五月
續*	殷虛書契續編	羅振玉	民國二十二年九月
佚*	殷契佚存	商承祚	民國二十二年十月
鄴二*	鄴中片羽 第二集	黄濬	民國二十四年二月 廿六年八月
柏*	柏根氏舊藏甲骨文字	明義士	民國二十四年
通別*	卜辭通纂 附別錄	郭沫若	民國二十四年五月
庫*	庫方二氏藏甲骨卜辭	方法斂、白瑞華	民國二十四年十二月
河*	河南通志館甲骨文錄	孫海波	民國二十六年
七*	甲骨卜辭七集	方法斂、白瑞華	民國二十七年
金*	金璋所藏甲骨卜辭	方法斂、白瑞華	民國二十八年
天*	天壤閣甲骨文存	唐蘭	民國二十八年
零*	鐵雲藏龜零拾	李旦丘	民國二十八年
誠	誠齋殷虛文字	孫海波	民國二十八年
珠*	殷契遺珠	金祖同	民國二十八年

簡名	書名	著者	備注
甲*	殷虛文字甲編	董作賓	民國二十九年（自此以下，均未出版）
明* 甲乙丙丁	明義士藏甲骨文字	容庚藏拓本	
卜* 上下	殷虛卜辭續編上下冊	明義士　容庚藏拓本	
善*	善齋所藏甲骨文字	劉體智　史語所藏拓本	
粹*	殷契粹編	郭沫若	民國二十六年五月
外*	殷虛文字外編	董作賓　採輯拓本	待刊
北*	北京大學藏甲骨刻辭	劉復藏拓本	
凡	凡將齋藏甲骨文字	馬衡　劉復藏拓本	
滇*	雲南圖書館藏骨（?）	何叙甫　採輯拓本	

加*號者，第一集已收入。

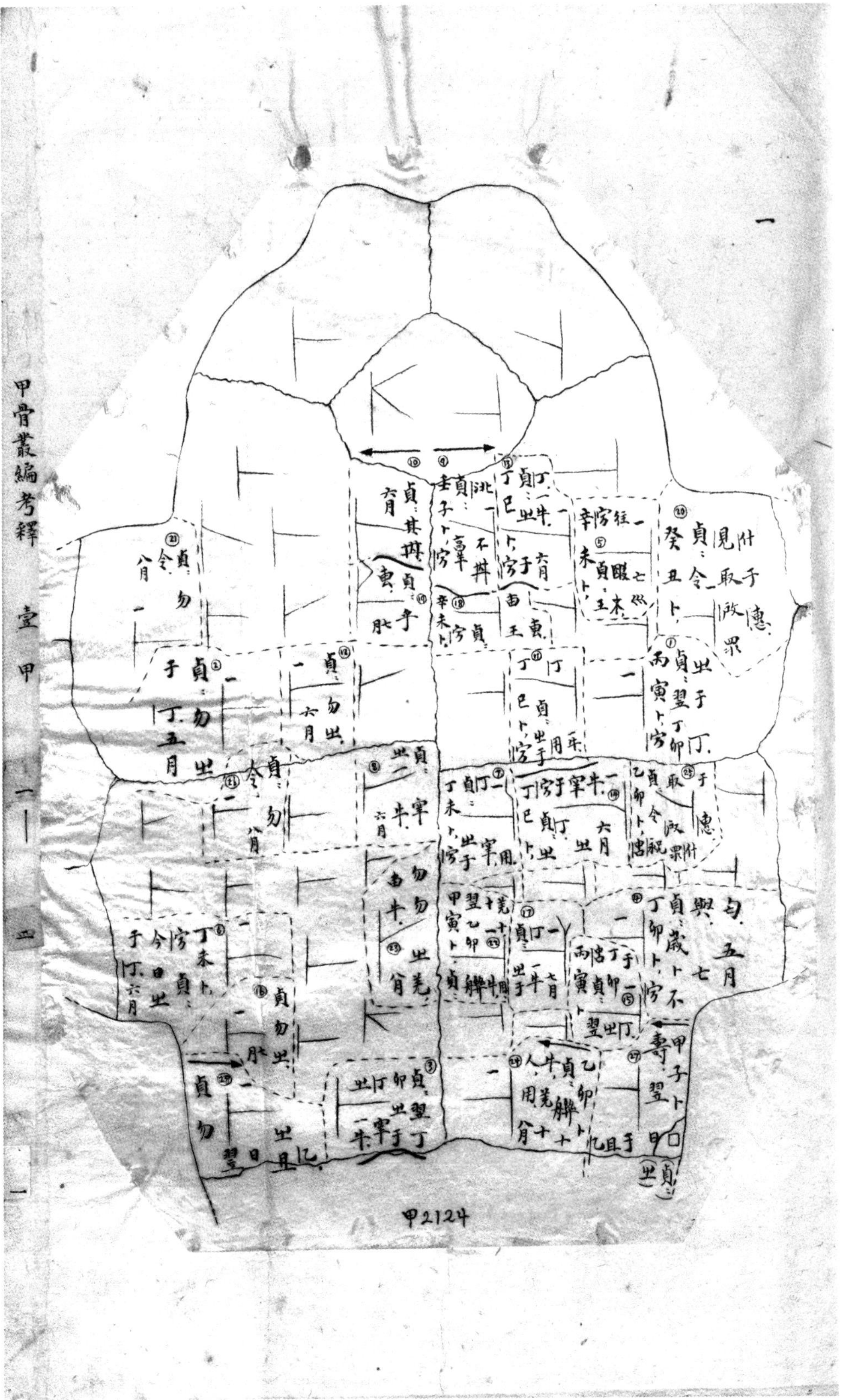
甲骨叢編考釋
壹甲
甲2124

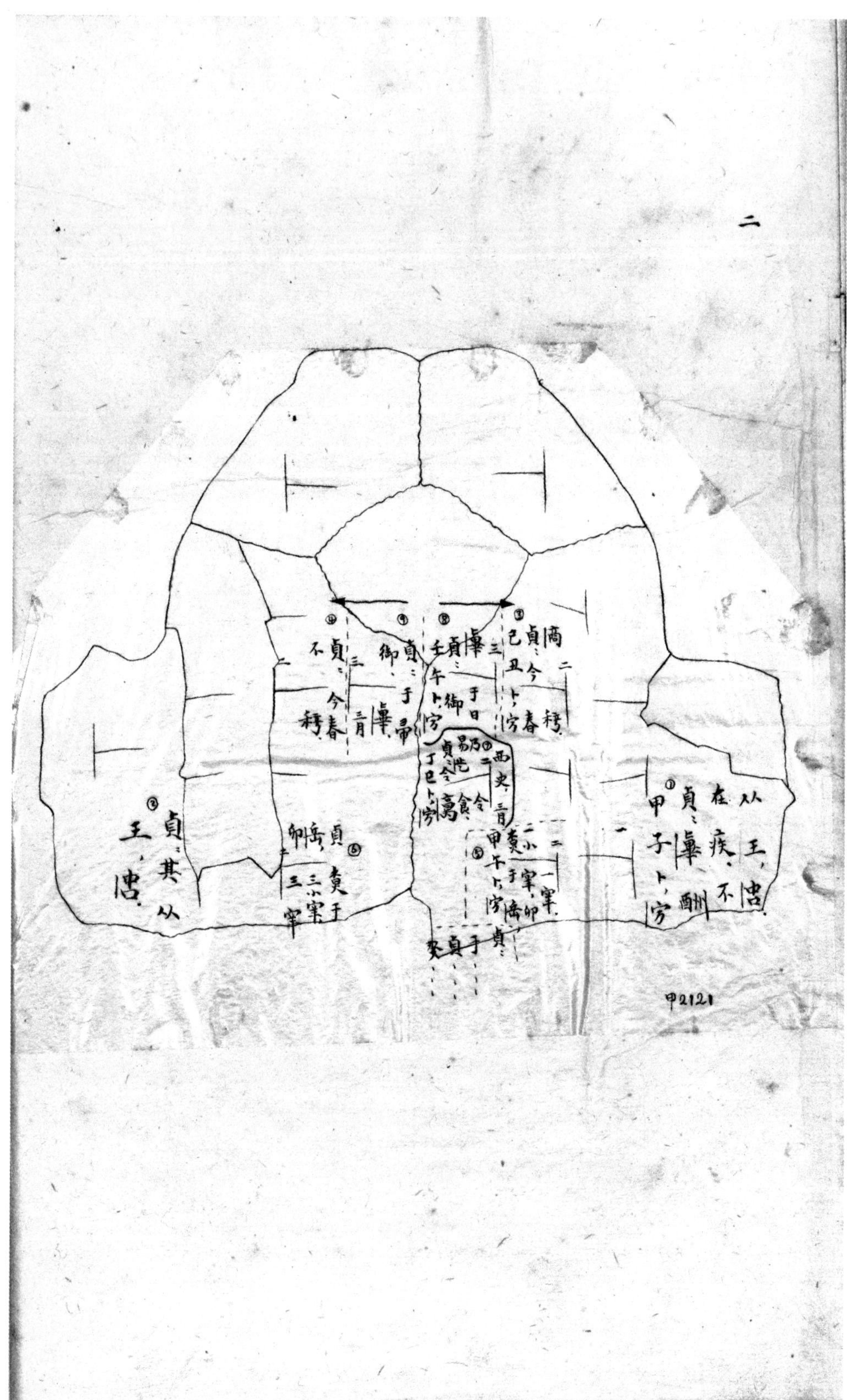
二
甲2121

甲骨叢編考釋　壹　甲　三一一四　二

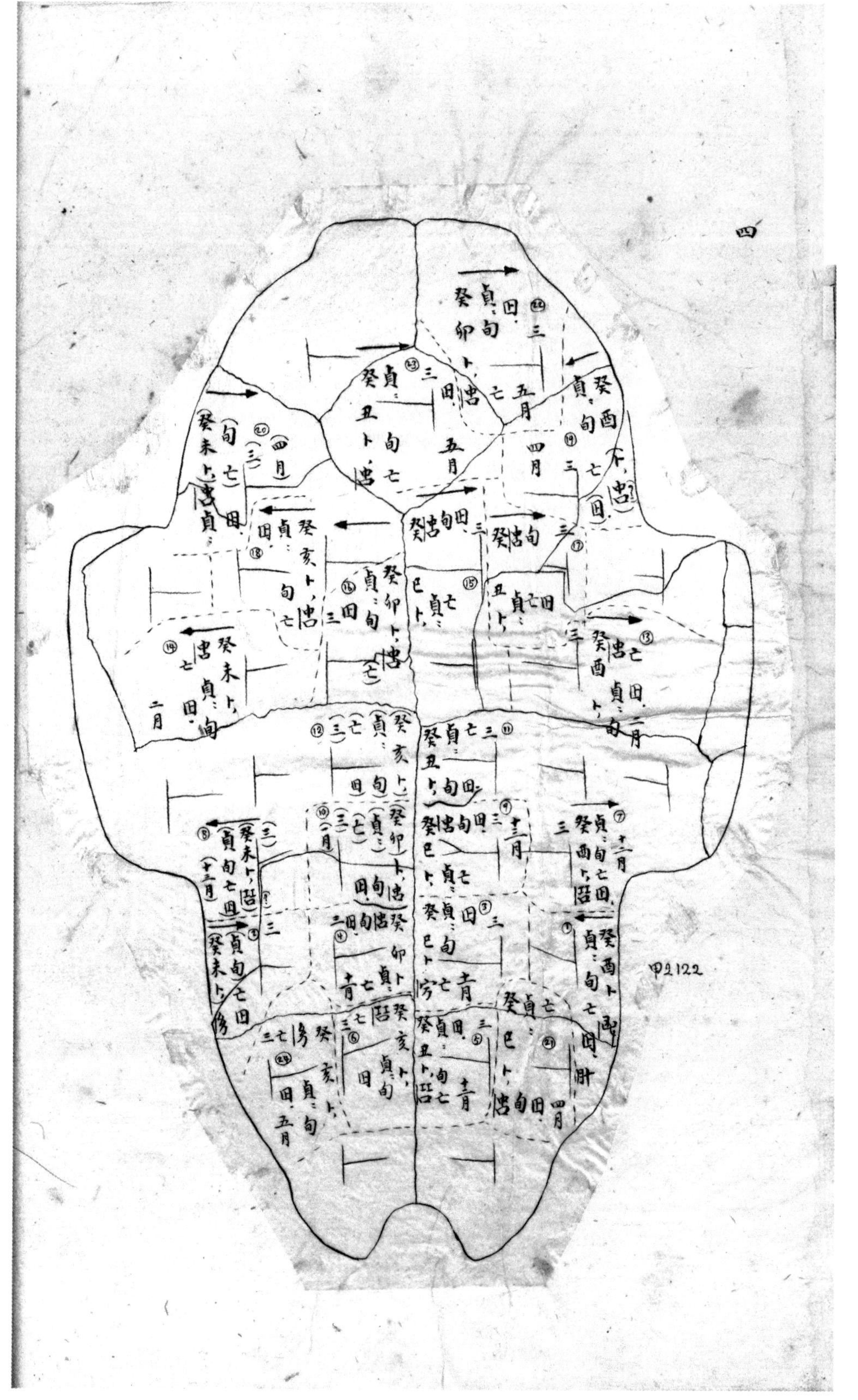
甲2122

壹甲四

由壹甲一至此，為殷墟發掘所得之大龜四版，著錄於殷墟文字甲編二一二一至二一二四。卜辭通纂別錄之一。詳細研究，見拙著大龜四版考釋。

兹補述第四版關於年曆之問題。

余作卜辭中所見之殷曆一文，曾舉此版為殷代有小月之證。謂小月必在十三月與一月之間，其分配有兩種可能，一種為

十三月大(甲戌朔)　癸未(十日)　癸巳(廿日)　癸卯(卅日)

一月小(甲辰朔)　癸丑十日　癸亥(廿日)　(二十九日壬申)

一種為

十三月小(甲戌朔)　癸未(十日)　癸巳(廿日)　(二十九日壬寅)

一月大(癸卯朔)　癸卯(一日)　癸丑(十一日)　癸亥(廿一日)

因此版十三月一月卜旬殘缺，而依前後各月推算，此兩月僅有五次卜旬，即五個癸日也。有此五癸之限，則其年必有閏月——十三月，十三月無論大小盡，其朔日必為甲戌。檢殷曆譜，年有閏而十三月甲戌朔者兩見，一在小乙十四年(公元前一三四七)，十三月甲戌大，合於第一種可能。一在武丁五十年(公元前一二九〇)，十三月甲戌小，合於第二種可能。由貞人為武丁時史，且出於同坑之他三甲，皆顯然為武

丁時物，故以後者為是。茲依譜排之。除此之外，武丁五十九年中，無第二「十三月甲戌朔」也。

武丁五十年（公元前一二九〇年　辛卯）

十月小（殷正）　乙巳（一日）（九月十九日）（儒略周日）（一二五〇五一三）　癸丑（九日）

癸亥（十九日）

癸酉（廿九日）　癸酉卜，㱿貞：旬亡囚。十月。

十一月大　甲戌（一日）（日食）（十月十八日）（一二五〇五四二）　癸未（十日）

癸巳（廿日）　癸巳卜，穷貞：旬亡囚。十一月。

癸卯（卅日）　癸卯卜，㞢貞：旬亡囚。十一月。

十二月大　甲辰（一日）（十一月十七日）（一二五〇五七一）　癸丑（十日）　癸丑卜，咠貞：旬亡囚。十二月。

癸亥（廿日）　癸亥卜，咠貞：旬亡囚。

癸酉（卅日）　癸酉卜，咠貞：旬亡囚。十二月。

十三月小　甲戌（一日）（十二月十七日）（一二五〇六〇二）（十六日乙丑）（一二八九年一月一日）　癸未（十日）

癸巳（廿日）　癸巳卜，㞢貞：旬亡囚。十三月。

武丁五十一年（公元前一二八九年　壬辰）

一月大　癸卯（一日）（一月十五日）（一二五〇六三〇）　癸卯（一日）

月	朔日	癸日	卜辭
		癸丑(十一日)	癸丑卜貞：旬亡𡆥。
		癸亥(廿一日)	
二月小	癸酉(一日)(二月十四日)(一二五〇六六〇)	癸酉(一日)	癸酉卜，㱿貞：旬亡𡆥。二月。
		癸未(十一日)	癸未卜，㱿貞：旬亡𡆥。二月。
		癸巳(廿一日)	
三月大	壬寅(一日)(三月十四日)(日食)(一二五〇六八九)(十六日丁巳 月食)	癸卯(二日)	癸卯卜，㱿貞：旬亡𡆥。
		癸丑(十二日)	癸丑卜，㱿貞：旬亡𡆥。
		癸亥(廿二日)	癸亥卜，㱿貞：旬亡𡆥。
四月小	壬申(一日)(四月十三日)(一二五〇七一九)	癸酉(二日)	癸酉(卜口)貞：旬亡(𡆥)。四月。
		癸未(十二日)	
		癸巳(廿二日)	癸巳卜，㱿貞：旬亡𡆥。四月。
五月大	辛丑(一日)(五月十二日)(一二五〇七四八)	癸卯(三日)	癸卯卜，㱿貞：旬亡𡆥。五月。
		癸丑(十三日)	癸丑卜，㱿貞：旬亡𡆥。五月。
		癸亥(廿三日)	癸亥卜，爭貞：旬亡𡆥。五月。

右表中十二月之癸酉，二月之癸酉，限制十三月，一月僅有五癸，雖有殘缺，此已爲堅強之證明矣。

曩有對余釋文補苴部分懷疑者，今更補充復原如下葉。其左右對稱，先下後上，先右後左，先中部後四隅或兩邊，為龜卜常例。全版皆於兆上註「三」，蓋卜旬不止一次，此其第三次，亦即第三版也。

月有大小，大月三十日，小月二十九日，故每月一日不能固定為甲日，此自然之理。關於一日非甲之確證，除貳骨二—六考釋所舉並此版四證外，尚有祖甲帝辛時祀譜日譜等足以證明者，具詳殷曆譜，茲不贅及。

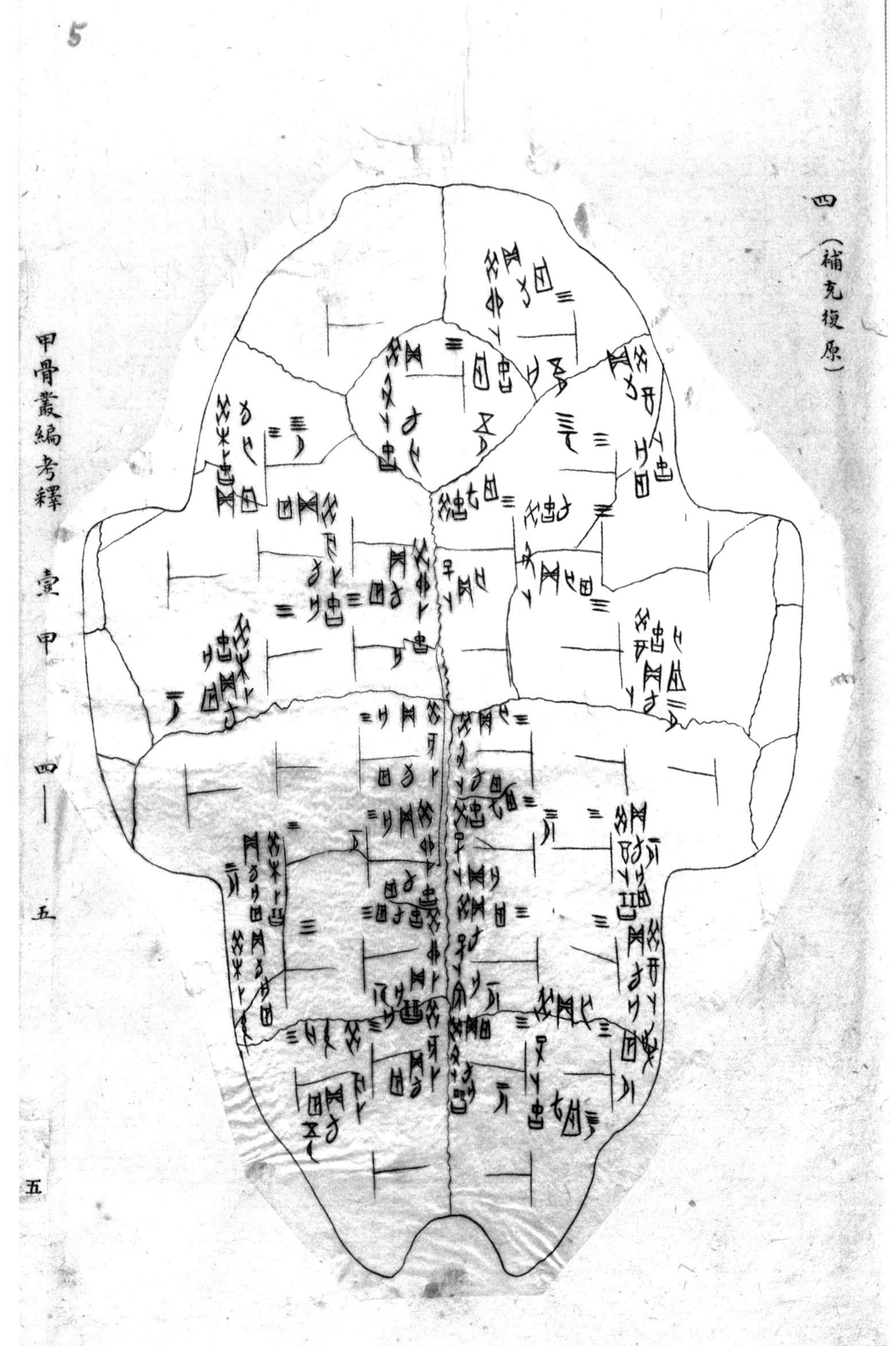
甲骨叢編考釋　壹甲　四—五
四（補充復原）
5
五

五（背甲）

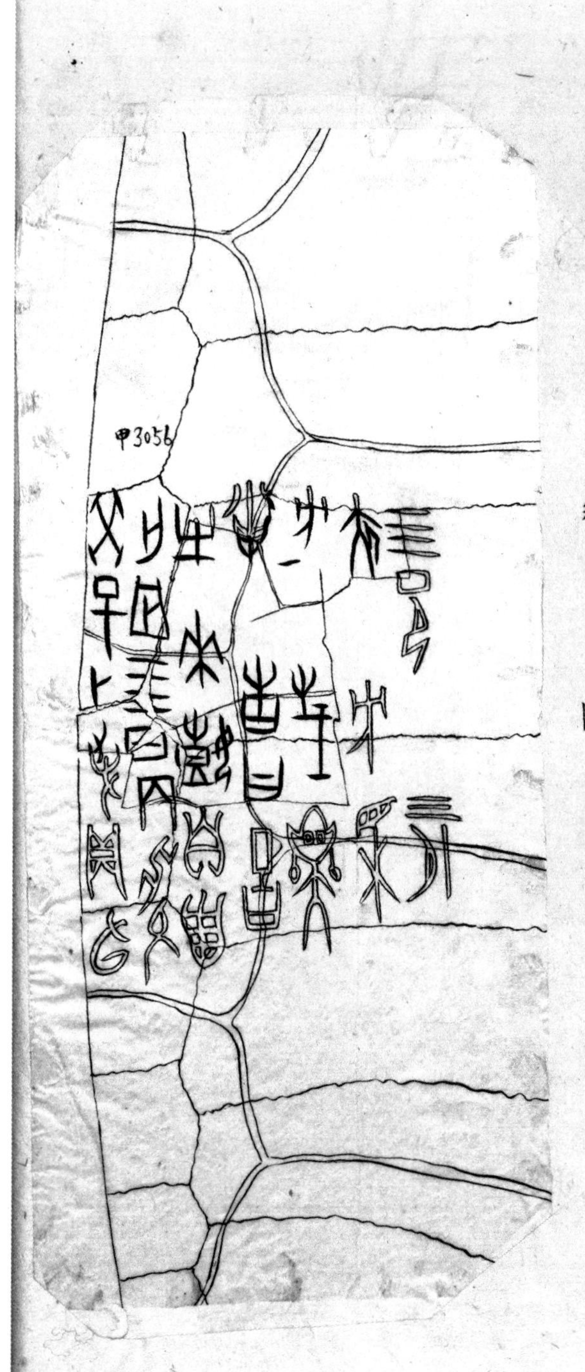

癸巳卜，㱿（貞：旬）
亡田。四日丙（申，允）
㞢來嬉，（自西：）
𠂤告曰：「（呂）
方一戈（魌），
陝，（方，杲，）
四邑」。（十三月）

甲骨叢編考釋　壹　甲　六——一三

六

珠1368　前5.6.4

(鐵114.1)

九

前3.24.4

一〇

鐵159.3

一二

鐵172.4

七

前6.11.5　前6.11.6

一一

(反面)

庫528

八

前6.11.4

一三

(反面)

北3.12.1(正,反)

(續4.30.8)

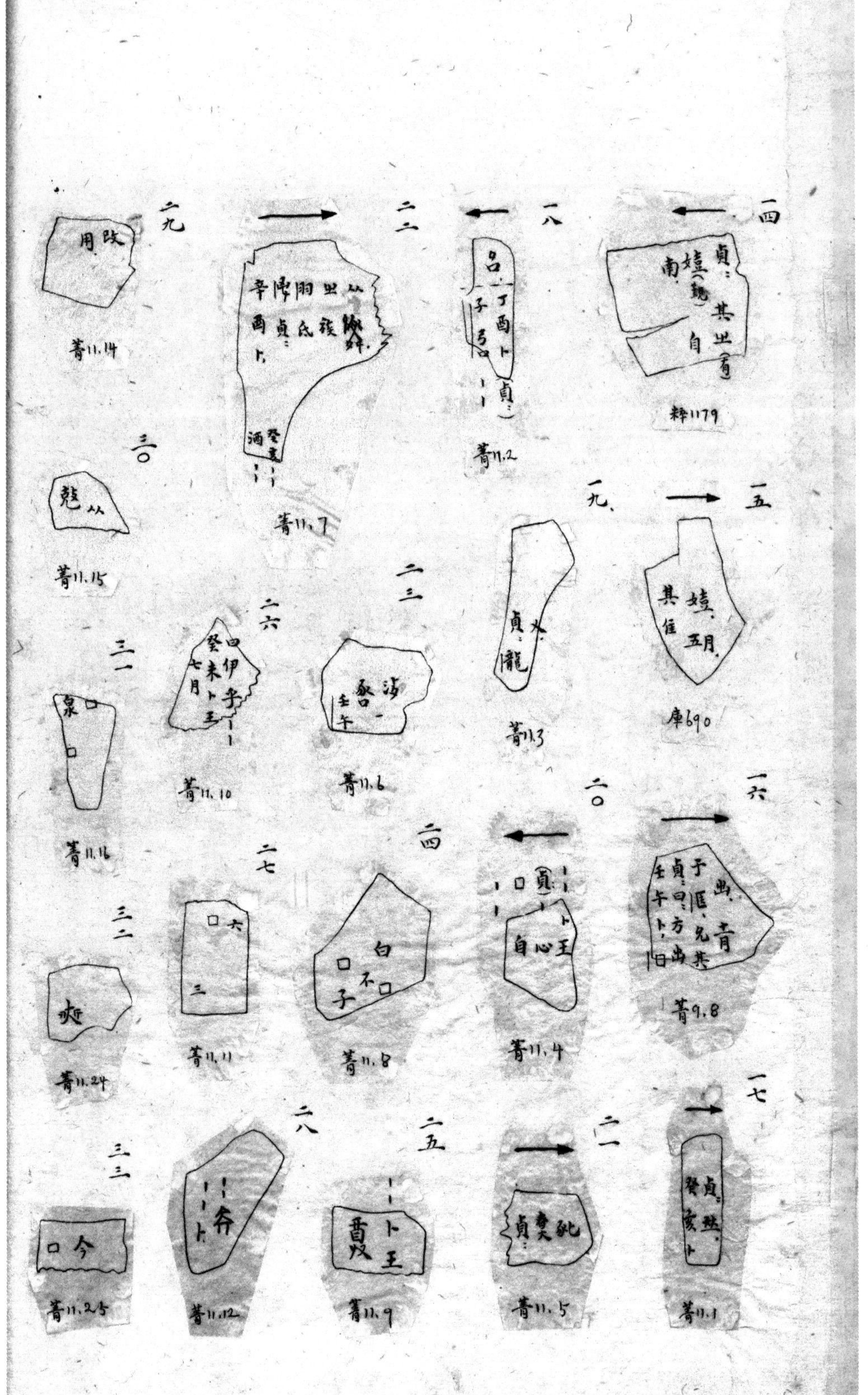

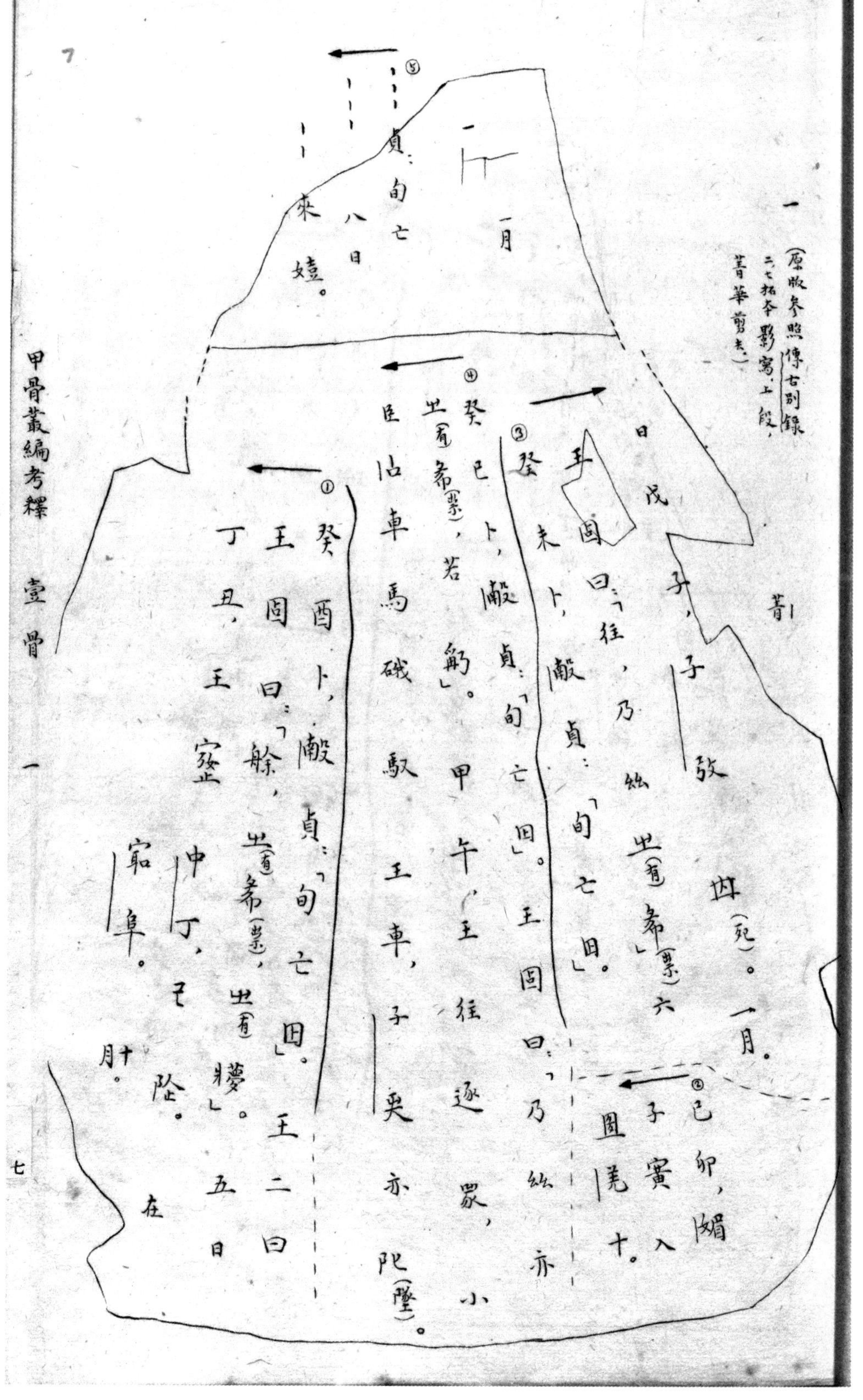
一
（原版參照傳古別錄二之拓本影寫上段，著華剪去。）
背1
日戊子，子㪔囚(死)。一月。
②己卯，媚子寅入，宜羌十。
王固曰：「往，乃丝㞢(有)希(祟)」六
③癸未卜，㱿貞：「旬亡𡆥。」王固曰：「乃丝亦
④癸巳卜，㱿貞：「旬亡𡆥。」甲午，王往逐兕，小
臣甾車馬硪馭王車，子央亦阺(墜)。
①癸酉卜，㱿貞：「旬亡𡆥。」王二曰
王固曰：「艅，㞢(有)希(祟)，㞢(有)夢。」五日
丁丑，王賓中丁，乞陟在
宿阜。十月。
⑤貞：旬亡
八日
来嬉。
一月

甲骨叢編考釋　壹骨　一　七

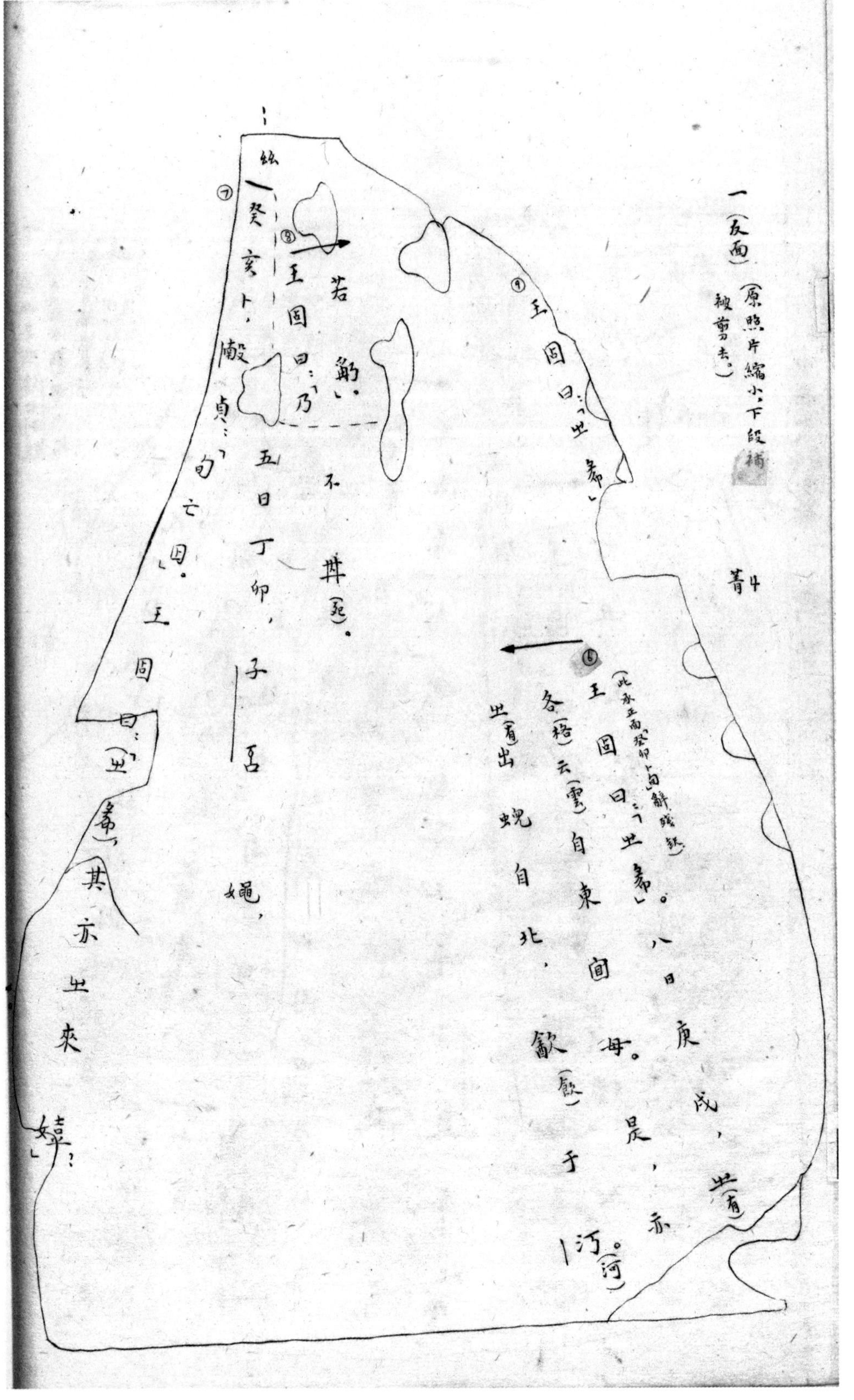
一（反面）（原照片縮小，下段補被剪去。）
菁4

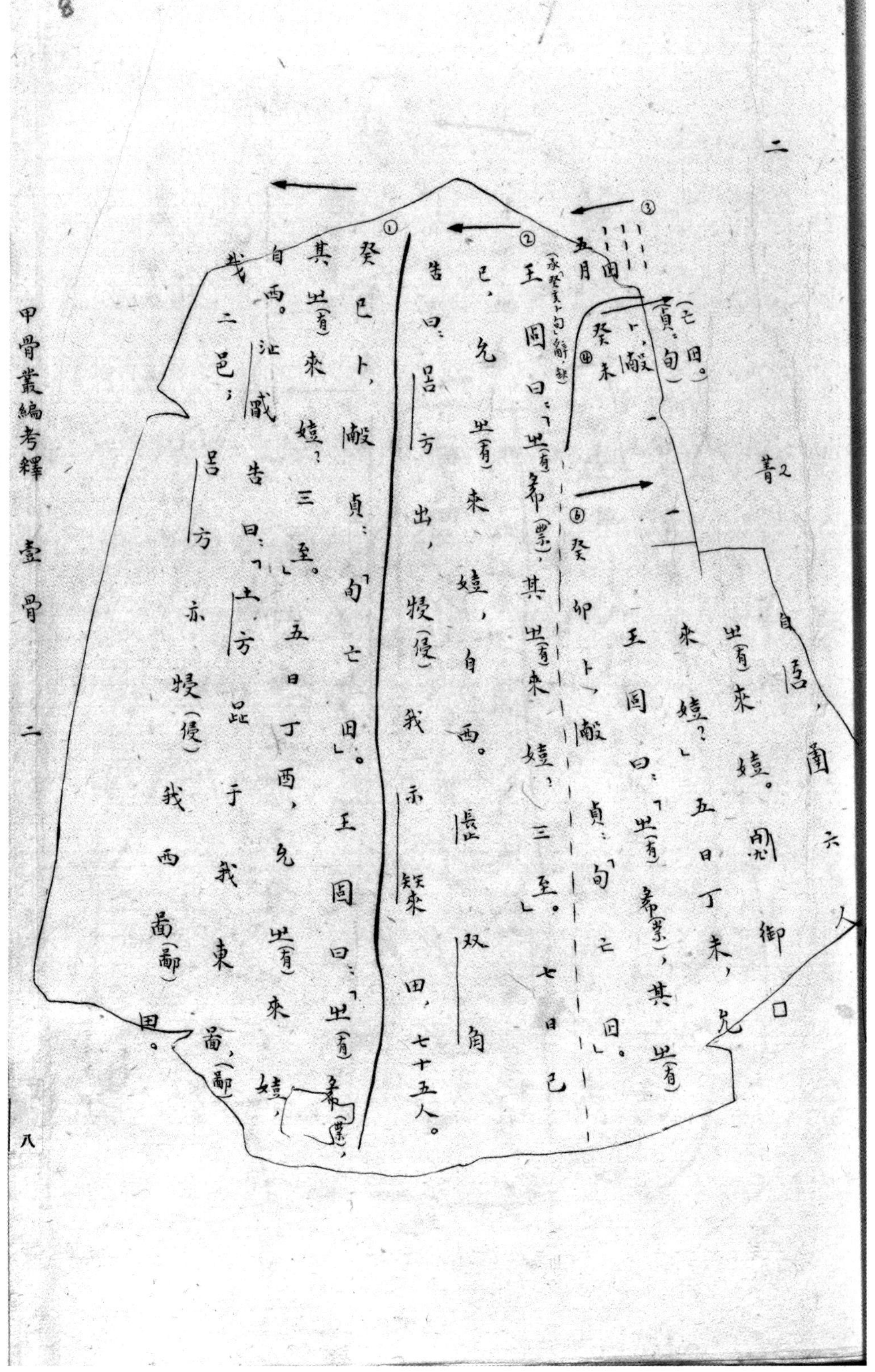

甲骨叢編考釋　壹骨　二
癸巳卜，㱿貞：旬亡𡆥。王固曰：㞢(有)希(祟)，其㞢(有)來嬄？三至。五日丁酉，允㞢(有)來嬄，自西。沚戓告曰：土方𢀛于我東啚(鄙)，𢦏二邑；𢀛方亦牧(侵)我西啚(鄙)田。
王固曰：㞢(有)希(祟)，其㞢(有)來嬄，三至。七日己巳，允㞢(有)來嬄，自西。長友角告曰：𢀛方出，牧(侵)我示𣏟田，七十五人。
八

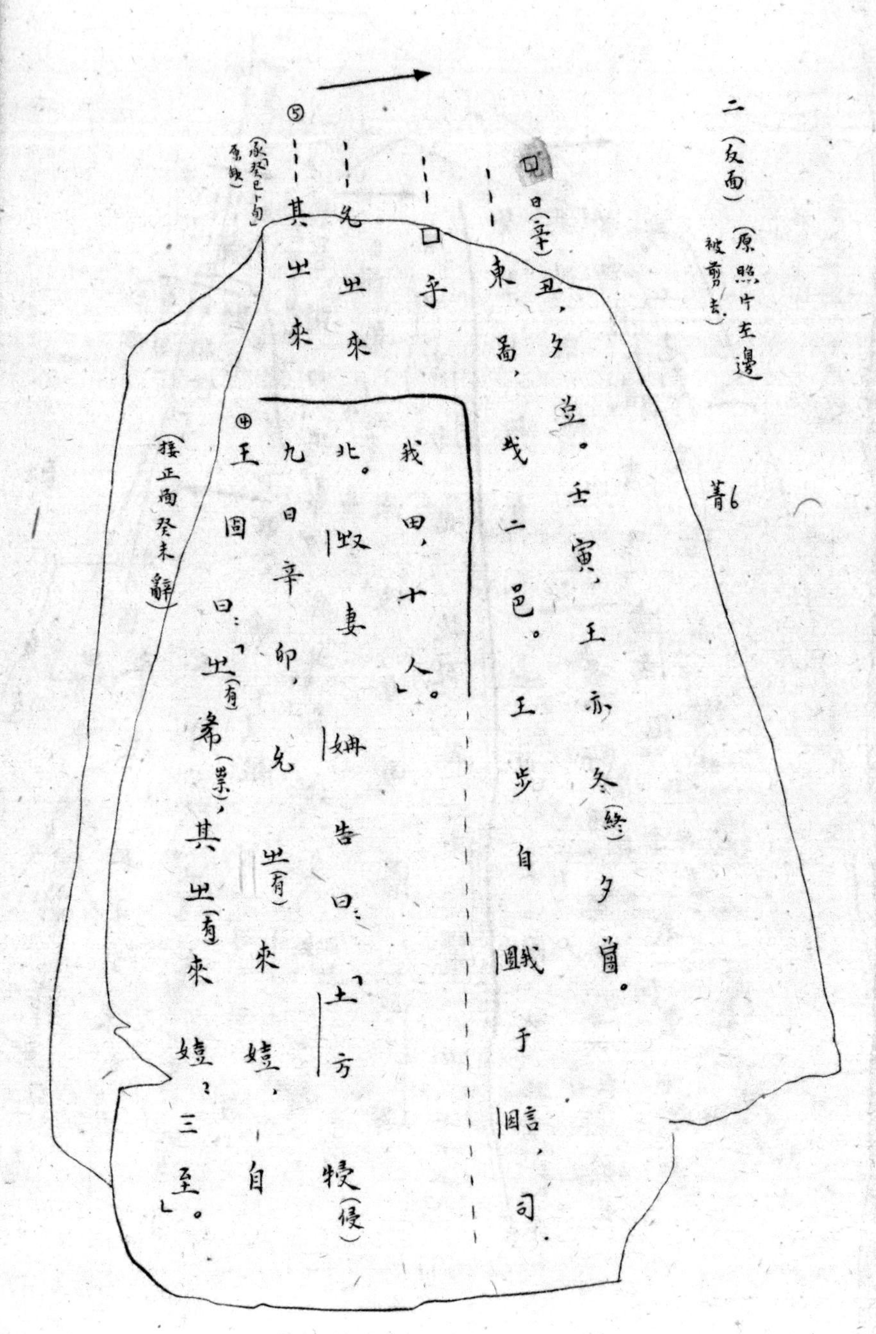

二（反面）（原照片左邊被剪去）
菁6
東啚，戈二邑。王步自圍，于圉言，司
我田，十人」。
王固曰：「㞢（有）希（祟），其㞢（有）來嬉？三至」。

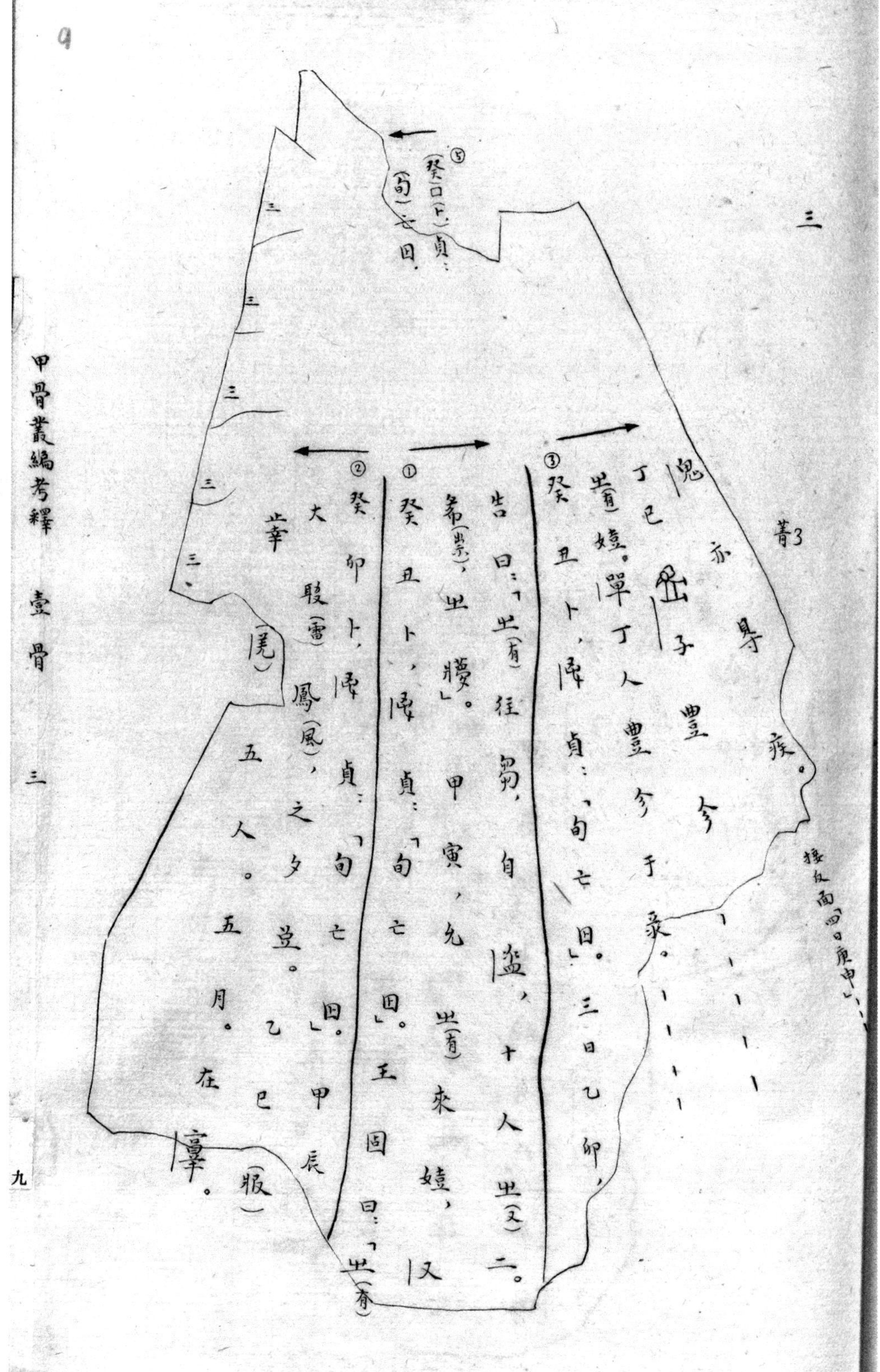
甲骨叢編考釋　壹骨　三
九
著3
接反面「四日庚申」
① 癸丑卜，㱿貞：「旬亡𡆥」。王固曰：「㞢（有）希（祟），㞢（有）夢」。甲寅，允㞢（有）來媗，又告曰：「㞢（有）往芻，自盜，十人㞢（又）二。
② 癸卯卜，㱿貞：「旬亡𡆥」。甲辰大𩇯（雷）鳳（風），之夕皿。乙巳𤰔（服）羍（羌）五人。五月。在𩫏。
③ 癸丑卜，㱿貞：「旬亡𡆥」。三日乙卯，㞢（有）媗。單丁人豐夕于彔。丁巳𡆥子豐夕。鬼亦得疾。
⑤ 癸□（卜），貞：（旬）亡𡆥。

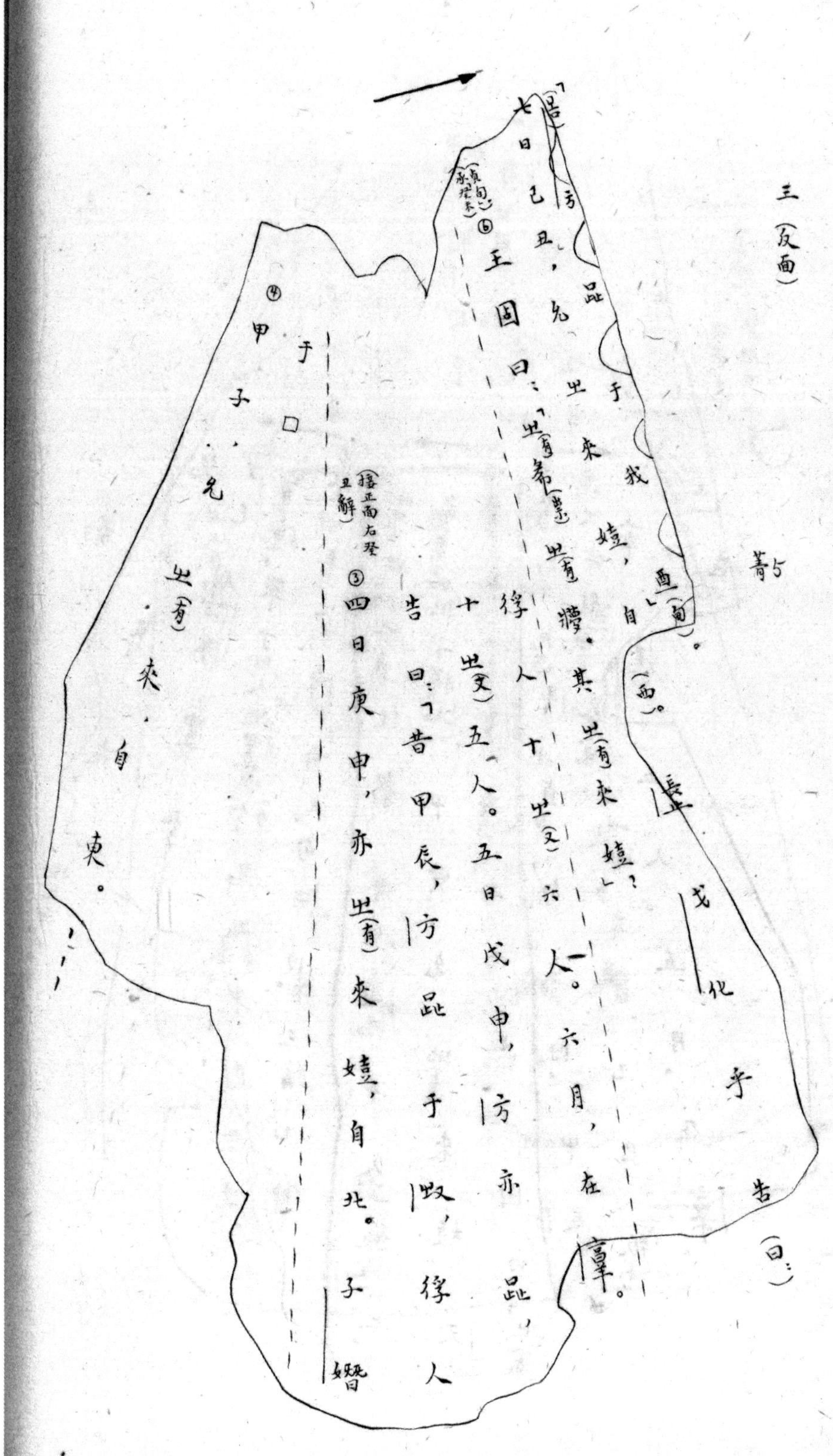
三（反面）
菁5
七日己丑，允㞢來嬄，自西。
王固曰：「㞢（有）祟（祟），其㞢（有）來嬄，乞至。
十㞢（又）五人。五日戊申，方亦正，俘人十㞢（又）六人。六月，在𩫏。
告曰：「昔甲辰，方正于蚁，俘人
四日庚申，亦㞢（有）來嬄，自北。子㛸
甲子，允㞢（有）來嬄，自東。
戈化乎告（曰：）

四

（原照片上，左，被剪去）

菁7

⑩丙午卜，永貞：射□（接反面「王固曰其隻」）隹隻（虎）。

⑨甲辰卜，𡆥貞：□娶冥。

⑪丁未卜，宕貞：今……

⑥庚子卜，㱿貞：「翌辛丑，啟」。（接反面「貞：翌辛丑」）

④己亥卜，㱿貞：王曰：「侯虎，余其𢀛女史受」。

③戊戌卜，㱿貞：王曰：「侯虎，母（毋）歸，御」。

⑤貞：王曰：「侯虎𢀛女史𢀛受」。

①丁酉卜，㱿貞：乎宅𣑵。

②戊戌卜，㱿貞：王曰：「侯虎，往！余不𣑵，其合（會）氏乃史，歸」。

二

一

四（反面）（原照片左右，上均剪過）

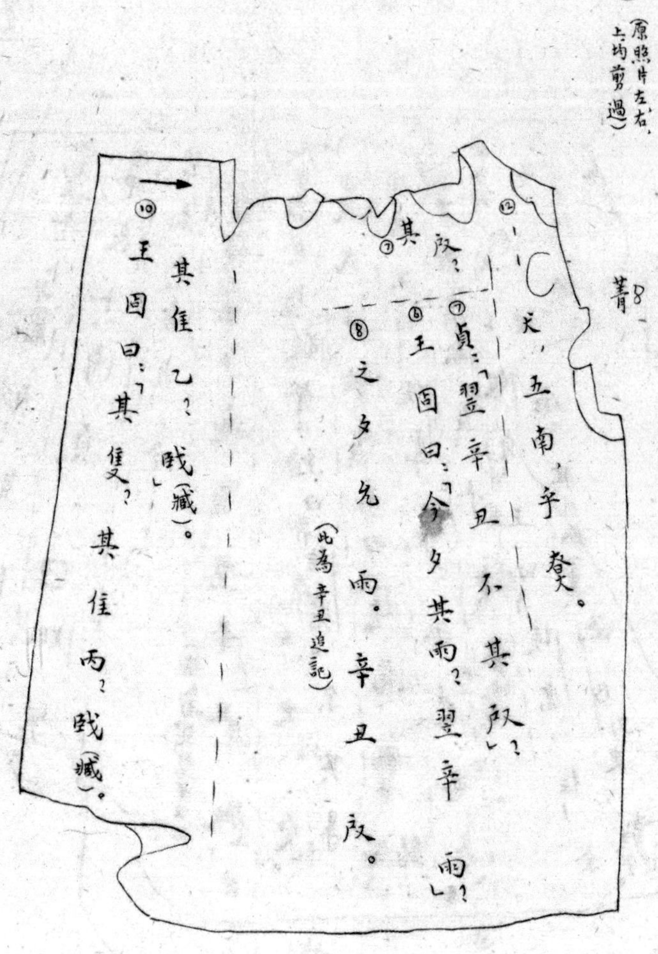

壹骨一—四

此為羅振玉氏所藏，著錄於殷虛書契菁華，凡八片，實則大胛骨三，普通胛骨一，共為四版之正反兩面也。皆為武丁中葉前後兩三年間之卜辭，同文同大之胛骨尚多，散見各書中之大字殘片皆是。惟不如此四版之保存完好耳。今精摹揭之，可注意者六事：

一、武丁時代之偉觀。此武丁中葉之極盛時代，其史臣書法，久經鍛煉，已達爐火純青之候，故能刀筆運用，得心應手，行款起承，自有氣韻，非拘謹者所敢為，一時之偉大作風也。取原拓影本審視之，可見其筆力之雄厚，為此後各期所無。余之摹本，僅具皮相而已。余於大連羅氏寓廬，曾目覩原物，字畫塗朱猶鮮，可想見三千年前之當日，史𢿱諸人，左操大骨，右執刀筆，書契既竣，潤色有加，骨版光澤，朱墨耀目，有不得意洋洋者乎？

二、大胛骨之復原。此中三大胛骨，余據殷虛古器物圖錄及中村不折氏大骨等，參訂復原。初余疑是象胛骨（羅氏亦云然），詢之古生物學者楊鍾健氏，則決其為大水牛之肩胛。第四版，則常見之普通牛胛骨也。所據影拓本或已縮小，故尺寸不必準確，覽之者，知其約略之輪廓而已。

三、追記占驗之辭。凡辭中「某日某干支」以下，皆為卜旬之後某日所追記，乃記事辭，非卜辭。亦有全辭記事者，如一版②，不見「卜」「貞」字也。追記辭，四版共二十一見。

一　①「五日丁丑」以下　④「甲午，王往」以下　③「六日戊子」以下

⑤「八日」以下　⑥「八日庚戌」以下　⑦「五日丁卯」以下

二　①「五日丁酉」以下　②「七日己巳」以下　⑭「九日辛卯」以下

⑤「卜予（告曰）」以下　「辛丑」以下　「壬寅」以下（三次追記）

⑥「五日丁未」以下

三　①「甲寅允出」以下　②「甲辰」以下　「乙巳」以下（二次追記）

③「三日乙卯」以下　「〔三〕日丁巳」以下　「四日庚申」以下（三次追記）

⑥「七日己丑」以下

四　⑧「之夕允雨」以下（此不繫日，當為辛丑記）

追記占驗，乃卜期之風習，他期不多見。

四、正反兩面文辭銜接之例。此亦緣追記之事項無定，正面原辭之下，為部位所限，乃續書於同版之反面也。此例四版皆有，具見釋文。此例之發見，為治契學者闢一新門徑，若干卜辭，日辰之連貫，月份之補足，事類之穿插，繫屬，皆賴以證明。考釋壹骨一七，即其例也。

五、每版卜辭之次第。各版皆取數字加圈以誌之。細加審辨，可見貞人書契，有恣情書寫，氣魄宏放者；有迴避委婉，將就局勢者；有加之界線，分其畛域者；有正面不足，繼以反面者，皆先後之序有以限之也。

六、同為前後三年間之物。四版除第三版已見考釋壹骨一七年表武丁廿九年之外，其一、二、四版，亦為武丁二十八年至三十年之物。詳載殷曆譜中。茲畧舉其年、干支、事類、月份，皆有互資聯絡之關係也。

一　①、②，武丁廿八年　③以下，廿九年（考釋七年表未收入）

二　①至⑥，廿九年（考釋七年表未收入）

三　①至⑥，廿九年

四　①至⑫　卅年

關於四版之出土地，據余所考知者，當在朱家十四畝地中部，殷墟發掘團所開E區之北，余第一次試掘之9坑，其原儲藏之窖穴矣。出土時，在清光緒三十年，據甲骨年表：

冬，小屯村地主朱坤，率領農佃，大舉挖掘甲骨文字於村北洹河南岸朱氏田中，搭蓆棚，起爐竈，工作甚久。所得甲骨盈數車。

此四版者，殆「數車」中之菁華矣。後六年，乃為羅振常所得。

羅振常於宣統三年春，奉乃兄振玉之命，偕范恒軒赴安陽購求甲骨文字。四版即此行所得，見羅著洹洛訪古游記，記四版來歷甚詳，摘錄之，亦可作四版之軼史觀也。

壹骨一。此版得於清宣統三年二月廿八日。羅記云：

二十八日。是日計所得龜骨已不少，而資斧將竭，其所餘僅可再收一二日。恒軒謂余：「此次大塊不多，前僅得大塊一，（原註：《書契菁華》第四葉（按：此註誤，《菁》四為一之反面，蓋事後追註，誤以為兩版也。））然骨雖大而字少（按：當指《殷虛古器物圖錄》所載之大骨）。昨得二片，則骨大字多，然有破缺（當指《壹骨》三、四兩版，二十七日得。），終不如昨見潼朱之大片。此片如京估至，必以善價將去。殊不能捨。不如以二日之資單購此片。」余亦謂然。餐後，渠獨至小屯，留余在寓，檢點包紮各物。並約：「如此片可得，明日即運物北行，再携資來購買。不成，明日續收一日，後日成行。」匆匆遂去。

恒軒去二三時，欣然歸來，隨一土人，提柳筐，卧大骨於中。恒軒出骨筐中，如捧圭璧，蓋即昨日議價未成者也。（原註：《書契》第一葉（按：即《壹骨》二））土人收資去，恒軒乃言：「初雖增價，彼愈堅持。後告以余等將他往，可售則售，不可則已，匆匆欲行。有一老者留其姑坐，而與其子及諸人密議，似欲買某姓之地，將以此為地價者。良久，乃議決售之。」此片有百餘字，數段皆文字完全，為骨片中所僅見。此家有此片已久，（按：已六年矣）小屯人及估客多知之，待價而估，不肯輕售。余等初至小屯時，即向索觀，時並無價，遂無可商。昨日忽出此，且有定價，即因欲購地之故。適逢其會，竟得成議，信乎物各有主也。彼之藏此，飢不可食，寒不可衣，易而為田，則取之無盡，為計良得。而我亦得此瓌寶，誠所謂「交易而退，各得其所」矣。恒軒之欣喜，與余得磬字無異。摩挲久之，因謚為「卜骨之王」。余亦以磬字示之，相與軒渠。

13

壹骨二。此版得於同年三月十三日。記云：

十三日。……乃提早午餐，邁步出門，至彼（小屯村）後，專議佳品，謂吾輩將他往，今將價加足，不成，則將舍旃。磋議良久，皆就緒。尋常品亦購數宗。最後僅餘二三筐未留，皆棄材也。滿載而歸，兩人均欣躍。

十四日。早起，檢昨日所得，大小相錯，分別之，則大者中者二百五十五塊，小者一千零三十塊，為到此收買最多之一日。有數大片，有一片滿字，雖非全文，所缺不多。（原註）書契菁華第二葉（按即壹骨二）此骨片之王猶多數字，彼稱王，此亦可稱公也。又一片，字不多，中間亦全文。（原註）書契菁華第六葉（按菁六，乃壹骨二之反面。羅氏記付印在民國廿五年，寫時參看菁華，已不知六葉與二葉原為一版之正反兩面，故有此誤。）

壹骨三、四。此兩版約得於同年二月廿七日。記云：

二十七日。檢視所得，視前日為多。因昨夕計議，佳者難成，每日所得太少，不如大小美惡兼收，可期迅速。故所得驟增，前日未成者，亦多議定。計大小一千數百塊，為到此得骨最多之一日。

二十八日。昨日所得，以小塊龜甲為多，中、大者少，然得二大骨。（原注）見殷虛書契菁華第三葉、第五葉。（按此亦羅氏之誤，菁三、五，即壹骨三之正反兩面，非二版。疑指菁華三與七葉，即壹骨三、四之正面也）尚有一塊全文，滿字而塗朱者，(按指滿一，本編壹骨二)索價過昂，未能購定。

一二兩版大骨，當為羅振常氏所能憶及者，其購入之經過，記載不致有誤，三、四兩版之記載則不免附會為之，蓋前者乃其特別注意之物，其敘述鋪張盡致，為當時實情。餘則取菁華所收，隨意註入。羅為經手購買之一人，所謂「摩挲久之」者，豈不知一骨之正反兩面有文字，而誤以菁華所收之八葉為八片大骨也。

羅氏於宣統三年二月二十一日，曾至小屯村調查甲骨出土情形。記云：

出(王)龜甲地，在村後田中，有二段。

一，為舊發掘地。在村(後)北偏東二三百步，掘於三十餘年前，今無骨矣。

一，為新發掘地。又在舊地北數百步，始掘於十餘年前，骨尚未盡。土人掘一次，取骨後即填平。新地有一穴正掘，云此為田主僱人發掘，已七八日，尚未得骨。由村後迤邐而北，中間為一帶高地，較平地高二三尺，龜甲多出此。及近水涘，地漸低削，土人謂出骨最多處，面積約十三畝云。

所謂舊坑，據其附圖，乃余等發掘之A區，為「劉家二十畝地」，鐵雲藏龜一書所收，出於此，皆一二期物。所謂新坑，乃在E區之北，余第一次發掘之2，6，9，10，11—18各坑所在，為朱坤之「十四畝地」，正如余所調查者。

五

庫1516

（亥）、魌、㳄、㝬、方、允、𢦏），

……（齒）三旬㞢（有）六日，虎，辛……

……石之齒，今之㞢𠂤，……

……昔我舊臣……

（丙子卜），㱿貞：𠂤（師）其（㞢（有）囚（禍））

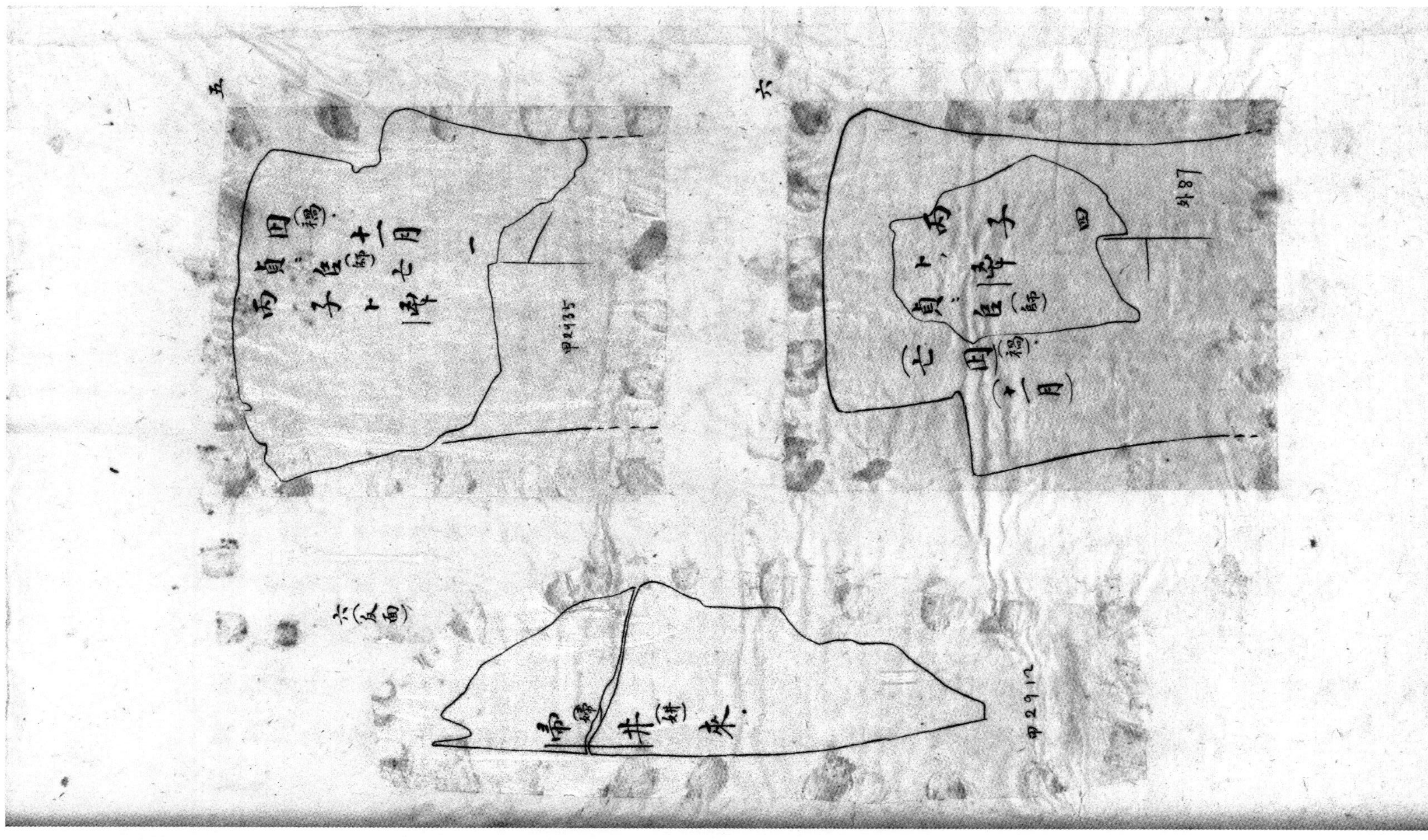
五
甲2935
六
外87
六（反面）
甲2912

15

六

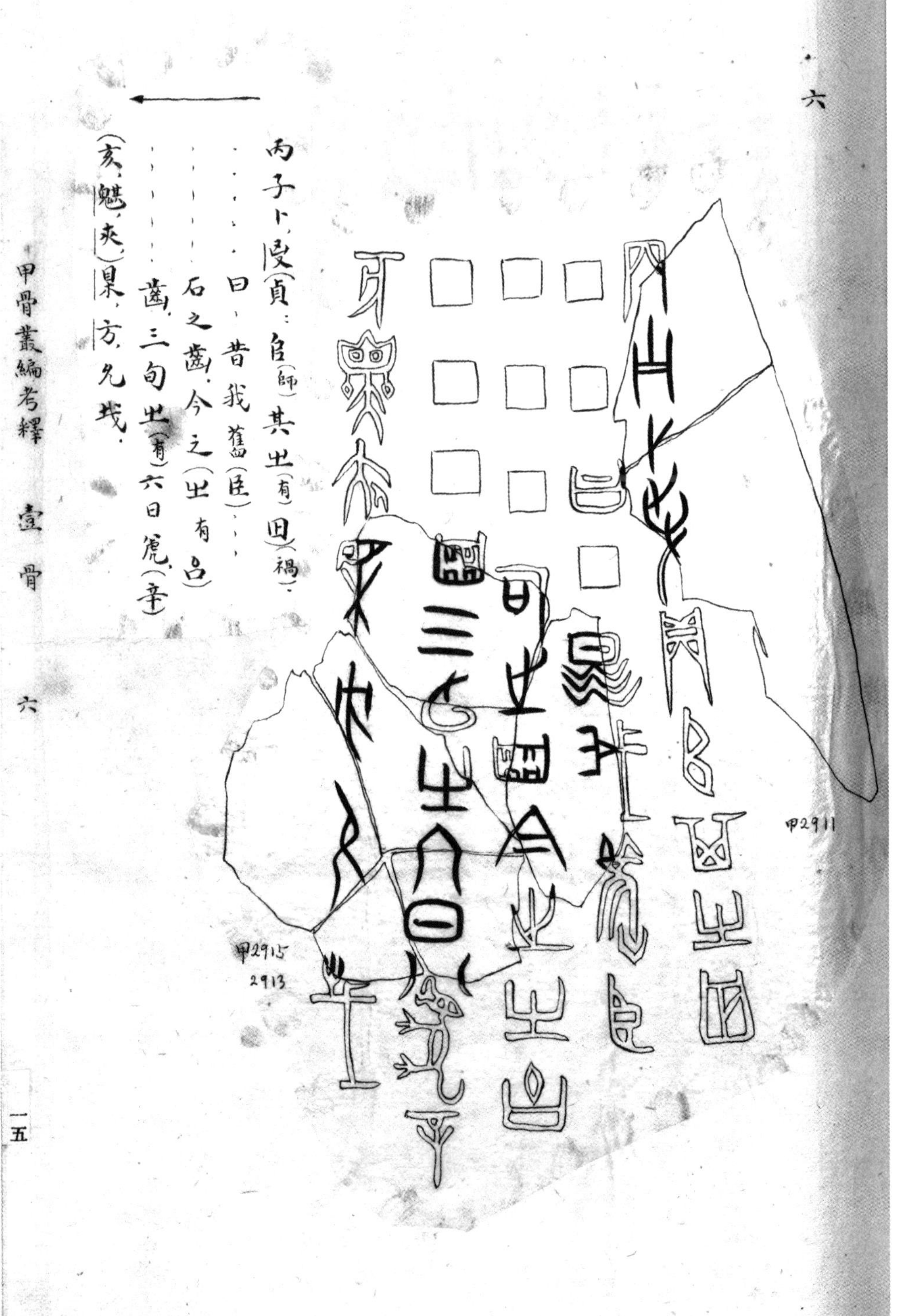

丙子卜，㱿（貞）：𠂤（師）其㞢（有）𡆥（禍）·
……曰：昔我舊𦣞（臣）……
……石之齒，今之（㞢有𠂤）
……齒，三旬㞢（有）六日虎（辛）
（亥）魁（夾）杲，方允𢦏。

甲骨叢編考釋　壹　骨　六

壹骨五｜六

此兩版太殘碎，補綴煞費匠心。初，余見壹骨五下段殘片，文有「昔我舊臣」，「二旬㞢（有）六日」，甚注意。繼於甲二九一三、二九一五（壹骨六下左），辭相似，合之，知二乃三之缺畫，蓋「三旬㞢（有）六日」也。五版下有辛之殘字，三十六日為辛，則卜之日必為丙，乃又發見「丙子卜㱿」（六）之一骨邊，而五版亦爭貞也。兩版字大，骨大，四部必大，得甲二九三五，文為「丙子卜，爭貞：旬亡囚」，十一月。「一」，乃大骨之上部，又得外八七，同部位而為第四卜，知此類大胛骨同文者至少為四版。凡骨之正反兩貞，分列上下，上貞「旬亡囚」，下必貞「旬㞢（有）囚（禍）」，而五版尚存「旬其」二字，知下缺「㞢囚」二字也。至此，兩骨之組成，已不成問題矣。（兩四部不必為下半之同版，然左右行恰為對稱，姑合繪之，以見全形）。

文辭之擬補，除兩版互足者外，則為「四邑之𢦏」（説詳壹骨一七考釋三）。六版左邊殘存「杲方先𢦏」四字，杲為邑名，僅武丁時出現，他處不有。以「魌夾方杲」被𢦏事例之，知所缺乃「魌夾」二字。此卜上為「旬亡囚」，下為「旬其㞢囚」，且有王固之語（昔我舊臣），知史爭必於十一月丙子卜後，進記發生之禍事以證其「有禍」也。十一月有丙子，則三十六日辛亥，必在十二月，而四邑被𢦏在十三月來嬉報告，則四邑被𢦏實即十二月之辛亥，故曰「三旬有六日虎辛亥，魌夾，杲方先𢦏」，而進記於丙子之卜，以證其驗也。以此擬補，字數亦合。餘詳後考。

16

七

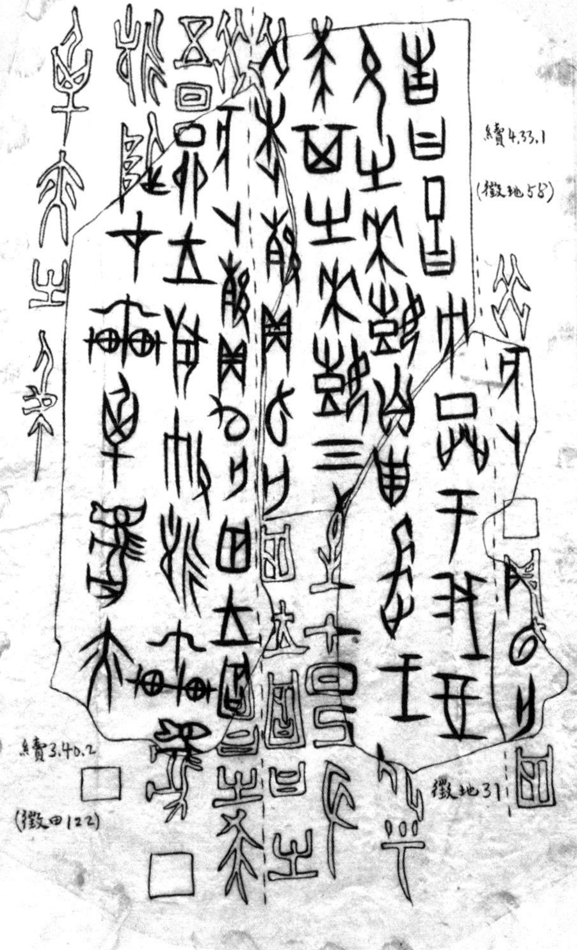

七（反面）

七

……亦焚面三。

⑥(曰：「)舌方)𢀛我奠，戋四邑」。

(四日)壬辰，亦㞢來，自西，𢦏乎告

②王固曰：「㞢希」。八日庚子，戈𦎫羌

人，改㞢圍，二人。

④王固曰：「㞢希，㞢見」。

③王固曰：

(其)㞢來嬉，其隹丙，不(吉)」

⑤(癸)亥卜□貞：旬亡囚

告曰：「舌方𢀛于我奠」。

允㞢來嬉，自西。長𢀛戈化(乎)告

希，其㞢來嬉，三至」。七日己(丑)，

⑥癸未卜，㱿貞：「旬亡囚」。王固曰：「㞢

①(癸)亥卜，㱿貞：「旬亡囚」。王固(曰：「㞢希」)

(五日)丁卯，王獸敝，𧿿車馬□

(𧿿)陷在車，𡕷馬亦□，

(𡕷亦㞢𠈉)。

壹骨七

此版正反兩面文辭銜接，如釋文。四日壬辰一段，本當與癸未卜旬辭連屬，追記於下，所以契於反面者，因甲骨刻辭皆先疏後密，左一癸亥先卜，右一癸亥次之，癸未卜時，中僅四行地位，第一次己丑之追記尚可容，第二次壬辰追記，乃不得不轉移於反面也。日次相貫，文皆下行而右，是其證。

補苴部分，皆有依據，分列如次：

正面　①　「曰出希」　據壹骨一二同文版　　「五日」　據壹甲六同文版

「祝陟」　據壹骨一三同文版　　「阜亦出徭」　據壹骨一二、一四同文版

⑤　「囚。王固曰：「出」　據常例　　「七日己丑」　據壹骨三反面同文

「化乎」　據壹骨三反面同文

反面　⑥　「四日」　據己丑至壬辰日數　　「䧹乎告」「四邑」　據殘餘部分

「呂方」　說見考釋一七、(一)2

八

（「癸巳卜𡧊」、「四日丙申」，據壹甲五同文補入，「𢀛方」說見考釋壹(一)2。）

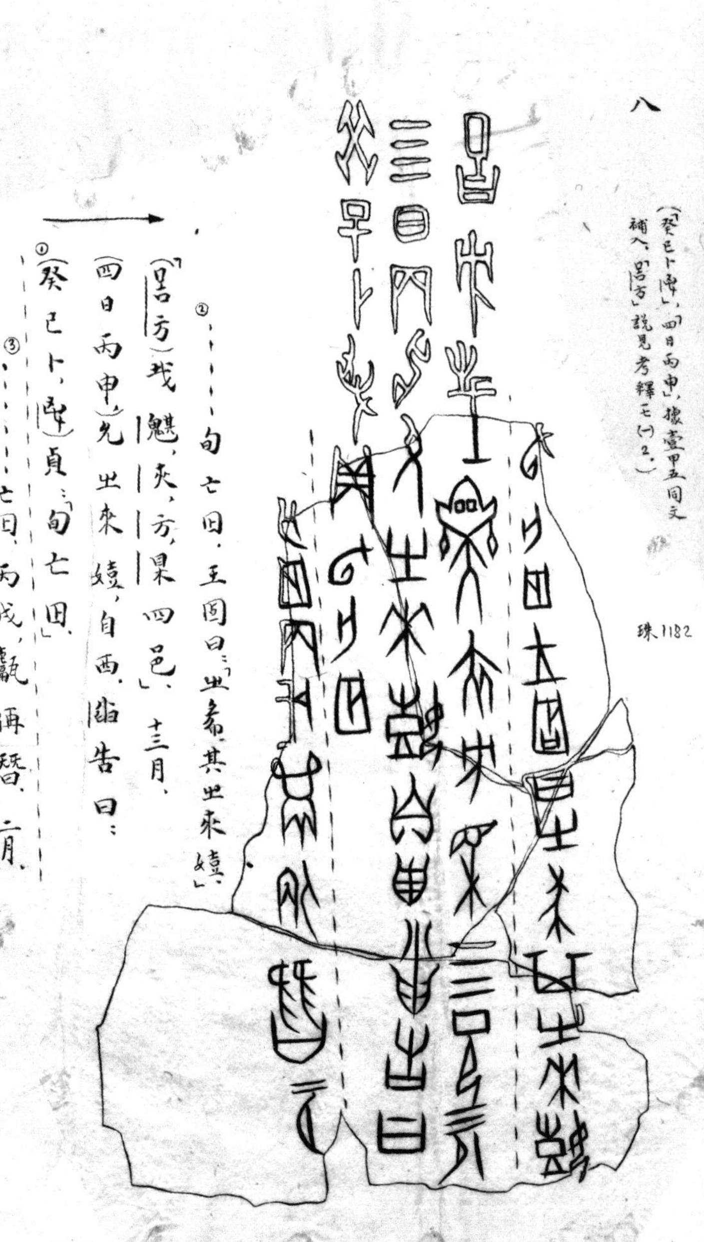

珠1182

② ……旬亡𡆥。王固曰：「㞢希，其㞢來嬄。」

「𢀛方」𢦏魅、夾、方、枼四邑」。十三月。

（四日丙申）允㞢來嬄，自西。𦣻告曰：

① （癸巳卜，𡧊）貞：「旬亡𡆥。」

③ ……亡𡆥。丙戌，𩰫侑……二月。

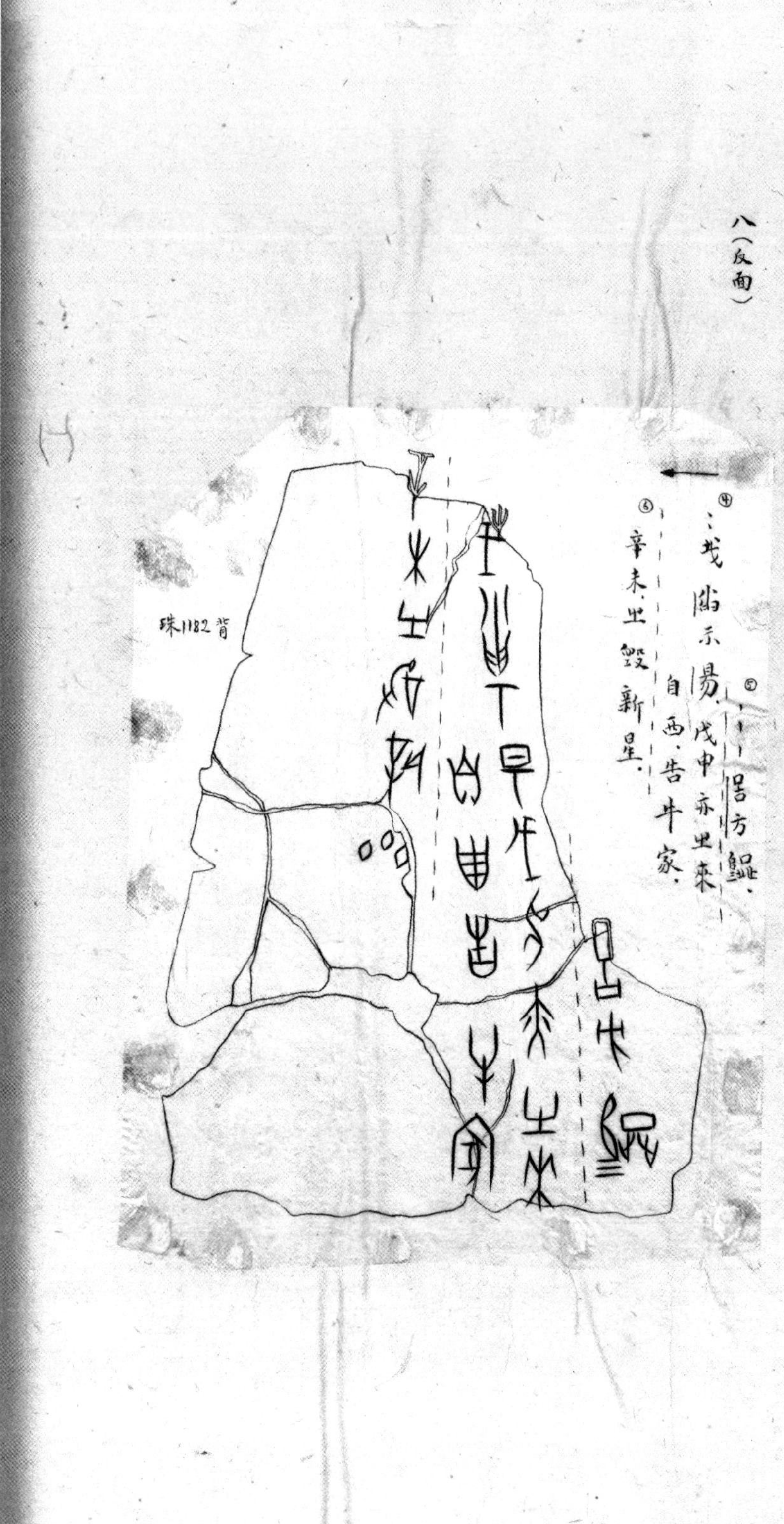
八（反面）
珠1182背

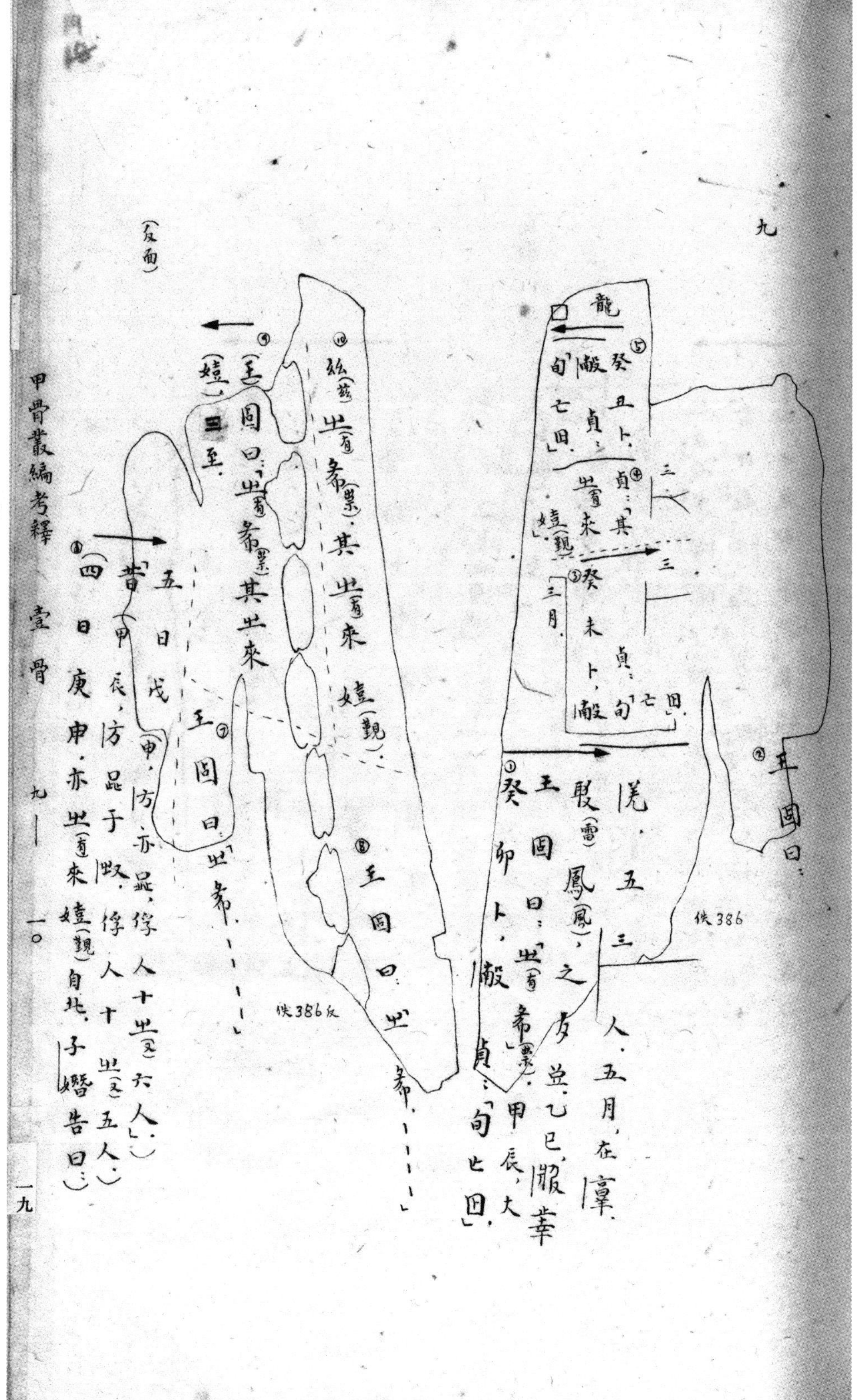
九
(反面)
甲骨叢編考釋　壹骨　九—一〇
佚386
佚386反
一九

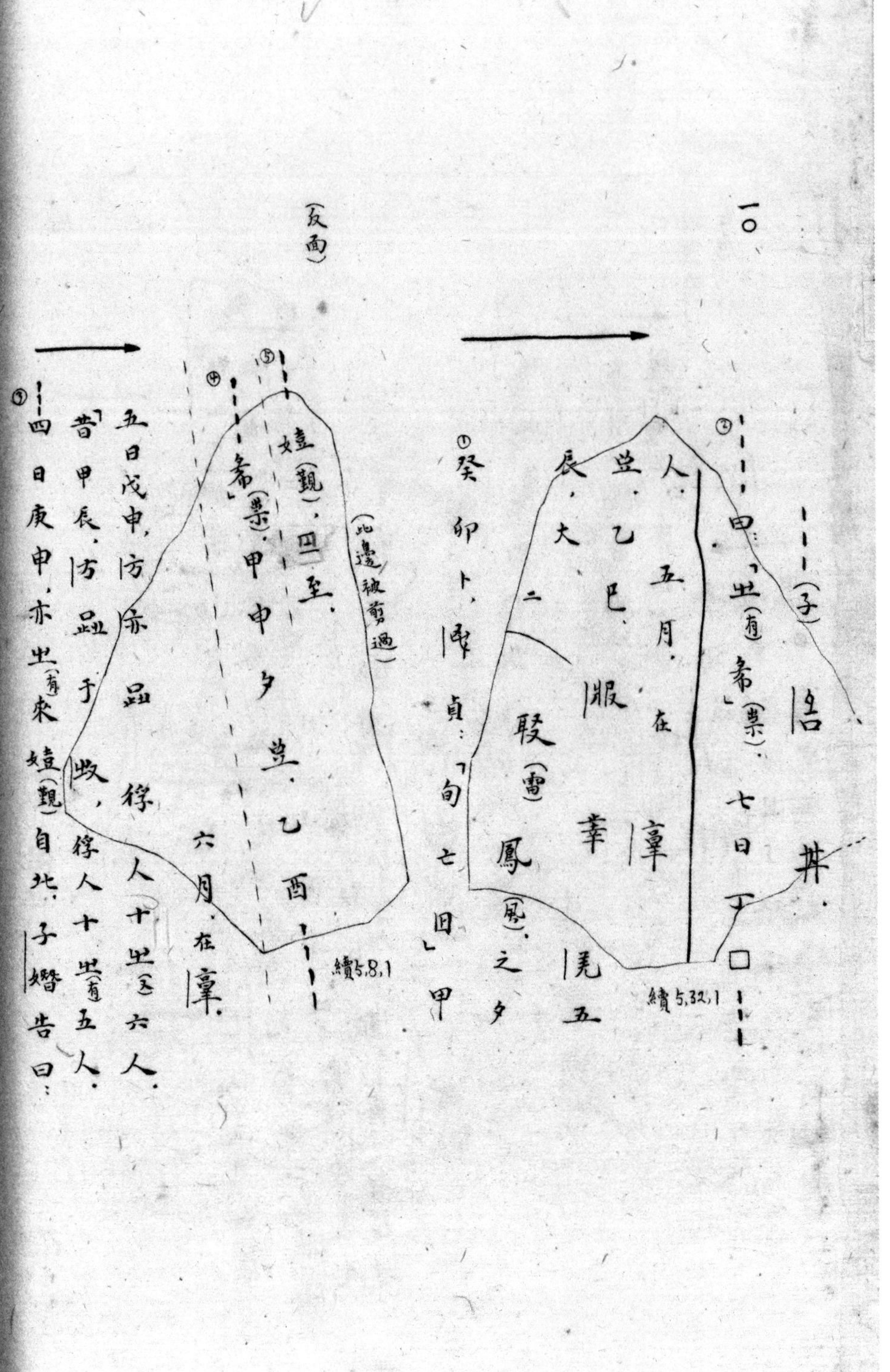
一〇
續5.32.1
續5.8.1
(反面)
(北邊被剪過)

二

②王固曰：「㞢(有)希(祟)，其㞢(有)來媗(艱)亖至」，七日己巳，允㞢(有)來媗(艱)，自西，長友角告曰：「𢀛方出，侵我示䕫田，七十五人」。

①癸巳卜，㱿貞：旬亡囚。王固曰：「㞢(有)希(祟)，其㞢來媗(艱)亖至」。五日丁酉，允㞢(有)來媗(艱)自西，沚戠告曰：「土方征于我東啚(鄙)，𢦏二邑；𢀛方亦侵我西啚(鄙)田。」

佚60(北3.13.4)

(反面)

③告曰：「……

④東啚(鄙)，𢦏二邑」。王步，自𪌗于䀎。

□日辛丑，夕㞢，壬寅，王亦冬(終)夕𡆥。

佚61(北3.13.4反)

壹骨七——一一

第一期卜辭同文異版者，所在多有，因一事不止一卜，卜若干次，即記卜辭若干次也。骨五、六，即同文之版，骨六上部有卜兆記數四，是同文者至少尚有兩版。又如下葉「狩微」之辭，見於骨版者三（壹骨一二至一四），龜版者一（壹甲六），皆其例也。武丁時大骨，同文者尚多，惟破裂太甚，不如骨一至三之完整耳。七至一一，有與之同文者，對照如次：

壹骨二	正面	①（第①辭）	一一	正①（同文）		
		②		②		
	反面	④		反③		
		⑤		④		
壹骨三	正面	②	一〇	正①	九	正①
	反面	⑥	七	正⑥		
		③	一〇	反③	九	反⑥

一二

亦口，畢亦㞢倦.
馬口，䄂阹在車，畢馬
五日丁卯，王獸㪔，䄂車
① 癸亥卜，㱿貞：「旬亡𡆥」，王固曰：「㞢希」.
② 癸口卜，口貞：「旬亡𡆥」，王固曰：「㞢
希……長，八月.

前7.5.3

一三

① 癸亥卜，㱿貞：「旬亡𡆥」，王固曰：「㞢希」，五日丁卯，
王獸㪔，䄂車馬口，䄂阹在車，畢馬亦口，
畢亦㞢倦.
② 王固曰：「㞢希，其㞢來嬉」，八日庚口，允㞢
來嬉自口，口口告曰：㽙.

前7.18.3

一四

畢亦㞢倦.
䄂阹在車，畢馬亦口，
卯，王獸㪔，䄂車馬口，
王固曰：「㞢希」，五日丁
癸亥卜，㱿貞：「旬亡𡆥」，

珠290

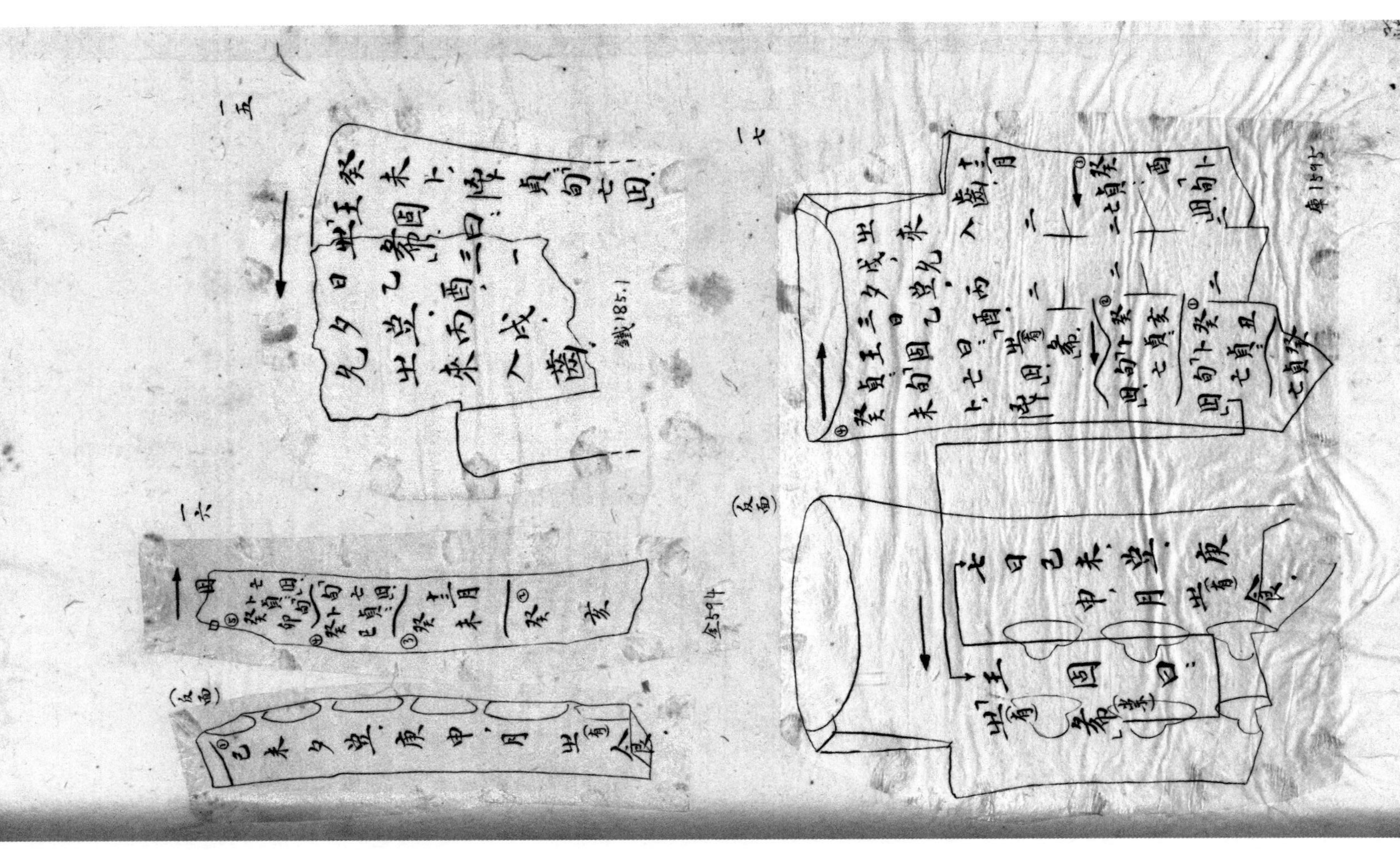

壹骨五—一七

此為一大組卜辭，尚包涵壹甲五—八及壹骨三各版，收藏分散於劉鐵雲、王襄、羅振玉、中央研究院、大英博物院、河井荃廬、三井源右衛門八處，殘破支離，昔為連綴，乃得武丁時代重要史實之聯絡，今揭之於此，可為治契學者示一新法例也。原為武丁日譜之一部分，摘舉如次。其年月日干，皆經推算正確，採自殷曆朔閏譜，可以覆按者。

武丁二十九年（公元前一三一一年　庚午）

一月小（殷正）　辛巳一日（公元前一三一二年十二月十九日　儒略周日一二四二五六八）（三日壬午　日食　酉日甲午　一三一一年一月一日）

二月大　庚戌一日（一三一一年一月十七日　周日一二四二五九七）

三月小　庚辰一日（二月十六日　周日一二四二六二七）

四月大　乙酉一日（三月十七日　周日一二四二五五六）

癸丑廿九日（上線示事類聯貫）

癸丑卜，𡧊貞：「旬亡𡆥」。王固曰：「㞢（有）希（祟），㞢（有）𡦹」。壹骨三（下線示甲骨同版）

甲寅卅日

甲寅，允㞢（有）來娃，𣪊告曰：「㞢（有）往芻自盜，十人㞢（又）二」。（以上追記）

五月小　己卯一日（四月十六日　周日一二四二五八六）

癸卯廿五日

（左傳）

癸卯卜，𡧊貞：「旬亡𡆥」。

甲辰廿六日

甲辰，大敔（雷）鳳（風），之夕皇。（是日𠂤方品𩰫，俘十又五人，見下月子𡚬報告）

乙巳 廿七日　乙巳(服)葦(羌)五人。五月，在(𦎫)。(以上乙巳追記)(括号内字據壹骨一〇同文補)　壹骨三

六月 大　戊申 一日　(五月十五日　周日一二四二七一五)(二日己酉 日食　十七日甲子　月食)　(本日土方又𢀛㪅，俘十又六人。見本月庚申子㛸報告)

癸丑 六日　癸丑卜，𡧊貞：「旬亡𡆥。」

乙卯 八日　三日(由癸丑至乙卯，此)乙卯，㞢(有)嬉，單丁人豊令于彔，……

丁巳 十日　丁巳，㽙子豊令……鬼亦得疾。

庚申 十三日　(在𦎫)　四日(由丁巳至此)庚申，亦有來嬉自北。子㛸告曰：昔甲辰，方𢀛于㪅，俘人十㞢(又)五人。(此五月廿六日事)　五日(由甲辰至戊申)戊申，方亦𢀛，俘人十㞢(又)六人。(此六月一日事)六月，在𦎫。　壹骨三反面

甲子 十七日　甲子允㞢(有)來自東。……　壹骨三反面

七月 小　戊寅 一日　(六月十四日　周日一二四二七四五)

八月 大　丁未 一日　(七月十三日　周日一二四二七七四)

癸亥 十七日　(狩㪤)　癸亥卜，㱿貞：「旬亡𡆥。」王固曰：「㞢希。」(有祟)(以下丁卯日追記占驗)五日丁卯，王獸(狩)㪤，𢦏車馬口，𢦏𨸏在車，𡆥馬亦口，𡆥亦㞢(有)𢓊。(本辭左行，壹骨九右行，壹骨一〇左行，壹骨一一右行，皆對稱。又壹甲五左行同文見五見。參五補足之，不備錄。)　壹骨七

(三)

乙丑 十九日

乙丑(卜,旧)貞:「翌(丁)卯,王其獸(狩)敝彔(麓),早(禽)。」八月。 壹甲六

乙丑(卜,旧)貞:「翌(丁)卯,其獸敝彔,弗早。」

乙丑(卜,旧)貞:「翌(丁)卯,王其獸敝彔早。」八月 壹甲七

丁卯 廿一日

五日(由癸亥至此)丁卯,王獸(狩)敝。祝車馬口,祝陷在車,阜馬亦口,阜亦㞢(有)徒。

九月小 丁丑 一日 (八月十一日 周曰一二四二八〇四)

十月大 丙午 一日 (九月十日 周曰一二四二八三三)

十一月大 丙子 一日 (十月十日 周曰一二四二八六三)

(四邑)

丙子卜,𠂤貞:「自(師)亡田(禍)。」十一月。一 壹骨五

(丙子卜,)𠂤貞:自(師)其(㞢田)……(此間當有「王固曰」之詞)……昔我舊臣……石之齒,今之㞢(有)㞢……(齒)。(以下乃史𠂤於十三月丙申,追來告四邑𢦏時追記𠂤㞢(有)田(禍)之占驗)三旬㞢(又)六日虎辛(亥)魁,庚𥂐,方允(𢦏)。(參壹骨六,同文補苴)

帚婦井妌來。(此在壹骨六反面,記骨版為婦妌貢來者。)

(癸巳卜,旧貞:「旬亡田。」)王固曰:「㞢(有)希(祟)。」(下接庚子) 壹骨七反面

癸巳 廿七日

庚子 廿五日　八日（自癸巳至此）庚子，戈羍羌人，改㞢（有）圉。二人。（以上追記）

癸卯 廿八日　王固曰：「（其）㞢來嬉，其隹丙，不（吉）」。

王固曰：「㞢希，㞢見」。

十二月小

丙午 一日（日食　十二月九日　周日一二四二八九三）（十五日庚申夕，月食）

辛亥 六日（四邑）三旬㞢（又）六日（自十一月一日丙子至此日）虎，辛（亥），魁，（夾），果，方，允戈。　壹骨五六

（此占驗之追記時日，當猶在辛亥以後，即十三月廿二日丙申也。彼時圉報告四邑之戈而不記戈之日，史佚乃著于丙子占驗，四邑被戈之日，賴以存焉。）

癸丑 八日（月食）癸丑卜貞：「旬亡田」。（以下反面）王固曰：「㞢希」。（以下庚申追記）七日

己未豈。庚申，月㞢（有）食。　壹骨一七

己未 十四日　七日（由癸丑至此）己未，豈。

己未夕豈。　壹骨一六

庚申 十五日　庚申，月㞢（有）食。　壹骨一六同文

癸亥 十八日　（癸）亥卜口貞：「旬亡（田）」。

癸亥卜貞：「旬亡田」。二

癸亥。

癸酉 廿八日　癸酉卜貞：「旬亡田」。二（此旬不屬于十三月，有同版「癸未十二月」可證。）

（七）（三）

十三月(閏)大　乙亥 一日 (十二月八日　周日一二四二九二二)(廿五日乙亥　公元前一三一〇年一月一日)

癸未 九日

(月食)癸未卜，𡧊貞旬亡𡆥。王固曰：「㞢(有)希」(祟)。(以下丙戌追記)三日

乙酉，夕皿。丙戌允㞢(有)來入齒。十三月。二　壹骨一五同文一下

癸未。十三月。

(四邑)癸未卜，㱿貞旬亡𡆥。王固曰：「㞢(有)希，其㞢來艱」，三至。(以下是追記)七日己(丑)，允㞢(有)來艱自西。長戈(化)乎(呼)告曰：「𢀛方征我奠。(以下壬辰又追記在反面)(四日)壬辰，亦㞢(有)來自西。𡆥乎告曰：「𢀛方征我奠，𢦏四邑。

王固曰：「㞢希，㞢夢，其㞢來艱」。七日己丑，允㞢來艱自(西)。長戈化乎告(曰)：「𢀛方征于我奠」。　壹骨三反面

乙酉 十一日　乙酉，夕皿。

丙戌 十二日　丙戌允㞢來入齒。十三月。

己丑 十五日　七日(由癸未至此)己丑，允㞢來艱自西。長戈化乎告曰：「𢀛方征于我奠」。

壬辰 十八日　(四日)壬辰，(由己丑至此四日)亦㞢來自西。𡆥乎告曰：「𢀛方征我奠，𢦏

(一五)(一七)(六)(三)

二四

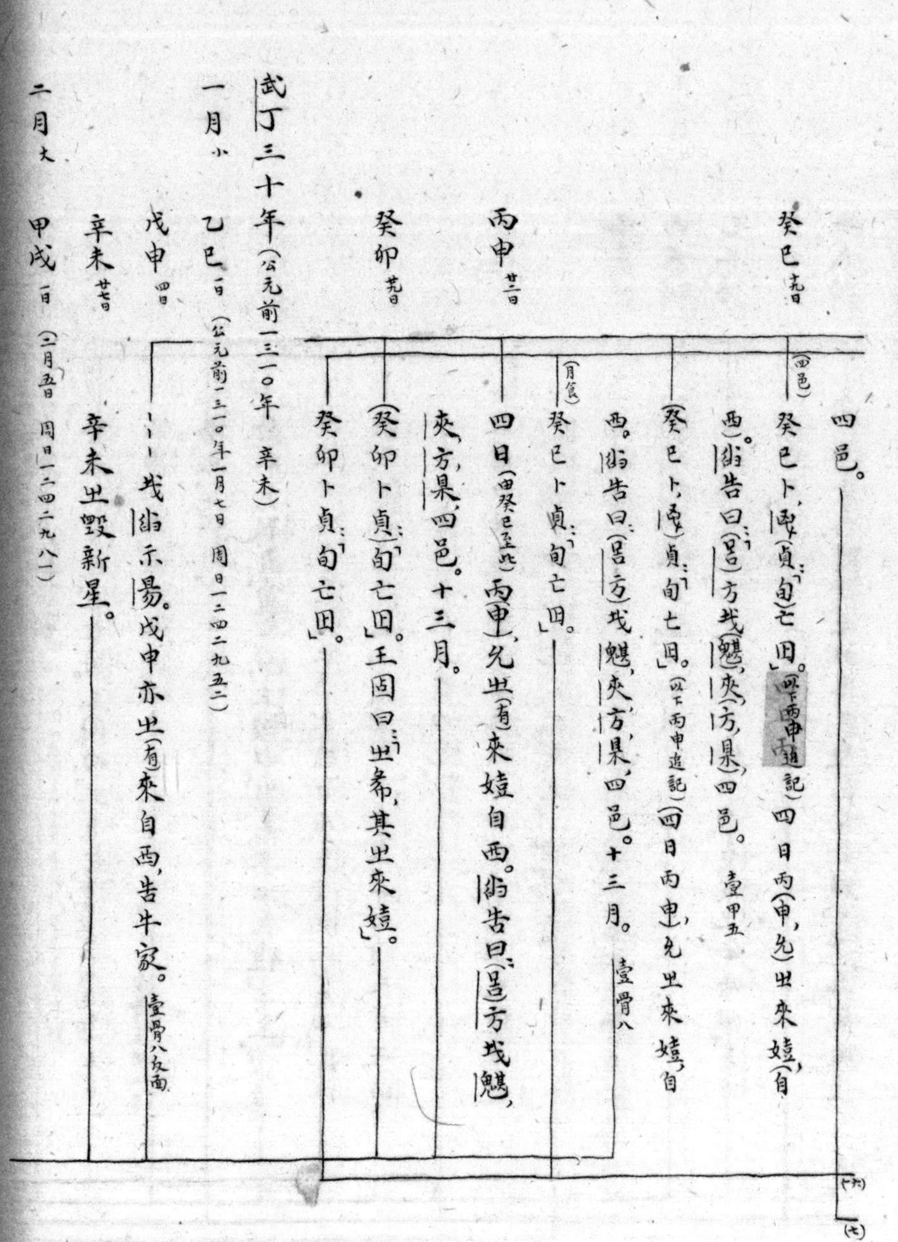

四邑。

癸巳 十九日 （四邑）癸巳卜，㱿，（貞）：旬亡𡆥。（以下丙申追記）四日丙（申），允出來嬉，（自）西。㞢告曰：（舌）方𢦏（魅），夾（方杲）四邑。 壹甲五

（癸巳卜，㱿）貞：旬亡𡆥。（以下丙申追記）（四日丙申），允出來嬉，自西。㞢告曰：（舌方）𢦏魅，夾方杲，四邑。十三月。 壹骨八

（月食）癸巳卜，貞：旬亡𡆥。

丙申 廿二日 四日（由癸巳至此）丙（申），允出（有）來嬉自西。㞢告曰：（舌）方𢦏魅，夾方杲，四邑。十三月。

癸卯 廿九日 （癸卯卜，貞）：旬亡𡆥。王固曰：出希，其出來嬉。

癸卯卜，貞：旬亡𡆥。

武丁三十年（公元前一三一〇年 辛未）

一月小 乙巳 一日（公元前一三一〇年一月七日 周日一二四二九五二）

戊申 四日 ……𢦏，㞢示易。戊申亦出（有）來自西，告牛家。 壹骨八反面

辛未 廿七日 辛未出毁新星。

二月大 甲戌 一日（二月五日 周日一二四二九八一）

丙戌吉　　一一七日。丙戌，龢侑習。二月。

右表年月之配置，為改訂合天之古四分術，上起殷庚，下接漢元，在千餘年之大系統中，乃不容更易之一節段。而此有月食及日干月份之一組卜辭，能嚴密嵌入，如天衣無縫，當非偶然也。其活動之範圍，向後僅可移一日，（如壹骨一六癸酉可為十二月廿九日而不能入十三月）向前則一日亦不能移也。（如丙子為十一月一日。壹骨五）

此十二個月中一大組卜辭，仍可分之為四小組，第一組為王在𩫖，第二組為王狩㪇，第三組為四邑之戋，第四組為庚申月食。再分述之。

一，在𩫖一組　此武丁中葉，東巡狩之一段史蹟，其時間為廿九年，五月六月，王皆在𩫖也。𩫖當今何地，尚待考，然知其為在殷都東南之田獵區域以內，一，四，五期皆曾田游之地也。此田獵區約在山東南部羣山中，為殷人歷代田獵之地。是時武丁方在𩫖駐蹕，忽有自北來覲報告邊患者，則六月庚申也。報告者為武丁之子名婿者。今假定子婿之行，在戊申以後，（上方第一次䀁（當讀圍）㪅，為甲辰，徙十五人，第二次䀁㪅為戊申，徙十六人。）必戊申以後或在其次日，子婿乃赴行在覲告，至庚申乃達，是由㪅至𩫖疾行亦須十二日，兩地相距在千里內外也。此版壹骨三，由四月癸丑，用至十三月癸未，如表。癸丑，乙卯，丁巳，庚申，各日記載，一篇卜辭在八十字以上，為武丁時長文之一，且為正反二面文字連接之一例。

二，狩㪇一組　此為武丁廿九年八月在㪇狩獵之故事。此時王猶在𩫖與否不可知，但仍遊獵在外，未歸殷都，則可以推知。此一節包涵一段軼史，乃田獵時從者兩人，因馬逸車顛而受傷也。殷人每旬必於癸日卜下旬吉凶，此乃例行公事。武丁喜親臨而占之，占每不吉，（王固曰㞢希）貞旬之史臣則必於其旬內所發生不幸事件附會之，以證王占之驗。正因其如此，乃遺吾人三千載下，以片斷之珍貴史料也。此一組主要之記事，乃「丁卯之日，王率侍從至㲋录（麓）狩獵，此行發生之禍事有二，其一，乃祝所乘之車因馬逸而傾覆，祝仆於車中；其二，乃阜（武丁子）車之馬亦逸，阜亦受傷也」。此辭殘片凡五，郭沫若氏舉其四，以為同文互足之例，而此故事，如百衲之衣，乃可屬讀。其月份，乃輯自殘甲三片，恰為此旬乙丑日卜丁卯田獵有所擒獲與否之辭，稱其地曰㲋录（第一期字，第五期則加繁為𣞤、𣡕、𧃝等形。即麓字。）知㲋為山阜也。得此，知癸亥卜旬在八月，乃依譜繫于是年。

三、四邑之𢦏一組　此一組之聯系，主要卜辭為壹骨五至八，壹甲五。壹骨七正反兩面記事銜接，極重要。壹骨八乃郭沫若氏所綴合，揭之通纂四九八片者，知有反面，則金祖同氏目驗之功也。余於甲三〇五六，本編壹甲五，得四邑被𢦏報告之日；又輯「丙子卜㠯」大骨，壹骨五、六；而此一段史實，乃從千劇百孔中，復現於世，亦奇緣也。此組以「四邑」為線索，可再分兩部分：

(一)前後五日之兩次報告。

1. 壬辰之報告。　此次在甲申旬之第九日，追記於癸未卜旬辭下，所以證王固，「其㞢來嬉三至」者。（三，郭釋川，余疑當讀如「南宮三復白圭」之三，短其中橫，所以別於數字者。）蓋此旬接連來嬉有二次，壬辰乃二次，故曰「亦㞢(有)來(嬉字)自西」。是日來者為𢀛所遣派之代表，故曰「爭告」，代表報告簡畧，僅言「呂方𢦏四邑」而不舉其名。

先四日，有𡆥戈化之代表來告呂方征亟之事，𡆥為國或地，戈化為其守土者。於此知𡆥之去四邑，在其東或南有三日之程也。邊境被侵，守土有責，在呂方當是同時進犯而來報有先後，蓋遠邇之別矣。𡆥之守將尚有𡆥角(壹骨二)則其遠廓可知。

2，丙申之報告。　後壬辰四日，𢀛乃親來報告，是為甲午旬之第三日，追記於癸巳卜旬辭下，故云「四日」也。𢀛本人報告為詳，且舉呂方所𢦏之四邑為𩲃、夾、方、𡿩，尚有𢦏此四邑之時日，見於壹骨五、六，惜此處未載耳。四邑被𢦏在辛亥(詳下節)距壬辰四十二日，知𢀛之代表至王行在(此時度武丁仍在東南巡狩，若返殷都，不當行如是之久)旅途經四旬以上也。𢀛又遲之四日，或部署善後，防衛之工作歟？

此類辭，皆缺敵國呂方之名。知為呂方者，一沿上辭𡆥戈化使者報告；一則他辭有「王曰𢀛，呂方其出」(鐵七一、二)「𢀛爭告呂方出」(前五、一七、七)𢀛與呂方，固為比鄰也。

(二)貞夂𡆥，附會占驗之追記。

貞人每每附會占驗，必追記卜貞以後所發生之事件以證明之，在旬月內猶易辯，若遲之過久，如「百日㞢(又)七旬」以上(鐵五三)，不惟記憶力須強，即甲骨檔案山積，翻檢亦非易事也。

此組中有十一月丙子卜「隹其㞢(有)田(禍)」之辭，其貞人為𠂤，其中「王固有田」之辭適殘缺，由「昔我舊臣」一語，知為王言。此次卜貞之後，𠂤乃默記之，注意其後發生之事，至十三月之丙申，𠂤來嬉告邊患，云「呂方於辛亥入寇，𨚃于邊地(𨚃當為奠，假為甸，非地名。)戋魁夾方泉四邑。」(此次亦𠂤貞卣。)乃取丙子一版而追記之曰：「三旬㞢(又)六日(自丙子至此)，𦥑辛亥，魁夾泉方允戋。」以證「隹㞢田」之驗。丙申去丙子已八十一日，在兩閏月以後，尚能憶及兩月前未記徵驗之一次卜事，其人之精明勤謹，有如此者。

四，庚申月食一組　此為武丁時月食記錄之一，有月份可推者僅此，至可珍也。月食之文，前此所以不注意者，一因誤以「夕皀」當之，一因月夕二字不辨，一因不知一期之㞢，即二期以後之又(有)。此十一月食見於殘骨二版(𡋊骨一六、一七)，由丑亥酉未之四次卜旬，而癸未註十三月，知丑亥酉之可能為十二月之三癸，庚申正可為十二月望也。初余檢殷曆譜，得武丁廿九年十二月丙午朔，十五日庚申，乃記此月食於上，繼倩陳遵嬀先生推之，果此日有月全食之可能，為之狂喜。余更據奧泊爾子氏日月食典依週期推步，知此一「月全食」，在公元前(史家年)一三一一年，儒略曆十一月廿三日，儒略周日一二四二九〇七，當中國殷武丁廿九年，干支紀年庚午，殷正十二月十五日庚申夜半，食甚為安陽〇時。惟此時武丁若東巡未歸，所見猶當早於安陽，不可考矣。

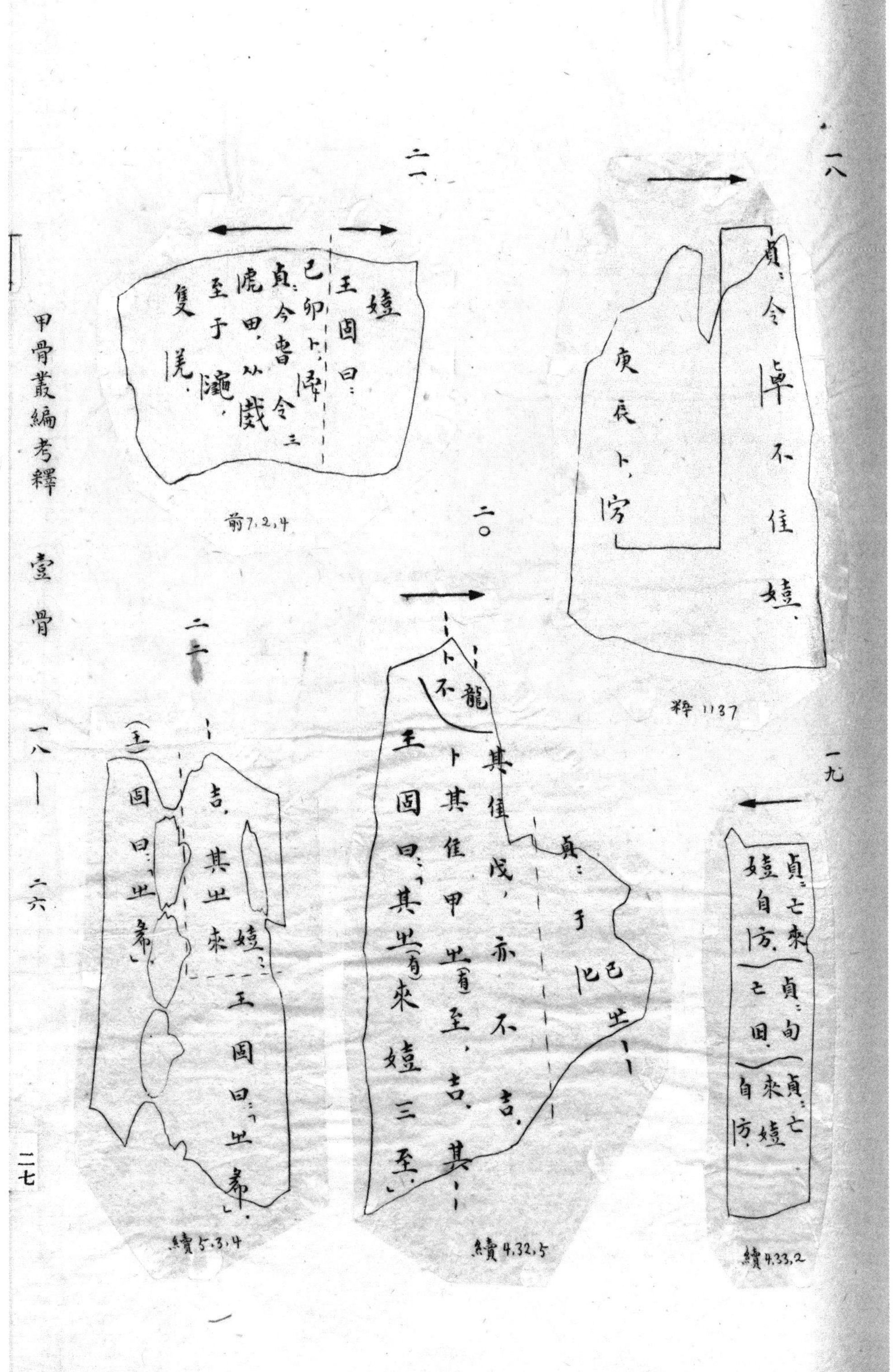

甲骨叢編考釋　壹　骨　一八—二六
二七
一八
粹1137
一九
續4.33.2
二〇
續4.32.5
二一
前7.2.4
二二
續5.3.4

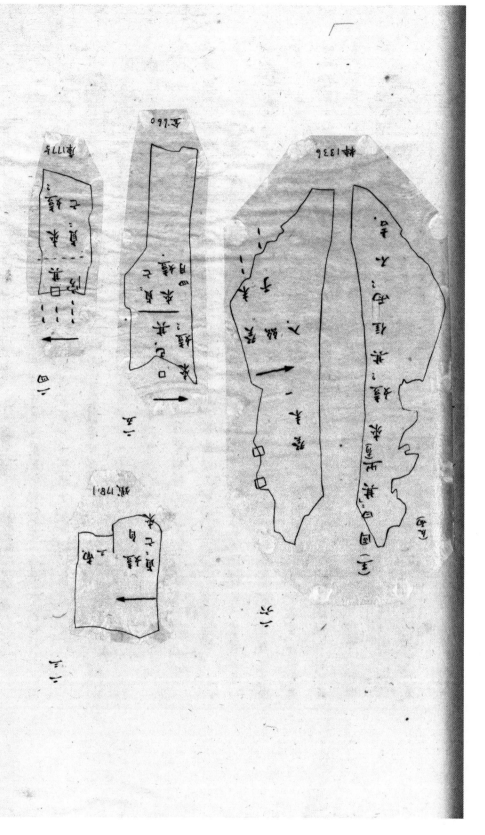

二三

鐵178.1

二五

金660

二四

庫1775

二六

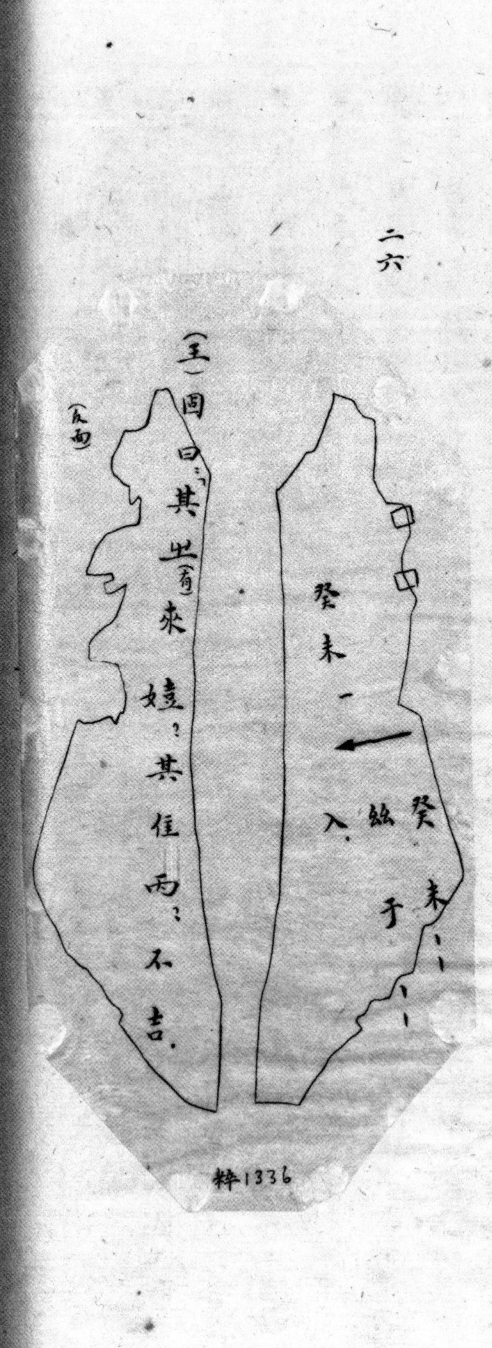

粹1336

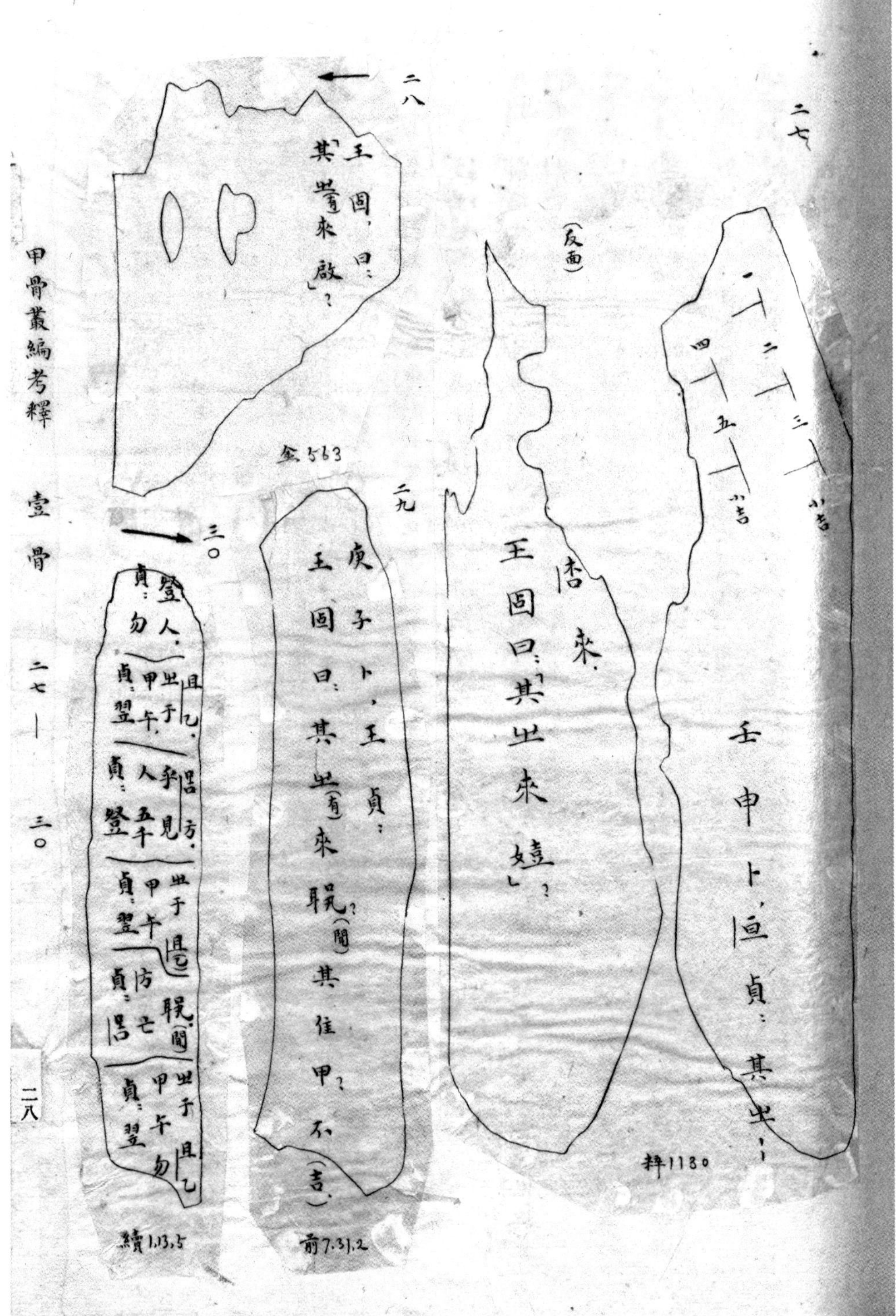
甲骨叢編考釋　壹　骨　二七—三〇
二八
二七
壬申卜，亘貞：其㞢
粹1130
(反面)
王固曰：其㞢來艱
二八
王固，曰：其㞢來艱
金563
二九
庚子卜，王貞：
王固曰：其㞢來艱？其隹甲？不(吉)
前7.31.2
三〇
續1.13.5

壹骨一八至三〇。（釋嬄）

卜辭中習見「嬄」字，亦作「鼓」，多屬於第一期武丁時。孫詒讓釋嬉，歖，喜，羅振玉釋僖，謂即豎字；郭沫若釋鼟，以為憂戚字；均不得真解。今由斷代法詳審之，此乃一時期所用之字，祖庚祖甲時已有沿變，蓋即朝覲字也。具論如次：

郭沫若卜辭通纂第四二六片（按即本編壹骨一反面）釋鼓字云：

卜辭用此字有一定之義例，大抵於癸日卜（下）旬之吉凶，而繫之以『王固曰㞢（有）希（祟）其㞢（有）來鼓』之文，下紀其應，則云『若干日某干某支允㞢（有）來鼓自□（東西南北字）』而繫之以事變，以關於疆理之事為多。是此鼓字必與希字相貫而含凶咎之意。

所謂「卜辭用此字有一定之義例」，是也。謂此字必含凶咎之意，則未見其然。卜辭中有舉此字而不與「㞢希」相貫者。如

王固曰「嬄」。 壹骨二一

王固曰：其㞢（有）來嬄，「吉」來。 壹骨二七

癸丑卜，𡧊貞：旬亡囚。三日乙卯㞢（有）嬄。 壹骨三

又有卜來嬄之日，吉或不吉者，果「來嬄」即為「來戚」，義同「有祟」，不必更問其吉若不吉矣。如

王固曰：「其㞢來嬄，三至」。卜其隹甲㞢至，「不吉。其……其隹戊」，亦不吉。 壹骨二〇

其出來嬉，其隹丙，不吉。　壹骨二六

更有稱「來嬉」為吉者：

吉，其出來嬉。　壹骨二二　此片上段殘，吉字斷句，亦有屬於上句可能。

至少「來嬉」為中和性之事件，其本身不含凶咎，因來嬉報告邊境被侵掠事項較多，故似含凶兆，實則其本身無吉凶之可言也。且釋為鼓，為戚，太覺抽象玄虛。嬉，有所來，有所至之日；有所自來之方向，繼之以所來為誰，為本人或所派遣之代表，事實昭然，非抽象之憂戚字所能概括者也。如

貞，翌甲辰，其出(有)至嬉？　壹甲一一　壹甲一三同文

亡來嬉自方。　壹骨一九　其自𠂤出(有)來嬉。不自𠂤出(有)來嬉。　壹甲三①②

允出(有)來嬉，自東。叀告曰……　壹骨四一

允出(有)來嬉，自西。沚戠告曰……　壹骨一

允出(有)來嬉自西。長双角告曰……　同上片

其出(有)嬉自南。　壹甲四

允出(有)來嬉，自北。𢦔妻㚢告曰……　壹骨二反面

允出(有)來嬉，自北。子𡚱告曰……　壹骨三反面

以上所舉之叀(武丁之子)，沚戠，双角，㚢(武丁婦)，𡚱(武丁子)，皆本人自來覲見者，其稱「某某予告」，則為其人遣

派代表覲見報告也。如

允坐(有)來嬉，自西。長戈化乎(呼)告曰……　　壹骨七　參壹骨三反面同文補足.

亦坐(有)來嬉，自西。𠭯乎告曰……　　壹骨七反面

𠭯則先呼人報告邊患，嗣即親來覲告，其史實別詳骨五至一七考釋。其文曰

允坐(有)來嬉自西。𠭯告曰……　　壹骨八

凡此皆足見非一「戚」字所能詮解，而來者為諸侯，為戍邊將領，為王之婦子，雖間有代表之使者，亦未可以僕豎論也。

考覲見之覲，在武丁時作嬉([illegible])、鼓([illegible])。至祖庚時仍之，亦或作鼓([illegible])、嬉([illegible])，或借𦰩([illegible])為之。祖甲時則一律改作為囍([illegible])、[illegible]([illegible])，具見下例。卜辭因時代之不同，用字有異，此為識字之大問題，尚待治斯學者再下一番工夫也。祖甲為一英睿之主，經其手改訂閏法，廢「十三月」置閏年終之制，整齊祀典，以彡、翌、祭、[illegible]、劦依日次祀其祖妣，稱唐為大乙，皆其大端。文字之更易，如以又(又有)為坐，以[illegible]([illegible])為[illegible]，以囍為嬉，皆其特著者也。此字四五兩期尚未之見。三期則沿用𦰩作，至周金未改，囍則引申為艱矣。其演化之大略如此。

覲之涵義，就字形結構言，確如郭沫若氏所云「象於壴(鼓)旁有人跽而(戍)守之」。其與壴(鼓)之關係尤切，無論其人為男([illegible])，為女([illegible])，為立，為跽([illegible])，為冠服交拜([illegible])，除段借𦰩字外，總不離乎壴(鼓)，是可以

深長思者。郭氏所引，有足資參證者：

說文「鼜，夜戒守鼓也。从壴蚤聲。禮「昏鼓四通為大鼓，夜半三通為戒晨，旦五通為發明。」讀若戚。」

周禮地官鼓人「凡軍旅夜鼓鼜。」鄭注「鼜，夜戒守鼓也。司馬法曰「昏鼓四通為大鼜，夜半三通為晨戒，旦明五通為發昫。」」

曰「夜戒守」，曰「凡軍旅夜鼓鼜」，疑古者王在軍旅，有進見報告邊事，必先鳴鼓而後覲，故覲字從鼓作也。卜辭中足證「㞢(有)來嬉」而武丁在外者有四：

癸丑……三日乙卯，㞢(有)嬉。……丁巳……四日庚申，亦㞢來嬉自北。……六月，在𩫖。

允㞢來嬉自西。　允㞢來自東。　癸丑……甲寅允㞢來嬉。　癸卯……五月在𩫖。　壹骨三

九日辛卯，允㞢來嬉自北。　允㞢來(嬉)……王步，自𨸏于𠤳。　壹骨二

其亦㞢來嬉。　癸酉……在𠖥阜。　壹骨一

此類記「來嬉」兼及王田遊所在者，甚為明晰，其餘多不可考。尚書堯典：

「歲二月東巡狩，至於岱宗，……肆覲東后。」

更於五月，八月，十一月巡狩南，西，北各地，而隨時覲見羣后。可為武丁時代「來嬉」各辭一重要說明也。

祖庚之世，制度文字，一從前朝之舊規，未嘗改易，知為祖庚者，貞人皆二期也。其時王字作太，又祭作㞢，大乙稱唐，沿用「十三月」置閏法。覲之字，亦沿作嬉，如：

辛亥(卜)，兄貞：今日亡來嬉自囗。　貳甲五

兄與大與出皆曾仕于祖庚之朝。其稱「今日亡來嬉」實開祖甲世「今日亡來鼓」之先例，為嬉鼓二字遞變之重要連鎖。其時亦有改嬉之偏旁，易女為男者，則僖與㚇是也。

癸卯卜，出貞：旬亡(咎)祟。自西來㚇。　貳甲三

貞：其自南來㚇。　同上

丁未卜，王貞：多鬼(畏)夢，亡來㚇。　貳甲四

㚇象女子跽坐形，此改從男，象男子跽坐之形也。易女為男，蓋亦沿自第一期，如壹甲一二，正作㚇形，此羅氏釋僖所本，不同者立與坐而已。祖庚時更有借嫨為之者，如

西土尹(君)嫨。　貳骨七

囗囗卜，大貞：來丁亥嫨。　貳骨九

丁亥嫨丁酉留亦一一　貳骨八

嫨當同莫，莫為饑饉字，本象人正立交臂，衣冠整齊，謹恭敬肅之義，歲歉則人必謹慎節儉，故引申為饉，加火作㷀，似為乾旱之象，如上引三辭則借為覲見字矣。(㷀字見壹甲九一〇)

祖甲時，前期覲見字，已有嬉，僖，㚇，嫨諸形，乃改作為鼓，半存壴(鼓)義，半借莫形，兼取其聲。觀於鼓字演化為鼓，為覲，可以上推其音讀之必為覲也。

嬉之與鼓，形音義之聯繫，已如上述，在文法上亦有其相通之點。茲表舉如下：

武丁時　(祖庚時)　祖甲時

亡(無)來嬉(覲)　壹骨一九　二三一二五　(今日亡來嬉)(貳甲五)　今日亡(無)來鼓(覲)　貳骨一二三一五、一四

其出(有)來嬉(覲)　壹骨二六、二七、九　又(有)來鼓(覲)　貳甲一五

由此可見嬉鼓兩字更遞之關係。至三期康丁時，則沿祖庚時借𦰩為之。

乙酉，小臣[illegible]𦰩。　叁甲四⑯

即其例也。金文女雙鼎：「女雙𦰩(覲)于王」，作𦰩，猶沿祖庚康丁之舊。

今列卜辭中覲字一、二、三期之因革，下及金文小篆，以見其孳乳之關係，為下表：

武丁時一期	祖庚時二期	祖甲時二期	康丁時三期	金文	小篆
[illegible](鍾)				[illegible](勤) 宗周鐘	[illegible](勤) 鐘
			[illegible](覲)	[illegible](覲) 女雙鼎	[illegible](堇)
[illegible](覲) 壴从女	[illegible](覲) 从壴从女	[illegible](覲) 壴从𦰩		[illegible](艱) 不嬰簋	[illegible]＝[illegible]
[illegible](覲) 壴从亻	[illegible](覲) 壴从卩				

據右表，由金文上溯，庚丁時之𦰩為覲，可謂毫無問題。而祖甲時從𦰩以配壴旁之鼓，證以後起之囍，其音為覲，亦無可疑。而武丁時之嬉、僖，祖庚時之鼓，固與鼓為同一法式下所製造之文字也。

壹骨二八，辭曰「其㞢(有)來㱿」，二九辭曰「其㞢來䎽(聞)」，與「其㞢來娃(艱)」為同樣句法，「㱿」、「聞」、「娃」亦當為同類事項也。「㱿」或如後世公文款式，為稟奏之類，「聞」亦當為文書一種，「娃」則面見奏告之類。如「夕月有食，聞」，直與漢以來日食記載「京師不見，郡國以聞」者全同，足見殷代禮制之繁重。

䎽(聞)之見於卜辭者數則，其字作人跽而以手掩口狀，附以耳，示所以聞也。舉如次：

庚子卜，王貞：其㞢來䎽(聞)，其隹甲，不(吉)？ 壹骨二九

貞：呂方亡(無)䎽(聞)。 壹骨三〇 此片有「登人五千見呂方」辭，則「無聞」猶絕信使往來也。

癸巳卜，㱿貞：旬亡(𡆥)。甲午，㞢(有)䎽曰「戌……吏𡆥夏」。七月。在囗。 續五·二·四

……貞：㞢(有)䎽曰…… 前七·七·三

……(貞)：允隹我䎽(聞)。 續一·一三·五 「我聞」、「余聞」，與盂鼎句法同。

……貞：䎽(聞)㞢(有)𡆥…… 餘五·五

……卜貞：方由䎽(聞)。 前六·一七·一 由，叀，有傳呼之義，此辭「傳聞」尤可證。

貞：余䎽(聞)𡆥…… 餘五·三

(癸口卜貞)：旬(亡𡆥)。(夕)月㞢(有)食。䎽(聞)。八月。 甲一二八九 以上皆第一期卜辭

金文盂鼎「我聞殷墜命」，聞作𦖞，沿甲文少變。說文引古文作䎽，玉篇作䎽，石經古文作𦖞，玉篇作𦔻，古鉩作𦖞。此字本為會意，其從耳從昏、米、門，則皆後起之形聲矣。

三一

貞：不子

菁9.1

三二

𣪘孜

菁10.6

三三

旬庚辛[illegible]虫日方

自卜，三日[illegible]，在㞢，己卯虫來

菁9.7

三四

貞：在麓 殸

田，萬年

貞：商 不

菁10.7

三五

甲午卜，殸貞：帝𧧷且

甲午卜，殸貞：乎阜

戊午卜，殸貞：由岳

戊午卜

菁10.8

三六

貞：今𠂤王珎

我見又（佑）

貞：今夕其雨？

貞：翌丁

三夕雨

菁10.9

三七

不同，叀一同

菁10.11

三八

甲子卜

菁10.12

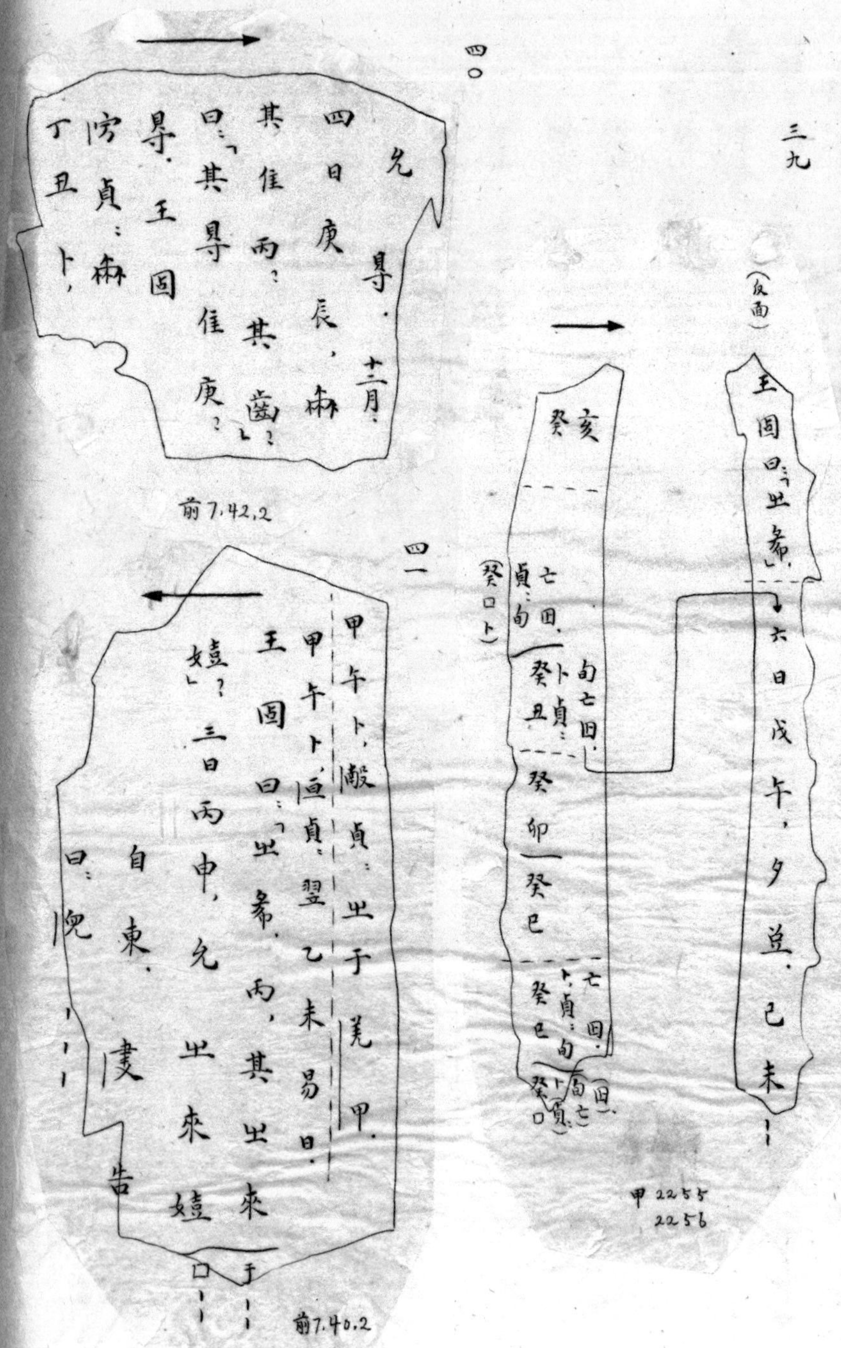

四二

（辛酉一段，右「一二三四」、上吉皆塗朱）

卜，韋貞：今夕不其(雨)。
辛酉
辛未卜，
亘貞：往
豕止(逐)豕，
隻(獲)

一　二　三　四　上吉
一　二　不啎黽

（辛未一段，左上「一」，皆塗墨）

甲3339

四二（反面）

（此段事後追記）

貞：帚
其隻。
之日王往
豕止(逐)，在
豕　允
隻(獲)九。

甲3340

四三

丁酉卜，㝊
貞：帚(婦)好
㞢(有)受生。

二　一　一　三　不啎黽

取白。
貞：乎雇
宅。
貞：侯

四三（反面）

貞：帚
(生)。
受
受生。
㞢(有)受
王固曰：「吉，其

外144　　外141

四四

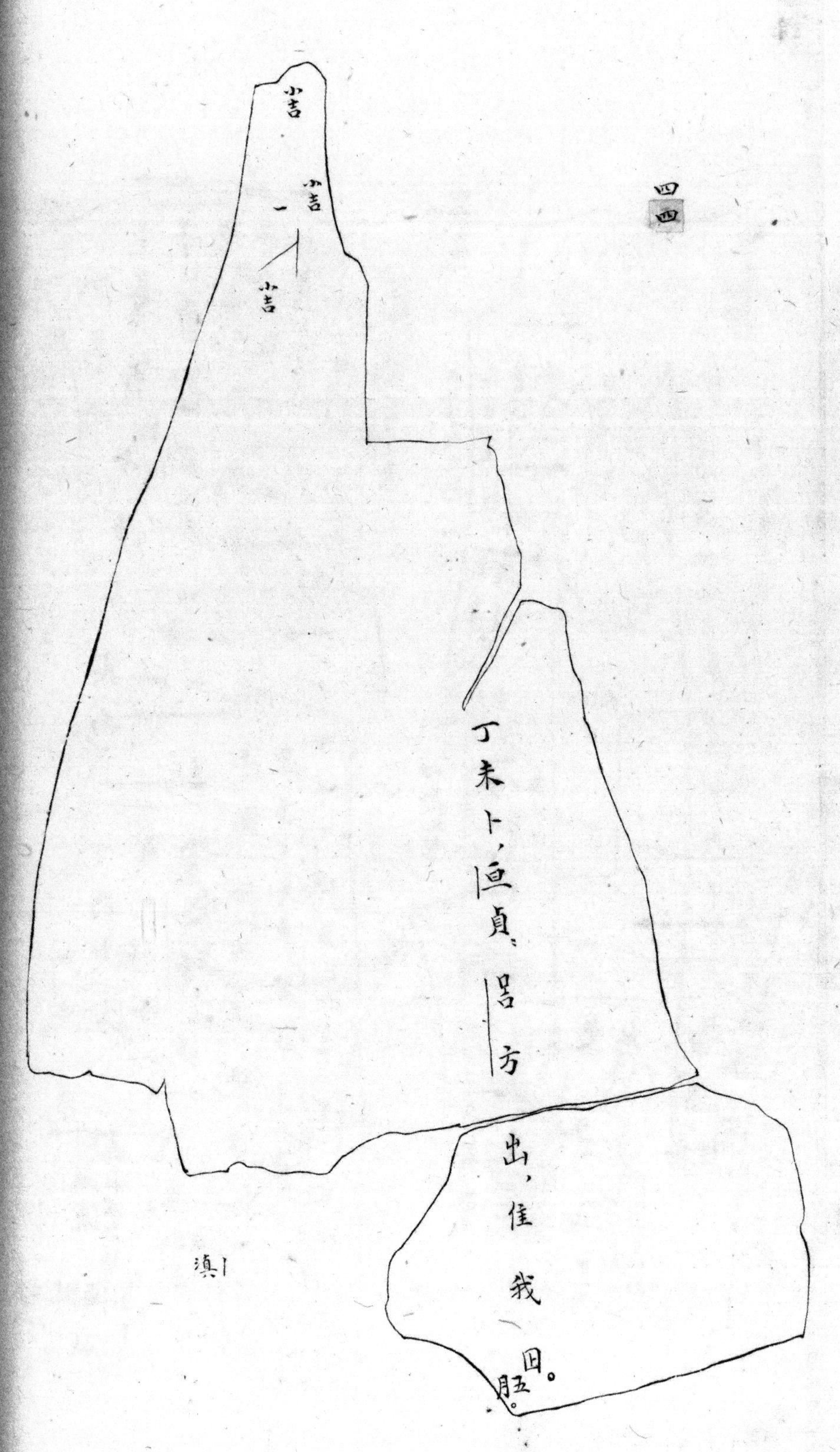

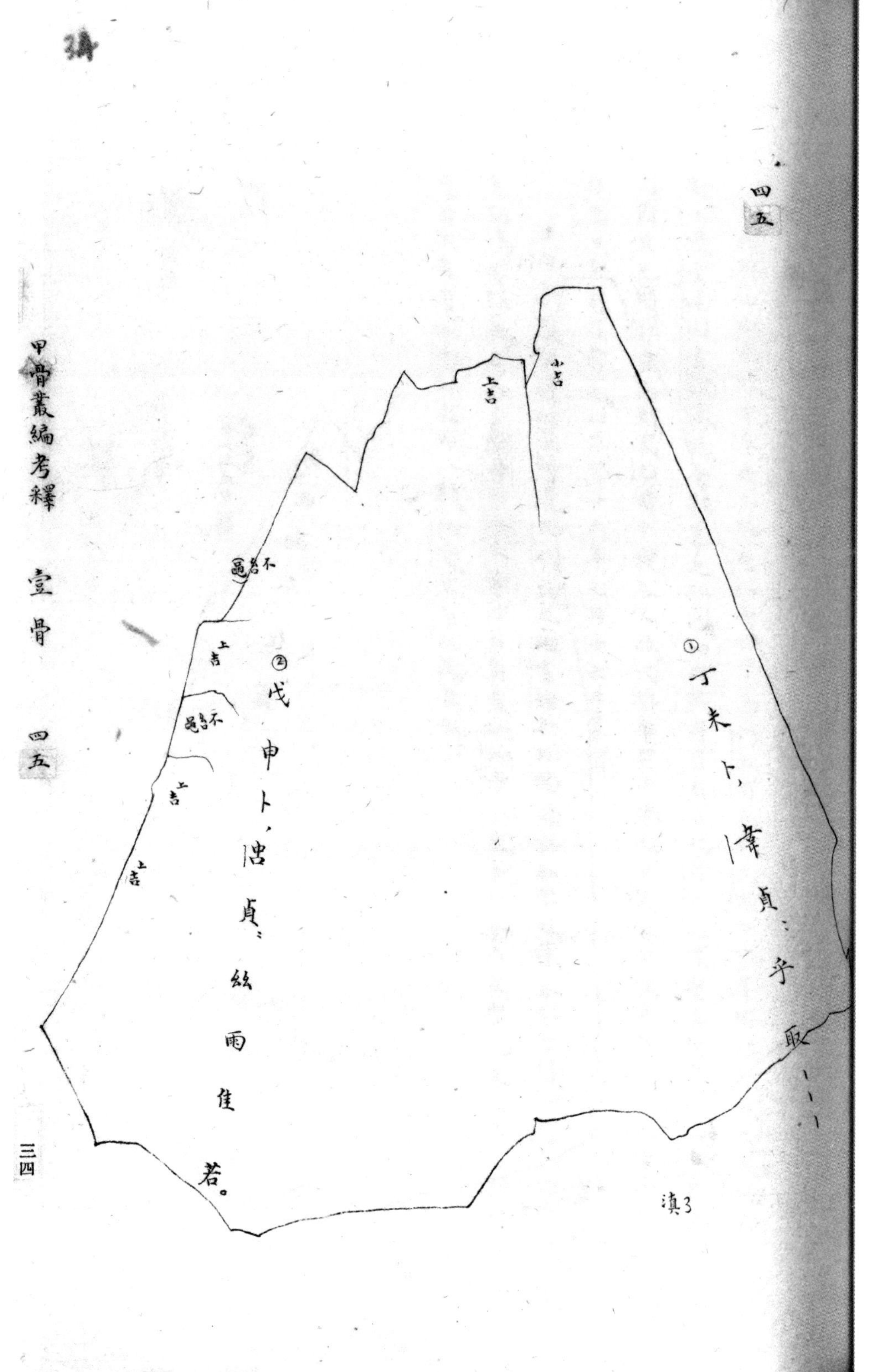
甲骨叢編考釋　壹骨　四五
四五
三四
① 丁未卜，…貞：予取
② 戊申卜，㞢貞：兹雨隹若。
上吉
小吉
上吉
上吉
上吉
滇3

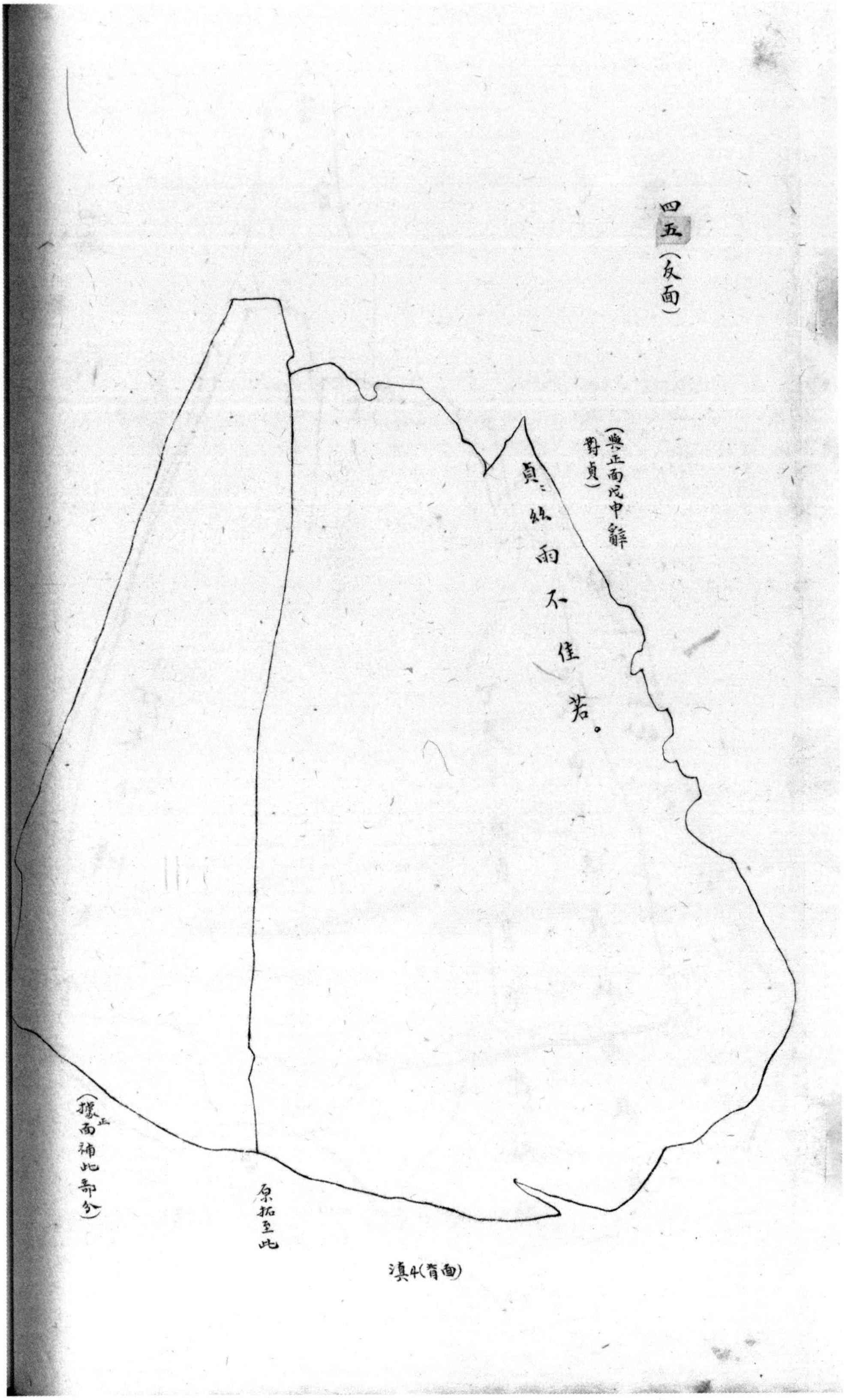

四五（反面）

（與正面戊申辭對貞）

貞：丝雨不隹若。

（據正面補此部分）

原拓至此

滇4（背面）

壹骨四五

此與四四及肆骨五，共三版，原拓本四片，為何叙甫氏於民國廿六年游滇所得，尚有偽刻小片十餘，云是雲南圖書館藏物，余影摹之如圖。四四版有月名，乃伐𢀛方之役重要材料也。四五版，為正反兩面對貞之例。肆骨五，則武乙時卜田之大版，戊與辛皆田獵之日（殷人田獵日為乙，丁，戊，辛，壬，餘五日為休息日，余别有考）也。四片，皆廿六年七月十六日摹寫。

廿七年春，余隨研究所遷昆明，詢之圖書館，無此物，徧訪私家收藏，亦不可得。然何氏固自滇得之，豈記憶有誤歟？原拓本壹骨四五反面右下角有「姚湘雲女史手拓金石文字記」朱文章一顆，肆骨五一片，右下角有「湘雲」白文印一顆。湘雲，其原收藏者歟？

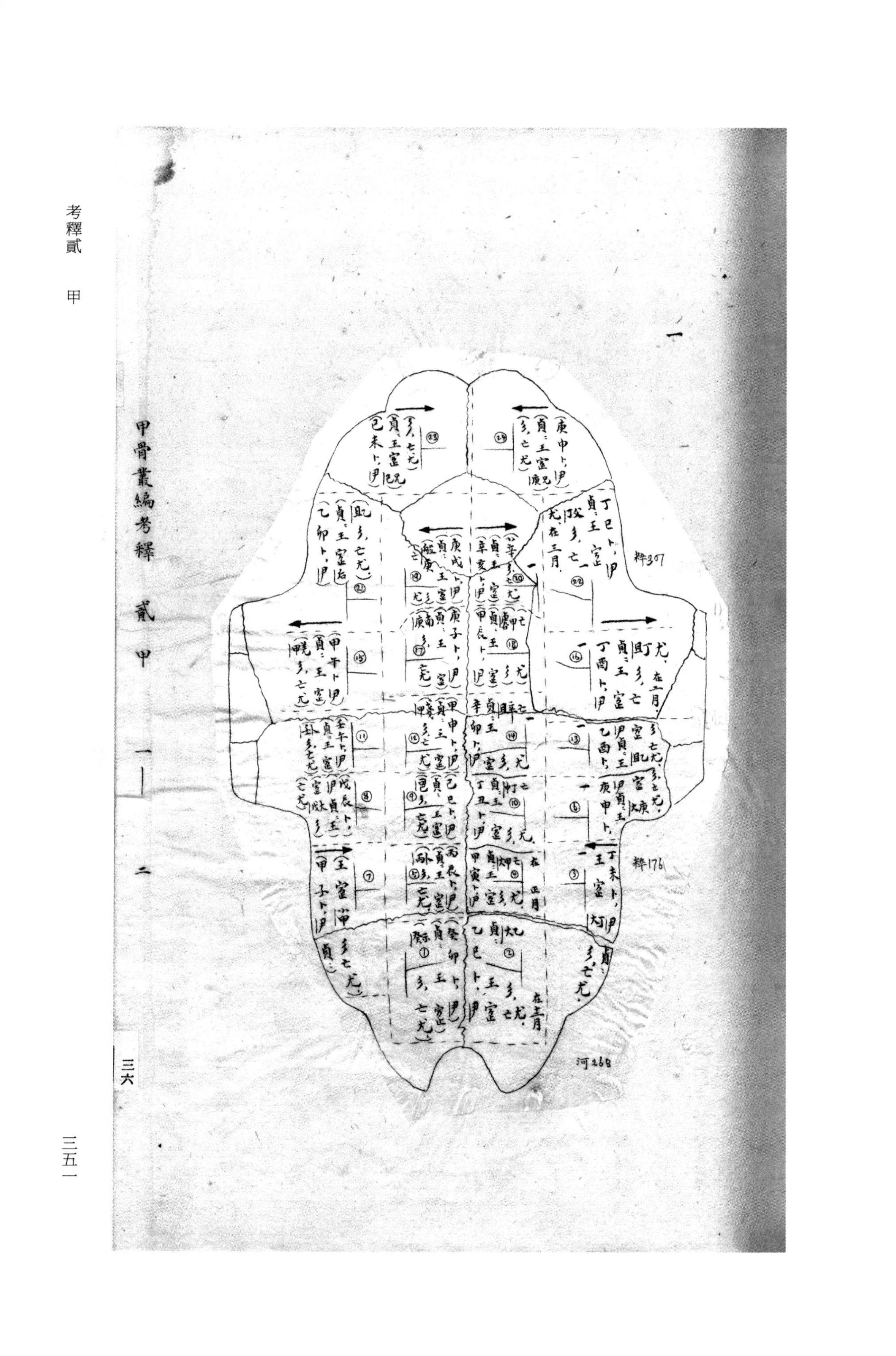

甲骨叢編考釋　貳　甲　一一二

一

粹307

粹176

河268

三六

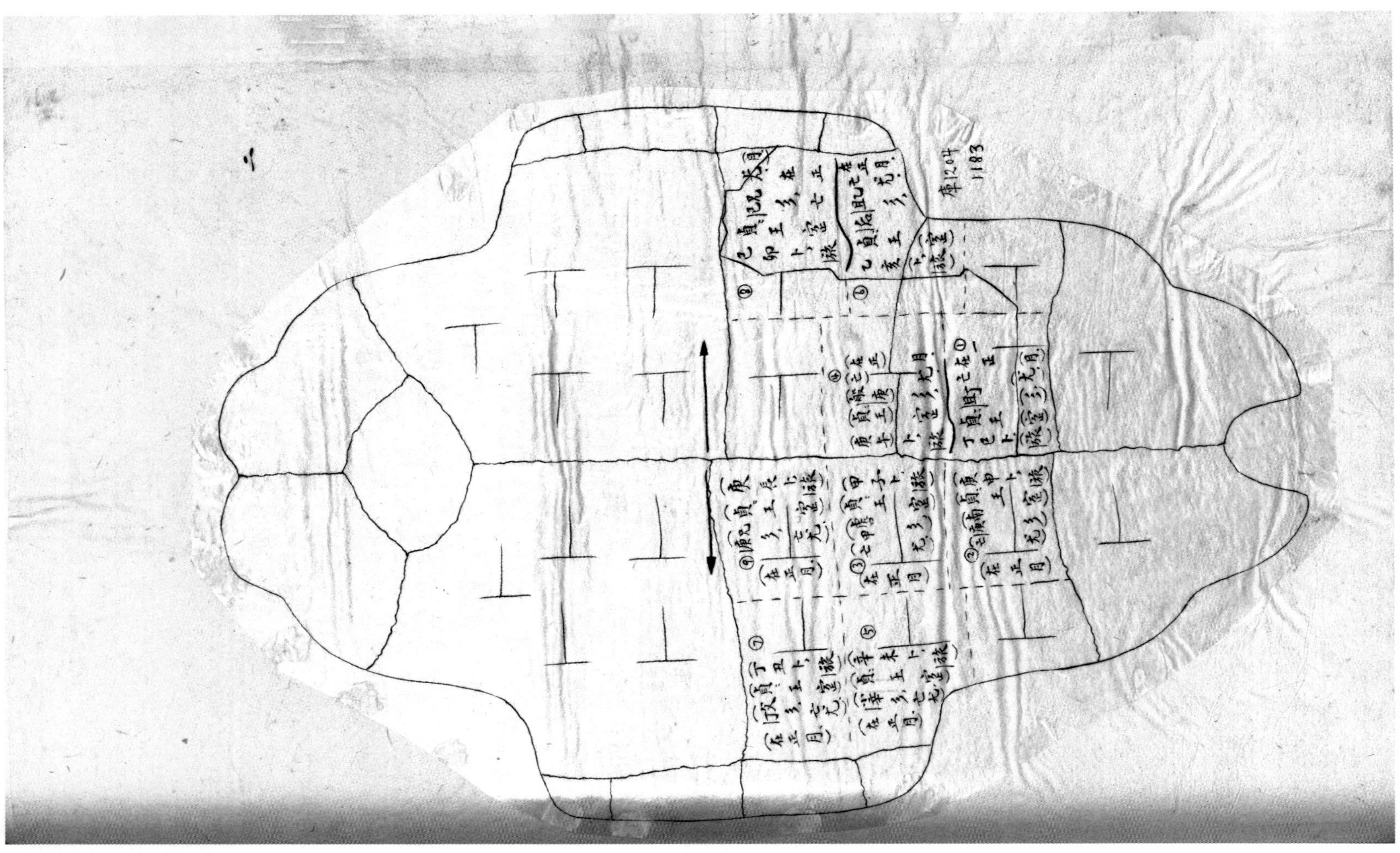

貳甲一—二

此龜腹兩版之復原，輯殘辭五片，祖甲時兩組彡祭卜辭也。三年前余理五期祀典，得彡，翌，祭，𡧊，𠬝五種祀典之關係，因祀典而求其年曆。嗣輯各期祀典，知五期蓋沿二期之舊，特二期彡，翌各佔九旬，祭𡧊𠬝錯一旬聯合舉行，佔十旬，並「工典」一旬，凡三十旬而五種祭祀一匝。五期則三十六旬而一匝，約相當於一年，故稱年為祀也。今舉彡祭系統示例。

貳甲一，為彡祭之甲午系，在祖甲祀譜列入三十至三十一年。對照如左：

祖甲三十年：十二月大（甲午系）　（卜辭）

十二月大丙子一日
甲午十九日　彡上甲
乙未廿日　彡匚乙
丙申廿一日　彡匚丙
丁酉廿二日　彡匚丁
壬寅廿七日　彡示壬
癸卯廿八日　彡示癸
乙巳卅日　彡大乙　　乙巳卜，尹貞：王賓大乙彡，亡尤。在十二月

三十一年：正月大丙午一日
丁未二日　彡大丁　　丁未卜，尹貞：王賓大丁彡，亡尤。

甲寅卜，尹貞：王賓大甲彡，亡尤。在正月。

庚申卜，尹貞：王賓大庚彡，亡尤。

丁丑卜，尹貞：王賓中丁彡，亡尤。

乙酉卜，尹貞：王賓祖乙彡，亡尤。

辛卯卜，尹貞：王賓祖辛彡，亡尤。

丁酉卜，尹貞：王賓祖丁彡，亡尤。在二月。

甲寅九日　彡大甲

丙辰十一日　彡卜丙

庚申十五日　彡大庚

甲子十九日　彡小甲

戊辰二十三日　彡大戊

己巳二十四日　彡雍己

二月小丙子一日

丁丑二日　彡中丁

壬午七日　彡卜壬

甲申九日　彡戔甲

乙酉十日　彡祖乙

辛卯十六日　彡祖辛

甲午十九日　彡羌甲

丁酉廿二日　彡祖丁

庚子廿五日　彡南庚

甲辰廿九日　彡㫚甲

38

三月大乙巳一日　庚戌六日　彡般庚

辛亥七日　彡小辛

乙卯十一日　彡后祖乙（即小乙）

丁巳十三日　彡父丁（即武丁）　丁巳卜，尹貞，王賓父丁彡，亡尤。在三月。

己未十五日　彡兄己（即祖己）

庚申十六日　彡兄庚（即祖庚）

此祖甲時彡祭先王先公之一組系統也。甲午系者，自甲午日開始。五種祀典，皆始於上甲，終於祖庚，此種依忌日之次序，排列規整，自祖甲創之。祖甲以前，祭唐亦以乙日，然無此系統組織，祖甲改稱唐曰大乙，為便於列入此系統組織者也。祖甲以下，垂為定制，絕無稱大乙為唐者矣。

貳甲二，為甲寅系之彡祭，彡上甲始自年前之十月，祖甲祀譜列入十三、十四年間。

祖甲十三年：

（甲寅系）

十月大丙戌一日　甲寅廿九日　彡上甲　乙卯卅日　彡匚

十一月小丙辰一日　丙辰一日　彡匚　丁巳二日　彡匚　壬戌七日　彡示壬

癸亥八日　彡示癸　乙丑十日　彡大乙　丁卯十二日　彡大丁

甲戌十九日　彡大甲　丙子廿一日　彡卜丙　庚辰廿五日　彡大庚

十二月大 乙酉一日

甲申廿九日 彡小甲

戊子四日 彡大戊　己丑五日 彡雍己　丁酉十三日 彡中丁

壬寅十八日 彡卜壬　甲辰廿日 彡戔甲　乙巳廿一日 彡祖乙

辛亥廿七日 彡祖辛　甲寅卅日 彡羌甲

十四年：正月小 乙卯一日

丁巳三日 彡祖丁　丁巳卜(旅)貞：王(賓)祖丁(彡)，亡(尤)。在正(月)。

庚申六日 彡南庚

甲子十日 彡虎甲

庚午十六日 彡般庚　(庚午)卜旅(貞)：(王)賓(般庚)彡，(亡)尤。(在正)月。

辛未十七日 彡小辛

乙亥廿一日 彡后祖乙　乙亥(卜)，(旅)貞：王(賓)后祖乙彡，亡尤。在正月。

丁丑廿三日 彡父丁

己卯廿五日 彡兄己　己卯卜，旅貞：王賓兄己彡，亡尤。在正(月)。

庚辰廿六日 彡兄庚

彡祭尚有甲子、甲戌、甲申、甲辰四系。翌、祭、壹、劦，皆可以此類推。五種祀典殘辭頗多，讀者試依次推尋排比之，當無往而不暢通也。

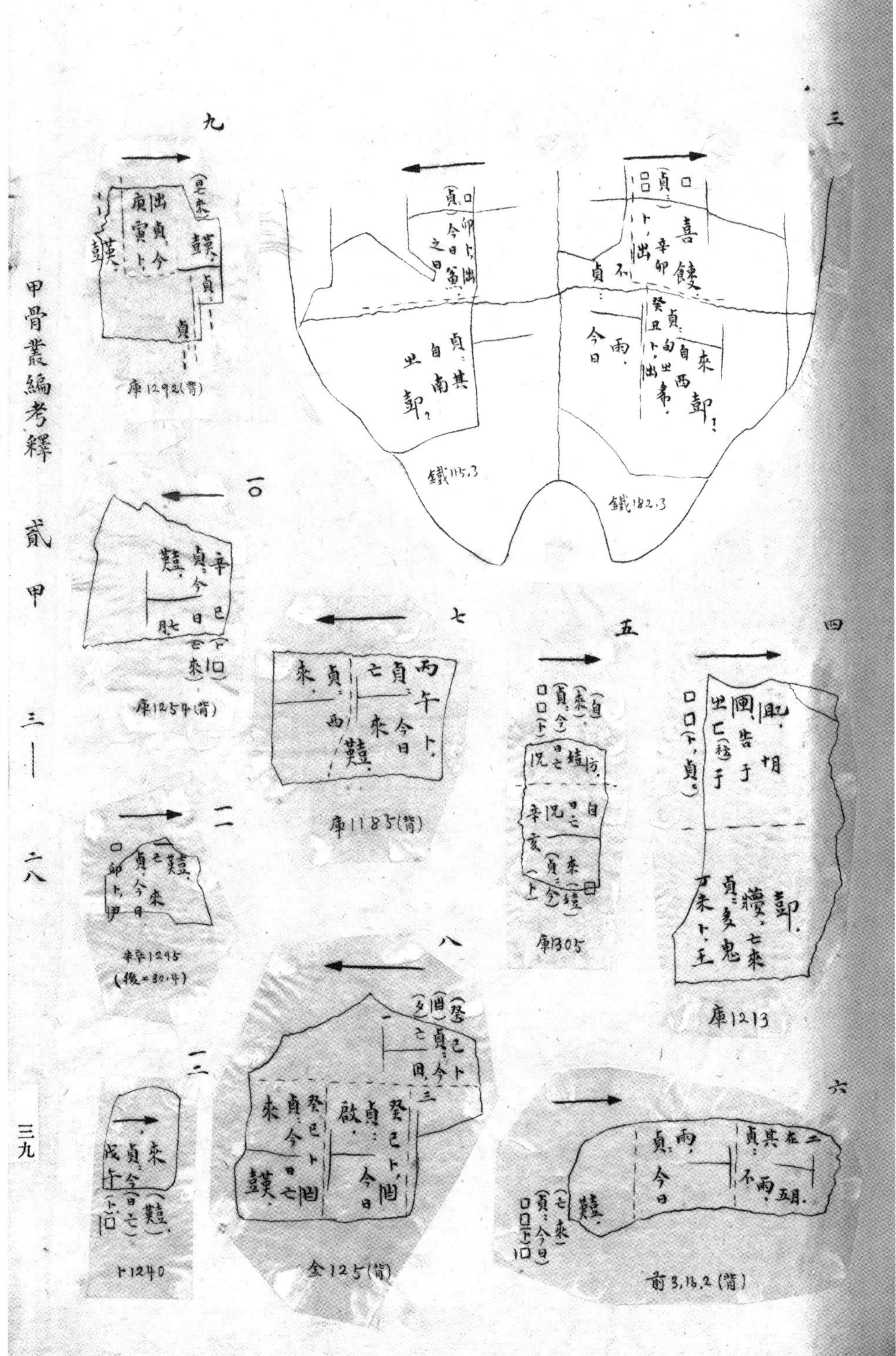
甲骨叢編考釋　貳　甲　三一—二八
三九
九
庫1292(背)
三
鐵115.3
鐵182.3
一〇
庫1257(背)
七
庫1183(背)
五
庫1305
四
庫1213
二
八
一二
卜1240
金125(背)
六
前3.16.2(背)

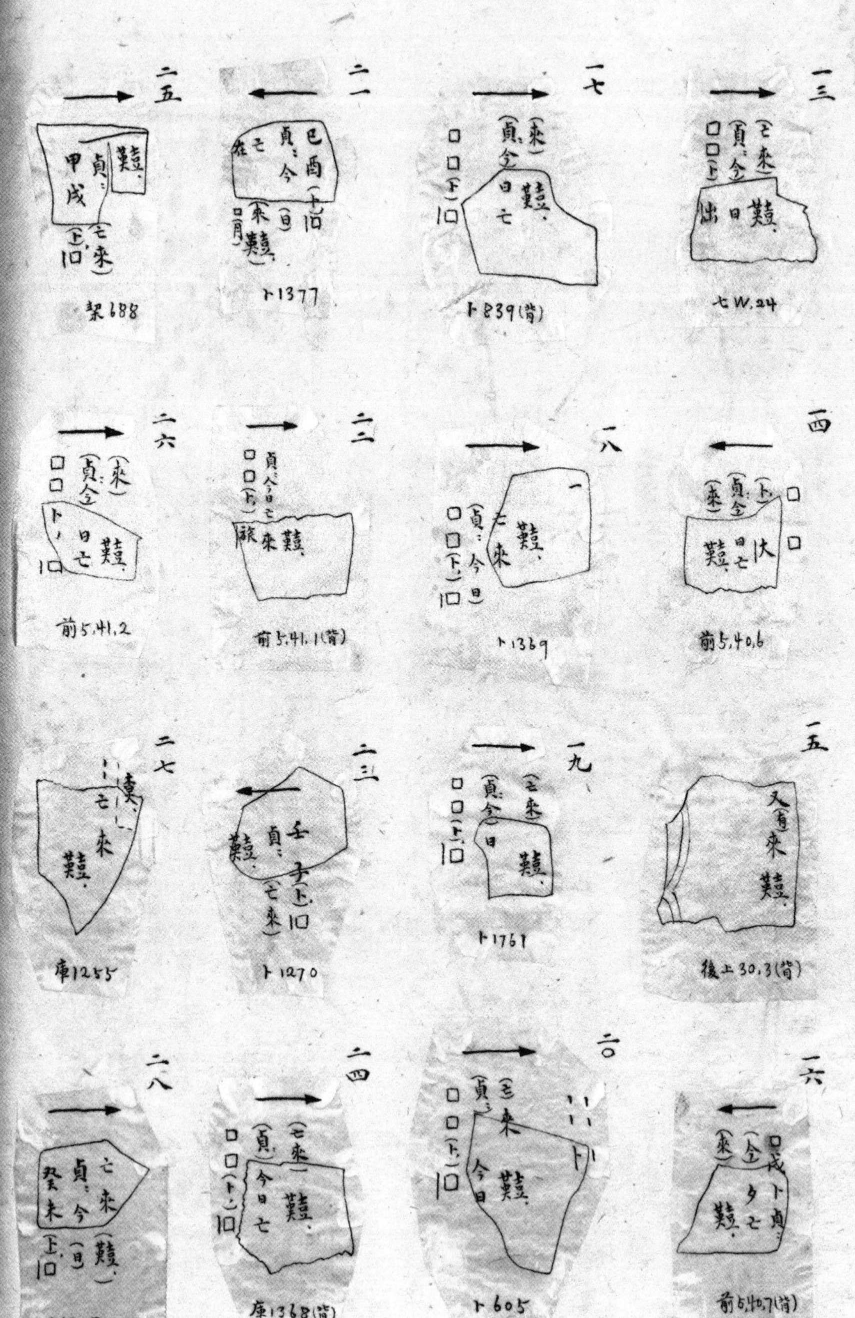
一三
七W.24
一四
前5.40.6
一五
後上30.3(背)
一六
前6.40.7(背)
一七
卜839(背)
一八
卜1369
一九
卜1761
二〇
卜605
二一
卜1377
二二
前5.41.1(背)
二三
卜1270
二四
庫1368(背)
二五
架688
二六
前5.41.2
二七
庫1255
二八
卜1307

甲骨叢編考釋　貳甲　二九—三一

二九

河669

①丙子卜，王。在𡉚卜。

②丙子卜，王。

③丙子卜，王。在𡉚卜。

④丙子卜，王。

河674

河672

⑤丁丑卜，王。

⑥丁丑卜，王。

⑦丁丑卜，王。在𡉚卜。

⑧丁丑卜，王。

⑨丁丑卜，王。

⑩丁丑卜，王。

⑪丁丑卜，王。

⑫丁丑卜，王。

⑬丁丑卜，王。

⑭丁丑卜，王。

⑮丁丑卜，王。

⑯丁丑卜，王。

河672

⑰丁丑卜，王。在𡉚卜。

⑱丁丑卜，王。

⑲丁丑卜，王。

⑳丁丑卜，王。

㉑丁丑卜，王。

㉒丁丑卜，王。

㉓丁丑卜，王。

㉔丁丑卜，王。

四〇

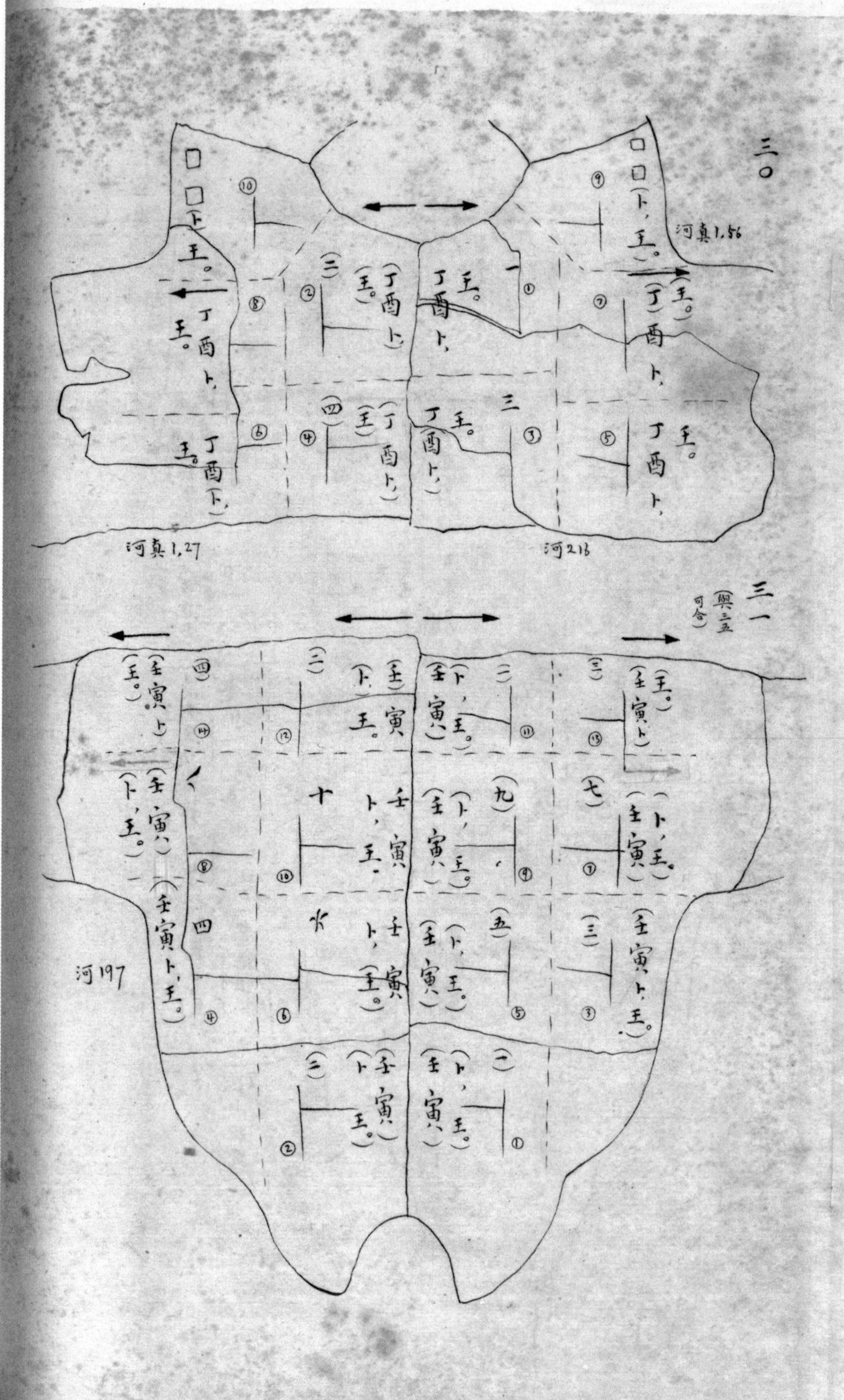

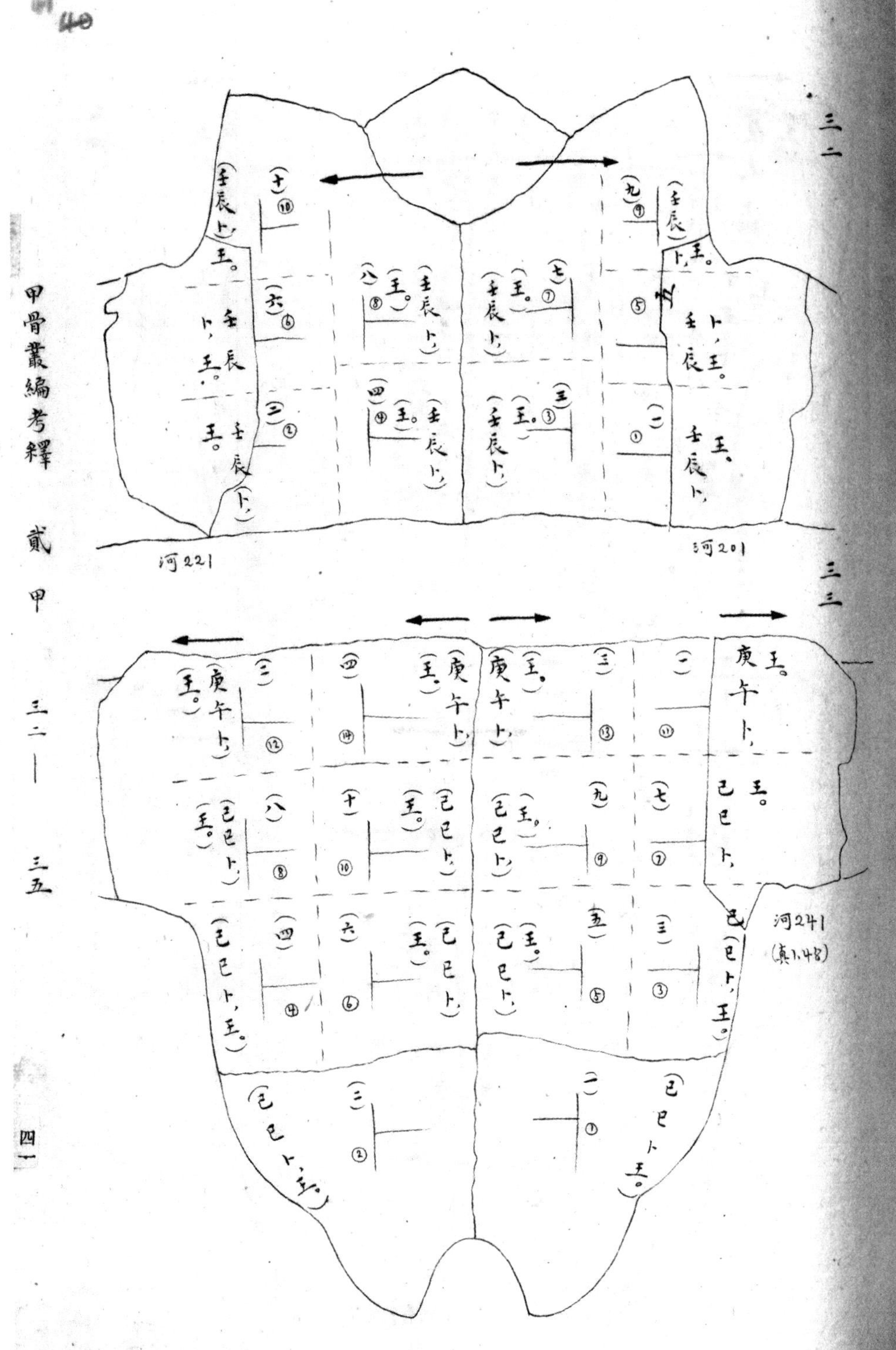
甲骨叢編考釋　貳　甲　三二—三五
四一
三二
三三
河221
河201
河241
(真1.48)

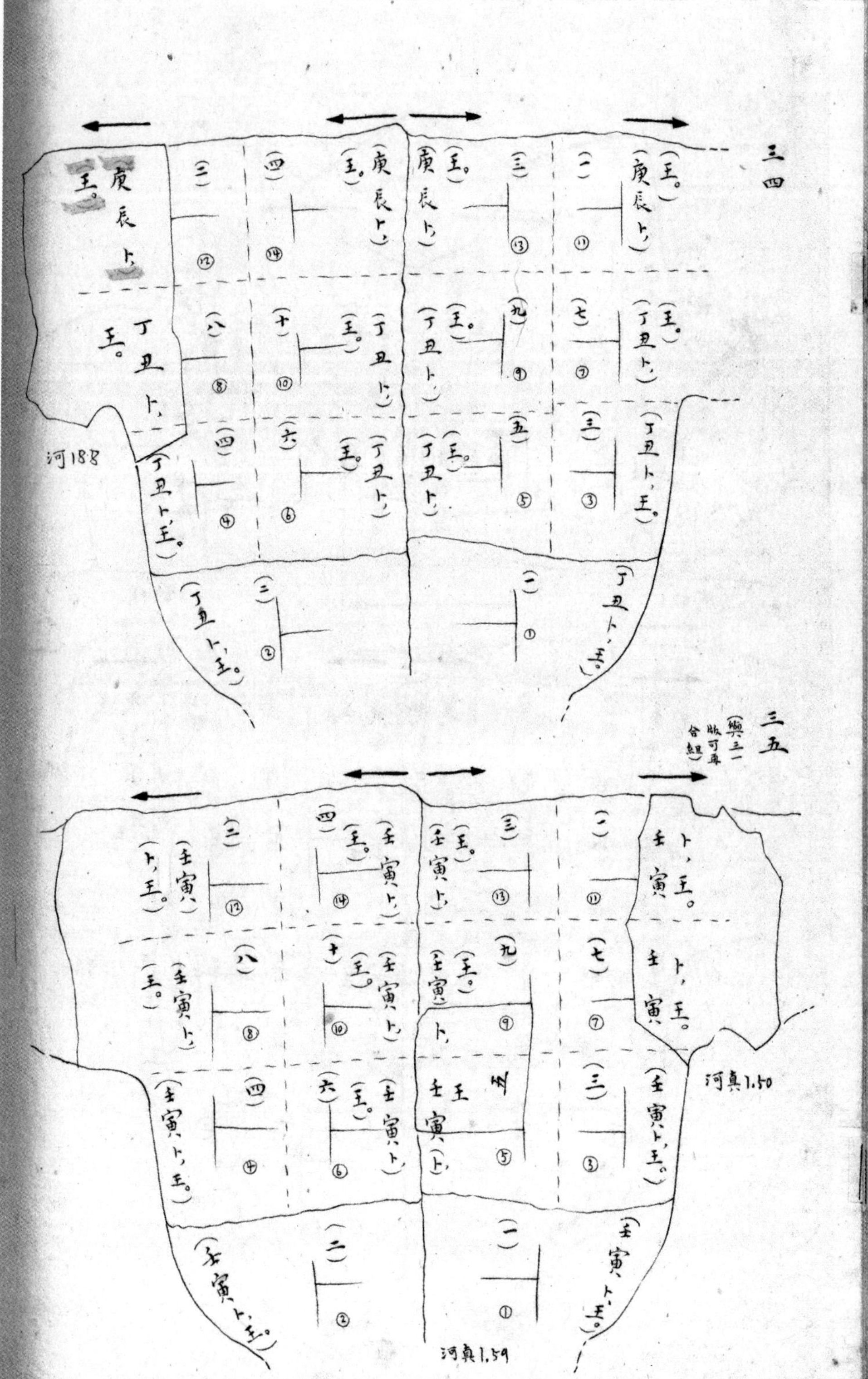

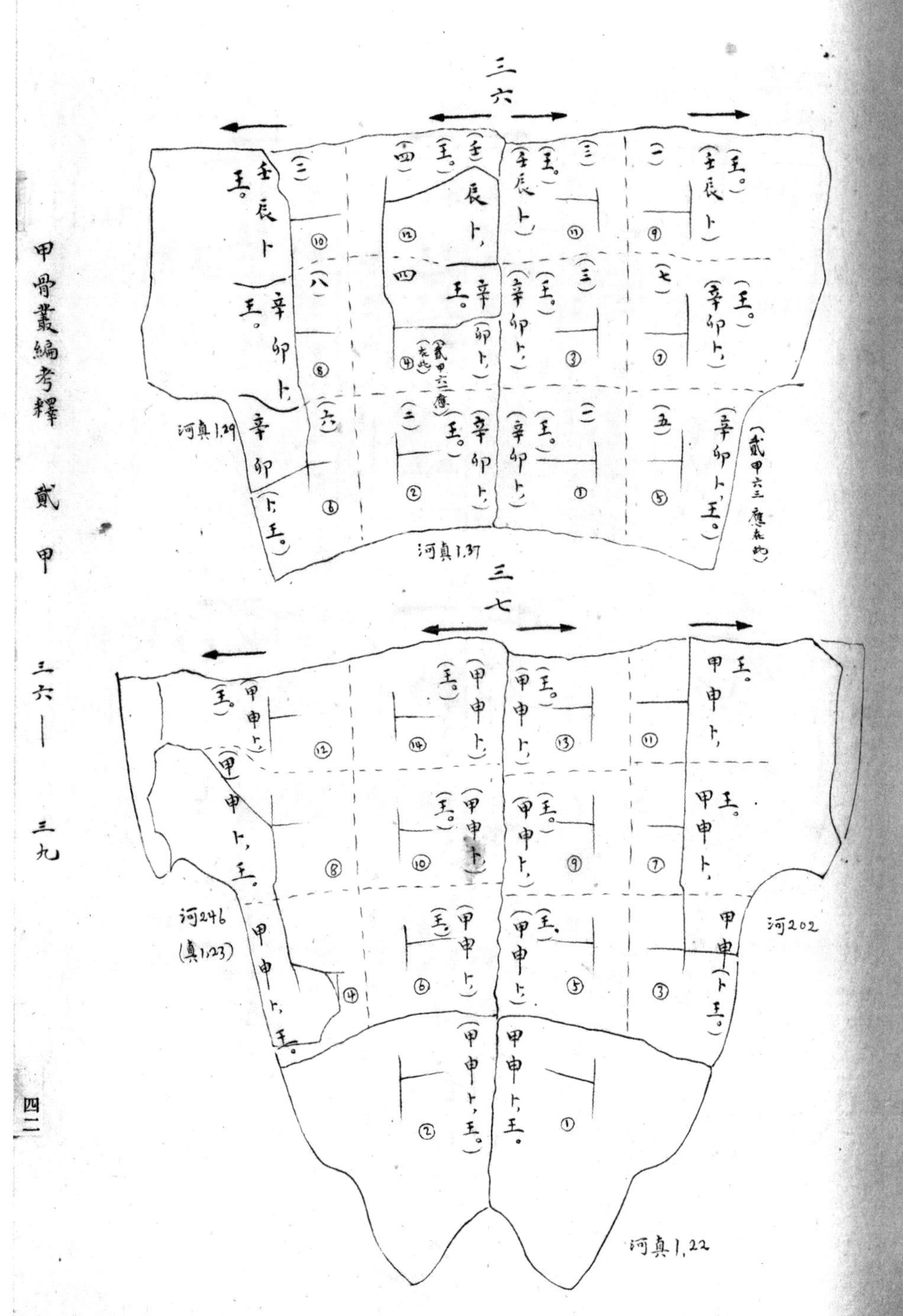
甲骨叢編考釋　貳　甲　三六一 — 三九
三六
河真1.29
河真1.37
(貳甲六三應表此)
三七
河246
(真1.23)
河202
河真1.22
四二

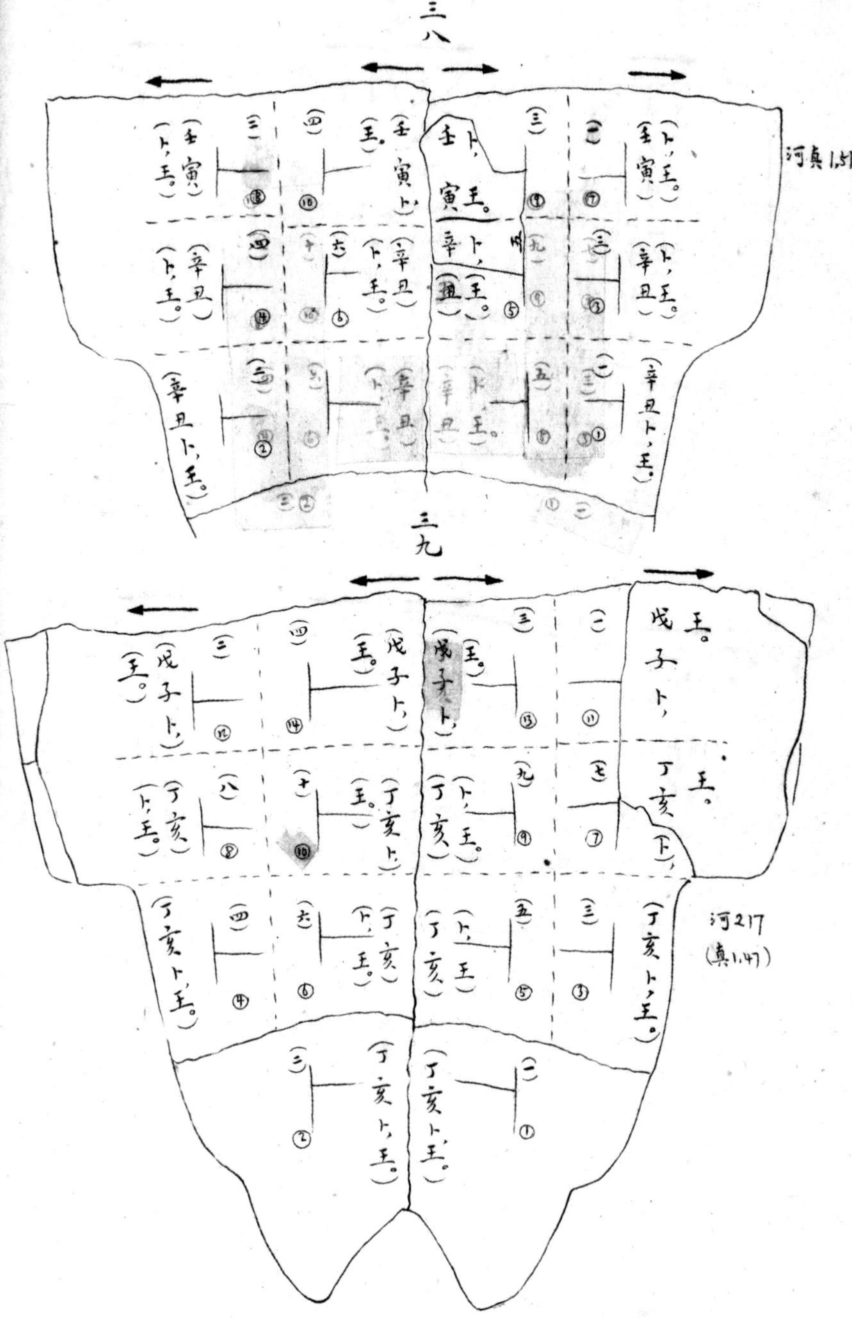
三八
河真1.51
三九
河217
(真1.47)

四三

四〇 甲子卜，王。 河真1.25

四一 甲子卜，王 河真1.21

四二 甲子王。 河真1.53

四三 甲子王。 河真1.54

四四 甲子卜，王。甲子卜，王。 河真1.20 河真1.24

四五 丙寅王 河真1.55

四六 卜，王。丙寅王。卜，丙寅王。卜， 河240 河233

四七 卜，王。丙寅卜，王。丙寅王。卜， 河196

四八 寅王。丙寅王。卜， 河208

四九 卯卜，王。丁卯卜，丁 河205

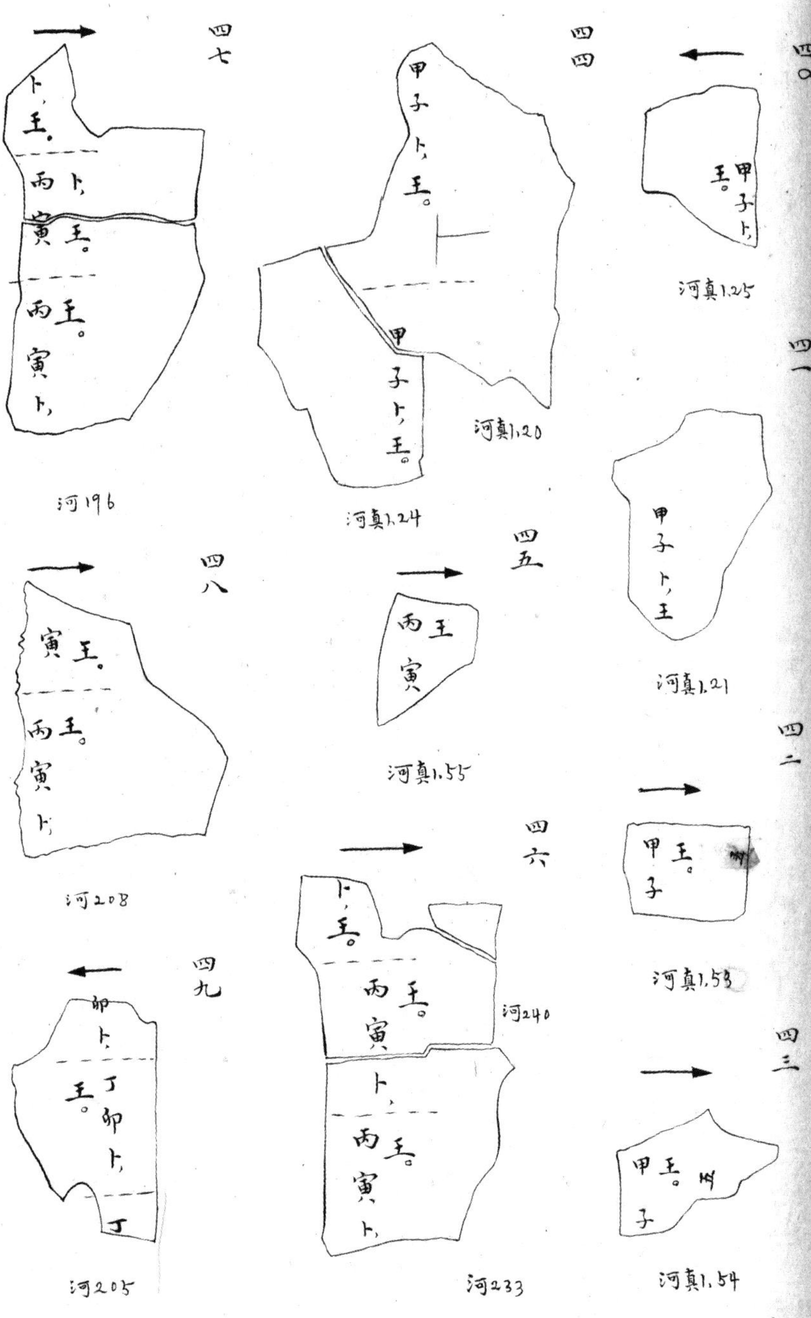

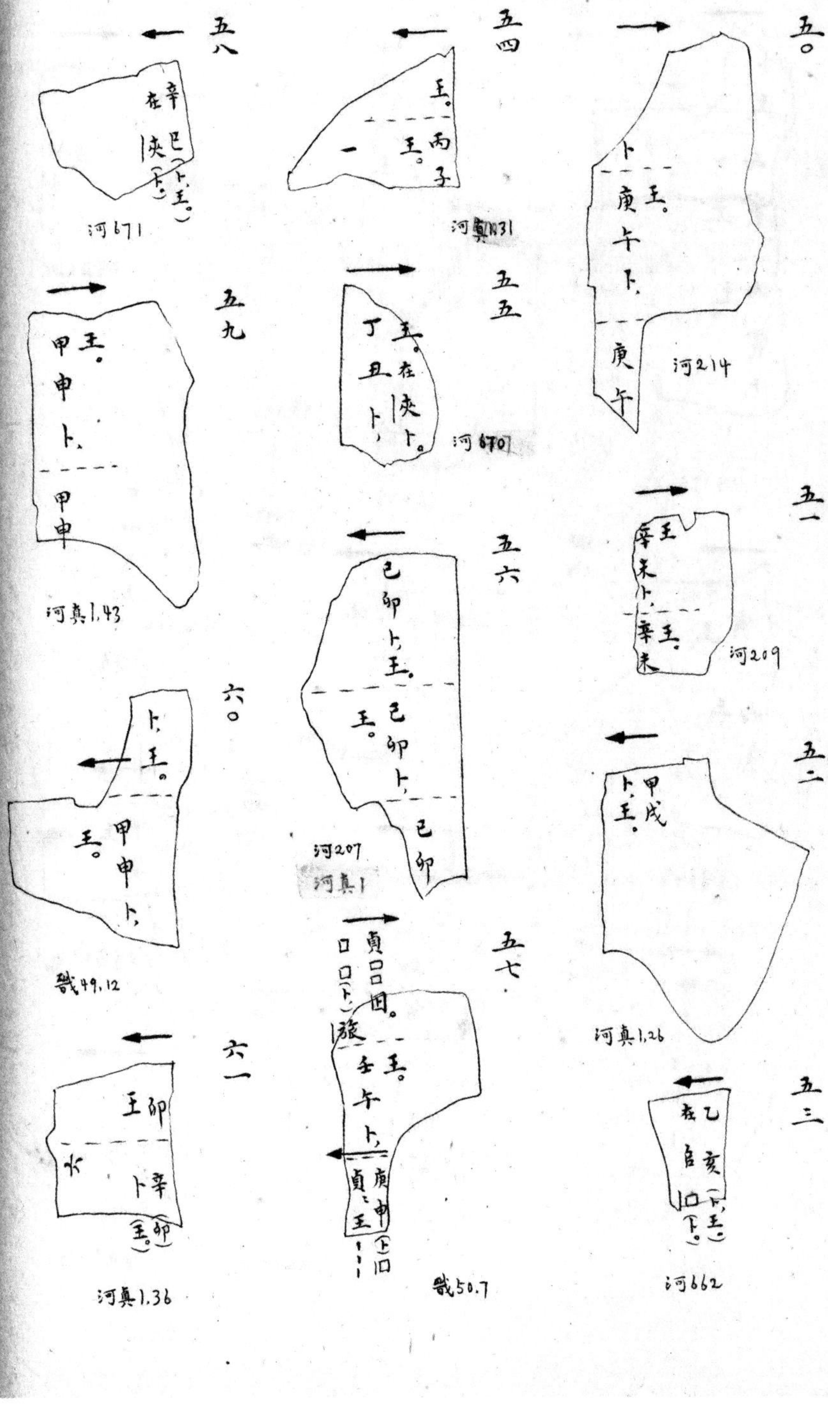

五〇
庚午卜，王。
庚午
河214

五一
辛未卜，王。
辛未，王。
河209

五二
甲戌卜，王。
河真1.26

五三
乙亥（卜，王。）
在自□（卜。）
河662

五四
丙子，王。
王。
一
河真1.31

五五
丁丑卜，王。
在|夾卜。
河670

五六
己卯卜，王。
己卯卜，王。
己卯
河207
河真1

五七
貞□□旬。
□□（卜）旅
壬午卜，王。
庚申（卜）□
貞，王
戩50.7

五八
辛巳（卜，王。）
在|夾（卜。）
河671

五九
甲申卜，王。
甲申
河真1.43

六〇
卜，王。
甲申卜，王。
戩49.12

六一
卯，王。
辛卯卜，（王。）
水
河真1.36

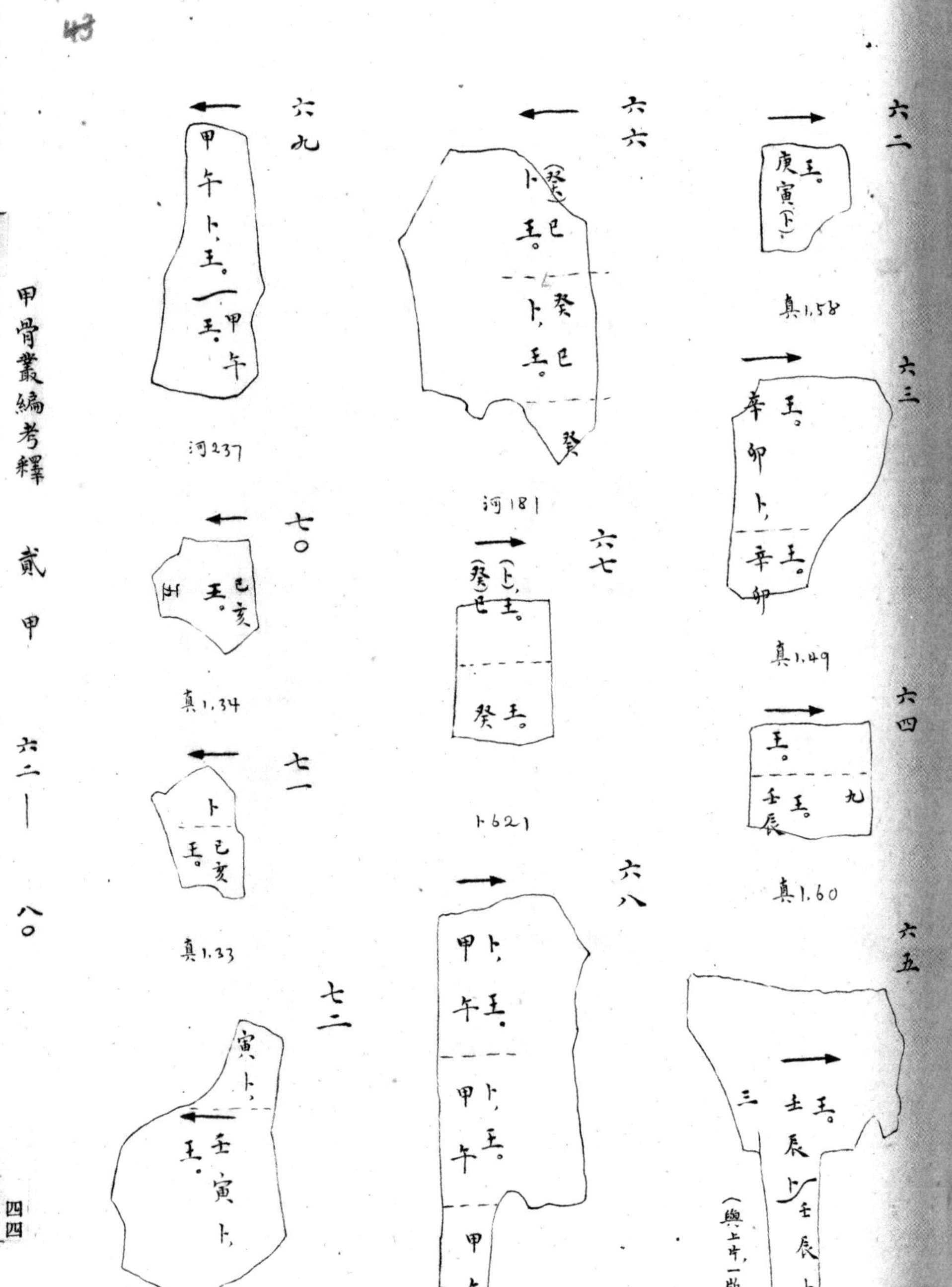
六二
庚寅(卜)王。
真1.58
六三
辛卯卜王。
辛卯王。
真1.49
六四
王。
壬辰王。九
真1.60
六五
壬辰卜王。三
壬辰卜王。
(與上片一版之折)
河218(真1.52)
六六
(癸)巳卜王。
癸巳卜王。
癸
河181
六七
(癸)巳(卜)王。
癸王。
卜621
六八
甲午卜王。
甲午卜王。
甲午
真1.42
六九
甲午卜王。
甲午王。
河237
七〇
己亥王。
真1.34
七一
卜
己亥王。
真1.33
七二
寅卜
壬寅卜王。
卜794

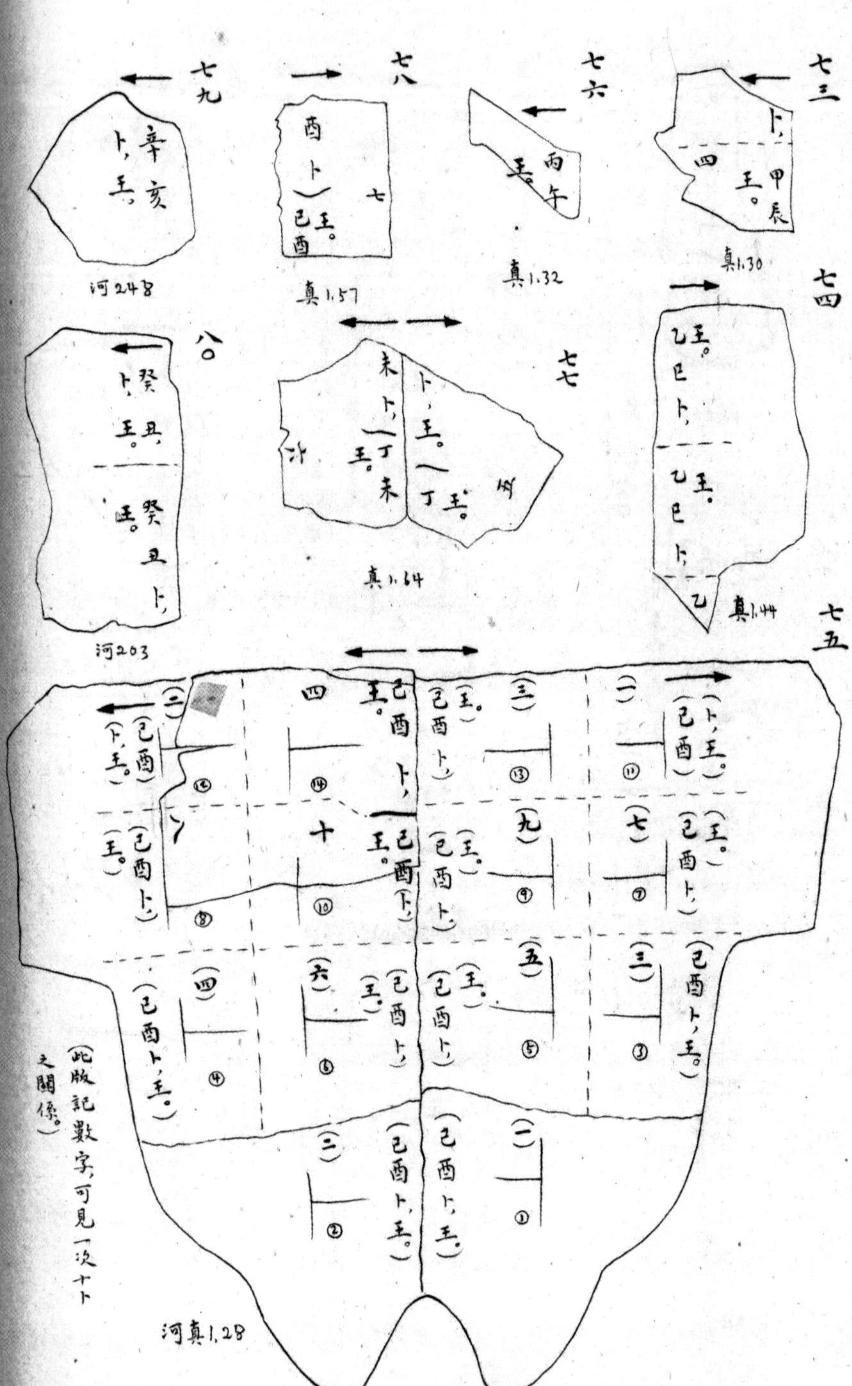
七三
甲辰卜，王。
真1.30
七四
真1.44
七五
河真1.28
（此版記數字，可見一次十卜之關係。）
七六
丙午王。
真1.32
七七
真1.64
七八
真1.57
七九
辛亥卜，王。
河248
八〇
河203

八一

甲申王。

甲申王。

河真1.63

八二

卜，

己未卜，王。

河199

八三

乙未卜，王。

（河南博物館藏卜辭見「卜王釋例」引）

河例1.9

八四

庚申王。

河真1.35

八五

戊卜，王。

壬戌卜，王。

壬王。

河192

八六

辛酉卜，王。

二

卜743

八七

亥卜，王。

卜748

八八

丁王。

河真1.39

八九

王。𢓊在自

河717

九〇

王。

王□未卜，

卜233

九一

卯卜，王。

卜217

甲骨叢編考釋　貳　甲　八一—一〇三

四五

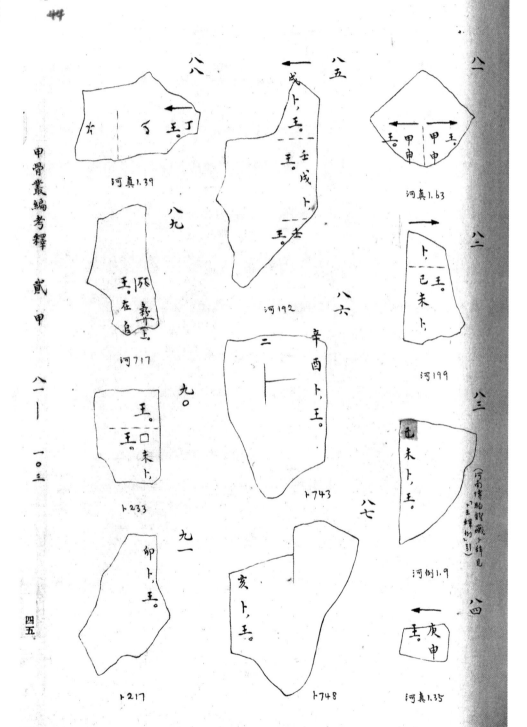

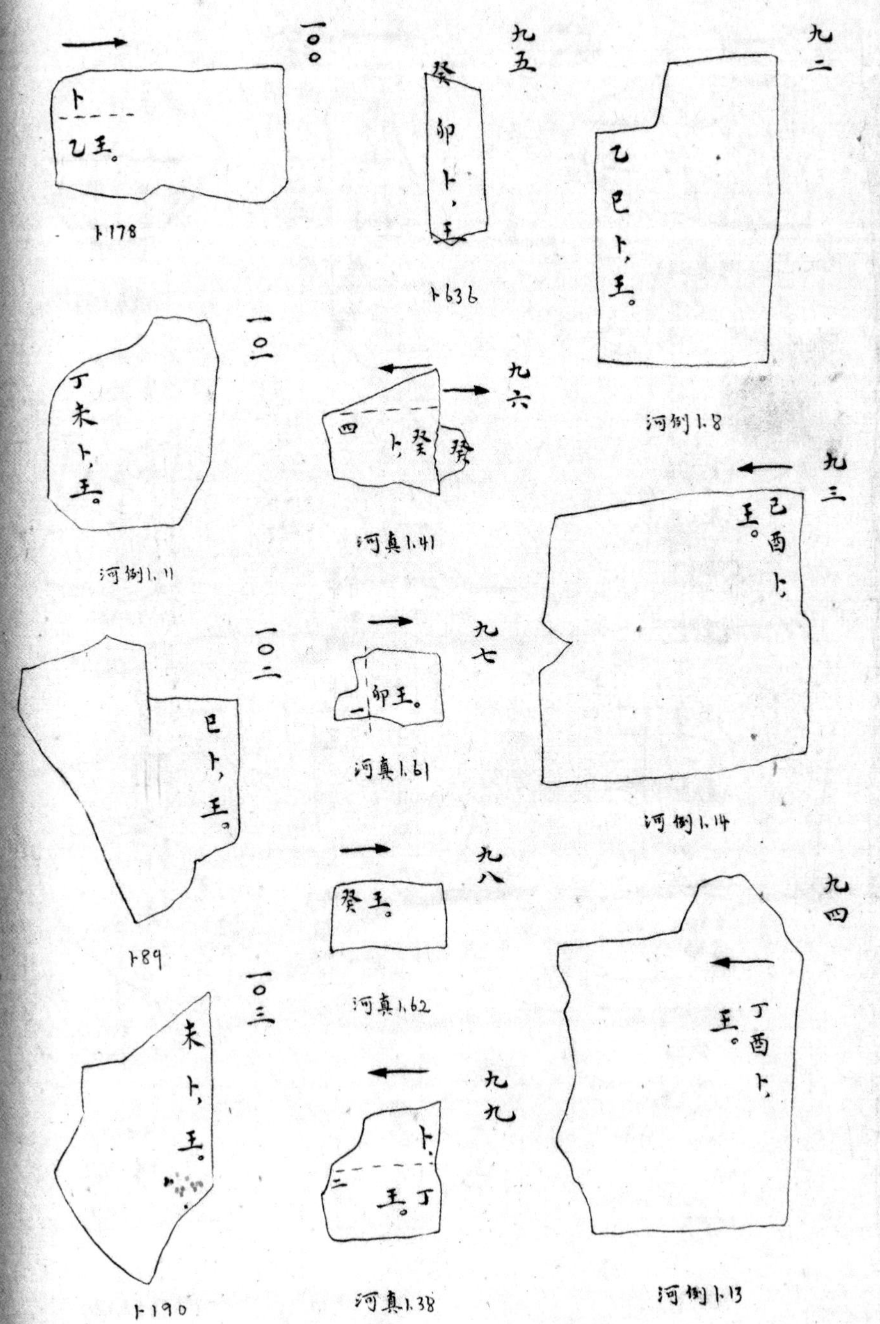
九二
乙巳卜，王。
河例1.8
九三
己酉卜，王。
河例1.14
九四
丁酉卜，王。
河例1.13
九五
癸卯卜，王
卜636
九六
四 卜，癸 癸
河真1.41
九七
一 卯王。
河真1.61
九八
癸王。
河真1.62
九九
卜
二 丁王。
河真1.38
一〇〇
卜
乙王。
卜178
一〇一
丁未卜，王。
河例1.11
一〇二
巳卜，王。
卜89
一〇三
未卜，王。
卜190

甲骨叢編考釋　貳　骨　一

①至⑯，示卜夕在骨版之次序

河36

① 癸酉卜，行貞：今夕亡田，在肚。
② 甲戌卜，行貞：今夕亡田，在肚。
③ 乙亥卜，行貞：今夕亡田，在肚。
④ 丙子卜，行貞：今夕亡田。
⑤ 丁丑卜，行貞：今夕亡田，在肚。
⑥ 戊寅卜，行貞：今夕亡田。
⑦ 己卯卜，行貞：今夕亡田。
⑧ 庚辰卜，行貞：今夕亡田，在肚。

河30

⑨ 辛巳卜，行貞：今夕亡田。
⑩ 壬午卜，行貞：今夕亡田。
⑪ 癸未卜，行貞：今夕亡田，在肚。
⑫ 甲申卜，行貞：今夕亡田。
⑬ 乙酉卜，行貞：今夕亡田。
⑭ 丙戌卜，行貞：今夕亡田。
⑮ 丁亥卜，行貞：今夕亡田。
⑯ 戊子卜，行貞：今夕亡田。

四六

貳骨一，示骨版卜辭文例。此為牛胛骨之左骨，凡胛骨，視上端鋸缺之部分，在左者為左骨，在右者為右骨。文例在卜夕，卜旬，最易分辨，依干支之順序，一望而知。大抵骨版刻辭與龜版同，皆先下後上也。卜旬卜夕，文辭簡整，骨之每邊可容六段乃至九段，此為八段。可容卜夕辭十六，如釋文。

河南博物館得大骨版六，此與貳骨四、五、六皆是，惜已多殘缺。卜夕辭無重要意義，但能依骨例輯録粘兑，使復原版，則有月份者於曆法之研究，功用極大。此版所涵十二月之干支，自癸酉至庚辰僅八日（補入者不計），在祖甲之三十三年中，有十年之十二月能容之。即據殷曆朔閏譜，為祖甲三、六、七、十、十一、十八、二十一、二十八、三十一、三十二等年也。兹舉三年示例：

祖甲三年，（公元前一二七一）殷正月，小，己未朔。（儒畧周日一二八七一八六）（是年閏九月小，乙酉朔）

十二月，大，癸丑朔。

癸亥（十一）

①癸酉（廿一）②甲戌（廿二）③乙亥（廿三）④丙子（廿四）⑤丁丑（廿五）⑥戊寅（廿六）⑦己卯（廿七）⑧庚辰（廿八）辛巳（廿九）壬午（卅）

是恰能容此八日也。餘不備舉。

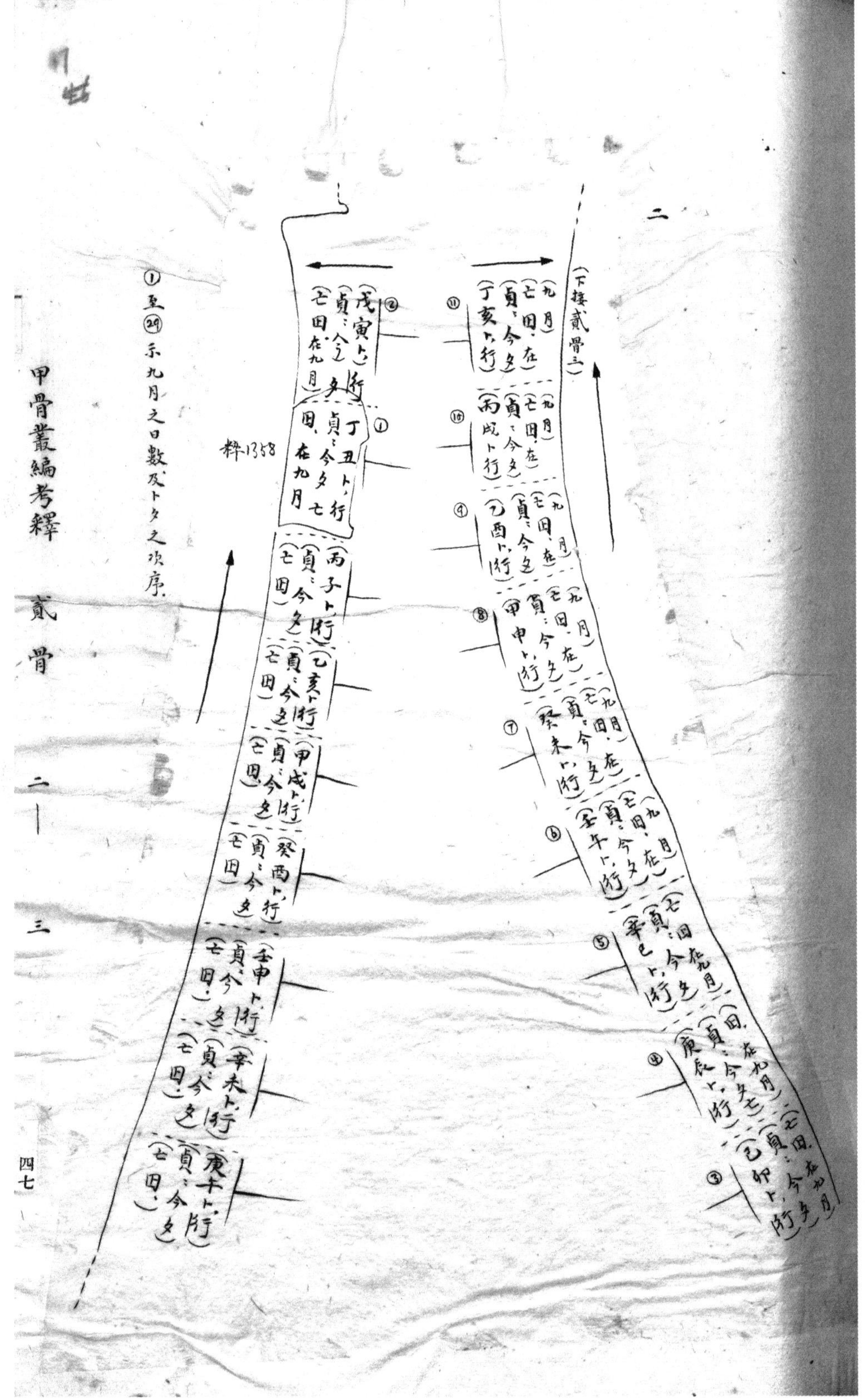

甲骨叢編考釋　貳骨　二一三
四七
①至㉙示九月之日數及卜夕之次序.
粹1358
(下接貳骨三)

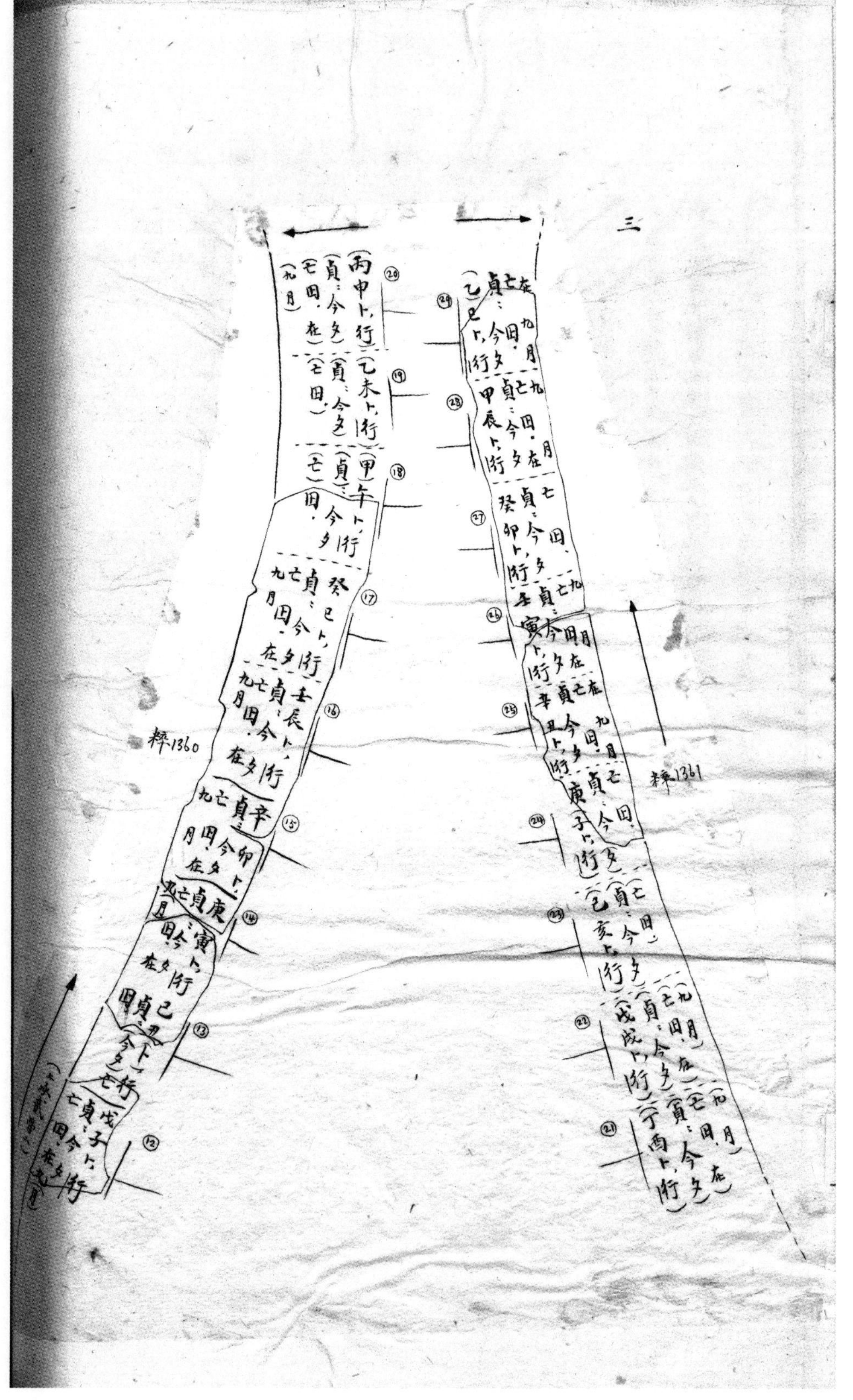
三
粹1360
粹1361

48

貳骨二—三

此兩骨版之補苴復原，由合殘骨三片，依文例每版可容之段落甚合，知當為日次相連之兩胛骨也。此種補苴非偶合可比，其嚴格之限制有五：骨版邊緣之部位，左右不可更易，一也；每邊不容九段以上之卜辭，二也；卜夕之干支密接，三也；月名連貫，四也；貞人皆第二期之行，五也。有此五種限制，欲事改動，殊不可能，補苴部分，或在人間，他日將有實物出為吾說證明者。

今但據殘存之三片，知九月有丁丑，更有乙巳，丁丑至乙巳為二十九日，恰足一小盡月之日數，此一巧合也。檢殷曆譜自武丁以來至於帝辛，九月丁丑朔凡五見，（依四分術同月同朔，約三十一年重見）。

武丁二十九年（公元前一三一二）　九月大丁丑朔

祖庚元年　（一二八〇）　九月大丁丑朔

祖甲二十五年（一二四九）　九月小丁丑朔

帝乙二十三年（一一八七）　九月大丁丑朔

帝辛十九年　（一一五六）　九月小丁丑朔

此版有貞人行，月名有「在」字，決為祖甲時卜夕之辭，而祖甲適得其一，又恰為小盡九月，此二巧合也。（如此版九月有丙午，是為大盡，則不合祖甲時之九月）。

茲節錄祖甲二十五年曆譜，以資對證。

祖甲二十五年（公元前一二四九年　壬申）

（殷正）正月大　辛亥一日（一二五〇年十二月二十四日儒略周日一二六五二一八）（九日己未一二四九年一月一日）

二月小　辛巳一日（一月二十三日　周日一二六五二四八日食）（十五日乙未　月食）

三月大　庚戌一日（二月二十一日　周日一二六五二七七）（二日辛亥日食）

四月小　庚辰一日（三月二十二日　周日一二六五三〇七）

五月大　己酉一日（四月二十日　周日一二六五三三六）

六月小　己卯一日（五月二十日　周日一二六五三六六）

七月大　戊申一日（六月十八日　周日一二六五三九五）（廿日丁丑日食）

七月閏小　戊寅一日（七月十八日　周日一二六五四二五）（十五日壬辰　月食）

八月大　丁未一日（八月十六日　周日一二六五四五四　日食）

九月小　丁丑①一日（九月十五日　周日一二六五四八四）……戊子⑫十二日　己丑⑬十三日　庚寅⑭十四日　辛卯⑮十五日

壬辰⑯十六日　癸巳⑰十七日　甲午⑱十八日……庚子㉔廿四日　辛丑㉕廿五日　壬寅㉖廿六日　癸卯㉗廿七日

甲辰㉘廿八日　乙巳㉙廿九日

十月大　丙午一日（十月十四日　周日一二六五五一三）

十一月大　丙子一日（十一月十三日　周日一二六五五四三）

十二月大　丙午一日（十二月十三日　周日一二六五五七三）（二十日乙丑　三四八年一月一日）

本年閏七月，閏法與無中氣置閏不同，蓋無節氣乃置閏也，説詳殷曆譜。朔用平朔，故三月日食在二日，七月日食在晦。然二月、八月，則皆為定朔，日食在朔也。故九月一日丁丑，廿九日乙巳，為最準確。

貳骨四—六

此與貳骨一同坑出土。皆河南博物院挖掘所得，此坑共出全整之牛胛骨六，茲所錄一、四、五、六殘版三，全骨一，皆是也。此為甲骨文字出土之一段軼史，詳採衆雜譚，錄之以供參閱。

軒家「大連坑」

民國十八年秋，中央研究院發掘殷墟第三次工作開始，河南博物院亦派人至小屯挖掘甲骨文字，時李濟博士主持研究院工作，乃劃出B區以北為彼等挖掘地帶，兩方同時工作。此次研究院得儲存甲骨最多之坑，因多坑連接，名曰「大連坑」，大龜四版（本編壹甲一—四）即出其間。

博物院主持者為軒某，在村北「二十畝地」內開採（小屯村人呼吾等發掘區之A區南北一条曰「劉家二十畝地」。地主劉姓，此地發現甲骨最早，皆一二期卜辭，鐵雲藏龜所收皆出于是，無五期卜辭，為其特點），於地北首亦得一儲積豐富之坑，村人艷稱之，呼曰「軒家大連坑」。

軒之挖掘甲骨也，以得物為主，每鼓勵工人隨地掘之，得甲骨則檢拾之，不計畫，不測量，不繪圖，不記錄，故遺物之出土情形無可考。

民國二十一年殷墟第七次發掘，余閱A區各坑，探視地下堆積情狀。A區在「劉家二十畝地」，乃集曾為博物院挖掘之工人，翻檢所謂「軒家大連坑」者，得其概略如下：

此坑範圍甚大，觀其形，似即儲藏器用之竇穴，竇穴之中又有竇窖，A區一帶之普遍現象也。據熟悉當時情形者言：（坑名參看附圖）

甲坑：「曾出六個馬蹄兒（村人稱牛胛骨曰「馬蹄兒」，因其骨臼處形似馬蹄，蓋倒而視之也）完整的，有字的。六個平排，小的一頭（指骨臼）向西，有兩塊互相擠壓，殘破了。」

按此坑即本編所錄貳骨一、四、五、六，出土地點，六版殆皆卜夕之辭，今則所謂「完整的」，只餘貳骨四之一版矣。

乙坑：「是一個東西濠（指發掘之坑，長形者。）長二米，寬一米。博物院卸姓看坑。深二米時候，出象牙器，狠長，如　形，一頭有孔（工人於地上，以指劃此形）共出十餘条。下邊有花骨（村人謂有文字之骨曰「字骨」，雕鏤花紋之骨曰「花骨」）。象牙器東西橫排在花骨上，花骨出黃土中。」

丙坑：「有兩丈深，出箭頭（指骨製者）、麵版」。

丁坑：「一人深，出有字龜甲。至八圈深，（村人謂轆轤上所繞之繩。一圈約二尺許，八圈約深二

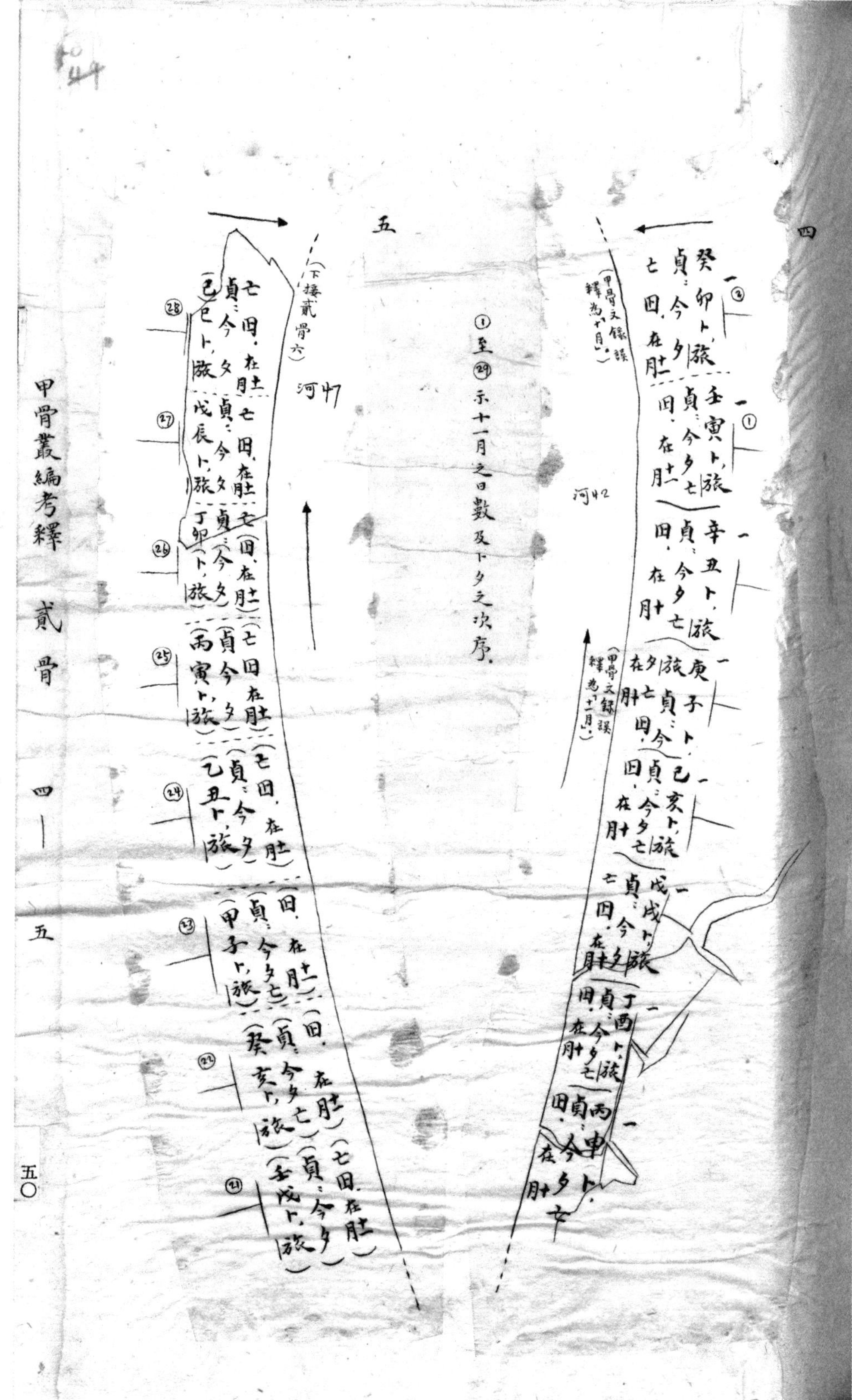
甲骨叢編考釋 貳骨 四一 五
五〇
四
② 癸卯卜，旅貞：今夕亡田，在肚
（甲骨文錄誤釋為「六月」）
① 壬寅卜，旅貞：今夕亡田，在十二月
辛丑卜，旅貞：今夕亡田，在十月
庚子卜，旅貞：今夕亡田，在十月
（甲骨文錄誤釋為「十月」）
己亥卜，旅貞：今夕亡田，在十月
戊戌卜，旅貞：今夕亡田，在十月
丁酉卜，旅貞：今夕亡田，在十月
丙申卜，貞：今夕亡田，在十月
河42
①至㉙示十一月之日數及卜夕之次序。
五
（下接貳骨六）
河47
㉘ 己巳卜，旅貞：今夕亡田，在肚
㉗ 戊辰卜，旅貞：今夕亡田，在肚
㉖ 丁卯（卜，旅貞：今夕）亡（田，在肚）
㉕ （丙寅卜，旅貞：今夕亡田，在肚）
㉔ （乙丑卜，旅貞：今夕亡田，在肚）
㉓ （甲子卜，旅貞：今夕亡田，在肚）
㉒ （癸亥卜，旅貞：今夕亡田，在肚）
㉑ （壬戌卜，旅貞：今夕亡田，在肚）

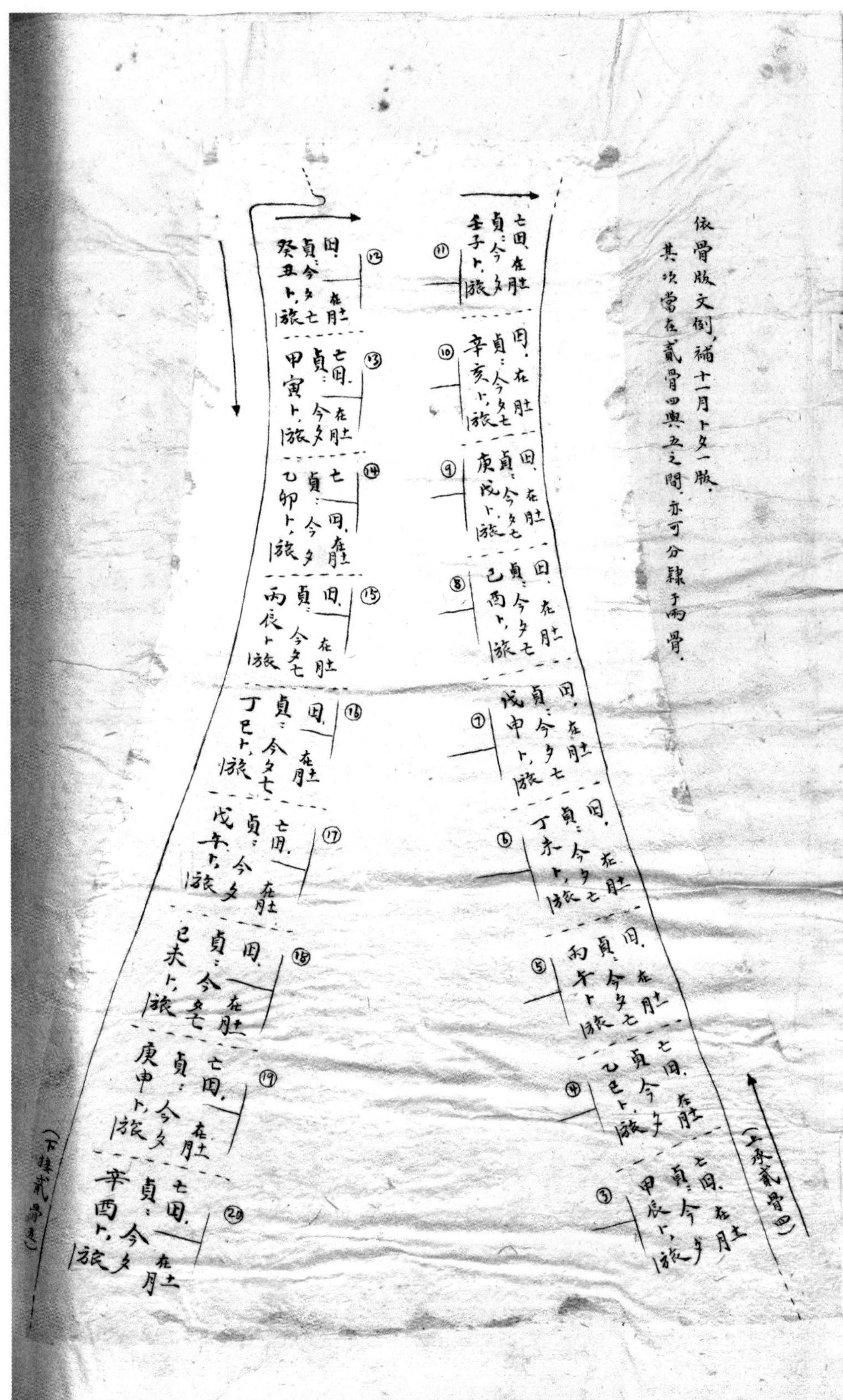
依骨版文例，補十一月卜夕一版。
其次當在貳骨四與五之間，亦可分隸于兩骨。
（上承貳骨四）
③ 甲辰卜，旅貞：今夕亡囚，在十一月
④ 乙巳卜，旅貞：今夕亡囚，在十一月
⑤ 丙午卜，旅貞：今夕亡囚，在十一月
⑥ 丁未卜，旅貞：今夕亡囚，在十一月
⑦ 戊申卜，旅貞：今夕亡囚，在十一月
⑧ 己酉卜，旅貞：今夕亡囚，在十一月
⑨ 庚戌卜，旅貞：今夕亡囚，在十一月
⑩ 辛亥卜，旅貞：今夕亡囚，在十一月
⑪ 壬子卜，旅貞：今夕亡囚，在十一月
⑫ 癸丑卜，旅貞：今夕亡囚，在十一月
⑬ 甲寅卜，旅貞：今夕亡囚，在十一月
⑭ 乙卯卜，旅貞：今夕亡囚，在十一月
⑮ 丙辰卜，旅貞：今夕亡囚，在十一月
⑯ 丁巳卜，旅貞：今夕亡囚，在十一月
⑰ 戊午卜，旅貞：今夕亡囚，在十一月
⑱ 己未卜，旅貞：今夕亡囚，在十一月
⑲ 庚申卜，旅貞：今夕亡囚，在十一月
⑳ 辛酉卜，旅貞：今夕亡囚，在十一月
（下接貳骨五）

六

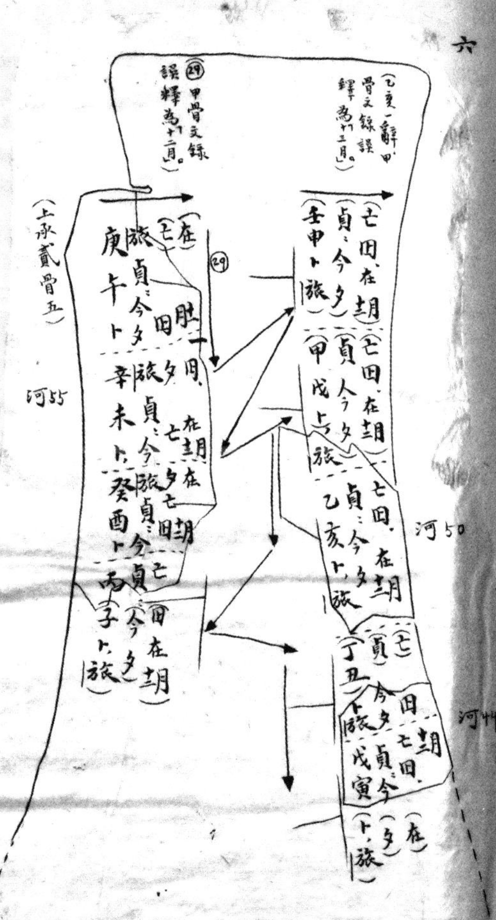

丈左右）。出元馬蹄兕（指未經人工鋸製之牛胛骨，蓋卜用骨之原料也）一層，無火號（指鑽灼處），無文字。又出獸面（村人稱饕餮形曰獸面）白石。」

戊坑：「此坑深一米時出馬蹄兕一層，平排甚整齊。」

所謂「衖家大連坑」者，即此五坑之外圍，連接之而擴成一長方形不規則之大坑也。坑在吾人第七次發掘A26與A29之間，乃一儲存之穴窖，特經破壞，不能知其原狀耳。附圖於次：

甲骨叢編考釋　貳　骨　六

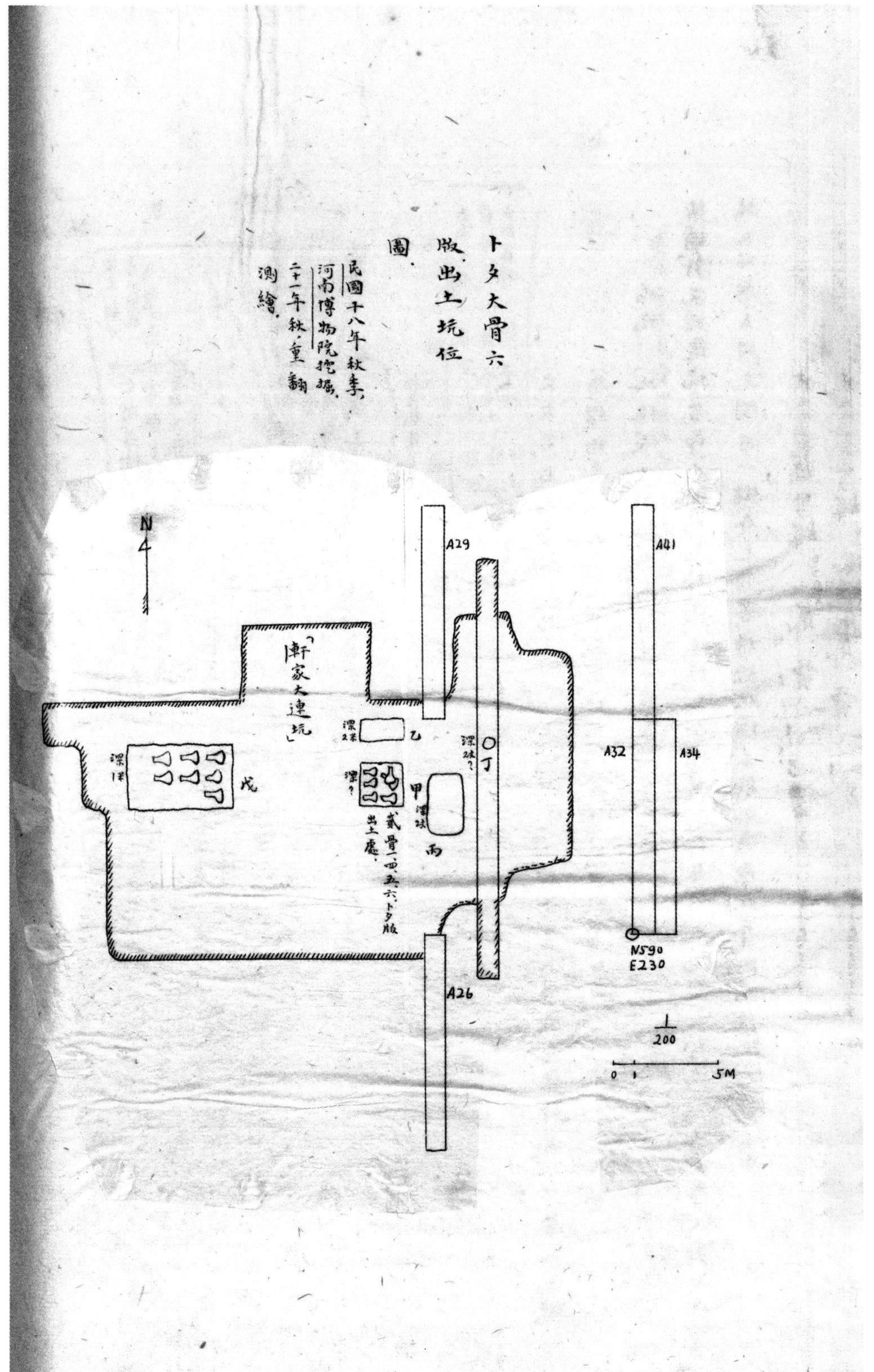
卜夕大骨六版出土坑位圖.
民國十八年秋季，河南博物院挖掘，二十一年秋，重翻測繪.
N
「斬家大連坑」
戊
深1米
深2米
乙
甲
丙
丁
貳骨一、四、五、六、卜夕版出土處.
A29
A41
A32
A34
A26
N590
E230
1/200
0
1
5M

為此四版卜夕之辭而不憚煩瑣考其出土之地及出土情形，正所以證明其卜夕月名之聯貫，乃同時存儲，且為同月所卜，非偶合可比也。

貳骨四，為一完全之版，可覘文例，其日次自十月丙申至十一月癸卯，兩月之接連處，十月辛丑，十一月壬寅，卜辭不著「朔」，實則壬寅即十一月之朔。貳骨五殘存丁卯，戊辰，己巳三日，而兩存「十一月」，依其部位，知下段闕壬戌至丙寅五日。自癸卯至壬戌，所闕凡十八日，適為骨版之兩行，每行九段，如所補之版。一骨不可兩邊用之，或分見于兩版，亦未可知，然其所闕則恰為兩行能容者，惜尚未能覓得其殘片耳。此種補苴之限制，如前版九月卜夕之辭，皆非可任意附會者。貳骨六有殘版三，文例稍異，乃先上後下，左右兩邊遞卜，其十一月庚午，十二月辛未，兩月分界幸存，則辛未十二月朔矣。十一月壬寅朔至庚午凡二十九日，恰合小盡月之日數，此絕不得謂為湊合，蓋文例可補，貞人亦一，月份銜接，日次連續，同屬骨版，同出一處，事事巧合，焉能如是乎？

由此四，五，六，三版，知其含有「十一月小壬寅朔」之一件曆法上史實，而貞人旅又屬於祖甲之世，則此「十一月小壬寅朔」乃祖甲時之曆日矣。

檢殷曆譜自武丁元年（公元前一三三九）至帝辛五十二年（一一一二），僅有一次「十一月小壬寅朔」在祖甲元年之前一年，即祖庚七年，（一二七四）余謂祖庚必崩於七年十一月之前，是時祖甲已即位，而次年乃改元也。月名加在，第一期偶亦有之，不自祖甲創作，祖甲時貞人多祖庚之舊，以此卜夕之版屬於祖庚，固亦可通。然祖甲時改「一月」為「正月」，廢「十三月」置閏之法，月名上普遍加「在」字，有時代性之特徵，故以在祖甲即位以後之解說，更為妥貼也。

茲以曆譜對證之。

祖庚七年（公元前一二七四年　丁未）

（殷正）一月大　丙午一日（公元前一二七五年十二月三十日　儒略周日一二五六〇九三）（三日戊申　一二七四年一月一日）

二月小　丙子一日（一月廿九日　周日一二五六一二三）

三月大　乙巳一日（二月廿七日　周日一二五六一五二）

四月小　乙亥一日（三月廿九日　周日一二五六一八二）

五月大　甲辰一日（四月廿七日　周日一二五六二一一）

六月小　甲戌一日（五月廿七日　周日一二五六二四一　日食）（十五日戊子　月食）

七月大　癸卯一日（六月廿五日　周日一二五六二七〇）

八月小　癸酉一日（七月廿五日　周日一二五六三〇〇）

九月大　壬寅一日（八月廿三日　周日一二五六三二九）

十月大　壬申一日（九月廿二日　周日一二五六三五九）

壬午十一日

壬辰　廿一日

丙申　廿五日　　丙申卜(旅)貞：今夕亡囚。在十月。

丁酉　廿六日　　丁酉卜，旅貞：今夕亡囚。在十月。

戊戌　廿七日　　戊戌卜，旅貞今夕亡囚。在十月。

己亥　廿八日　　己亥卜，旅貞：今夕亡囚。在十月。

庚子　廿九日　　庚子卜，旅貞：今夕亡囚。在十月。

辛丑　卅日　　辛丑卜，旅貞：今夕亡囚。在十月。

十一月小

壬寅　一日　(十月廿二日)(周日一二五六三八九)　　壬寅卜，旅貞：今夕亡囚。在十一月。

癸卯　二日　　癸卯卜，旅貞：今夕亡囚。在十一月。　以上貳骨四

壬子　十一日　　(甲辰至辛酉見補版)

壬戌　廿一日　　(壬戌至丙寅見釋五補)

丁卯　廿六日　　丁卯(卜，旅)貞：(今夕)亡(囚。在十一月)。

戊辰　廿七日　　戊辰卜，旅貞：今夕亡囚。在十一月。

己巳　廿八日　　(己)巳卜，旅貞：今夕亡囚。在十一月。　以上貳骨五

庚午　廿九日　　庚午卜，旅貞：今夕亡囚。在十一月。

十二月大　辛未一日（十一月廿日 日食）（周日一二五六四一八）　辛未卜，旅貞：今夕亡𡆥。在十二月。

癸酉三日　癸酉卜，旅貞：今夕亡𡆥。在十二月。

乙亥五日　乙亥卜，旅貞：今夕亡𡆥。在十二月。

戊寅八日　戊寅（卜，旅）貞：今（夕）亡𡆥。（在）十二月。以上貳骨六

辛巳十一日（十六日丙戌 月食 十二月四日 周日一二五六四三四）

辛卯廿一日

十三月小　辛丑一日（十二月廿日 周日一二五六四四八）（十三日癸丑 一二七三年一月一日）

祖甲元年（公元前一二七三年 戊申）

正月大　庚午一日（一月十八日 周日一二五六四七七）

（下略）

祖庚七年六月十二月，皆有日食，雖中國在夜，亦可證朔日之準確。其年之「十三月」，為最末一次歲終置閏之法，至祖甲三年，則置閏於九月矣。

此一組卜夕之譜，證明十一月一日為壬寅，十二月一日為辛未，足破數年來殷曆「一甲十癸」之疑案，（卜辭足證一日非甲，固不止此。）其重要之價值在此。

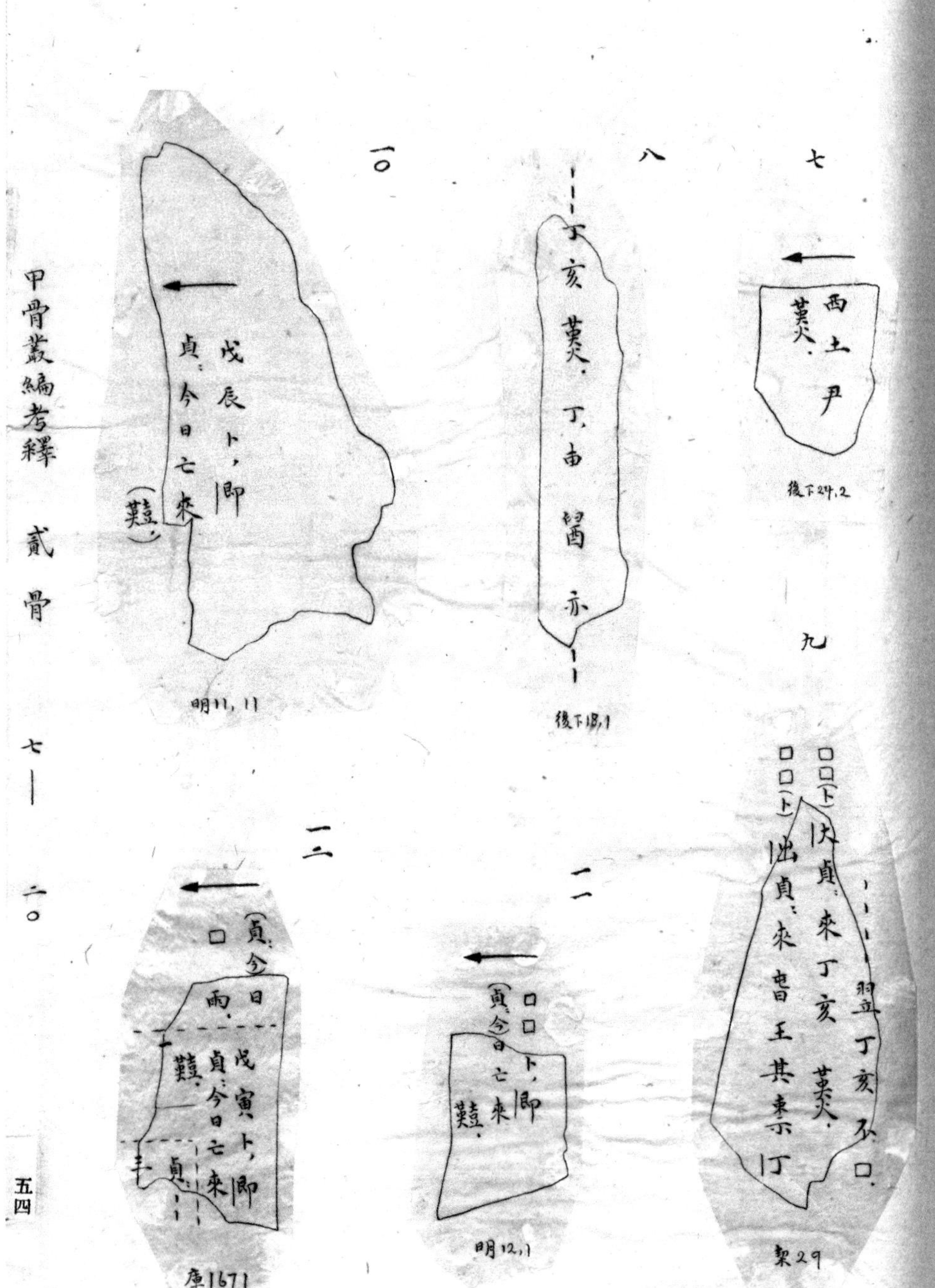

甲骨叢編考釋　貳骨　七一—二〇
七
八
一〇
九
一一
一二
後下24,2
後下18,1
明11,11
架29
明12,1
庫1671
五四

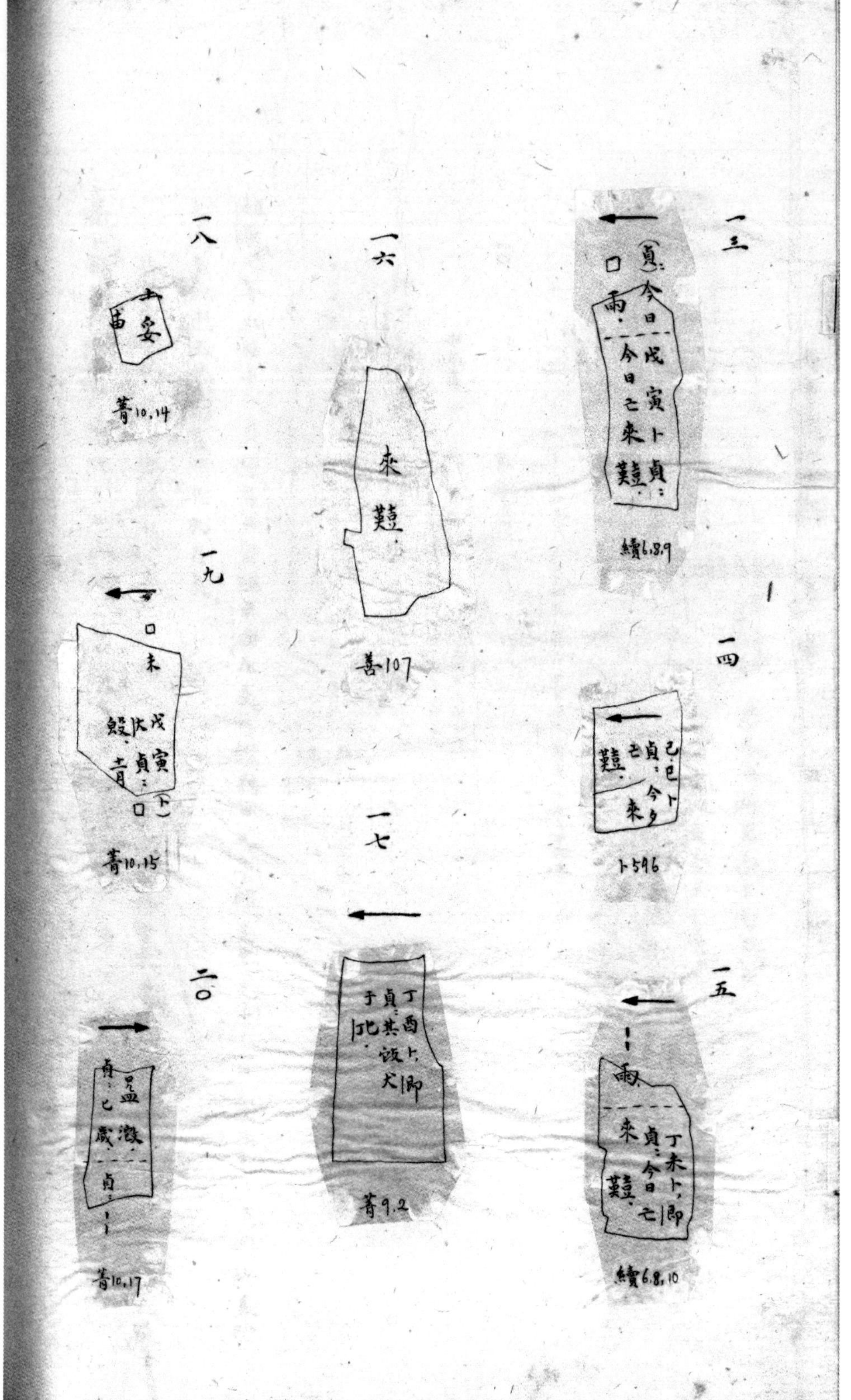
一三
續6.8.9
一四
卜596
一五
續6.8.10
一六
善107
一七
菁9.2
一八
菁10.14
一九
菁10.15
二〇
菁10.17

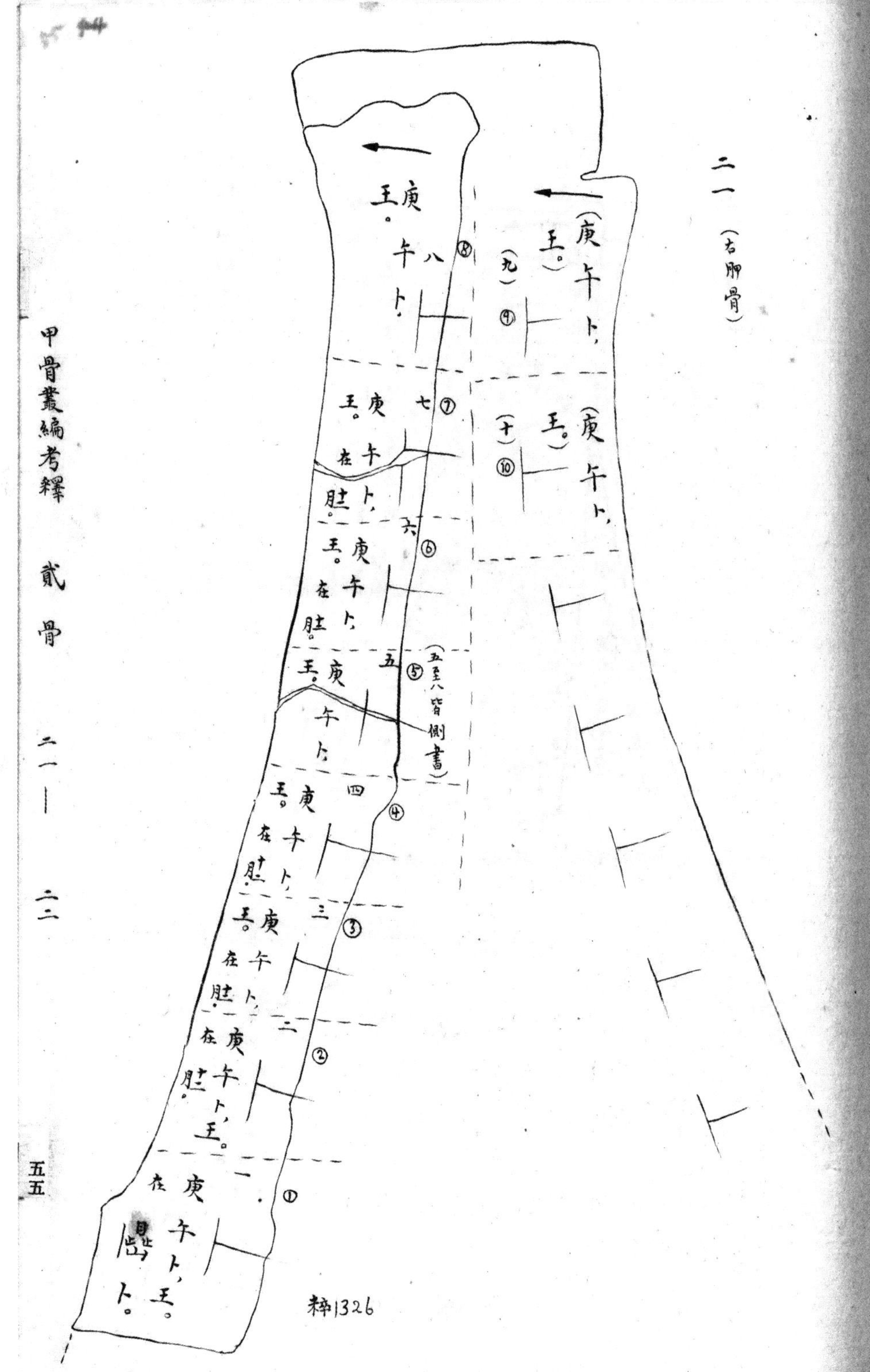
甲骨叢編考釋　貳　骨　二一—二二
五五
二一（右胛骨）
（五至八皆側書）
粹1326

二二（左胛骨）

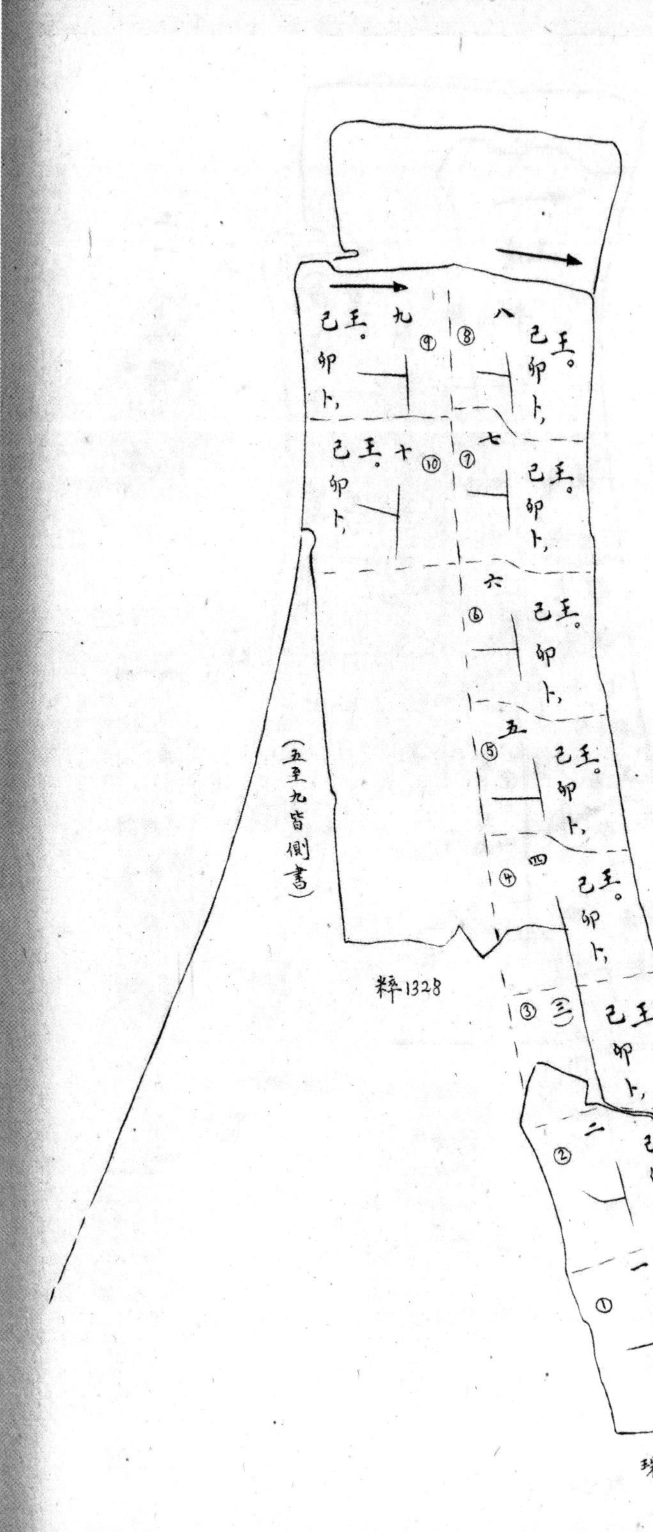

甲骨叢編考釋　貳　骨　二三—二六

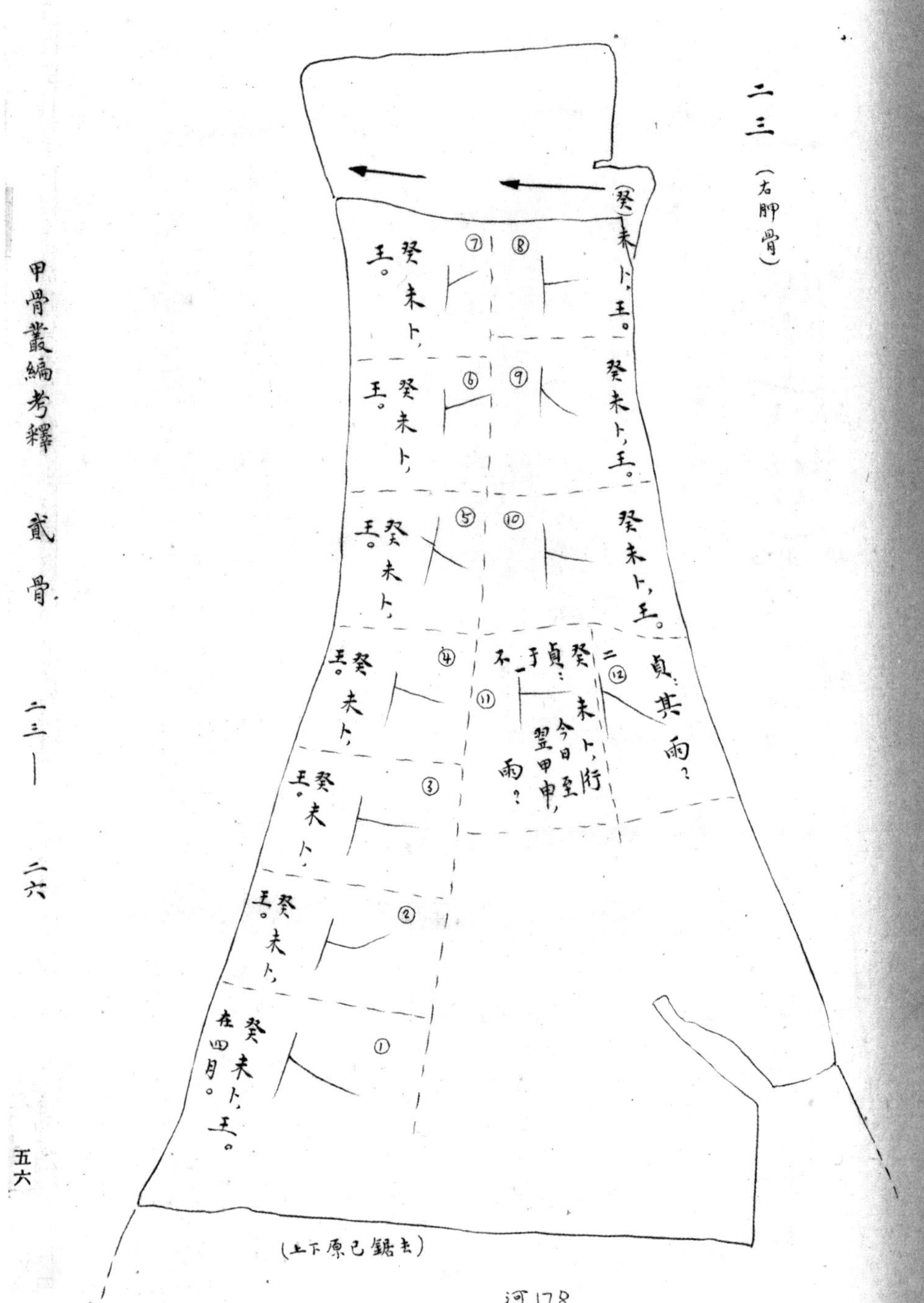

五六

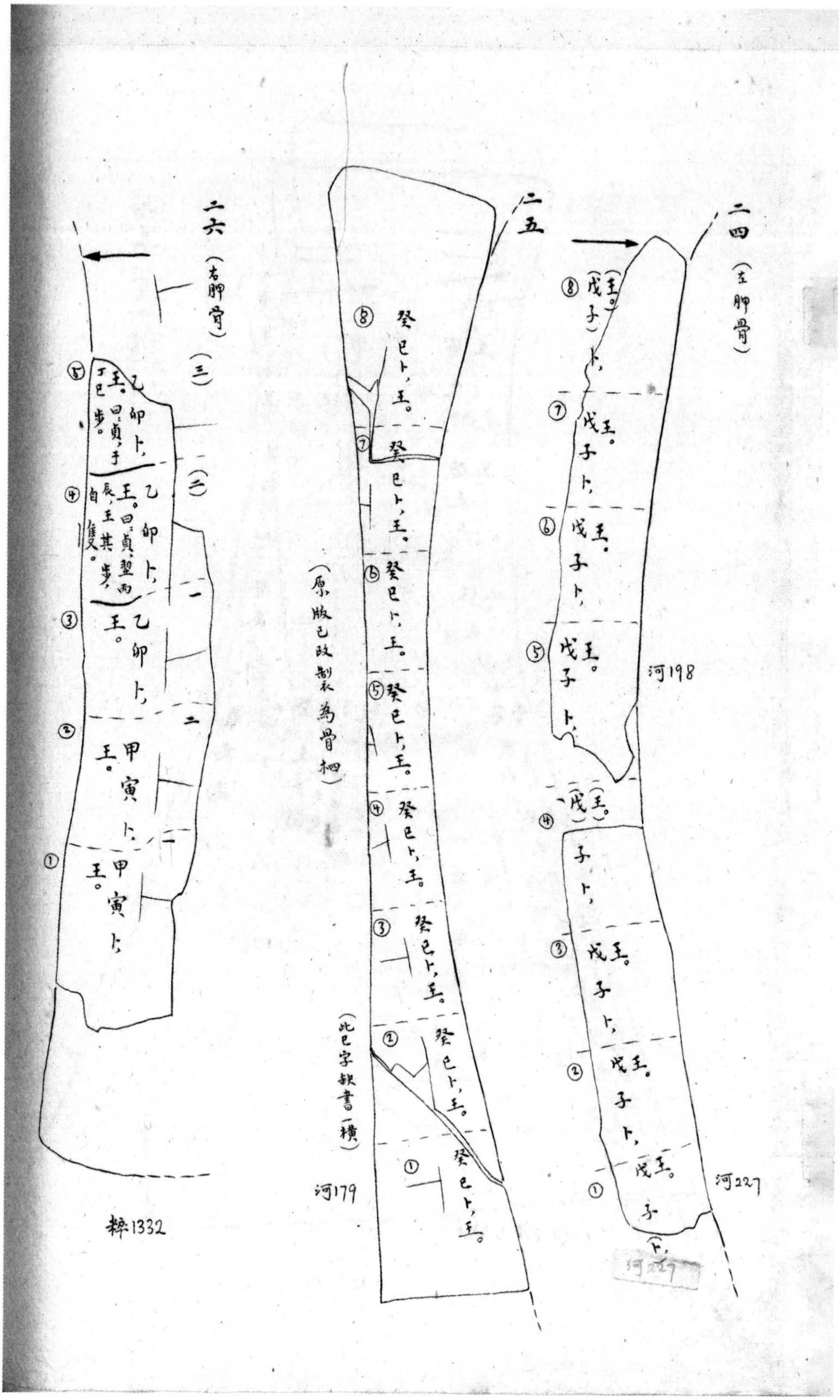
二四
（左胛骨）
(王。)
(戊子)卜，
戊子卜，王。
戊子卜，王。
戊子卜，王。
(戊)(王。)
子卜，
戊子卜，王。
戊子卜，王。
戊子卜，王。
(卜，)
河198
河227
二五
癸巳卜，王。
（原版已改製表為骨柶）
（此巳字缺書一横）
河179
二六
（右胛骨）
(三)
(二)
乙卯卜，王。
甲寅卜，王。
甲寅卜，王。
粹1332

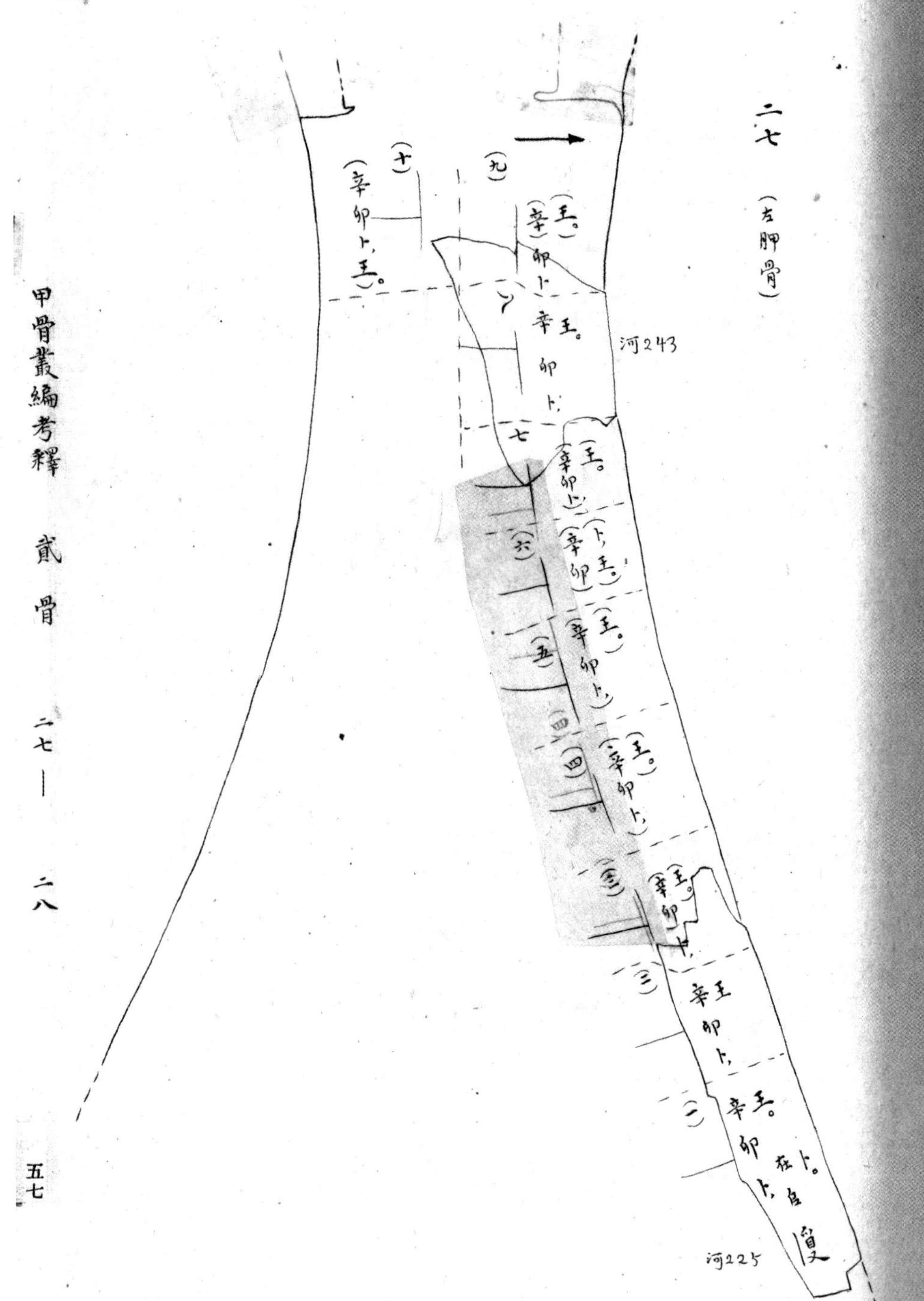
二七
（右胛骨）
河243
河225
（一）
辛卯卜，在白
（二）
辛卯卜，王。
（三）
（四）
（五）
（六）
七
（九）
（十）
（辛卯卜，王。）

二八（右胛骨）

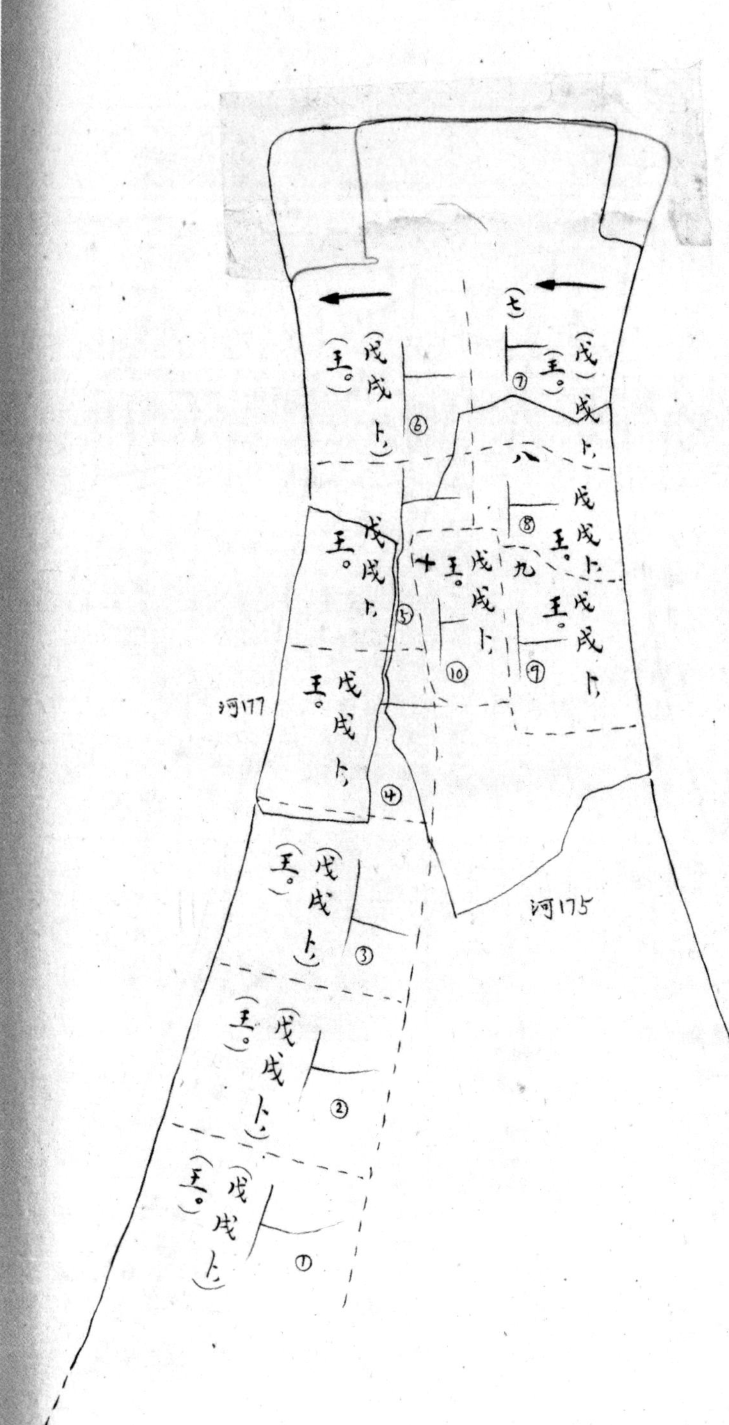

甲骨叢編考釋　貳　骨　二九—四六

二九

（四）甲子卜，王。在肚。

甲子卜，王。在肚。

甲

河235

三〇

王

① 甲子卜，王。

② 乙丑卜□ 貞：□

卜97

三一

② 甲子卜，王。

① 己未卜□ 貞：小王歲，牢。

河204

三二

甲子卜，三月。

卜245

三三

甲子卜，王。

河例1.7

三四

乙丑卜，王。

乙丑卜，王。

乙丑卜，

河194

三五

己□卜，王。

（二）乙丑卜，王。

乙丑卜，王。

乙丑卜，王。

伊卜。

己巳

河184

三六

自䝉卜。在乙丑卜，王。

乙丑卜，王。

粹1208

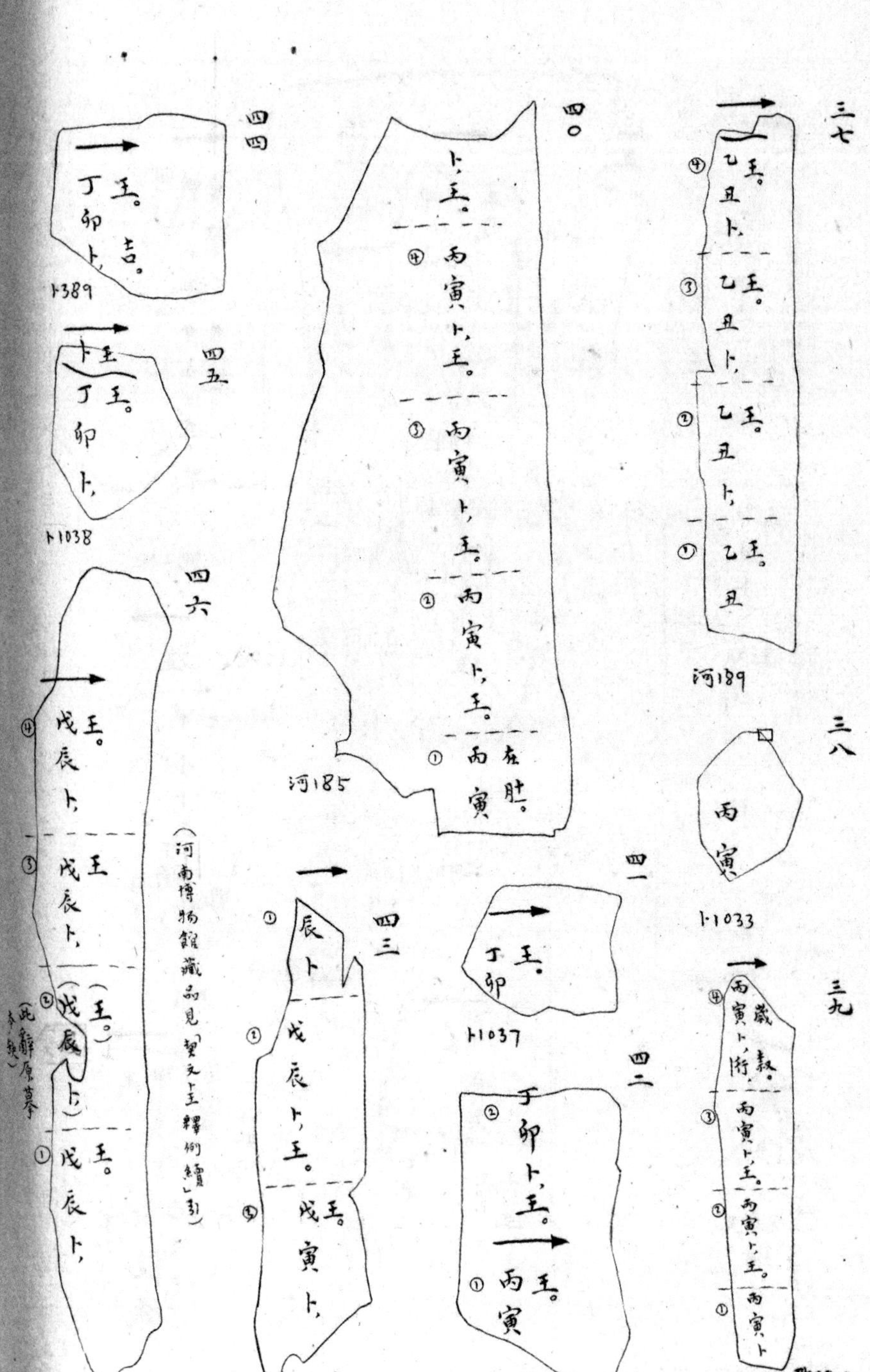
三七
乙丑卜，王。
乙丑卜，王。
乙丑卜，王。
乙丑卜，王。
河189
三八
丙寅
卜1033
三九
丙寅卜，王。
丙寅卜，王。
丙寅卜，脐，𢦏。
戬49.14
四〇
丙寅在肸。
丙寅卜，王。
丙寅卜，王。
丙寅卜，王。
卜，王。
河185
四一
丁卯王。
卜1037
四二
丙寅王。
丁卯卜，王。
卜79
四三
辰卜
戊辰卜，王。
戊寅卜，王。
戬50,2
四四
丁卯卜，王。吉。
卜389
四五
丁卯卜，王。
卜1038
四六
戊辰卜，王。
戊辰卜，（王。）
戊辰卜，王
戊辰卜，王。
（河南博物館藏品見「望文卜王釋例續」引）
河例2,6

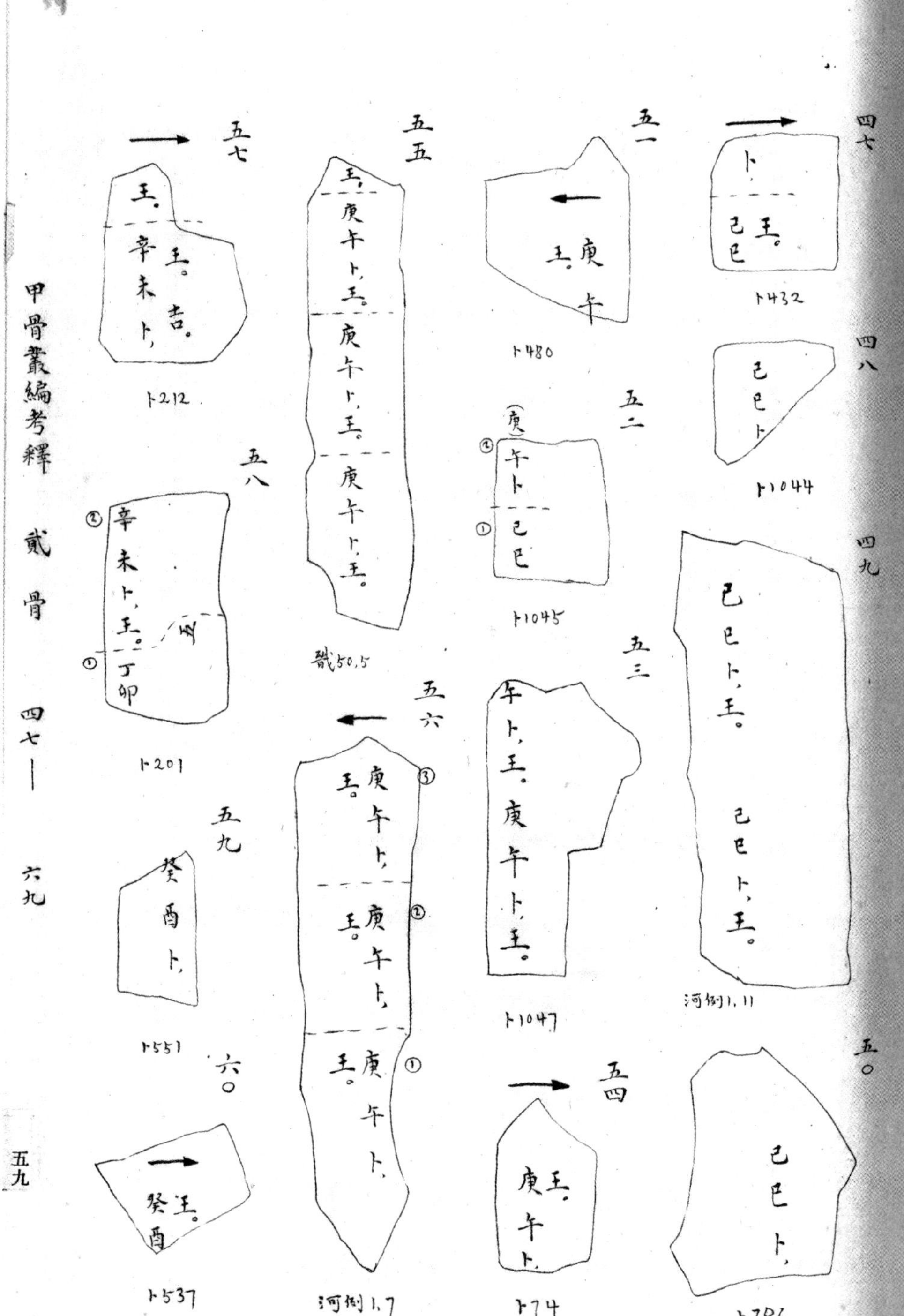

四七
卜
己巳 王。
卜432
四八
己巳卜
卜1044
四九
己巳卜，王。
己巳卜，王。
河例1.11
五〇
己巳卜，
卜786
五一
庚午 王。
卜480
五二
(庚)午卜
己巳
卜1045
五三
午卜，王。庚午卜，王。
卜1047
五四
庚午卜，王。
卜74
五五
王。
庚午卜，王。
庚午卜，王。
庚午卜，王。
戩50.5
五六
庚午卜，王。
庚午卜，王。
庚午卜，王。
河例1.7
五七
王。
辛未卜，吉。王。
卜212
五八
辛未卜，王。
丁卯
卜201
五九
癸酉卜，
卜551
六〇
癸酉 王。
卜537

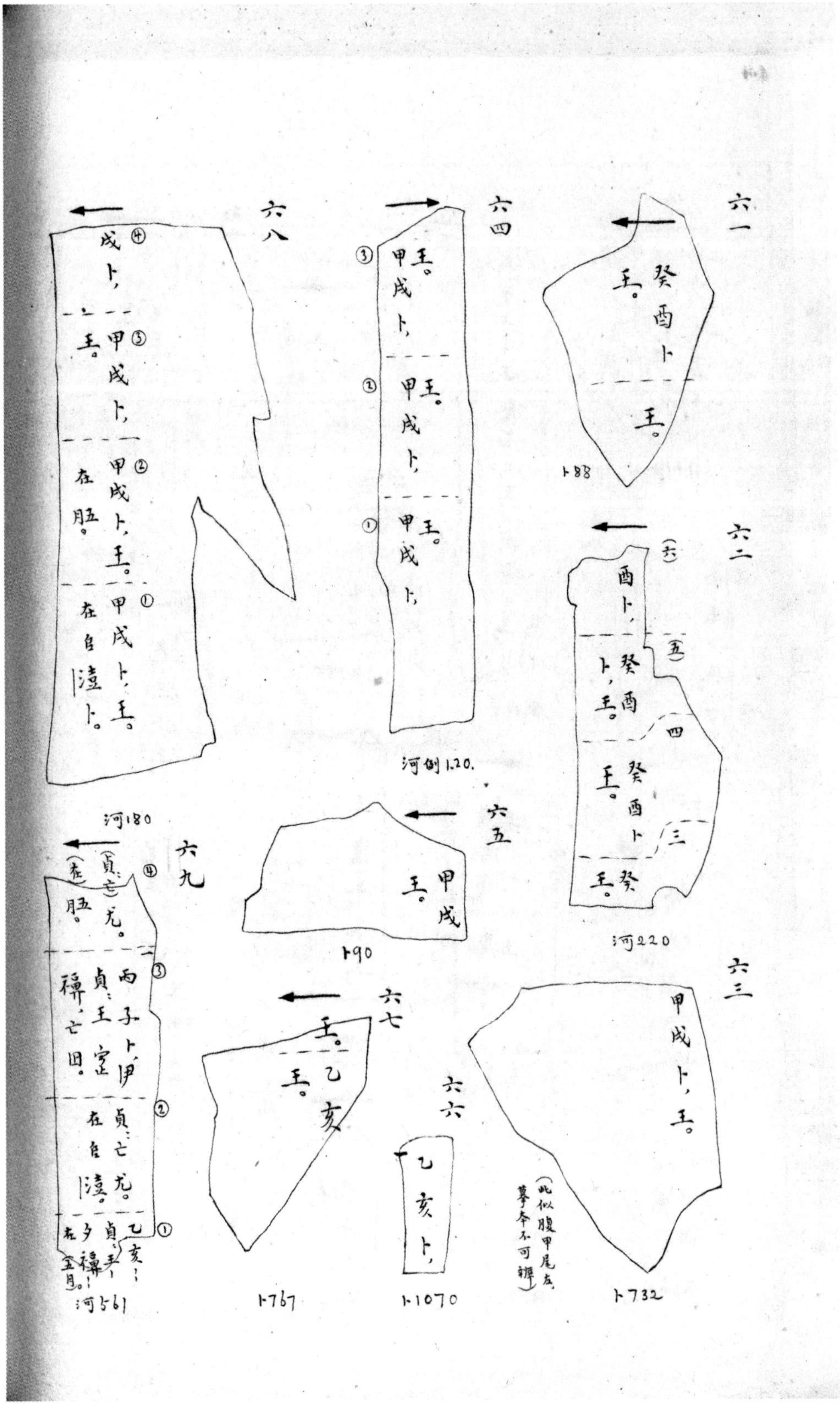

六一

癸酉卜，王。

王。

卜88

六二

(六) 酉卜，

(五) 癸酉卜，王。

(四) 癸酉卜，王。

(三) 癸 王。

河220

六三

甲戌卜，王。

（此似腹甲尾左，摹本不可辨）

卜732

六四

③ 甲戌卜，王。

② 甲戌卜，王。

① 甲戌卜，王。

河倒1.20.

六五

甲戌 王。

卜90

六六

乙亥卜，

卜1070

六七

乙亥 王。

王。

卜767

六八

④ 戊卜，

③ 甲戌卜，王。

② 甲戌卜，王。在[illegible]。

① 甲戌卜，王。在自[illegible]卜。

河180

六九

④ （貞：亡）尤。（在）[illegible]。

③ 丙子卜，尹貞：王賓禘，亡田。

② 貞：亡尤。在自[illegible]。

① 乙亥卜，貞：王賓禘，亡尤。在[illegible]月。

河561

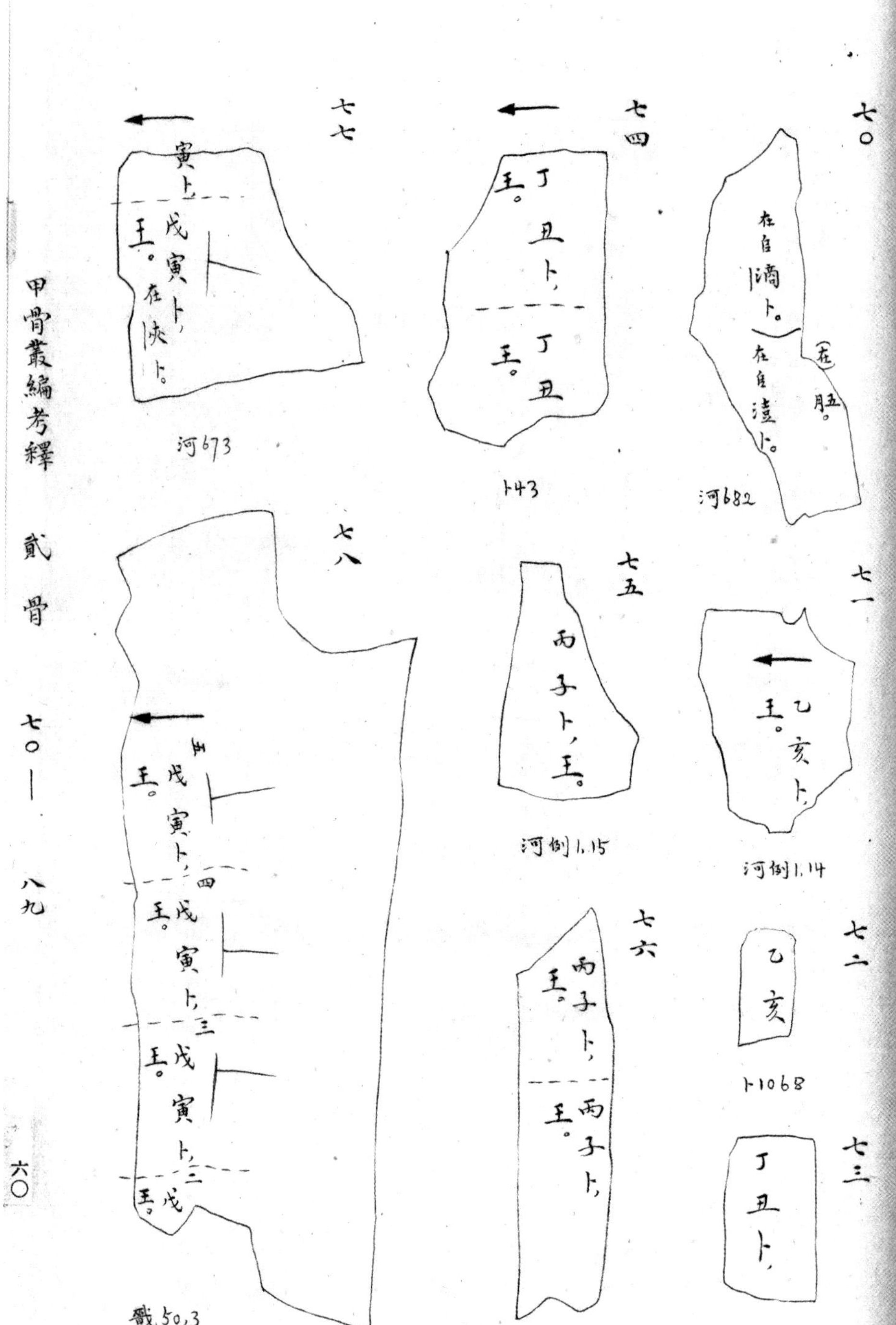
七〇
在自灣卜。
在自澅卜。
（在）肚。
河682
七一
王。乙亥卜，
河倒1.14
七二
乙亥
卜1068
七三
丁丑卜，
卜1075
七四
王。丁丑卜，
王。丁丑
卜43
七五
丙子卜，王。
河倒1.15
七六
王。丙子卜，
王。丙子卜，
河倒1.8
七七
寅卜，
王。戊寅卜，在汏卜。
河673
七八
王。戊寅卜，
王。戊寅卜，
王。戊寅卜，
王。戊
戩50.3

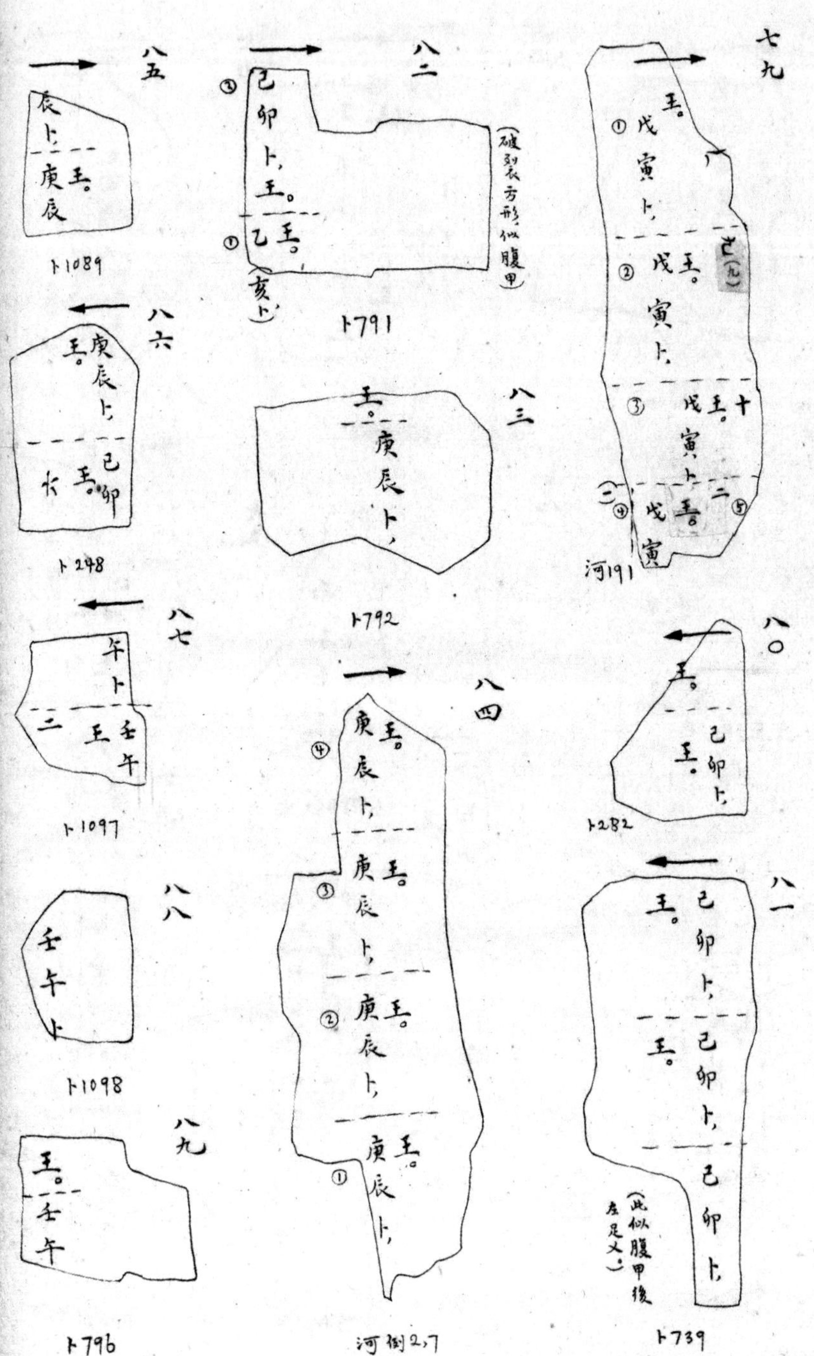
七九
河191
八〇
卜282
八一
（此似腹甲後左足又。）
卜739
八二
（破裂長方形，似腹甲）
卜791
八三
卜792
八四
河例2,7
八五
卜1089
八六
卜248
八七
卜1097
八八
卜1098
八九
卜796

九〇
壬午卜，王。
卜616

九一
癸未卜
卜1099

九二
① 癸未卜，王。
② 癸未卜，王。
③ 未卜，
河195

九三
甲申卜，王。
卜42

九四
① 癸未卜
② 甲申卜，王。
③ 丙戌卜，王。
(似腹甲左足文)
卜747

九五
① 丙寅卜，王。
② 甲申卜，王。
③ 申卜，
卜162

九六
甲申卜，王。
河例1.20

九七
乙酉卜，王。
河例1.13

九八
乙酉卜，王。
河例2.1

九九
丙戌卜，王。
丙戌卜，王。
丙戌卜，王。
河例2.3

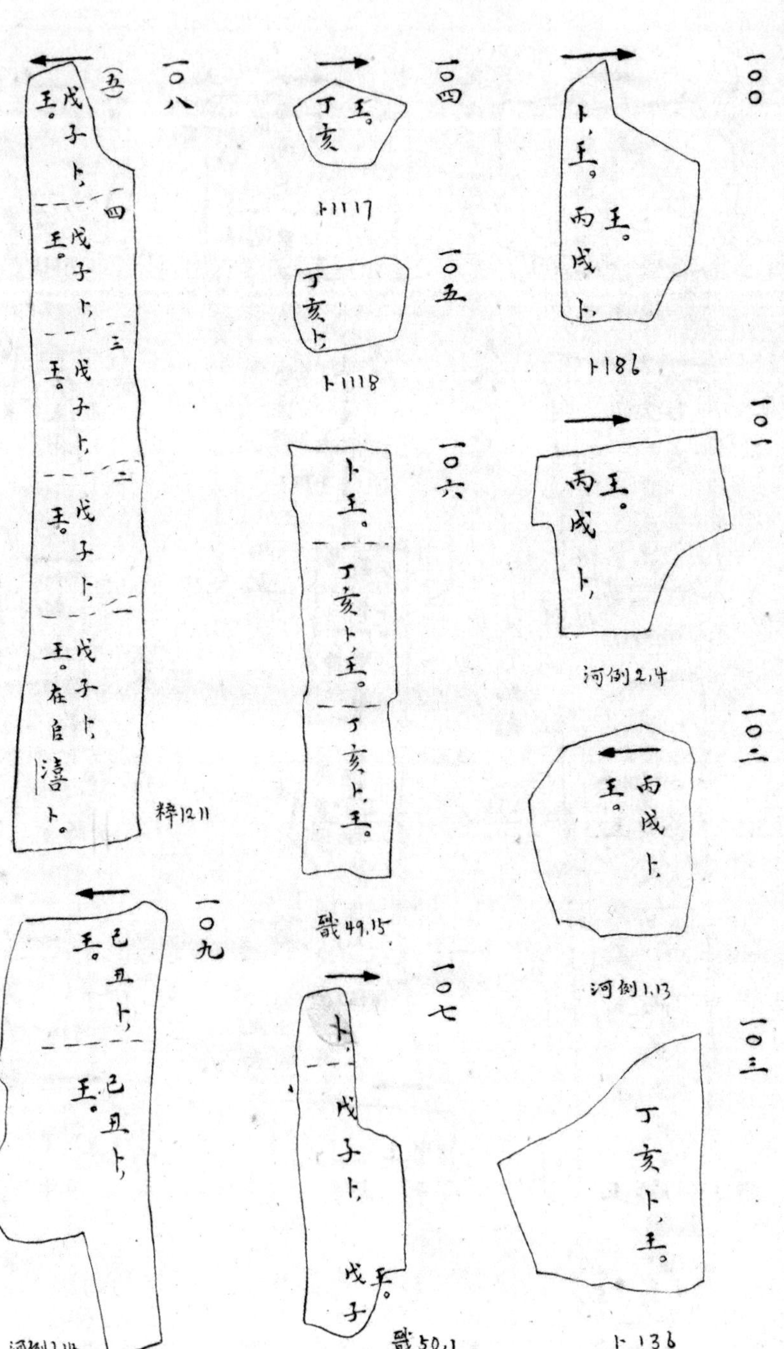

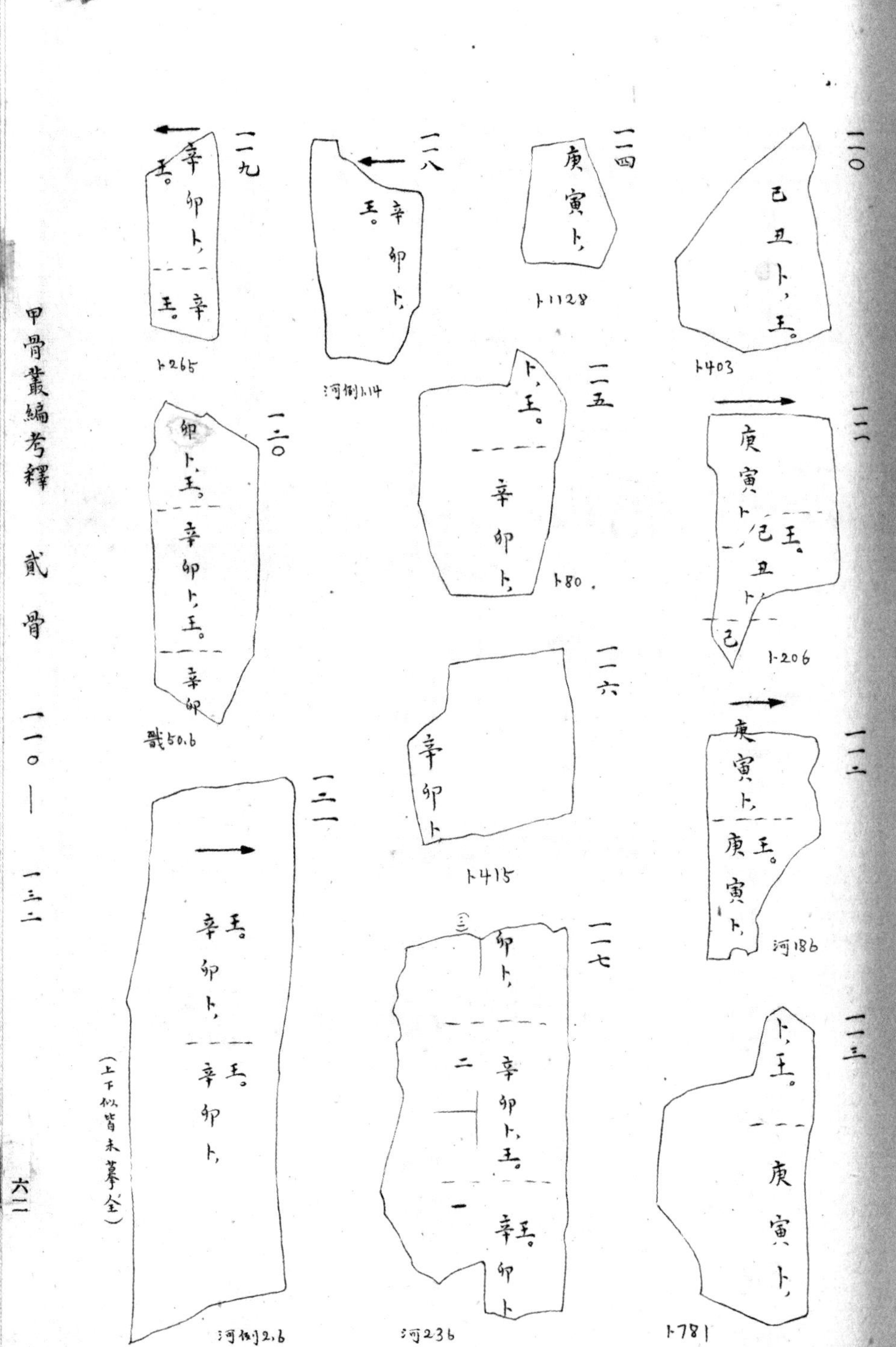
一一〇
己
丑
卜，
王。
卜403
一一一
庚
寅
卜
己
丑
卜
己
王。
卜206
一一二
庚
寅
卜，
庚
寅
卜，
王。
河186
一一三
卜，王。
庚
寅
卜，
卜781
一一四
庚
寅
卜，
卜1128
一一五
卜，王。
辛
卯
卜，
卜80
一一六
辛
卯
卜，
卜415
一一七
卯
卜，
二
辛
卯
卜，
王。
一
辛
王。
卯
卜
河236
一一八
辛
卯
卜，
王。
河例1.14
一一九
辛
卯
卜，
王。
辛
王。
卜265
一二〇
卯
卜，
王。
辛
卯
卜，
王。
辛
卯
戩50.6
一二一
辛
卯
卜，
王。
辛
卯
卜，
王。
（上下似皆未摹全）
河例2.6

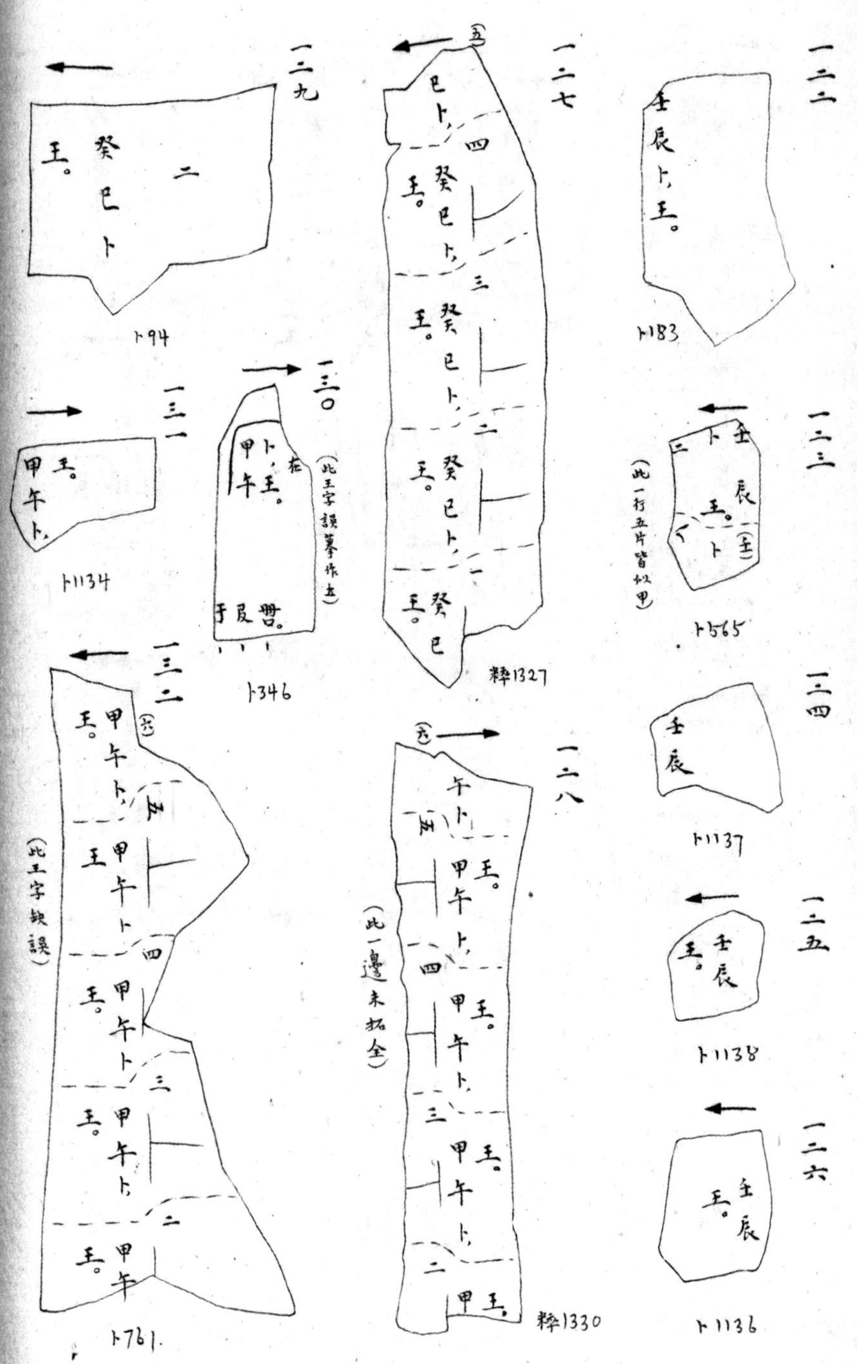
一二二
卜183
一二三
（此一行五片皆似甲）
卜565
一二四
卜1137
一二五
卜1138
一二六
卜1136
一二七
粹1327
一二八
（此一邊未拓全）
粹1330
一二九
卜94
一三〇
（此王字誤摹作五）
卜346
一三一
卜1134
一三二
（此王字缺誤）
卜761

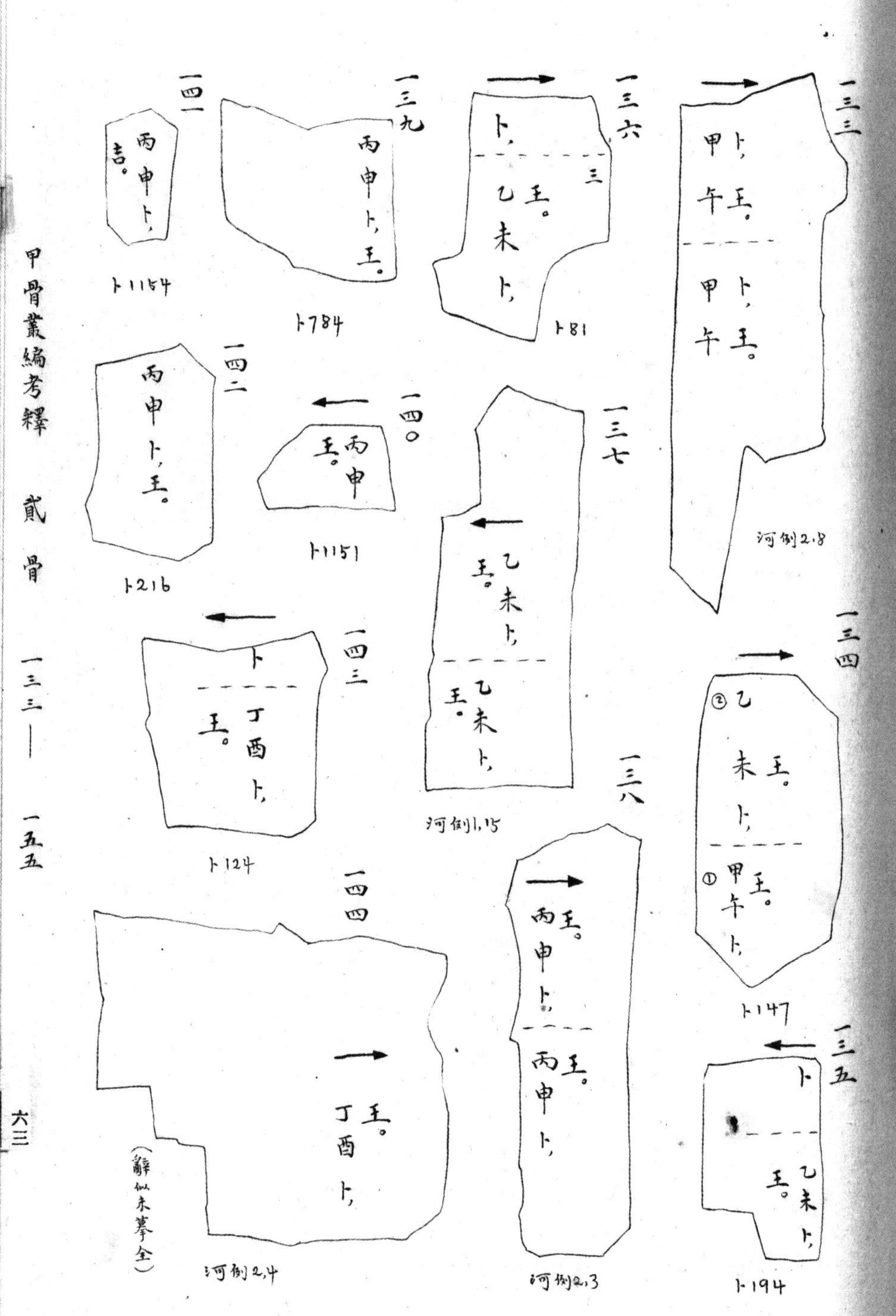
一三三
甲午卜，王。
甲午卜，王。
河例2.8
一三四
② 乙未卜，王。
① 甲午卜，王。
卜147
一三五
卜
乙未卜，王。
卜194
一三六
卜，
乙未卜，王。
三
卜81
一三七
乙未卜，王。
乙未卜，王。
河例1.15
一三八
丙申卜，王。
丙申卜，王。
河例2.3
一三九
丙申卜，王。
卜784
一四〇
丙申王。
卜1151
一四一
丙申卜，吉。
卜1154
一四二
丙申卜，王。
卜216
一四三
卜
丁酉卜，王。
卜124
一四四
丁酉卜，王。
河例2.4
（辭似未摹全）

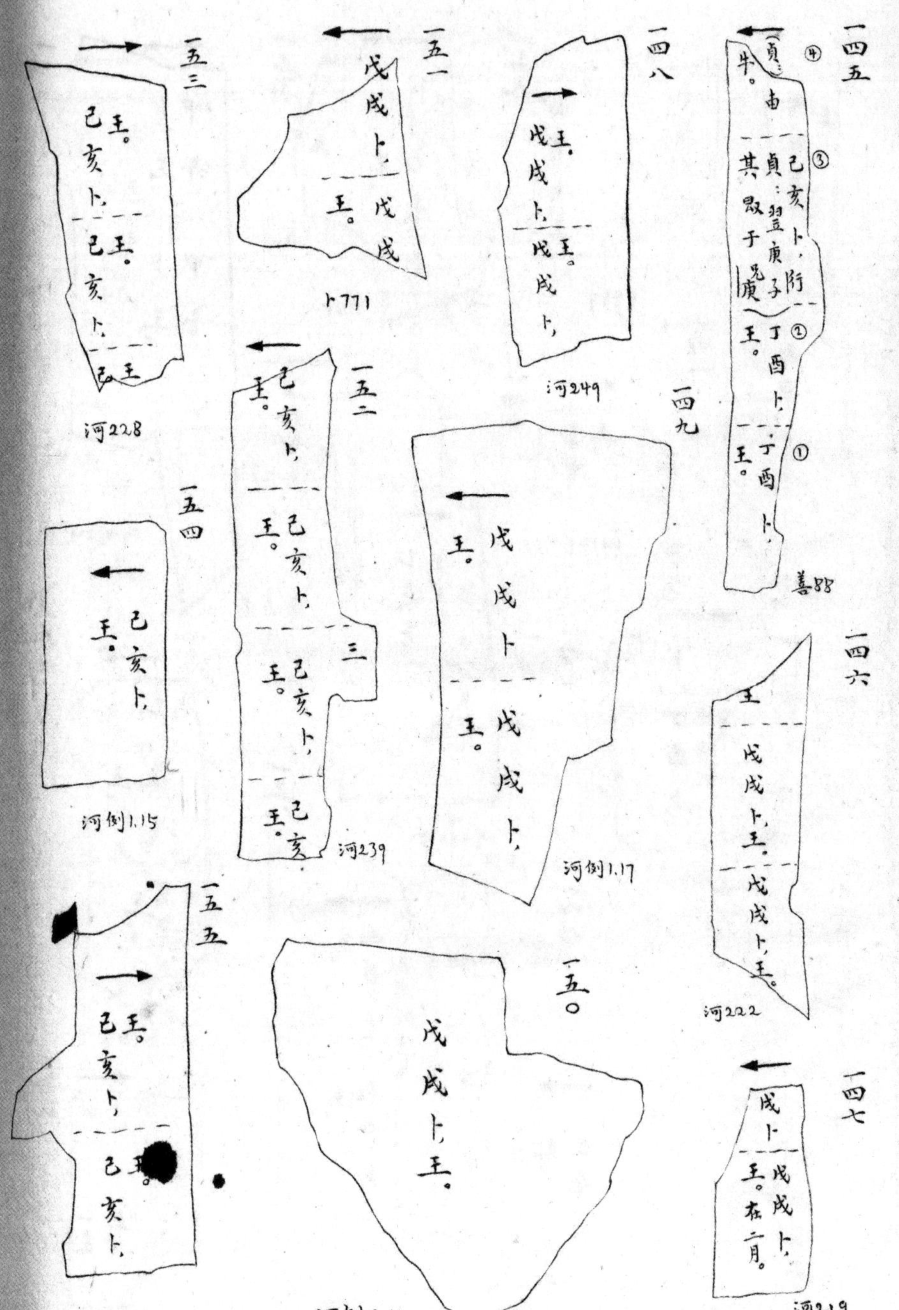
一四五
善88
一四六
河222
一四七
河219
一四八
河249
一四九
河倒1.17
一五〇
河倒1.11
一五一
卜771
一五二
河239
一五三
河228
一五四
河倒1.15
一五五
河倒2.5

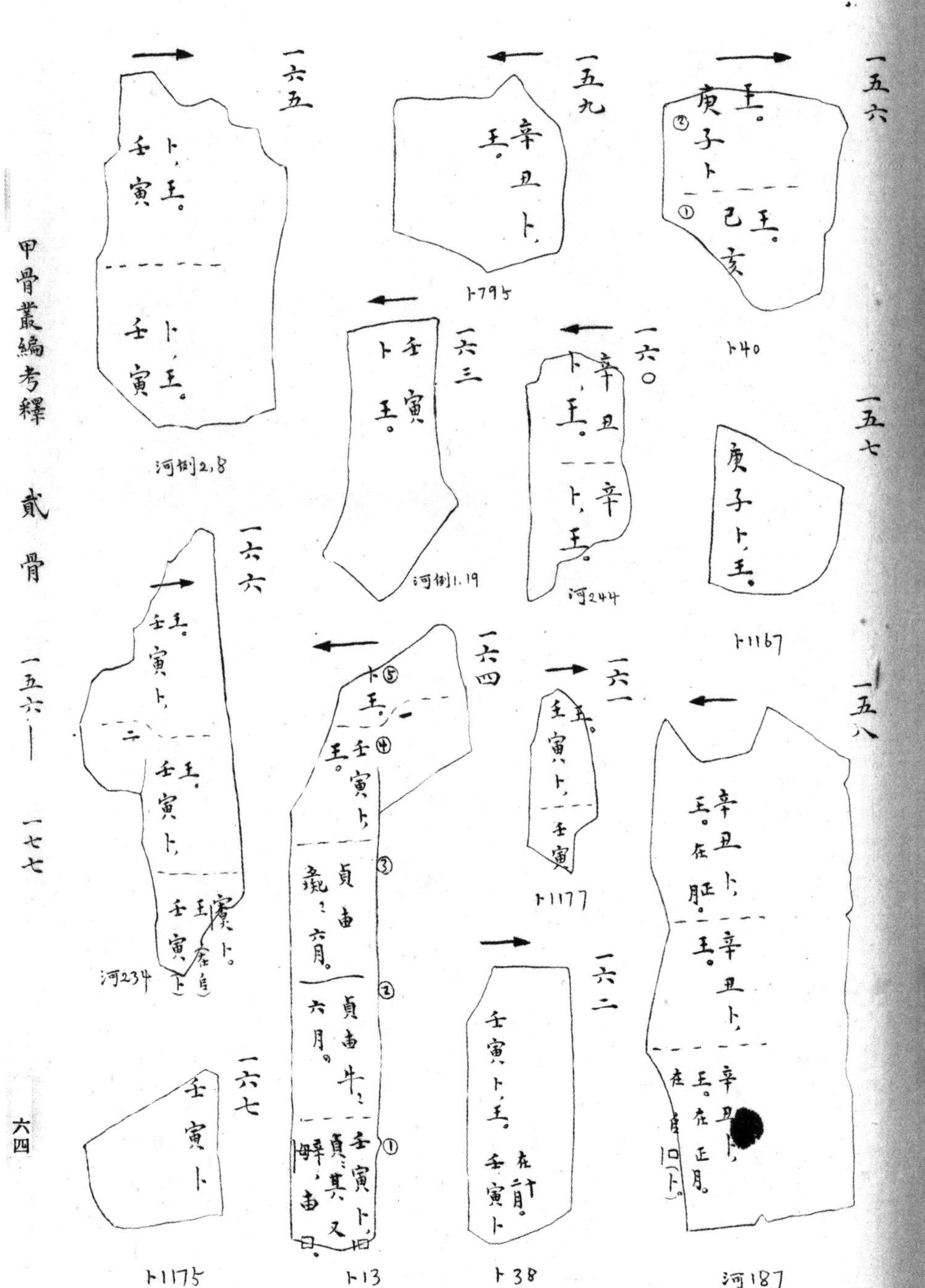
一五六
卜40
一五七
卜1167
一五八
河187
一五九
卜795
一六〇
河244
一六一
卜1177
一六二
卜38
一六三
河倒1.19
一六四
卜13
一六五
河倒2.8
一六六
河234
一六七
卜1175

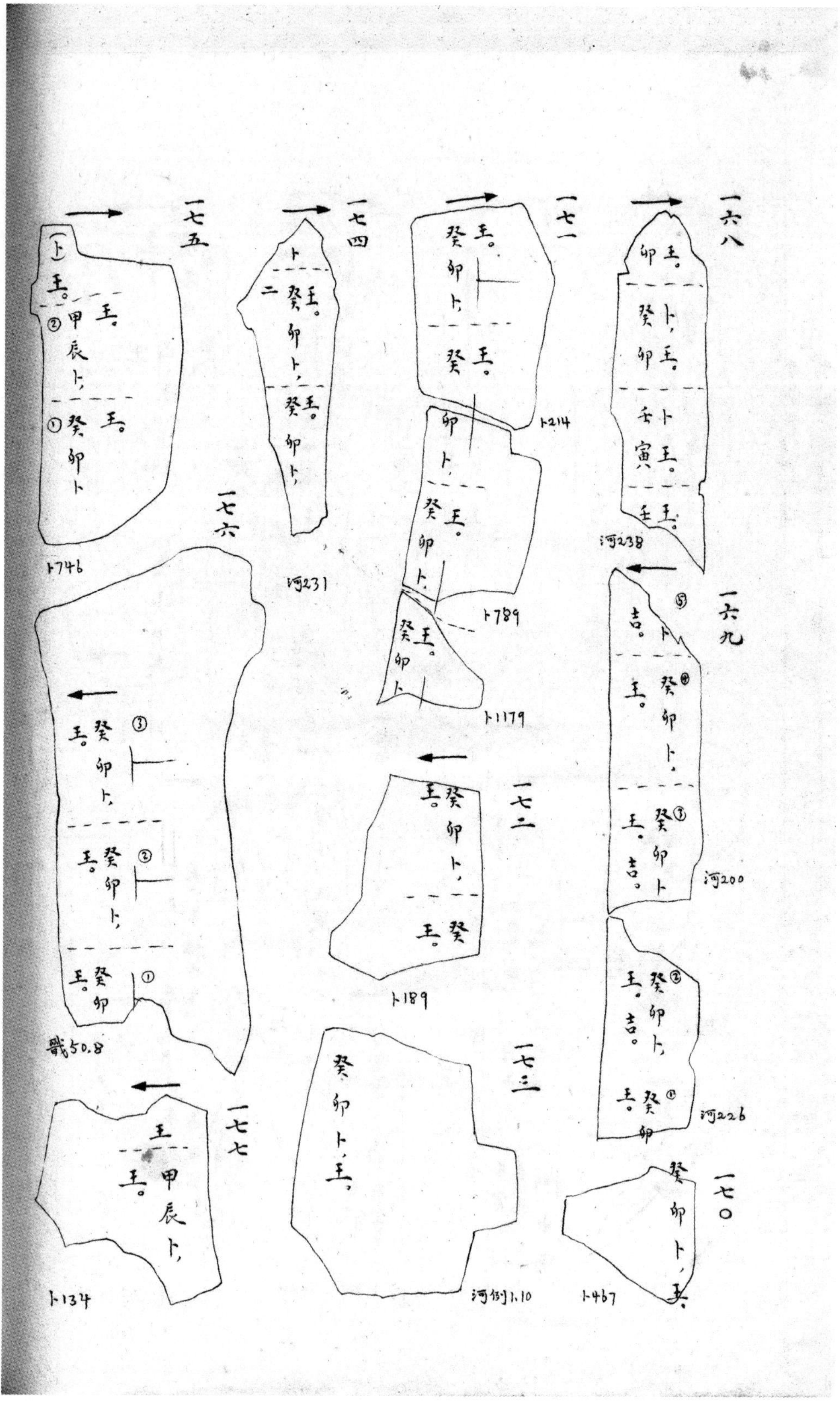
一六八
卯 王。
癸 卜，王。
卯
壬 卜
寅 王。
壬 王。
河238
一六九
⑤ 吉。卜
⊕ 王。癸
卯
卜，
③ 王。癸
吉。卯
卜
河200
② 王。癸
吉。卯
卜，
① 王。癸
卯
河226
一七〇
癸
卯
卜，王
卜467
一七一
癸 王。
卯
卜
癸 王。
卜214
卯
卜，
癸 王。
卯
卜，
卜789
癸 王。
卯
卜
卜1179
一七二
王。癸
卯
卜，
王。癸
卜189
一七三
癸
卯
卜，王，
河佚1.10
一七四
卜
二 癸 王。
卯
卜，
癸 王。
卯
卜，
河231
一七五
（卜）
王。
② 甲 王。
辰
卜，
① 癸 王。
卯
卜
卜746
一七六
③ 王。癸
卯
卜，
② 王。癸
卯
卜，
① 王。癸
卯
戩50.8
一七七
王
王。甲
辰
卜，
卜134

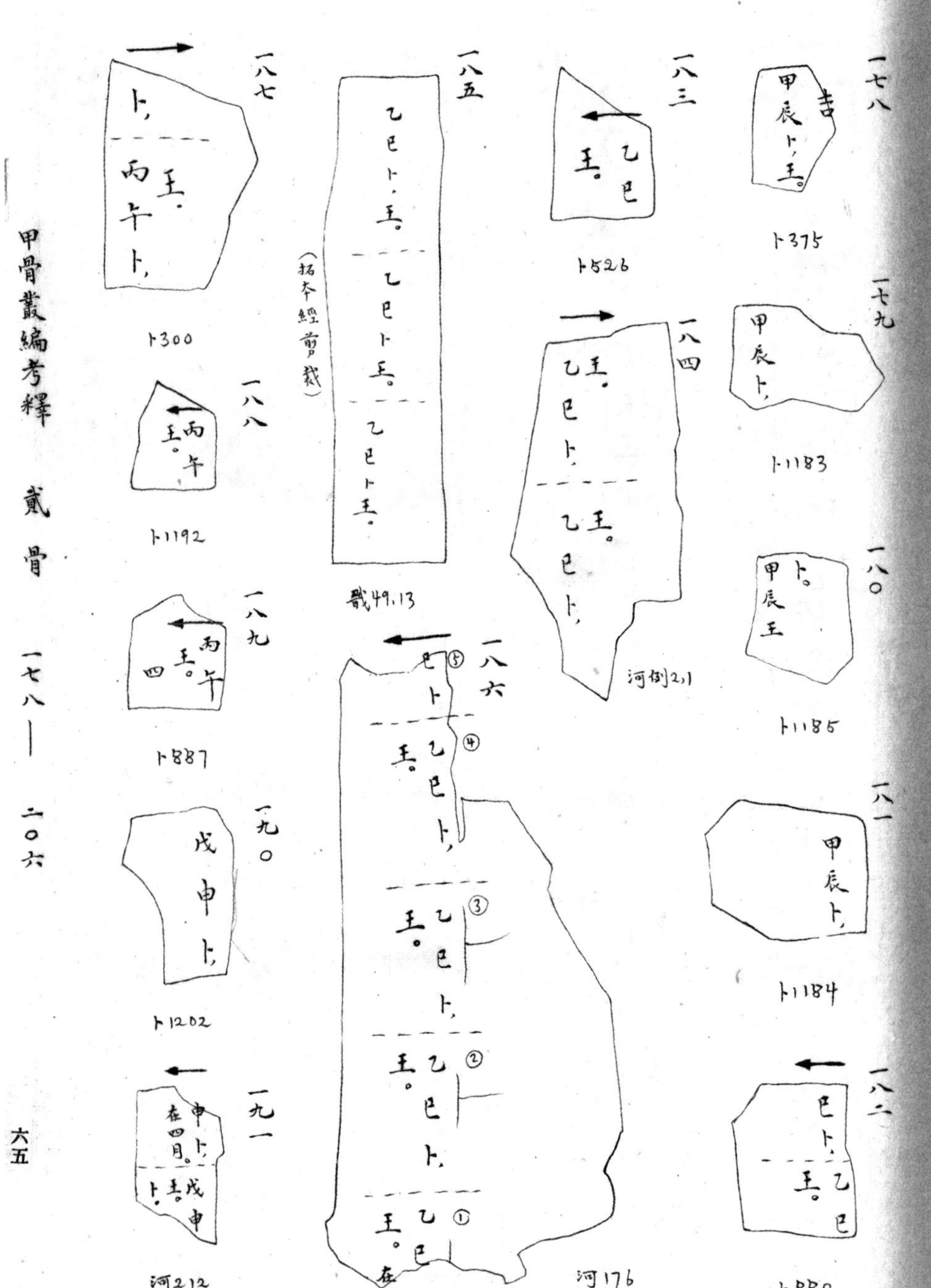
甲骨叢編考釋　貳　骨　一七八—二〇六
六五
一七八　甲辰卜，王。吉　卜375
一七九　甲辰卜，　卜1183
一八〇　甲辰王卜。　卜1185
一八一　甲辰卜，　卜1184
一八二　巳卜，乙巳王。　卜880
一八三　乙巳王。　卜526
一八四　乙巳卜，王。乙巳卜，王。　河例2,1
一八五　乙巳卜，王。乙巳卜王。乙巳卜王。（拓本經剪裁）　戩49,13
一八六　⑤巳卜　④乙巳卜，王。　③乙巳卜，王。　②乙巳卜，王。　①乙巳王。在　河176
一八七　卜，丙午卜，王。　卜300
一八八　丙午王。　卜1192
一八九　丙午王。四　卜887
一九〇　戊申卜，　卜1202
一九一　甲卜，在四月。戊申卜，王。　河212

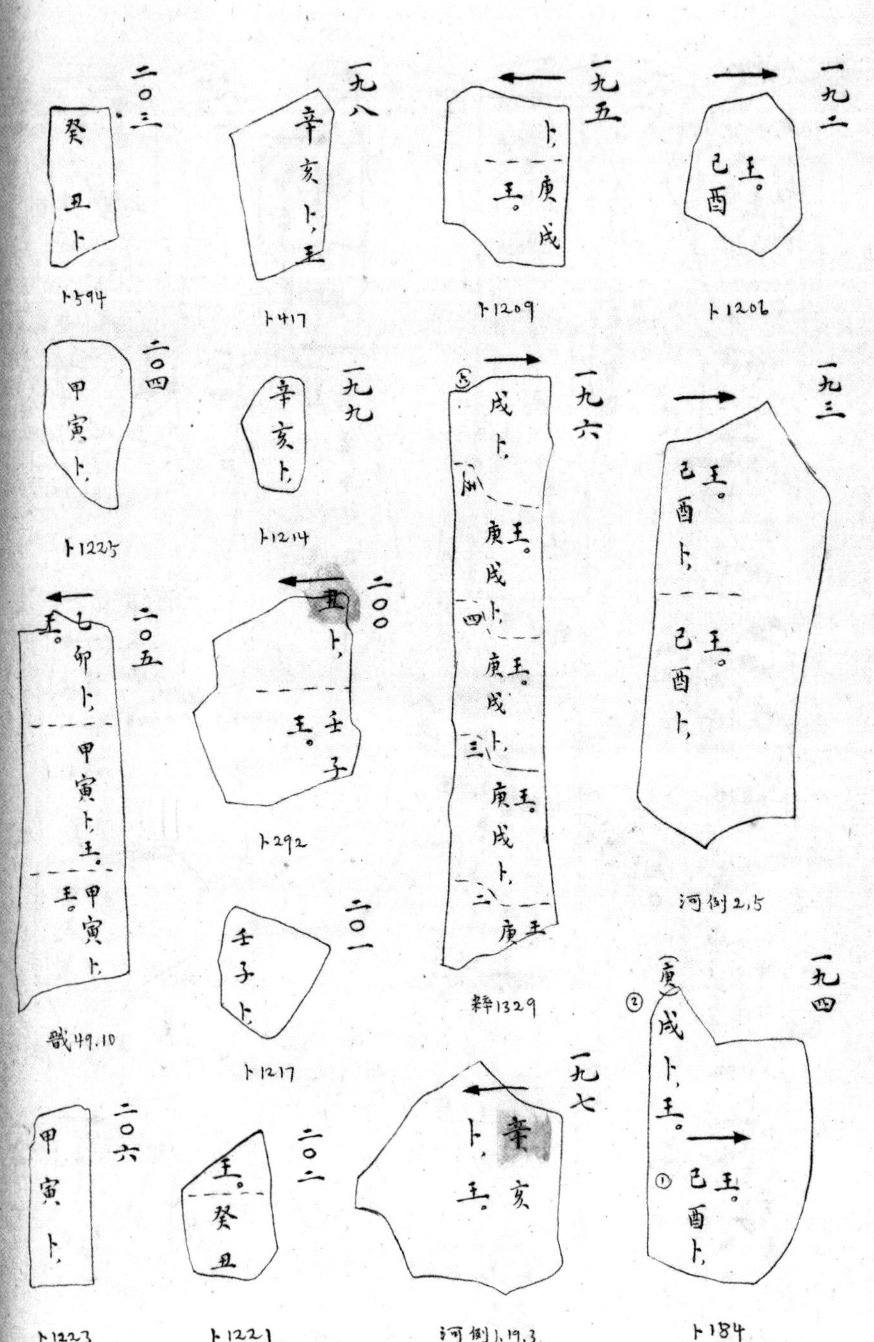
一九二
卜1206
一九三
河倒2,5
一九四
卜184
一九五
卜1209
一九六
粹1329
一九七
河倒1,19,3
一九八
卜417
一九九
卜1214
二〇〇
卜292
二〇一
卜1217
二〇二
卜1221
二〇三
卜594
二〇四
卜1225
二〇五
戬49.10
二〇六
卜1223

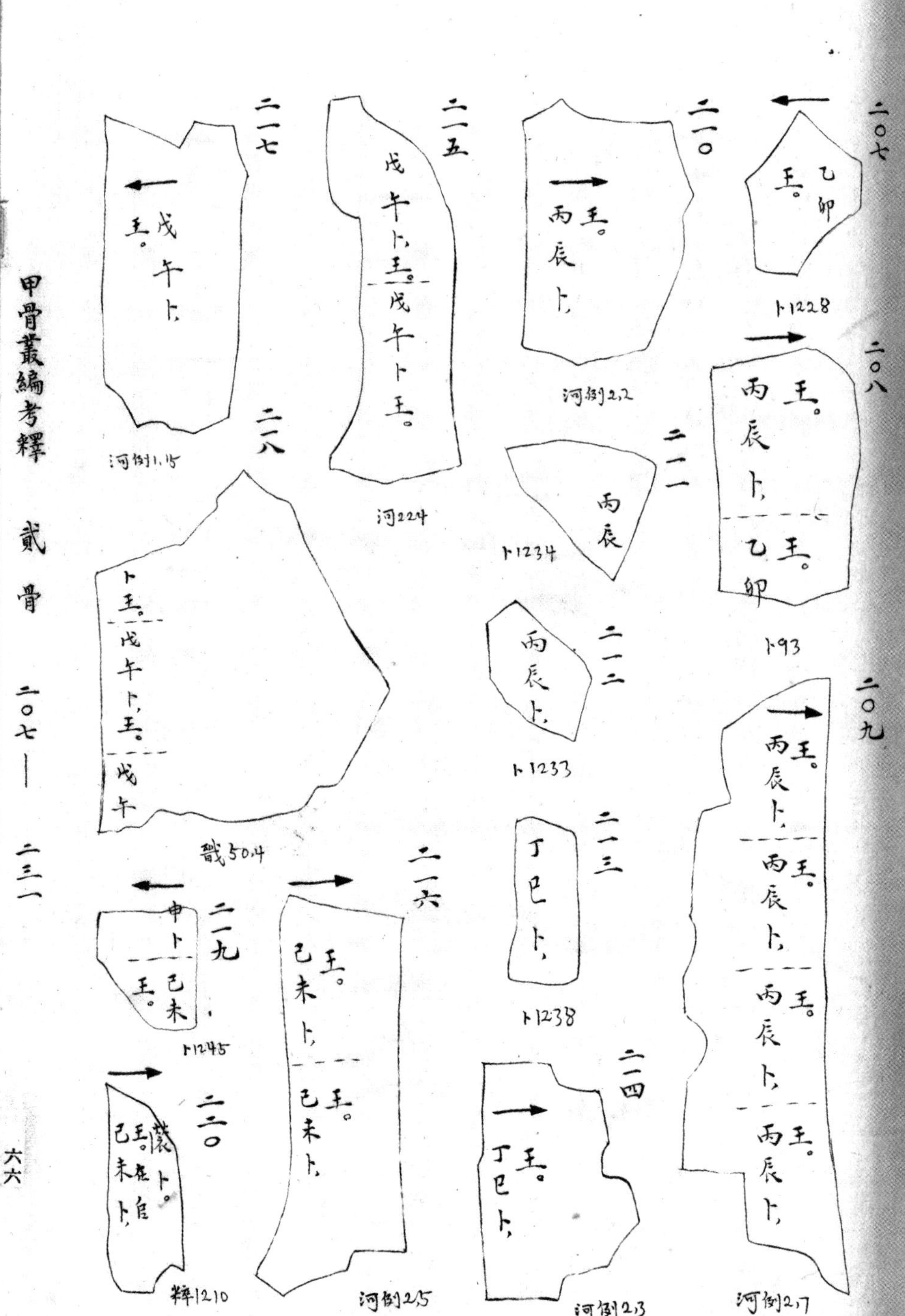
甲骨叢編考釋　貳　骨　二〇七——二三一
二〇七
乙卯
王。
卜1228
二〇八
丙辰卜，王。
乙卯王。
卜93
二〇九
丙辰卜，王。
丙辰卜，王。
丙辰卜，王。
丙辰卜，王。
河例2.7
二一〇
丙辰卜，王。
河例2.2
二一一
丙辰
卜1234
二一二
丙辰卜，
卜1233
二一三
丁巳卜，
卜1238
二一四
丁巳卜，王。
河例2.3
二一五
戊午卜，王。
戊午卜王。
河224
二一六
己未卜，王。
己未卜，王。
河例2.5
二一七
戊午卜，王。
河例1.15
二一八
卜王。
戊午卜，王。
戊午
戩50.4
二一九
申卜
己未王。
卜1245
二二〇
己未卜，王在自蒙卜。
粹1210
六六

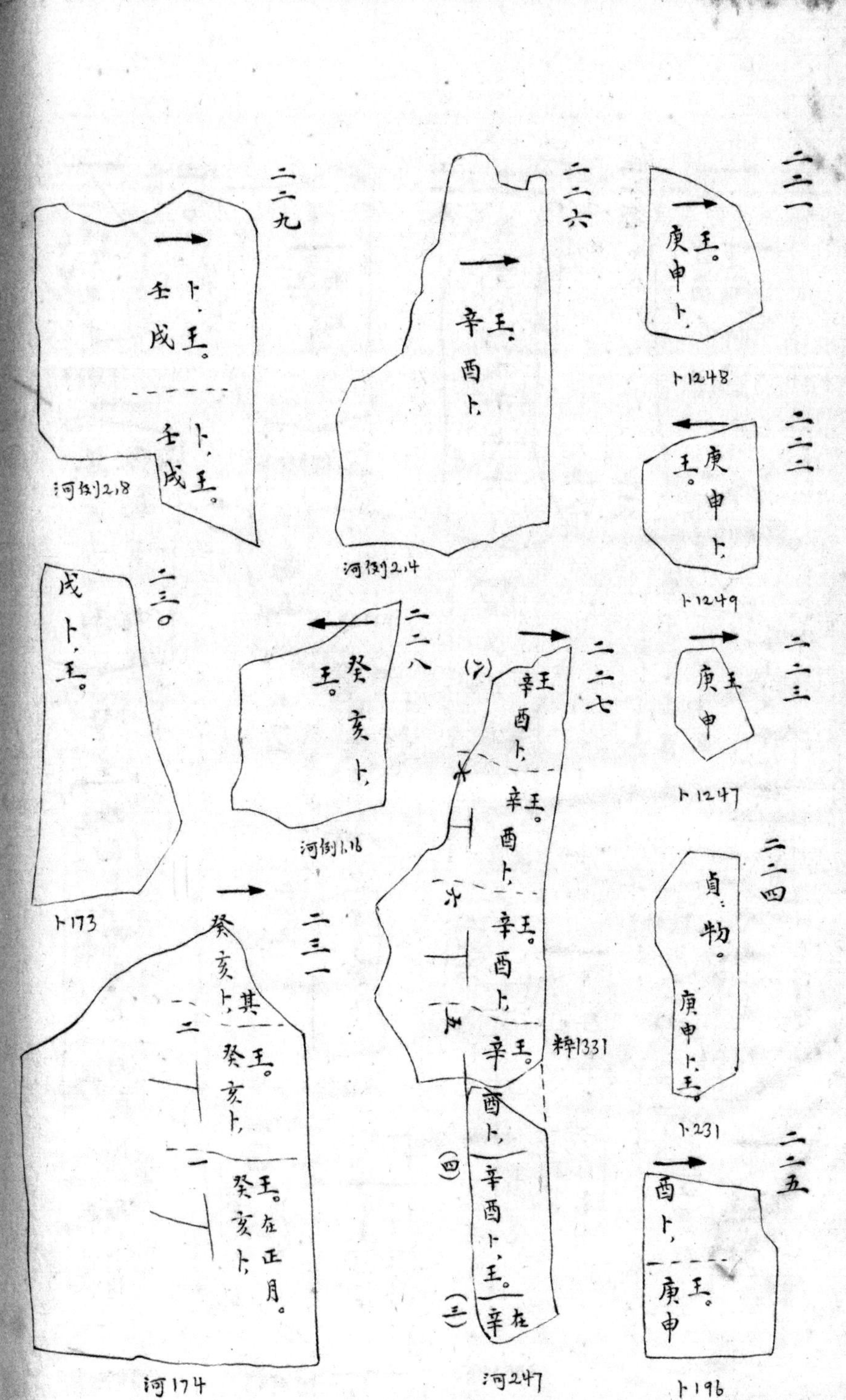

二二一
卜1248
二二二
卜1249
二二三
卜1247
二二四
卜231
二二五
卜196
二二六
河例2.4
二二七
粹1331
河247
二二八
河例1.16
二二九
河例2.8
二三〇
卜173
二三一
河174

貳甲二九一一〇三　貳骨二一一二三一

右甲骨所輯為「卜王」之辭，尚未完備。計龜腹甲七四號，牛胛骨二一一號。

「卜王」辭甚簡單，向不為著錄者所注意。聞封許敬參君曾作契文卜王釋例一文，發表一部分於河南博物館館刊第四、五集。今理出已摹寫者，畧加分別，論述如次。

一、「卜」「王」乃王所親貞，而省畧貞辭者。

「卜」與「貞」在卜辭中顯然為二事，「卜」乃太卜為之，灼龜骨以見兆，視兆以定吉凶是也。「貞」乃問事，所貞問之事每記于貞字之下者是也。每卜必有人，多不記其名。貞字上所記之人，乃貞問其事者，余所稱「貞人」者也。「貞人」非必有其職掌。自時王以下，方國君侯，史官小臣，凡參與卜事而問及某事者，其名列于卜之下，貞之上者，皆可謂之貞人。普通卜辭，卜貞二字並用，第二期以下或省卜字。第三期有但用「卜」而省「貞」者，第四期有但用「貞」而省「卜」者，皆特殊之例也。卜人貞人皆記名者，僅第二期祖甲時一見。其辭曰：

丙寅卜，𡧊貞：卜冉曰：「其𨑌于丁寀。」王曰：「从，壽（禱）。」翌丁卯，𡧊若。八月。河五一九（甲骨文錄收入）

𡧊乃貞人，冉乃卜人，王（祖甲）亦參與其間。是蓋丙寅卜後，太卜冉、王祖甲，次第發言，𡧊乃並記于貞辭，𡧊固執筆書契之史也。

「卜」「王」乃某日卜，王貞：某事如何云云，而省去貞字及所貞之事者。此可借用第三期貞人𢀛所記之一版證之。影釋於下：

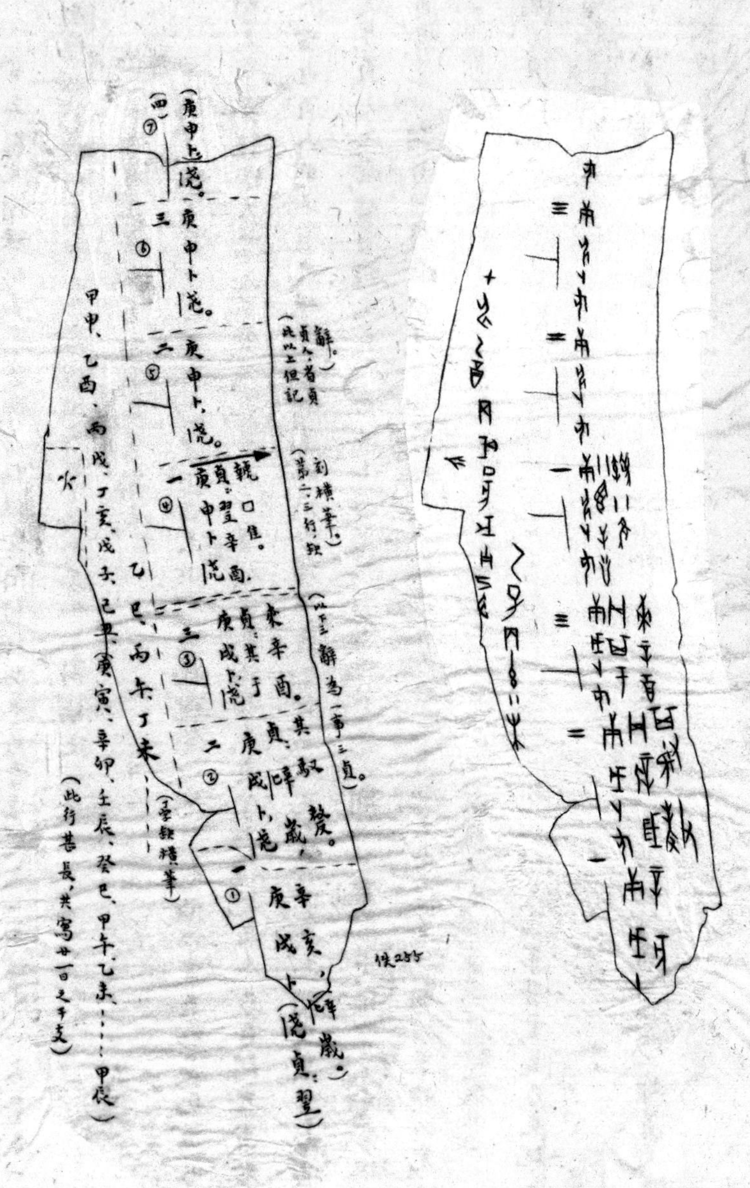

細審右片文辭，於例至為明晰。①至③為卜祭妣辛之事，貞人㱿也。凡三卜。④至⑦為卜另一事，貞人亦㱿也。凡四卜。此四卜，除第一卜外，皆省畧貞字及貞問之事，與「卜王」例同。故「庚申卜，㱿。」者庚申卜，㱿，貞云」云，而省去貞以下之記述辭者也。猶貳甲八四、貳骨二一一｜二二五之但記「庚申卜，王」，而不記王所貞問之事也。

「卜王」之版，亦有記貞辭者廁其間，如貳骨二六是。此版殘存左邊一行五段卜辭。①②乃甲寅日卜。③至⑤乃乙卯日卜。乙卯三卜，皆先書「乙卯卜，王」。四字，細審可辨。蓋三卜皆王所親臨貞問，所問何事，初未宣布，史乃依慣例書之。書「乙卯卜王」者，乙卯日王命太卜卜之（如為王所自卜，則當似五期「王卜貞」之例而書為「乙卯王卜」。貳骨三五書「伊卜」可證）。王自問事而未知所問何事，王不告，史不書耳。三卜既畢，書「卜王」畢，王謂史曰：「今日第二卜，余所問者，擬于明日丙辰，自隻啟行也。」史唯唯，乃秉筆書于「乙卯卜王」第二卜之下曰：「曰貞：翌丙辰，王（有此王字，已為史官語氣矣。知為史官轉述王所貞也）其步，自隻。」王更謂史曰：「余欲再留此間一日，擬後日丁巳行，故有三卜之貞。」史又振筆書于「乙卯卜王」第三卜之下曰：「曰貞：于丁巳步。」至于第一卜所貞何事，王不言，史不敢問，無由書也。此一段王史對話，恍如目覩，非同演義，依理推之，當如是耳。

王何以不以親貞之事，事事命史書之？不外：一、不甚信任卜事；二、愛惜人力物力。二期卜辭，不貞疾病、雜事，僅于祭祀祖妣，恭謹為之。「卜王」之辭，王既不明言貞事，則可任情反復徵驗，以窺卜事之隱。故「卜王」一日有至二十次者，考驗有得，祇自知之，不肯道破也。至於例行卜夕、卜旬、卜行止、風雨，則命史循例舉行，奉祖宗之成法也。此其一。由二六版有記貞辭者，所貞亦例行事，而不告史命書者必有之。此則愛惜人力與物力，不似第一期之事事張大其辭也。此其二。以此期其他卜辭證之，則祖甲固一英睿仁厚之賢王也。二期卜辭之不甚繁縟者，亦以此。

二、「卜王」皆祖甲時辭之證。

斷定「卜王」屬於第二期祖甲時，余久已有此意見，未嘗寫出而已。最惹人注意者，為王字作王，月名上有「在」字。而重要之標準，則仍為同版之「稱謂」與「貞人」。據本册已收之辭：

稱謂：

兄庚（即祖甲之兄祖庚）與「丁酉卜王」同版，己亥卜，後丁酉二日。貳骨一四五

母辛（即武丁配妣辛，祖甲之母）與「壬寅卜王」同版，同日卜。貳骨一六四

貞人：

旅。與「壬午卜王」同版。貳甲五七

行。卜雨。與「癸未卜王」同版，同日卜。貳骨二三

行。卜祭。與「丙寅卜王」同版，同日卜。貳骨三九

行。卜祭兄庚。與「丁酉卜王」同版，己亥卜。見第一例

尹。卜祭。與「甲戌卜王」一版。貳骨六八同地（在自𨓚）同月（在五月）卜。丙子卜，後甲戌二日。貳骨六九

即此已足證明「卜王」之辭皆在祖甲時矣。除此之外，無可為非「祖甲時」之反證卜辭也。

三、「卜王」各例。

1. 次數之多少。

69 68

「卜王」之辭，殘缺者多，接對尚需工夫。今就可知者言之。大抵每日卜二次以上，多則十次為止，同日已卜十次，再卜則仍從一起。（下批記數）

二次者：骨二六　甲寅，二卜

三次者：骨一一七　辛卯三卜　上有殘缺，恐不止三次。

五次者：骨五八　丁卯五卜　此確為五次，其上乃辛未卜。

骨七八　戊寅五卜　　骨一〇八　戊子五卜　上有殘缺。

骨一二七　癸巳五卜　上有殘缺。

六次者：甲三八　辛(丑)五卜　上為壬寅。以例推之，多則六或八次。　骨一二八　甲午六卜。上有殘缺。

骨一三二　甲午六卜　上有殘缺。　骨一九六　庚戌六卜　上有殘缺。

八次者：甲三六　辛卯八卜　參釋文。　骨二一　庚午八卜　右有殘缺，如釋文或十次。

骨二四　戊子八卜　左有殘缺。　骨二五　癸巳八卜

骨二二七　辛酉八卜　上有殘缺。

十次者：甲三二　壬辰十卜　參釋文。　骨二二　己卯十卜　有數字，最準確。

骨七九　戊寅，十卜　有數字。　骨二七　辛卯十卜　缺左行第十辭

骨二三　癸未十卜　無數字。

十次以上者：甲二九　丁丑　依部位推之，中部凡丁丑可容二十次，上部殘餘七，九兆兆記數字，知凡十辭者兩組。參看釋文。

甲三一　壬寅　下十次有記數字，上又有同日卜辭。

甲三五　壬寅　甲三七　甲申

甲七五　乙酉　此版為重要之證，證明同版有兩組十次卜辭，卜兆記數滿十數，仍由一起。參看釋文。

骨七九　戊寅　由上而下，已足十次，另由一起，如上例。

由上諸例，可見「卜王」之辭，在一日之內，有卜二次者，卜五次者，多則有十次者，十次以上，則卜兆記數仍由一起，故可能至二十次，無一定之標準也。

2，日之距離。

前後兩次「卜王」辭，日之距離，以相接連者為多，知在祖甲時，王親貞而不記貞辭者為平常事。亦有兩辭相距二日，三日，四，五日者，十日者，十八日者。例如下：

兩次「卜王」之日干相連者：辛卯—壬辰　甲三六　辛丑—壬寅　甲三八　丁亥—戊子　甲三九

己巳—庚午　甲三三　丙寅—丁卯　骨四二　己巳—庚午　骨五二　癸未—甲申　骨九四

己丑—庚寅　骨一一一　甲午—乙未　骨一三四　己亥—庚子　骨一五六　壬寅—癸卯　骨一六八

癸卯—甲辰 骨一七五 壬子—癸丑 骨二〇〇 甲寅—乙卯 骨二〇五 己未—庚申 骨二一九

乙卯—丙辰 骨二〇八 己酉—(庚)戌 骨一九四

相距二日者： 甲申—丙戌 骨九四 丁酉—己亥 骨一四五

相距三日者： 丁丑—庚辰 甲三四

相距四日者： 乙丑—己巳 骨三五 丁卯—辛未 骨五八 乙亥—己卯 骨八二

相距五日者： 己未—甲子 骨三一

相距十日者： 戊辰—戊寅 骨四三

相距十八日者： 丙寅—甲申 骨九五

此距日之可考者也。

3，記時者。

「卜王」之辭，每於第一卜下記此日在幾月，亦有記月在二，三卜以上者。例如

戊戌卜王。在二月。骨一四七 癸未卜王。在四月。骨二三 (戊)申卜(王)。在四月。骨一九一

壬寅卜王。在十二月。骨一六二 甲子卜王。在十一月骨一九 丙寅(卜王)。在十一月。骨四〇

4，記地者。

此類記月之辭，將來輯錄多時，可據以求其年代也。

記地，亦每于第一卜下書之，此可證「卜王」之辭，多為祖甲在外時所作。故曰「在𠂤口卜」也。𠂤，即五期之「𠂤」，師所止之地也。「卜王」辭所記地名甚多，據其月日之聯貫，為研究殷代地理之重要材料。今就已收者舉之。

在𠂤澅卜：五月甲戌 骨六八 戊子 骨一〇八

在𠂤𣪊卜：己未 骨二〇。乙丑 骨三六 己卯 骨二

在[illegible]卜：丙子 丁丑 甲二九 辛巳 甲五八 戊寅 骨七七

在[illegible]卜：庚午 骨二一

（在追[illegible]卜：壬寅 骨一六六

所記地名及在其地之月日，皆待整理研究，而後知其關係者也。

5、記吉者。

卜遇吉兆，史每喜記于兆下，第三期為較多。此記于卜王辭下。如

辛未 骨五七 丙申 骨一四一 癸卯 骨一六九②③⑤ 甲辰 骨一七八

皆于「卜王」字下，注一「吉」字，是其兆吉也。惜卜兆已不可見，無由知其作何形狀耳。

6、夾雜他事卜貞之辭者。

龜骨有全版純粹為「卜王」之辭者，亦有書契其他卜貞事項于其間者。賴有此，乃能由稱謂貞人以定

其時代耳。本冊已收之辭有

貳骨三一　①己未卜囗貞：小王歲，宰。②甲子卜王。此於己未後五日有卜王辭也。

三九　①②③丙寅卜王。④丙寅卜，行(貞)：歲，叙。此丙寅卜王之同日卜祭也。

二三　①至⑪癸未卜王。⑪癸未卜，行貞：今日至于翌甲申，不雨。一　⑫貞：其雨。二

此癸未卜王，十卜之後，于同日卜雨也。

一四五　①②丁酉卜王。③己亥卜，行貞：翌庚子，其賁于兄庚。④(貞)：㞢牛。

此丁酉卜王之後二日，卜祭兄庚也。

一六四　①壬寅卜囗貞：其又母辛，㞢(宰)。②貞㞢牛。六月。③貞㞢𢑚。六月。④壬寅卜王。

此壬寅卜祭母辛之後，同日有卜王辭也。

此類「卜王」與他辭同版者尚多，因未能一一接對，致殘辭失其聯繫。將來一番整理之後，必更有所發見也。

7，「卜王」之下，補記王之貞辭者。

此例如貳骨二六，已具詳前說。此版殘辭五段，由下而上，①②甲寅卜王。③④⑤乙卯卜王。④⑤皆已先書「乙卯卜王」四字，行式皆與③同，細審可辨。曰貞云云，皆補記也。並因補記字多，恐與下辭相混，皆作界劃以區分之。

四，由「卜王」辭，整理所得之甲骨文例。

甲骨文例，吾人當求其全。全龜全骨不易得，就其卜辭之有干支連繫者，推而求之，一斑之窺，如見全豹也。故卜夕，卜旬辭，於文例研究，最為重要。「卜王」辭多為同日卜，或前後二日所卜，有卜兆數字，於研究文例亦至便。今就本冊所收之甲骨數版，其文例明晰者舉之，得公式二。

1. 凡龜腹甲，分為四行五段，或四行七段。卜貞刻辭，皆先下段，後上段。自甲之中縫分，先右後左，先外後內。辭在中縫左者左行，兆右向；右者右行，兆左向。四隅刻辭反之。甲二九 一三九 七五

2. 凡牛胛骨，皆近邊兩行刻辭，每行可容八段。右胛骨，從左一行起，先下後上。右一行繼之，先上後下。兩行文皆左行。左胛骨反是。右骨 二一 三三 二六 左骨 二七 四四 二二 六

此二期甲骨普通之公例也。五期龜甲有用六行七段式，或八行九段式者，皆見序論文例圖。

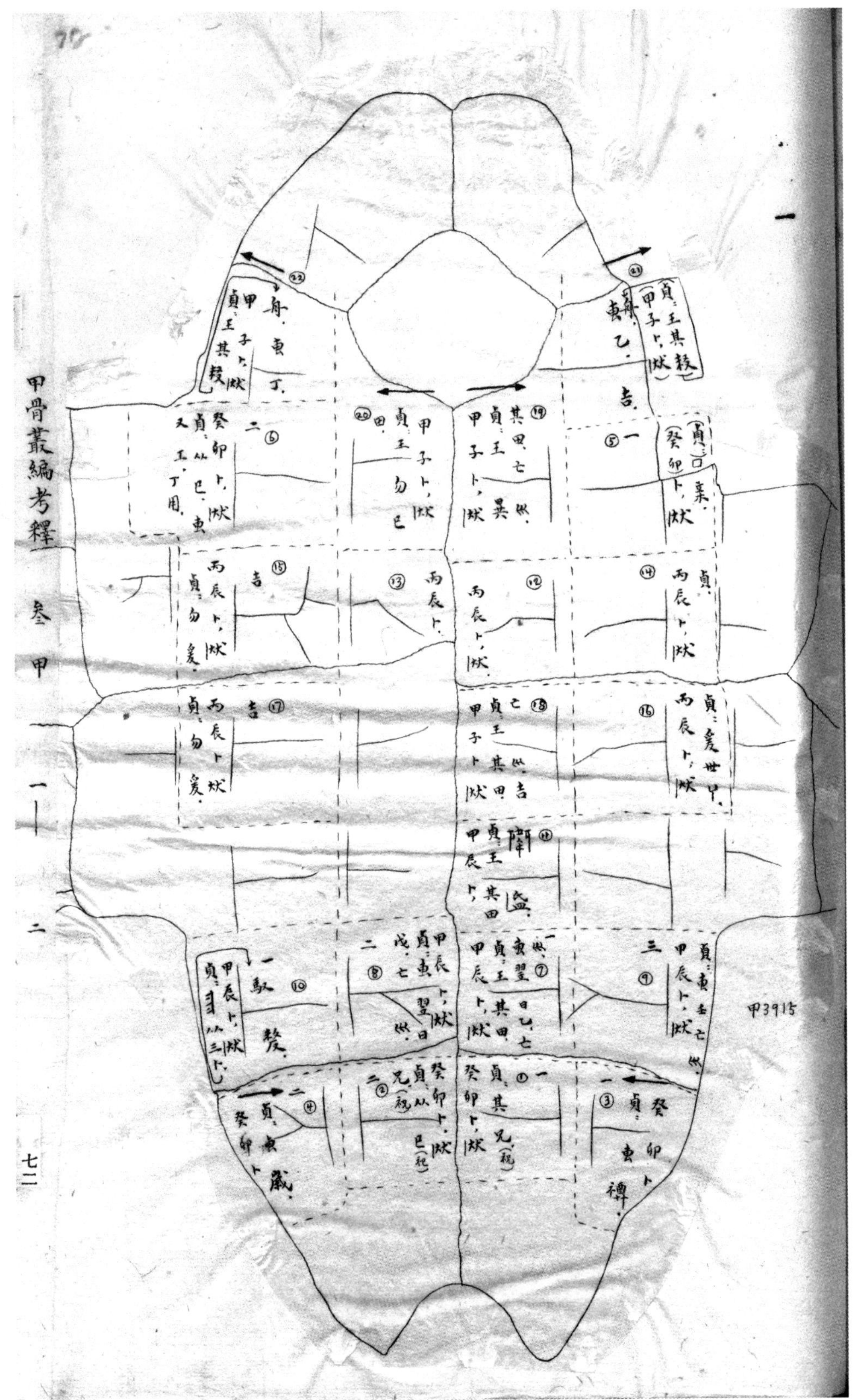
甲骨叢編考釋　叁　甲　一一二　七二
甲3915

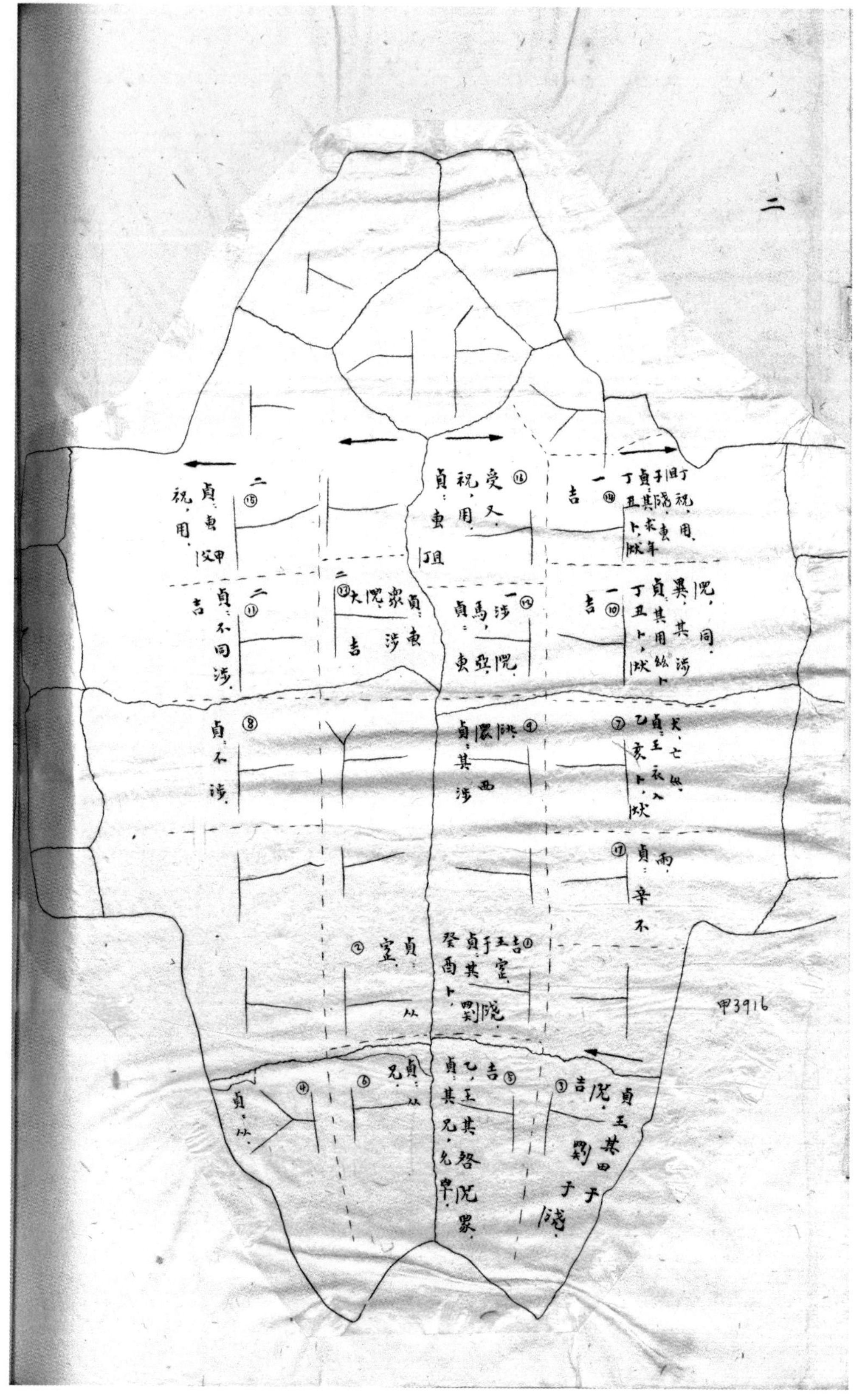
二
甲3916

73

三

甲骨叢編考釋　叁　甲　三一一四　七三

甲3917

① 己亥卜，狀，貞：今夕亡田。

② 庚子卜，狀，貞：今夕亡田。

③ 辛丑卜，貞：今夕亡田。

④ 壬寅卜，貞：今夕亡田。

⑤ 癸卯卜，狀，貞：今夕亡田。

⑥ 甲辰卜，狀，貞：今夕亡田。

⑦ 乙巳卜，貞：今夕亡田。

⑧ 丙午卜，貞：今夕亡田。

⑨ 丁未卜，狀，貞：今夕亡（田）。

⑩ 戊申卜，口，貞：今夕亡田。

⑪ 己酉卜，狀，貞：今夕亡田。

⑫ 庚戌卜，貞：今夕亡田。

⑬ 辛亥卜，狀，貞：今夕亡田。

⑭ 壬子卜，狀，貞：今夕亡田。

⑮ 癸丑卜，狀，貞：今夕亡田。

⑯ 甲寅卜，狀，貞：今夕亡田。

⑰ 乙卯卜，狀，貞：今夕亡田。

⑱ 丙辰卜，狀，貞：今夕亡田。

⑲ 丁巳卜，狀，貞：今夕亡田。

⑳ 戊午卜，口，貞：今夕亡田。

㉑ 己未卜，狀，貞：今夕亡田。

㉒ 庚申卜，狀，貞：今夕亡田。

㉓ 辛酉卜，狀，貞：今夕亡田。

㉔ 壬戌卜，狀，貞：今夕亡田。

㉕ 癸亥卜，狀，貞：今夕亡田。

㉖ 甲子卜，狀，貞：今夕亡田。

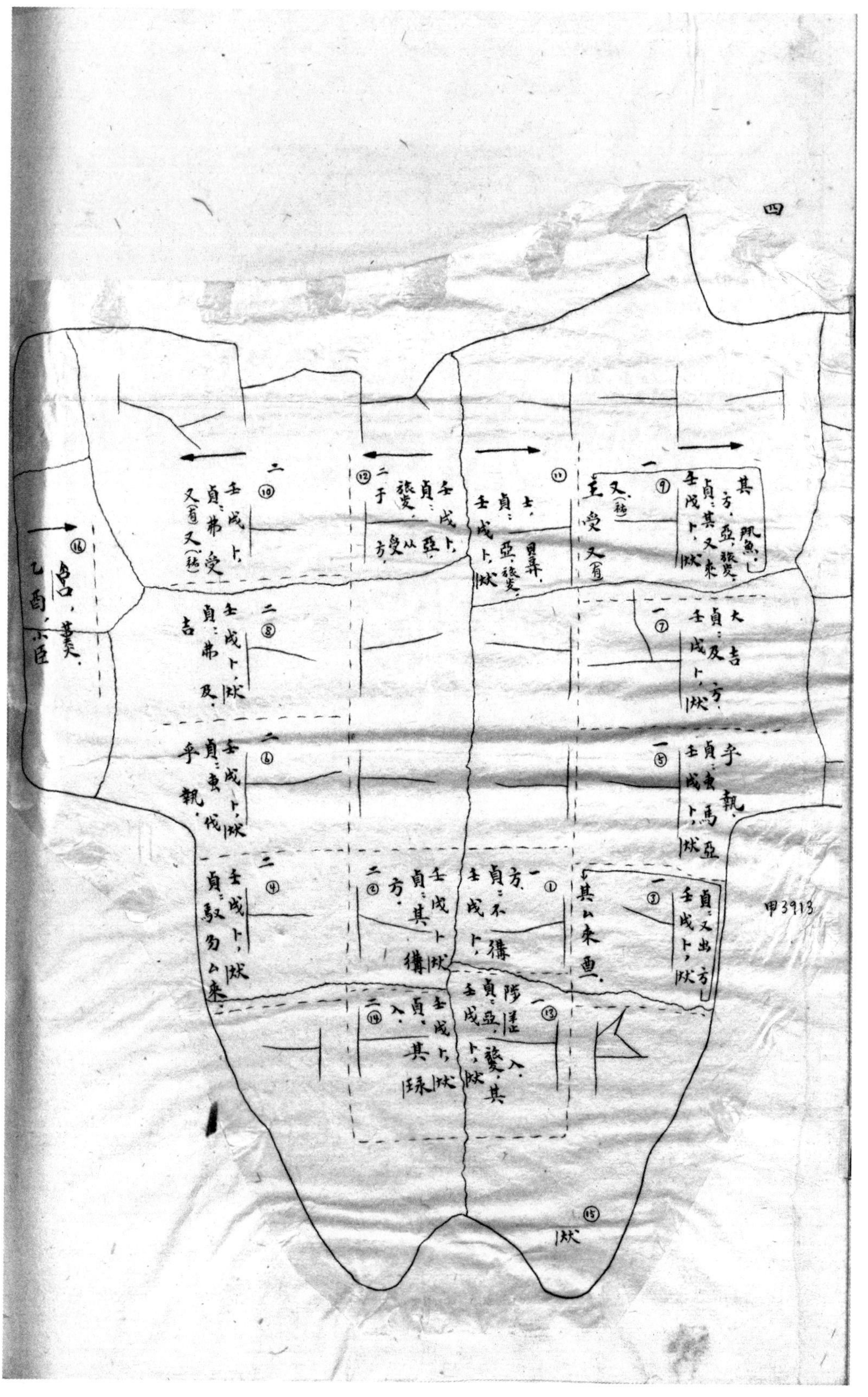
甲3913

甲骨叢編考釋　叁甲　五一六

七四

甲3914

五

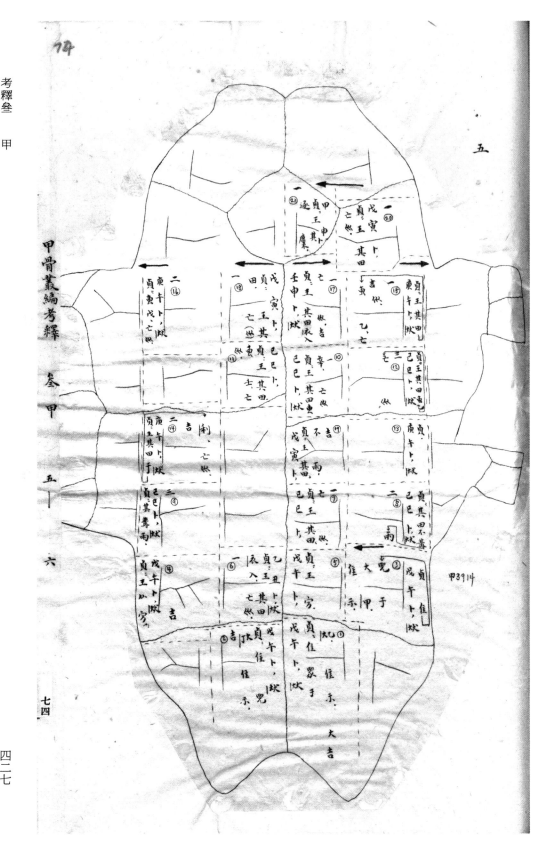

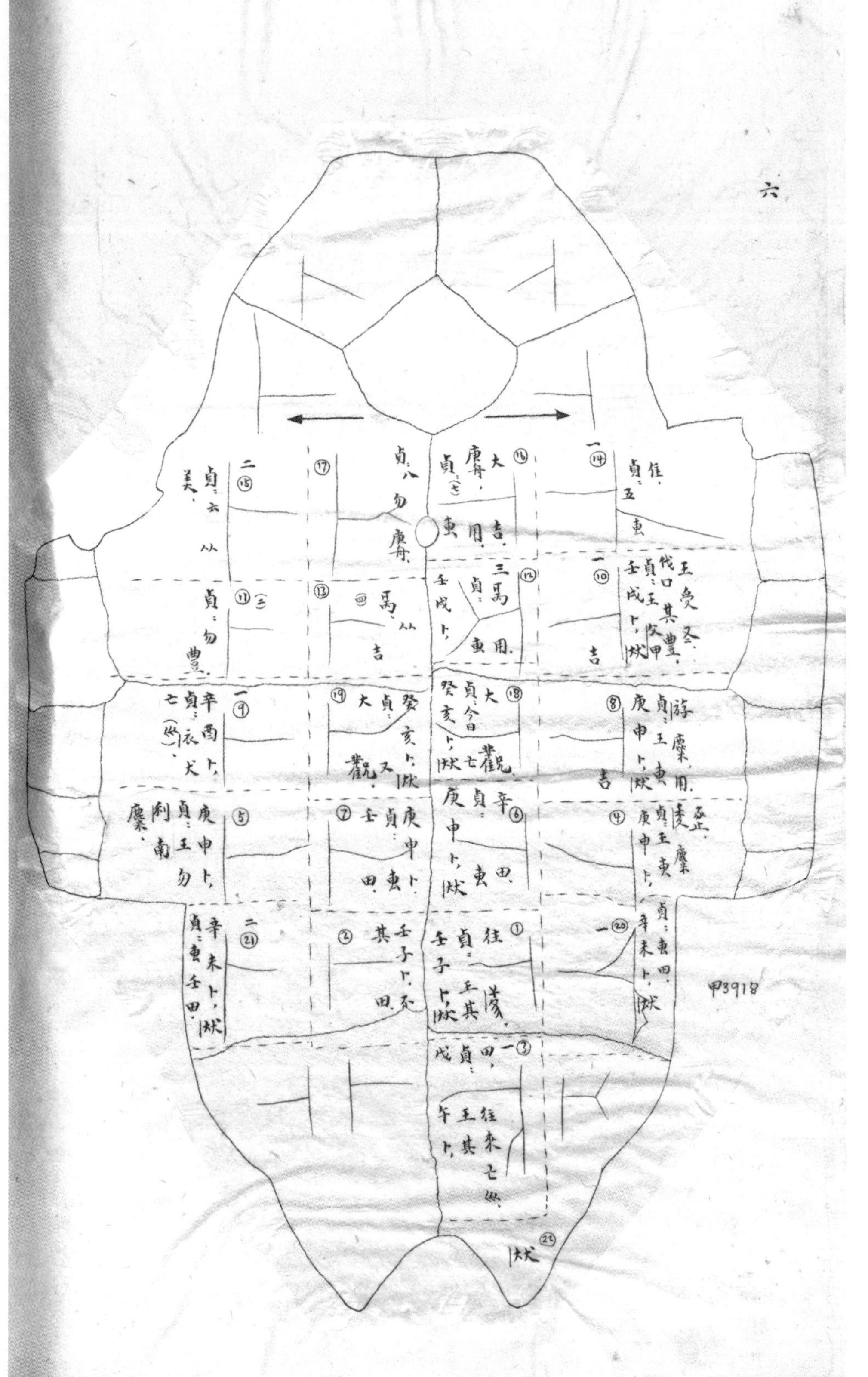
六
甲3918

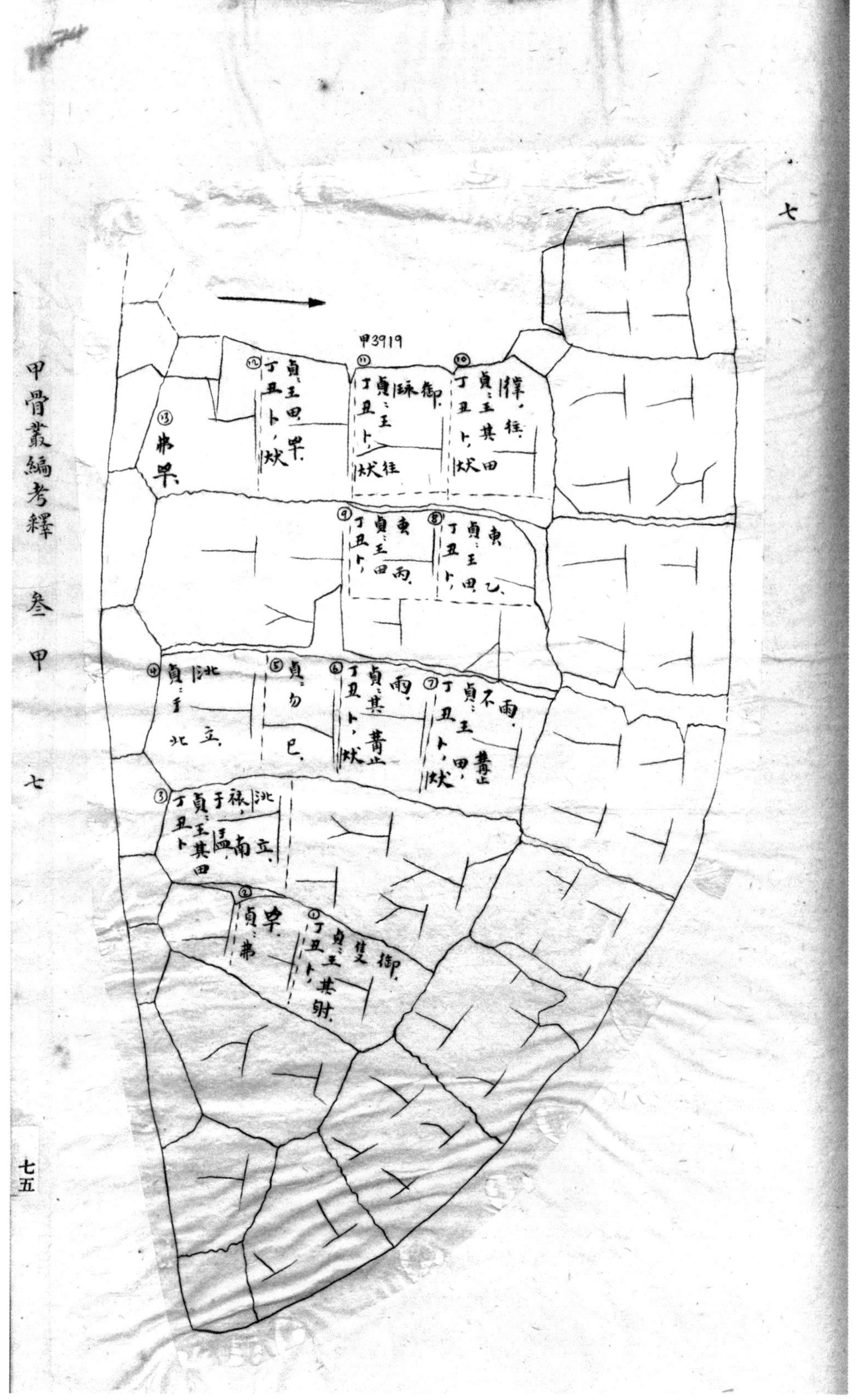
甲骨叢編考釋　叁　甲　七
七
甲3919
七五

叁甲一—七

以上七版，出土於安陽城西北洹河北岸之侯家莊。去小屯西北隔河約五六華里。再北二里許，有地稍高曰西北岡，乃殷代帝王陵墓所在也。此地在其南，有建築遺址，其版築台基，陶竇，陶穴，竇窖之類，一如小屯，為第三期廩辛康丁以後之離宮別館所在。其出土情形，文字詮考，具詳拙作安陽侯家莊出土之甲骨文字一篇中，茲不複述。

书籍 1002
洋
04845

76

一

③ 小王父己。

② 癸酉卜：于父甲求，[字形]。

卜2.32

① 癸酉卜：其求[字形]，父甲，一牛。

卜下20

叁骨一

此為第三期廩辛康丁時之標準片。有下兩辭「父甲」可證。原破為二，今合之。在字體上，有可注意者二事，即「酉」與「卜」。酉字在第一期皆作[字形]。祖庚仍之，祖甲時加一橫作[字形]。第三期乃有此[字形]形也。卜字，一二期皆橫坼向上，作[字形]或[字形]形。此一平列作[字形]，一下向作[字形]，皆其異也。

最可注意者則為「小王父己」之稱，帝丁時之父己，即武丁之子，祖庚祖甲之兄，武乙以下所稱之祖己。祖己而有「小王」之稱，是祖己生時常稱小王矣。王為生稱，殷人死後無稱王之例，故知為祖己生稱也。

在第二期祖庚祖甲時，祭祖己因稱「兄己」，但亦有僅稱「小王」者，以此畋例之，是亦祖己也。二期有兩片，一為祖庚時：

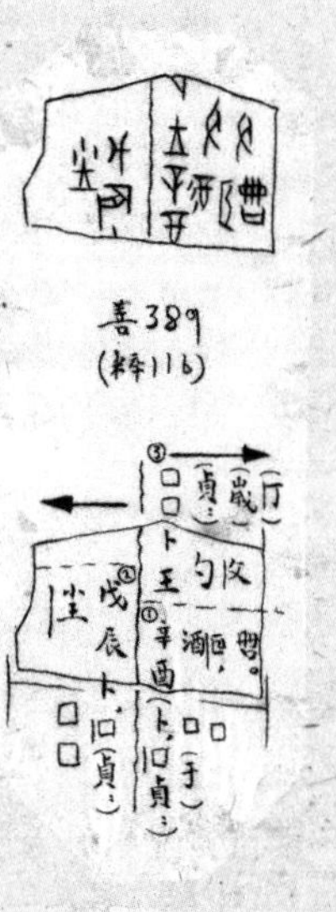

善389
（粹116）

右片疑亦祖庚時卜辭。善齋一片，承張政烺先生見告，已經收入粹編二六號，並由郭氏考釋所示，更得此片。

鐵90.2

此片為腹甲中部，未經著錄，乃劉晦之氏所藏。由字形王字因襲第一期，而辰字較晚，證之，且有下片祖甲時可資參考也。一為祖甲時：

河204

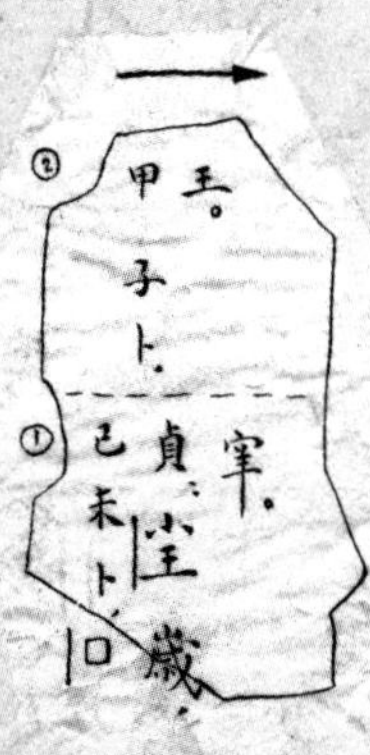

見本編貳骨三一，重錄于此，可對照庚甲兄弟卜辭之別。「小王」二字皆合文，而王字寫法不同。此上有「卜王」，為祖甲時代之確證。兩辭皆卜祀，一為乙巳前一日卜，一為己未日卜，可知所祭者為「己」，有「小王父己」之證，則此「小王」之為兄己，無疑問矣。

余於甲骨文斷代研究例中，考定祖己為漢書古今人表所列之孝己，在卜辭中當即子漁。今更列其異名為下表：

武丁時	祖庚時	祖甲時	廩辛康丁時	武乙至帝辛時	晚周諸子
子漁(3)	兄己	兄己	父己	祖己	孝己
	小王	小王	小王父己		

卜辭「王」皆稱「當今」之王，即時王。如壹骨一「王往逐豕」，王即武丁。武丁稱王，王之子（太子）稱小王（小即少也）。於名為正，是「小王」者乃武丁之子之生稱。武丁之子甚多，而稱「小王」者只一人，是小王必其嫡長之子，所謂大子（太子）矣。由此知殷人有立大子之制，父在則稱「小王」，父死即稱「王」矣。祖己不幸早死，以「小王」終其身，其弟祖庚、祖甲，相繼立為王，於祭祖己時，自當稱曰兄己，然有時不忍己之獨稱王也，乃舉祖己生時之「官」稱曰小王。小王生時有名，或即子漁；死有神主，則為己；此其別矣。第三期於父己冠以小王之稱，沿二期之制也。

今之通俗劇文，每有「老王晏駕，小王登極」之語，不圖於三千年前之高文典册中見之，亦一饒有趣味之發見也。記載中見於後漢書明德馬皇后紀者有「小王」之稱：

常與帝旦夕言道政事及教授諸小王，論議經書，述敘平生，雍和終日。

漢時，君王已稱「帝」，諸子之分封者始稱「王」、「小王」，非對時王而言，與卜辭之稱祖己不同。所謂「諸小王」，蓋諸王之年少者耳。卜辭埋藏地下者三千餘年，今經分別時期，乃能知祖己為「太子」時有「小王」之稱，前此不能知也。故周秦以降，記述罕聞，縱有稱説，亦偶同耳。

甲骨叢編考釋　叁　骨　二一　九　七八

78

二

酒・日，日，酒，正。兄，叀今用。吉

王受又。其三牢。大吉

癸亥卜：父甲夕歲，二牢。吉

佚166

三

戊午卜：其兄于父甲，叀己。

甲801

四

(7) 以剛

(6) 其剛父甲俾，又雨。

(5) 叀羊。

(4) 其剛祖乙俾，叀豚，又雨。

(3) 以剛。

(2) 其剛祖乙俾，又雨。

(1) 从叔，又雨。

下下22

五

(3) （叀）牛。

(2) 癸酉卜：叀羊。

(1) 叀西。叀冊用。

粹472

六

(2) （甲）子卜：父甲豊。

乙

(1) □□卜：父杏歲，即月

（此為牛肋骨，未經製作，無卜兆、鑽灼，乃卜於他骨記辭於此者。僅此一見。）

甲3627

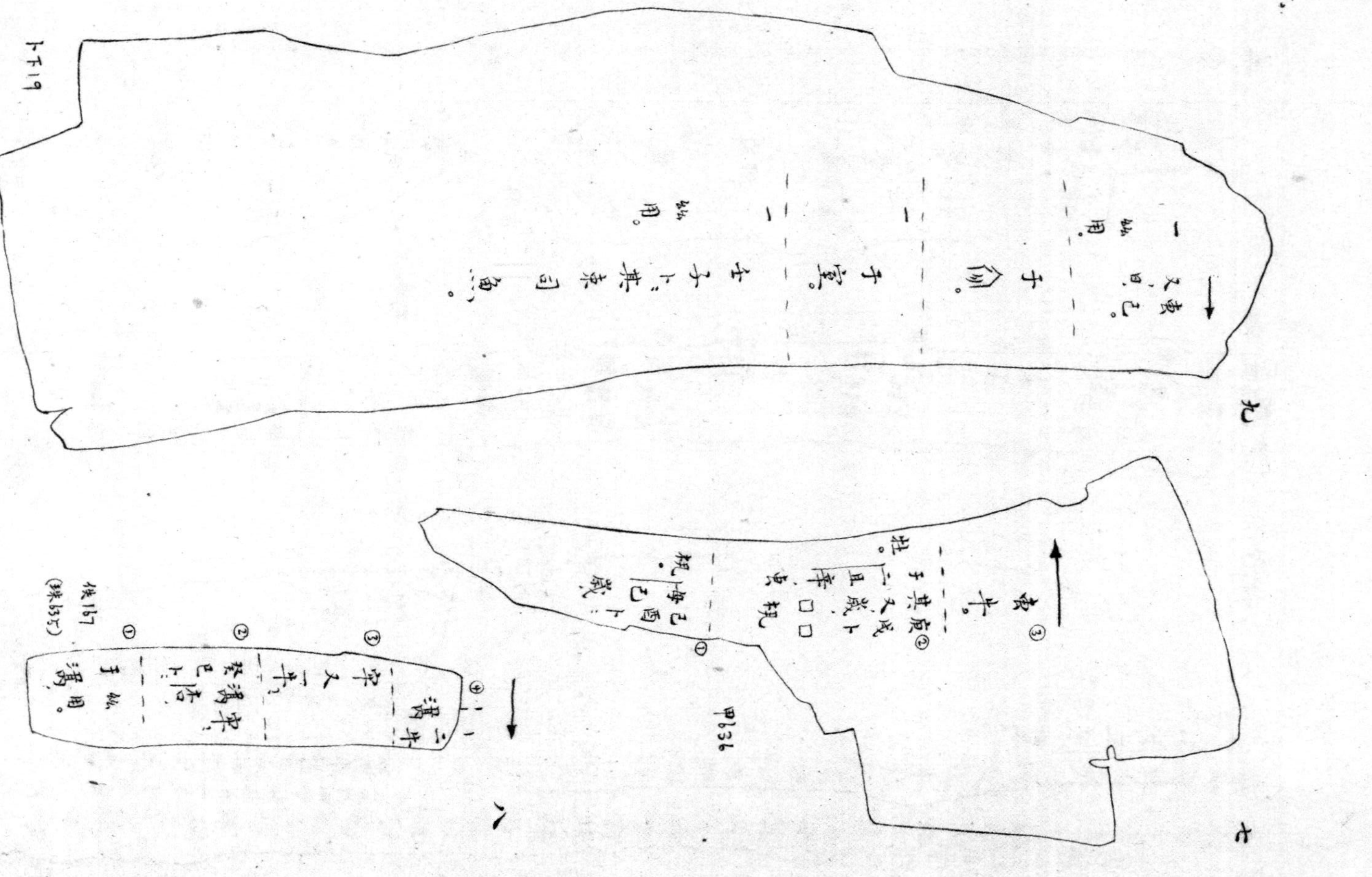
九
七
甲636
八

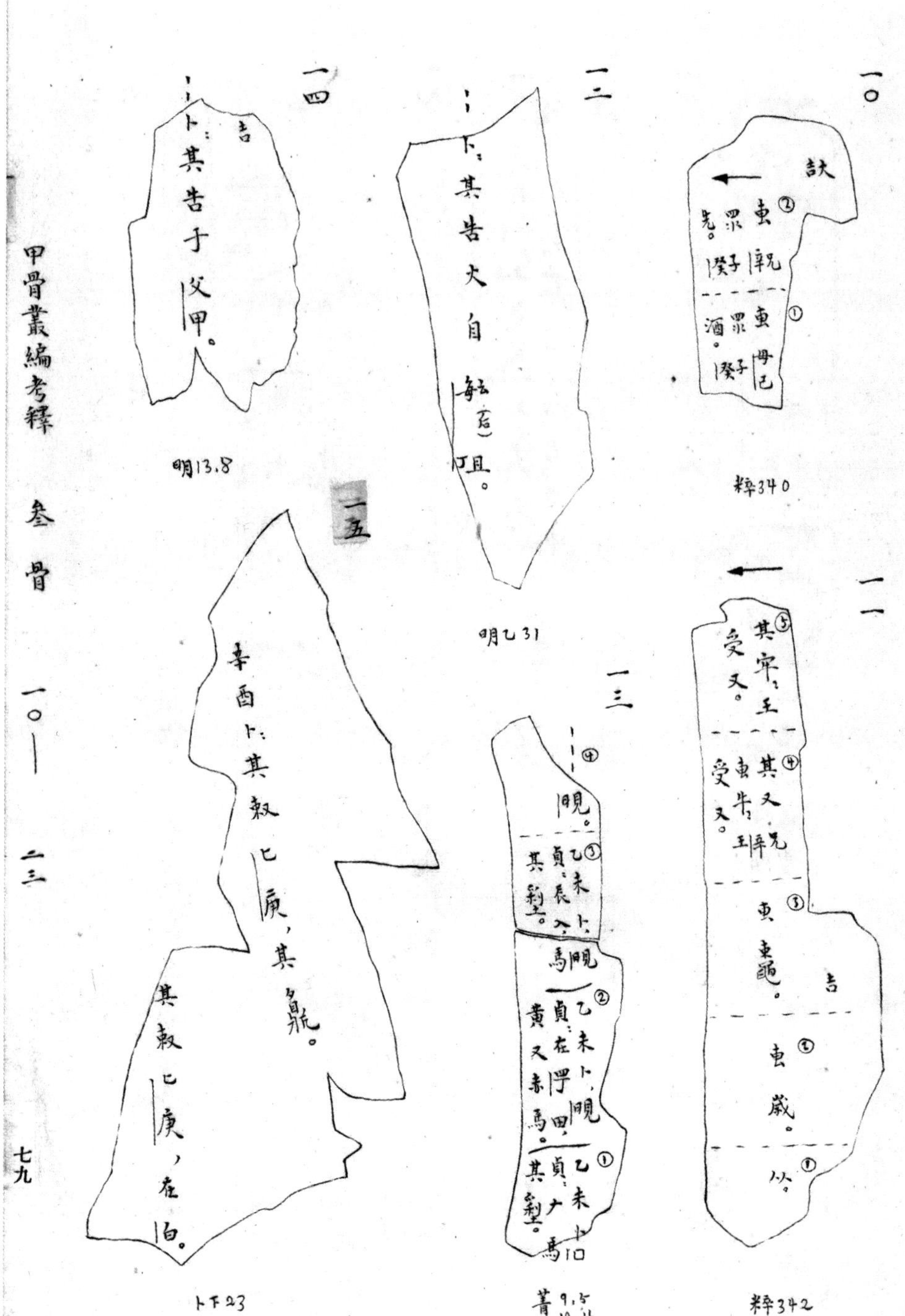
甲骨叢編考釋　叁　骨　一〇一　二三
七九
一〇
粹340
一一
粹342
一二
明乙31
一三
菁9.5 10.16
一四
明13.8
一五
卜下23

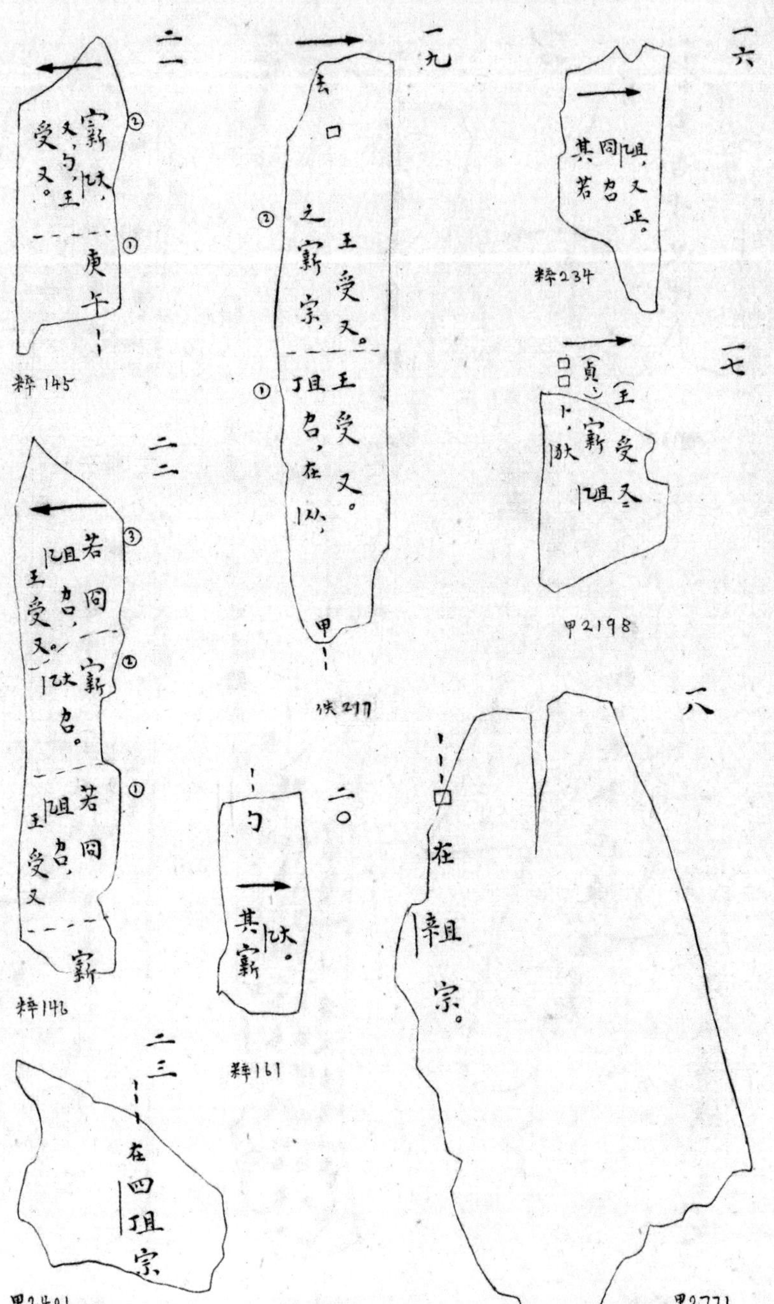
一六
粹234
一七
甲2198
一八
甲2771
一九
佚277
二〇
粹161
二一
粹145
二二
粹146
二三
甲2401

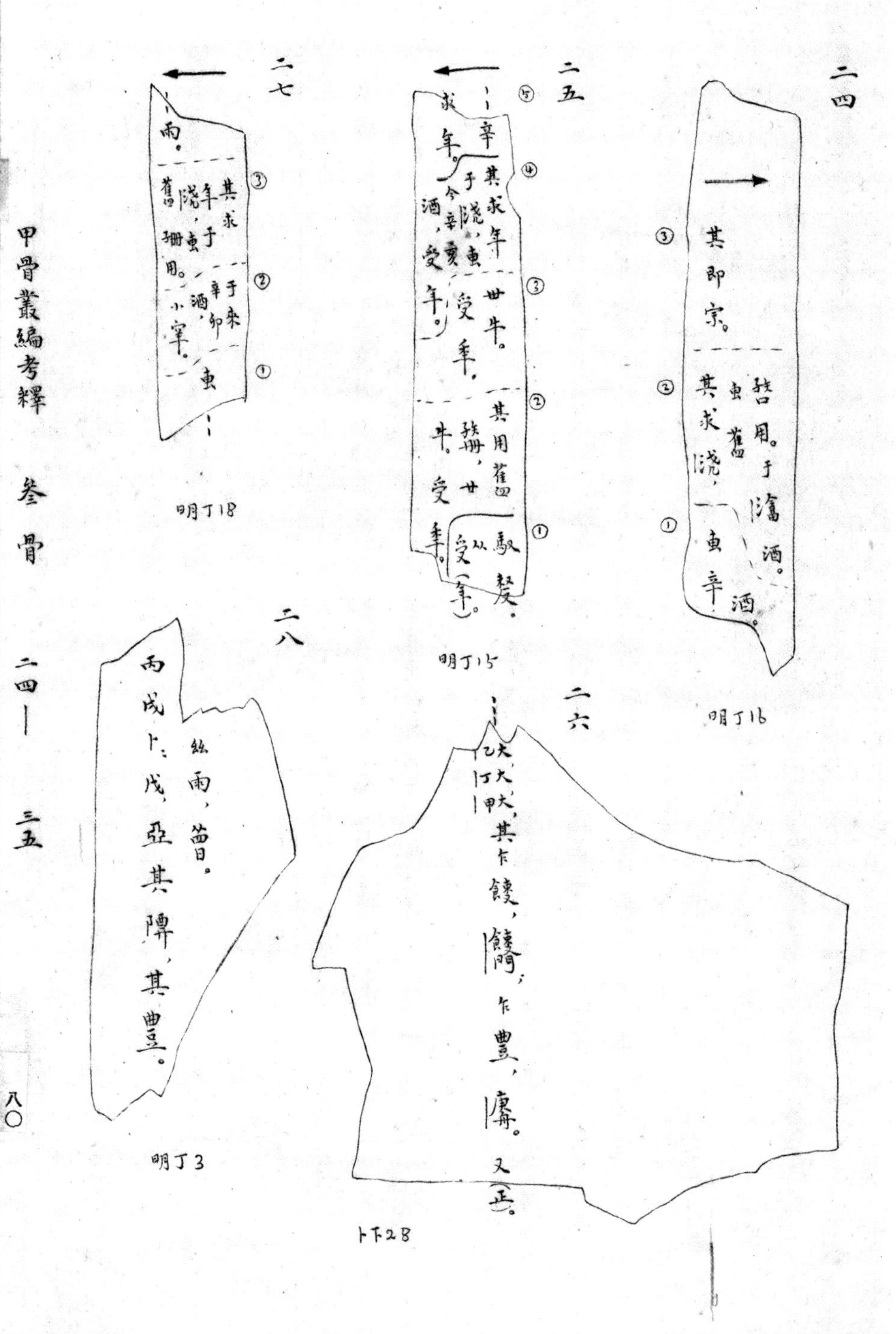
甲骨叢編考釋　叁　骨　二四—三五
八〇
二四
明丁16
二五
明丁15
二六
卜下28
二七
明丁18
二八
明丁3

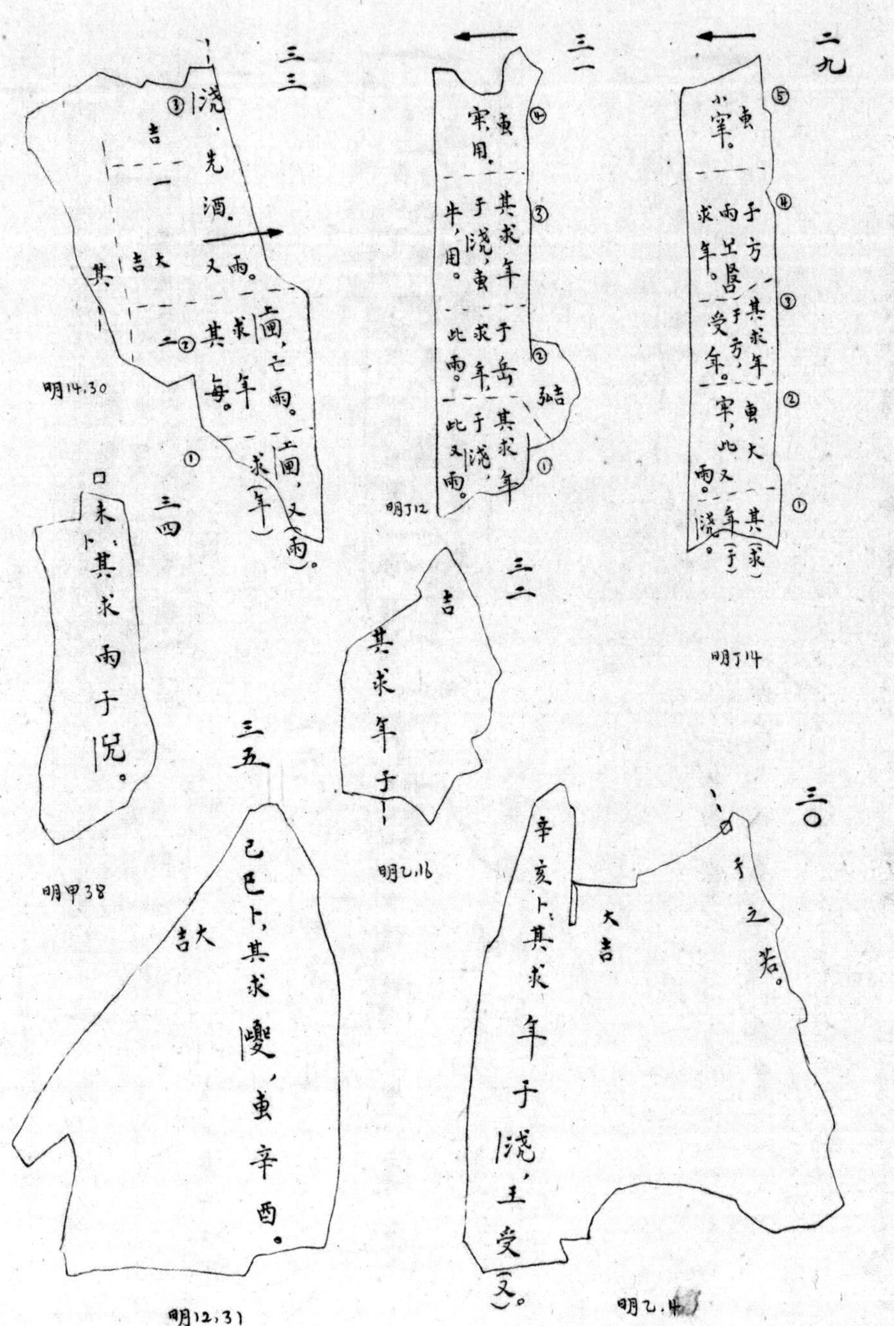
二九
明丁14
三一
明丁12
三三
明14.30
三四
明甲38
三二
明乙16
三五
明12.31
三〇
明乙4

叄甲一—七　叄骨一—三五

全部卜辭，以第三期康辛康丁時之數量為最少。據余所知，第三期卜辭之出土地帶有三：

一、小屯村之村中及村前。此一帶出土者，在民國十七年以前，多為明義士及劉晦之購去。明氏一部有拓本，但未著錄。劉氏著錄于殷契粹編者亦少數。十七年以後，則為中央研究院發掘得之，全已收入殷墟文字甲編中。

二、小屯村北地之「大連坑」。此坑民國十八年秋季中央研究院發掘得其大部分，亦入殷墟文字甲編。一小部分流入估人手，為美國施美士購得，商錫永氏編入殷契佚存中。(二五五—三一六)

三、侯家莊村南。此坑民國二十三年春季，中央研究院發掘得之。全部發表於田野考古報告第一冊。並收入殷墟文字甲編。本書叄甲一至七即是。

其餘各家亦間有收藏，為數寥寥，而出土地大抵皆為村中也。

三期卜辭辨別之標準，坑位最為重要，如上所述，其出土有一定區域也。其本身，仍以「稱謂」與「貞人」為斷，能選出稱謂貞人之片為三期標準片，然後更進而依據之以求其字形，書體，文法，詞類，禮制與他期之異同，則得之矣。

稱謂之可為標準者，在三期為稱祖己，祖庚，祖甲曰父己，父庚，父甲。更因同版之辭以及其他稱謂。

如康丁稱康辛曰兄辛，叁胄一〇有兄辛，則康丁之辭也。其同版有母己，有子癸，則母己子癸亦標準矣。叁胄七有母己，同版有二且辛（即小辛），是二祖辛亦標準矣。余于甲骨文斷代研究例舉何（今舊釋冘，今從郭沫若氏說）為三期貞人，即據稱謂定之。所舉之辭：

丁未卜，何貞：御于小乙奭妣庚，其賓鄉。

癸巳卜，何貞：翌甲午登于父甲，鄉。

壬子卜，何貞：翌癸丑其又妣癸，鄉。甲二七九九

丙午卜，何貞：翌丁未，其又勺歲后祖丁（武丁）。

庚子卜，何貞：翌辛丑，其又妣辛，鄉。甲二五〇二

因父甲之稱，定何為三期貞人，三期稱武丁為祖，是后祖丁乃武丁，加「后」字，以別于小乙之父祖丁也。是后祖丁又可為標準也。與何曾在同版之貞人為彭，三·二〇七〇六、佚二八 為宁；三·二〇七〇六 佚二六六 彭之同版有口，三·二〇五一七 有狄，三·二〇五〇一 佚二七八 口之同版有逄；佚二六七 狄之同版有卯；三·〇·二七〇三 卯之同版有𠦪；三·〇·〇七六〇 由此連鎖關係，知𠦪，卯，狄，口，彭，宁，何，逄，皆為第三期之貞人矣。此八人者所貞之辭皆三期之標準片也，因其字形，書體等等，以求三期之卜辭，未有不中者矣。

本冊所收三期甲七，骨三五，為例尚少，故畧述鑒別之法。殷墟文字甲編已出版，讀者依此法求之可也。

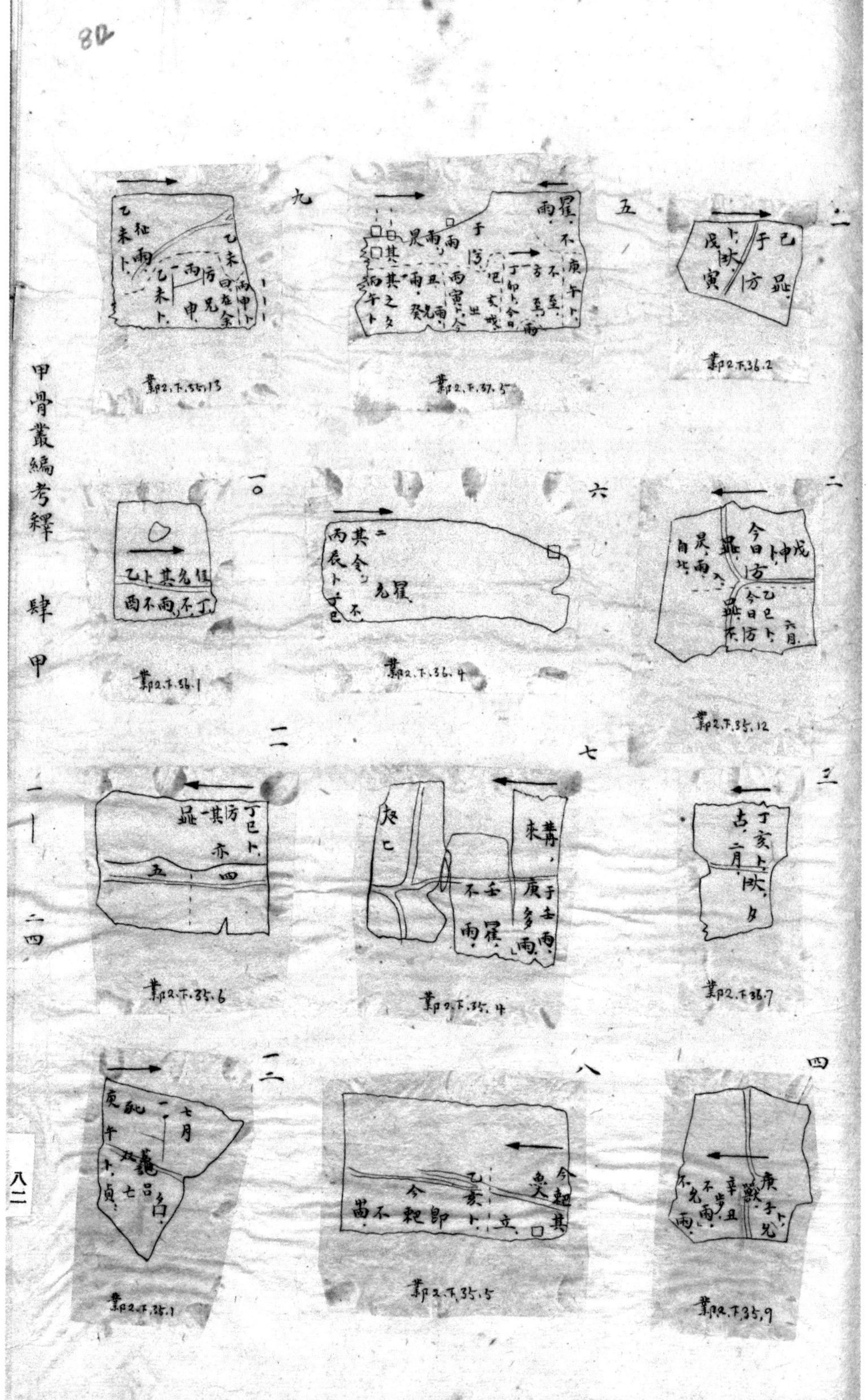

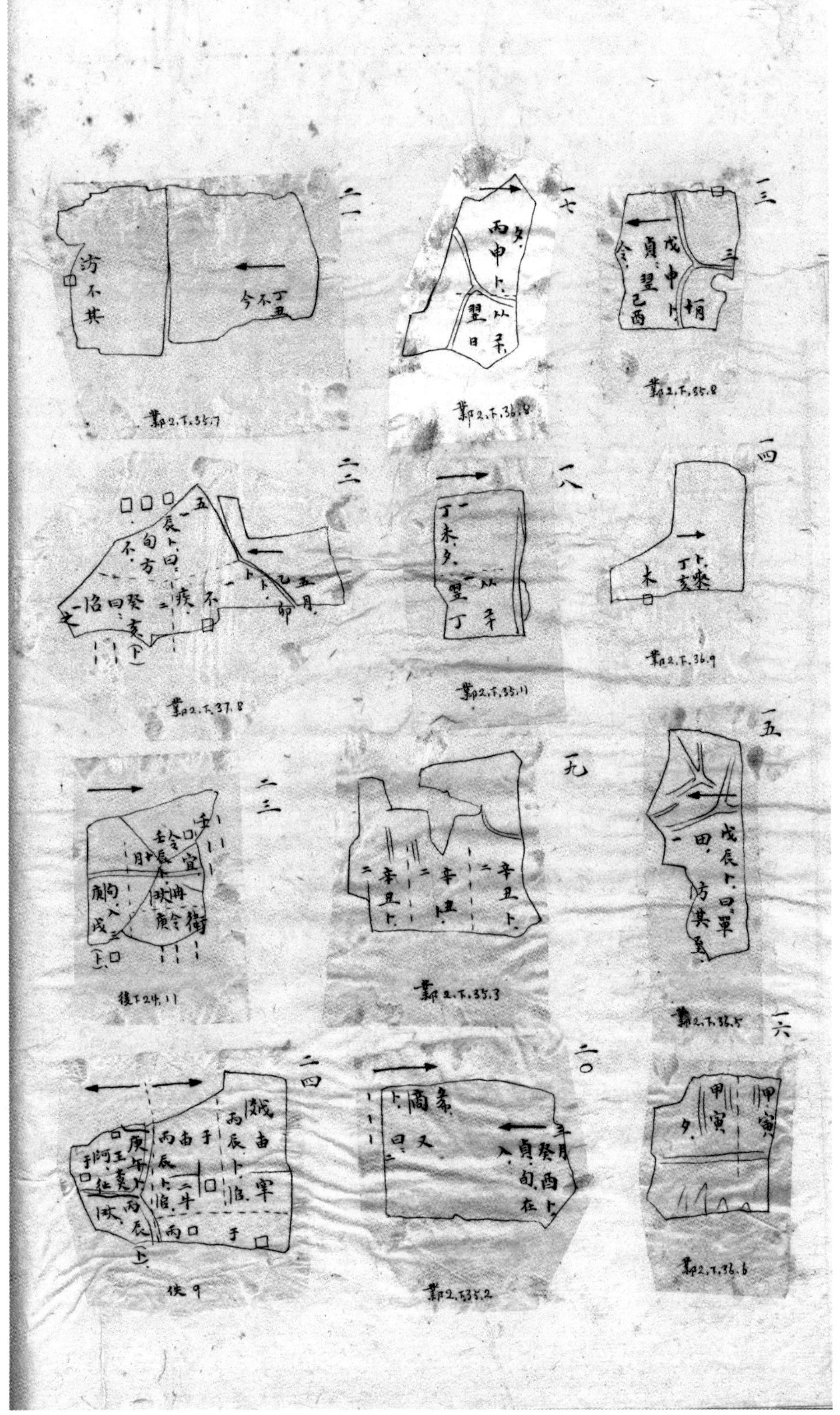

二五
甲454

二六
甲249

二七
甲210

二八
甲264

二九
佚599

三〇
甲955

三一
甲3483

三二
佚777

三三
甲234

三四
甲280

三五
甲207

三六
甲254
甲248

三七
新302

三八
甲281

三九
甲2407

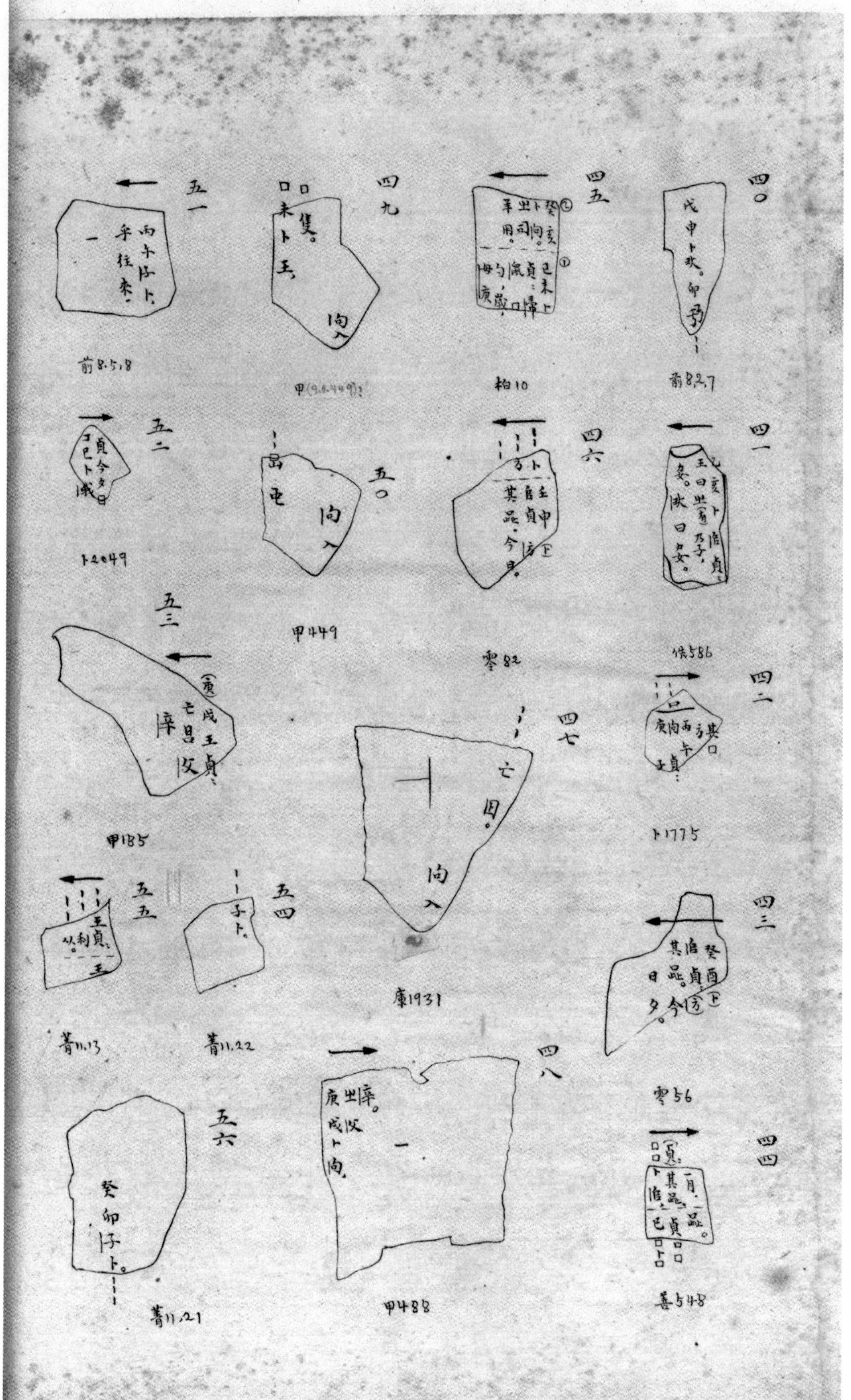
四〇
前8.2.7
四一
佚586
四二
卜1775
四三
零56
四四
四五
柏10
四六
零82
四七
庫1931
四八
甲488
四九
五〇
甲449
五一
前8.5.18
五二
卜2049
五三
甲185
五四
菁11.22
五五
菁11.13
五六
菁11.21

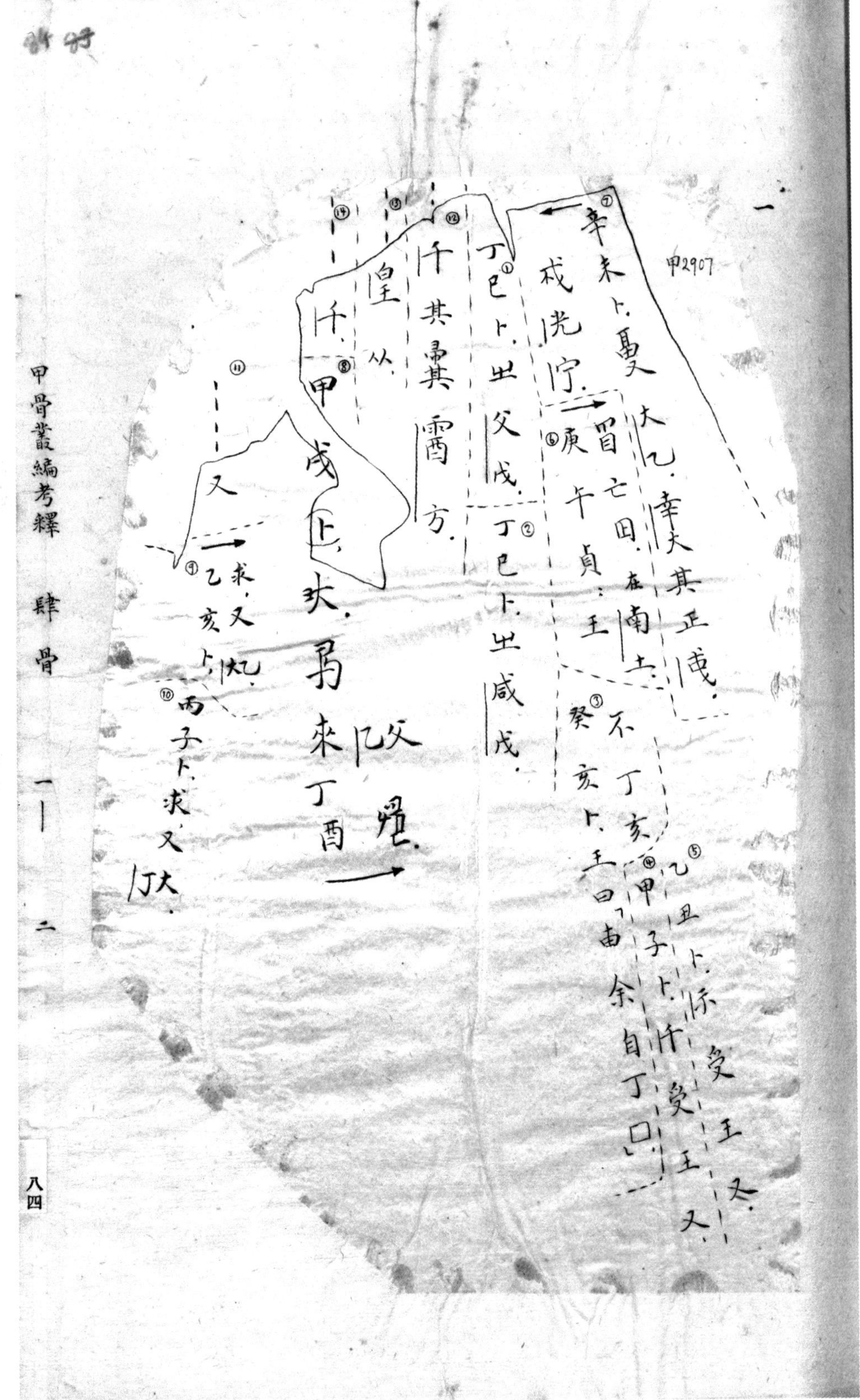
甲骨叢編考釋　肆　骨　一一二
八四
甲2907

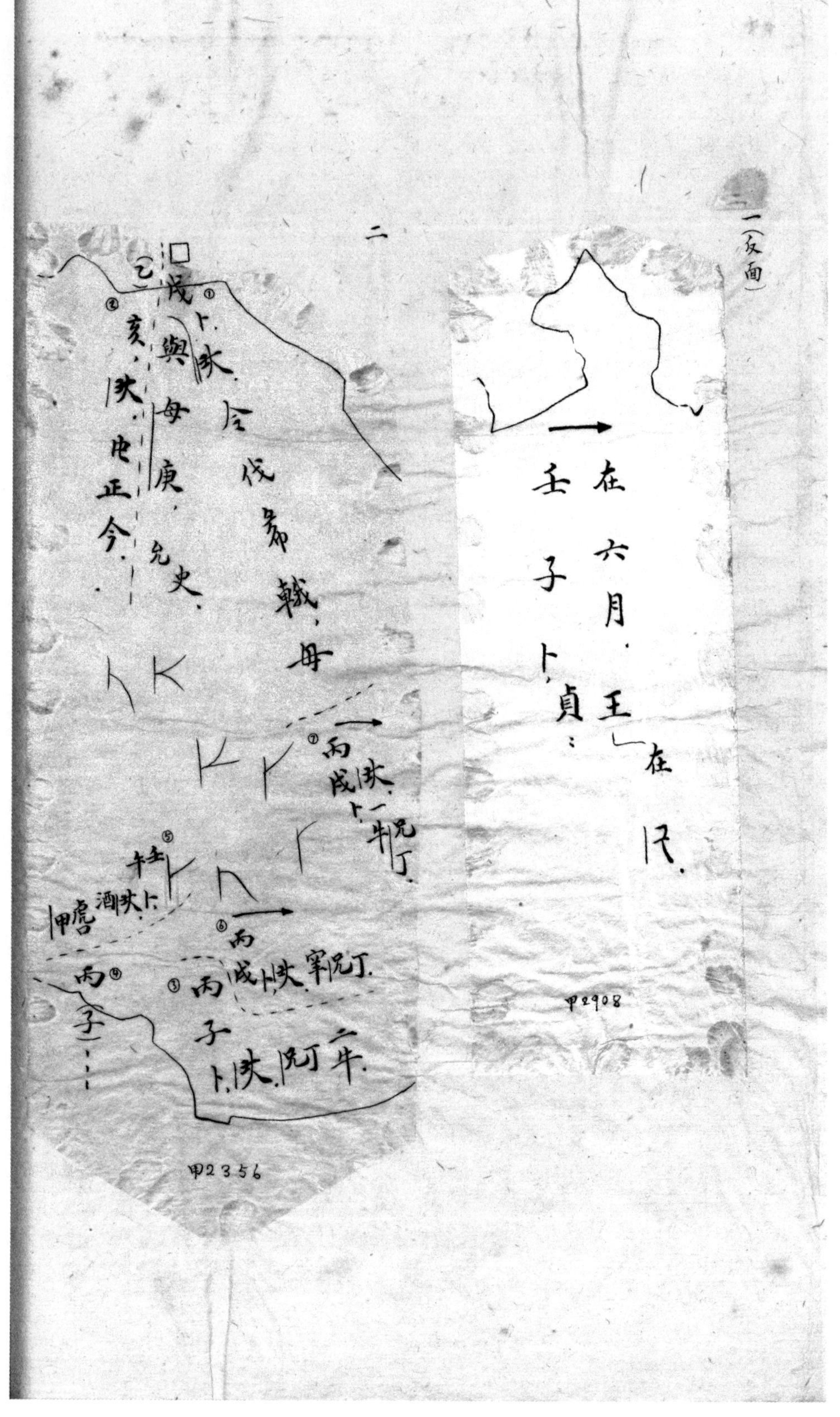
一（反面）
在六月，王在
壬子卜，貞：
甲2908
二
甲2356

甲骨叢編考釋 肆 骨 三一五

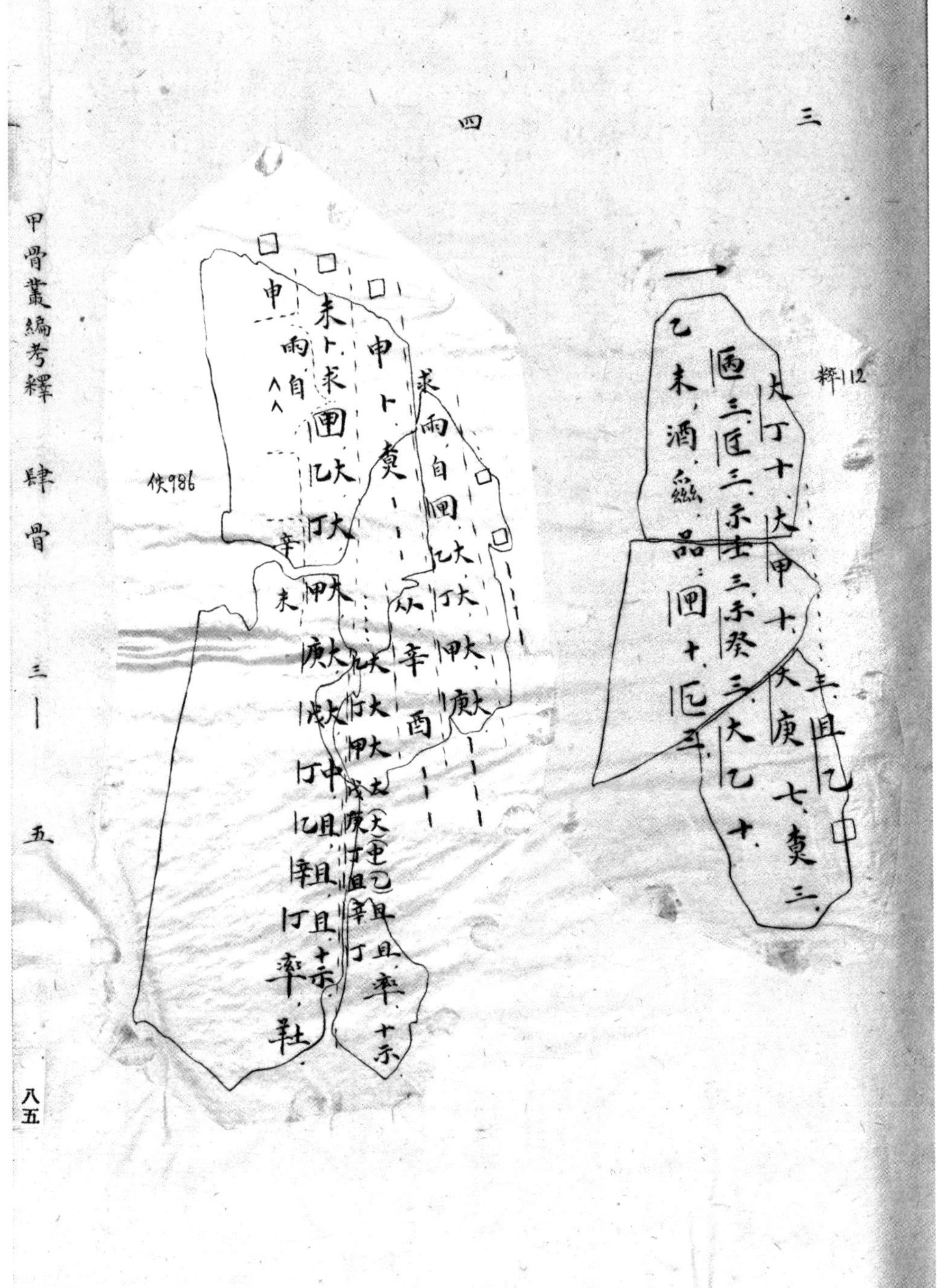

八五

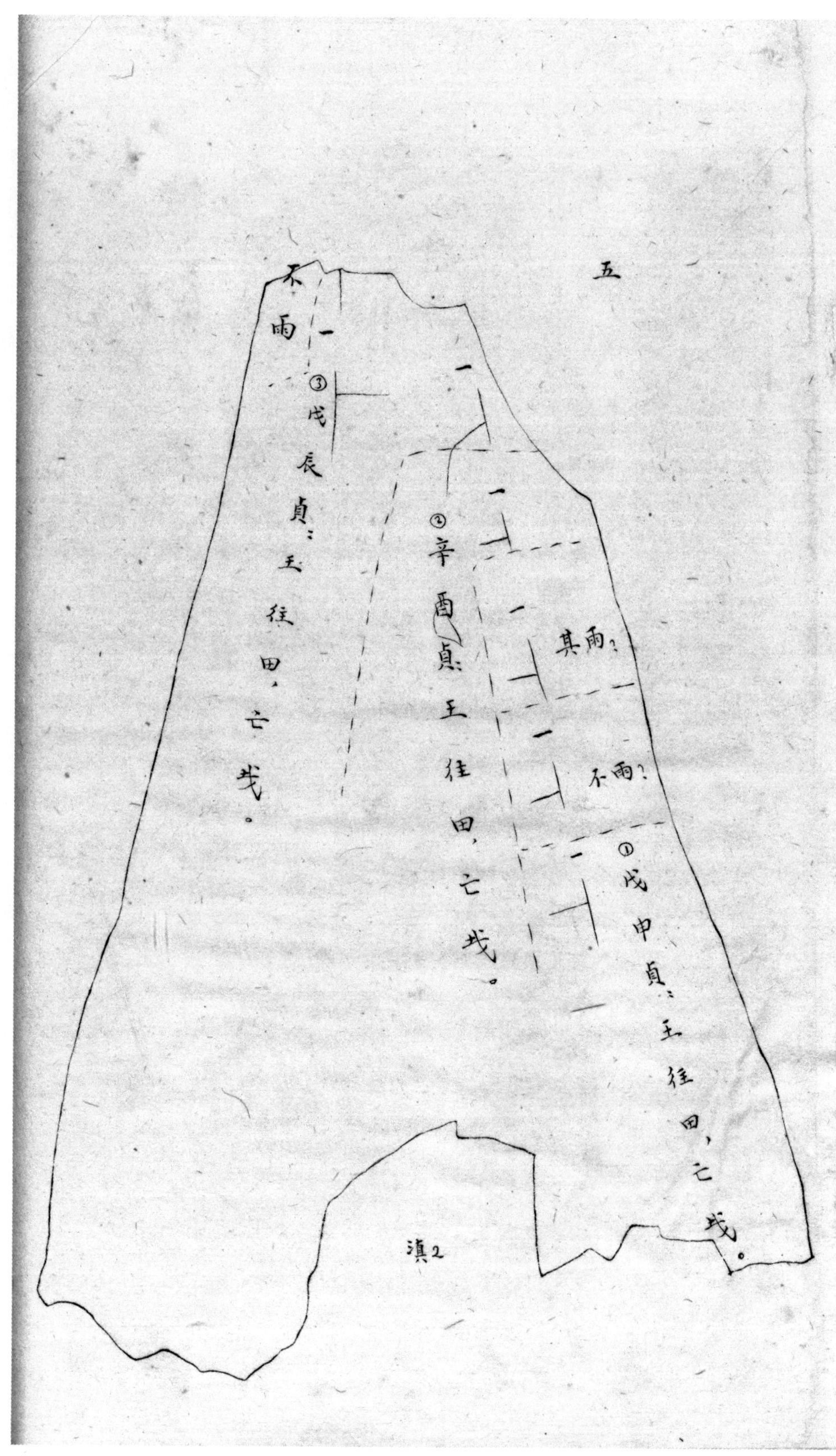

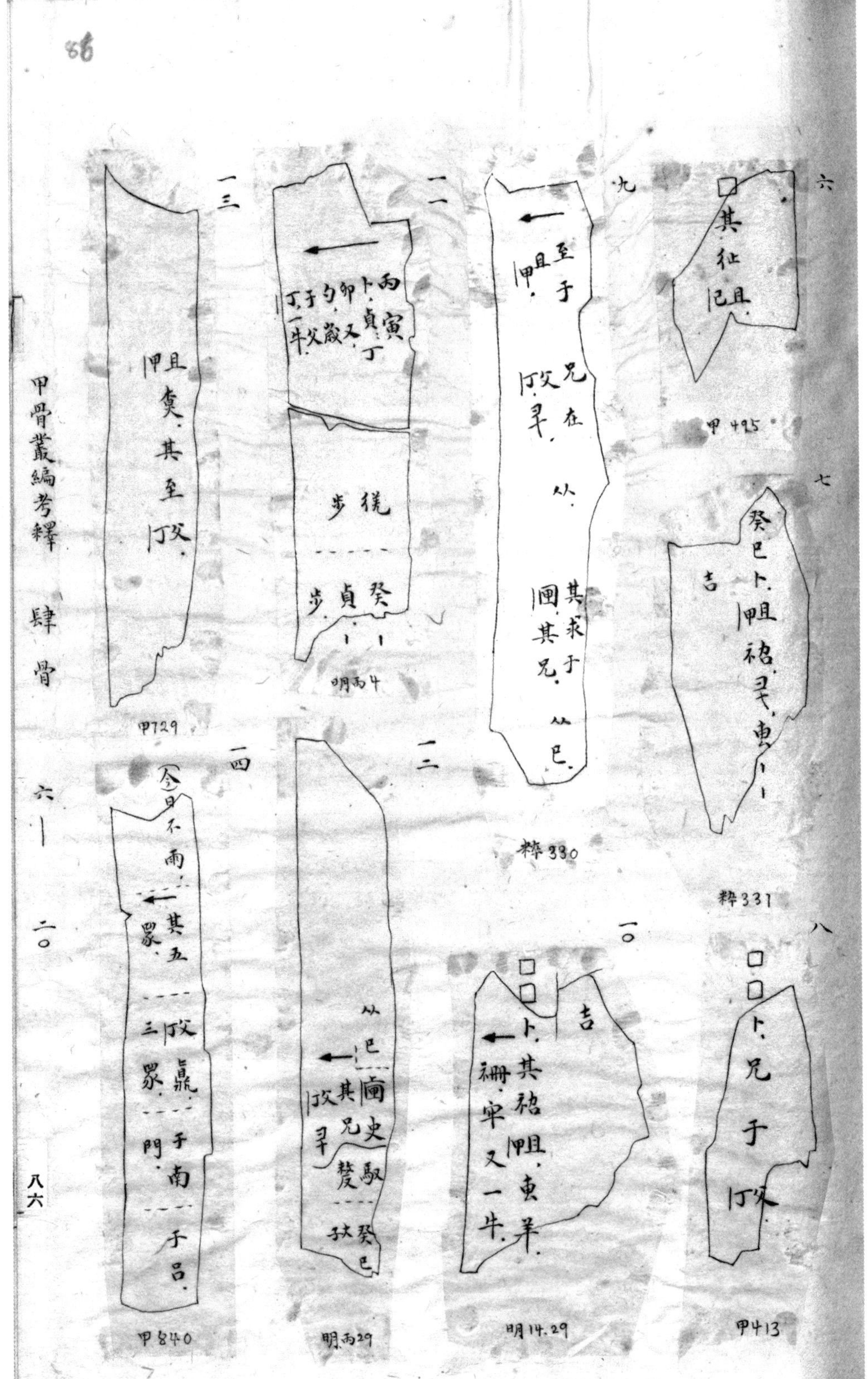

甲骨叢編考釋　肆　骨　六一—一〇

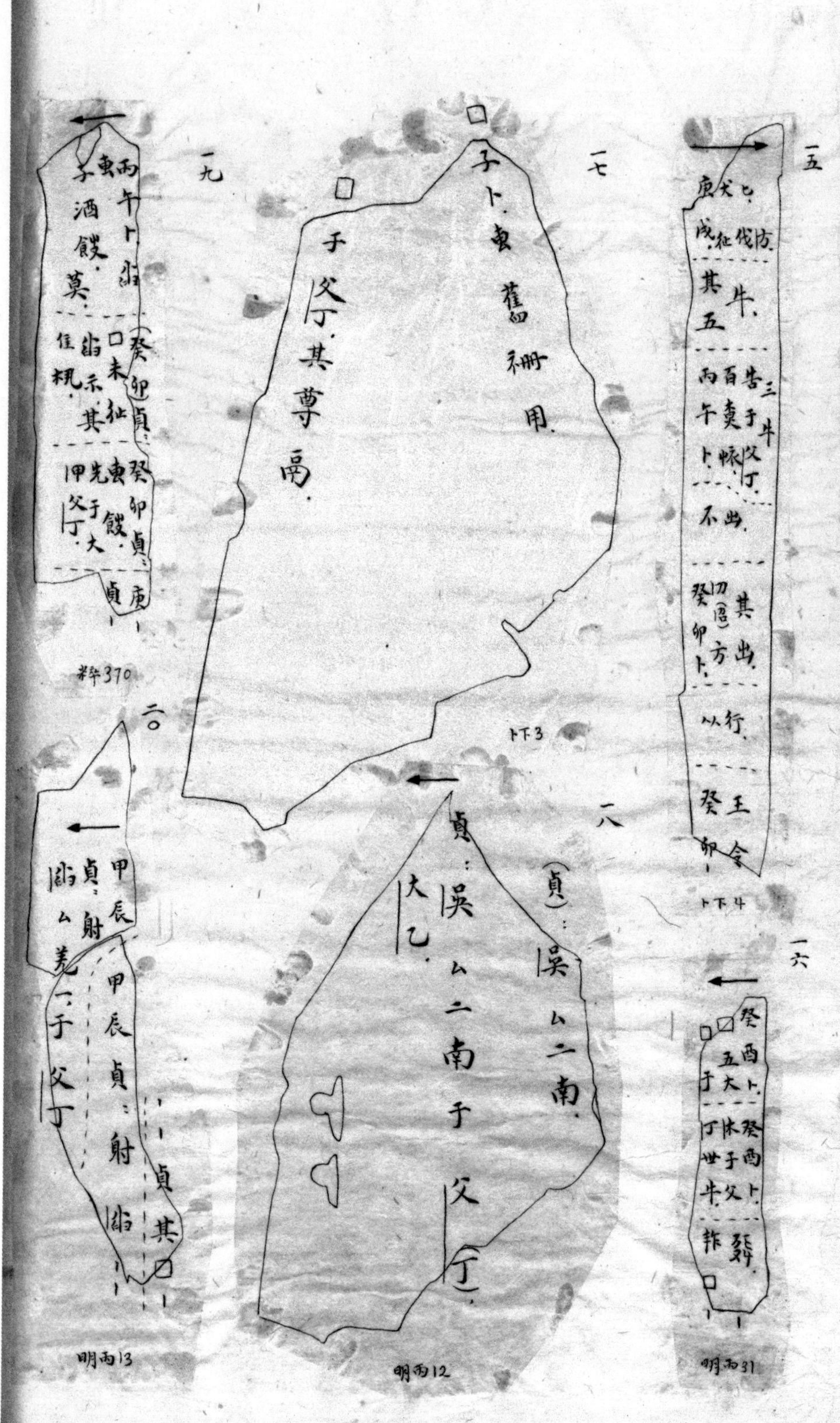

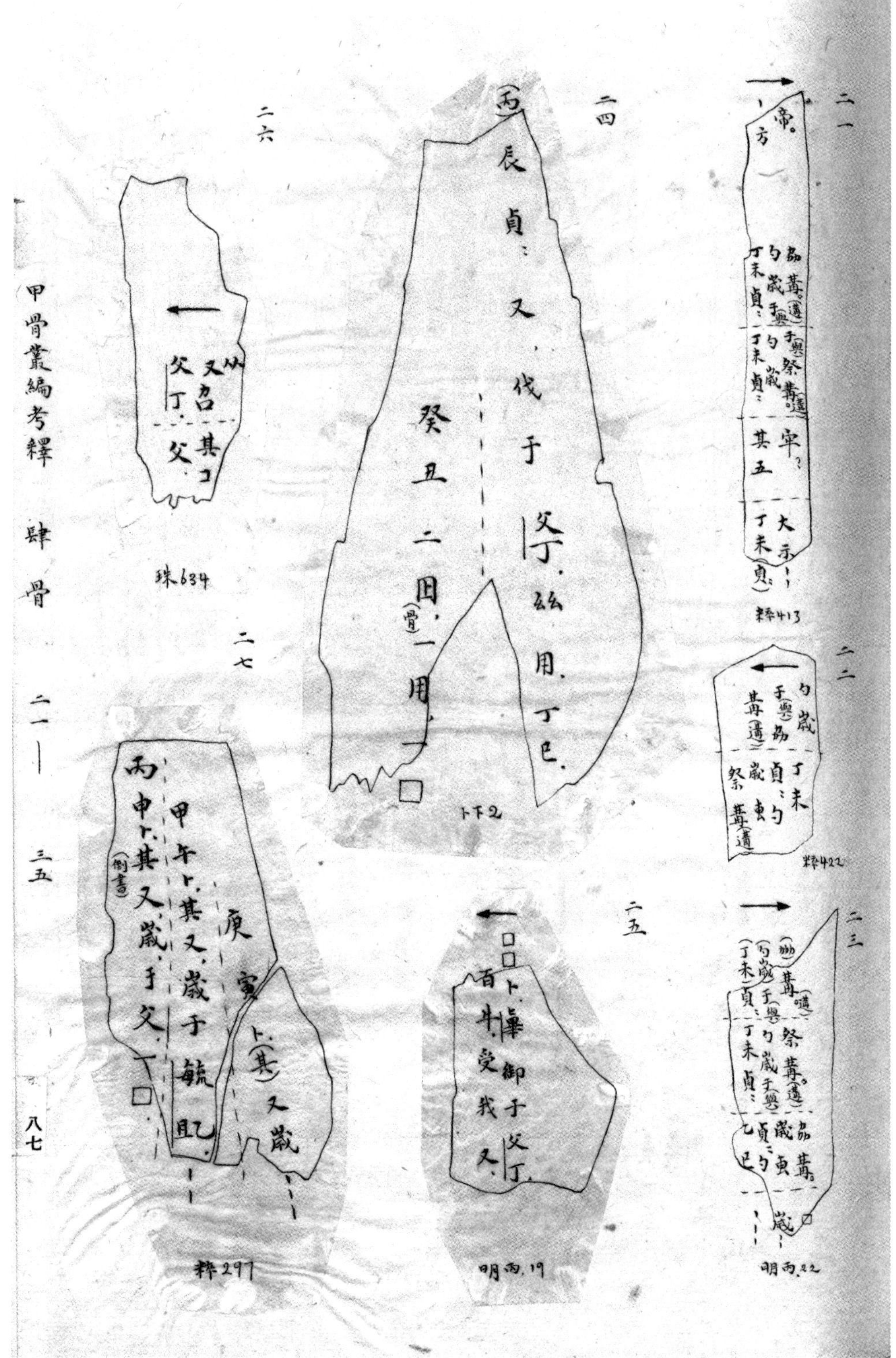
89
甲骨叢編考釋　肆　骨　二一一　三五
八七
二一
粹413
二二
粹422
二三
明丙22
二四
卜下2
二五
明丙19
二六
珠634
二七
粹297

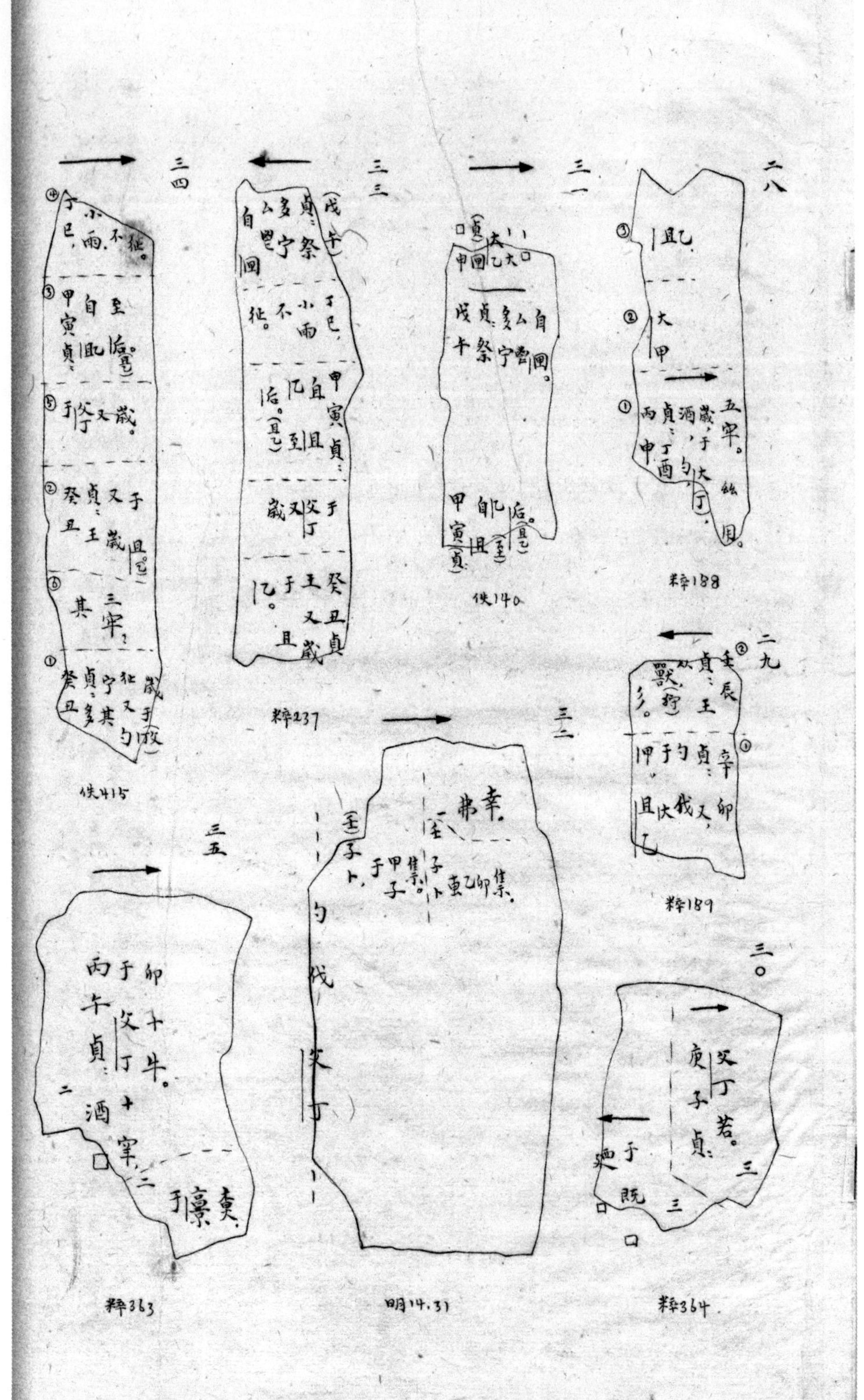

二八
粹188
二九
粹189
三〇
粹364
三一
佚140
三二
明14.31
三三
粹237
三四
佚415
三五
粹363

甲骨叢編考釋　肆　骨　三六一—四七

八八

三六

① 丁未貞:王其令望乘帚(婦),其告于父丁一牛。
② 丁未貞:王其令望乘帚(婦),其告于祖乙一牛。
③ 乙卯貞:又勹伐于伊。
④ 乙卯貞:
⑤ 癸亥貞:㞢方厶牛,其𢍏。于來甲申。
⑥ 其自圃。

明1921　粹506

三七

雨　不其遘
丙子貞:父丁彡。
从至三且。

明丙18

三八

丙子卜,父戊歲叀牛。
从又。

明丙38

三九

乙亥貞:又勹伐,自圃卯,至父丁。于乙酉。
(乙)亥貞:來甲申酒求

粹99

四〇

方出,从北土,弗戈北土。
(方出)从北土。其𢍏,告
貞:又來告。
(且)乙、父丁。

粹366

四一

① 乙亥貞:又勹伐,自圃,至父丁。于乙酉。
② 乙亥貞:來甲申酒求禾于𢍏。
③ 丙子,又人𨸏于河。其用。
④ 戊寅貞:王叀黍。
⑤ (戊)寅貞:从令。

(三九同文)

甲690

四二

辛亥卜,其又歲于三且辛。

粹341

四三

① 癸(未貞)又勹口且乙宰。翌日。
② 丁亥貞:用望𢆶,自圃。
③ 丁亥貞:用于父丁。
貞:牛

佚875

四四

① 丁卯貞:其告于父丁,其𣪊(豰)一牛。
② 戊辰卜,乙亥
丁

粹374

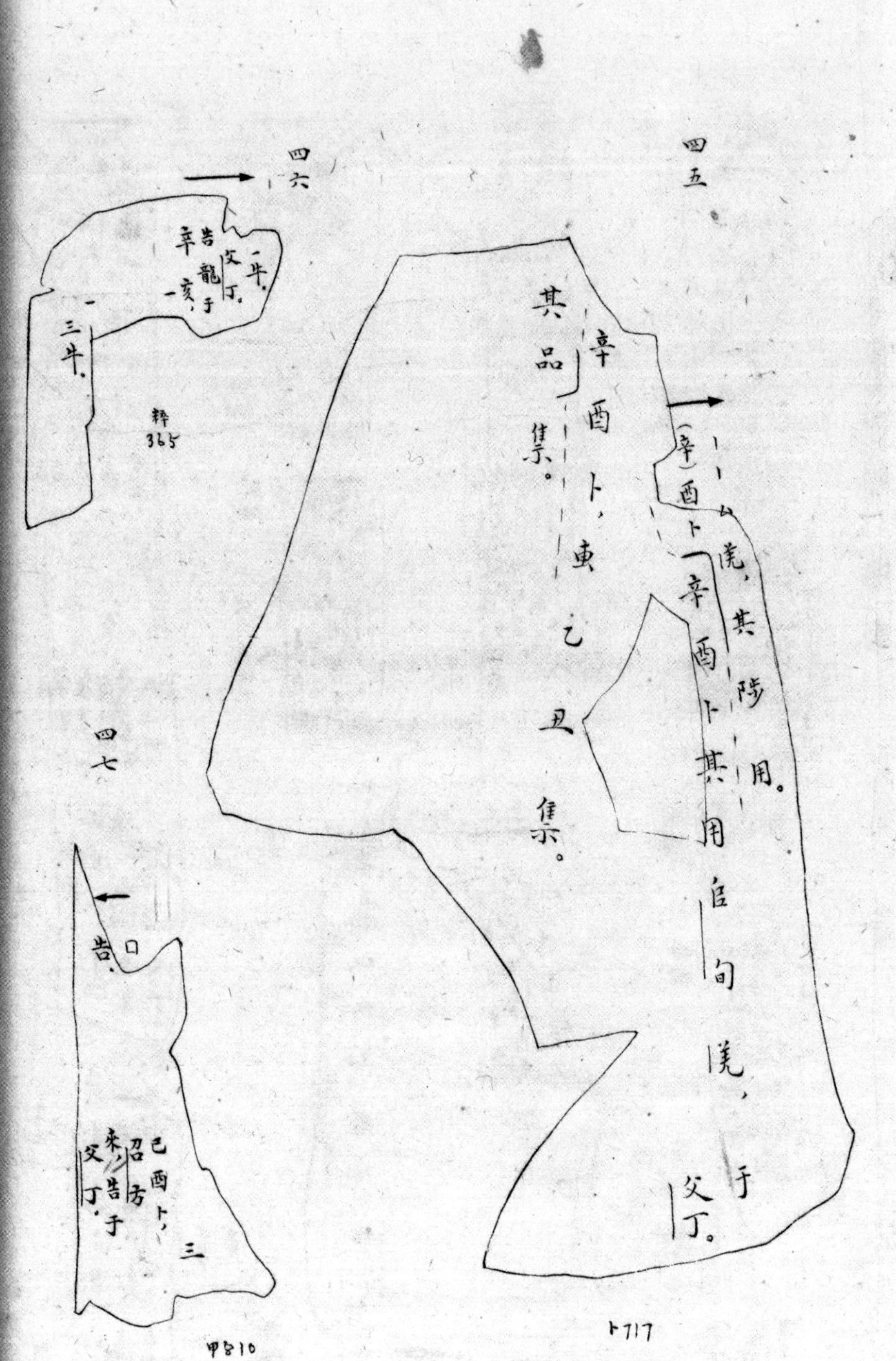
四五
四六
四七
粹365
卜717
甲810

四八

不冓雨。

大庚，日。

己丑貞：

不

从又。

从又。

明14.34

四九

(甲)申貞：小乙，日。亡巷。

亡巷。

明14.35

五〇

其雨

日。𠬝。

丁未卜，父丁

从又。

明丙15

五一

(甲)戌貞：乙大，日。亡巷。

卜下33

五二

辛卯卜，御，彡，酒，其又于四方。

明丙37

五三

甲申貞：其孳丰

出伯于父丁。

明丙16

五四

丁巳卜

于来丁

且

口宗

沓。

从即宗。

明丙36

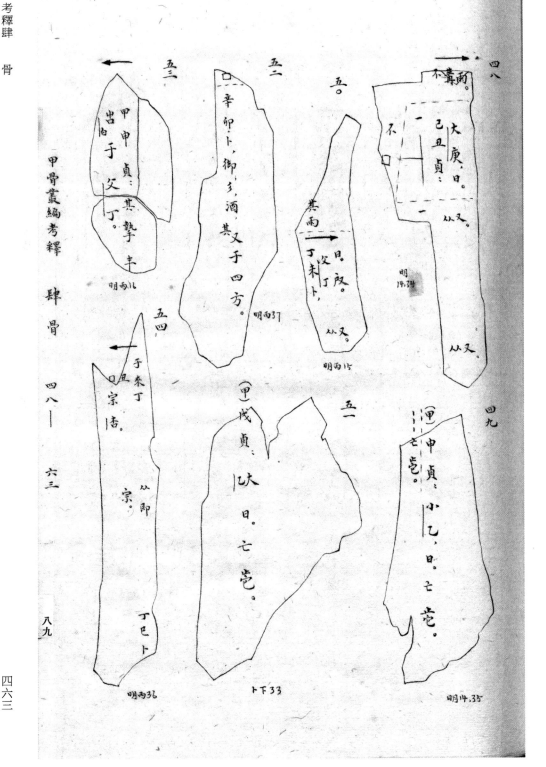

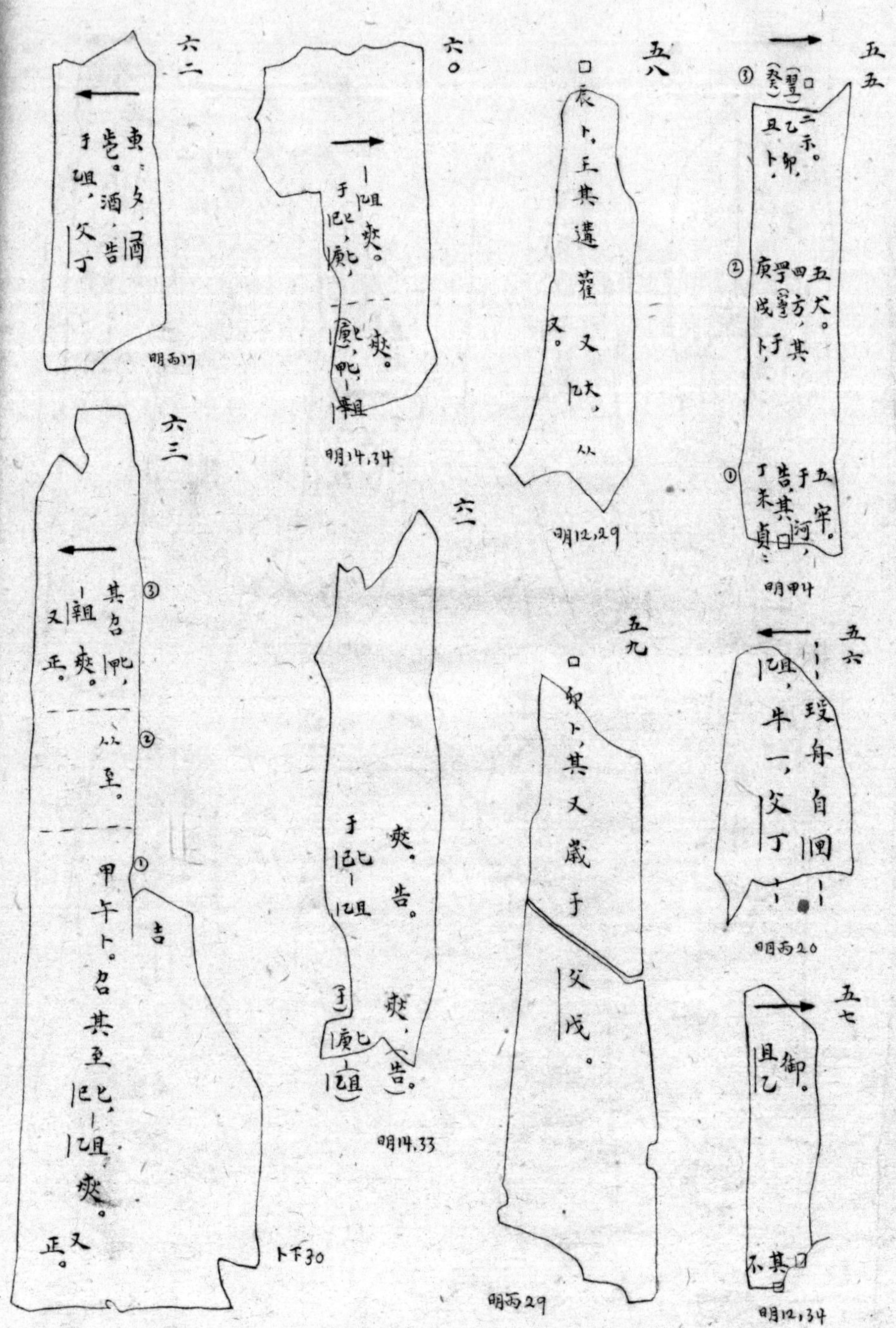

六四

十羊。
伊尹歲
三牛。

明丁6

六五

五
叀伊尹。

明乙20

六六

大吉
(乙)亥卜，王其又小乙，王受(又)。

明乙2

六七

乙巳卜。
㞢，至伊尹。

明甲31

六八

吉
卜
且夕歲

明14.5

六九

牢
甲子卜。
其又歲，又。
于高且，三牢。
甲

明19.11

七〇

馭
𩫖。
丁未卜。其又小丁，王
吉

明12.22

七一

其又𩰫，
叀羊，王受又。
牢
受

明丁9

七二

𡆥
于
小丁𠂤

明18.31

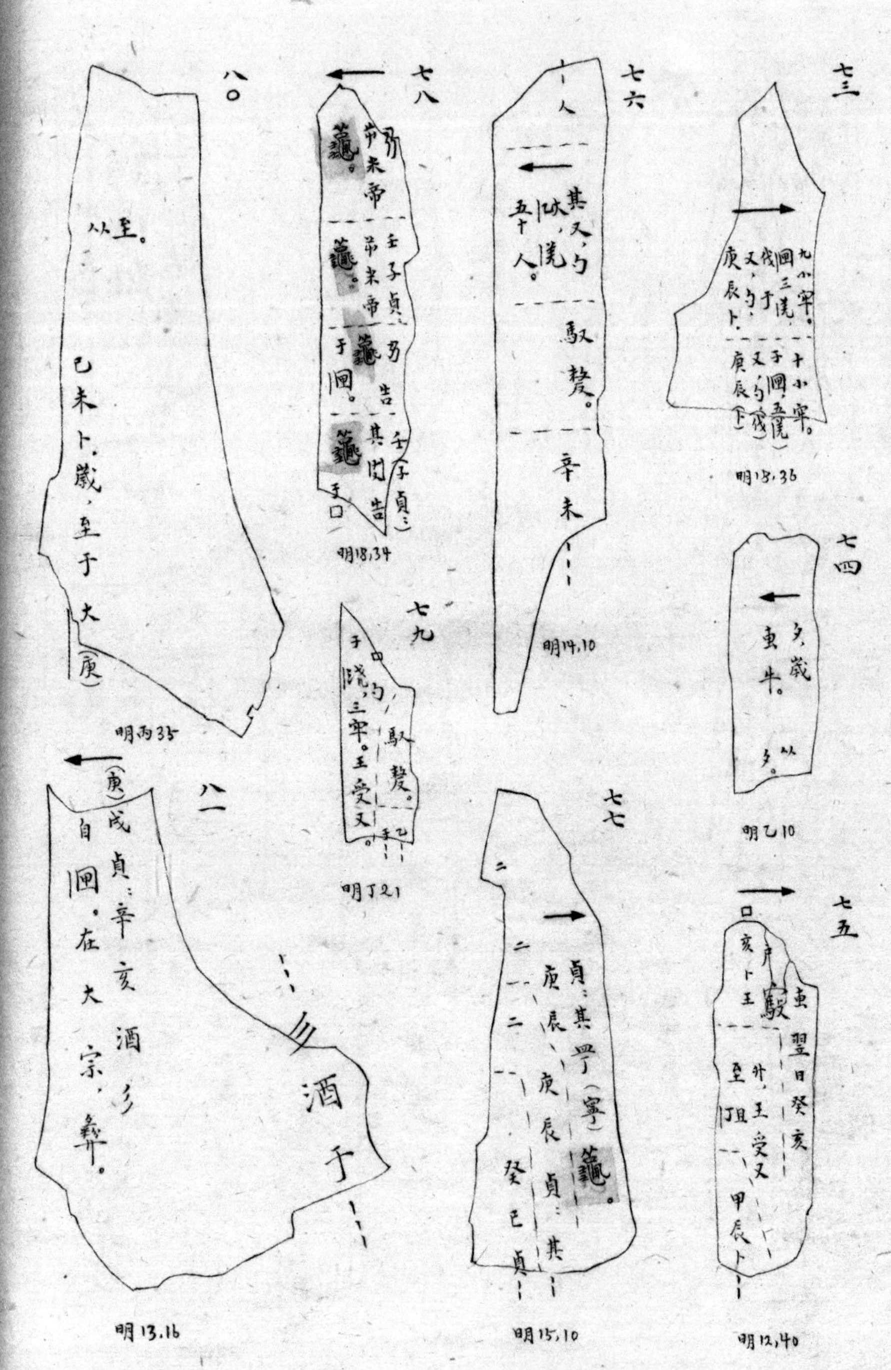

七三
明18.36
七四
明乙10
七五
明12.40
七六
明14.10
七七
明15.10
七八
明18.34
七九
明丁21
八〇
明丙35
八一
明13.16

甲骨叢編考釋　肆　骨　八二—九〇

91

八二

乙卯貞：勺伐黽示，五㲋，三牢。牢。

明14.1

八三

①□□貞：來丁丑，又歲于伊示。黽

②貞：于乙亥，伊口人。

③日其取伊口人。

丑

卜下15

八四

①乙未卜，其又歲于高且。

②叀㲋祝。

③庚子

④庚子卜，王往田于向。

明13.28

八五

乙丑貞：又甲口□

冓雨。

明13.35

八六

貞：又勺歲于

卜2334

九一

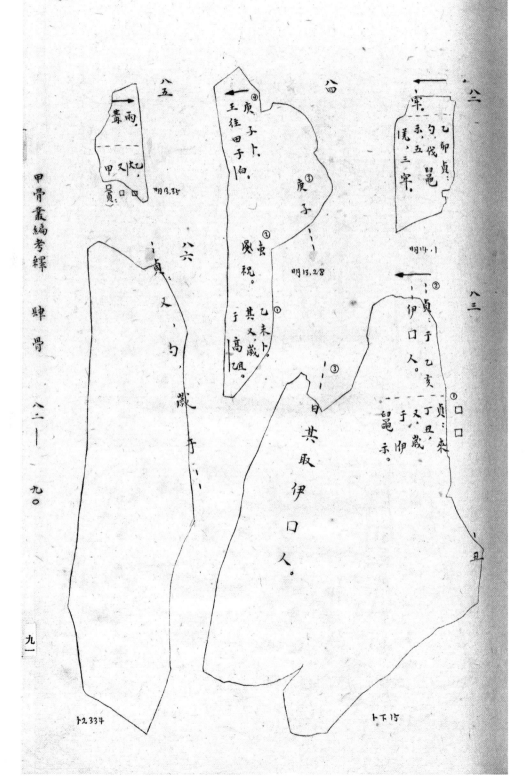

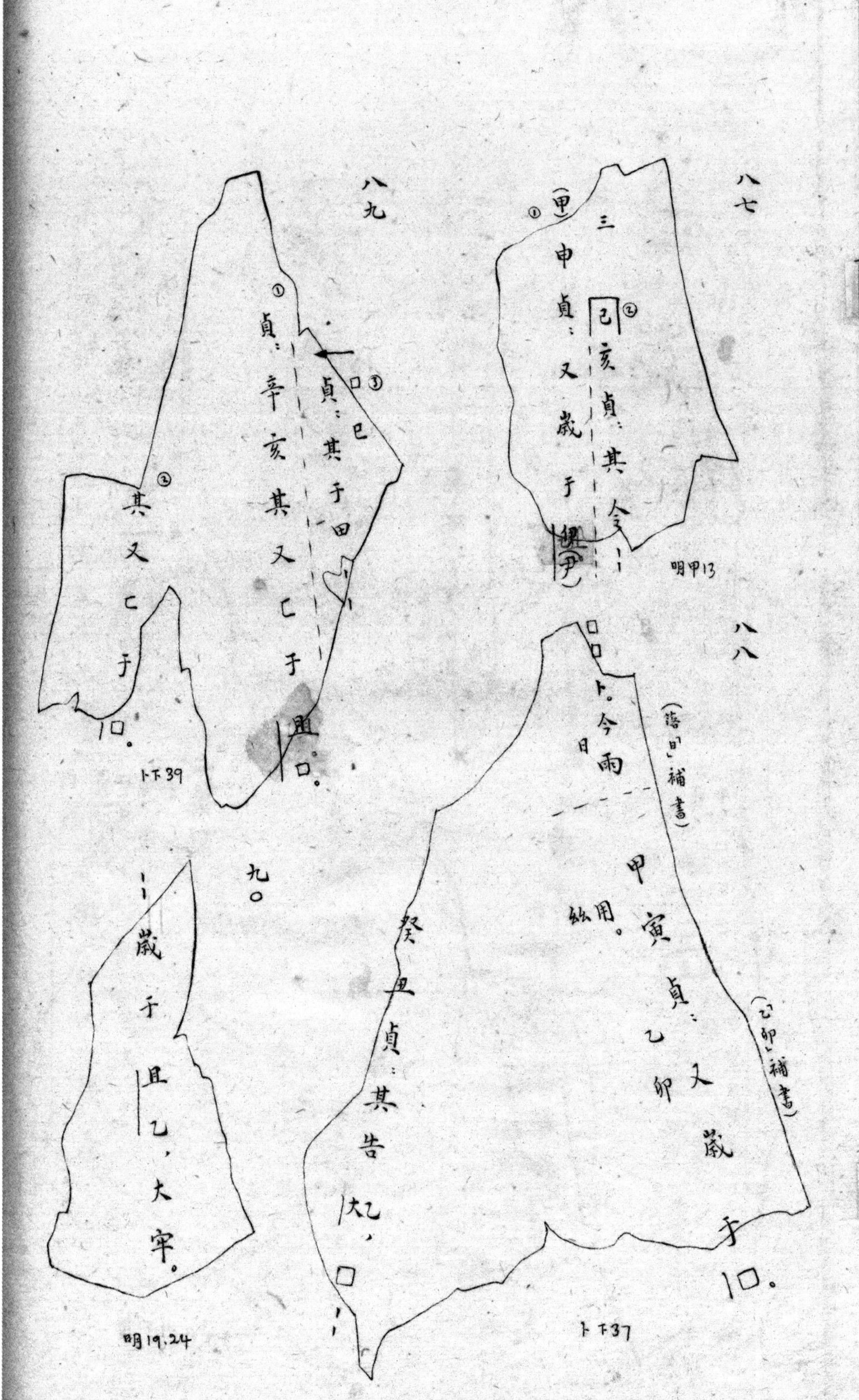

九一

畐
貞：

亡矢殹。
隹其
羽異
戊戌貞：
其告。
其歲
其告。
畐
三牛。
沉
三牢。
沉

卜下10

九二

己亥貞：其令
鼻。
又歲于伊尹

（與八七同文異版）

明甲3

九三

⑤ 亥貞：
又，勹，于
雨。茲用。
④ 十
牢？
③ 五
牢？
② 三
牢？
① 从
又。

卜下8

九四

歲，二牢。

明甲10

九五

邑。
大丁
丁卯貞：
彡，七
冓
雨。
其
甲

明15.9

九六

歲于
丮，三牢。
癸巳貞：
其冓

卜下38

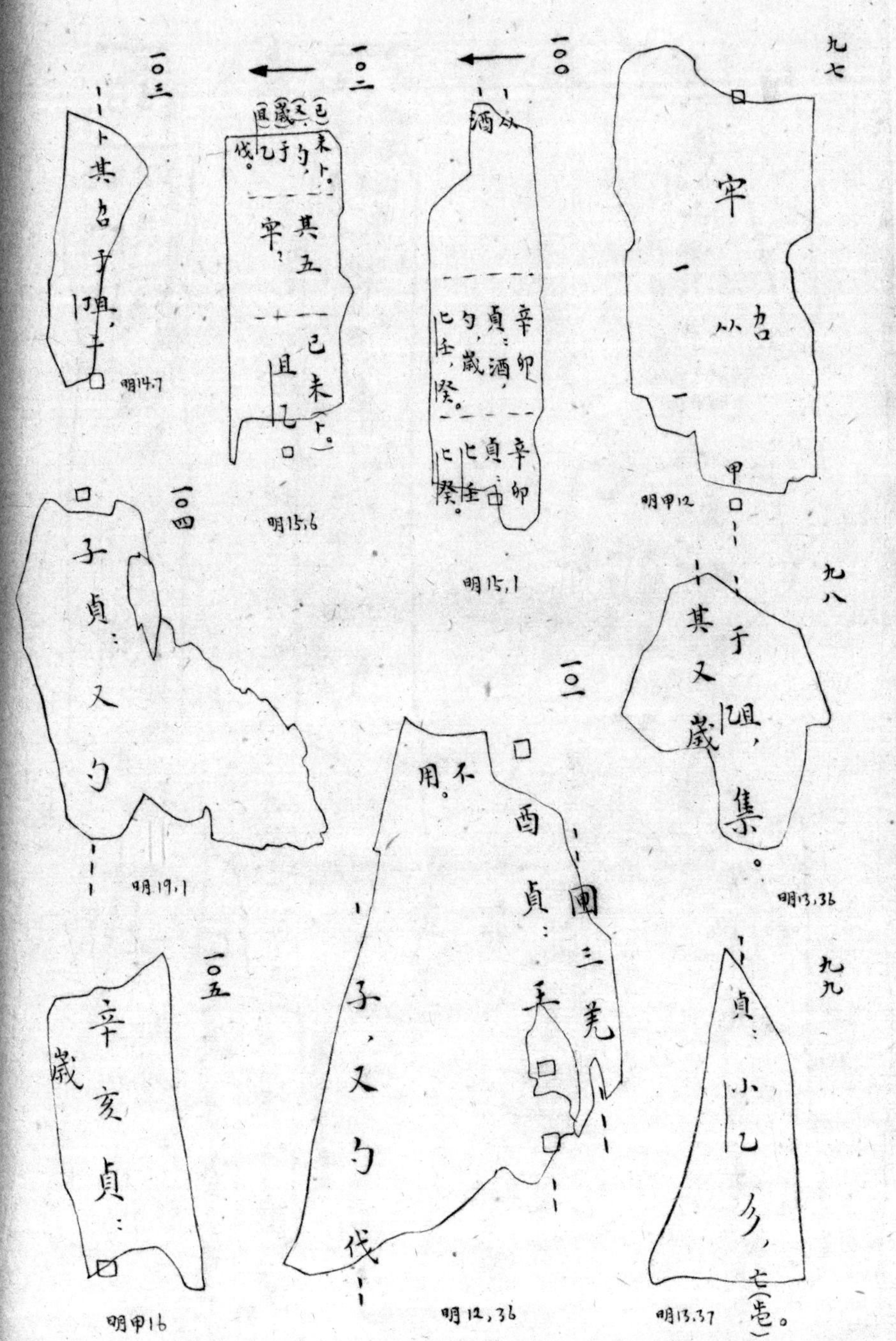
明甲12
明13.36
明13.37
明15.1
明15.6
明12.36
明14.7
明19.1
明甲16

一〇六

于高且乙，□
戊貞：其告龜

粹2

一〇七

□□
沔宗。
卽𡨦宗。
从。
其告龜𠙵，
其立于。
从。
戊申

粹4

一〇八

四牛？
三牛？
吉
二
二牛？
其告龜𠙵，
吉大
二

粹88

一〇九

□□
牢
其酉
于帝五丰臣
左且乙宗卜。
庚午貞：龜大𢆶，
兹用。
集。

粹12

一一〇

不祉雨。
毋歲祭雨。
兹用，羞
世牢，□
歲且乙
乙未（貞：）

明19,3

一一一

囲歲，叀犬。
辛酉卜，

明15,7

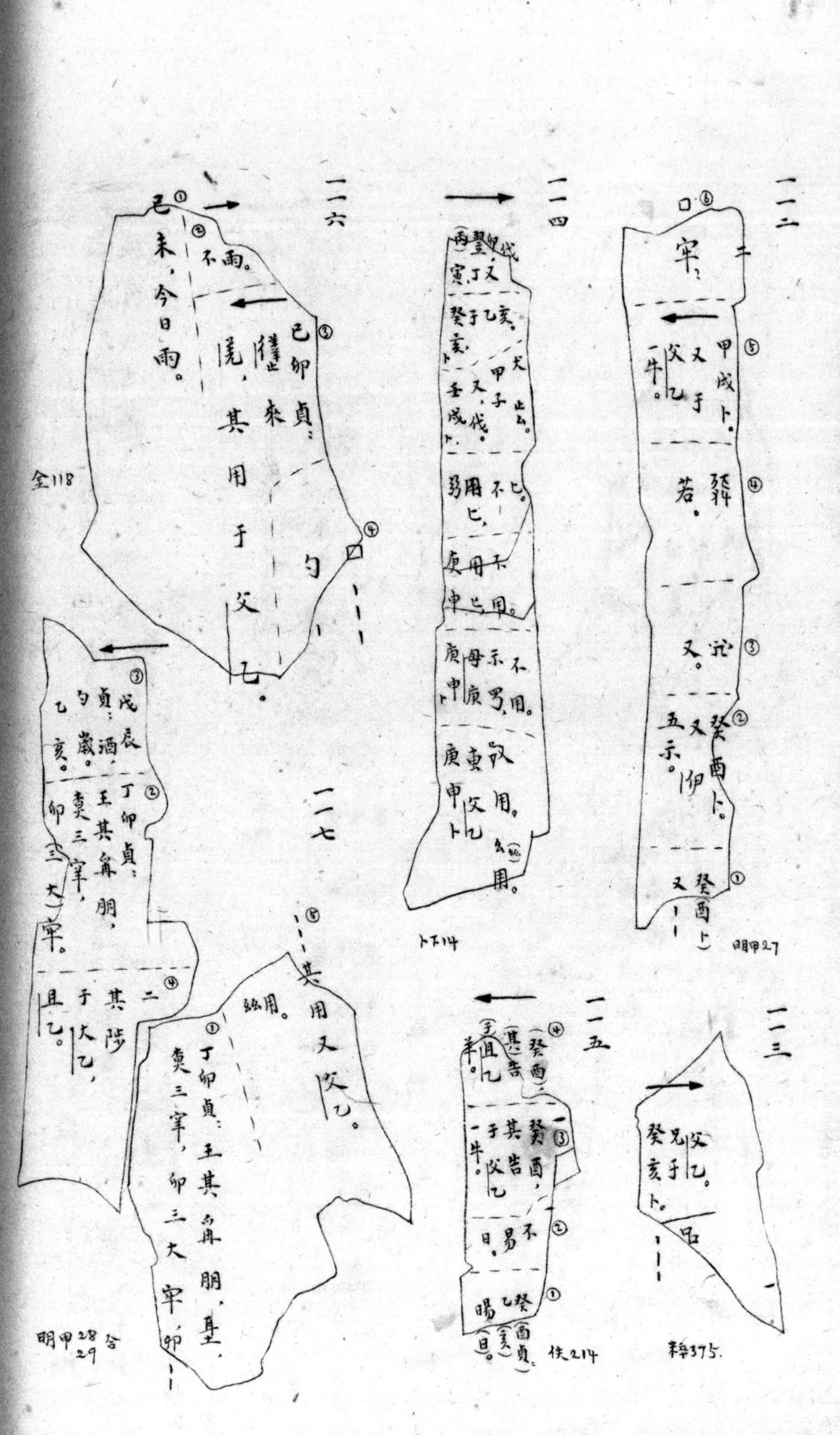

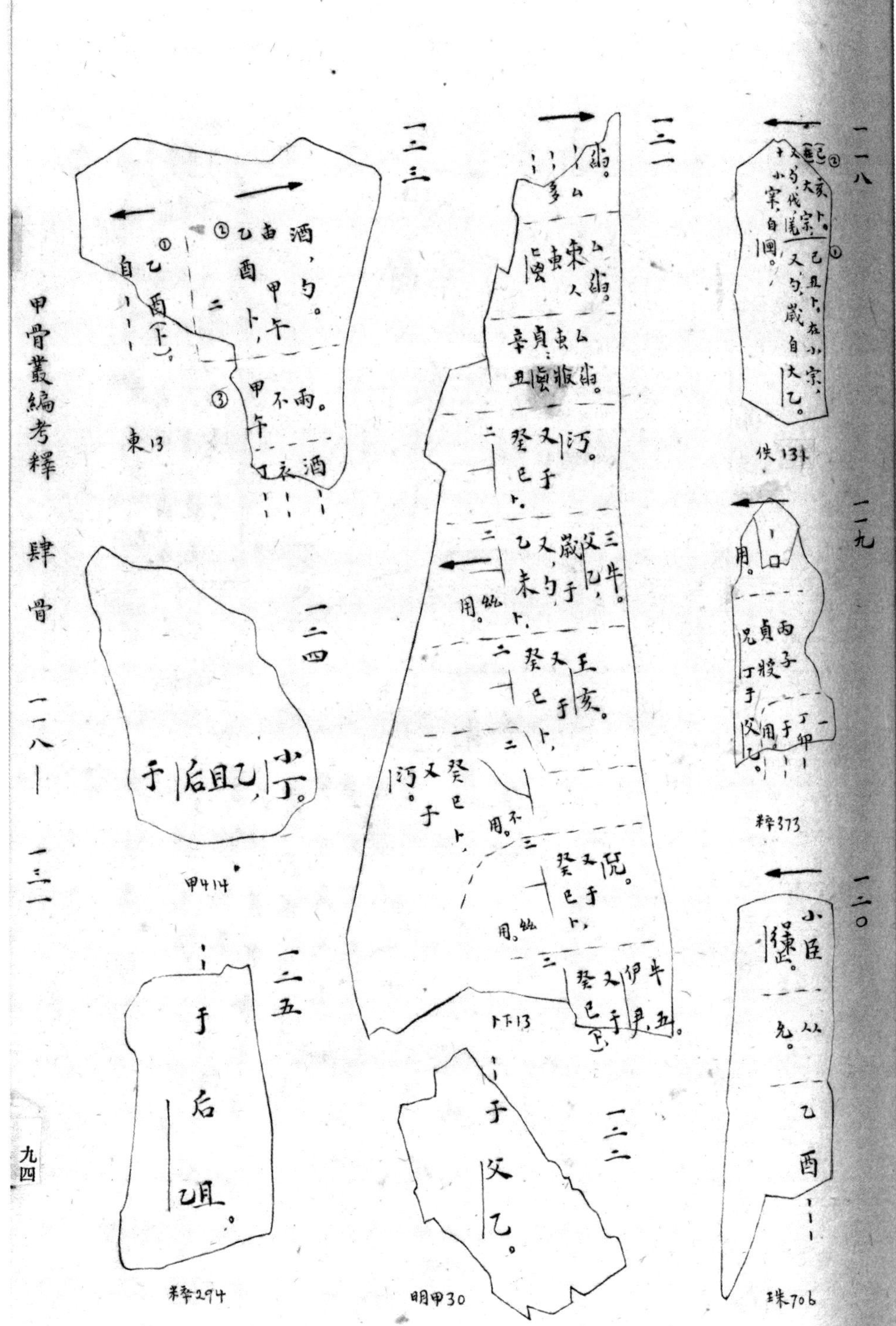
甲骨叢編考釋　肆　骨　一一八—一三一
一一八
佚131
一一九
粹373
一二〇
珠706
一二一
下下13
一二二
明甲30
一二三
東13
一二四
甲414
一二五
粹294
九四

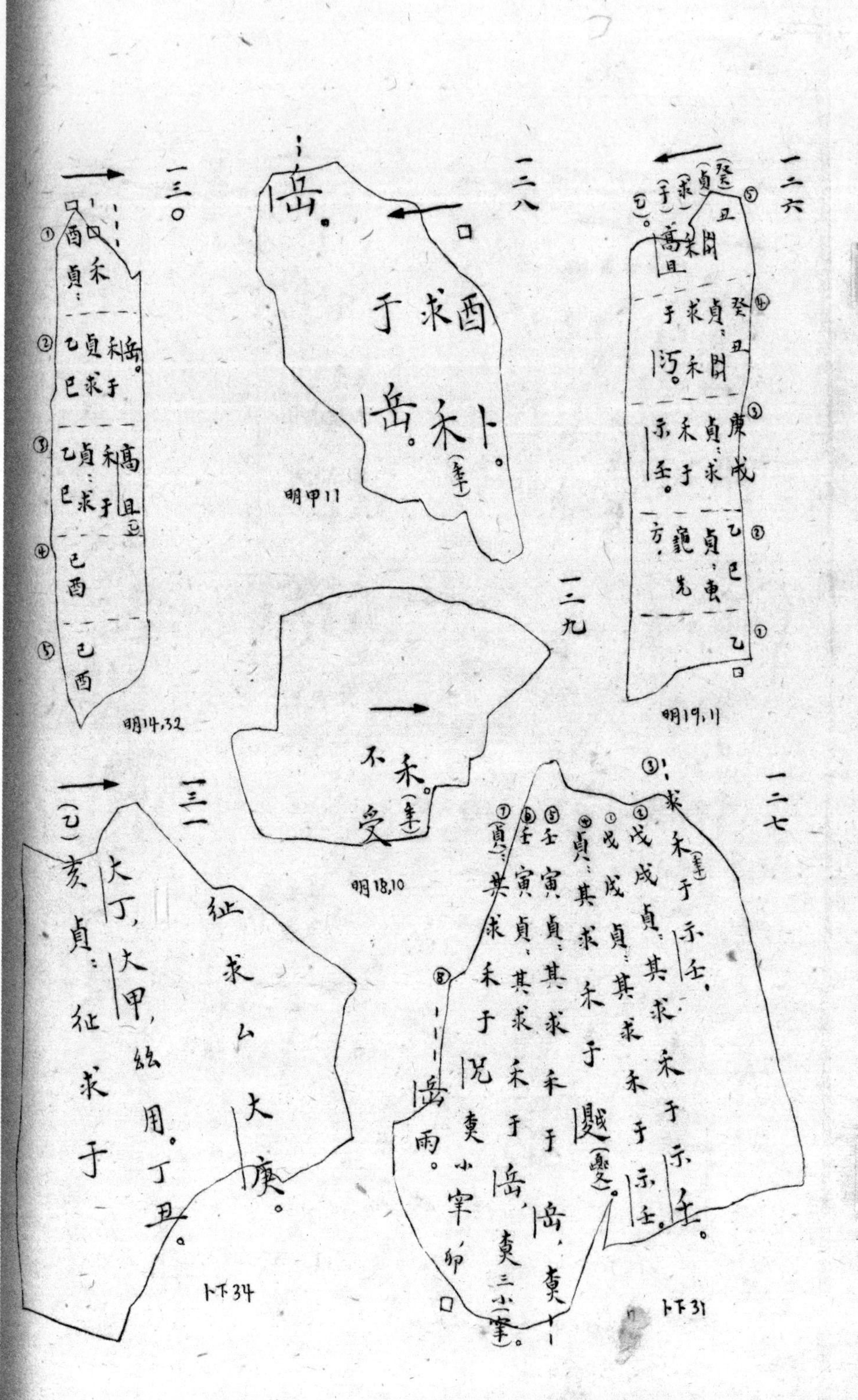
一二六
明19.11
一二七
卜下31
一二八
明甲11
一二九
明18.10
一三〇
明14.32
一三一
卜下34

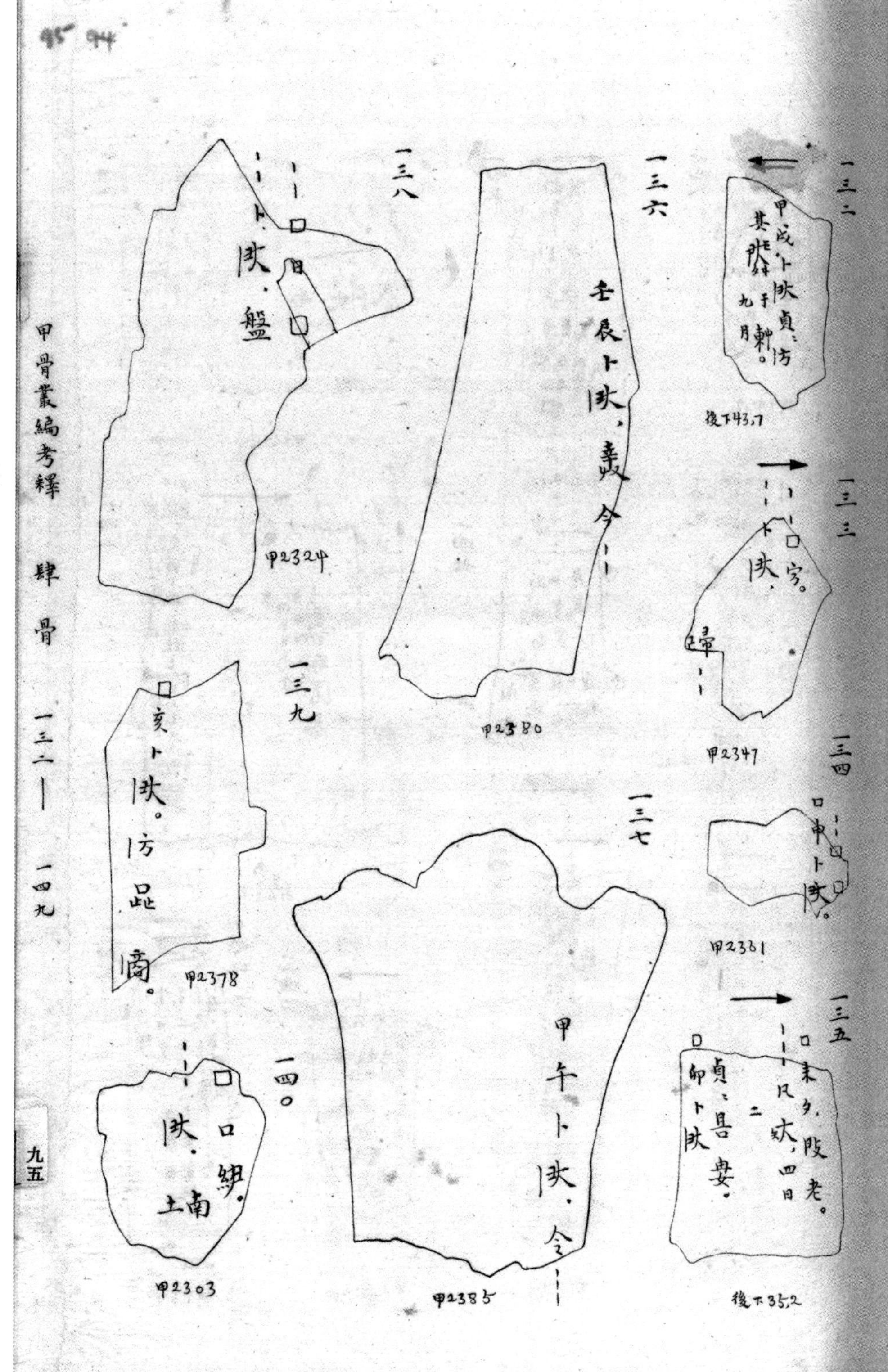

一四一

甲2314

一四二

前8,8,1

一四三

前8,6,1

一四四

前8,12,5

一四五

前8,14,1

一四六

前4,42,5

一四七

前8,9,1

一四八

後下42,9

一四九

菁11,19

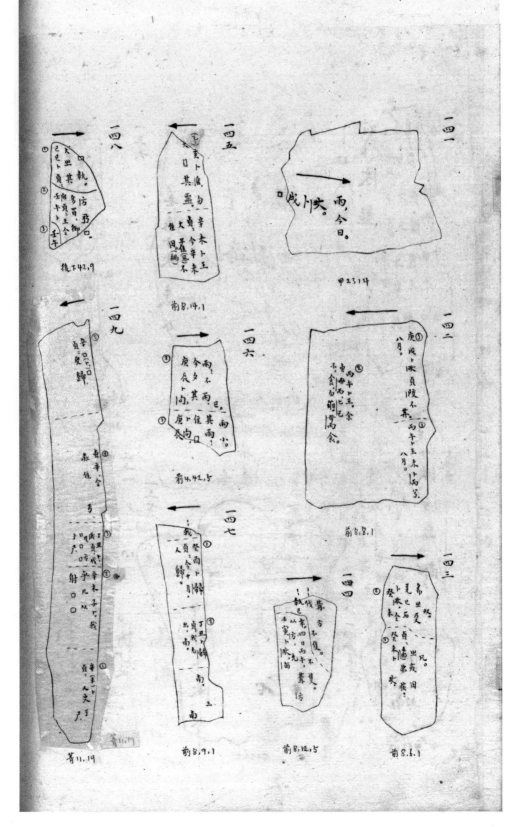

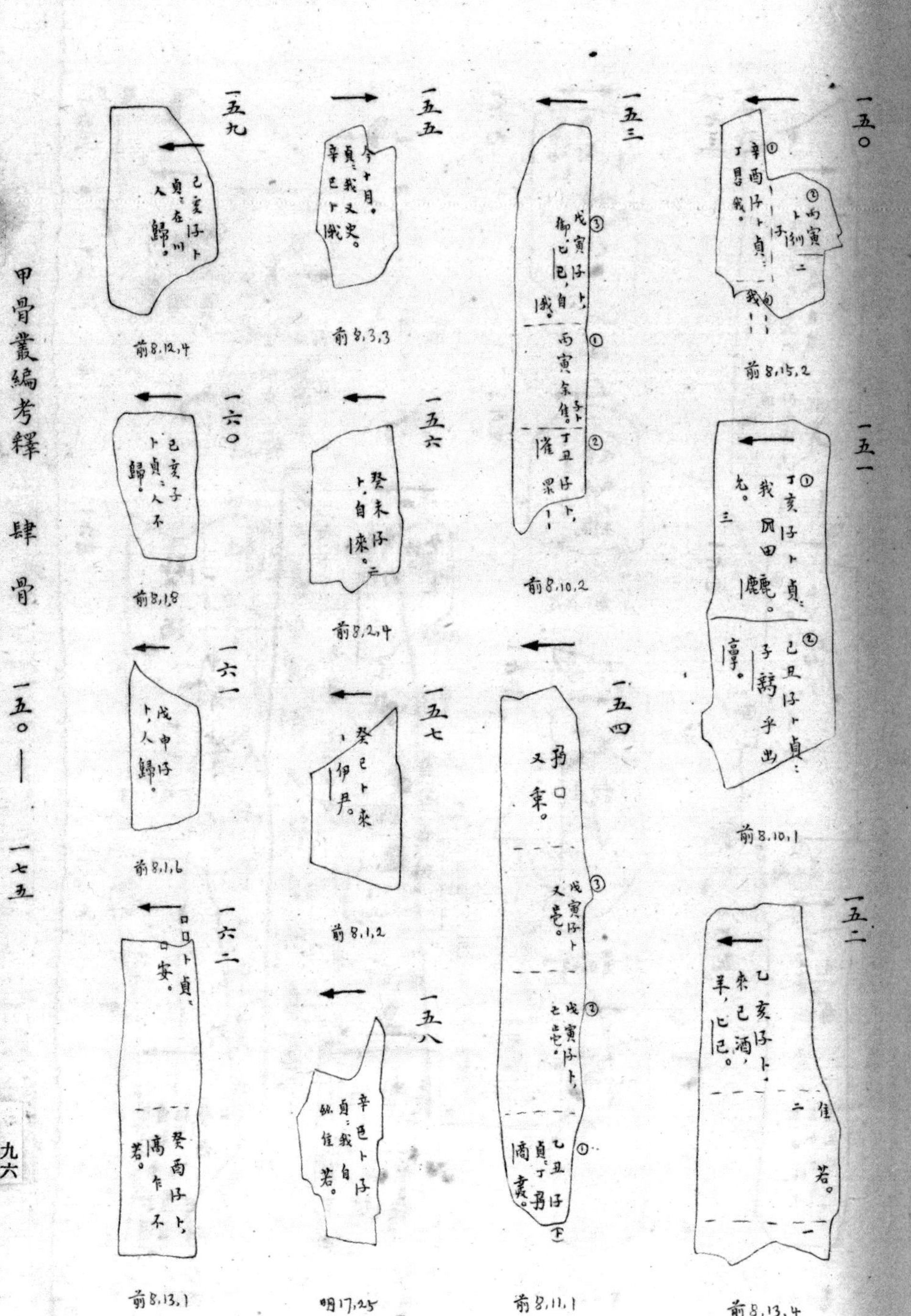
甲骨叢編考釋　肆　骨　一五〇——一七五
九六
一五〇
前8.15.2
一五一
前8.10.1
一五二
前8.13.4
一五三
前8.10.2
一五四
前8.11.1
一五五
前8.3.3
一五六
前8.2.4
一五七
前8.1.2
一五八
明17.25
一五九
前8.12.4
一六〇
前8.1.8
一六一
前8.1.6
一六二
前8.13.1

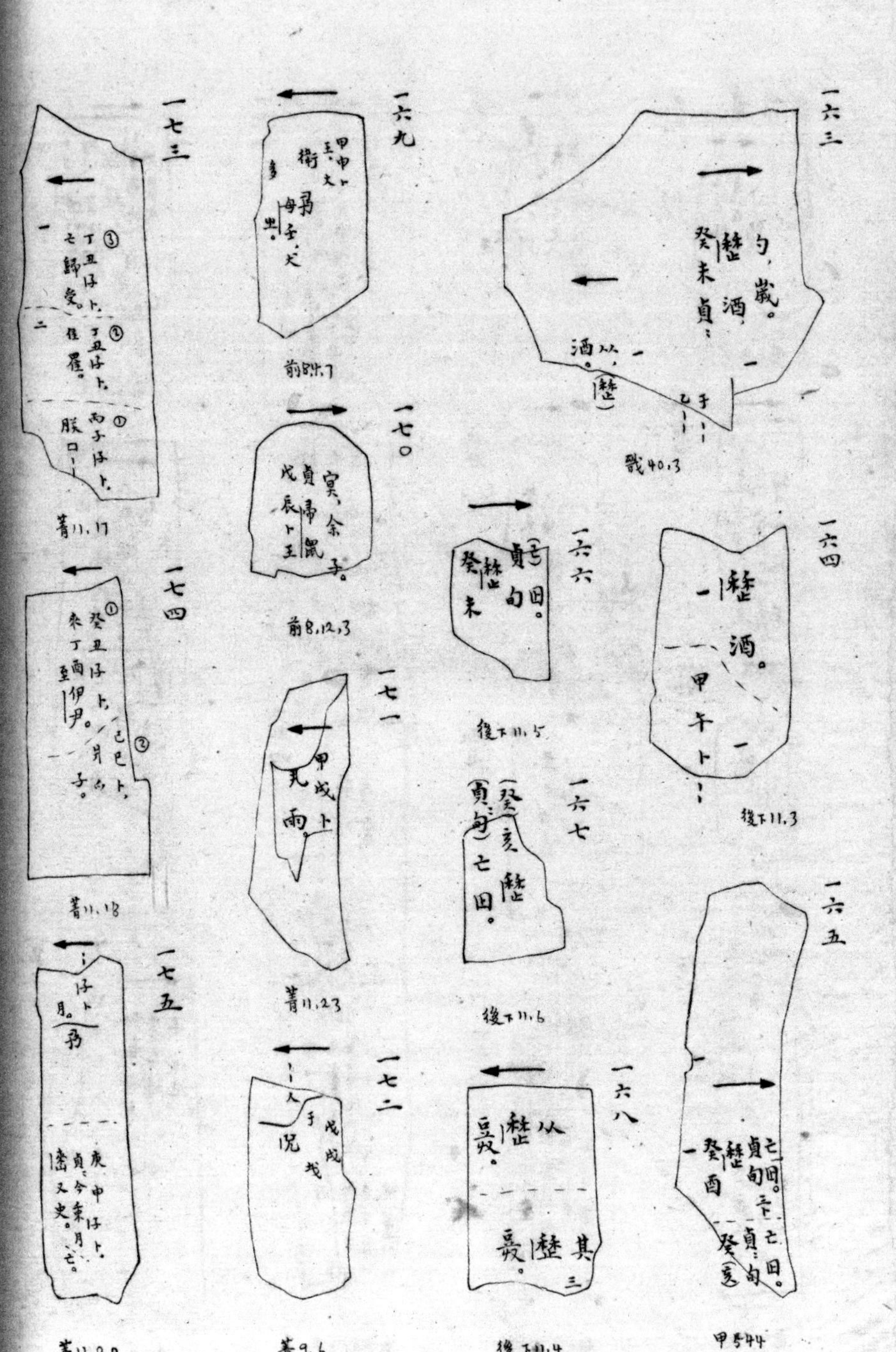

一七六

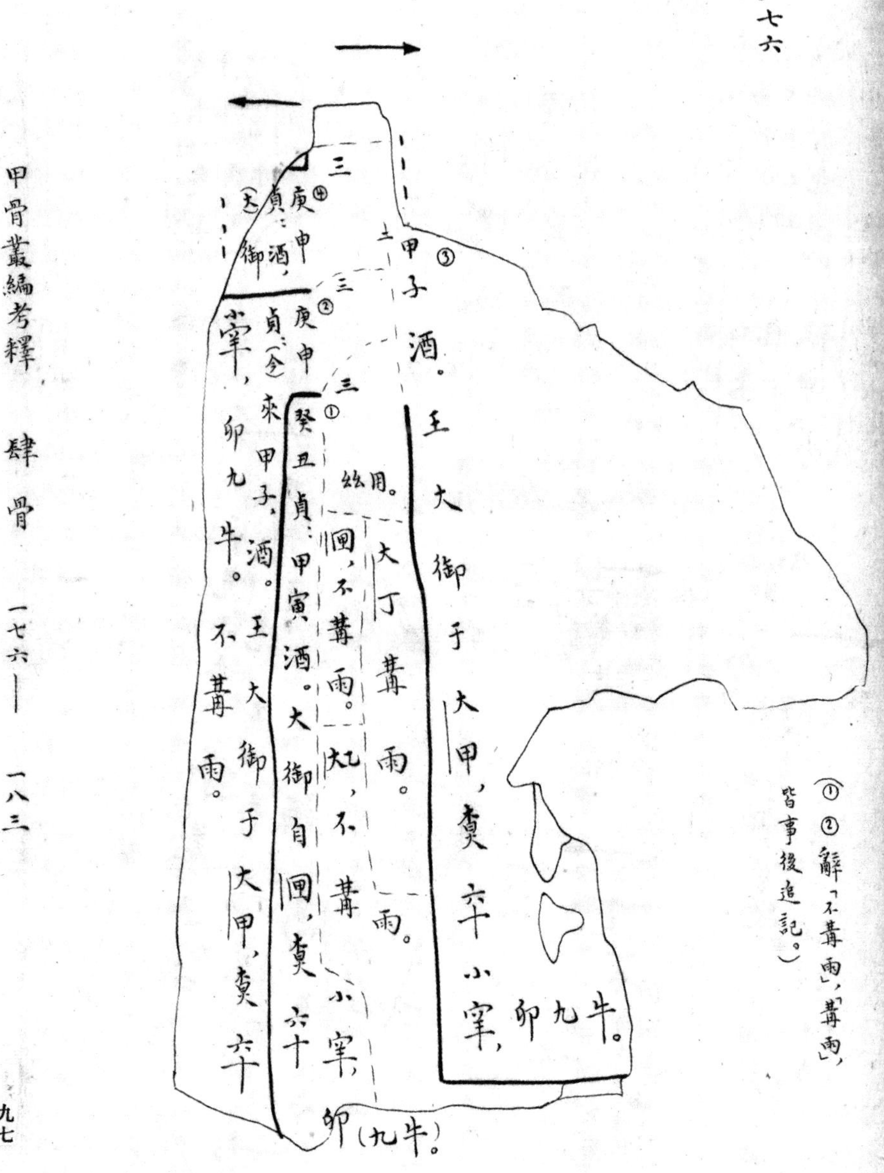

①②辭「不冓雨」、「冓雨」，皆事後追記。

卜下，41

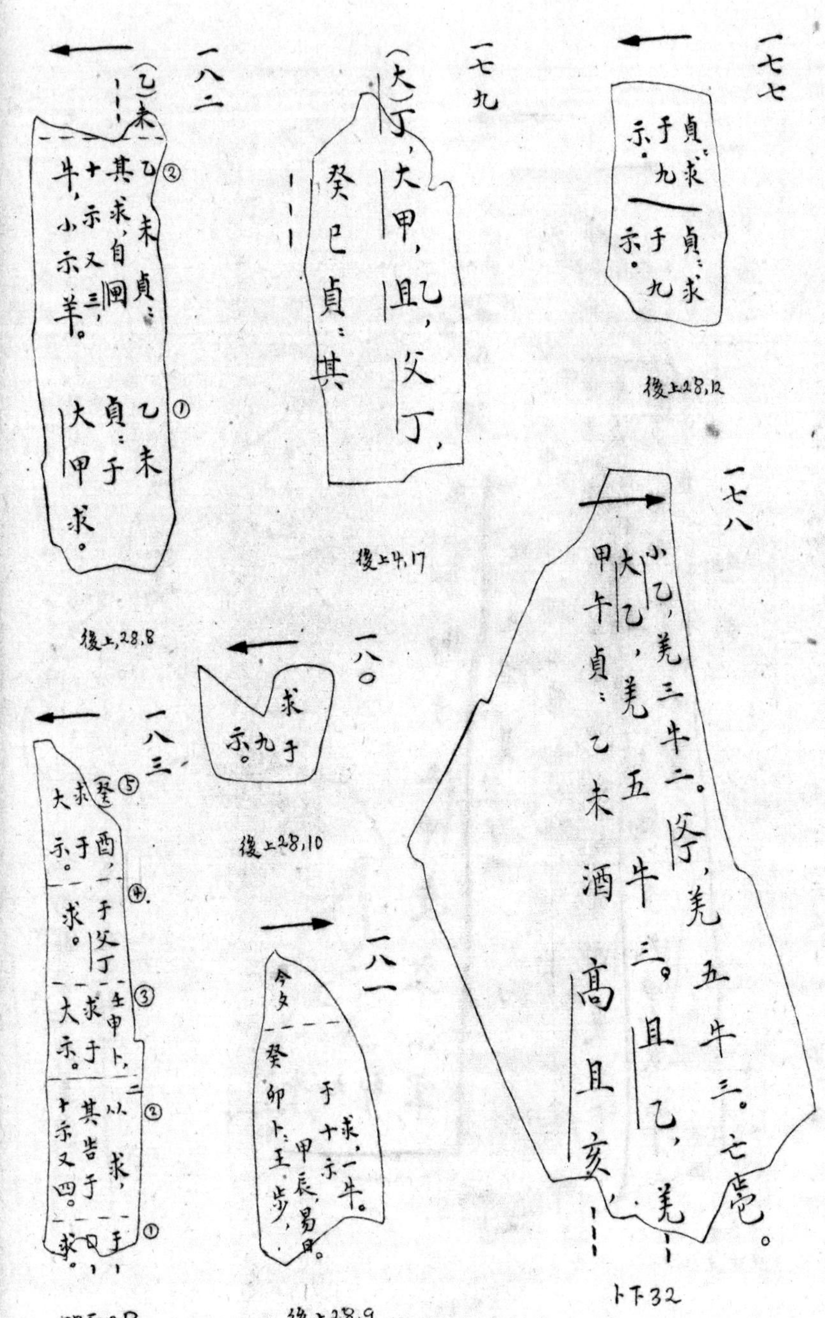

肆甲一—五六　肆骨一—一八三

於此總説第四期卜辭。

余作甲骨文斷代研究，迄今十年，而第四期卜辭之鑒別，猶疑不能決者亦且十年。初余發掘殷墟田村中出土物之特異，曾於新獲卜辭寫本後記中，揭舉「𢦏」字。繼於斷代例中，以村中出土甲骨為三、四期物。然又時感不安。蓋余初以四期不著貞人為特點，又覺稱謂，字體，每與一期相混，如父乙，母庚，兄丁，如干支字之寫法，皆是。其故仍因分理第一期卜辭，不能詳且盡也。全部整理甲骨，余雖抱此願而力有未逮，今編此冊，乃初步工夫也。

四期卜辭，包括武乙文丁兩世，前後不過十餘年（今定武乙四年，文丁十三年）。而十餘年間卜辭，則情形極為複雜。武乙，文丁亦有可別者，在武乙稱康丁曰父丁，文丁稱武乙曰父乙。文丁易與二期混，父乙，易與一期混，則又須因書法，字形以別之，且兩世亦著貞人，惟不書貞字，故未發見耳。

今舉一標準片為例，如肆骨一。

此版有父乙⑧，有王字作太④⑤⑥，甚類第一期武丁時物，背面大字亦類一期，然武丁世不惟無此書寫稚弱之史，無此未（未）子（巳），中（戌），𡆥（子），㐭（酉）字之寫法，亦絕無大乙（稱唐，祖甲時始改稱大乙），父戊（武丁有兄戊）之稱謂也。此版既非第一期物，亦非五期帝辛時物，仍由父乙之稱謂而確定為文丁時也。此版⑧辭有貞人㺇（作𤞞），但省去貞字，知㺇乃文丁時之史也。稱㺇為貞人，因其本人書辭，亦有不省貞字者，如肆甲二九：

甲申卜，𠬝貞：出父乙一牛。用。八月。

即其例。其省去貞字者，亦可由此推知之。知𠬝為文丁時人，文丁時卜貞，不並用，（少數並用）凡卜下人名，與𠬝同版者亦文丁時貞人，故知

㕯　肆甲二三　與𠬝同版

𠂤　肆甲二四　與𠬝同版

亦皆文丁時史也。肆甲四一有辭曰：

乙亥卜𠂤貞：王(大)曰：出(有)孕，㓜。𠬝曰：㓜。

此王，即文丁矣。㕯亦嘗仕于武乙之朝，肆甲四八

庚戌(卜)卜，㕯(耳)：出父辛。

父辛，乃廩辛也。由此推求，則肆骨二有史𠬝，同版有虘甲，虎甲即陽甲，祖甲以後之稱謂也。武丁時稱父甲，故知絕非武丁之辭，亦文丁之辭也。又有兄丁，有母庚，此兄丁乃文丁之兄，母庚乃文丁之母也。

以稱謂定時代，更由稱謂定貞人，無貞人者定其書法，字形，詞類，禮制，依此種種以求四期卜辭，未有不得者也。今就研究結果，略述於次。

一曰：四期書史之有多派也。

四期書法多種，可見其書史之衆。蓋承三期文風彫敝之餘，舊史多已死亡，新史派別分立，各不相謀，以人才缺乏之故，乃兼收並納之。此由書法之龐雜，可以推知者也。就本冊所收，約略分之，有

謹飭體　承三期之作風，似狄、宁、彪等史成熟作品　骨六一〇　六三等

豪放體　骨二七　一二八　一七六等

瘦勁體　骨九三　一〇九　一一〇等

肥圓體　骨一四一　一三九　一三八等

稜方體　骨五　一七六　一七八等

秀弱體　骨一四四

細小體　骨一四二等

幼稚體　骨一　二

以上八體，審視影寫各版，已可見其各異，讀者多檢拓本，自能知之。此中大別，可分三派：

第一派，為三期舊史。此派因襲三期舊法，書契尚能規整，遠承一期二期之作風者。此派作品不多。其代表作品：武乙時　骨六一〇　一二一四　文丁時　骨一一三　一一七

第二派，為新興之史。此派書契各逞其才，發展個性，有恣情豪放，肆意峭拔各體，皆不記貞人，為其特點。其代表作品：武乙時　骨一五　一七　二四　一七九　文丁時　骨一二一

九九

第三派，復古之徒。此派於武丁舊史，有所師承，追慕武丁之盛世，以文藝復興之責自任者。亦記貞人，而多省貞字。其代表作品，武乙時 骨四五 九六 一七八 甲四八 文丁時 骨一 二 甲元

以上三派，武乙文丁兩世皆有之，而第一派作品甚少，第二派則武乙之世為多，第三派則文丁之世為多也。

二曰：武乙之好田獵也。

在斷代研究例中，余曾舉武乙時卜田遊辭之特徵三：

卜田　慣用「五其田」，亡巛作「亡𢦏」。

卜游　慣用「于某亡𢦏」。

出土　皆在小屯村中。

由第一二次發掘材料中，理出田游之辭計六十五見：

卜田　一次發掘　八　二次發掘　三十四　共四十二見

卜游　一次發掘　四　二次發掘　十九　共二十三見

此乃村中出土物之一部分，其由村人自掘而為劉晦之明義士及其他收藏家所得之物，猶多未入統計中也。「𢦏」字之為四期標準字，於三期五期不用此字證之。

三期　檢叁甲一、二、五、六諸卜田「亡巛」字，皆作≋，沿一二期，不用𢦏。

一〇〇

五期 檢伍骨一三，諸卜田「弋（从）」字，皆作「冉」，不作「戈」。此例極多，本冊尚未收耳。因同出於村中四期咸有稱謂可證，故決此「戈」字之用，為四期卜辭，無可疑也。

四期有武乙文丁二世，何以獨分此田獵辭於武乙？此亦讀者所當問。欲答此語，請先釋肆骨七一一辭。

原文：[illegible]

釋文 其又兄癸，叀羊。王受又。（佑）

兄癸者康丁之子也。叁骨一〇辭曰：

叀母己眔子癸酒。 叀兄辛眔子癸先。

粹編尚有一辭：

子癸歲，王室叙。 壬申卜：毋戊歲，叀牡。 叀牝。

郭沫若氏說「子癸為康丁之子，在武乙則為兄」，是也。並舉後編上，七，一二，一辭：

原文 [illegible]

釋文 叀□兄癸，叀又（有）遘。王受又。（佑）

兄辛者康丁之稱康辛也。故母己亦當為祖甲之配，特不見於五期之祭系耳。母戊即「祖甲奭妣戊」也。此六辭中之稱謂，更列表如次。

祖甲＝妣戊＝母己

康辛 康丁（兄辛；母戊、母己） 子癸（兄癸） 武乙 （文丁）

知兄癸之為武乙時辭，此表已足以明之。四期王字有兩種寫法，一作王，沿承二、三期之舊，一作太，復武丁時之古寫也。文丁時王字皆復古，武乙時則兩種寫法皆有，兄癸兩辭之王字作王，即其堅證。知此，則武乙文丁之別，王字之寫法，即一標準。

四期卜田辭，本冊僅收入一版，即肆骨五，有三辭：

壬子貞王其田亡𢦏

辛酉貞王其田亡𢦏

壬戌貞王其田亡𢦏

戌，四期之證也。「王」武乙之證也。四期卜田辭之王字皆如此作，故不憚煩瑣，於此辨證之。

武乙之好田獵，見于史記殷本紀：

武乙獵于河渭之間，暴雷，武乙震死。

是武乙之好田獵，田而遘大雨，觸電而死，古必有此傳說也。四期卜田每及「其遘大雨」，粹一〇〇六「不冓雨」，粹一〇〇八「其雨」，粹一〇一一「不雨」粹一〇〇九等天氣之貞，而武乙竟以此殞其身，亦可謂「防不勝防」矣。

余主殷人以日干為名，乃其忌日之說，今於武乙亦得一證，即武乙以乙日死也。殷人田獵有定日五期皆然，今揭於此，讀者檢各期田狩之日，當自知之。其田狩與休息，在十日中為固定者。

田狩之日：乙　丁戊　辛壬

休息之日：甲　丙丁　己庚　癸

蓋乙田，丙息，丁戊田，己庚息，辛壬田，癸甲息，有田狩而休息者，未有休息日而田狩者，此律信守極嚴，終殷之世，未嘗有所更易也。武乙之死于「乙」，正田狩之日矣。

武乙之號，乃帝乙時所定，在文丁世則僅稱「父乙」。古者田獵所以練兵，尚武之精神寄焉，武乙之美謚，意在此與？

三曰，文丁之銳意復古也。

復古派佔優勢於文丁之世，前已言之，史之所以復古，必其「上有好者」。文丁時，有父曰乙，有母曰庚，有兄曰丁，與武丁同，此文丁所以發思古之幽情與？於是以狄為史，司卜貞之事，事々以武丁盛世為師法。其大要有五：

1、禮制　於此略述殷人祀典。五期祀典，可分兩大派：一為武丁派，二為祖甲派。武丁時規模宏大，遠祖如夔、亥，祭尚御、𡆥，兮及河、岳。祖甲則廢除雜祀，奉上甲為始祖，以彡、翌、祭、𡆥、𩁹五種祀典為主幹，上甲以上遠祖不祭也。上甲以下，大小宗及大宗之配偶皆入祀典也。整齊劃一，井然有序。此其大別。廩辛康丁，猶疑二者之間而兼採之。四期武乙時已有復古之傾向，文丁繼之，崇拜武丁尤甚。故祭名御、𡆥，先祖夔、亥，皆復一期舊觀。河、岳之祀，亦並及之。檢本冊所錄各辭，已可概見。至五期帝乙、帝辛，又恢復祖甲之制矣。

2、字形　由武丁至康丁，已百有餘年，字形變易，前後多有不同。今就干支字言之，干支日用之常字也，除不變者外，如

	一期	三期
戊	[illegible]	[illegible]
辛	[illegible]	[illegible]
巳	[illegible]	[illegible]
酉	[illegible]	[illegible]
戌	[illegible]	[illegible]
亥	[illegible]	[illegible]

等字，已略有變易。至於四期，則又變本加厲，而猶間存古體者，復古之史所為也。表如下：

一期	三期（以上據于支演化表）	四期 新體（多在武乙時）	復古體（多在文丁時）
		骨一七　骨一三 三二　骨一四 二九	骨二(郑書) 七八
		甲四　骨三五(郑)　骨一　骨一 文	
		甲六　甲二 三(郑)	
		甲山 三十 一　甲三五(郑)　骨七七 三一	
		骨一〇九　甲五 一二 二四(伯)　骨三五	骨二(郑)
		骨八 一六　甲九	甲一八 三九(郑) 四五(丙)
		甲七 二九(郑) 四六(隹) 三二(郑)	甲四〇(郑) 骨四九 六八
		甲二〇　骨一六　骨四七　骨四五	甲一〇 四三(隹)
		骨一二 一五	
		甲四八(白) 骨二　甲三〇(郑)	骨一二
		甲一三	甲五
		骨八四　骨五五　骨四二(郑)　骨一四	甲五
		甲四 一九　骨八一	骨四五

甲骨叢編考釋　肆　骨　一八三　一〇二

觀右表，可見武乙文丁時古今體字之一斑。此時今體新字，已屬約定俗成，有積重難返之勢，雖如醉心於復古運動之史臣，亦每於不自覺中而寫出俗體之字，雖處處摹擬武丁時古體，而一段卜辭，仍不免有新體字之羼入，此武丁時之所無，一望而辨者也。干支字外，最惹人注目者為「王」字，此字首經祖甲改製，於頭上加一橫畫，易「太」為「王」。三期遵循不變。四期改回古寫，多作「太」形，而武乙卜貞田獵之史，猶沿俗書，仍書為「王」，此又為吾人留遺一分斷乙丁兩世卜辭之標準也。

3，追記占驗　一期史官，好以卜貞之後發生事端附會占驗而記之，所謂「幾日某干支，某事云云」，如壹骨一①③④⑥⑦，二①②④⑤⑥，等，皆是。四期史臣亦喜仿為之，如

壬寅卜，狄：湄从方幸。四日丙午（不自壬寅起算，自癸卯起算）雚方，不隻。　骨一四四

又如：

乙卯卜，狄貞：昔安口只戈。四日（己）未（不自乙卯起算，自丙辰起算）夕改，老　骨一三五

所追記之日數，皆將繫屬之卜日除外，此小異於第一期者。

4，大骨大字　大骨版書契大字，偉偉壯麗，武丁時敵、亘、永諸人之傑作也。狄乃不自揣量，起而效之，如骨一、二，骨大字大矣，其如工力氣魄之不逮何？取壹骨一至四而比較，一則堂閣堂皇之文，一則小學生之信筆塗鴉也，刻鵠類鶩，畫虎成犬，此之謂矣。

5，月名　如改回「正月」為「一月」，月上不加「在」字（骨一及偶沿二期加在字），月名合書，皆復一期之舊。

此文丁時代復古而開倒車之一事也。殷人曆術，武丁時置閏於當閏之年之末，謂之「十三月」，其置閏也，必節氣月與太陰月，差至一個月，乃補一閏以整齊之，「十三月」之閏法，又必待至年終，故氣候與太陰月可差至四十餘日，將及半季，此其弊也。祖甲改訂歷術，置閏不待年終，在一年之內，何時節氣差至一月，何時置閏，使氣候之差異，在一個月內，而滿一個月，即閏以齊之，此進步之歷法也。祖甲以後，無「十三月」，即以此。同時改「一月」為「正月」，正，正也，合於天象節氣之正者也。月名加以「在」字，確定此一日所在之月也。今並此而復武丁之舊，是已不解祖甲改定「正」「閏」之初旨矣。

以上所舉，乃其概要，詳審分析，須待材料輯全之後，非今日所能從事也。

又文丁之名，亦有可說者，吾人須知武丁之名，自帝乙整訂祀典始定之，前乎此，則為父丁（三期）為毓（后）祖丁，（三、四期）為祖丁也。文丁之稱文武丁，文武帝，文武宗，由帝辛定之，帝乙時稱父丁也。帝辛時已有武丁之稱，帝辛以文丁之崇拜武丁，復古情殷，而又有振刷文風之志，故以文武丁謚之，殆亦「小武丁」之意與？美之，所以刺之也。蓋乙辛又皆崇拜祖甲，志趣各異耳。

吾人分別四期卜辭，自以稱謂，坑位，書法等，為重要標準。其可注意者尚有下列各事：

貞人：　敹 骨一　向 甲四二　㠯 甲四一　我 甲五二　子 甲五四　歸 骨一四七　㣥 骨五〇　㱿 骨一六三

稱大乙不稱唐　此與一期之別　甲三六　骨一　五一　五八　七六　八八　九六

稱小乙或后祖乙　此與一期之別詒自二期者　骨四九　六六　九九　一二七　一三四

稱伊尹　一期作黄(衡)尹　骨六四—六五　六七　九二　一二一　一七四

月，夕，同作D　此為一二期月D，夕D，五期月D夕D之過渡期，月夕無別也。　甲二　骨六八　七四　一四六　一四七

好横行書寫　甲三六　骨二　一二四

好作界畫　甲三六　三九　四一　四二

文例左右行相雜　甲三二

好祭咸戊　甲二八　三九　骨一

好合祭先祖，或列舉或舉其示數　骨三四　一七七—一八三

伍甲一

甲骨叢編考釋　伍　甲　一

通64
（通別2.2）

一〇四

右龜腹甲一版，日本河井氏藏。此類卜辭，舊不得其解，蓋在誤認口、口諸形為「丁」也。自斷代方法研究之，則第五期「日」字作「口」，第三期即有作◇或口者（甲三九一五，本書卷甲一第⑦⑧辭），乃日字省去其中之一畫者，五期日祭之日字，皆用此減寫作「口」，頗與「丁」之作「口」者同。更由同類卜辭，知其舉行日祭，每旬遍其日必卜之，六旬而遍，如日祭祖甲，必於癸日卜其用牲之數與色，癸酉卜，甲戌「日」祭，則下旬癸未卜甲申之「日」祭，次及甲午、甲辰、甲寅、甲子，六甲日皆遍，所謂日祭也。日祭在帝乙時，自武丁始，至文丁及母癸而止，帝辛因之，亦至文武丁而止，具詳後說。

此版殘右下方，殊可惜。然由此已可推知貞卜之次序及日祭卜法。日祭之五世，為武丁、祖甲、康丁、武乙、文丁，皆大宗，並及文丁之配母癸。三丁各佔六旬，共十八旬而一週，其祖甲、武乙、母癸，皆隨武丁日祭舉行，此版是已。茲擬其日次並補苴如下：

甲戌旬　丙子　卜武丁日祭（皆前一日卜祭則次日）　癸未　卜祖甲日祭

甲申旬　甲申　卜武乙日祭　丙戌　卜武丁日祭　癸巳　卜祖甲日祭

甲午旬　甲午　卜武乙日祭　丙申　卜武丁日祭　癸卯　卜祖甲日祭

甲辰旬　甲辰　卜武乙日祭　丙午　卜武丁日祭

……

丙午以下，此版不能容，不備舉。此版無母癸之辭，亦從略。日祭之卜法，先卜用牲之數，在右方，曰「其宰」，即其用一宰中之牝牡二牛也。更於左方對稱處貞「其宰又一牛」，即一宰之外，再加一牛也。決其數，則註以

「兹(茲)用」二字，亦有省略之者。次卜其二牛或三牛之毛色，於右卜「叀革(騂)」，於左卜「叀牟(犁)」，決其色，亦間註「兹用」字。一次卜日祭，必有四辭，本版補足之得四十辭，知所卜為十次日祭矣。更分列之：

(第一卜) 貞問用一牢(三)　(第二卜)(三) 貞問一牢又一牛　(第三卜) 貞問用騂色牛(二)　(第四卜) 貞問用犁色牛(三)

① a1 丙子卜，貞：武丁(日)其(牢)？一　a2 其牢又一牛？二　a3 叀革？一　a4 叀牟？二

② b1 (癸未)卜，貞：(祖甲)日，其(牢)？(三)　b2 其牢又一牛？二　b3 叀革？(三)　b4 叀牟？兹用(三)

③ c1 (甲申卜，貞：武乙宗，日，其牢)？　c2 其牢又一牛？兹用　c3 叀(革)？一　c4 叀牟？兹用　二

④ d1 (丙戌卜，貞：武丁，日，其牢？兹用)(三)　d2 其牢又一牛？二　d3 (叀革)？(三)　d4 叀牟？二

⑤ e1 癸巳卜，貞：祖甲，日，其牢？一　e2 其牢又一牛？二　e3 叀革？一　e4 叀牟？二

⑥ f1 甲午卜，貞：武乙宗，日，其牢？一　f2 其牢又一牛？二　f3 叀革？(三)　f4 叀牟？兹用　二

⑦ g1 (丙)申卜，貞：(武)丁，日，(其)牢？(兹)用(三)　g2 其牢又一牛？二　g3 叀革？(三)　g4 叀牟？二

⑧ h1 癸卯(卜，貞：祖甲，日，其牢)？　h2 其牢又一牛？兹用　h3 叀革？　h4 叀牟？

⑨ i1 甲辰卜，(貞：武乙)宗，日，(其牢？兹用)一　i2 其牢又一牛？二　i3 叀革？一　i4 叀牟？兹用

⑪ j1 (丙午卜，貞：武丁，日，其牢？兹用)　j2 (其牢又一牛)？　j3 (叀革)？　j4 叀(牟)？兹(用)

⑩辭為別種祀事，故不列入。所補②③④⑪四辭，不能確證其必為某干支日祭某祖，而其必佔此四辭部位，則可斷言也。此版於日祭相互關係極明瞭，故舉以為例。

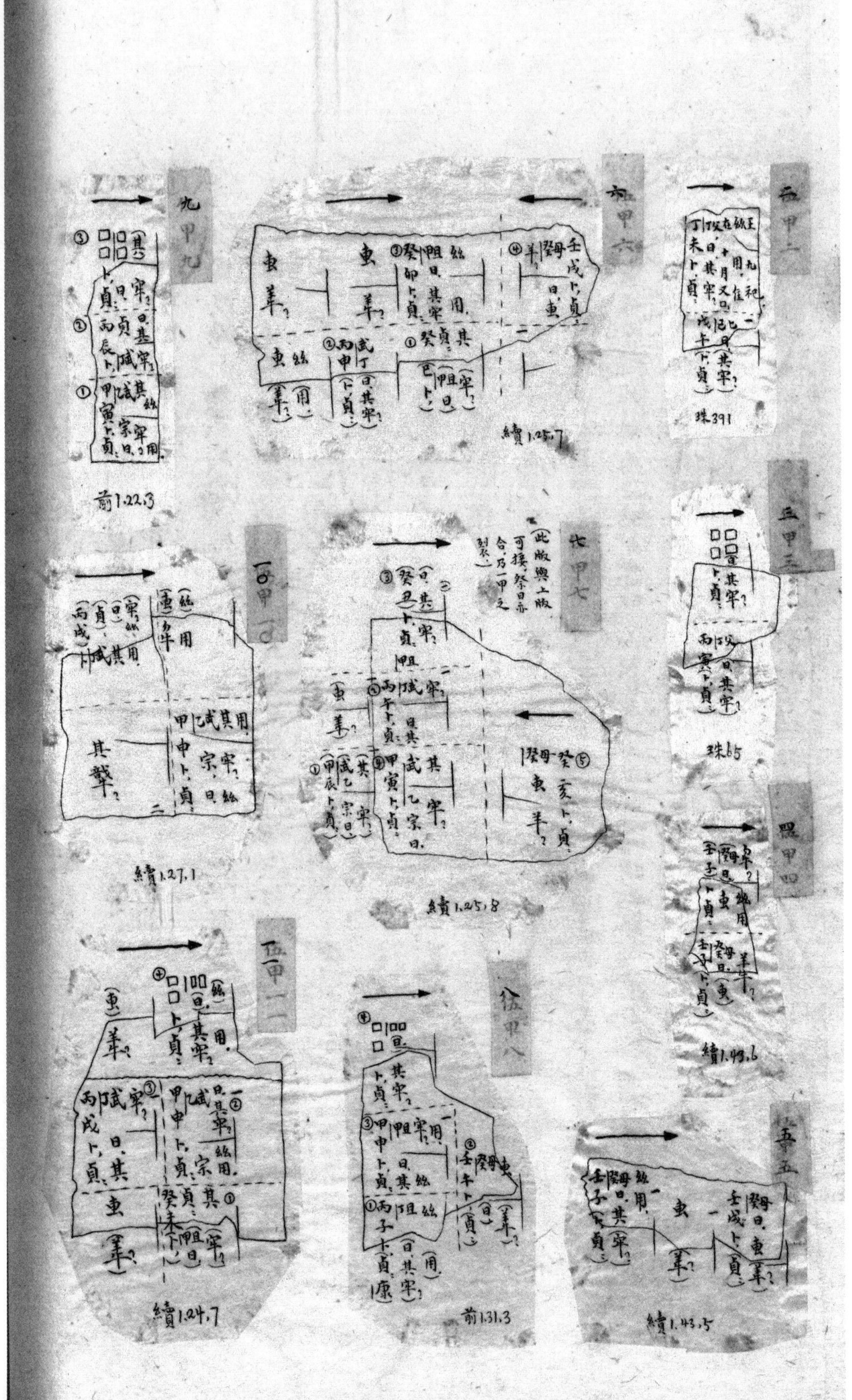

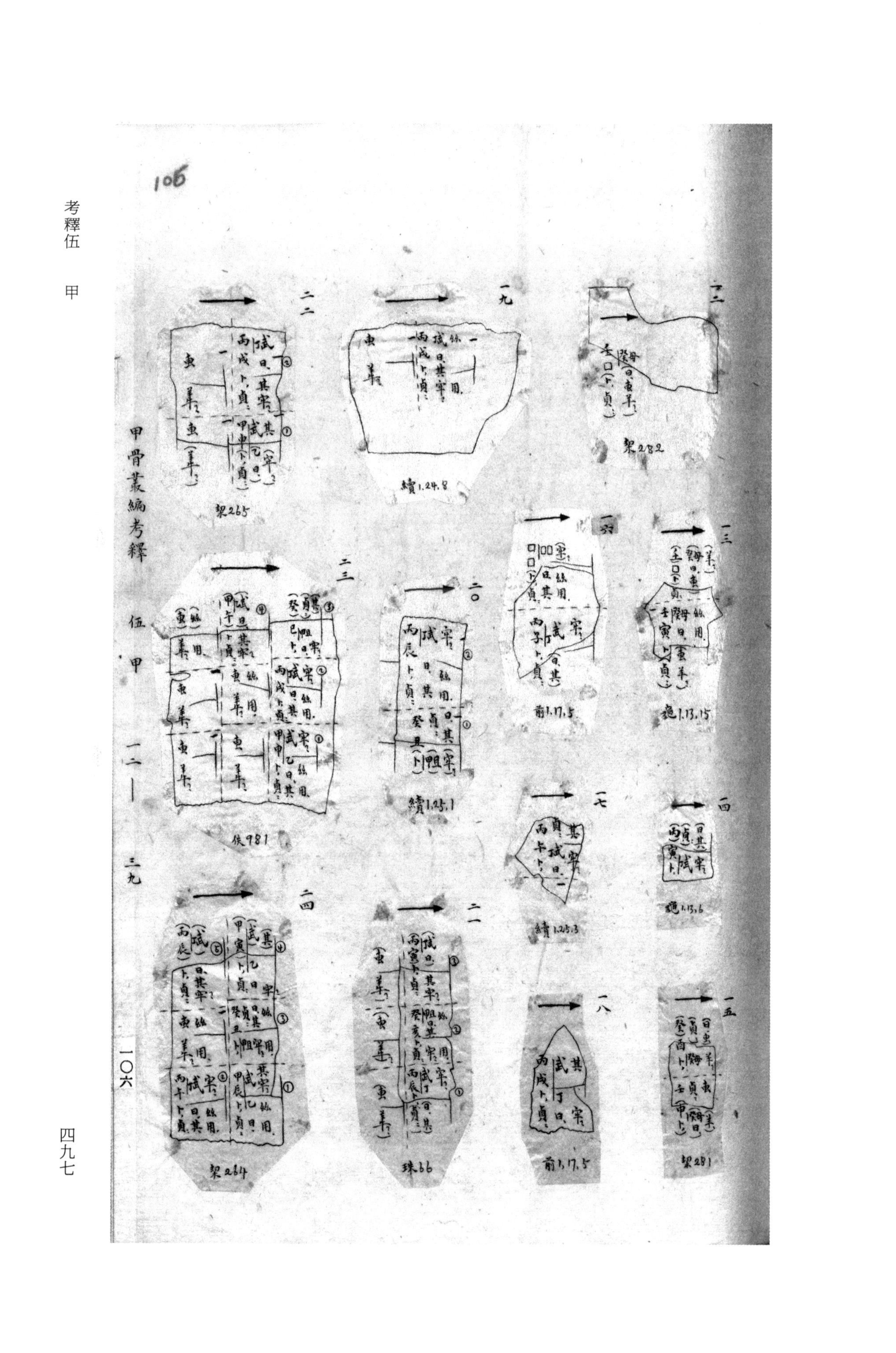

甲骨叢編考釋　伍　甲　一二一

三九

一二 契282

一三 遺1.13.15

一四 遺1.13.6

一五 契281

一六 前1.17.5

一七 續1.25.3

一八 前1.17.5

一九 續1.24.8

二〇 續1.25.1

二一 珠66

二二 契265

二三 佚981

二四 契264

一〇六

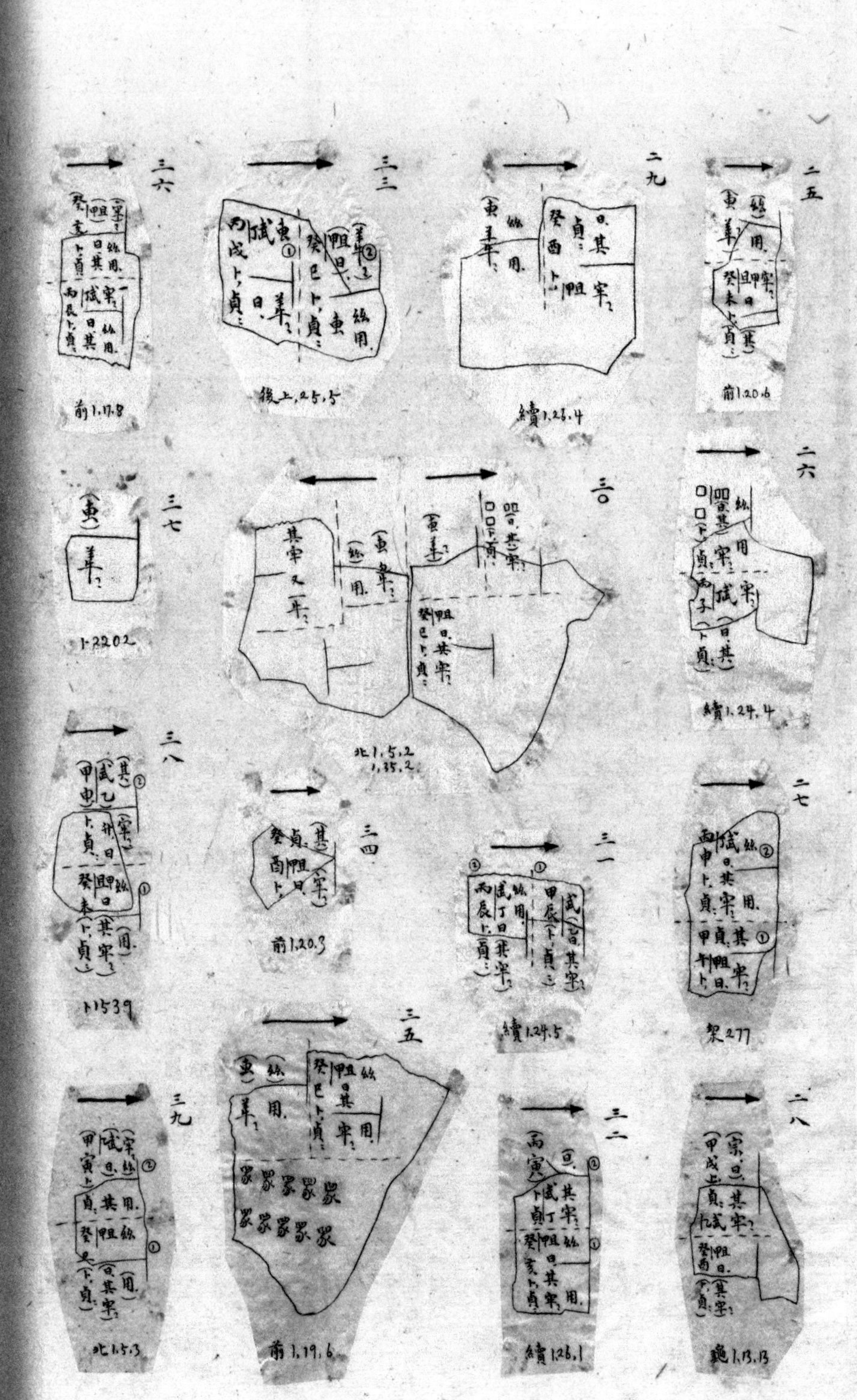

107

甲骨叢編考釋　伍　甲　四〇—七〇

一〇七

四〇
卜311

四一
續1.24.6

四二
前1.21.3

四三
續1.24.9

四四
卜1349

四五
珠61

四六
卜1737

四七
前1.13.1

四八
珠66

四九
卜2263

五〇
卜1533

五一
續1.26.2

五二
珠77

五三
卜1404

五四
卜534

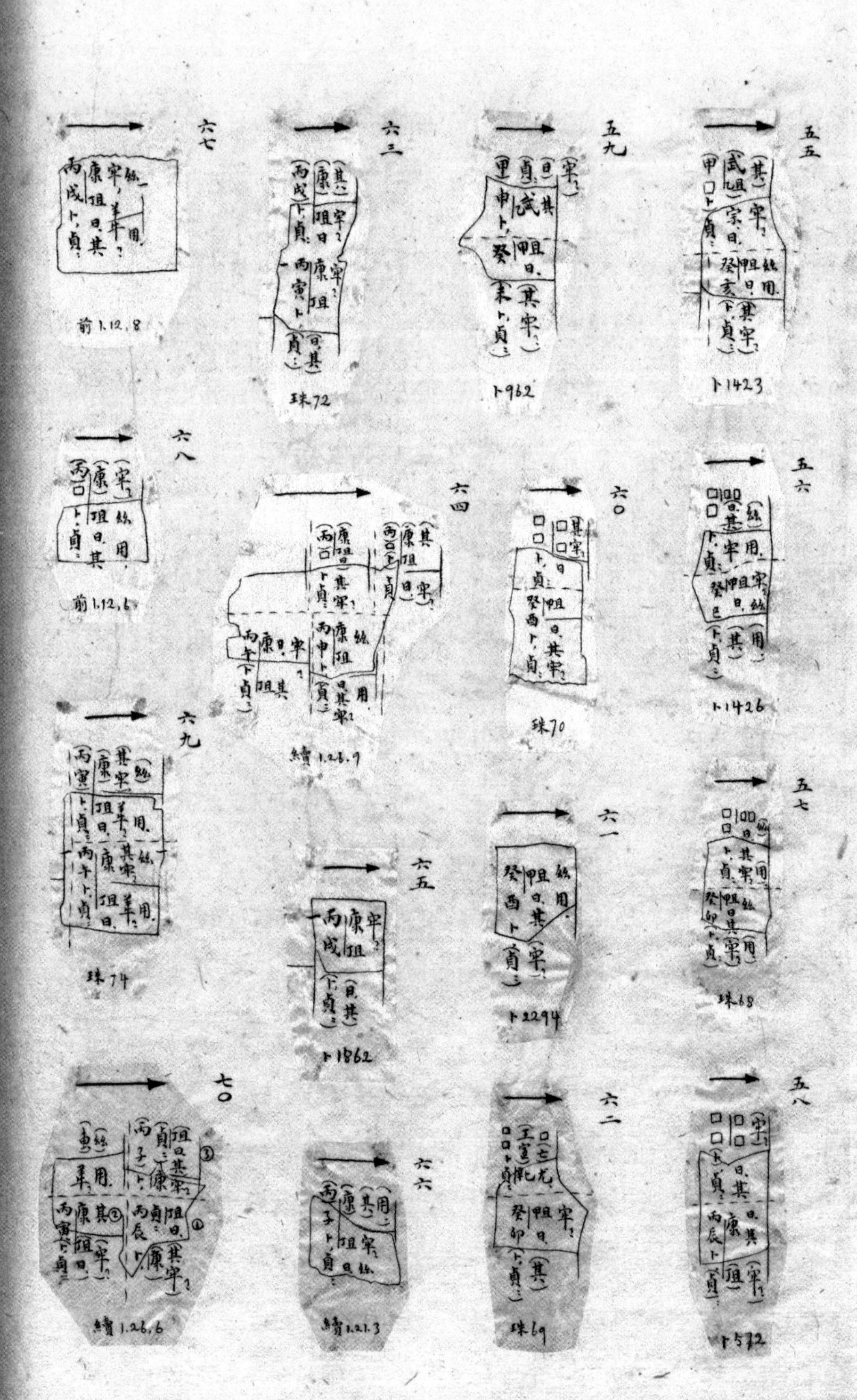

甲骨叢編考釋　伍　甲　七一—九五

七一
此版左右上皆經剪裁
前1.12.7

七二
卜1963

七三
續1.21.5

七四
卜2315

七五
珠71

七六
卜1783

七七
卜1975

七八
卜2104

七九
卜2302

八〇
卜1019

八一
續1.27.4

八二
續1.27.5

八三
珠73

八四
前1.21.1

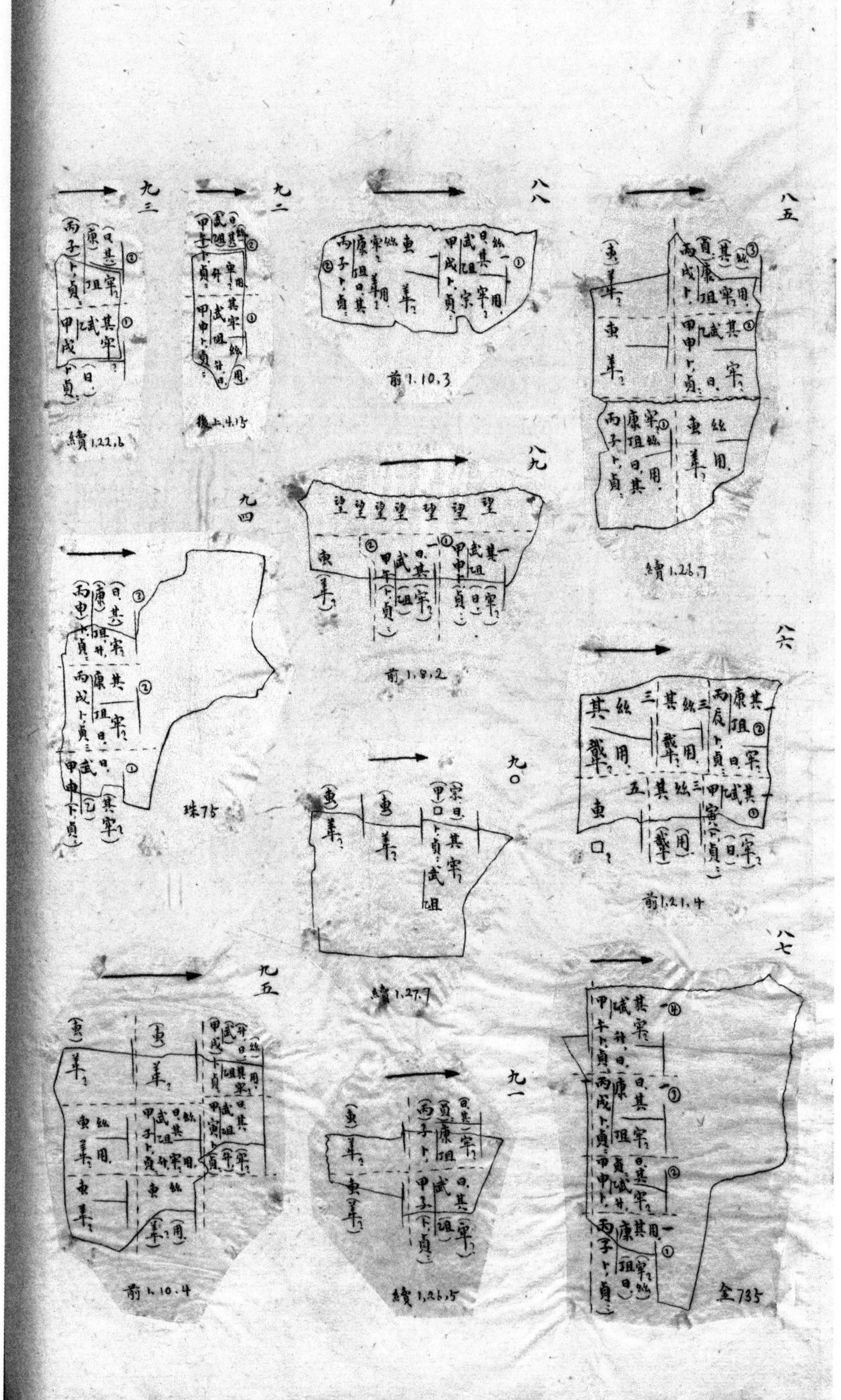
八五
續1.26.7
八六
前1.21.4
八七
金735
八八
前1.10.3
八九
前1.8.2
九〇
續1.27.7
九一
續1.26.5
九二
九三
續1.22.6
九四
珠75
九五
前1.10.4

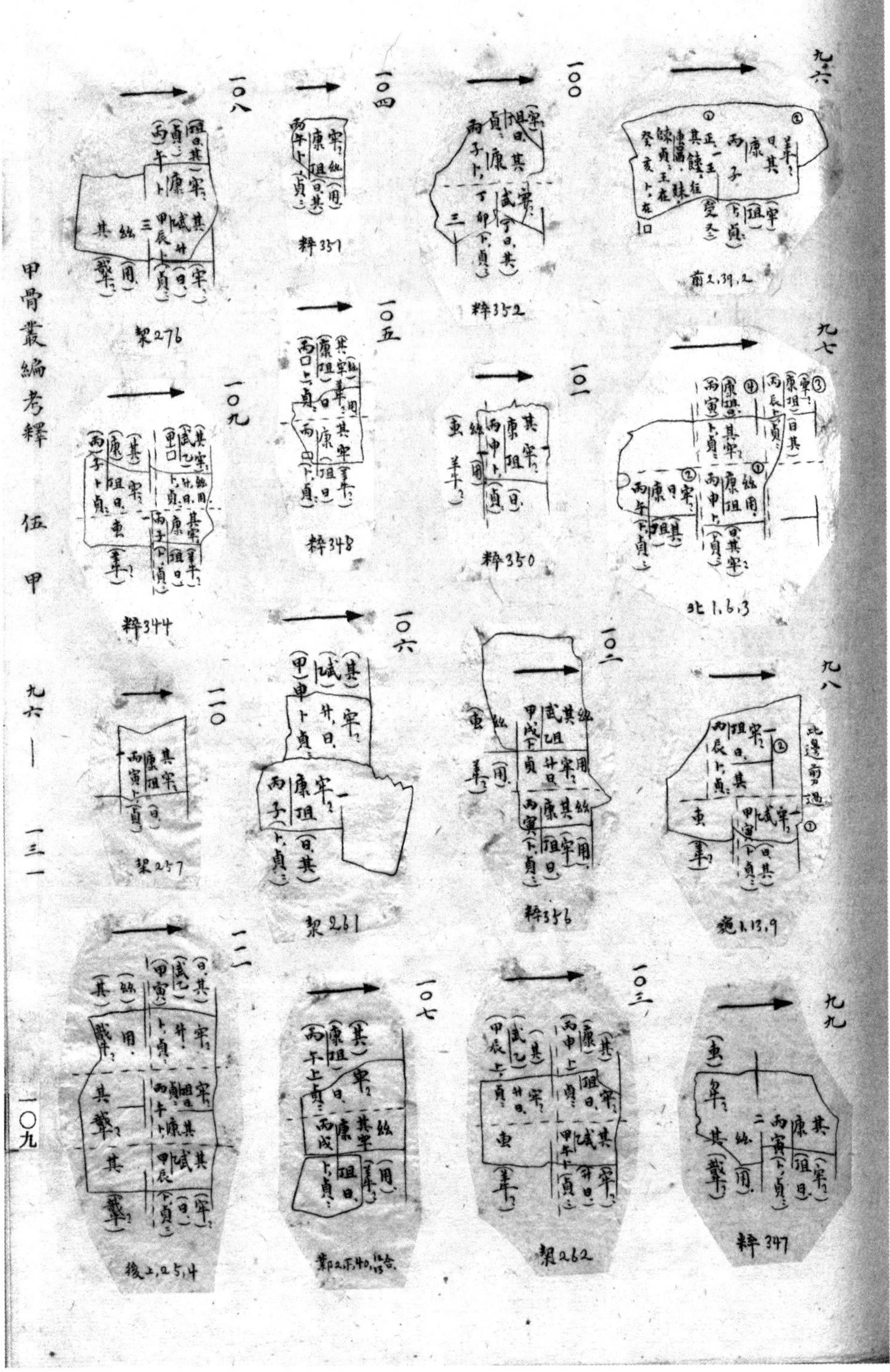
甲骨叢編考釋　伍　甲　九六——一三一
九六
前2.39.2
九七
北1.6.3
九八
此邊剪過
摭1.13.9
九九
粹347
一〇〇
粹352
一〇一
粹350
一〇二
粹356
一〇三
契262
一〇四
粹351
一〇五
粹348
一〇六
契261
一〇七
鄴2下40.13合.
一〇八
契276
一〇九
粹344
一一〇
契257
一一一
後上25.4

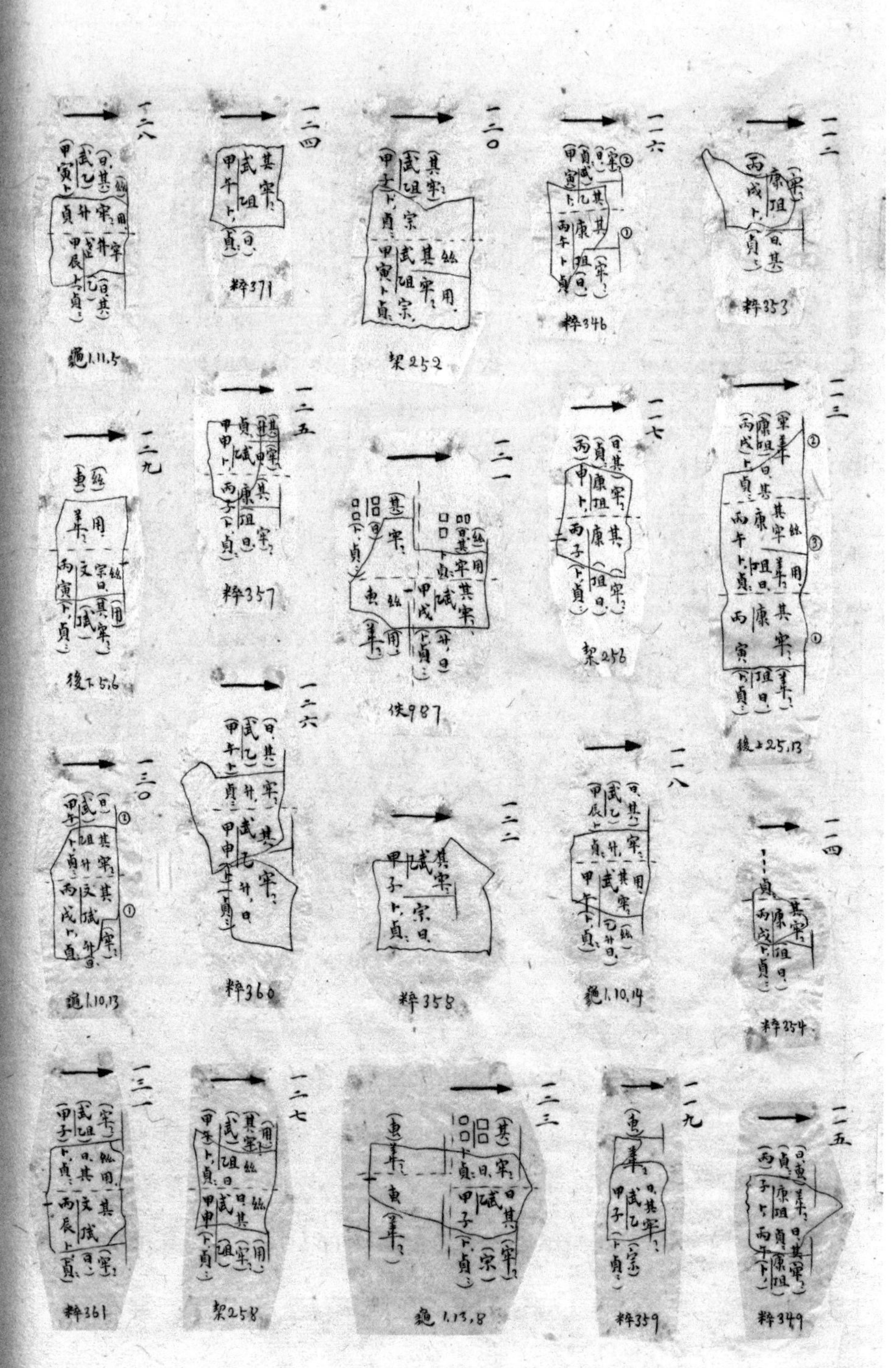

甲骨叢編考釋　伍　甲　一三二—一六〇　一一〇

一三二　前1.18.1　前1.11.1

一三三　續1.15.7

一三四　續1.26.8

一三五　續1.24.10

一三六　續1.27.6

一三七　珠76

一三八　卜1680

一三九　卜1331

一四〇　卜867

一四一　卜1390

一四二　卜2047

一四三　卜881

一四四　卜842

一四五　卜800

一四六　卜1747

一四七　卜558

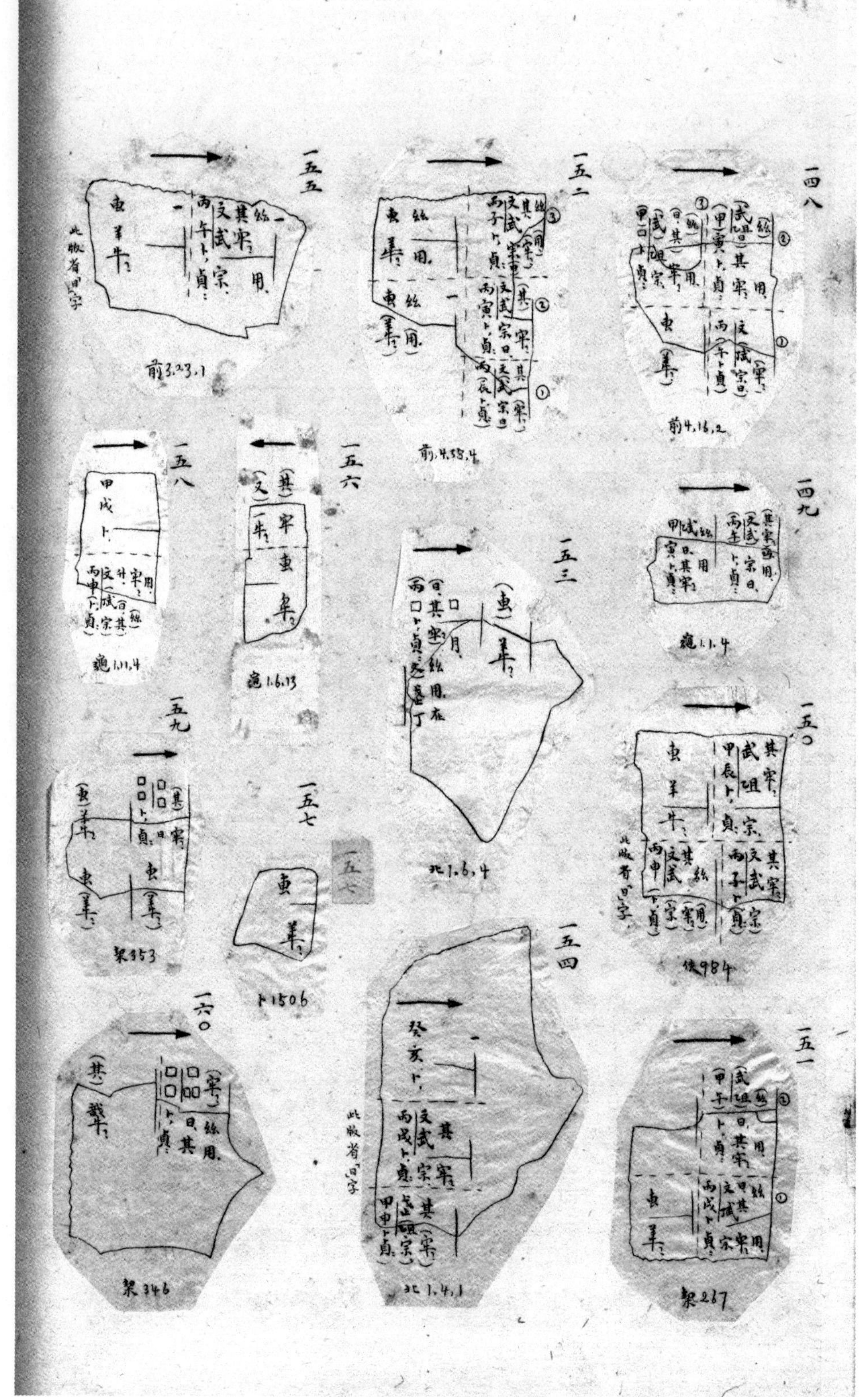

自伍甲一至伍甲一六〇，皆卜日祭之辭。其時代為帝乙、帝辛二世。

帝乙時重修祀典，復祖甲之舊規，卜祭之辭多工整嚴肅，與前代卜辭，迥有不同。其書契文字，小如蠅頭，筆畫細於毫髮，吾人在三千年後之今日，執淨雞狼毫而精心臨摹之，猶自愧不得其神情也。殷人於父不稱謚，祖乃稱謚，右列一六〇版中，有稱父丁者（二、三），稱母癸者（四—八），皆帝乙時之確證。帝辛之世則改稱文武丁（一三〇、一三一、一三二、一三五）文武丁宗（一五二）或文武宗（一五二—一五四），而不祀母癸。（帝辛當稱妣癸）此其別也。又與母癸同版之辭，稱武乙曰「武乙宗」，是乃帝乙時物，則改稱武乙（六五）武祖乙（八九、九〇）武祖乙宗（八八）者，當為帝辛時物矣。其餘如武丁，如祖甲，如康祖丁，乙辛兩世稱謂全同，則不易劃分。

日祭之認識，遠在六年以前，在南京時摹前一、二七之片（七二）旁有小註云「此由丙辰至丙午，六旬中遇丁日即祭康祖丁而於先一日丙卜之，可知其為日祭也。口舊釋丁，誤，蓋日之省寫。廿四、十、八」。當時無暇輯錄研究之。近作叢編，細審通纂別錄河井藏龜，得日祭之例，乃檢舊摹本著於篇。僅依類排比，為之釋補，拚合工夫，猶未能做。如伍甲七八，可拚對，乃腹甲之右上部，齒縫相接，編成後始發現之。今舉研究方法及結果如次。

一、文例。「日」祭卜辭行文之例，與一般腹甲辭例略同，即先下後上，先右後左，先外後內，（有時或先內後外，）至補填空隙之卜辭，則為少數之例外。

二、接對。接對殘片，使復原龜，殆屬絕不可能。其故：1，出土時，但取有字部分，無字部分悉被捨棄。

2、拓印時，無字部分不拓全形。3、編録者，時無字部分剪去。每一龜版，無字者佔大半，此大半不存，何從復原。又龜版卜兆繁密，殘破術甲，全辭一組，中間必騎一兆紋，故辭之殘半者尤多。然正因其如此，吾輩研究之者，乃可以充量運用其匠心也。依腹甲之部位，日祭之順序，分剪比合，使復舊觀，是在讀者。

三、祭法。 在理得祖甲時及帝乙帝辛時彡、翌、祭、壹、劦五種祀典之嚴密程序之後，吾人深感祀典之探索，有其重要之意味，而不容籠統淺忽視之。即此種「日」祭，所舉僅及五世，以帝乙時論，則為其：

父	祖	曾祖	高祖	五世祖
＝父丁（文丁）母癸附入	＝武乙	＝康祖丁	＝祖甲	＝武丁

伍甲二下一辭有妣己日祭，戊午卜之，祭法相同，不詳為某祖之配，且五世之中僅母癸日祭用羊，妣之日祭只此一見，尚待考。所謂「日」祭者，遇此五世之祖若父忌日必祭之。祭文丁、康祖丁、武丁，皆以丁日，丁日配合十二支，凡不同之丁有六，六丁日皆有日祭，而皆於前一日丙，卜其祭牲之數及毛色。亦有於丁日更卜之者，如伍甲二於丁未卜文丁日祭，伍甲四九於丁酉卜武丁日祭是。此或丙午、丙申未卜，而於丁補卜之。然三丁無同日卜祭者，當有次第，準彡翌等祭之例，先遠而後近，故其次當為武丁、康丁、文丁。此三丁每人佔六旬，須十八旬而遍，遍則更重新舉行，故每年每人可祭二次，一次六祭，每年每人十二祭。每癸、武乙、祖甲，則與三丁同時舉行，先後次序，

微有變易，而每人每年祭二次，一次六祭，則一也。帝辛時相沿不改，除母癸未見之外，亦祭此五世而不及帝乙。其大要如此。兹據所見材料，韓成乙辛時代日祭格，如下：

日祭格甲種

(下祭之日)				(五世) 第一式 以祖甲、武乙、母癸，隨武丁日祭，於前六旬彈行之。	第二式 以祖甲、武乙、母癸同時日祭，於前十旬內彈行，不必全隨武丁者。
癸酉	甲戌	丙子	壬午	祖甲 武乙 武丁 母癸	武丁
癸未	甲申	丙戌	壬辰	祖甲 武乙 武丁 母癸	武丁
癸巳	甲午	丙申	壬寅	祖甲 武乙 武丁 母癸	祖甲 武乙 武丁 母癸
癸卯	甲辰	丙午	壬子	祖甲 武乙 武丁 母癸	祖甲 武乙 武丁 母癸
癸丑	甲寅	丙辰	壬戌	祖甲 武乙 武丁 母癸	祖甲 武乙 武丁 母癸
癸亥	甲子	丙寅	壬申	祖甲 武乙 武丁 母癸	祖甲 武乙 武丁 母癸
癸酉	甲戌	丙子	壬午	康祖丁	祖甲 武乙 康祖丁 母癸
癸未	甲申	丙戌	壬辰	康祖丁	祖甲 武乙 康祖丁 母癸
		丙申		康祖丁	康祖丁
		丙午		康祖丁	康祖丁
		丙辰		康祖丁	康祖丁

丙寅　康祖丁　康祖丁
丙子　父丁（帝辛時稱父武丁）　父丁
丙戌　父丁　父丁
丙申　父丁　父丁
丙午　父丁　父丁
丙辰　父丁　父丁
丙寅　父丁（文武丁）　父丁

（丙次日癸之相接）
癸酉　甲戌　丙子　壬午　祖甲　武乙　武丁　母癸（一三五）
癸未　甲申　丙戌　壬辰　祖甲　武乙　武丁　母癸
癸巳　甲午　丙申　壬寅　祖甲　武乙　武丁　母癸
癸卯　甲辰　丙午　壬子　祖甲　武乙　武丁　母癸
以下畧　以下畧

以上為甲種，凡二式。其武丁日祭之起始，不必定是丙子，或為其他丙日，故丙式皆可變易為六式也。如伍甲四二，甲子甲戌武乙，丙寅，丙子武丁，為前二式所不容，必武丁始祭於丙戌以後，始能容之。甲種有母癸之祭，定為帝乙時，乙種則當為帝辛時也。伍甲一三五，應列乙種，附此以見父丁母癸之關係。

113

日祭格乙種

(卜祭之日)

		第一式 祖甲武乙各佔六旬接排於前十二旬。 (五世)	第二式 祖甲武乙各佔六旬分列於首尾。
癸酉	丙子	祖甲 武丁	祖甲 武丁
癸未	丙戌	祖甲 武丁	祖甲 武丁 (三三)
癸巳	丙申	祖甲 武丁	祖甲 武丁 (二七)
癸卯	丙午	祖甲 武丁	祖甲 武丁 (二〇)
癸丑	丙辰	祖甲 武丁 (二〇)	祖甲 武丁 (四八)
癸亥	丙寅	祖甲 武丁	祖甲 武丁
甲戌	丙子	武乙 康祖丁 (三)(三)	康祖丁
甲申	丙戌	武乙 康祖丁	康祖丁
甲午	丙申	武乙 康祖丁	康祖丁
甲辰	丙午	武乙 康祖丁 (四)	康祖丁
甲寅	丙辰	武乙 康祖丁	武乙 康祖丁
甲子	丙寅	武乙 康祖丁	武乙 康祖丁 (七〇)
甲戌	丙子	文武丁	武乙 文武丁 (一〇二)

甲申 丙戌	文武丁	（一三二）武乙 文武丁
甲午 丙申	文武丁	（一三六）武乙 文武丁
甲辰 丙午	文武丁	（一三二）武乙 文武丁
甲寅 丙辰	文武丁	武乙 文武丁
甲子 丙寅	（一三五）文武丁	武乙 文武丁
（兩次日祭相接）癸酉 丙子	祖甲 武丁	—
癸未 丙戌	祖甲 武丁	
癸巳 丙申	祖甲 武丁	
以下略	以下略	

武乙 文武丁（一三二）
武乙 文武丁（一三六）
武乙 文武丁
武乙 文武丁
—

以上為乙種，凡三式。日祭開始之旬，皆可變易，如伍甲七一康丁日祭為丙辰至丙午之六旬，則武丁日祭亦當自丙辰始也。是為第二式之改從丙辰始祭者。再有發現新辭，以此類推。

日祭一遍，歷時十八旬，接連舉行，循還無已，伍甲一三五一版文丁武丁相接，可以說明之。伍甲一〇〇版，可證武丁日祭之後繼以康丁。文丁日祭，既在下次武丁祭日之前，必在此次康丁祭日之後，亦可推知。表中例證，舉原辭有聯系者，餘不一一。

本編伍骨六一版，有「昔乙卯，武(武乙)升，勺(曰)。癸亥其至于妣癸廿日」。此帝辛稱母癸之辭。説詳原片。

甲骨叢編考釋　伍　甲　一六一—一七四

一六一
北 1.34.1—2
1.36.4

一六二
絜 349

一六三
粹 560

一六四
絜 360

一六五
龜 1.6.10

一六六
絜 361

一六七
菁 9.10

一六八
菁 9.11

一六九
菁 9.12

一七〇
菁 9.14

一七一
菁 10.2

一七二
菁 10.13

一七三
菁 11.26

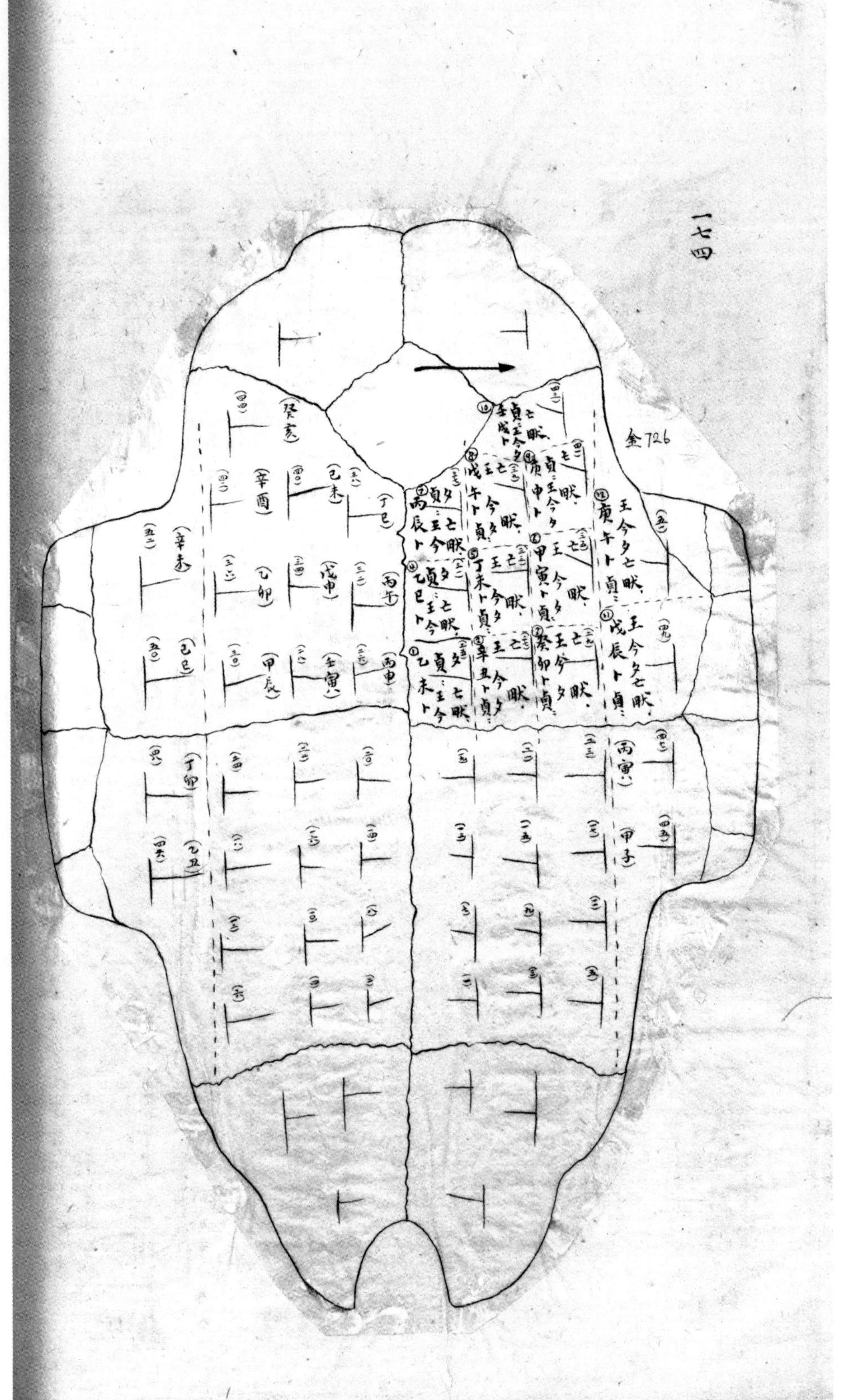
一七四
金726

一七五

新46

一七六

卜54

一七七

新5

一七八

卜64

一七九

新7

一八〇

卜1844

一八一

北1,38,1

一八二

新126

一八三

卜1853

一八四

新15

一八五

北1,38,4

北1,38,5-6

一八六

北1,34,4

北1,38,3

一八七

卜1569

一八八

粹364

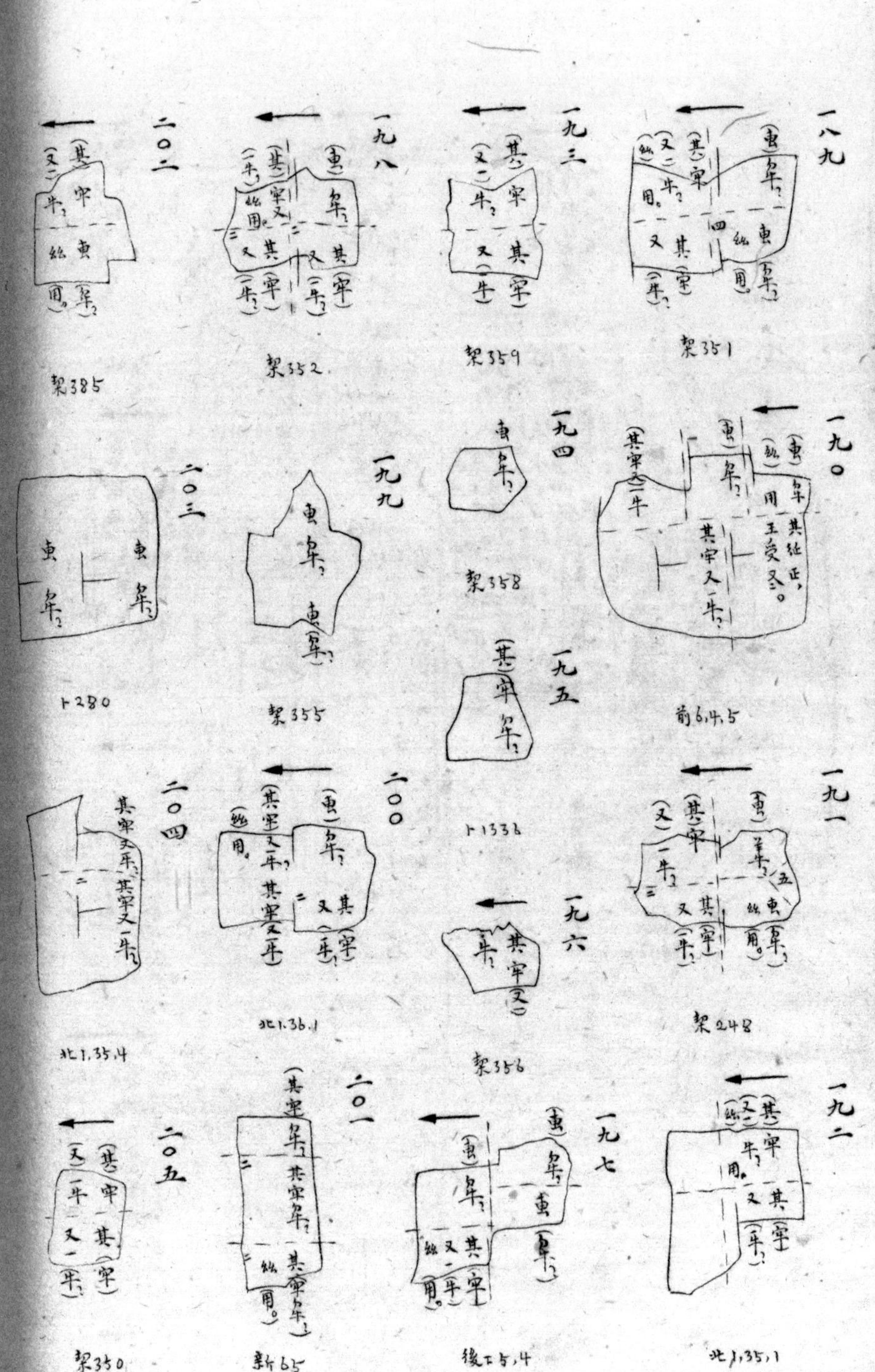

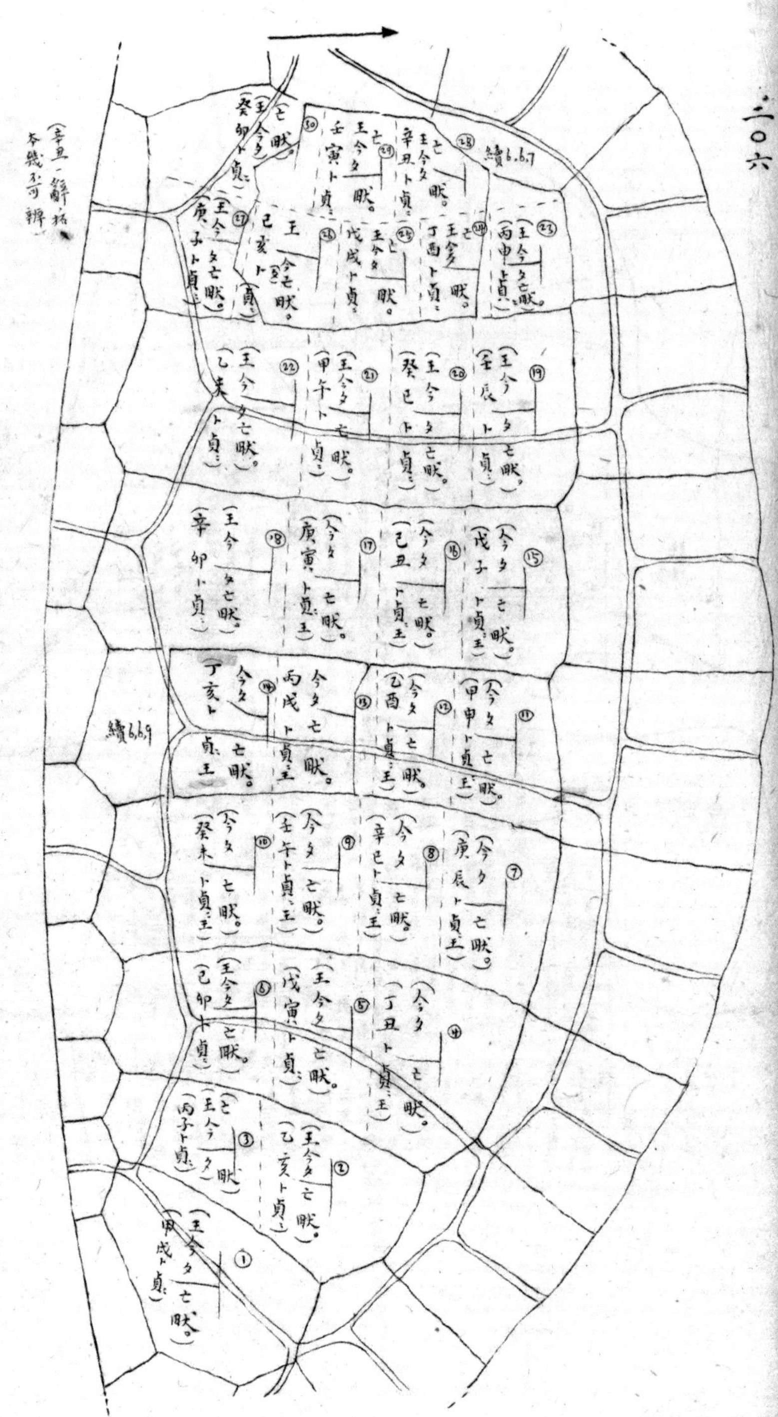

二〇六
續6.6.7
續6.6.9
（辛丑一辭，拓本幾不可辨）
①甲戌卜貞：王今夕亡畎。
②乙亥卜貞：王今夕亡畎。
③丙子卜貞：王今夕亡畎。
④丁丑卜貞：王今夕亡畎。
⑤戊寅卜貞：王今夕亡畎。
⑥己卯卜貞：王今夕亡畎。
⑦庚辰卜貞：王今夕亡畎。
⑧辛巳卜貞：王今夕亡畎。
⑨壬午卜貞：王今夕亡畎。
⑩癸未卜貞：王今夕亡畎。
⑪甲申卜貞：王今夕亡畎。
⑫乙酉卜貞：王今夕亡畎。
⑬丙戌卜貞：王今夕亡畎。
⑭丁亥卜貞：王今夕亡畎。
⑮戊子卜貞：王今夕亡畎。
⑯己丑卜貞：王今夕亡畎。
⑰庚寅卜貞：王今夕亡畎。
⑱辛卯卜貞：王今夕亡畎。
⑲壬辰卜貞：王今夕亡畎。
⑳癸巳卜貞：王今夕亡畎。
㉑甲午卜貞：王今夕亡畎。
㉒乙未卜貞：王今夕亡畎。
㉓丙申卜貞：王今夕亡畎。
㉔丁酉卜貞：王今夕亡畎。
㉕戊戌卜貞：王今夕亡畎。
㉖己亥卜貞：王今夕亡畎。
㉗庚子卜貞：王今夕亡畎。
㉘辛丑卜貞：王今夕亡畎。
㉙壬寅卜貞：王今夕亡畎。
㉚癸卯卜貞：王今夕亡畎。

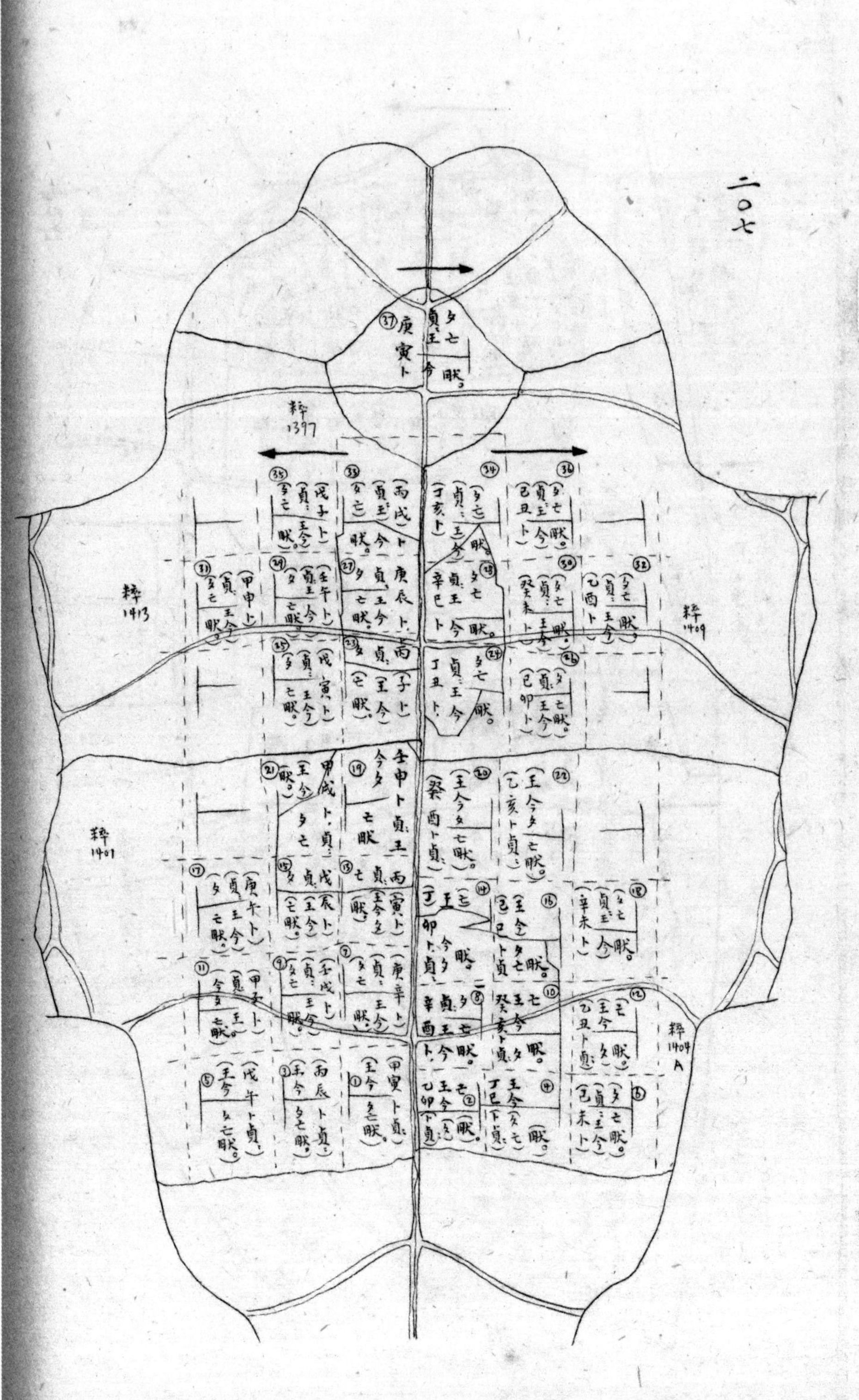
二〇七
粹1397
粹1413
粹1409
粹1401
粹1404A

117

一（右胛骨）

前2.16.4

前2.16.3

菁9.10

金574

② 辛巳卜。

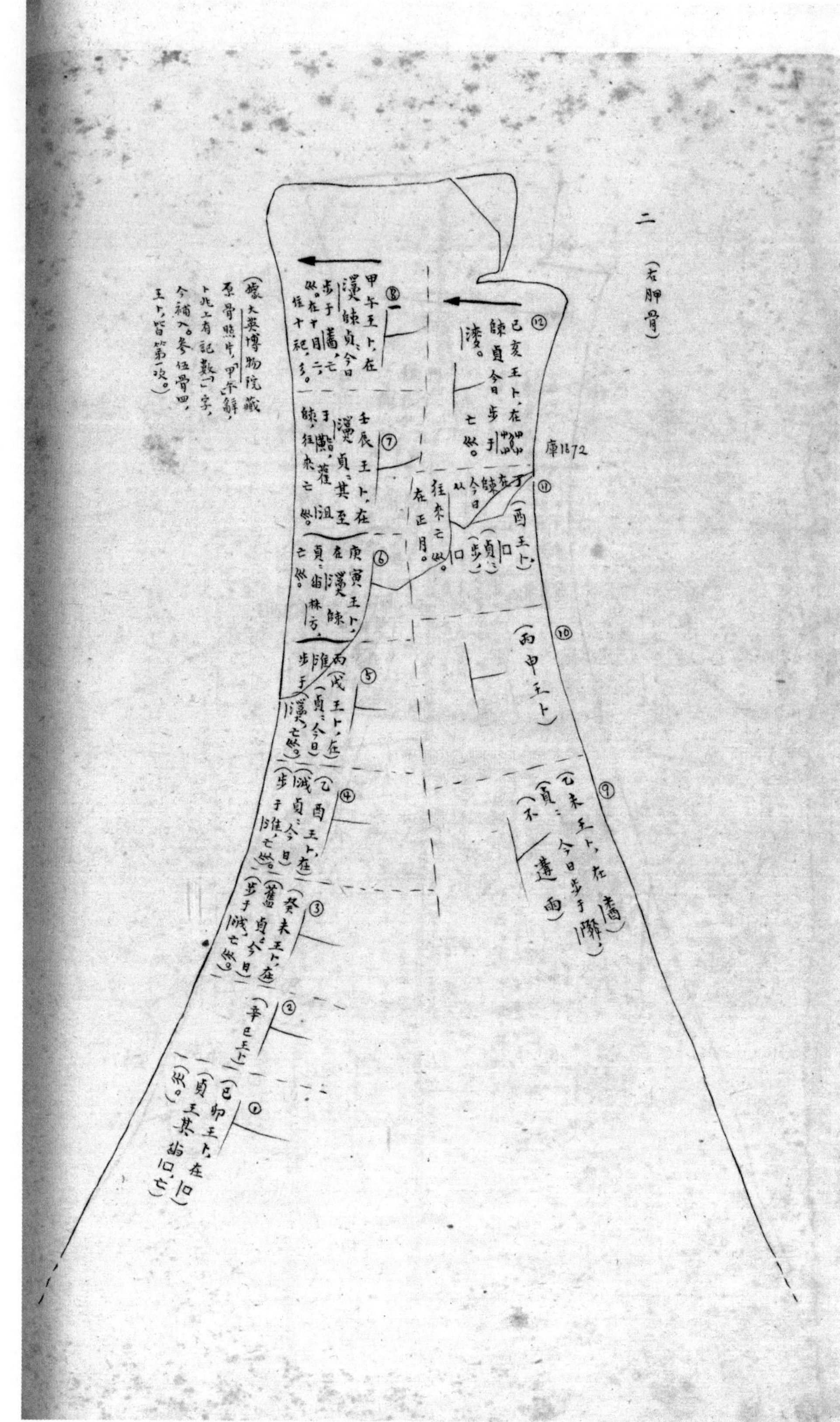
二
（右胛骨）
庫1872
（據大英博物院藏
原骨照片，甲午辭
卜兆上有記數「一」字，
今補入。參任骨四，
王卜，皆第一次。）

三　（左胛骨）

後上15,14

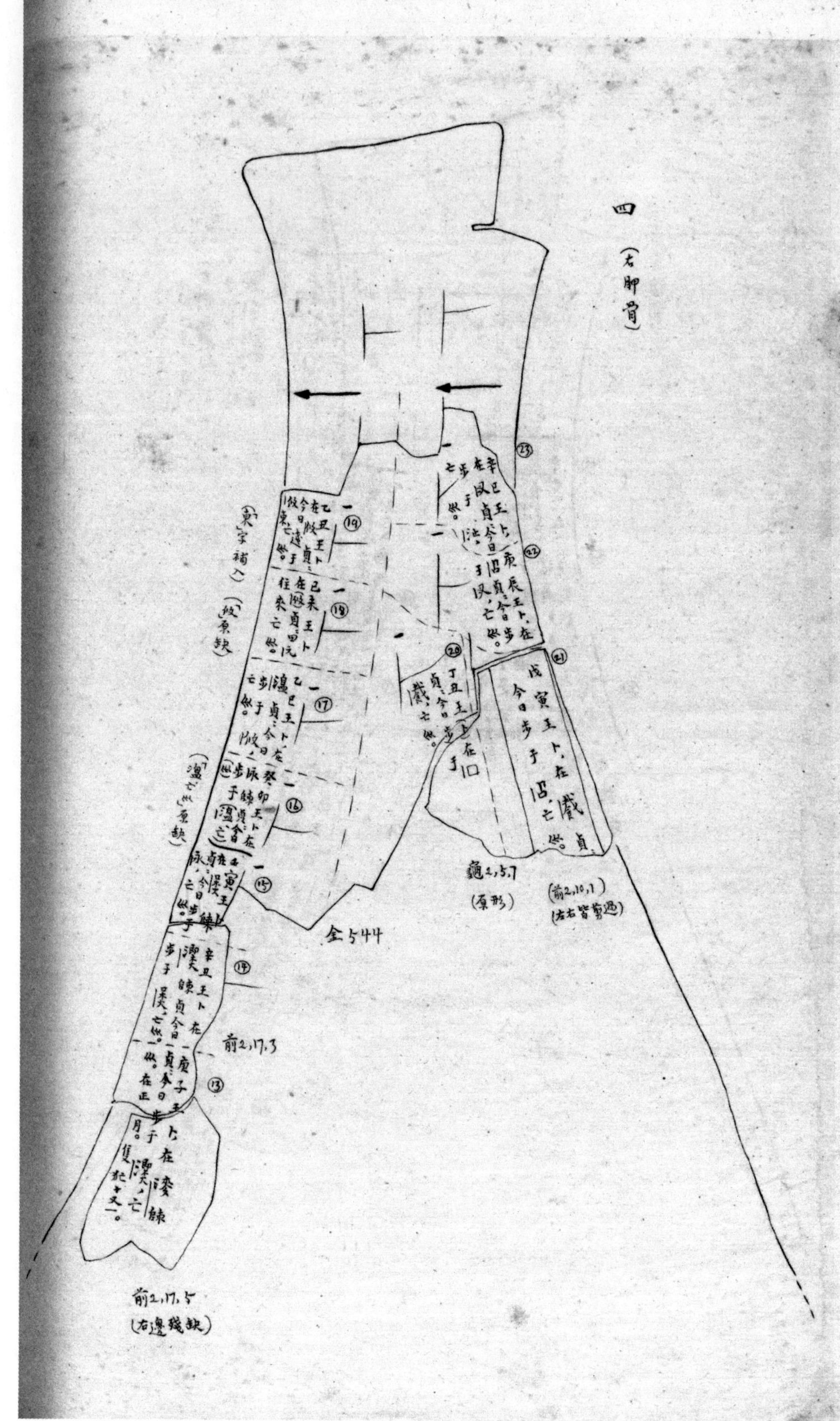
四
（右脚骨）
金544
前2.17.3
前2.17.5
（右邊殘缺）
龜2.5.7
（原形）
前2.10.1

伍骨一、二、三、四

右四版，全文曾發表於方法歛博士對於甲骨文字之貢獻一文中，此其左右胛骨各二版之全形也。二、四為右胛骨，皆王親卜貞者，卜之次序為第一卜。一與三當史官所貞，一④有立，乃史之書名者，餘史為誰，不可知矣。王乃帝辛，是四版其正人方時行程中一組重要卜辭也。

四版合十殘片而成，釋文中全辭，多由對稱之版互補之。前文所錄大小月有誤，茲據譜更列如次。卜辭錄原有者，補足部分不錄。

帝辛正人方日譜節鈔　殷曆譜

帝辛十祀（公元前一一六五年　丙申）

十二月（殷正）　小　戊辰　一日　儒略周日一二九六二五五（一一六五年十二月廿五日）

己卯　十二日

辛巳　十四日

癸未　十六日

乙酉　十八日

第一卜　右胛骨，王卜貞之辭

第二卜（三）　左胛骨，史貞之辭

己①卯卜，在□貞：王其翁口，亡巛。

辛②巳卜。

癸③未卜，在𦪽貞：王步于𣶒。亡巛。

乙④酉卜，在𣶒，立貞：王步于淮，亡巛。

丙戌 十九日 ⑤丙(戌王卜，在)淮(貞：今日)步于(漢。亡
(一一六四年一月一日) 㞢。)

⑤丙戌卜，在淮貞：王步于(漢)。亡㞢。

庚寅 廿三日 ⑥庚寅王卜，在漢餗貞：㞢林方。亡㞢。

⑥庚寅卜，在漢餗貞：王㞢林方，亡㞢。

壬辰 廿五日 ⑦壬辰王卜，在漢貞：其至于𪊔雚沮
餗。往來亡㞢。

⑦壬辰卜，在漢貞：王其至于𪊔雚，亡
㞢。

甲午 廿七日 ⑧甲午王卜，在漢餗貞：今日步于𬒳。
亡㞢。在十月(又)二，隹十祀。彡。
(此彡字關係極大，為甲午彡上甲之日)

⑧甲午卜，在漢餗貞：今日王步于𬒳。
亡㞢。

乙未 廿八日

⑨(乙)未卜，在𬒳貞：王步于𬒳。不遘雨。

(以上，伍骨一)

帝辛十一祀（公元前一一六四年 丁酉）

正月 大

丁酉 一日 ⑪丁(酉王卜)在囗餗(貞)：今日(祉)从囗。
一二九六八四 (一月十一日) 往來亡㞢。在正月。

己亥 三日 ⑫己亥王卜，在𦼯餗貞：今日步于淒。
亡㞢。

(以上伍骨二)

庚子四日　庚子⑬王卜，在漊餗貞：今日步于漊。庚子⑬卜，在漊餗貞：王步于漊。亡巛。

亡𡿧。在正月。隻狖十又一。（以上伍骨三）

辛丑五日　辛丑⑭王卜，在漊餗貞：今日步于溴。

亡𡿧。

壬寅六日　壬寅⑮王卜，在溴餗貞：今日步于永。

亡𡿧。

癸卯七日　癸卯⑯王卜，在永餗貞：今日步于溫。

亡𡿧。

乙巳九日　乙巳⑰王卜，在溫貞：今日步于攸。亡

𡿧。

己未廿三日　己未⑱王卜，在（攸）貞：田𤜥。往來亡𡿧。

乙丑廿九日　乙丑⑲王卜，在攸貞：今日從，从攸東。

亡𡿧。

二月小

丁卯一日　（一二九六三一四）（三月十一日）

丁丑十一日　丁丑⑳王卜貞：今日步于㦽。亡𡿧。

㉑戊寅王卜，在𢦏貞：今日步于㫖。亡巛。

戊寅吉

㉒庚辰王卜，在㫖貞：今日步于𡧊。亡巛。

庚辰吉

㉓辛巳王卜，在𡧊貞：今日步于沚。亡巛。

辛巳吉

（以上伍骨四）

以上為帝辛正人方時兩閱月行程中關於卜行止之版。尚有卜夕、卜旬可資印證之版，別詳日譜。以卜夕、卜旬之版參證之，知帝辛於十一祀正月己酉（十三日）至攸，二月戊寅（十二日）離去，前後在攸駐蹕一月之久，即他辭王卜貞所謂「余从攸侯喜正人方」也。

由四版，可見骨版刻辭先後，及左右行，在左右胛骨上之款式。讀者細審之，即知其異常規整也。

又右表中⑥至⑧各辭，上為王貞，下為史貞，比較之，便可見語氣之不同。王所貞乃自己事，史則處處必稱「王」，其恭謹崇敬之情態，可以想見。

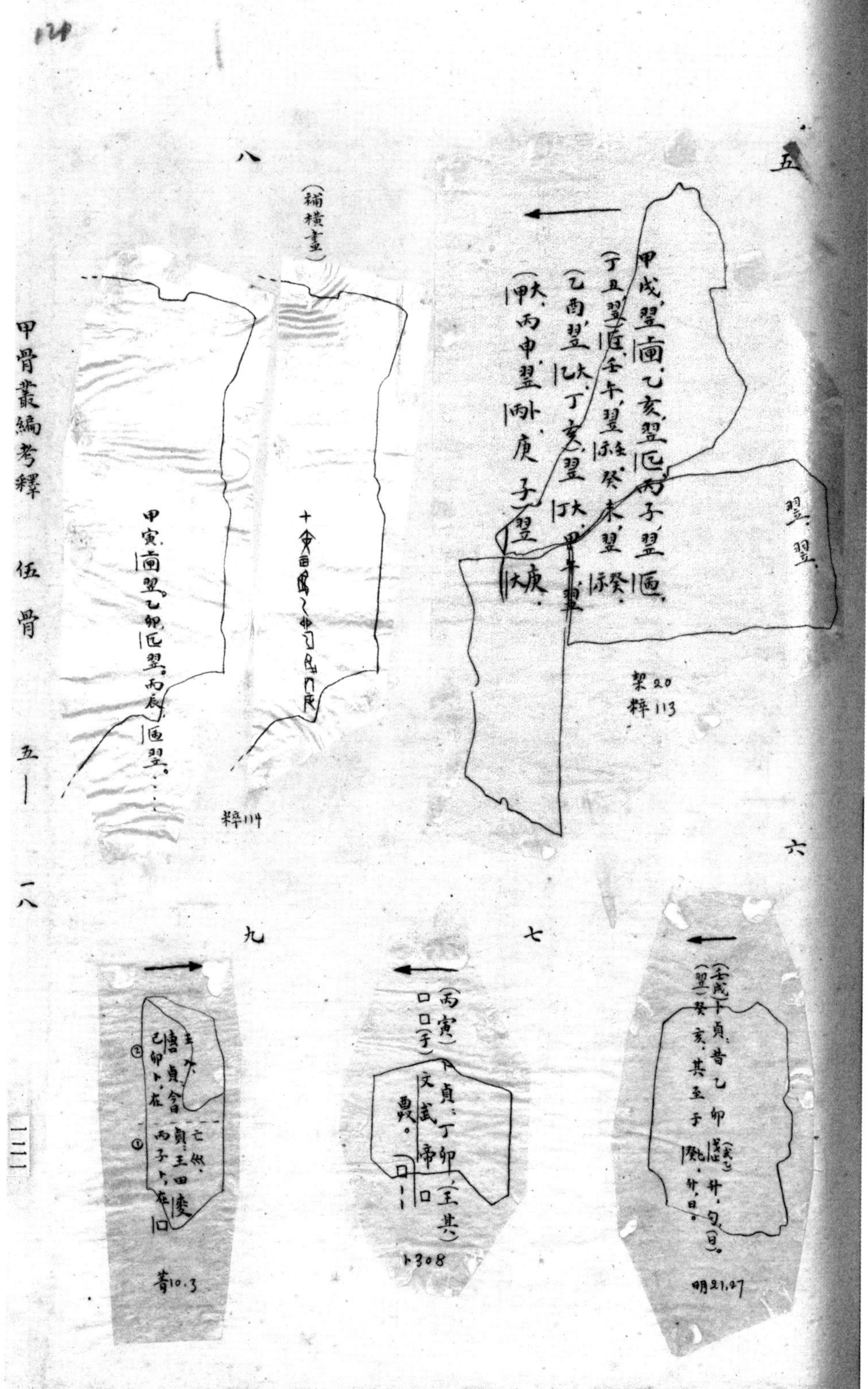
甲骨叢編考釋　伍　骨　五一　一八
二三
五
六
七
八
九
絜20
粹113
粹114
卜308
菁10.3
明21.27
(補橫畫)

一〇

菁10.18

一一

菁9.16

一二

菁10.10

一三

菁9.15

一四

菁9.9

一五

丙戌卜貞：翌日丁亥，王其又勺，于文武帝，正，王受又（祐）。

方地山藏骨
陳松苑摹本

一六

菁9.3

菁9.4

一七

菁10.4

一八

菁10.5

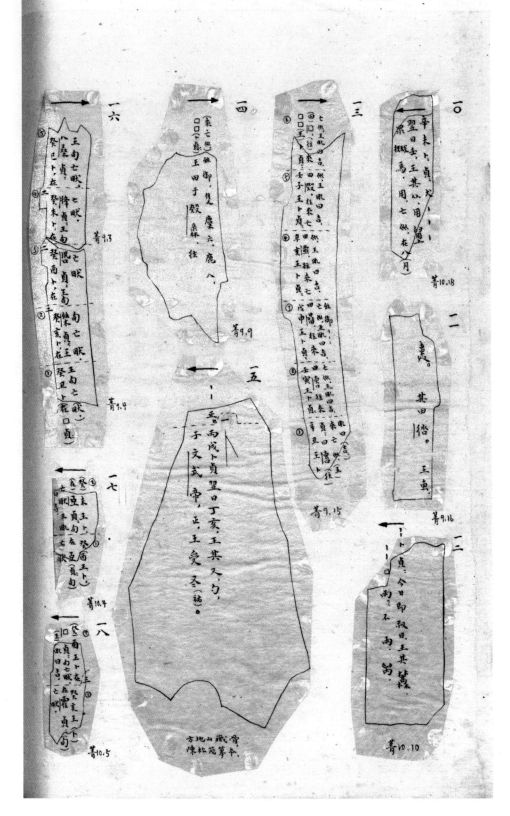

伍骨五、八

此兩版乃研究祭祀典禮之基本材料，余理出二期及五期祀典系統之出發點也。二期、五期於舉行彡、翌、祭、壹、劦五種祭祀之先，必有「工典」之禮，工字意義不甚瞭然，或當假為共，即供奉之義，典則其時先祖若先妣之譜牒，有日干，有祭法，有祖妣之名次者也。典，冊，原為簡編之形，其質竹木，今已毀滅，此殆自典冊譜牒抄錄之一部分，幸藉骨質而存，吾人乃得因之參稽卜祭之辭而推求其祭法之大系也。

翌為五種祀典之一，此其甲戌系及甲寅系，尚有甲申、甲午、甲辰、甲子各系也。此為其先祖翌祭之典，其先妣之典，遺文雖不可得，亦可由卜辭祖妣之祭日連貫，推而知之。茲揭兩系之全，如次表，作帝乙、帝辛時之祖妣譜牒觀可也。

「翌」譜（亦稱「翌日」）

(1) 甲戌系祭日	(2) 甲寅系祭日	當祭之先祖	先妣
甲戌（甲戌旬第一）	甲寅（甲寅旬第一）	上甲（先祖自此始）	
乙亥	乙卯	匚乙	
丙子	丙辰（伍骨八殘文止此）	匚丙	
丁丑	丁巳	匚丁	
壬午	壬戌	示壬	

癸未	癸亥	示癸	
乙酉（甲申旬第二）	乙丑（甲子旬第二）	大乙	
丁亥	丁卯	大丁	
庚寅	庚午		示壬奭妣庚（先妣自此始）
甲午（甲午旬第三）	甲戌（甲戌旬第三）	大甲	示癸奭妣甲
丙申	丙子	卜丙	大乙奭妣丙
戊戌	戊寅		大丁奭妣戊
庚子（伍骨五璲文止此。）（翌大庚左旁有畀書。）	庚辰	大庚	
辛丑	辛巳		大甲奭妣辛
壬寅	壬午		大庚奭妣壬
甲辰（甲辰旬第四）	甲申（甲申旬第四）	小甲	
戊申	戊子	大戊	
己酉	己丑	吕己	
壬子	壬辰		大戊奭妣壬
丁巳（甲寅旬第五）	丁酉（甲午旬第五）	中丁	

甲骨叢編考釋　伍　骨　五一一八　一二三

己未	己亥		中丁奭妣己
壬戌	壬寅	卜壬	
癸亥	癸卯		中丁奭妣癸
甲子（甲子旬第六）	甲辰（甲辰旬第六）	戔甲	
乙丑	乙巳	祖乙	
己巳	己酉		祖乙奭妣己
庚午	庚戌		祖辛奭妣庚
辛未	辛亥	祖辛	
甲戌（甲戌旬第七）	甲寅（甲寅旬第七）	羌甲	祖辛奭妣甲
丁丑	丁巳	祖丁	
庚辰	庚申	南庚	祖丁奭妣庚
辛巳	辛酉		祖丁奭妣辛
甲申（甲申旬第八）	甲子（甲子旬第八）	虎甲	
己丑	己巳		祖丁奭妣己
庚寅	庚午	般庚	

辛卯	辛未	小辛	
癸巳	癸酉		祖丁奭妣癸
乙未（甲午旬第九）	乙亥（甲戌旬第九）	小乙	
丁酉	丁丑	武丁	
己亥	己卯	祖己	
庚子	庚辰	祖庚	小乙奭妣庚
辛丑	辛巳		武丁奭妣辛
癸卯	癸未		武丁奭妣癸
甲辰（甲辰旬第十）	甲申（甲申旬第十）	祖甲	
丁未	丁亥	康丁	
戊申	戊子		武丁奭妣戊
乙卯（甲寅旬第十一）	乙未（甲午旬第十一）	武乙	
丁巳	丁酉	文丁（帝乙時稱父丁）（先祖至此止）	
戊午	戊戌		祖甲奭妣戊
辛酉	辛丑		康丁奭妣辛

戊辰(甲子旬第十二)　戊申(甲辰旬第十二)　武乙奭妣戊

癸酉　癸丑　文丁奭妣癸(帝乙時稱母癸)(先妣至此止)

此丙系翌祭，先祖自上甲始，至文丁止，前後需時十一旬，並先妣自妣庚(示壬奭)始，至妣癸(文丁奭)止，共需時十二旬，約當四閱月也。翌與彡，皆單獨舉行之，祭、𠩫、𣪊，連續重疊舉行之，别詳殷曆譜，此一例也。

大乙之名，自祖甲定之，祖庚及武丁之世，則皆稱唐。武丁之名，自帝乙定之，帝乙以前，則四期三期多稱后祖丁(别於兄之父祖丁也)，二期稱父丁也。

「奭」字二、三、五期皆用之，其書寫多異體，其義當為配偶。舊以祖妣合祭解之，誤也。如「武丁奭妣辛」「武丁奭妣癸」「妣戊」，以今語釋之，猶言「武丁元配妣辛」「武丁繼配妣癸」「武丁繼配妣戊」也。辛、癸、戊之次，依祭日推知之。其譜牒中凡先祖有兄弟行者，依其長幼之序；先妣有姊妹行者，依其嫡庶之别，(帝元配、繼配之先)體例嚴明，不容少紊。其間有與史傳大異者，即外丙之祭，列於大甲之後，是外丙與大甲為兄弟行，且不能即位於大甲以前。是孟子「外丙二年，仲壬四年」及殷本紀「太子太丁未立而卒，于是乃立太丁之弟外丙」之說，皆成問題矣。揭此待考。

在第二期祖甲時，翌祭之系統亦如此，惟先祖僅至祖庚(祖甲稱兄庚)，先妣僅至武丁奭妣辛(祖甲稱母辛)，祖妣九旬而遍祭。彡祭，𠩫、𣪊皆然。五期實因二期之成規，續修祖妣譜牒而已。

祖甲時有卜祭附入卜旬一辭，舊多誤以其中妣甲為羌甲之配偶，實則羌甲與妣甲，在一種祀典

124

之下，同日而祭也。辭見後編上，第四葉，第一片，摹釋如下。

(癸)丑卜，尹
(貞)：甲寅，
(翌)于羌甲
(眔)妣甲。

此於癸丑卜旬之後，記次日甲寅應祭之祖與妣，五種祭名適缺，姑補以「劦祭」，「眔」亦可為「于」，即「羌甲與妣甲」也。此「妣甲」乃「祖辛奭妣甲」之省文。檢前表甲寅系之祭日，在第七旬之甲寅日，翌祭羌甲，同日亦翌祭妣甲（祖辛奭），即可知在五種祀典中，羌甲，妣甲，皆同日而祭，非妣甲為羌甲配偶也。

又見於佚存五六六，亦此類殘辭。

(甲口卜旧)貞：
(王賓祖)奭妣劦
(眔)羌甲劦，亡
尤。

此為甲日卜劦祭妣甲，羌甲之辭，妣甲上可容「祖辛奭」三字。由上兩片，足證妣甲羌甲同日而祭之關係，否則誤以叔嫂為夫婦，厚誣古人矣。

伍骨六

此片足爲帝辛時代之特徵，父丁母癸之稱，乃帝乙之對文丁及其配偶也。至帝辛，不稱父丁而稱「文武丁」、「文武宗」、「文武帝」。龜甲卜辭，不見妣癸，故於日祭格乙種一二式未列入。今得此辭，知帝辛亦祭妣癸也。

茲補易如下表：

日祭格乙種　第一式之二。卜武丁日祭開始，自丙寅。

（下祭之旦）		（五世）	
癸亥	丙寅	祖甲	武丁
癸酉	丙子	祖甲	武丁
癸未	丙戌	祖甲	武丁
癸巳	丙申	祖甲	武丁
癸卯	丙午	祖甲	武丁
癸丑	丙辰	祖甲	武丁
甲子	丙寅	武乙	康祖丁
甲戌	丙子	武乙	康祖丁
甲申	丙戌	武乙	康祖丁

「(壬戌)卜貞：昔乙卯武(乙)升，勺(日)。
(翌)癸亥，其至于妣癸升，日。」

甲午　丙申　　武乙　康祖丁
甲辰　丙午　　武乙　康祖丁
甲寅(乙卯)　丙辰　　武乙　康祖丁
壬戌(癸亥)　丙寅　　妣癸　文武丁
壬申　丙子　　妣癸　文武丁
壬午　丙戌　　妣癸　文武丁
壬辰　丙申　　妣癸　文武丁
壬寅　丙午　　妣癸　文武丁
壬子　丙辰　　妣癸　文武丁

辭曰「昔乙卯」祭武乙，明武乙日祭，至乙卯而畢也。曰「癸亥其至于妣癸」，明妣癸日祭，當自癸亥起始也。三丁之日祭十八旬，配以甲乙癸之祖妣，如此排比，更為整齊矣。(龜二·三·六有妣癸，亦帝辛時辭。)

伍骨七，一五

兩辭皆稱「文武帝」，又皆以「丁」日卜祭，(丙日卜丁日之祭)知即「文武丁」，亦即文丁，帝辛時之稱謂也。

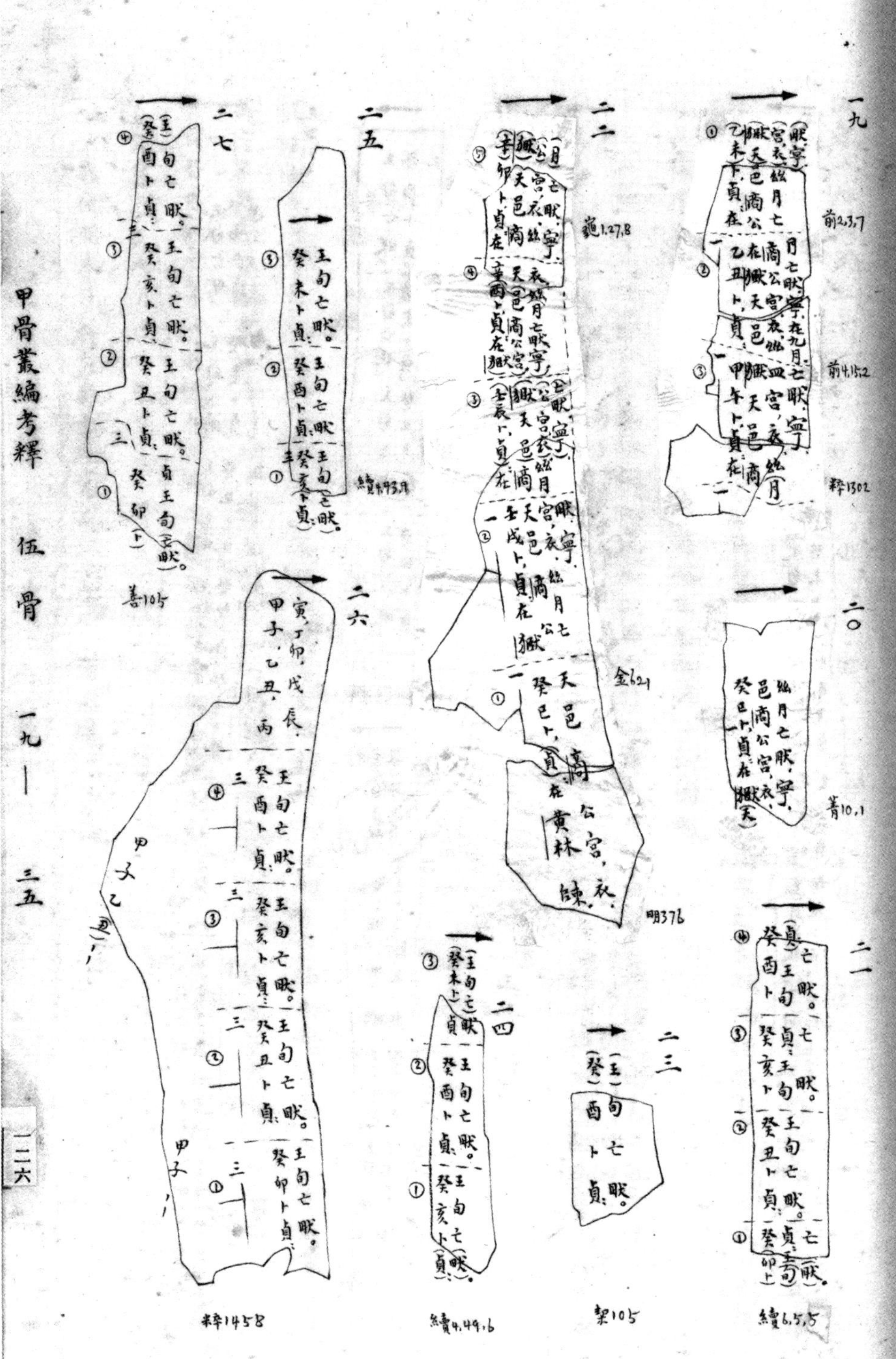
甲骨叢編考釋　伍　骨　一九—二五
一九
二〇
二一
二二
二三
二四
二五
二六
二七
前2.3.7
前4.15.2
粹1302
菁10.1
鐵1.27.8
金621
明376
續4.43.9
菁10.5
粹1458
續4.49.6
契105
續6.5.5
一二六

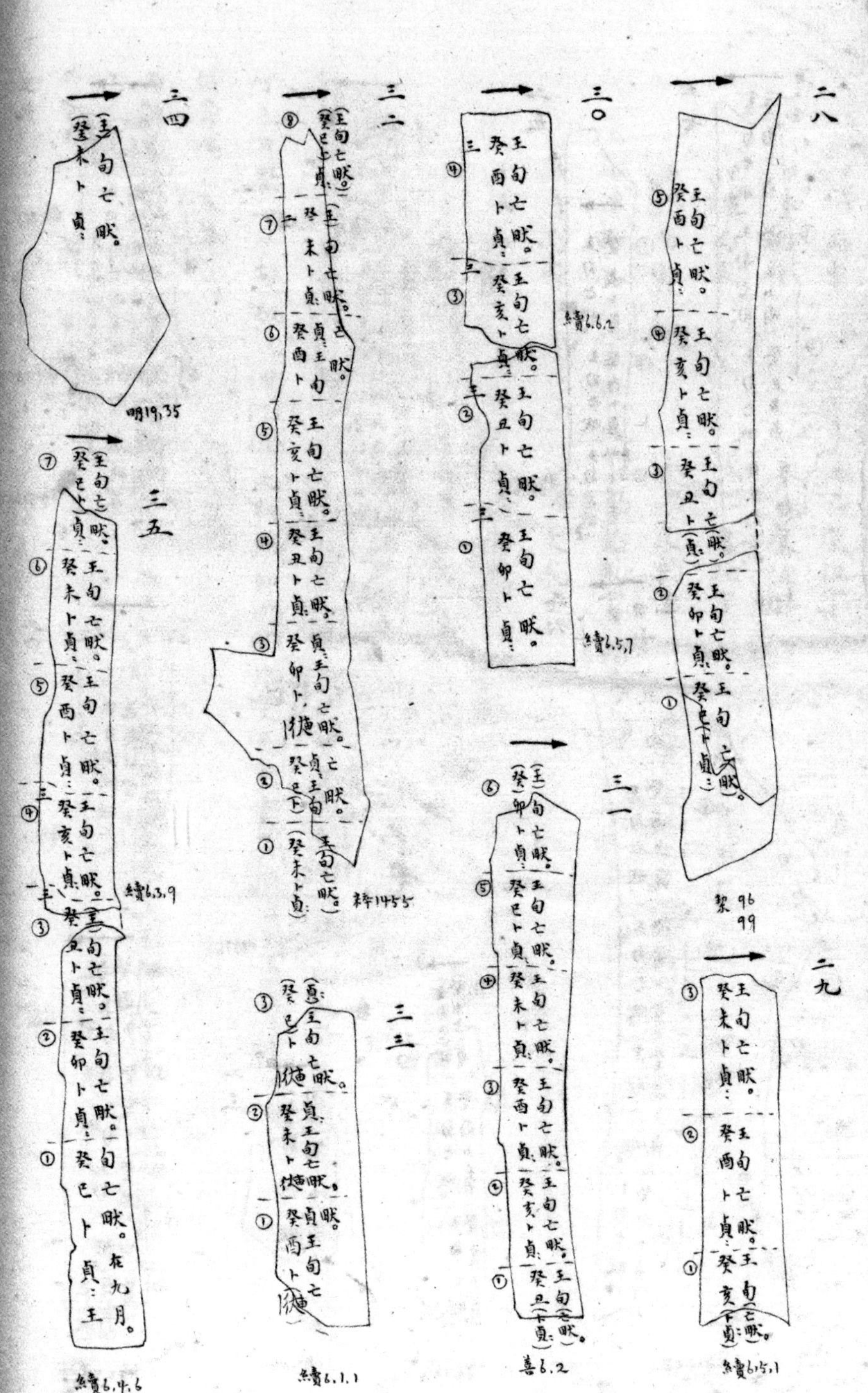

伍骨一九、二〇、二二

卜辭中卜夕、卜旬，最常見。卜夕，於每日晚間舉行之，卜當夜之安寧與否也。卜旬，於每旬之末日舉行之，卜下一旬之吉凶禍福也。卜月，於每月一日舉行之，卜一月內之吉凶禍福，安否也。卜月最少見，僅此三殘片，又為一時期之物，蓋帝乙田游在外所作，一新例也。

卜月三片，又殘而為七，分藏五家（羅振玉、劉體智、明義士、林泰輔、金璋諸氏）明義士氏曾復其形為一胛骨之右邊，錄其六（見所著表較新舊版殷虛書契前編並記所得之新材料一文）郭沫若氏又見合善齋所藏一片（見粹編一三〇二），共為七片。明氏原排之次第（參看附圖）：

(七)	(六)	(缺)	(五)	(四)	(三)	(缺)	(二)	(一)
菁華10.1 (菁)	林1.27.8 (龜)		前2.3.7	前4.15.2	(未到) (粹1302)	(無)	H621 (金)	明376

菁、前、金原片皆有記卜兆次序之「一」字，明氏遺落。又明氏將(二)(四)兩片密接，今發見善齋一片，是當分離，其下且有兩缺辭也。以每月一卜計之，則(二)(三)之間，缺二辭。全部共缺四辭，並癸巳、壬戌、甲午、乙丑、辛口、口口、癸巳，此一骨邊共須有卜月之辭十一段，骨側每邊刻辭，少者六、七段，多者八、九段，十段以上則絕不能容之，是此七片，不能列為一骨之一邊也。

茲依明氏法，補苴缺文，附圖如次，以見一骨右邊之不容。

且如右之接兑排列法，其次序，在一骨之一邊，自當全部一致，先下後上，則其「卜月」之日，必在每月之一日乃至六日之間，證以每日初昏「卜夕」，每周（十日）癸日「卜旬」，卜有定時之例，不應參差錯亂如此。

今分為三段讀之，如釋文，則由乙丑至甲午，由癸巳至壬戌，皆為二十九日，恰足一小盡月之日數，於每月初吉（一日），卜衣祭之時，兼卜「兹月」之安寧，一如昏時「卜夕」，癸日「卜旬」，於例於理，皆甚暢通也。

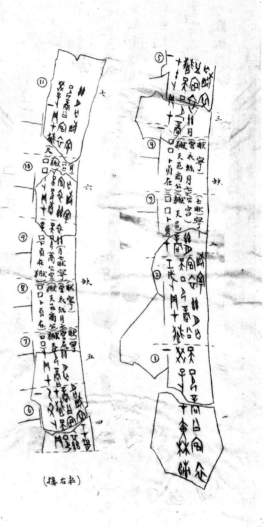

卜月各辭，僅「乙丑」一辭有「在九月」之記錄，今如以「九月小乙丑朔，十月大甲午朔」為標準，在殷曆譜中，僅帝乙廿年有之，其月朔如由九月乙丑，前後推求，所估時日，當為廿年八月至廿一年六月，十一個

月之間。其餘，在第五期帝乙帝辛時代之曆譜中，不二見也。

殷曆譜　　卜辭節錄

帝乙廿祀（公元前一一九〇年　辛未）

八月大　乙未一日（儒略周日一二八六九八二）（一一九〇年七月二十六日）　（乙未）——（在獄）———茲月亡（畎，寧）。

九月小　乙丑一日　乙丑——在獄———茲月亡畎，寧。在九月。

十月大　甲午一日　甲午——在獄———茲月亡畎，寧。（以上一九版）

十一月小　甲子一日

十二月大　癸巳一日　癸巳——在獄———茲月亡畎，寧。（以上二〇版）

帝乙廿一祀（公元前一一八九年　壬申）

正月大　癸亥一日（周日一二八七〇一三〇）（一一九〇年十二月廿日）　十二日甲戌（一一八九年一月一日）

二月小　癸巳一日　癸巳——在黃林——

三月大　壬戌一日　壬戌——在獄———茲月亡畎，寧。

四月小　壬辰一日

五月大　辛酉一日　辛（酉）——（在獄）———茲（月亡畎，寧）。

六月小　辛卯一日　（辛）卯——在（獄）———茲（月）亡畎，寧。（以上二一版）

如右之排列，正月為頻大，則前後兩組先小後大之月朔，安排甚為妥貼，所有之干支，即一殘餘之「辛」字「卯」字筆畫，亦皆不落空，而骨邊刻辭先下後上及先上後下，俱為恒例，以後再有同版卜月之殘片出現，必更足證成此說也。

此類卜辭，為時王田游在外之際，於該地之行在，即所稱「天邑商公宮」或「皿宮」者，舉行「衣祭」，祭之日，當月之一日（朔，初吉），故兼卜及「兹月亡畎寧」也。此為每月一日卜一月之安寧者，毫無疑問，五期夕字作D，月字作D，無例外，又有本片（一九）中「九月」之D，更足證明之。故如右之排次，而得六、七月朔之干支，安排妥當，實為一最完善之解說也。

三六

癸未卜貞：王旬亡畎。

（癸）酉（卜貞）：王旬（亡畎）。

明19.32

三七

（癸）卯卜貞：（王）旬亡畎。

二　癸巳卜貞：王旬亡畎。

明19.33

三八

癸巳卜貞：王旬亡畎。

續6.5.12

三九

③（癸）卯（卜）貞：（王旬亡）畎。

②癸巳卜貞：王旬亡畎。

①癸未（卜貞）：王（旬亡畎）。

契95

四〇

⑤（癸）卯卜貞：（王旬）亡畎。

④癸巳卜貞：王旬亡畎。

③癸未卜貞：王旬亡畎。

②癸酉卜貞：王旬亡畎。

①癸亥卜：王旬亡

善62

四一

（非一版，誤合）

貞：王……畎。

②癸丑卜貞：王旬亡畎。在三月。

①癸卯（卜貞：王）旬亡（畎）。

粹1460

四二

②（癸丑卜貞：王）旬亡畎。

①癸卯（卜貞：王旬亡畎）。

明21.33

四三

（癸）卯卜貞：（王）旬亡畎。

明19.31

四四

癸卯卜貞：（王）旬亡畎。

續6.4.8

四五

③（癸丑卜）貞：王旬亡畎。

②癸卯卜貞：王旬亡畎。

①（癸）巳卜貞：王旬亡畎。

王

明20.2

四六

⑥（癸）卯卜貞：（王）旬亡畎。

⑤癸巳卜貞：王旬亡畎。

④癸未卜貞：王旬亡畎。

③癸酉卜貞：王旬亡畎。

②癸亥卜貞：王旬亡畎。

①癸丑（卜貞）：王旬（亡畎）。

善62

四七

癸丑卜貞：王旬亡畎。在十月又二。

明21.24

四八

②（癸）亥卜貞：（王）旬亡畎。

①癸丑卜貞：王旬亡畎。

續4.49.7

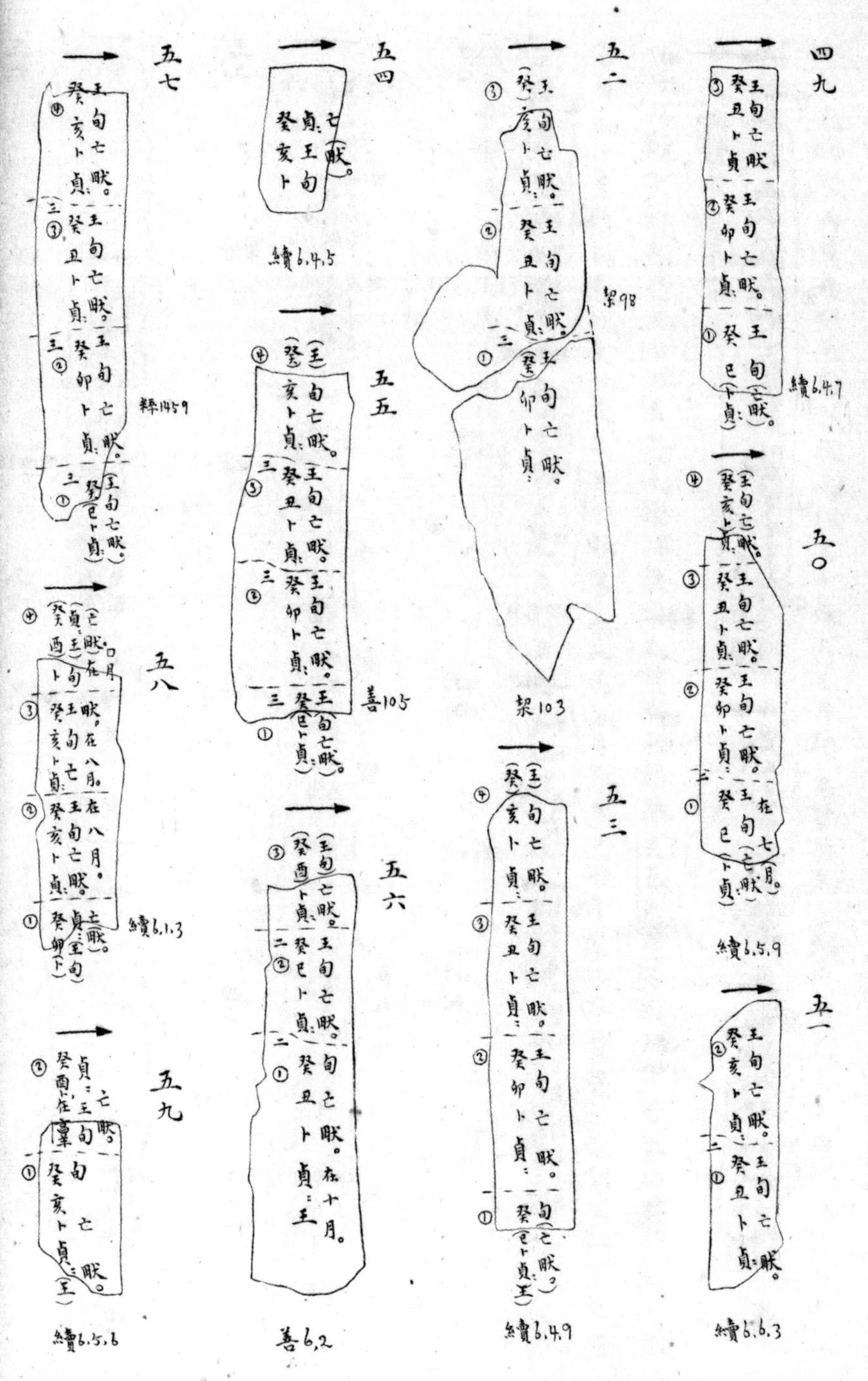

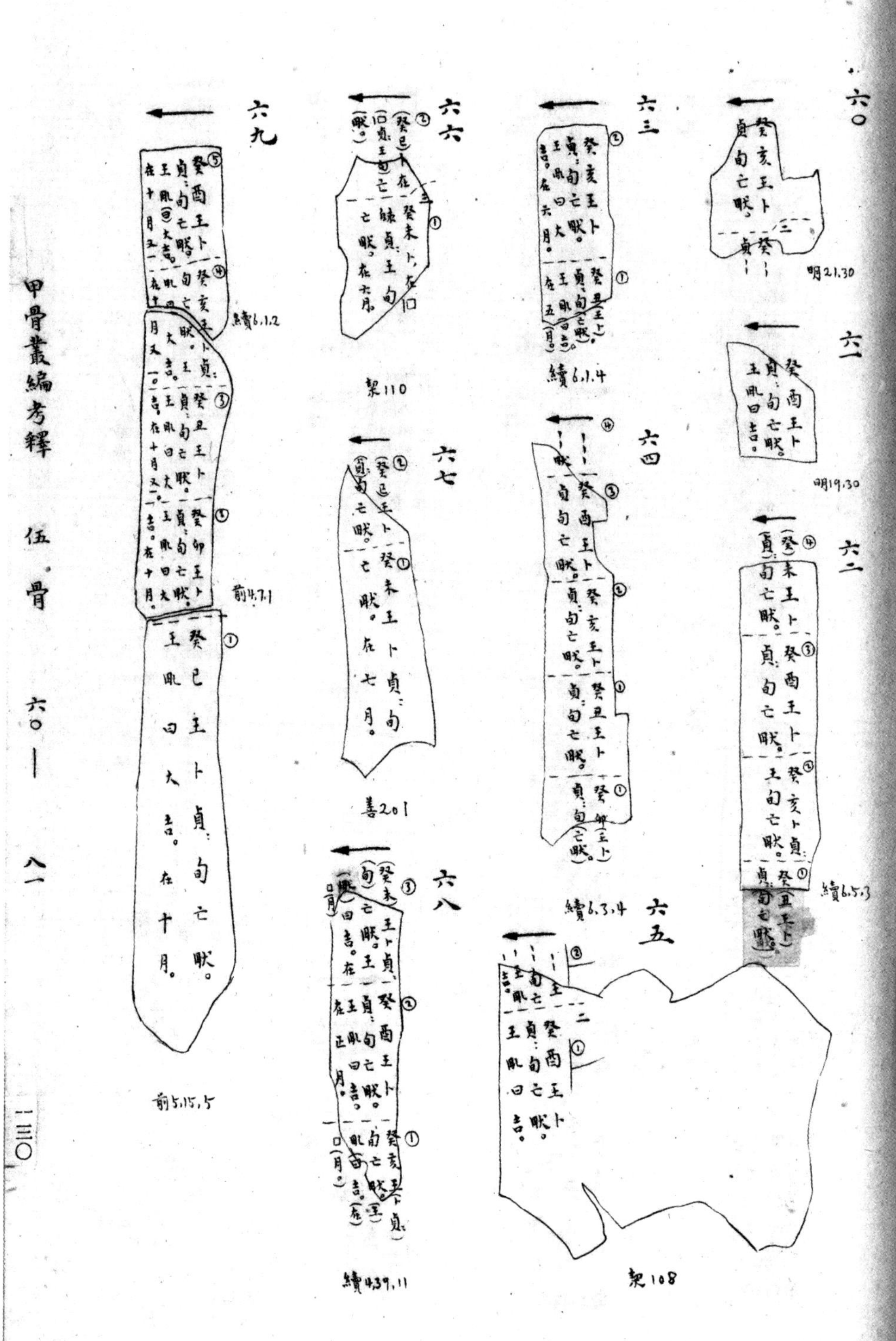
甲骨叢編考釋　伍.骨　六〇—八一
一三〇
六〇
明21.30
六一
明19.30
六二
續6.5.3
六三
續6.1.4
六四
續6.3.4
六五
契108
六六
契110
六七
善201
六八
續4.39.11
六九
續6.1.2
前4.7.1
前5.15.5

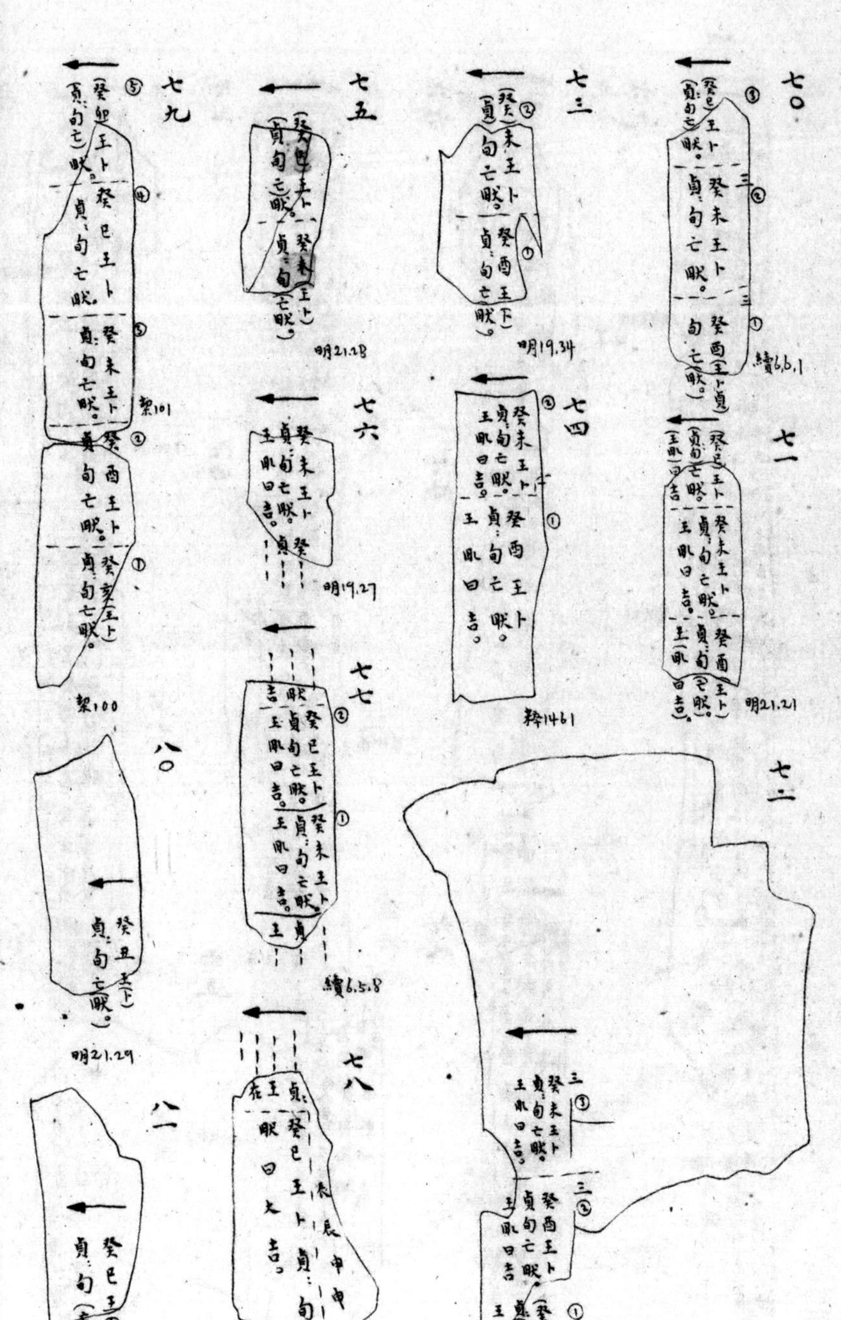
七〇
續6.6.1
七一
明21.21
七二
梨107
七三
明19.34
七四
粹1461
七五
明21.28
七六
明19.27
七七
續6.5.8
七八
前5.16.3
七九
梨101
梨100
八〇
明21.29
八一
明21.20

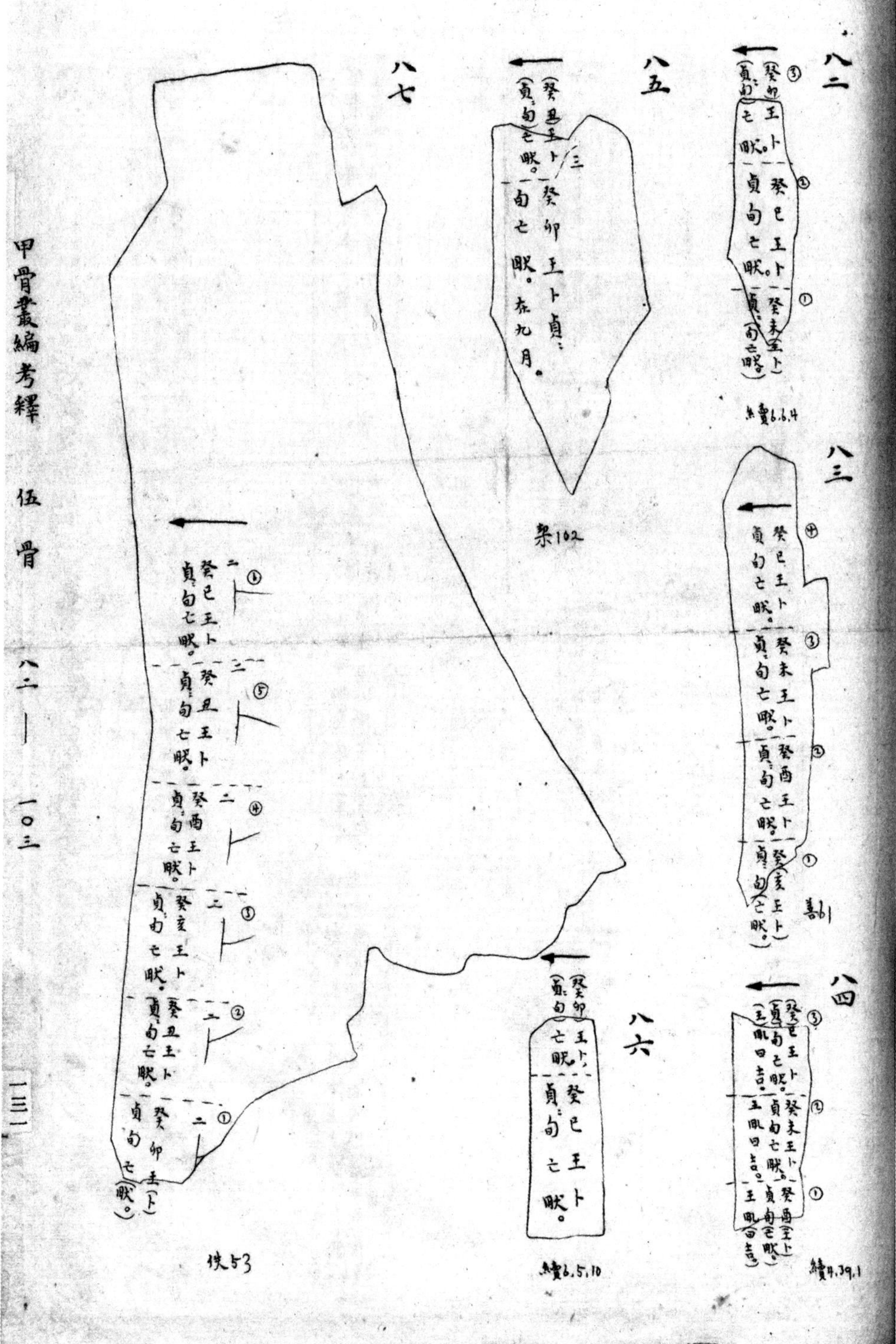
131
甲骨叢編考釋　伍　骨　八二—一〇三
一三一
八二
續6.6.4
八三
嘉61
八四
續4.39.1
八五
粹102
八六
續6.5.10
八七
後53

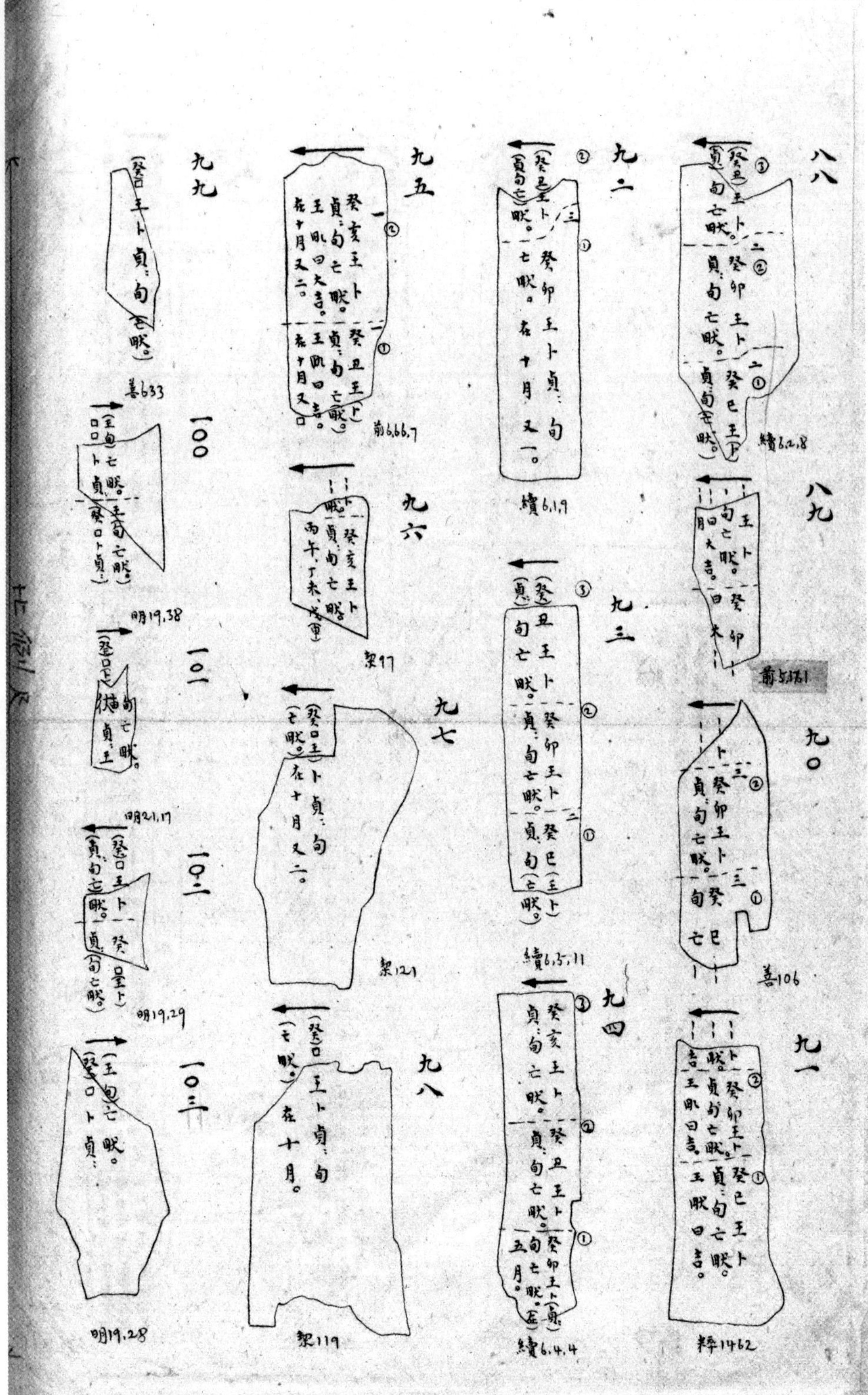
八八
續6.2.8
八九
前5.17.1
九〇
善106
九一
粹1462
九二
續6.1.9
九三
續6.5.11
九四
續6.4.4
九五
前6.66.7
九六
契17
九七
契121
九八
契119
九九
善633
一〇〇
明19.38
一〇一
明21.17
一〇二
明19.29
一〇三
明19.28

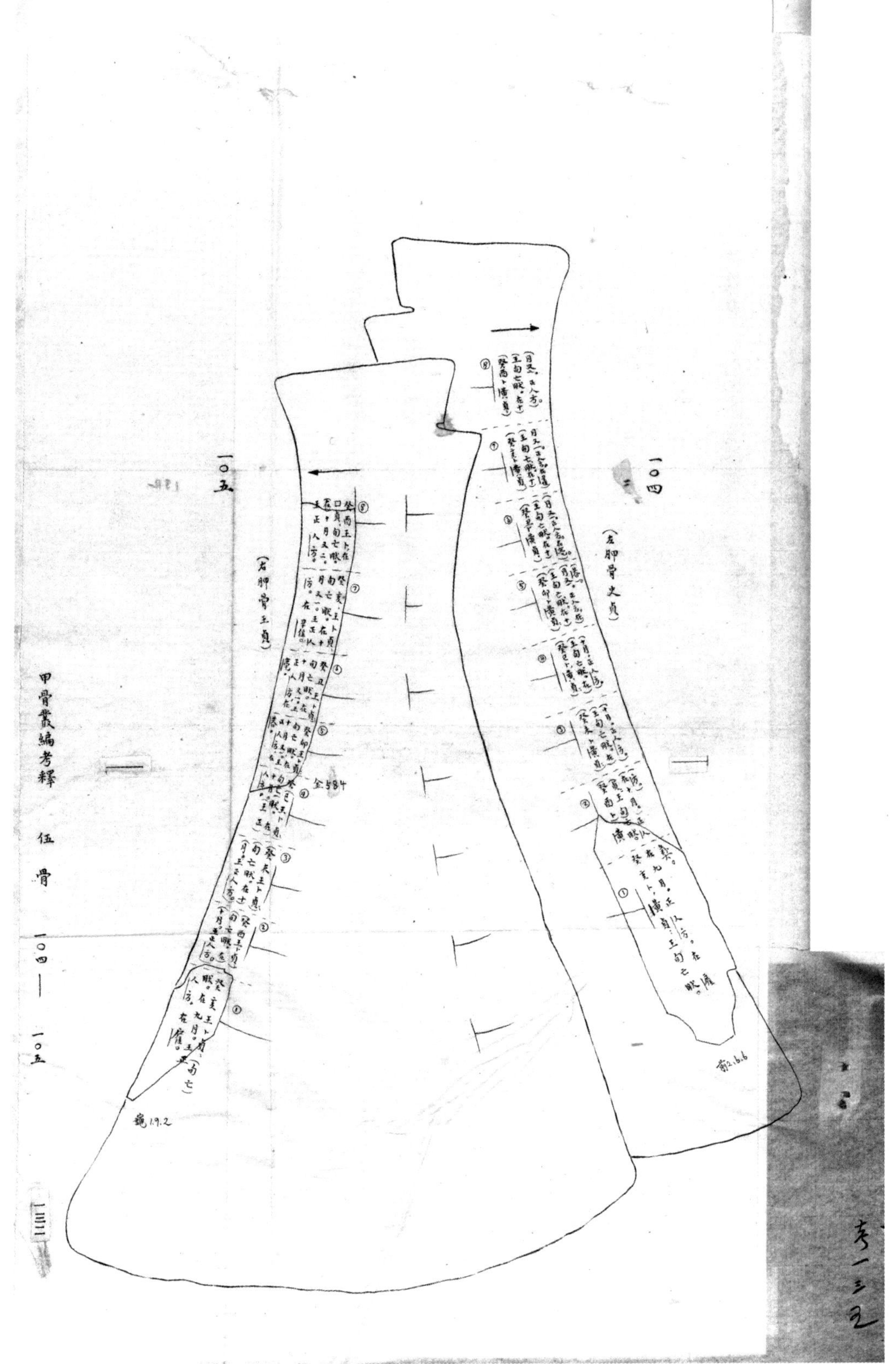

甲骨叢編考釋　伍　骨　一〇四——一〇五
一〇四
(右胛骨文貞)
前2.6.6
一〇五
(右胛骨王貞)
金584
龜1.9.2

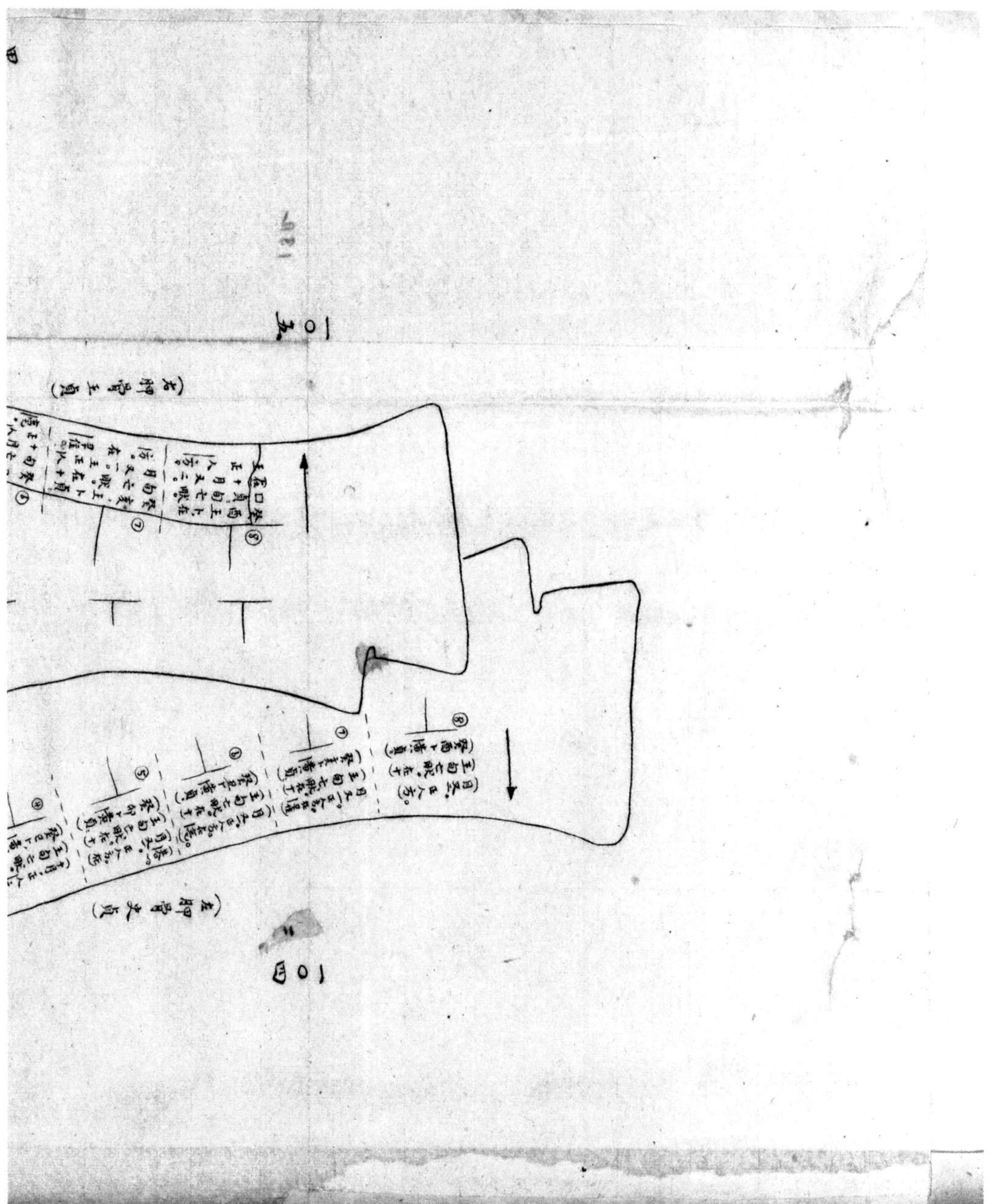

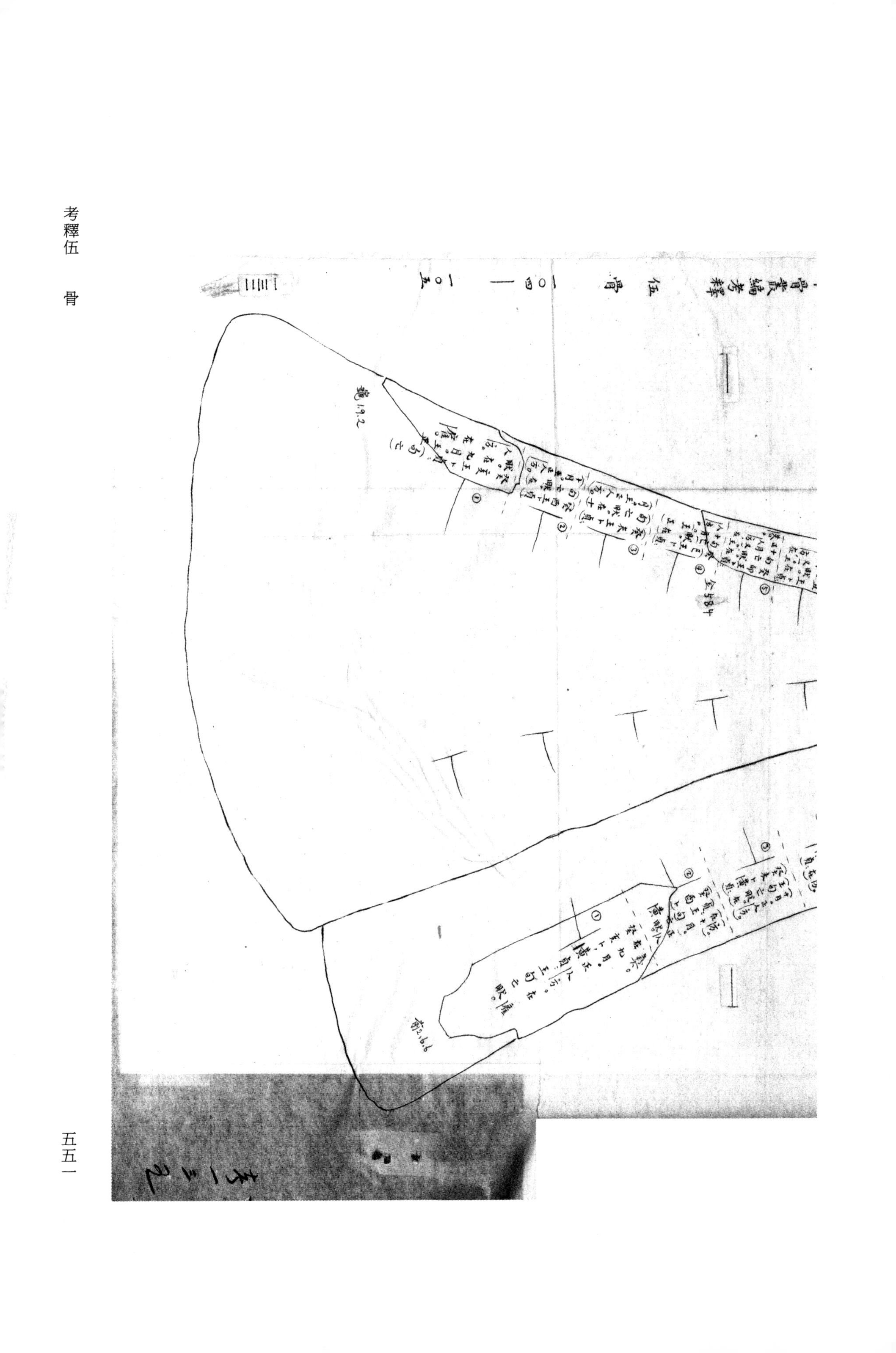

骨叢編考釋　伍　骨　一〇四—一〇五

三

龜1.9.2

金584

前2.16.6